A History of African Linguistics

Bringing together a team of leading scholars, this volume provides the first global history of African linguistics as an autonomous academic discipline, covering Africa, America, Asia, Australia, and Europe. Defining African linguistics and identifying important forerunners, the volume describes its emergence from a 'colonial science' at the turn of the twentieth century in Europe, where it was first established mainly in academic institutions of former colonial powers. Its riddance from the 'colonial project' is traced, following its 'decolonization' and subsequent spread from imperialist Europe across all inhabited continents, with particular reference to its academic establishment in the various regions of Africa. Providing inside views of African linguistic research and its ramifications over time, active researchers in its various sub-fields present highly informative accounts of current and past research priorities and achievements. The 26 authors are themselves representatives of the various regions of both the world and Africa, in which African linguistics has become entrenched in academic institutions.

H. EKKEHARD WOLFF is Professor Emeritus at Leipzig University, where he retired from the Chair of African Linguistics (Afrikanistik) in 2009. He has taught previously at Hamburg University and extensively also in Ethiopia, Niger, Nigeria, South Africa, and Finland. He has published over 25 books, including *Sprachkunst der Lamang* (1980), *Die Sprachen Afrikas* (1981), *Referenzgrammatik des Hausa* (1993), *The Lamang Language and Dictionary* (2 vols., 2015), *Language and Development in Africa: Perceptions, Ideologies and Challenges* (2016), *Multilingual Education for Africa: Concepts and Practices* (2016), *Multilingualism and Intercultural Communication: A South African Perspective* (2017), and *The Cambridge Handbook of African Linguistics* (2019).

A History of African Linguistics

Edited by

H. Ekkehard Wolff

CAMBRIDGE
UNIVERSITY PRESS

CAMBRIDGE
UNIVERSITY PRESS

University Printing House, Cambridge CB2 8BS, United Kingdom

One Liberty Plaza, 20th Floor, New York, NY 10006, USA

477 Williamstown Road, Port Melbourne, VIC 3207, Australia

314–321, 3rd Floor, Plot 3, Splendor Forum, Jasola District Centre,
New Delhi – 110025, India

79 Anson Road, #06-04/06, Singapore 079906

Cambridge University Press is part of the University of Cambridge.

It furthers the University's mission by disseminating knowledge in the pursuit of
education, learning, and research at the highest international levels of excellence.

www.cambridge.org
Information on this title: www.cambridge.org/9781108417976
DOI: 10.1017/9781108283977

First published 2019

Printed and bound in Great Britain by Clays Ltd, Elcograf S.p.A.

A catalogue record for this publication is available from the British Library.

Library of Congress Cataloging-in-Publication Data

Names: Wolff, Ekkehard, editor.
Title: A history of African linguistics / edited by H. Ekkehard Wolff.
Description: New York : Cambridge University Press, 2018. I Includes
    bibliographical references and index.
Identifiers: LCCN 2018041010 I ISBN 9781108417976 (alk. paper)
Subjects: LCSH: Linguistics—Africa—History. I African languages.
Classification: LCC P61 .H575 2018 I DDC 418.009—dc23
LC record available at https://lccn.loc.gov/2018041010

ISBN 978-1-108-41797-6 Hardback

Contents

Figures

Tables

Contributors

AKINBIYI AKINLABI
Professor, Department of Linguistics, Rutgers University,
New Brunswick, NJ, USA

SONJA E. BOSCH
Professor, Department of African Languages, University of South Africa, Pretoria,
South Africa

MARIA BULAKH
Research Fellow, Institute for Oriental and Classical Studies, Russian State University
for the Humanities, Moscow, Russia; and National Research University Higher School
of Economics, Moscow, Russia

G. TUCKER CHILDS
Professor and Chair, Department of Applied Linguistics, Portland State University,
Portland, OR, USA

BRUCE CONNELL
Associate Professor, Linguistics and Language Studies Program, Glendon College,
York University, Toronto, ON, Canada

YAMINA EL KIRAT EL ALLAME
Professor and Vice-Dean for Research and Cooperation, Faculty of Letters and Human
Sciences, Mohammed V University, Rabat, Morocco

ABDERRAHMAN EL AISSATI
Assistant Professor, Department of Culture Studies, Tilburg University, Tilburg,
The Netherlands

ANNE-MARIA FEHN
Researcher, Department of Linguistic and Cultural Evolution, Max Planck Institute
for the Science of Human History, Jena, Germany; Institut für Afrikanistik, Johann-
Wolfgang-Goethe Universität, Frankfurt am Main, Germany; Human Evolutionary
Genetics Group, CIBIO/InBIO: Research Center in Biodiversity and Genetic
Resources, Vairão, Portugal

JOHN HAJEK
Professor of Italian Studies and Director of the Research Unit
for Multilingualism and Cross-cultural Communication
(RUMACCC), School of Languages and Linguistics, University of Melbourne,
Melbourne, Australia

ARVI HURSKAINEN
Professor (emeritus) of African Studies, Institute of World Cultures, Faculty of
Humanities, Helsinki University, Helsinki, Finland

ANGELIKA JAKOBI
Senior researcher (retired), Institut für Afrikanistik und Ägyptologie, Universität zu
Köln, Cologne, Germany

SHIGEKI KAJI
Professor, Department of Sociology, Kyoto Sangyo University; Kyoto University
(emeritus), Kyoto, Japan

ROLAND KIEßLING
Professor, Afrikanistik, Asien-Afrika-Institut, Universität Hamburg,
Hamburg, Germany

INGE M. KOSCH
Professor, Department of African Languages, University of South Africa, Pretoria,
South Africa

AMANI LUSEKELO
Senior Lecturer, Department of Languages and Literature,
University of Dar es Salaam, Dar es Salaam, Tanzania

RONNY MEYER
Maître de conférences (Amharique), Institut National des Langues et Civilisations
Orientales (INALCO) and Langage, Langues et Cultures d'Afrique (LLACAN),
Paris, France; former Associate Professor, Department of Linguistics, Addis Ababa
University, Addis Ababa, Ethiopia

PHILIP NGESSIMO MATHE MUTAKA
Professor of Linguistics, University of Yaoundé I, Yaoundé, Cameroon

NINA PAWLAK
Professor, Department of African Languages and Cultures, University of Warsaw,
Warsaw, Poland

MARGARIDA PETTER
Professor, Department of Linguistics, Universidade de São Paulo, São Paulo, Brazil

MARIE-CLAUDE SIMEONE-SENELLE
Directrice de Recherche (emerita), Langage, Langues et Cultures d'Afrique (LLACAN),
CNRS, INALCO, Université Sorbonne Paris Cité, Villejuif, Paris, France

WOLBERT G. C. SMIDT
Director of 'Ethiomap', Forschungszentrum Gotha, Universität Erfurt, Germany; Associate Professor in Ethnohistory, PhD advisor and teacher in the PhD programme 'History and Cultural Studies', Mekelle University, Mekelle, Ethiopia

SUN XIAOMENG
Professor, School of Asian and African Studies, Beijing Foreign Studies University, Beijing, P. R. China

RAINER MARIA VOIGT
Professor (emeritus), Seminar für Semitistik und Arabistik, Fachrichtung Semitistik, Freie Universität Berlin, Germany

H. EKKEHARD WOLFF
Professor and Chair (emeritus) of African Linguistics, Institut für Afrikastudien, Universität Leipzig, Leipzig, Germany

YANG CHUL-JOON
Humanities Korea (HK) Research Professor, Institute of African Studies, Hankuk University of Foreign Studies, Yongin, South Korea

ALEXANDER ZHELTOV
Professor and Chair/Head of Department, Department of African Studies/Department of African Ethnography, St Petersburg State University/Museum of Anthropology and Ethnography, St Petersburg, Russia

Preface

African linguistics, as we accept it today as being a separate and autonomous field of academic research and teaching, had its origins in colonial Europe and was without parallels in other parts of the world. It partly pre-dated but mainly accompanied the imperialist regime of European colonial expansion and Christian mission in Africa, boosted by the notorious 'Scramble for Africa' that preceded and followed the Berlin Congo Conference of 1884/1885. Obviously, early African linguistics used to serve the colonial project by taking care of its linguistic dimension, in the beginning fostering but later and currently challenging the hegemonic dominance of the 'North' over the Global South. Thereby, it continues to weigh in on postcolonial national language policies and planning in Africa until this day.

Hence, African linguistics has come of age and has rid itself almost completely of the missionary and colonial paradigm. Today, it prides itself on its global academic representation as an autonomous academic discipline, as witnessed by the World Congress of African Linguistics, which has met triennially since 1994. Based on the early and ground-breaking work of its precursors, professional African linguistics arose during the peak period of European colonialism in Africa. It eventually also established itself outside the former European colonial powers, namely in Eastern and Northern Europe. Another boost followed decolonization and African independence after 1960. Since then, African linguistics has found an academic home not only across Africa, but also in the Americas and eventually in parts of Asia and in Australia.

Increasingly in recent years, if for a long time rather hesitantly, members of the scientific community of African linguistics have begun to turn their attention to their own academic history, not least with a view to challenging the prevailing 'Northern' by a complementary, if not alternative, 'Southern' perspective. The fact that African linguistics is not everywhere established as a separate academic discipline apart and distinct from 'general linguistics', on the one hand, and 'African studies', on the other, has tended to slow down the emergence of critical concern with not only its academic but also its ideological history. Further, with only few exceptions, there is little information available that would be reliable, comprehensive, and easily accessible on where, when, by whom, and how African linguistics emerged and became entrenched in institutional structures of academia in the various parts of the world, including Africa herself. In its early days at the turn of the twentieth century, particularly in Europe, it remained in the shadow and under the influence of already established disciplines such as Egyptology and Semitic philology. For reasons of the geographic proximity of its object of study to languages and cultures in the Near and Middle East, it was administratively located near, or as part of, 'Oriental studies'. Later, by the middle of the twentieth century and in the wake of African independence from European colonialism, it had to set itself apart from the intrusive and much more general African studies that had some of its roots in black studies and the modern human rights movement, mainly in the USA. In this volume, the authors trace the motivations for the establishment and subsequent growth of African linguistics, often beginning with simply providing language instruction for practical needs, if not for nostalgic purposes (as in the case of early black studies). Today, this academic field is pursued in autonomous and titular university departments of 'African languages' or 'African linguistics' in some parts of the world, or as an integral part of more encompassing institutions such as 'general linguistics', 'African and Asian studies', 'foreign studies', and 'world cultures' in others.

For this volume, and for the first time in history, 26 experts from Africa, the Americas, Asia, Australia, and Europe have come together to tell the story of African linguistics, namely how it emerged as an academic field more or less of its own accord in their various world regions. They tell the story from within, being actively involved themselves as researchers in various sub-fields of African linguistics in different places. They are not looking at matters from a distance as historians or archivists.

As a rule and characteristically for Africa as a whole, research on African languages began and was stimulated by impetus from outside Africa, often tainted by a Christian mission and colonial agenda. This linked African linguistics 'in the field' intimately to research activities that were conducted simultaneously outside Africa. The current volume takes a focused view on matters. Rather than sketching out research history according to language groupings or individual languages in particular regions of Africa, for which a growing literature is already available, it focuses on research activities from the perspective of the origin of researchers and institutions. The structure of the book, therefore, reflects different world regions as much as sub-regions of Africa, where African linguistics emerged under quite different conditions, involving both African and non-African individuals and institutions.

The absence of previous worldwide surveys, the selective availability of digitalized historical documents available via the Internet, and presuming that relevant sources still remain undiscovered and hidden in archives that are difficult, if not impossible, to access from where today's researchers live and work, mean that gaps in knowledge and information persist. This must be accepted for the time being. The editor and the contributors share the hope that this volume may stimulate local in-depth research into the history of the study of African languages and linguistics in the various parts of the world. This should then subsequently allow for a broader and critical review of African linguistics, which would link up with current general debates on colonial and postcolonial continuities and their impact on knowledge production in and about Africa. Against this backdrop of persisting lacunae, the present book pilots a broad approach to the complex history of African linguistics in a global perspective. It does so by providing expert 'inside' views on the academic history of African linguistics within and outside Africa, which may serve as a first fact-finding and fact-describing vade mecum to the global history of African linguistics since its inception as a 'colonial science' in imperialist Europe more than 130 years ago.

This volume accompanies *The Cambridge Handbook of African Linguistics* (Wolff 2019), for which a survey of the regional histories of African linguistics was considered an essential topic. The restricted space available in the *Handbook* allowed only for abridged summarising treatments. This companion volume, therefore, provides the necessary space needed for a more detailed treatment including extensive bibliographical references. It is compiled by the same editor in cooperation with mainly the same authors, who contributed historical accounts of different length and detail to both volumes.

Abbreviations and Acronyms

AATA	American Association of Teachers of Arabic
AAU	Addis Ababa University
ACACIA	Arid Climate, Adaptation and Cultural Innovation in Africa, 1995–2007
ACAL	Annual Conference of African Linguistics
	Association of Contemporary African Linguistics
ACALAN	African Academy of Languages
ADEA	Association for the Development of Education in Africa
AIDA	Association Internationale de Dialectologie Arabe
AJL	*Australian Journal of Linguistics*
AL	*Africana Linguistica*
ALS	African Linguistics School
	Australian Linguistic Society
	Arabic Linguistic Society
ALSEC	Afar Language Studies and Enrichment Center
ALUPEC	Alfabeto Unificado para a Escrita do Cabo-Verdiano
ALUSTP	Alfabeto Unificado para a Escrita das Línguas Nativas de S. Tomé e Príncipe
ARAL	*Australian Review of Applied Linguistics*
ARAS	*Australasian Review of African Studies*
a.r.t.e.s.	Graduate School for the Humanities Cologne (AGSHC, Cologne)
ASAFAS	Graduate School of Asian and African Area Studies
ATR	advanced tongue root
AAVE	African American Vernacular English
BA	baccalaureus artium, bachelor of arts
BaFraLe	Colloquium on Berber Languages
BAKITA	National Swahili Council
BFSU	Beijing Foreign Studies University
BICCL	Biennial Colloquium on the Chadic Languages
BIGSAS	Bayreuth International Graduate School of African Studies
BLR	Bantu Lexical Reconstruction

BRICS	Brazil, Russia, India, China, South Africa
CALL	Colloquium on African Languages and Linguistics
CAR	Central African Republic
CERD	Centre d'Études et de Recherches de Djibouti
CFS	Côte française des Somalis
CIBIO/InBIO	Research Centre in Biodiversity and Genetic Resources
CIDA	Canadian International Development Agency
CLARIN	European Research Infrastructure for Language Resources and Technology
CLO	*Cahiers de Littérature Orale*
CMS	Church Missionary Society
CNRS	Centre National de la Recherche Scientifique
CODESRIA	Council for the Development of Social Science Research in Africa
CPLP	Comunidade dos Países de Língua Portuguesa (Community of Portuguese Language Countries)
CRI	China Radio International
CRLD	Centre for Research on Linguistic Diversity
CRUD	Centre de Recherches de l'Université de Djibouti
CSIR	Centre for Scientific and Industrial Research
CVCP	Canadian Volunteer Cooperation Program
DaF	Deutsch als Fremdsprache (German as a Foreign Language)
DEL	Documenting Endangered Languages
DELL	Department of Ethiopian Languages and Literature
DLING	Department of Linguistics
DMG	Deutsche Morgenländische Gesellschaft
DoBeS	Dokumentation Bedrohter Sprachen
DOBES	Documentation of Endangered Languages Program
DRC	Democratic Republic of the Congo
E.C.	Ethiopian Calendar
EHESS	École des Hautes Études en Sciences Sociales
ELDF	Endangered Languages Documentation Fund
ELDP	Hans Rausing Endangered Languages Documentation Program
ELRC	Ethiopian Languages Research Center
ENLOV	École Nationale de Langues Orientales Vivantes
EPHE	École Pratique des Hautes Études
ESL	English as a Second Language
EST	extended standard theory
FLAS	Foreign Language and Area Studies
FOCAC	Forum on China–Africa Cooperation

FQRNT	Fonds Québécois de la Recherche sur la Nature et les Technologies (formerly FCAR)
FQRSC	Fonds Québécois de la Recherche sur la Société et la Culture
FQRSC	Fonds Québécois de la Recherche sur la Société et la Culture
G.C.	Gregorian Calendar
GDR	German Democratic Republic
GILLBT	Ghana Institute of Linguistics, Literacy and Bible Translation
GLECS	Groupe Linguistique d'Études Chamito-Sémitiques
GLOW	Generative Linguistics of the Old World
HUFS	Hankuk University of Foreign Studies
IAAS	Institute of African and Asian Studies
IAI	International African Institute
ICT	Information and Communication Technology
IES	Institute of Ethiopian Studies
IKS	Indigenous Knowledge System
ILCAA	Research Institute for Languages and Cultures of Asia and Africa
ILD	Institut des Langues de Djibouti
ILS	Institute of Language Studies
INALCO	Institut National des Langues et Civilisations Orientales
INDE	Instituto Nacional de Desenvolvimento da Educaçao (National Institute for Education Development)
INE	Instituto Nacional de Estatistica
INEAS	Institute of Near Eastern and African Studies
IPA	International Phonetic Alphabet
IRICA	Institut de Recherche Indépendant de la Corne de l'Afrique
ISCED	Instituto Superior de Ciências de Educaçã (Higher Institute for Educational Studies)
ISE	Instituto Superior de Educaçao
ISERST	Institut Supérieur d'Études et de Recherches Scientifiques et Techniques
ISNTD	Institut des Sciences et des Nouvelles Technologies de Djibouti
JALL	*Journal of African Languages and Linguistics*
JCU	James Cook University
JOLAN	*Journal of the Linguistic Association of Nigeria*
JWAL	*Journal of West African Languages*
LACITO	Langues et Civilisations à Tradition Orale
LAN	Linguistic Association of Nigeria

LBT	Lutheran Bible Translators
LCRC	Language and Culture Research Centre
LLACAN	Langage, Langues et Cultures d'Afrique
LoT	Languages of Tanzania Project
LREC	Language Resources and Evaluation
MaLEX	Malawi Lexicon Project
MIT	Massachusetts Institute of Technology
MoI	medium of instruction
MPhil	magister philosophiae, master of philosophy
NACALCO	National Cameroonian Languages Committee
NC	Niger-Congo
NECAAS	Network of European Centers of Asian and African Studies
NELIMO	Núcleode Estudos de Línguas Moçambicana (Institute for the Study of Mozambican Languages)
NEPAD	New Partnership for Africa's Development
NGO	nongovernmental organization
NINLAN	National Institute for Nigerian Languages
NISA	Nilo-Saharan - Linguistic Analyses and Documentation
NISALICO	Nilo-Saharan Linguistics Conference
NRF	National Research Foundation
NSF	National Science Foundation
NTNU	Norwegian University of Science and Technology
NUC	National Universities Commission
NUFU	Nasjonalt Utvalg for Utviklingsrelatert Forskning og Utdanning (National Committee for Development-Related Research and Education)
OPSL	Occasional Papers in the Study of Sudanese Languages
ORSTOM	Office de la Recherche Scientifique et Technique d'Outre-Mer
PALOP	Países Africanos de Língua Oficial Portuguesa (Officially Portuguese-Speaking African Countries)
PANMAPAL	Pan-African Master's and PhD Programme in African Languages and Applied Linguistics
PhD	philosophiae doctor
RCLT	Research Centre for Linguistic Typology
REST	revised extended standard theory
RIÉ	*Recueil des inscriptions de l'Éthiopie* (Bernand et al. 1991)
RMA	Language Resource Management Agency
RMCA	Royal Museum for Central Africa (Musée Royal de l'Afrique Centrale)
RTP-Afrika	Rede de Televisao Portuguesa
RUD	Revue Universitaire de Djibouti
RUEPUS	Research Unit for Experimental Phonology of the University of Stellenbosch

SAJAL	*South African Journal of African Languages*
SAL	*Studies in African Linguistics*
SELAF	Société d'Études Linguistiques et Anthropologiques de France
SIDA	Swedish International Development Cooperation Agency
SIL	Summer Institute of Linguistics
SNU	Seoul National University
SOAS	School of Oriental and African Studies
SSHRC	Social Sciences and Humanities Research Council
ST	standard theory
SUNY	State University of New York
SUSO	Unified Orthography of a Unified Language called Shona
SyWAL	Symposium on West African Languages
TAM	tense, aspect, and mood
TFAI	Territoire Français des Afars et des Issas
TGG	transformational-generative grammar
TUFS	Tokyo University of Foreign Studies
TWB	Translators without Borders
UBS	United Bible Societies
UCB	University of California, Berkeley
UCLA	University of California, Los Angeles
UD	University of Djibouti
UDC	Union pour le Développement Culturel
UNICEF	United Nations Children's Fund
UQAM	Université du Québec à Montréal
USC	University of Southern California
VAD	Vereinigung der Afrikawissenschaften in Deutschand
WALS/SLAO	West African Linguistic Society/Société Linguistique de l'Afrique Occidentale
WOCAL	World Congress of African Linguistics

1 The History of African Linguistics

H. Ekkehard Wolff

1.1 African Linguistics

'African linguistics' can be defined by a specific triple research focus, i.e. 'African languages', 'language in Africa', and 'the applied dimension of linguistics in Africa'. It deals primarily with the scientific study of 'African languages'. These are in turn defined, in a purely technical sense for non-ambiguous reference, as languages that are assumed to belong to one of the four language phyla, which were originally postulated by Joseph H. Greenberg in his seminal classification *The Languages of Africa* (1963), namely NIGER-CONGO, AFROASIATIC, NILO-SAHARAN, KHOISAN. Secondly, African linguistics focuses on the role, status, functions, and use of both indigenous and imported languages in African cultures and societies, past, present, and future, and deals with the ideology-laden views and attitudes on 'language in Africa', as seen both from outside and from within Africa. To these two fundamentally different yet related perspectives, we can add a third and 'applied' focus that links up with the 'language in Africa' perspective. This would be the application of robust sociolinguistic research for purposes of societal transformation, socio-cultural modernization, and economic development in the independent African countries as, most of them, postcolonial polities. These three research foci lie at the core of a well-defined autonomous academic discipline that we have come to refer to under the label 'African linguistics'. For a more detailed treatment of these research foci, the reader is directed to *The Cambridge Handbook of African Linguistics* (Wolff 2019). The present book is a complementary volume to the *Handbook*, the latter containing but short historical sketches ('Part I: Short Regional Histories of African Linguistics'). Here in this volume, the same authors provide additional and more detailed information and references on the asymmetrical and relatively short global history of African linguistics as it emerged and grew in the various world regions.

With its first focus on 'African languages', African linguistics deals primarily with the more than 2,000 languages, conveniently grouped in language phyla and families, that are indigenous to Africa and which amount to almost one-third of all living languages on our planet. African linguistics, as it emerged first in predominantly German-speaking academia at the turn of the twentieth century in Europe, sees itself as a separate and autonomous academic discipline. In this tradition, it does not represent merely a geographically focused sub-field of modern general linguistics, despite the fact that it owes much of its theoretical and methodological foundations to it and, vice versa, contributes challenging insights from the analysis of African language data. Since its early days of traditional Eurocentric and rather narrow positivist and taxonomic approaches based on nineteenth- and early twentieth-century Northern scholarship, African linguistics maintains a strong focus on the four Greenbergian major language phyla, namely NIGER-CONGO, AFROASIATIC, NILO-SAHARAN, and KHOISAN. Fifty and more years after Greenberg (1963), his classification still serves as a convenient reference system for lack of a more recent and generally accepted modified classification, despite considerable criticism questioning whether some of his language families are valid genealogical units.[1] Traditional narrow African linguistics tended not to take into account foreign languages brought to Africa in historical times, at least not beyond their source value as donors of lexical and possibly grammatical loans. Likewise, it tended to marginalize concern with language varieties that emerged within Africa in historical times, when they were considered as based on non-African languages, like so-called Arabic-based Nubi, Dutch-based Afrikaans, English-based Krio, etc. In the course of time, the received and rather narrow view on languages in Africa has considerably broadened, particularly under the more recent 'language as resource' (Ruíz 1984) paradigm. This goes to the extent of even questioning the theoretical notion of 'named language' in the light of recent studies of multilingual language use, particularly in urban environments and among the African youth, which is currently discussed under labels such as 'fluidity' and '(trans)languaging', linking up with a more recent and originally non-linguistic notion of 'super-diversity'. This ties up with a position long discussed and popular, not only in African intellectual circles, that the plethora of distinct African languages parallel to the notions of 'tribes' or 'ethnic groups' (cf. the often invoked 'Tower of Babel' metaphor), reflects only the Eurocentric distortion and 'invention' by missionaries and colonialists for the purposes of effective divide-and-rule policy under the colonial project. This leads to the second research focus of African linguistics, namely the role of language in African cultures and societies, including a critical review of the received notion of 'languages' as discrete entities and/or ideology-laden artefactual reifications and constructs (see the relevant chapters in Wolff 2019).

---

[1] This is particularly true for Khoisan and with regard to a number of isolates within the other three language phyla. For a nutshell account of current African languages classification, see Wolff (2016:300–304); for details see the respective chapters in 'Part II: Comparative and Descriptive African Linguistics' of *The Cambridge Handbook of African Linguistics* (Wolff 2019).

With its second and complementary focus on 'language in Africa', African linguistics deals with dimensions of language use, whether in monolingual or multilingual patterns of practice in different contexts such as rural versus urban, generational and/or educational, as much as in the various cultures and societies in Africa, both past and present. Allowing widely for interdisciplinary perspectives, African linguistics here views languages as embedded in the ever-changing cultures and societies of Africa, with which they entertain dynamic interaction. This places African linguistics (aka Africanistics) at the interface of linguistics and philology on the one hand, and various cultural and social sciences on the other, including comprehensive and fashionable 'global studies' and 'development studies'; see the respective chapters in 'Part III: African Languages in Cultures and Societies' of *The Cambridge Handbook of African Linguistics* (Wolff 2019). Modern African linguistics embraces the 'language as resource' paradigm and views languages in relation to the aspirations of their speakers in their quest to master their daily routines and to meet the social, cultural, political, and economic challenges of sustainable, including mental, decolonization and development (see Wolff 2016).

Third, and in terms of applied science linking up with the research focus on 'language in Africa', African linguistics addresses, among others, issues of language policy and planning, in particular with regard to language(s) in education used as either medium or subject of instruction. It is concerned, occasionally joining hands with human rights activism, with language 'empowerment' through 'intellectualization' as part of comprehensive language planning. Embracing a focus on economic development, it also deals with the potential of human language technology and digital humanities in Africa. For details see the respective chapters in 'Part IV: Applied Perspectives in African Linguistics' of *The Cambridge Handbook of African Linguistics* (Wolff 2019).

1.2 Learning from History

Why read and write about the history of African linguistics? At least four answers immediately come to mind.

First, it is an essential part of human nature and curiosity to wish to explore where 'we' come from, where and how it all started, and what the directions of development were over periods in the past. 'We' would here encompass two groups of human beings, namely humankind in general, and scholars of African linguistics in particular. Humankind ultimately originated from Africa, and who among us modern language-using representatives of *homo sapiens sapiens* wouldn't like to know since when our human ancestors spoke, and possibly what languages they spoke, and at what time in history. We would also like to know whether there was only one language from the start (*monogenesis* hypothesis) – if there ever was a point in time in the very distant past, most likely in Africa, that would qualify to be considered the 'start' of human language capacity in general. Or, are there better arguments for proposing a *polygenesis* hypothesis, according to which different human languages, i.e. including the beginnings of language families as we know them today, emerged independently several times in different regions of the then inhabited globe?

Second, as Africanists, we might wish to know more specifically: How old are the language phyla of Niger-Congo and Afroasiatic, how old are established linguistic units within Nilo-Saharan and within what used to be called Khoisan? And, if we were willing to assume that linguistically reconstructed proto-languages were spoken at all at one period in the past: What would be the estimated periods when such proto-languages would have been spoken, i.e. what is the actual time depth of language families as we accept them today? Unfortunately, the history of African linguistics as such will not be able to provide conclusive answers to these far-reaching questions, nor will historical research within African linguistics. The chronological horizon of sound historical linguistic research remains limited because of constraints of methodology, and only a few professional linguists venture to allow their linguistic comparisons to reach into assumed time depths beyond 10,000 years from the present.

Third, as members of both an interested public and, in particular, also the group of researchers in African linguistics worldwide, whether living and working in Africa or elsewhere, we would definitely take a strong and possibly professional interest in the history of the study of African languages. We would be interested to learn where, when, why, and how scholars became interested in the languages, conserved in written documents or still spoken, in Africa, and whether they first met with African languages in Africa or elsewhere. What was the nature and development of concepts and ideas that dominated scientific and intellectual debate at their time, and which have, as the case may be, promoted or impaired progress of knowledge in this field of science? What was the impact of ideologies virulent at certain periods in the past (e.g. abolitionist, humanitarian, missionary, racist, Social Darwinist, colonialist)? Where and when did certain schools of thought in different (sometimes more or less 'national') contexts emerge? What were the prevailing degrees of distance or nearness to political agendas of governments (like the notorious apartheid in South Africa, but also membership in global postcolonial political pressure groups such as the Commonwealth of Nations, the Organisation Internationale de la Francophonie, Países Africanos de Língua Oficial Portuguesa alongside the Comunidade dos Países de Língua Portuguesa)?

Fourth, and again particularly for researchers in the field, knowing about the history of one's discipline helps to conceive and develop untrodden paths of investigation and research. These are guided by disregarding directions of research of the past that have proven to be less fertile or unyielding, and by identifying certain models and theories as just currently fashionable rather

than opening up promising directions for sustainable progress in the acquisition of new knowledge. Insights into the history of one's science may help
to unearth forgotten or overlooked scientific treasures, so to speak, that lay
covered under temporarily more fashionable approaches but now are likely to
stimulate renewed interest in old questions. Possibly and in an applied dimension, this could make feasible the exploitation of such knowledge for the benefit of those who, in the past, had been excluded from the benefits of a science.
This, namely, is particularly true for African linguistics. Having begun as an
applied 'colonial science' in the heyday of European colonialism in Africa,
African linguistics clearly was conceived to serve the needs and interests of
the colonialists, not necessarily those of the colonised populations. Even or
particularly in education, the choice of the language(s) of instruction in schools
was governed by concerns about the efficiency of colonial administration and
economic exploitation rather than by pedagogical concerns about efficiency
of learning. Concern with African languages under the colonial regime was
basically 'extractive', just like all other colonial activities.[2] African languages
were considered tools for the benefit of the colonizers that could be used to
run colonial exploitation more smoothly, if and to the extent that they were
considered useful at all. More or less reluctantly, it was accepted that there
was a spin-off benefit for those Africans who became literate and 'educated',
the colonialists fearing or foreseeing that this would foster anti-colonial attitudes, which indeed later fed into movements for political independence. In the
British colonial model of 'indirect rule', but also in some of the German colonies before 1918, competencies in African languages on the part of colonial
officers were deemed useful, if only in order not to be drastically 'cheated' by
'native interpreters', who might have had an agenda of their own. The colonial
administrations were dependent on the emergence of a small class of moder-
ately literate and bilingual 'natives', who would function as the link between
the ruling expatriate minority, who governed 'their' territories through the
hegemonic official language of the colonial motherland, and the largely illit-
erate masses of the potential labour force, who were almost exclusively using
indigenous vernaculars. Mainly Protestant Christian missions became instrumental in creating and establishing low-level literacy not only in the colonial
language of power, for instance, English, but also in some of the indigenous

---

[2] Likewise, even the purely academic interest in African languages was largely, and remains until
this day, extractive by serving, not least, the needs of expatriate researchers for empirical linguistic data on which to base their academic degree work and publications at home that would
further their academic career. Concerns about how to 'reintroduce' their research results and
potential applications, for instance, in terms of assisting in the development of orthographies,
providing readable grammars and dictionaries for speakers and practitioners, creating literacy
and post-literacy materials, etc. in African languages, are usually of secondary concern, if any at
all. There are, however, notable exceptions.

African languages that had a wider regional distribution, like, for instance, Swahili. In the franco- and lusophone colonial territories, however, not even this was an option. Here, African languages were given no room to serve any practical purpose.

Much later, that is towards the end of the twentieth century, a conceptual paradigmatic shift occurred from mainly 'extractive' to 'inclusive', i.e. following an agenda of increasing international cooperation and mutual benefit. To no little extent, its theoretical basis is the more recent notion of 'language as resource' (see Ruíz 1984). This new perspective, which is still shared by only a minority section of Africanists and members of the wider African studies community, values African languages as highly instrumental. This is true particularly in the educational systems, at the same time presupposing and fostering the 'intellectualization' of indigenous languages that were and are not used regularly in higher domains.[3] It is also argued to be true, as part of the on-going and necessary processes of societal and economic transformation in the African post-colonies, for sociocultural modernization and economic development, which would be effected by the re-empowerment of indigenous languages that had been disempowered under the colonial project (see Wolff 2016). In this context, applied African (socio-)linguistics is challenged to take on an important role as a lead science in the twenty-first century.

The individual chapters of this volume provide, in some detail, answers to questions that relate to the history of the research foci 'African languages' and 'language in Africa' in terms of academic theoretical interests. A book on the history of African linguistics would, however, be incomplete without confronting the inherent applied dimension of African linguistics of the past, i.e. under a prevalent colonial ideological and political regime, with the current and future challenges of finally 'decolonizing the mind'. In an activist perspective, this amounts to the attempt to put African languages on a par, by so-called intellectualization, with hitherto more prestigious languages of European provenance, and Arabic, in terms of both local and global relevance. Targeted are both practical applications and political discourse, which both need underpinning by scientific arguments and a critical stance on underlying ideologies. In other words, it is about 'bringing African linguistics home' to Africa by changing the primary motivation from 'extractive' to 'inclusive' in terms of a global knowledge society that would, on equal terms, embrace both former colonial powers and the independent postcolonial states.

---

[3] By intellectualization, we refer to processes of language planning and language standardization that lead to the use of indigenous (or any disempowered) languages for all educational matters from kindergarten to university, i.e. vernacular languages that have hitherto not been used in these domains, and thereby make them educational competitors to international standard languages (Wolff 2016:326).

This volume would appear to be the first to attempt to do justice to African linguistics research that happens outside the long-established and globally best centres in the North, i.e. Western Europe, whose origins tend to coincide with former colonial activities in Africa (see Chapter 2, this volume), and later the United States of America (see Chapter 11, this volume). Rather, it also turns the focus on Central and Eastern European as well as the Nordic countries, which are devoid of a history of colonial activities in Africa (Chapter 3, this volume). It also addresses more or less late-comers to African language studies in Asia and Australia (Chapter 12, this volume), and – as a world region of rather specific interest in its own linguistic African heritage – in Latin America (also in Chapter 11). In particular, however, Africa herself is moved into historical focus. A number of chapters deal in some detail with the continent's major regions and the persisting linguistic impact of colonial history. African linguistics in North Africa is dealt with in Chapter 4, North-Eastern Africa in Chapter 5. Southern Africa is the topic of Chapter 6, and Eastern Africa in Chapter 7. Official English-speaking West Africa is treated in Chapter 8, official French-speaking West and Central Africa in Chapter 9, and official Portuguese- and Spanish-speaking Africa in Chapter 10. Leading figures, past and present, affiliated to the West European and US centres tend to be more widely known in informed circles, not least because of the wider distribution and availability of their research, which finds support among international publishing houses. This is, as a rule, not the case outside their own narrow circles for currently active researchers in the lesser-known locations, between Trondheim (Norway) and Beijing (China), or Rabat (Morocco) and Melbourne (Australia). This volume sets out to fill such gaps of knowledge about past and current activities in various parts of the world. Authors are concerned with established institutions as much as with individual researchers who, in various historical periods, may occasionally have shouldered the burden of almost single-handedly representing their home country in the concert of nations. For quite some time during the nineteenth and twentieth centuries, this was the case with Leo Simon Reinisch (1832–1919) in Austria, or with Hiob Ludolf (Leutholf, 1624–1704), Carl Meinhof (1857–1944), and Diedrich Westermann (1875–1956) in Germany, not forgetting the outstanding Danish expert on the language(s) of the Tuareg, Karl-G. Prasse (b. 1929), to name a very few. On the other hand, some countries and universities pride themselves on a comparatively long and successful history of African linguistics. Some institutions may even claim the distinction of having established this field as an autonomous discipline besides Oriental and Semitic studies at the turn of the twentieth century, such as the universities in Berlin, Leipzig, and Hamburg in Germany, and the University of Vienna in Austria. Others take particular pride in having provided dominant theoretical models, like some stemming from North American general linguistics after the Second World War, or for having kept practical applications in mind most of the time, as could be said in respect of important contributions by British scholarship.

In the chapters of this book, insiders whose origins lie or who work in the various corners of the globe, sketch out historical developments, leading institutions and personalities, research priorities and underlying political motivations, and enumerate relevant contributions by individual researchers in their world region. The authors are active researchers in various sub-fields of African linguistics rather than professional historians or archivists. The absence of established traditions of research into the history of African linguistics in the various parts of the world, together with the fact that relevant archives may remain unidentified and/or inaccessible, makes the task a challenging one. Sometime, it is very difficult to do much more than scratch at the surface of things. The editor and authors, however, remain convinced that the pioneering efforts in this volume unearth valuable facts, which will stimulate other researchers to delve more deeply into the subject and, eventually, provide more comprehensive and critical studies on the emergence and development of African linguistics on this planet.

1.3   Origins: Language Learning for Practical Purposes

Bluntly speaking, African linguistics – theoretically and methodologically located at the interface of the humanities and social sciences – owes its present existence as a globally accepted scientific discipline to the darker days of Christian missionary activities in, and colonial exploitation of, African territories by European powers before and after the turn of the twentieth century.

There were notable precolonial forerunners, who were seeking information and knowledge about African peoples and their cultures, some also taking interest in their languages. They were travellers and explorers driven mainly by individual intellectual curiosity, or they were sponsored by members of the European aristocracy, who developed some kind of whimsical interest in 'exotic' artefacts in order to boast with treasures to be displayed in their fashionable 'cabinets of curiosity' (see Chapters 2 and 3, this volume). To some extent, too, the language philosophy of Wilhelm von Humboldt (1767–1835), to be discussed later in terms of linguistic relativism and determinism, provided an additional impetus to study 'exotic' languages in the attempt to uncover how they linguistically encode their culture cum language-specific 'world-views' (see Wolff 1975, 1981).[4]

---

[4] This line of research eventually became dominated by American linguistics, mainly with data from Amerindian languages, and is linked above all to the names of the Pomerania-born immigrant to the USA Edward Sapir (1884–1939) and Benjamin Lee Whorf (1897–1941), laying the foundations of modern ethnolinguistics.

A majority of the forerunners, however, had a missionary agenda, appropriating and using indigenous languages in overseas territories for the proselytization of 'pagans' and aiming at the civilization of 'savages'. An additional motivation came from attempts to make contact with potential representatives of a mysterious Christian empire linked to the mythical Prester John, which was identified by some, among others, with the early Christian empires in Ethiopia (Aksum, Lalibela). This is true for the earliest known texts, vocabularies, and grammatical descriptions of African languages, such as for liturgical Geez in Ethiopia, first published in 1513 by the monk Johan Potken from Cologne (*Psalterium et Canticum Canticorum et Alia Cantica Biblica Aethiopice et Syllabarium Seu de Legendi Ratione*) to be later followed by the first European grammar of Geez (*Chaldea seu Aethiopicae Linguae Institutiones*) by Fr. Marianus Victorius (1518–1572), published in Rome in 1552 (see Chapter 5, this volume). A vocabulary of a precursor to present-day Akan in Ghana was contained in a Portuguese source of 1523. Often mentioned is Fr. Giacinto Bruciotto di Vetralla's early grammar of Kongo (*Regulae quaedam pro difficillimi Congensium idiomatic faciliori captu ad grammaticae normam redactae*), published in Rome in 1659. Much less known is the first grammar of Kimbundu (*Arte da lingua de Angola oeferecida a Virgem Senhora N. do Rosario, Mãy & Senhora dos mesmos Pretos*), written by the priest Pedro Dias of the Company of Jesus in Brazil (published in Lisbon in 1697). Early Catechisms were published in Kongo (1624), Kimbundu (1643), and Gɛ (1658). A Coptic-Arabic dictionary was translated into Latin by the Jesuit Athanasius Kirchner in 1636; the Franciscan Arcangelo Carradori collected more than 7,000 words of the Nubian language (1638). A first Kongo vocabulary is mentioned for the year 1652, likely produced by the Belgian Capucin Georges de Gheel (Joris van Gheel). In the early and mid-seventeenth century, continuous focused work on Geez and Amharic began, and we must here mention the name of Hiob Leutholf alias Job Ludolf from Erfurt in Germany.[5]

Clearly, and soon after the first travellers and explorers came back with their first-hand information, the initial interest in African languages, long before the scientific, i.e. linguistic study of African languages entered the agenda, was a practical one. Language learning for missionaries and colonial agents and the military was deemed useful and so was basic literacy for the speakers of these languages, both for proselytization and the creation of a low-skilled labour force, and for recruiting members of low military rank into the services of the colonial powers (see Chapter 2, this volume). This applied and largely extractive dimension of African language studies prevails in part up to the present day; Chapter 12 (this volume) describes this as also being at the bottom of the more recent initiatives to

---

[5] For the early period, see Wolff 1981, Connell and Akinlabi (Chapter 8, this volume), and Petter (Chapter 11, this volume).

establish and expand research on African languages in Asia (see Chapter 12, this volume).

In the end, the extractive strategy of dealing with African languages for missionary and colonial benefits contributed to the development of both African languages and African linguistics. The outright extractive strategy, however, had an 'exclusive' corollary. The idea of colonial administrations, later to be continued by postcolonial African elites, was to keep the masses of the African populations down by no or only limited access to quality education, which was managed through a European language in mostly private institutions of learning. The characteristic feature of this type of education was exclusiveness via highly restricted access, often accompanied by fee paying, and thus accessible only for a chosen few. Exclusiveness was the explicit idea also behind 'Bantu Education' under the apartheid regime in South Africa (see Chapter 6, this volume). Until this day, it remains the implicit motivation for 'elite closure' and the 'status maintenance syndrome', which characterizes the postcolonial African elites who are currently in power. Hence, the strongly expressed will and strategy by many stakeholders to establish and maintain bottle-neck systems which would allow children only restricted access to education based on English (or any other foreign, usually ex-colonial, language). European languages-based education is implicitly assumed to be superior to education through African languages, which in turn are implicitly assumed to be inferior.

Therefore, it is widely assumed generally that there is little intrinsic value in African languages, particularly not in African countries and in the eyes of their governments and influential intellectual circles. Outside Africa and outside rarefied academic circles, public and political interest in African languages, and thus in the research-based teaching and learning of these languages, was and still is widely based on their perceived instrumental value primarily for non-African powers and economies in order to more easily access African commodities in negotiations with postcolonial African governments. As long as training colonial officers and postcolonial diplomats or agents of North–South development or military cooperation (from American Peace Corps in the 1960s to Development Aid Programmes run by present-day parastatal organizations or NGOs) in African lingua francas served the purpose, African linguistics found support 'at home'. This included capacity building, initially by expatriates, for Africans to teach (and to do research into) their own languages. This was supported by grants and scholarships for this purpose, or by employing African students of any subject matter as 'teaching assistants' for lessons in their mother tongues or in the lingua francas they happened to speak well (see also Chapters 3 and 11, this volume). Again, this strategy was mainly extractive. The prime interest was not, for a very long time, to strategically invest in a generation of emerging African scholars for purely academic purposes, even though this eventually came about, with African professors and lecturers finally taking over from expatriate professors and lecturers at universities in Africa (see the relevant chapters for African regions in this volume). The main interest was to create advantages for expatriates in dealing with African 'counterparts'. To achieve this, educational institutions in the colonial motherlands were equipped and supported by governments to offer African language courses for practical purposes. This was also true for the oldest of such institutions in Germany, namely the university in Berlin (later named after Wilhelm von Humboldt) and the pre-university Colonial Institute in Hamburg, with Carl Meinhof taking up the first professorial positions in both institutions. In Africa, on the other hand, teaching African languages, in particular to non-native speakers as a second language, was hardly ever considered an educational necessity.

In Africa, 'educated' (which practically always must be construed to mean educated in Western ways in Western-type educational institutions) opinion leaders often dismiss the academic need to study African languages *in situ* as obviously irrelevant, particularly at institutions of higher education like universities. One has often heard it said in African political and intellectual circles: 'Why study African languages – we speak them already?!' Again, and as widely also elsewhere, the value of African languages studies is reduced to the instrumental value of acquiring a practical command of a given language, for whatever purpose. Most people do not expect studying African languages to serve any possible other purpose, including purely scientific ones.

There are many university departments across Africa that offer degree programmes and deal with the linguistics of African languages, usually restricted to the major so-called national languages or those of the immediate catchment area. As a rule, however, African universities pay little if any attention to the practical teaching of African languages, be it for mother tongue speakers or non-speakers of particular languages – with a few notable exceptions. Outside Africa, programmes, for instance, for ESL (English as a Second Language) or DaF (*Deutsch als Fremdsprache* – German as a Foreign Language), not to forget the teaching of Mandarin to foreigners in the mushrooming Confucius Institutes, not least across Africa, are academic routine at universities. Very much to the contrary, in Africa very few institutionalized programmes exist at local universities that target the teaching of non-native speakers in the major African languages. It is also as surprising as it is deplorable that there is little interest, if any, in establishing a culture of translation into African languages. Both measures, i.e. professionally teaching African languages as second/additional/foreign languages and massive translation into African languages, would at the same time boost the desirable intellectualization of the target languages. As has been widely propagated by members of the African linguistics scientific community, such intellectualization would re-empower African languages by putting them on an equal footing with global languages and thus provide a necessary intellectual and educational foundation for sociocultural modernization and economic development (see Wolff 2016).

1.4   The Colonial Legacy: Disempowerment of Local Languages and Hegemonic Dominance of Foreign Languages

Under the colonial regimes as much as after independence, and parallel to the falsely assumed minimal political and economic potential of African languages for nation building and development, the former colonial and present global languages became structurally deeply entrenched in the educational systems in Africa. Their purported supremacy and status from colonial times as official language of the postcolonial state, either alone or combined with one or two so-called national and co-official languages, is never questioned nor jeopardized. Thus, the instrumental value of African languages, and with it the inherent applied dimension of African linguistics, for formal education beyond the lower primary grades (and mostly in former British colonies only) tends to be neutralized under a regime of subtractive bilingualism in favour of English. As a rule, African mother tongue languages are phased out as soon as possible after early alphabetization and literacy in lower primary, to be replaced by English as medium of instruction. In other words, African languages, where they are used in lower primary, continue to be stigmatized as a 'necessary evil', something undesired but an important stepping-stone to the acquisition of English. In former French and Portuguese colonial territories, African languages are usually disallowed completely in formal education, even at the lowest levels. The narrow and purely instrumental focus on language instruction in selected African languages, limited as it is to the years of lower primary education in so-called anglophone countries of Africa, excludes relevant debate on language issues, policies, and politics, for societal transformation and economic modernization and development in current mainstream development discourse.[6] As most enlightened and inspired scholars would claim, adequate educational systems for Africa must rest on high-quality mother tongue education, combined in a multilingual scheme involving both Arabic and the European official language (*mother tongue-based multilingual education*), through secondary and even tertiary education. Modern sociolinguists and educationists consider the lack of these issues in public debate an irresponsible oversight, accompanied by a tremendous waste of valuable resources, both material and immaterial, in the underperforming educational systems that are currently in place across most of Africa (see Kaschula & Wolff 2016 and Wolff 2016).

For most of the past and up till the present day, African linguistics has been primarily conceived by the general public as providing the basics of, or being restricted to, teaching African languages to mainly expatriates, who do so outside Africa and seek to profit from acquiring them for their

---

[6] Post-revolutionary Ethiopia is a notable exception by allowing mother tongue education through the whole primary cycle for a number of selected regional languages.

own purposes. In this practical extractive application for the benefit of largely expatriates, African linguistics – originally a colonial science – has survived decolonization and is still going strong or even expanding – even if persistently of little if any inclusive benefit to the speakers of these languages themselves. African linguistics, for a long time, was not meant to challenge the supremacy and hegemonic dominance of the official exoglossic languages in the African post-colonies; there was hardly any attempt to attribute status and prestige to African languages on an equal footing with the languages of European provenance, or Arabic, Swahili in Tanzania coming close to being a counterexample but always relied on English as co-official language. This situation prevailed in the colonial period and still persists today. In the words of the late South African educationist, sociolinguist, and language activist Neville Alexander (1936–2012), current language policies and politics across Africa foster a kind of 'neo-apartheid'. Under neo-apartheid conditions, speakers of the former colonial languages are allowed to maintain a privileged status, and the speakers of African languages remain somewhat exiled in their own countries, having limited if any access to the privileged high-quality foreign language education. The privileged foreign-language-based type of education would almost guarantee access to positions in government, administration, and the formal sector of the economy; however, it is usually restricted to private schools, access to which the persistently underprivileged masses cannot afford for their children. They are widely forced to make do with low(er)-quality education, which is dispensed by low(er)-quality teachers with low(er)-quality command of the eternally foreign medium of instruction, i.e. the language of the former colonial masters (see Kaschula & Wolff 2016 and Wolff 2016).

1.5   The Postcolonial Challenge: Intellectualization and Re-empowerment of Languages

The former colonial purpose of African language teaching and learning, particularly outside Africa, has largely survived unquestioned, even after the formal independence of the African colonial territories. It continues in language programmes offered by 'Centers of African studies' at American universities as well as through agencies employed by the US Army. The beginnings of institutions which pre-dated the establishment of academic institutions across Asia and are now devoted to more general 'foreign studies' also go back to teaching and learning African languages. The question to be asked is whether, in the twenty-first century and 50 years after official decolonization in Africa and formal independence of sovereign African states, alternative benefits of the applied dimension of African language study can be sought, whether for practical or scientific purposes, i.e. besides the (post-)colonial extractive approach. The idea would be that Africans, who are the speakers and owners, so to speak, of these languages, should themselves profit in terms of accelerating their way out of 'underdevelopment' towards societal transformation, cultural modernization, and economic progress. Sociolinguists and educationists, turned language activists, have long suggested that any serious drive to overcome mass poverty and underdevelopment presupposes mother tongue-based quality education for the masses. Indeed, worldwide applied sociolinguistic and educationist research indicates that mother tongue-based multilingual education is the most effective strategy for the Global South, particularly for Africa. The effects would be seen on both the local level at home and on the global level. At home, young Africans graduating from high schools and universities would do so thoroughly well educated, having profited from education in a fully familiar language from beginning to end, opening their way into all kinds of challenging careers. Currently, education through mainly foreign media of instruction in Africa is underperforming: it does not create the necessary number of sufficiently trained school-leavers because formal education through a poorly mastered foreign language medium must remain deficient and non-competitive. On the other hand, on the global level and in terms of professional and academic quality, graduates from mother tongue-based multilingual education would in all likelihood be highly competitive with peers elsewhere on this planet, who all tend to benefit from mother tongue education through all educational cycles. School-leavers under the current foreign-language-based educational systems in Africa tend to remain non-competitive, unable to facilitate Africa's access to modern knowledge-based global societies.

The question of adequate language policies for education in Africa, even though the answer is obvious to experts in applied (socio-)linguistics and education, still fuels heated debates among some sections of Africa's intellectuals and politicians today. These debates are stimulated by countless studies and publications from applied (African) sociolinguistics. The issue is not only whether African languages should play any role at all in national communication and education, but whether their role in education should reach minimally into secondary or, ideally, into the tertiary cycle. By taking important contributions from sociolinguistic research by both African and non-African researchers seriously, the history of African linguistics teaches us how to harvest the potential resourcefulness of indigenous languages. By running inclusive rather than exclusive strategies in language policies, both for national communication in general and education in particular, the *local* value lies in improving the living conditions of speakers. Language policies need to respond to the fact that the vast majority of Africans, and particularly those in sub-Saharan Africa, perform their daily routines by communicating almost exclusively through African languages, often using more than one or two simultaneously, and possibly also accessing non-African languages, at least occasionally. They do so to such an extent that recent sociolinguistics speak of 'translanguaging' and linguistic 'fluidity', rather than 'code-switching' between discrete 'languages', in the sense of modern European standard languages. Only an – admittedly growing – largely urban minority would appear to rely exclusively on global languages like English, French, and Portuguese.[7] Further and widely deplored, the underperforming educational systems currently in place in most parts of Africa alienate school-leavers from their immediate social and cultural environment, in which English, French, or Portuguese have little currency outside the classroom and the school premises. Current poor schooling tends to provide little achievement in terms of the targeted competencies in the ex-colonial languages and thereby creates masses of class-repeaters and dropouts, adding little if anything in terms of producing, for example, better farmers and gardeners, cattle herders, small-scale merchants, and artisans for whom primary education is final. The implicit assumption appears to be that all students enrolled in primary school will continue schooling in the secondary cycle, which would be run through a foreign language medium anyway. This simply is not the case; for many if not most children in school, primary education is final. African learners would be much better off if their formal education was grounded in the persistent use of the mother tongue or a well-mastered lingua franca medium of instruction, as routinely happens with great success in all so-called developed societies and economies. Counter to generally held fears, this in no way diminishes the value of 'the window to the world' that was purportedly opened for Africans when the languages of European provenance were introduced and established as the official medium for national communication and education. Members of African elites feel very strongly about this. They fear, wrongly so for lack of accepting competent advice from African (socio-)linguistics, that the instrumental value of European languages for *global* communication is interfered with negatively by the continued use of African languages for *local* communication. This fear, however, has no substance in the context of the almost natural multilingualism of many, if not most, Africans even at home, not only in urban agglomerations but also in the more rural areas. There is no reason why access to the global languages of the former colonial masters must necessarily be paid for by the rejection if not annihilation of the local African languages. On the contrary, experts are convinced that sound grounding in the mother tongue through its constant use as medium of instruction is conducive

---

[7] There is considerable uncertainty about the functional value of the former colonial languages in Africa as lingua francas, i.e. for those speakers who use English, French, and Portuguese, for instance, as more or less regular means for inter-ethnic communication. Figures range from considerably below 20 per cent (for French) to up to 70 per cent (for Portuguese). Quoting higher or lower numbers may depend on one's own position and agenda in the debate regarding official mono- or multilingualism and endo- or exoglossic strategies for language policies. Usually, the figures available contain no indication as to the degree of language competency, nor on how linguistic competencies were tested and evaluated, and whether speakers use the exoglossic language only (to the exclusion of African languages) or as part of multilingual repertoires (including one or several African languages).

to learning other languages as subjects, including that of the former colonial master, during the school career. Interestingly and from a theoretical point of view, this long-discussed and highly ideologized issue remains independent of the actual communicative performances of multilingual individuals. Modern sociolinguistics describes this with more recently coined terms like linguistic 'fluidity', speaking of '(trans)languaging' and 'linguistic repertoires' rather than discrete 'languages' in contact (cf. the received notions of 'code-mixing', 'code-switching', and 'code-meshing'). The new notions are based on new empirical data, which possibly render traditional definitions of language contact in terms of interference phenomena between discrete languages obsolete. Such recent research into the complexities of linguistic performance in Africa provides a body blow for proponents of the ideological position that bedevils and forbids code-switching in class as being detrimental to learning, since it 'contaminates' the 'purity' of the language of instruction of European provenance (or Arabic, for that matter). Clearly, modern pedagogy favours using already pre-existing multilingual competencies in class to enhance mutual comprehension and better learning results through translanguaging across the linguistic repertoires shared by learners and teachers, disregarding the traditional pedagogical fetish that relates to highly ideological notions of purity of language with regard to mother tongue or other tongue.

1.6   The Uphill Battle: Fears Concerning Official Usage of African Languages

A likewise unfounded fear by governmental authorities concerns purportedly outrageous costs for providing textbooks and teacher training for hundreds of local languages. To address this fear, one only needs to point out that, first of all, teacher training is a continuing governmental task independent of the medium of instruction; the actual running costs for providing training in both African languages and global languages amount to little extra. Further, given the widespread individual multilingualism in African mother tongues and lingua francas even among school-beginners, the number of African languages that are actually required to be used in schools is considerably reduced in contexts of territorial multilingualism as prevailing in the catchment areas of schools, in both rural and urban areas. A lingua franca medium of instruction, as long as the learners are competent speakers upon school entry, can render redundant the need to use a plethora of mother tongue languages from the school's catchment area as transitory or continuous medium of instruction. This fact, too, considerably reduces the overall extra costs of running mother tongue- or lingua franca-based multilingual education programmes.

As for providing literacy and educational materials in several, not to say many, different African languages, the idea that this involves exorbitant printing costs still lingers despite the fact that the ways of printing during the colonial period, when printers had to rely on the old letter-press technology which involved special phonetic symbols being manually carved out to the needs of individual languages (like the 'hooked' and 'dotted' letters in Standard Hausa and Yoruba orthography, for instance) have long since been replaced by digital technology. Indeed, the availability of desktop publishing and print-on-demand facilities means that publication costs for African language books and educational materials have been minimized; this includes all special fonts for phonetic symbols, as may be required by particular languages. Globally active publishing houses in the former colonial motherlands, however, are strongly opposed to what would be a serious threat to their postcolonial monopoly on, for instance, profitable textbook production for Africa. Since colonial times, an increasing number of African languages have been blessed with sufficient linguistic groundwork and standardization efforts in order to allow the emergence of community-based literacy and post-literacy activities, which could feed into the use of local languages for educational purposes throughout ideally all educational cycles. For those languages which have not, it should be at the top of the agenda of African universities and their African linguistics departments to provide such groundwork – for the benefit of scholarship and, not least, the speakers of these languages (see also Chapters 8 and 9, this volume).

Another misconception needs to be addressed. The 'numerical muscle' of languages is a Eurocentric obsession and cannot count in serious discourse on development and language planning worldwide. In the light of the fact that three-quarters of all languages on our planet, including Africa, count fewer than 100,000 speakers, the majority of them having fewer than 50,000 speakers, there is no excuse for not providing linguistic support for so-called minority communities of linguistic practice. Europeans, in particular, are used to believing that 'proper languages' must have several millions of speakers lest they be called negligible minority languages. They tend to overlook the fact that many national official languages, even in Europe, count far fewer than a million speakers. There are only some 11,000 speakers of Standard German in Luxembourg (despite there being more than 80 million across the border), and barely 40,000 speakers of Romansh in Switzerland. There are about 330,000 speakers of Icelandic in Iceland. One might wish to add the about 300,000 speakers of Maltese on Malta, and under 1 million speakers of Estonian in Estonia (Wolff 2016: 296). Why, therefore, should we disregard more than 2,000 languages with fewer than 1 million speakers in Africa as somewhat irrelevant minority languages, not worthy of any effort at intellectualization and empowerment for the purposes of national communication and education and thus treat them differently from other African or non-European languages? Do we implicitly accept that smaller groups of speakers of European languages are more relevant than any size groups of speakers of

African languages, and be found guilty of racial discrimination? A vision for the recognition of universal linguistic human rights would foresee a world in which every human being possesses the right and possibility to read and write in their own language, and others, for whatever purpose they please. If we were to take an arbitrary threshold of a minimum of only 1 million mother tongue speakers to make investment in language planning and standardization 'feasible' in political and economic terms, this would amount to depriving 96 per cent of the world's population, meaning also 96 per cent of Africans, of their linguistic rights. Applied African linguistics offers the appropriate strategies to avoid this by accepting multilingualism as a societal 'given', and by designing and implementing adequate mother tongue-based multilingual policies for each individual country and society within. As can be underpinned by available worldwide research, such policies and strategies in no way interfere with the acquisition and use of global languages, which open the desired 'window to the world' for hitherto deprived and underprivileged people in the Global South, including Africa. On the contrary, research results suggest that solid foundations in the mother tongue facilitate learning of additional languages, whether endoglossic or exoglossic (see Kaschula & Wolff 2016). This, to conclude, is one way of having one's cake and eating it, too.

1.7   Conclusion

Studying the history of African linguistics has a high potential for increasing knowledge about Africa, her languages, the role of language in society, language ideologies and attitudes, and the relationship between the North and the Global South. In particular,

1. it offers the chance of discovering new and promising lines of innovative research particularly into hitherto under-researched fields, in both theoretical and applied practical dimensions;
2. it broadens our intellectual and academic horizon with regard to the ever-increasing global spread of African linguistics since its inception as an autonomous discipline in German-speaking European academia at the turn of the twentieth century;
3. it illuminates the similarly increasing depth of scientific analysis of African languages with regard to their phonetics, phonology, syntax and semantics, not to forget their pragmatic dimension, which is deeply embedded in the local cultures of their speakers;
4. it underlines the cross-fertilization effects on neighbouring sciences, in particular general and theoretical linguistics;
5. it further helps to unearth its inherently rich transdisciplinary interface, since colonial times, with neighbouring social, cultural, and historical

sciences, which made it a forerunner of the much younger notion of broader African studies, in which African languages tend to play only a marginal, often plainly practical-instrumental, role;

6. and, most importantly, it provides the basis for understanding the manifold and changing ideological impact on science according to the prevailing Zeitgeist; for Africa in particular, how over the last five centuries since precolonial via colonial into postcolonial periods it shaped public prejudice and attitudes towards Africa, both within and outside the continent.

The history of African linguistics should make us humble. It illuminates changes in attitude towards African languages from more or less 'innocent' curiosity via extractive instrumental exploitation to unfavourable if not hostile attitudes even in the eyes and minds of African intellectuals and members of the postcolonial elite, which makes it an exclusive exercise for the benefit of non-African expatriates. It illustrates how the value of African languages and their potential role for a self-determined future of postcolonial Africa remains disputed, if not negated, in favour of neocolonial exclusive exoglossic monolingualism. This highly ideologized attitude uncritically copies Eurocentric preconceptions regarding monistic nation-state definitions along the lines of *one state – one people – one language*. It disregards the potential resourcefulness of pre-existing and often combined endo- and exoglossic multilingualism, which is corroborated by not only most findings of African sociolinguistic research on language policies, but also applied linguistic research in multilingual contexts, often also postcolonial, outside Africa. It thereby tends to perpetuate the ideological position of the supremacy of the North over the Global South.

Learning from the history of African linguistics, and strongly relying on the emerging sub-field of applied African sociolinguistics, means to recognize the current and prospective relevance of African languages for sustainable sociocultural modernization and economic development in Africa. It allows us to reflect on changing ideological positions and attitudes, and thus recognizes both the *local* and the *global* relevance of African languages. The history of African linguistics can teach us about potential strategies to overcome 'mass poverty' and economic 'underdevelopment', and attain sociocultural 'modernization'. Studying the linguistics of African languages over time provides essential yet often overlooked robust foundations for comprehensive and sustainable development planning, which needs to encompass not only social and economic planning but also linguistic planning. In fact, linguistic planning is social planning in the context of the almost ubiquitous multilingualism which is an essential characteristic of African societies, namely as territorial, institutional, sociocultural, and individual multilingualism.

Multilingualism, therefore, remains one of the core research issues in African linguistics. In its applied dimension, studies of multilingualism offer strategies for overcoming the underdevelopment of speaker communities of African languages. Such research has an impact on descriptive, comparative, and typological linguistics through studying language contact, and identifying areal convergence zones by *sprachbund* features, which potentially challenge received notions of genetic units of languages. The history of African linguistics amply testifies to the overall importance of studying multilingualism in its various manifestations, i.e. territorial, institutional, sociocultural, and individual. This is not surprising, given the fact that almost one-third of all living languages on this planet have their present distribution on African soil and that it is 'normal' for languages on our planet to have rather small numbers of speakers, that is, below 100,000, if not below 50,000. This, however, challenges the prevailing and hegemonic wisdom based on Eurocentric ideas about 'language' and language use in modern nation-states in the North, where there is little practice and experience of everyday natural multilingualism as it prevails over much of Africa. Increasing global migration whether for ecological, economic or security reasons, may before too long mean that the North will have to face similar problems and issues of multilingualism that are essential characteristics of much of the Global South. It is here where the South can teach the North, if the North is at all willing and able to be taught, and African linguistics will have a relevant role to play in such discourse.

2 Western Europe: African Linguistics and the Colonial Project

Roland Kießling

This chapter presents a historical overview of decisive periods in the study of African languages and linguistics as conducted by the former European colonial powers Britain, France, Germany, Netherlands, Belgium, as representing those countries in which Afrikanistik/African linguistics was 'invented' as an autonomous academic discipline and was, at the same time, linked to their respective colonial projects. Setting out from a concise account of the leading figures, their seminal publications and the national institutions involved, it traces the development of research priorities, their academic underpinnings and their political motivations, from the early exploration years up to the current stage of modern linguistics – with the ultimate goal of identifying regional 'schools' of African linguistics and their (dis)continuities.[1]

2.1 General Introduction

While recordings of word lists and idioms, and attempts at monographic descriptions of African languages based on the model of Latin grammar alongside translations of Christian-religious texts, authored by missionaries and explorers, reach back to the sixteenth century (Werner 1930; Cole 1971; Wolff 1981; Doneux 2003), the discipline termed *Afrikanistik*, i.e. African linguistics (Möhlig & Winter 1983), was established as late as in the nineteenth century in a number of European countries with a colonial past, more precisely Britain, France, Germany, Netherlands, and Belgium. Among the colonial powers of Western Europe, Portugal, Spain, and Italy paid considerably less attention, if any, to African languages. A special case is Austria, where the interest in African languages grew in academic interchange with neighbouring Germany but was devoid of a colonialist dimension, since Austria did not

---

[1] Sections 2.2 and 2.3 of this chapter roughly follow earlier synopses of the history of African-istics, as contained in Möhlig (2000), Doneux (2003), and Wolff (1981). Portions of section 2.4 relating to German Africanistics follow Wolff (2013, 2014). Note that African linguistics in Austria, despite being closely interlinked with academic developments in Germany both during the colonial period and later, will be treated for systematic reasons outside the colonial context in Chapter 3.

21

entertain colonies in Africa. In initimate intertwining with world history, its research targets and ideological orientations have been changing drastically over the past 200 years. So it makes sense to organize the present chapter according to decisive periods as follows: starting from the establishment of the discipline of Africanistics in the precolonial era in section 2.2, section 2.3 traces the establishment of research priorities, their academic underpinnings and their political motivations in the colonial period, which is roughly marked by two divergent concepts in colonial language policy, i.e. assimilation versus indirect rule. Section 2.4 unfolds the development and proliferation of Africanistic discourse in the postcolonial period, as enshrined in (national) histories of leading figures, their seminal publications, the (national) institutions involved, regular journals and academic conferences, up to the current stage informed by modern linguistics and characterized by convergence via advanced globalization in research agendas and densification of interdisciplinary networking, as fleshed out in section 2.5. Finally, section 2.6 draws a conclusion.

2.2   Precolonial Era

The precolonial study of African languages was mainly carried by humanitarian motives, i.e. the Christian mission, the abolishment of slavery, and the resocialization of liberated slaves. As a necessary precondition for an effective and sustainable dissemination of the gospel, basic Christian literature, i.e. the Bible and catechism, had to be translated into African languages. Before this task could be achieved, the languages, most of them unwritten, had to be analysed thoroughly for their lexical and grammatical structures and be 'reduced to writing'. Inevitably, the intense study of African languages also revealed first glimpses of the immense treasury of oral literatures (myths, fables, songs, proverbs, and riddles) enshrined in these languages. As a consequence, early pioneers in missionary service came up with not only remarkable monographic studies of individual African languages but also anthologies of oral literature.

Leading figures who shaped the outlines of the discipline at this early stage were Johann Ludwig Krapf (1810–1881), Heinrich Barth (1821–1865), Sigismund Wilhelm Koelle (1823–1902), Wilhelm Heinrich Immanuel Bleek (1827–1875), Johann Gottlieb Christaller (1827–1895), and Simon Leo Reinisch (1832–1919).

Krapf produced the first Swahili grammar (1850) plus dictionary (1882) and must be regarded as the founding father of modern Swahili studies (Vierke 2014). On his extended travels in large parts of the Western Sudan, Barth collected – beside ethnographic, historiographic, and geographic data – abundant language materials (1862–1866). Owing to his accurate methodological standards in data processing and presentation, these data still serve as the basis for modern linguistic research in Central Western Africa. Koelle compiled the

Polyglotta Africana (1854), a unique compendium of 300 words and sentences from more than 200 African languages which he had collected from liberated slaves in Freetown (Sierra Leone). This work also provides a preliminary attempt at grouping African languages on the basis of criteria of lexical and typological similarity. Bleek coined the term Bantu and must – by virtue of his comparative grammar of this African language family (1862, 1869) – be regarded as the founder of modern Bantuistics. Christaller was the first to recognize the crucial role of tone and ATR (advanced tongue root)-based vowel harmony ('euphony') in Twi and to systematically describe its lexical and grammatical functions in his Twi grammar (1875) and dictionary (1881), laying the foundation of the systematic study of tone in various other West African languages. Reinisch provided the first accurate descriptions of several North-East African languages, based on his extensive fieldwork in Sudan and Eritrea in 1875/1876 and 1879/1880, and must be viewed as the founder of Cushitic and Omotic studies (Mukarovsky 1983; Kießling 2008).

Since this early phase the study of African languages was regarded as part of Oriental studies. While today Africanistics has become established as a discipline in its own right, the traditional Orientalistic symbiosis still lingers on in institutional labels such as School of Oriental and African Studies (SOAS) in London, Institut National des Langues et Civilisations Orientales (INALCO) in Paris, and Deutsche Morgenländische Gesellschaft (DMG) in Germany.

2.3 Colonial Era

Following the 'Scramble for Africa' and its division among European colonial powers in the Berlin Conference of 1884–1885, new agendas and applied perspectives began to emerge for Africanistics. In order to warrant a neat and effective administration of their newly acquired colonies, it became necessary for some of the colonial powers to learn more about the African cultures and societies which had happened to end up in their respective domains. Thus, the ensuing boom in the study of African languages was due to new practical national interests, that is, to teach the basics of African languages for wider communication to new target groups such as colonial service cadets, administrators, and military officers, beside commercial people and missionaries. In order to meet these new requirements of colonial practice, new institutions were founded, such as the Seminar für Orientalische Sprachen (1888) with a sizeable Africa department at the Friedrich-Wilhelms-University (later Humboldt University) in Berlin and the Hamburgische Kolonialinstitut (1908) (later University of Hamburg) with a department for African linguistics as well.

The necessity for colonial powers to build an efficient administration in their respective colonies fuelled the interest in African languages to different degrees, though, depending on ideological underpinnings and divergent concepts of language policies spinning out in a spectrum between the poles of assimilation versus indirect rule. Roughly speaking, the policy of assimilation, as pursued by colonial powers such as Portugal, Spain, France, and Italy, versus the policy of indirect rule which was characteristic of Britain, the Netherlands, and Germany produced different effects with respect to the academic interest in African languages.

While the 'Romance' colonial practice was basically geared towards exporting language and culture to the colonies and assimilating the population, the 'Germanistic' colonial practice rather aimed at indirect control of local hierarchies. Under the former approach, indigenous languages had no practical importance but rather posed an obstacle to the project of 'civilization'. As a consequence, their exploration had no immediate point, apart from satisfying the esoteric pleasure of Orientalists. Therefore, the establishment of specialized chairs for African languages and linguistics was rather late in France, Italy, Portugal, and Spain, as compared to in England and Germany whose indirect rule principle made it necessary for many administrators to acquire full fluency in local vehicular languages so as to avoid the risk of manipulation by translators and acquire respect from local chiefs. This was a powerful incentive to produce a considerable amount of early lexical compilations and practical grammars.

In England, the beginnings of Africanistics go back to Alice Werner (1859–1935). In 1896 she started giving private lessons in African languages until they were officially integrated into the teaching programme of King's College in London in 1901, and from 1917 onward into the newly founded School of Oriental and African Studies. With a focus on Bantu languages, she authored a number of general introductions to African languages (1915) and African oral literature (1933), in particular Swahili poetry (1917). With the establishment of a separate department of African languages and cultures at SOAS in 1937 under Ida C. Ward (1880–1949) as its first director, the new discipline of Africanistics visibly emerged from the Orientalistic shadow. Ward specialized in West African languages and advanced descriptive standards by a high degree of phonetic and tonetic accuracy (1933). In cooperation with Diedrich Westermann, she published a ground-breaking handbook of phonetics which adopted IPA (International Phonetic Alphabet) conventions (Westermann & Ward 1933). This line of descriptive groundwork based on solid empirical foundations was continued by Archibald Norman Tucker (1904–1980), who specialized in East African languages in nearly 40 years of research at SOAS (Arnott & Mann 1974). Apart from a series of monographic studies on various Non-Bantu languages (Dholuo, Maasai, Murle, Shilluk, Zande), he contributed to the classification debate by coining concepts such as Paranilotic, Fringe Cushitic, and Erythraic in various compendia and handbooks co-authored by Margaret Bryan (e.g. 1966). Independent from SOAS, the International African Institute (IAI) had already been founded in 1926 under a private initiative with French and German participation, a manifestation of an early joint European venture in Africanistics which had considerable impact on European research into African languages and cultures by its initiatives and publications such as the *Handbook of African Languages* and the language map of Africa (Dalby 1977).

Owing to different priorities in the colonial project in France and its orientation towards the assimilation of Africans under the concept of francophony, the institutionalization of the study of African languages only began in postcolonial times. Before that, research into African languages developed within the confines of Orientalistic circles, most prominently represented by Marcel Cohen (1884–1974), or remained the hobby horse of individuals such as Maurice Delafosse (1870–1926) and Henri Labouret (1878–1959). Delafosse and Labouret, originally engaged in colonial administration and language instruction for colonial staff, acquired international recognition for their studies of West African languages. Cohen, starting out from (Ethio-)Semitic and founder of the Groupe Linguistique d'Études Chamito-Sémitiques, became an important pioneer of comparative Afroasiatic. In East Africa, the missionary Charles Sacleux (1856–1943) laid the foundation for Swahili lexicography with his monumental *Dictionnaire Swahili–Français* (1939/41) which still remains unexcelled today.

Throughout the colonial period, the development of Africanistics was dominated by two (partly antagonistic) leading figures, Carl Meinhof (1857–1944) and Diedrich Westermann (1875–1956). While neither of them ever fleshed out a coherent theory of the emerging discipline of Africanistics, they succeeded in establishing it as a discipline in its own right, beyond the service role as a colonial language school, with three proper academic agendas: (a) description and analysis of African language structures under strictly linguistic perspectives, (b) language classification and historical reconstruction, (c) understanding of the conceptual organization of thought which underlies African poetry, art, religion, and law, as is manifest in language.

An important achievement in the struggle for descriptive adequacy under (a) was the insight to develop analytical categories from the language data itself, without imposing European preconceptions of grammar onto African language structures. Among many monographs conducted in this spirit, probably the most impressive ones are Westermann's monumental studies on Ewe (1905–1906, 1907, 1930, 1954) which were, in contrast to most of Meinhof's work, based on his own fieldwork, forming the basis of modern standardized Ewe in Togo and representing an invaluable source until today.

With respect to classification (b), it was Meinhof (1899, 1906) who laid the foundation of modern Bantuistics. In the transfer of Neogrammarian inductive methods of historical linguistics, he succeeded in reconstructing the sound system, grammatical structure, and vocabulary of Proto-Bantu, the hypothetic predecessor of modern Bantu languages. Westermann, working on the considerably more heterogeneous zone of the Sudan, recognized the important relations of several 'Sudanic' languages to Bantu (1911, 1927), pre-shaping Greenberg's concept of the overarching phylum of Niger-Congo.

Aim (c) indexes the holistic approach of a culturally integrated African linguistics to which most European Africanists still subscribe today and which continues in the spirit of Wilhelm von Humboldt's philosophy of language. According to this view, language forms the central key to the understanding of all other aspects of human cultures. This conviction is most prominent in Westermann's work, which includes anthropological, sociolinguistic, and ethnolinguistic aspects, e.g. in his classical study on African customs of taboo and their impact on language (1940).

Two important implications of this axiom characterize originally colonialism-driven Africanistics up to the present. First, the study of African languages cannot be isolated from the study of their social, cultural, and historical backgrounds. This is reflected in most European traditions of Africanistics, e.g. in the strong French school of African oral literatures (see section 2.4.2), in a series of special interdisciplinary research programmes in Germany since the 1970s with considerable Africanistic participation, and in curricula such as 'African languages in context' (Hamburg), 'Swahili studies' (Bayreuth), and 'Language and cultural transfer in Africa' (Cologne), which integrate the study of African languages into their wider social, cultural, and historical contexts. Second, the study of African societies and cultures, in reverse perspective, cannot dispense with a central consideration of African languages on all levels, in order to avoid an inadequate reduction of focus on discourse conducted in the ex-colonial languages and the resulting imposition of elitarian filters on African communication (Wolff 2013:38-41). Unfortunately, this aspect has not gained the wider acceptance it deserves, especially in modern contexts of development discourse and the fight for sustainable African futures (Wolff 2016).

As a consequence of the holistic Humboldtian approach to language, the scope of Africanistics was expanded to include issues such as language planning (standardization) and language policy, e.g. the analysis of the social functions and dynamics of African languages of wider communication. Also new fields of practical application emerged from the claim to contribute to educational projects of colonial cultural policy such as 'Eingeborenenlenkung', that is, the guidance of Africans in the process of cultural transformation, which was under way in the colonies as a confrontation of African and European civilizations to an unprecedented extent. Ideologically, this claim was based on a mixture of humanitarian ideals including a neo-romantic valorization of African cultures on the one side and on Eurocentristic beliefs in superiority on the other side, merging in a paternalistic attitude which saw the European masters, by virtue of their superior position, responsible for counterbalancing the exploitation of the colonies with efforts at preserving and developing African languages (Westermann 1941).

Colonial involvement and racist conceptions about the inferiority of African cultures and languages which characterized the spirit of the time produced a weird and aberrant academic construct, the 'Hamitic' theory (Pugach 2012:101–114), propagated and linguistically elaborated by Meinhof 1912, but soon discarded and tacitly ignored due to its inacceptable racist preassumptions and highly inadequate methodological underpinnings. Much more successful was Meinhof's launching of the first Africanistic journal in 1910, published as *Zeitschrift für Kolonialsprachen* (up to volume 9), renamed *Zeitschrift für Eingeborenensprachen* in 1919, and continuing, since 1952, as *Afrika und Übersee* (volume 36).

After the Second World War, the leading role in Africanistics was taken over by SOAS in London, which assembled experts for nearly all major linguistic groupings in Africa. The consistent application of structuralist methods to the description of African languages led to more adequate analyses, allowing for comparability across various language groups. This descriptive quantum leap, alongside a pragmatic approach, inspired new classifications and referential groupings which, like Guthrie's referential classification of Bantu languages (1948a), are still used today.

2.4 Postcolonial Era in Countries with a Colonial Project Involving African Languages

With the independence of African states since the beginning of the 1960s, most colonial powers retained economic links to their former colonies, under new agendas of cooperative partnership in development, and increased and expanded their institutions for the study of African languages. While the macro-regional focus, inherited from colonial times, could be seen to linger on in national Africanistic academics in France, Italy, Belgium, and the United Kingdom, Africanistic research in Germany followed a less constrained regional course of orientation from the beginning, because of colonial disruption after the First World War.

In general, the development of Africanistics in the postcolonial era is characterized by massive adoption of modern linguistic methods, the proliferation of interdisciplinary discourses, and intensification of institutionalized international cooperation. Methodological refinement, empirical rigour, and analytical accuracy advanced the quality in descriptive studies of many African languages and produced major discoveries which fed into the general debate on language typology, crucially expanding the image of the human language capacity in the domains of phonology (e.g. clicks, ATR vowel harmony), tonology (concepts such as downdrift, downstep, floating tones), and the development of analytical models to accommodate these phenomena (autoseg-mentalism), systems of nominal categorization, morphologicization of infor-mation structure (e.g. Somali). Empiricism and pragmatism together with the Humboldtian undercurrent prevented most Africanists from delving deeply into decontextualized experiments; rather, the holistic view on African lan-guages within their cultural and historical settings allowed for a growing range of cross-disciplinary ramifications in respect of sociology, philology, cultural anthropology, and genetics – targeted at the study of multilingualism, lan-guage ecology, language standardization, oral and written literatures, and the reconstruction of the genetic relationship of languages, historical contacts, and migration history.

In terms of genetic classification, the model elaborated by American Joseph H. Greenberg (1963) remains the most influential and sustainable model and still serves as a comprehensive referential framework for scholars today. Based on the pragmatic principle of shared similarities in combination with mass comparison, Greenberg assigns all African languages to four overarching phyla, i.e. Niger-Kordofanian (today Niger-Congo), Afroasiatic, Nilo-Saharan, Khoisan, and pro-vided detailed dendrograms of genetic sub-branching for each of them, with three most salient innovations: (a) the internal subdivision of Afroasiatic into five par-allel branches, i.e. Old Egyptian, Berber, Semitic, Cushitic, and Chadic, manifest-ing the dismissal of the previously postulated genetic unity of so-called Hamitic languages and the full incorporation of Chadic; (b) the recognition of a Nilo-Saharan phylum whose genetic unity, in spite of large-scale efforts at reconstruc-tion, still remains controversial today; (c) the relegation of the Bantu family which had played such a prominent role in all previous debates about classification to a single sub-branch low down in the genealogical tree of Niger-Congo.[2]

Fuelled by the progress in broad-scale synchronic description of under-researched African language groups, Greenberg's classification was put to the test by low-level reconstructions based on the rigid application of the historical-comparative method, including in Benue-Congo (de Wolf 1971), Bantu (Meeussen 1967, 1969; Guthrie 1967–1971), Plateau (Gerhardt 1983), Kwa (Stewart 1973), Gur (Manessy 1969, 1975, 1979), Cushitic (Heine 1978; Sasse 1979), and Nilotic (Rottland 1982; Voßen 1982). Eventually, these efforts led to a higher resolution and refinement in sub-branching as well as to reshuf-fling of subgroupings or branches at lower levels within the phyla, while the study of language contact phenomena such as pidginization and creolization processes increasingly came to raise fundamental doubts about the adequacy of the unilinear genealogical model (Bennett & Sterk 1977; Möhlig 1981).

---

[2] For a very detailed account of the history of the classification of African languages up to the 1970s, see Köhler (1975).

2.4.1   England

In England, Africanist expertise was concentrated in London, at the School of Oriental and African Studies (SOAS), which advanced to the most influential center of Africanistics after the Second World War. Following the recommendations of the Scarbrough report, the African department of SOAS was considerably expanded by recruitment of staff from the ranks of colonial officials as well as former missionaries, such as David W. Arnott (West African languages), Frederick W. Parsons (Hausa), Lyndon P. Harries (Swahili), Ewan C. Rowlands (West African languages), Gordon Innes (West African languages), and Edward Ullendorff (Ethiopian studies) (Brown 2016:128, 131–132). This expansion was part of SOAS's ambition to strive for large-scale academic coverage of world cultures, reaching beyond the satisfaction of the demands of government and the practical needs of colonial administration. Still, with respect to Africa, coverage at the level of linguistic groupings remained largely restricted to the British territories because of diffculties in finding qualified staff. According to the general organization at SOAS, Africanistics followed the 'cultural studies' model; that is linguistics was balanced with anthropology, history, law, and the social sciences. The postwar expansion of SOAS was followed by a period of contraction after the 1980s, which hit the African department particularly hard as it led to a reduction of staff to nearly half the number of the 1950s (Brown 2016:213–214).

An outstanding figure was Malcolm Guthrie (1903–1972), chair for Bantu languages from 1951 to 1970. In adapting structuralist methods of general linguistics, he insisted on a strict separation of synchrony and diachrony, which is reflected in his 'two-stage method' of reconstructing Proto-Bantu by (a) the establishment of Common Bantu via an inventory of comparative series based on regular synchronic sound correspondences, and (b) the historical interpretation of the Common Bantu series in relation to their geographical distribution in his referential classification, as condensed in his monumental four-volume work *Comparative Bantu* (1967–1971). While Guthrie's appearance clearly marks the end of the Meinhof era in Bantuistics, the impact of his methods and hypotheses remains limited, except for his concept of Common Bantu and his practical referential classification of Bantu languages (1948). His comparative series form the basis of the Bantu Lexical Reconstructions (BLR) website housed at Tervuren (Bastin et al. 2002). Guthrie's rigidity in handling phonological and morphological detail contrasts sharply with the neglect of semantic concepts such as polysemy and the resultant failure to integrate semantic change in his diachronic interpretation, as is reflected in a large number of semantically 'osculant series' (Möhlig 1976; Bostoen 2002) – which became re-aggregated and subsumed in BLR.

Wilfred Howell Whiteley (1924–1972), successor of Guthrie to the chair for Bantu languages, established and consolidated an East African focus

(Carter 1973; Guthrie 1973). Beside monographs on Bantu languages such as Yao, Gusii, and Kamba, he also laid the foundation for Southern Cushitic studies by his seminal work on Iraqw. More important still is his broader contribution to the emergent field of Swahili studies, which includes dialect surveys of Zanzibar and Pemba and descriptions of Swahili varieties such as Mtang'ata, Mvita, and Chimiini. As secretary of the East African Swahili Committee and editor of the journal *Swahili*, he was an active editor and translator of Swahili literature and critical observer of the process of Swahili standardization and its impact on the linguistic landscape in East Africa, thus pioneering in East African sociolinguistics. His devotion to Swahili cumulates in his study of Swahili transitivity (1968) and his monograph on the rise of Swahili as a national language (1969).

Another outstanding researcher was South Africa-born Archibald N. Tucker, who became an expert with regard to the non-Arabic languages in the Sudan. He had obtained an MA from the University of Cape Town in 1926, and a PhD from the University of London in 1929 (DLitt in 1949). In 1932 he became Reader at SOAS.

One of the most remarkable figures was Roy Clive Abraham (1890–1963), a linguistic all-rounder with major achievements both in the study of West African languages such as Tiv, Idoma, Yoruba, and Hausa and in North-East African languages such as Amharic and Somali.

A strong tradition of Hausa studies, initiated by George Percy Bargery, has been continued by F. W. Parsons, among whose important contributions was the analysis of Hausa verbs in terms of a 'grade system'; Philip J. Jaggar (see especially his comprehensive grammar, 2001); and Graham Furniss (1995), an expert on Hausa literature, both oral and written.

Another strong tradition of Cushitic studies was founded by Bogumił Witalis 'Goosh' Andrzejewski (1922–1994) and his ground-breaking work on fundamental categories of Somali and Oromo grammar (Orwin 1996; Samatar 1998) and on Somali poetry (Andrzejewksi & Lewis 1964). He also played 'a crucial role in the development of a phonetically accurate and convenient Roman script for Somali' (Brown 2016:309), which formed the basis of the official orthography finally adopted in 1972 and accompanied the further development of Somali by analyses of its terminological expansion and its role in the media. Cushitic studies were continued in David Appleyard's work on Agaw (2006), Martin Orwin's work on Somali (1995), Richard Hayward's contributions to Eastern Cushitic (e.g. 1984) and his seminal work on Omotic (1990).

Mention must be made of the strong SOAS input to the Handbook of African Language series embarked upon by the IAI in the 1940s, which was factually a SOAS publication series. These volumes remained authoritative reference works, which were later challenged by the new classification of African languages by Joseph H. Greenberg (1963).

· SOAS has been editing an impressive range of journals, including *African Language Studies* (1960–1980), *African Languages and Cultures* (1988–1997), and, the oldest one, the *Bulletin of the School of Oriental and African Studies* (since 1917), which continues in print today. Another important journal published in the UK was the *Journal of African Languages* (1962–1972).

2.4.2 France

While individual African languages of wider communication had been taught in France since colonial times for largely practical purposes, i.e. language instruction for colonial administrators and missionaries, a broader institutionalization of African linguistics – besides a long-standing Orientalistic tradition of Berberology (Basset 1952) – only started in the 1960s with the establishment of a series of specialized chairs at the École Nationale de Langues Orientales Vivantes (ENLOV), today's Institut National des Langues et Civilisations Orientales (INALCO). This included senior academic positions for Bantu (Pierre Alexandre), Ful (Pierre Francis Lacroix), Hausa (Claude Gouffé), Mande (Maurice Houis, Gérard Dumestre) – beside two chairs for African linguistics: one was installed in Paris (Serge Sauvageot), the other in Aix-en-Provence (Gabriel Manessy), later transferred to Nice (Thomas & Behaghel 1980). While Sauvageot's functionalist studies of Wolof (1965) and Sereer formed the basis for a broader study of the Atlantic languages, Manessy (1923–1996) became most influential in two respects. Building on accurate descriptive groundwork on several Gur languages, conducted by himself (1961) and André Prost (1964), his comparative analyses (1969, 1975, 1979) truly make him the founding father of Gur studies. Furthermore, he initiated the study of language contact and multilingualism in Africa (Nicolaï 2001) – which lives on in the sociolinguistic orientation at Nice with particular foci on the creolization history of Songhay (Robert Nicolaï) and Cameroonian Pidgin English and Camfranglais (Carol de Féral).

Claude Gouffé, first professor of Hausa at INALCO (1960–1994), established a strong school of Chadicists including scholars such as Bernard Caron, Daniel Barreteau, Jean-Pierre Caprile, Henry Tourneux, Véronique de Colombel, as well as Sergio Baldi and Herrmann Jungraithmayr – which eventually crystallized as an informal Groupe d'Études Tchadiques parallel to the pre-existing network of the International Colloquium on the Chadic Language Family initiated by Paul Newman (then Leiden) and Ekkehard Wolff (then Hamburg) in the mid-1970s. Both have been replaced since 2001 by the network of the Biennial International Colloquium on the Chadic Languages (BICCL), jointly created and organized by Henry Tourneux (Centre National de la Recherche Scientifique, CNRS), Dymitr Ibriszimow (Bayreuth), and Ekkehard Wolff

(Leipzig), whose location alternates between CNRS at Villejuif in France and universities in Germany (Leipzig and Bayreuth, from 2019 on Hamburg and Vienna, Austria).

With respect to research, Africanistics became institutionalized in largely independent research units ('laboratoires') such as Langues et Civilisations à Tradition Orale (LACITO) and Langage, Langues et Cultures d'Afrique (LLACAN), both affiliated to the CNRS. With respect to teaching, besides INALCO, leading institutions today are the Africa department of the École Pratique des Hautes Études (EPHE) and École des Hautes Études en Sciences Sociales (EHESS).

Principally devoted to the interdisciplinary study of languages and cultures of oral tradition worldwide, LACITO has, since its foundation in 1976, substantially contributed to the description, documentation, and analysis of under-documented languages of Africa. This is particularly due to the prominent participation of leading Africanists such as Jacqueline Thomas and Luc Bouquiaux. Apart from their studies of Aka and Birom, both authored a three-volume compendium for documenting and analysing unwritten languages (Bouquiaux & Thomas 1976), which has widely been used as a guideline for linguistic fieldwork in Africa, long before guides to linguistic fieldwork came to flourish. LACITO's focus on orality also fostered a tradition of the study of oral literatures and the verbal arts, as manifest in the works of Christiane Seydou (Seydou & Paulme 1972), Jean Derive (1975), Denise Paulme (1976), Geneviève Calame-Griaule (1987), and Veronika Görög-Karady (1992).

Since 1994, major Africanist expertise has been concentrated at LLACAN, which manifests, by virtue of its thematic organization along the axes of grammatical analysis, typology, reconstruction, and literature and linguistic practices, a truly Humboldtian perspective with an impressive coverage of language families such as Atlantic (Stéphane Robert, Guillaume Segerer, Konstantin Pozdniakov), Benue-Congo (Michel Lafon, Mark van de Velde), Berber (Mena Lafkioui), Semitic (Martine Vanhove, Marie-Claude Simeone-Senelle), Chadic (Bernard Caron, Henri Tourneux), Cushitic and Omotic (Yvonne Treis), Central and Eastern Sudanic (Pascal Boyeldieu, Pierre Nougayrol), Egyptian (Elsa Oréal), Nubian and Meroitic (Claude Rilly), Kordofanian (Nicolas Quint), Mande (Valentin Vydrin, Dmitry Idiatov), Adamawa (Raymond Boyd), and Ubangi (Paulette Roulon-Doko).

Beside Paris and Nice, the research centre Laboratoire Dynamique Du Langage, established in 1994 in Lyon, has also developed a strong focus on African linguistics with Denis Creissels and Jean-Marie Hombert, specializing in the exploration of language diversity from a typological and a historical perspective with a multidisciplinary approach integrating linguistic reconstruction with molecular and cultural anthropology.

Many protagonists of French Africanistics, including Claude Gouffée, Maurice Houis, and Serge Sauvageot, were influenced by André Martinet's functionalist school (Doneux 2003:216–221) as well as by general linguists contributing to Africanistics, such as Claude Hagège who stands out with his descriptive studies of West African languages such as Mbum (1970).

Following the first major outlet for French Africanist research, i.e. the *Bulletin de SELAF* (Société d'Études Linguistiques et Anthropologiques de France, formerly Société d'Etudes des Langues de l'Afrique), installed in 1967 under the directorship of Jacqueline Thomas and Luc Bouquiaux (Thomas & Behaghel 1980:79; Doneux 2003:226), several specialized Africanist journals have emerged since the 1970s. Established by Geneviève Calame-Griaule in 1976 and dedicated to the study of the verbal art of oral cultures worldwide, the *Cahiers de Littérature Orale* (*CLO*) has a strong focus on African oral literature. The journal *Mandenkan*, founded in 1981, specializes in the study of Mande linguistics. Since 2015, LLACAN has edited a general Africanist journal *Linguistique & Langues Africaines*. The institute ORSTOM (Office de la Recherche Scientifique et Technique d'Outre-Mer), mainly focused on development policy, publishes on Africanistic topics as well, e.g. language atlases, language profiles of African countries, and issues regarding the sociology of language.

2.4.3   Germany

In Germany, five new departments in Bayreuth, Cologne, Frankfurt, Mayence, and Munich[3] were installed in addition to the already existing ones in Berlin, Leipzig, and Hamburg, resulting from the postwar East–West divide and federal particularism. While there is considerable curricular overlap, for example with regard to teaching big vehicular African languages such as Swahili, Hausa, Bambara, Somali, and Amharic, all departments have developed complementary research profiles, the larger ones with an internal differentiation according to macro-regions and language families. In Hamburg, the Bantu tradition founded by Carl Meinhof was continued by Emmi Kähler-Meyer and Ludwig Gerhardt. August Klingenheben introduced research foci on Hausa, Fulfulde, Amharic, and Vai. His work on Fulfulde and Hausa were important both in themselves but also for broader issues in African linguistics, such as demolishing the linguistic foundations of Meinhof's postulated 'Hamitic' language family by his insightful reanalysis of the Fulfulde noun class system, and laying the foundations of Hausa diachronic linguistics (part of which was later referred to as 'Klingenheben's Law'). Johannes Lukas continued

---

[3] Since the retirement of Klaus Schubert, Munich has disappeared from the German map of Africanistics again.

Westermann's integrated cultural linguistics with a focus on West African languages, especially Kanuri and Hausa, elaborated and extended by Ekkehard Wolff (Gerhardt et al. 2008). In Cologne, Bernd Heine continued Nilotic and Khoisan studies, established by Oswin Köhler, while Wilhelm Möhlig specialized in Bantu. Today, the Nilotic focus is continued by both Anne Storch and Gerrit Dimmendaal. In Bayreuth, there is a split of Niger-Congo (Carl Hoffmann, Gudrun Miehe, Gabriele Sommer) versus Non-Niger-Congo (Franz Rottland, Dymitr Ibriszimow). In Leipzig, an Afroasiatic strand that started with Berber (Hans Stumme), shifted to Amharic and Hausa (August Klingenheben), and expanded, after breaks, to Chadic (Ekkehard Wolff), still continues today (Ari Awagana). Besides a general orientation towards various languages of wider communication such as Bambara and Shona during the period of the German Democratic Republic (GDR) (1945–1989) (Siegmund Brauner),a strong emphasis on Swahili (Karsten Legère, Irmtraud Herms, Rose Marie Beck) also continues today. In Berlin, Westermann's broad orientation towards Niger-Congo became focalized on Swahili (Ernst Dammann, Hildegard Höftmann), Kwa, and Gur (Brigitte Reineke), before it shifted to South and East African Bantu and Khoisan (Tom Güldemann). Departments with a single chair in Africanistics have experienced more dramatic shifts in terms of regional research foci, depending on individuals, e.g. from Chadic (Herrmann Jungraithmayr) to Nilotic and Khoisan (Rainer Voßen), to Bantu and Berber (Axel Fleisch) in Frankfurt and from Saharan (Norbert Cyffer) to Mande and Adamawa (Raimund Kastenholz) in Mayence. The larger departments in Bayreuth, Cologne, and Hamburg have additional chairs with dedicated specializations, regional or disciplinary or both. In Cologne, Africanistics is supplemented by cultural anthropology and goes together with Egyptology in curricular symbiosis. Africanistics in Hamburg harbours a chair for Ethiopian studies with a prominent philological orientation. Bayreuth has installed a chair for literatures in African languages, which adds – after the cancellation of Rainer Arnold's post in Leipzig – a unique note to the concert of African literature studies in European ex-colonial languages as established elsewhere in Germany, such as in Leipzig, Berlin, and Mayence (Veit-Wild 2003).

The added value of complementary linguistic specializations in the bigger Africanistic departments is clearly manifest in regionally defined cooperative projects, for example on the Kenyan language and dialect atlas (Heine & Möhlig 1980–1986) in Cologne and on the Chadic-Benue Congo contact zone (Wolff & Gerhardt 1977) in Hamburg. In other cases, convergent research specializations entailed inter-departmental national cooperations such as the one between Berlin and Bayreuth on the Gur languages.

Intensified contacts and cooperation with African socialist countries such as Tanzania and Ethiopia during the GDR period in the former East Germany entailed a strong involvement in practical issues of applied Africanistics at the departments in Berlin (van der Heyden 1999) and Leipzig (Brahm & Jones 2009:313; Geider 2009) with a focus on politically relevant languages of wider communication, development of didactically adequate teaching materials, and terminological elaboration.

The institutional affiliation of Africanistics within the faculties was different in East versus West Germany. The departments of the former Eastern part (Berlin, Leipzig), were organized according to a macro-regional and multi-disciplinary principle still maintained today, i.e. Africanistics was grouped with other disciplines such as history, politology. and economics for the common focus on Africa. In West Germany, Africanistics often constitutes a separate department, integrated into larger units at a higher level, e.g. alongside non-European philologies in the Asien-Afrika-Institute (Hamburg) or with linguistics and cultural studies (Frankfurt).[4]

2.4.4   *The Netherlands*

In the Netherlands, the Vakgroep Afrikaanse Taalkunde at the University of Leiden established itself in the 1960s as a very active centre of Africanistics with a core group of eminent scholars such as Jan Voorhoeve, Achille Émile Meeussen, John Stewart, Tom Cook, Thilo Schadeberg, Paul Newman, Paul Polydor de Wolf, Maarten Mous, and Felix Ameka.

Jan Voorhoeve (1923–1983) crucially shaped the evolving field of tonology by his seminal contributions to the analysis and representation of tone in the Cameroonian languages of the Grassfields Bantu group, especially Bangangte-Bamileke (1971) and Saramaccan, a Surinamese Creole language (Elias 1983). He was founding member of the Benue-Congo Working Group and organized the international Grassfields Bantu project 'in which linguists from the Netherlands, France, the United States, and Cameroon jointly tried to tackle the Bantu Border enigma' (Elias 1983:107), i.e. put Greenberg's hypothesis of the external classification of Bantu within Benue-Congo on sound methodological footings, and to explore the dividing line between Bantu and non-Bantu languages, which entailed meticulous descriptive groundwork on the little-known languages of the fragmentation belt in the Nigerian-Cameroonian borderland, alongside accurate, low-level reconstruction, e.g. in the Mbam-Nkam group of Grassfields Bantu (Elias et al. 1984). Considerable weight had already been added to the Benue-Congo focus by Paul Polydor de Wolf's (1936–2003) dissertation on the noun class systems in Benue Congo (1971), which remains a milestone in comparative Benue-Congo.

In a wider Niger-Congo perspective, John Stewart's (1926–2006) work became extremely important for both synchronic and diachronic phonology.

---

[4] For a detailed overview, see Wolff (2014a:47–48).

He introduced the concept of vowel harmony of the ATR type (1967) and its autosegmental representation. In tonology, he was very influential 'in arguing for a unified approach to (intonational) downdrift or automatic downstep and (phonologized) downstep' (Mous 2007:72). Starting from Akan and other Kwa languages, he headed towards systematic reconstruction of Volta-Congo and ultimately Niger-Congo, based on the strict application of the comparative method. The Niger-Congo focus was continued by Thilo C. Schadeberg's work on Kordofanian (1981) and on Bantu, with both comparative (2002) and descriptive studies, e.g. on Umbundu (1990) and Swahili (1992), and Stefan Elders' work on Mundang (2000) and Kulango (2008).

Besides the long-established Niger-Congo tradition, an Afroasiatic track of research has been growing strong recently, with a focus on Berberology (Kossmann 1999) on the one hand and on Cushitic and Omotic on the other hand, as is visible in Maarten Mous's work on Iraqw (1993) and Mbugu/Ma'a (2003), Harry Stroomer's work on Oromo (1987), and a series of descriptive PhD studies, e.g. on Maale, Benchnon, Dime, and Sheko.

Since 1970, Leiden has hosted the annual Colloquium on African Languages and Linguistics (CALL), the major venue for European Africanists/Linguists. It is also the home of the ongoing *Journal of African Languages and Linguistics (JALL)*, founded in 1979 by Paul Newman along with Thilo Schadeberg in a spirit of 'theoretically-informed empiricism' (Newman 2010:3).

2.4.5   Belgium

While African languages had been taught at the universities of Ghent and Leuven since the 1920s, the main centre of Belgian Africanistics evolved at the Royal Museum of Central Africa (Musée Royal de l'Afrique Centrale, RMCA) in Tervuren. Its linguistic department, founded in 1950 by Achille Émile Meeussen (1912–1978), became one of the leading centres in Bantuistics. Meeussen produced highly accurate grammatical analyses, e.g. of Rundi, and developed the important concept of tonal downstep, based on his findings in Lega. He also founded the Lolemi programme focused on comparative Bantu, which enabled him to provide condensed revisions of Meinhof's Bantu reconstructions (1967, 1969). Continued by Jean Doneux, André Coupez, Claire Gregoire, and Yvonne Bastin, this formed the starting point of the website of Bantu Lexical Reconstructions (BLR), hosted at Tervuren, which presents a continuously growing database with several thousand entries that have been proposed as Proto-Bantu reconstructions (Bastin et al. 2002). Today's leading Belgian Africanists are Koen Bostoen (Ghent) and Jacky Maniacky (Tervuren). Since 1962, Tervuren has edited the journal *Africana Linguistica* with a special focus on Bantu.

2.5 The Postcolonial Era in Countries with a Colonial Project Not Involving African Languages

2.5.1 Italy

Apart from specializations on Swahili language and literature (Elena Bertoncini, Flavia Aiello) and Hausa (Sergio Baldi, Gian Claudio Batic), Italian Africanistics in its main centres at the universities of Naples (L'Orientale), Rome (Sapienzà), and Torino is mainly focused on the regional languages of the Horn of Africa, as a result of its colonial ambitions in Eritrea, Ethiopia, and Somalia. Deeply rooted in the philological Orientalistic tradition, which is manifest in the focus of the main journals *Rivista di Studi Orientali* (Rome) and *Rassegna di Studi Etiopici* (Rome, Naples), most Italian Africanist scholars are still either Semiticists or Somalists. Their major contributions pertain to the study of Ethiosemitic, Cushitic, and Omotic (Lamberti 2003). The early extension of the scholarly scope beyond Ethiosemitic towards Cushitic, Omotic, and Nilo-Saharan, such as in the œuvre of Carlo Conti Rossini, Enrico Cerulli, and Martino Mario Moreno, was probably spurred by divide et impera motives in the colonialistic struggle with the Amharas who had subjugated most of these groups. The Somali and Cushitic tradition continues with leading Italian Africanists such as Giorgio Banti, Mauro Tosco, Marcello Lamberti, Annarita Puglielli, and Graziano Savà.

2.5.2 Portugal and Spain

As countries with the longest colonial engagement in Africa, both Portugal and Spain are still at the beginning of establishing Africanistics as a discipline. Owing to a rigorous politics of assimilation and elitarian education in Portuguese in PALOP (Países Africanos de Língua Oficial Portuguesa) countries, Portugal was rather occupied with disseminating Portuguese in its colonies via instruments such as CPLP (Comunidade dos Países de Língua Oficial Portuguesa), RTP-Afrika (Rede de Televisao Portuguesa), and the Instituto Camões (Bunk 2000) so that engagement with local African languages started only very late as compared to the other colonial powers. Major scientific contributions, until recently, were restricted to language policy issues in lusophone African countries, almost exclusively targetting the situation of Portuguese and largely ignoring African languages. One notable exception to this rule is the recent establishment of regular Swahili courses at Lisbon University. Interestingly, (lusophone) Angolan and Mozambican literatures are represented, while languages of Angola and Mozambique seem to be absent still. An Africanist association, based in the Colegio Mayor Nuestra Señora de África, at the University of Madrid, seems to be focused on African issues at large with no specific linguistic orientation.

2.6   Current Trends

The current situation of Africanistics in most former colonial powers is characterized by a wide proliferation in thematic scope with expanding ramifications into various disciplines such as linguistic typology, historical linguistics, cognitive linguistics, anthropology, sociology, politology, discourse studies, philology, and media sciences – the common denominator being the interest in how communication works in Africa.

Monographic language studies continue to form a priority. While considerable descriptive progress has indeed been made during the past 50 years, many African languages still remain uncharacterized or only poorly described. For historical reasons, these white spots on the map are unevenly distributed across Africa. While the languages in former British colonies are comparatively well investigated, large gaps in linguistic documentation remain in the former Portuguese colonies. Language endangerment and death (Brenzinger 1992, 2007), resulting from large-scale reorientation of linguistic minorities towards African languages of wider communication, upgrade the urgency of this descriptive task considerably, as is reflected in various projects on African languages in programmes of language documentation such as DoBeS (Dokumentation Bedrohter Sprachen) in Germany and ELDP (Endangered Languages Documentation Programme) in England.

The debate on classifying African languages continues. However, the focus has shifted from defining larger phylogenetic units in the Greenbergian sense to providing methodologically accurate reconstructions at lower levels, e.g. Khoe (Voßen 1997), Eastern Nilotic (Voßen 1982), Southern Nilotic (Rottland 1982), Chadic (Jungraithmayr & Ibriszimow 1994), West Mande (Kastenholz 1996), East Mande (Schreiber 2008), Eastern Grassfields (Elias, Leroy & Voorhoeve 1984 et al.), Eastern Cushitic (Heine 1978; Sasse 1979,), Central Cushitic (Appleyard 2006) and Southern Cushitic (Kießling & Mous 2003), and to the exploration of historical relations via distribution of linguistic features within more restricted areal confines (Wolff & Gerhardt 1977; Zima 2000; Dimmendaal 2001; Kießling et al. 2008) or across larger regions such as the Macro-Sudan belt (Güldemann 2008).

On the synchronic level, comprehensive descriptive coverage in areas such as North-Eastern Bantu allowed for the adoption of rigid dialectological principles and inspired the development of a new method, dialectometry (Guarisma & Möhlig 1986), for an accurate calculation of synchronic linguistic distance across dialect continua. Apart from fertilizing the discussion of low-level subclassification, its results serve increasingly important ends in Applied Africanistics, i.e. providing solutions to notoriously tricky issues in language standardization, e.g. in the delimitation of linguistic varieties subsumed for unification under the umbrella of a common standard.

Since independence, necessities of language planning, with respect to both corpus and status, established a thread of critical discourse on the standardization of African languages (Cyffer et al. 1991), African language policies in general (Reh & Heine 1982; Pasch 1994), and the practical implications of linguistic diversity management, especially in the educational sector (Ouane & Glanz 2010).

Postcolonial sociolinguistic realities and the challenges of linguistic diversity management in African educational systems, in particular, bring the issue of multilingualism vehemently to the fore, from the perspective of both its social functions (Manessy & Wald 1979; Calvet 1992; Juillard 1995; Miehe et al. 2007) and the phenomena it generates. Thus, inspired by Carol Myers-Scotton's work, code-switching practices (Parkin 1974; Haust 1995, Thomanek 1996) have come to be studied systematically, while their consolidation in emergent new codes in African megacities gains attention, for example in urban vehicular languages (Beck 2010) in general and in juvenile codes in particular (Kießling & Mous 2004; Nassenstein & Hollington 2015) such as Sheng, Indoubil / Yanké, Nouchi, Camfranglais, and *Lugha ya mitaani*. Furthermore, the study of African multilingualism also includes its written manifestations – multilingual literacy (Reh 2004).

More recently, studies on the type of multilingualism imported into European megacities by transcontinental migration increasingly come to converge in a shift of paradigm away from the rather static and compartmentalized Western view of languages as normatized systems. This shift is towards a more dynamic and interactional view which focuses on language practices such as multilingual languaging (Juffermans 2015) and crossing (Rampton 1995) and the deliberate choices speakers make when they draw on their repertoires in different types of multilingual settings. Africanistics claims to make crucial contributions to this field as well (e.g. Lüpke 2013), given the fact that communication in most African settings is characterized by a much higher degree of language diversity and density of interaction, as resulting from internal migration, and a much lesser degree of language standardization and normatization. In Africa, this goes hand in hand with more relaxed attitudes regarding the fluidity of codes, revealing various types of underlying ideologies of multilingualism (Lüpke 2016) that challenge Eurocentric framings of academic discourse on multilingualism.

While the classificatory debate about modifying and refining Greenberg's dendrograms continues to be fuelled by low-level reconstructions on the basis of the rigid application of the historical-comparative method, the adequacy of the unilinear-genealogical model has been seriously called into question, resulting in the development of alternative representations of language history, such as via the stratificational model as applied to Bantu (Möhlig 1981), which is notorious for resisting rigid internal subgrouping according to the unilinear-genealogical model due to the impact of large-scale multilateral patterns of multilingualism.

As the outlines of a model of historical sociolinguistics crystallize in Thomason and Kaufman's (1988) seminal work on structural reflexes of different types of language contact, reconstructions have been proposed for various contact areas in Africa, including Nubian (Bechhaus-Gerst 1996), Northern Songhay (Nicolaï 1990; Wolff & Alidou 2001), and Southern Cushitic (Kießling 2002), which qualify as sociolinguistically more adequate due to their effort at counterbalancing divergent changes by due consideration of language convergence with support from ethno- and sociohistorical evidence. More recently still, social network models have been introduced to Africanistics to come to terms with mechanisms of linguistic innovation at the micro level (Schreiber 2009; Beyer & Schreiber 2013; Lüpke 2016).

One domain of particular historical and typological relevance which has profited substantially from Africanistic contribution in terms of data analysis and concept formation is grammaticalization (Heine 1976; Heine & Reh 1984; Heine, Claudi & Hünnemeyer 1991 et al.), i.e. the study of the emergence and development of grammatical units and its underlying cognitive motivations (Heine 1997).

In semantics, the elaboration of specific lexical fields is studied in an interdisciplinary perspective, e.g. ethnobotanics (Heine 1985; Heine & Legère 1995), smithing (Klein-Arendt 2004), pottery (Bostoen 2005a), traditional crafts (Broß & Baba 1996). Particularly in Bantu, the relatively high resolution of lexical coverage across a vast area, combined with an advanced stage of reconstruction, allows for fine-grained studies pertaining to entire lexical fields such as mammals (Bastin 1994) or to individual concepts, including bone (Bastin 2001), oil palm (Bostoen 2005b), and canoe (Grégoire 1976b). The comparative perspective in enterprises such as these increasingly upgrades the need to develop models of semantic change by generalizing from the observation of recurrent patterns of polysemy (Bostoen 2002; Fleisch 2008; Vanhove 2008), in an attempt to fertilize historical linguistics from an African perspective.

While the exploration of ethnobotanic taxonomies follows semasiological lines of inquiry, another trend, rather onomasiologically oriented, emerges from the cognitive approach, investigating the expression of concepts within a semantic domain, for example emotion and experience (Reh et al. 1998; Ameka 2002; Becher 2003) and (loco-)motion (Sitoe 2001).

Inspired by the paradigm of ethnopragmatics (Goddard 2006), the study of African languages is expanded to include linguistic routines (Ameka 1987; Kießling et al. 2011) and the way they are framed by specific cultural patterns of communication (Ameka 2004).

Extensions into the realm of text linguistics focus either on the structures of dialogic discourse (Klein-Arendt 1992) or on the architecture of narratives

(Paulme 1976; Bremond 1980; Möhlig 1986). This latter field links up with the study of oral literature and verbal art. While collections have been compiled since the beginning of the nineteenth century, principled scientific analysis started only in the 1970s (Finnegan 1970; Derive 1975). Approaches focus on either particular figures, such a animal characters (Steinbrich 1982), the ogre (Paulme 1976; Geider 1990), the enfant terrible (Görög-Karady et al. 1980; Geider 2003), helper animals (Seydou & Paulme 1972), specific narrative types (Görög-Karady 1992), entire cultures and their epic matrices (Schott 1993; Reuster-Jahn 2002) or the areal comparison of motifs (Schmidt 1989; Schott 1990). As literacy and written literature in various African languages of wider communication keep expanding, the study of creative writing in languages such as Swahili has evolved as a comparatively new field (Kitereza & Möhlig 1991; Vögele et al. 2014).

Beside the study of the contents and the linguistic forms of discourse in African languages, it is the study of their usage in and transformation by media which emerges as another new field in Africanistics (Beck & Wittmann 2004). The spectrum here reaches from films (e.g. Böhme 2006) to music, e.g. Bongo Fleva (Krings & Reuster-Jahn 2014), 'speaking' objects, written messages on clothes such as *leso* and *kanga* in Eastern Africa (Beck 2001), manuscripts (Bondarev 2014), and urban linguistic landscaping (Reh 2004).

Topics such as health care (Dilger 2005; Drescher & Klaeger 2006; Tourneux & Métangmo-Tatou 2010) and development (Tourneux 2006; Bearth 2008; Beck 2011, 2013), which could effectively be tackled via discourse, media, and metaphor analysis as well as via ethnopragmatical methodologies, allow – to an increasing degree – for fertile interdisciplinary crossover between Africanistics, African studies, ethnology, Anglistics and Romance studies.

Last, but not least, the indispensable relevance of the study of African languages for sustainable economic development in Africa is articulated ever more forcefully to gain the attention of stakeholders and decision makers in both the European donor countries and African recipient countries (Bearth & Fan 2006), demanding the overdue linguistic turn in development discourse (Wolff 2016:155–171) by pointing to the gross underdevelopment of communicative aspects in the underpinnings of failed technologically driven development projects (Tourneux 2006). In continuation of the approach of applied Africanistics (Doneux 2003:232ff.) which attempts to overcome the out-dated paternalistic attitude in development discourse, these aspirations and demands recently crystallized into a call for applied African sociolinguistics to emerge as a new sub-field of study (Wolff 2013:41–44, 2016).

After the postwar and early postcolonial period of institutional expansion, the new millennium is characterized by an accelerated pace of compression and contraction for Africanistics. This seems to be caused by two converging trends in academia: the transnational institutionalization of teaching and research and a rigorous economicization of learning, inspired by neoliberal austerity policies, which tend to measure the value of academic disciplines by parameters such as student demand, student output, and immediate impact factors.

Contractions such as these instigated and eventually exacerbated latent antagonisms between language-based Africanistics on the one side and protagonists of African studies, who rather focus on politology or the social sciences, on the other side. While at SOAS in the 1960s and 1970s the conflict took the form of a general defence of linguists and philologists against what was perceived as an expansion of the social sciences at their expense (Brown 2016:189–192), another outburst in the early 2000s in Germany rather took the opposite direction in a battle for limited resources under austerity conditions and looming budget cuts, that is, as an attack from the politologists' side on what was perceived as an imbalanced status quo with under-representation of non-language-based African studies in Germany's universitarian landscape (Engel 2003). The ensuing academic debate (Bierschenk 2003; Reh 2003) came to stimulate a more rigid form of self-organization in the corporation Fachverband Afrikanistik in delimitation from the Vereinigung der Afrikawissenschaften in Deutschand (VAD) including an explicit declaration in the form of a constitution of the discipline of Africanistics in delimitation to non-language-based approaches.[5]

With respect to transnational academic institutionalization, centres of Africanistics such as London, Paris, Leiden, Naples, Hamburg, Vienna, and Lisbon – apart from their integration into European network programmes for student mobility and staff exchange (SOCRATES, ERASMUS) – are linked by the Network of European Centers of Asian and African Studies (NECAAS) with the agenda of maximally harmonizing curricula. While this type of European-scale internationalization contributes to facilitate student mobility at BA and MA levels, the transcontinental globalization of training and capacity building had already been established in Africanistics, as most centres have, since the postcolonial era, increasingly attracted African linguists working on their own languages, the most prominent exponents being Ayọ Bamgboṣe (Nigeria), Florence Dolphyne (Ghana), and Leonidas Sibomana (Rwanda).

At the local level, the economicization of learning and teaching triggered by the Bologna process, forces single-standing chairs of Africanistics into institutionalized symbiosis with bigger partners such as general linguistics (e.g. in Frankfurt) and ethnology (e.g. in Mainz), eventually resulting in contraction and erosion, as currently observed in the fusion of Africanistics at Frankfurt and Mainz.

---

[5] See www.uni-koeln.de/phil-fak/afrikanistik/fv/.

In terms of research, funding formats become increasingly clustered, on both national and European levels. Thus, a series of projects on the documentation of endangered African languages has been realized in the context of globalized research in internationalized programmes such as DoBeS and ELDP. In agreement with the Humboldtian approach, Africanistics has increasingly contributed to cooperative schemes of interdisciplinary research such as the German Sonderforschungsbereiche (i.e. Special Research Programmes) in Bayreuth (Identity in Africa, 1984–1997), Frankfurt (Kulturentwicklung und Sprachgeschichte im Naturraum Westafrikanische Savanne, 1988–2002), Cologne (ACACIA – Arid Climate, Adaptation and Cultural Innovation in Africa, 1995–2007), Berlin/Potsdam (Information Structure: The Linguistic Means for Structuring Utterances, Sentences and Texts, 2003–2015), Hamburg (Dealing with Social Transformation in African Societies, 1999–2003; Multilingualism, 1999–2011; Manuscript Cultures in Asia, Africa and Europe, since 2011). It is involved in various graduate schools, including a.r.t.e.s. Graduate School for the Humanities Cologne (AGSHC, Cologne), and the Bayreuth International Graduate School of African Studies (BIGSAS, Bayreuth). Having a graduate programme *in Germany*, but with teaching *in English* has allowed Bayreuth and other German universities to overcome the language barrier and promote graduate education for Africans.

Apart from conferences dedicated to individual language groups or areas such as the Symposium on Cushitic and Omotic Languages, the Biennial International Colloquium on the Chadic Languages (BICCL), the Nilo-Saharan Linguistics Conference (NISALICO), the International Symposium on Khoisan Languages and Linguistics, the Bantu Conference, the Symposium on West African Languages (SyWAL), and the Colloquium on Berber languages (BaFraLe), regular conferences with general dedication to African linguistics have become installed at the national level. The oldest one is the annual Colloquium on African Languages and Linguistics (CALL) in Leiden. Another one is the Afrikanistentag in Germany/Austria. Unique in its dedication to a single African language is the annual Swahili Colloquium, established in Bayreuth in 1987.

Keeping track with progress in information technology and coping with future challenges of big data accessibility and corpus management, Africanistics has started to develop electronic archives and search tools such as Bantu Lexical Reconstructions (Bastin et al. 2002), the Reference Lexicon of Africa (Segerer & Flavier 2011–2016), and Tsammalex (Naumann et al. 2015).

2.7   Conclusion

The common denominator in the history of Africanistics, which sets some Western European countries apart from other world regions, is the impact of colonialism on the formation of academic institutions and – to some extent – on concept formation in the discipline itself. The colonial project lent a strong incentive of practical application to Africanistics in these countries, which was absent elsewhere. Having grown from the earlier missionary project, the colonial boom of interest in African languages was fuelled by the practical purpose to effectively gain and exert administrative (and military) control over the colonies and to economically exploit them. Crucial differences in conceptual underpinnings of colonial policies entailed different effects on the development of Africanistics. While the 'Romance' colonial policy of assimilation kept the interest in African languages confined to small groups of individuals, the 'Anglo-German' indirect rule approach produced an earlier incentive for the acquisition of comprehensive knowledge in African vehicular languages across a larger group of colonial staff such as officers, clerks, and administrators, crystallizing in institutions of imperial training such as SOAS at London (Brown 2016), the School of Oriental Languages in Berlin (Stoecker 2008), and the Colonial Institute in Hamburg (Meyer-Bahlburg & Wolff 1986; Paul 2008).

In terms of methodological orientation, Africanistics was linked to the philological tradition of Oriental studies, still reflected in names such as the Institut National des Langues et Civilisations Orientales (INALCO) in France and the School of Oriental and African Studies (SOAS) in England. With the rise and development of structuralism, the methodological pacemaker in Africanistics soon became linguistics. Owing to the constant refinement of descriptive tools, Africanistics even advanced to become one of the conceptual pacemakers itself in various fields, e.g. in tonology. In contrast to the US focus on theory in the study of African languages which tends to be adopted in many African academic settings, the Africanist orientation in Western Europe is rather towards empiricism. Indeed, the impact of formalized theoretical models was short lived. The Humboldtian undercurrent prevented most Africanists in Western Europe from delving deeply into decontextualized generative experiments. Instead, empiricism in Africanistics has spurred the proliferation of various transdisciplinary discourse paradigms at the interface of linguistics, anthropology, sociology, politology, history, archaeology, genetics, and media studies. This is testified by the integration of Africanistic expertise in a wide range of interdisciplinary research networks. Further, the spirit of Humboldtian ethnolinguistics lives on in curricula that target African languages within their cultural, social, and historical settings.

Borderlines between particular national schools of Western European Africanistics become increasingly blurred and submerged by globalized research agendas and international networking. Apart from the orientation of regional research specializations towards former spheres of colonial influence, particularly prominent in Belgium, France, and Italy, echoes of the colonial past could be seen in the long-standing (only recently abandoned) practice, both in England and in France, of dedicating specialized chairs to the study of a single African language of wider communication, such as Swahili or Hausa. This is in contrast to the practice in Germany with its shorter colonial past. While specializations such as these do exist, they do not surface in denominations, in order to avoid undue inflexibility when it comes to refilling the posts. In fact, the Africanistic dedication of a chair in Germany often entails the requirement of a broader qualification in terms of regional and linguistic foci in sub-Saharan Africa.

Practical applications of Africanistics in Western Europe have changed from serving the administrative necessities of governing in the colonial 'project', being replaced by the challenges of development discourse in the postcolonial period, that is, the need to inform and advise stakeholders and decision makers, both in the former colonial powers and in Africa, about the basic concepts of communication and linguistic diversity management. Outside development discourse, applied Africanistics becomes increasingly relevant with respect to the African diaspora in the former colonial motherlands. However, while sizeable African immigrant and refugee groups have stimulated a research focus on the linguistic strategies of African diaspora communities in various European cities such as London, Paris, Amsterdam, Rotterdam, Den Haag, Utrecht, and Hamburg (e.g. Hoff 2014), their immediate relevance to communal concerns does not seem to have encouraged stakeholders to invest in sustainable institutionalized support in academia anywhere.

While traditional threads of discourse such as basic research on individual languages, the documentation of endangered languages, and language classification issues still continue, the scope of Africanistics has widened considerably since the 1990s to include 'research on language as resource for African individuals, social groups and even whole states' (Wolff 2016:21–22), resulting in a shift of paradigms that characterizes Africanistics as an emergent discipline dedicated to the study of communication in African languages at large.

Acknowledgements

I want to express my sincere thanks to Guillaume Segerer, Maarten Mous, Friederike Lüpke, Lutz Marten, Alessandro Bausi, an anonymous reviewer, and the editor for valuable comments and locating relevant sources.

3 African Linguistics in Central and Eastern Europe, and in the Nordic Countries

Roland Kießling, Nina Pawlak, Alexander Zheltov, and Arvi Hurskainen

3.1 African Linguistics in Austria (Roland Kießling)

Outside colonial contexts, but quite obviously in close academic exchange with parallel developments in neighbouring imperial Germany, Austrian Africanistics in Vienna emerged from Orientalist traditions in symbiosis with Egyptology (Sommerauer 2010). The foundation was laid by Leo Reinisch (1832–1919): holding a chair for Egyptology from 1868, he developed vital interests well beyond the southern fringes of traditional Egyptologists' domains in the Horn of Africa, providing an enormous number of descriptive studies of hitherto undocumented Cushitic, Omotic, and Nilo-Saharan languages, accompanied by dictionaries and extensive text collections (Böhm 1987; Kießling 2008).

While Friedrich Müller's (1834–1898) work on Bari and Harari had come to independently boost the visibility of African languages beyond the Orientalistic orbit, Africanistics still remained institutionally 'undercover'. Institutional recognition was achieved by Reinisch's successor Hermann Junker (1877–1962), who established the name Institut für Ägyptologie und Afrikanistik in 1923 and appointed his direct successor, Wilhelm Czermak (1889–1953), as professor for Egyptology and Africanistics in 1925. Beyond his main œuvre on Egyptian phonology, Czermak continued the Nubian research tradition (1919) and focused on the interface of language, psychology, and cultural history, as reflected in his psychologically oriented study of Ewe (1924) and his contribution on 'Sprachgeist und tieferer Wortsinn in Afrika' (1951). He left a sustained impact by inspiring pupils such as Ernst Zyhlarz (1890–1964), Johannes Lukas (1901–1980), and Herrmann Jungraithmayr (b. 1931).

The succession of Czermak seems to have been marked by an explicit separation of Egyptology on the one side, represented by Gertrud Thausing (1905–1997) and followed by Inge Hofmann (1939-2016), and Africanistics on the other side, since 1969 represented by Hans G. Mukarovsky (1922–1992). Starting out from the Atlantic, with languages such as Kisi and Ful, Mukarovsky established a focus on West African languages with a special interest in comparative Niger Congo (1976–1977) and historical language contact between Mande and Chadic (1987).

Beginning in the 1970s Africanistics was constantly expanded in Vienna with a proliferation of research foci including Jukun and Adamawa (Kiyoshi Shimizu), Atlantic (Walter Pichl, Peter Gottschligg), Mande (Erwin Ebermann), general Afroasiatic (Gerhard Böhm), Hausa and West Chadic (Franz Stoiber, Georg Ziegelmeyer), and Swahili (Walter Schicho). The West African focus was continued by Mukarovky's successor, German-born Norbert Cyffer, and his specialization in Saharan (1974, 1998). Norbert Cyffer was followed to the chair by Ghana-born Adams Bodomo in 2013.

3.2   African Linguistics in Eastern Europe
(Nina Pawlak and Alexander Zheltov)

3.2.1   Introduction

As a region, Eastern Europe carries geopolitical rather than geographic con-notations. Throughout history, the boundaries of this region have undergone fluctuations, and distinct sub-regions have been identified as separate units, such as Central Europe or South-Eastern Europe. The definition of these terms varies according to their historical connotations. For example, Central Europe, which includes Poland, the Czech Republic and Hungary, refers to a broader concept that emerged in the first decades of the twentieth century. The political definition of the region is strongly associated with the formerly communist European states termed as the Eastern Bloc, which included Eastern Germany, whereas Russia (formerly the Soviet Union) is either part of it or represents a separate sub-region.

From a historical perspective, the region lying in the eastern part of the European continent has much in common in respect of its relationship with Africa, mostly because it covers countries without a colonial past in Africa. This fact strongly determines its ties with African countries and the develop-ment of African studies as an academic discipline in these particular countries.

3.2.2   The Interest in Africa Evoked by Travellers and Ethnographers

In all countries of the region, an interest in African languages (and Africa in general) was initially part of a more general interest in other peoples' lan-guages and cultures. Since the Middle Ages, there have been scientific expe-ditions from Eastern European countries and Russia that were mainly oriented at exploring virgin areas, but that were also conducive to research on African languages. Notes accompanying geographic and ethnographic observations (rarely exhaustive descriptions) left by travellers and adventurers in the period from the seventeenth century to the beginning of the twentieth have so far not been fully investigated.

The first pieces of information about Africa obtained by Russian travellers date back to the sixteenth and seventeenth centuries. In 1745, a map of Africa was published by the Russian Academy of Sciences. A major contribution to the study of African peoples in Russia was made by nineteenth-century Russian voyagers such as E. P. Kovalevsky, who travelled to Egypt in 1847 to develop gold fields there, V. V. Junker, who travelled across Central Africa, as well as two Russian army officers: A. V. Eliseev, who attempted to reach Sudan through Egypt, and A. K. Bulatovich, an explorer of Ethiopia, the first European to provide a scientific description of the Kaffa Province. The descriptions and notes they left benefited the Russian geographical society first, but they also became a foundation for scholarly activities whose purpose was to extend knowledge about the particular regions and to develop African studies in Russia. The famous Russian poet N. S. Gumilev is worthy of special mention. He made four trips to Africa as a traveller (mainly to Ethiopia) and created the poetic 'African cycle', which evoked a substantial 'romantic' interest in Africa among the Russian intelligentsia (his influence may be compared with that of Rudyard Kipling on British society). In Russia his poetry still encourages an interest in Africa, but his fate was tragic: in 1921 he was arrested and shot as a member of an anti-revolutionary organization.

According to Olderogge (1993:113–116), it was Mikhail Lomonosov (traditionally considered the father of Russian science) who took the earliest steps towards the beginning of African linguistics in Russia when he mentioned the 'Hottentot' language in one of his manuscripts. He is also believed to have been interested in the Ethiopian script.

The significant moment in the early development of Russian studies focused on languages was the publication, in 1790–1791 of the *Comparative Dictionary of All Languages and Dialects*. It includes data from 33 African languages including Coptic, Fula, Wolof, Mandingo, and Kongo (Zheltov 2011:197). At the beginning of the nineteenth century, B. A. Dorn started to teach Geez in Kharkov University (1829); seven years later he moved to St Petersburg University to continue his academic career. However, systematic studies which date back to the second part of the nineteenth century were closely connected with the Semitic and Ancient Egyptian tradition represented by such scholars as V. S. Golenishchev, O. E. Lemm, B. A. Turaev, P. K. Kokovtsev, and I. Y. Krachkovsky. All of them worked in St Petersburg University and since that period St Petersburg has become the leading centre of African studies in Russia. Compared to African studies in the countries which had their colonies in Africa, African studies in Russia at the early stage of its development drew from the academic tradition of Oriental studies rather than from the practical needs of missionaries and colonial officials and concentrated on Egypt and Ethiopia. This specific sphere of interest could also have been motivated by the Orthodox branch of Christianity which spread both in Russia and in Ethiopia and Egypt (although the directions of the Orthodox Church were different). To that period also belong the lexicographic writings of the aforementioned traveller V. V. Junker. During his second voyage to Central Africa (1879–1896), he compiled 1,000-word dictionaries of Madi, Barambo, Zande, Mangbetu, Bangba, and several 450-word dictionaries of other languages. These dictionaries were published in the *Journal of African Languages* (Junker 1888–1889) in Berlin and constituted the first evidence about most of these languages to appear in Europe. The words in those dictionaries were systematized in groups according to parts of speech and lexical semantic groups (Olderogge 1993:117–118). As far as theoretical linguistic books are concerned, particular attention was devoted to Africa by A. L. Pogodin in his book *Language at Creation*. He analysed the problems of language origin and the psychology of 'primitive peoples' and their languages. He knew quite well the contemporary European literature on African languages (Bleek, Meinhof, Torrend), and his book was the most comprehensive review of the information on African languages to appear in Russia before 1914 (Olderogge 1993:118–119).

As far as the Polish interest in Africa is concerned, it may be traced back to the sixteenth century and for a long time it was focused on ethnographic studies. The best-known Polish ethnographer and anthropologist, the father of social anthropology, was Bronisław Malinowski (1884–1942), who was associated with British and American universities, and studied the indigenous cultures of many regions of the world, including Africa (Gikuyu and Kulurami). Polish expeditions to Africa in the second half of the nineteenth century and at the beginning of the twentieth century (e.g. those of Jan Czekanowski to Central Africa in 1907–1909) extended the focus to languages, but linguistic data were not abundant, with the most elaborate source being the grammar of Bakwiri by Szolc-Rogoziński that was the result of an expedition to Cameroon in 1882–1890.

Understanding of Africa in the latter half of the nineteenth century in the Czech lands and the rest of the Austro-Hungarian Empire was shaped by the expeditions of travellers. The greatest among them was Emil Holub, who travelled around Southern and Central Africa. In 1875 he reached present-day Zimbabwe near the Zambezi River. The result was the first ever detailed map of the Victoria Falls region and accounts of the area, published in English four years later. However, the bulk of travelogues, maps, and other materials usually disregarded language documentation.

Among the first Czech travellers in Africa, one should mention Václav Remedius Prutký. He was a missionary who visited Ethiopia between 1751 and 1753 and not only did he describe his travels but he also compiled a vocabulary of the Amharic language in his heretofore unpublished *Vocabularium linguae Gallicae, Arabicae et Abyssiniacae* (Záhořík 2006).

Hungarian travellers or adventurers also contributed to scientific knowledge about Africa during the eighteenth, nineteenth, and the beginning of the twentieth centuries. A well-known traveller, Móric Benyovszky (1741–1786), who went twice to Madagascar in the 1770s and 1780s, is recognized as a representative of three nations: Hungary, Slovakia, and Poland.[1] Other Hungarian travellers, such as László Magyar (1818–1864), who reached contemporary Angola, and Sámuel Teleki (1845–1916), who went to Kenya, as well as travellers who explored the areas of Uganda and Tanganyika, left geographic and ethnographic observations, but their linguistic content is not rich. African language data may be found in some missionary sources, such as those compiled by the Jesuit father István Czimmermann (1849–1893), who wrote linguistic studies on Mozambique (Szabó 2013).

In conclusion, one may remark that the interest in Africa evoked by travellers and ethnographers was not directly transferred to the institutional level by providing a basis for studies on languages. Indeed, the foundations for national scholarly activities in the field of African studies that included studies of languages formed out of the attention devoted to the Orient, which was later extended to the countries of Africa, and Northern Africa in particular. The history of African linguistics as grounded in the tradition of Oriental studies goes back to the middle of the eighteenth century in Russia, and the nineteenth century in Poland, Hungary, and the Czech Republic (the former Czechoslovakia). The interest in African languages developed as an extension of studies on Arabic or Semitic languages that represented the most ancient philological schools in Europe, less commonly of Egyptian studies. In this context, Amharic and Geez were the first African languages to be studied in a comprehensive manner at the universities. Initially, the teaching of these languages was a supplementary discipline within Christian theology and Bible research.

3.2.3   The Early Development of African Linguistics as a Discipline

The first academic institutions dealing with Africa were affiliated with centres of Oriental studies. Teaching Oriental disciplines has a long tradition at Moscow University, having started as early as in the mid-eighteenth century, but the history of African studies in Russia dates back to St Petersburg, where the Faculty of Oriental Languages was established in 1854 (later becoming the Oriental Faculty). The studies originated in the Semitic and Ancient Egyptian tradition and focused on Egyptian monuments (V. S. Golenishchev), also Coptic and Ethiopian manuscripts (O. E. Lemm, B. A. Turaev, P. K. Kokovtsev) and were

---

[1] Slovaks consider Benyovszky to be their own, and Poles regard him as a national hero (Maurycy Beniowski).

also connected with Old Egyptian, Arabic, Geez and Amharic languages (I. Y. Krachkovsky, N. V. Yushmanov, among others). The scholars who made an important contribution to the formation and development of Soviet African studies have contributed to the establishing of both non-university research institutions and (later) university departments. Indeed, often the same scholars worked in both research institutes and universities.

Russian studies on African languages, both at the institutional level and in terms of research inspirations, have a basis in the activities of the leading Soviet Africanist, Dmitri Olderogge (1903–1987), the 'founding father' of African anthropology in the mid-1930s (and African studies in general) in the USSR.

In 1927–1928 D. A. Olderogge, a specialist in Egyptology, ethnology, and ancient languages, who worked in the Museum of Anthropology and Ethnology, was sent abroad (Germany, Belgium, and the Netherlands), where he studied the organization of museums in these countries and African languages and associated with such famous scholars as D. Westermann. After his return to St Petersburg (*illo tempore* Leningrad), he became head of the African Department at the Museum of Anthropology and Ethnology (where a considerable African collection already existed by that time) and together with a famous Semitologist, N. V. Yushmanov, and an Assyriologist, A. P. Riftin, he put forward the initiative to reorganize the Department of Semitic Languages into the Department of Semitic and Hamitic Languages (at that time this term was still in use), which was a part of Leningrad (present-day St Petersburg) State University. In the 1934–1935 academic year, two groups of students were admitted to this department. The first was headed by N. V. Yushmanov and studied Hausa and Amharic, and the second was headed by D. A. Olderogge and studied Swahili and Zulu as well as pursuing some general courses. When, in 1944–1945, the Faculty of Oriental Studies (one of the oldest in the university, which opened in 1854) was re-established, it included the Department of African Studies and Egyptology headed by N. V. Yushmanov and, after his death in 1946, by D. A. Olderogge. It received its modern name, the Department of African Studies, in 1950–1951, after separating from Egyptology. In 1934 a group of specialists in the field of African languages (N. V. Yushmanov, I. L. Snegirev, P. A. Alekseev) also worked in the Institute of Language and Thought (Leningrad). Another group on African languages, headed by G. K. Danilov, existed at that time in Moscow (the Linguistic Committee of the African Chamber at the Research Association of National and Colonial Problems). In January 1934 the Workshop on African Languages at the Research Association of National and Colonial Problems was organized, and it became the first Russian conference on African languages. Leningrad (present-day St Petersburg) was represented by D. A. Olderogge, N. V. Yushmanov, and I. L. Snegirev, and Moscow by G. K. Danilov and P. S. Kuznetsov. It was a complicated time in Russian history and the fates of the participants were different: Yushmanov died in 1946, Kuznetsov switched to general linguistics, Danilov was arrested and shot in 1937, Snegirev took part in the Second World War, but in 1946 was arrested and died in prison. Only Olderogge (he survived the years of Stalin's terror but was not allowed to go abroad for many years in the late Soviet years) continued as an Africanist and contributed greatly to the development of African studies in the USSR (Olderogge 1937, 1949, 1977). The materials of this workshop were to be published, but this plan was not realized. They were discovered just recently and published under the editorship of N. V. Gromova (1999).

Studies in languages initiated in St Petersburg became a significant contribution to the development of African language study not only in Moscow but also in other centres outside the Soviet Union (e.g. in Warsaw). Quite numerous graduates of Leningrad/St Petersburg University worked and are currently working in Moscow, Paris, Hamburg, and elsewhere.

In Poland, institutes of African language studies are located mainly at the universities. Their origin may be traced back to the first decades of the twentieth century, when some attempts at conducting research on African languages were undertaken in Krakow at the Jagiellonian University. They were initiated by Roman Stopa (1895–1995) with his dissertation on clicks (1935) and courses in Swahili, Hausa, Ewe, and Khoisan. African studies as an academic field officially started in 1945 and was affiliated to Arabic studies, established in 1919. In Warsaw, African studies were initiated by Stefan Strelcyn (1918–1981) as an extension of Semitic studies within the Institute of Oriental Studies, and studies focused on Geez and Amharic.

In the Czech Republic, the tradition of Oriental studies at the Charles University in Prague (founded in 1348 as the first university in Central Europe) dates back to 1849 when Czech Oriental Philology was distinguished as a separate unit. In the first half of the twentieth century, three professors of Semitology at Charles University, A. Dvořák, K. Růžička, and A. Musil, started to study Ethiopian languages and history (Záhořík 2006) to lay the groundwork for the subsequent introduction of African and Ethiopian studies at Charles University. As for linguistics-based studies on African languages, they are closely connected to the Oriental Institute in Prague. The institute was established in 1922 as one of the oldest institutions dedicated to the study of Oriental cultures in Central and Eastern Europe. It became a non-university research institution which integrated researchers who actively participated in the so-called Prague Linguistic Circle that has been operating since the 1930s. It was one of the most influential schools of linguistic thought in pre-war linguistics in which typology was assigned a significant role. Owing to linguistic inspirations, several researchers were directed towards the African field (Zima 2013). Vladimir Skalička included the Bantu languages in the typological investigations (published in the *Archiv Orientální* in 1945), whereas Karel František Růžička has developed his specialization in Bantu linguistics (research on class systems and locatives). Czech African studies was institutionally established in 1950 when the Department of the Near East and Africa in the Oriental Institute was created. Since 1992, the institute has come under the administrative leadership of the Academy of Sciences of the Czech Republic.

Teaching Oriental disciplines in Hungary started with Semitic languages when a relevant department was established at Budapest University in 1873. The development of African studies in Hungary has been motivated by an interest in learning about the Arab world and studying Arabic sources, which include data related to early Hungarian history. At the University of Budapest, separate units focused on Egyptology as well as Semitic and Arabic studies have been established to deal with questions related to the peoples of North Africa and North-Eastern Africa.

In the first half of the twentieth century, African languages did not figure prominently in academic fields in any of the East European countries with the exception, at least to a certain extent, of the USSR. However, activities undertaken in terms of teaching and research formed a basis for the transformation of African studies from a complex discipline consisting of the history, anthropology, sociology, linguistics, and politics of the peoples living in sub-Saharan Africa into studies on languages with the methodology of linguistics.

3.2.4   African Linguistics of the Postcolonial Period in the Eastern Bloc

A dynamic period in the development of scholarly activities in all countries under discussion began after the Second World War, especially after the so-called Year of Africa (1960).

Various scientific research centres focused on Africa were created in almost all of the socialist countries of the region. Their research interests concentrated mostly on history, politics, ethnography, and less commonly on anthropology, but they also succeeded in arousing interest in the teaching of African languages. When initiated as a separate academic field within the scholarly system (such as in the case of the Soviet Union, Poland, and Czechoslovakia), African studies was pursued at the greatest state universities, which had a long tradition in the fields of the humanities and philological studies. The research on Africa conducted both at the universities and in Academy institutions received official support because of the Soviet stance on helping the so-called Third World and developing countries (Szabó 2013). The liberation of the peoples of Africa and the development of ties between African countries and the USSR and socialist countries created new opportunities to undertake research on Africa, including studies on languages.

St Petersburg University (in collaboration with some institutions of the Soviet Academy of Science) played a leading role in the process of introducing languages into the university curricula and preparing the teaching materials. The Department of African Studies, headed by D. A. Olderogge between 1946 and 1987, became a university unit which offered language courses, whereas the African Department in the Institute of Anthropology and Ethnology (also headed by Olderogge) coordinated lexicographic works on the first African language dictionaries to be published in the Soviet Union, e.g. the Swahili–Russian dictionary (1961), Hausa–Russian dictionary (1963), Luganda–Russian, Russian–Luganda Dictionary (1969), and grammatical sketches of Hausa, Swahili, Luganda, and Zulu. Common knowledge of Russian in the Eastern Bloc secured easy access to the dictionaries and teaching materials in Russian in other countries too.

Throughout this period, studies in African languages were conducted in close collaboration with the departments of the institute and the university.[2] Scholars from the institute taught at the university, and university graduates replenished the staff of the institute. During this inter-institutional cooperation, works on the written sources on African history whether Ancient Greek and Roman (Y. K. Poplinsky), Arabic (V. V. Matveev), Chinese (V. A. Velgus), Amharic (S. B. Chernetsov, V. M. Platonov), Swahili (V. M. Misyugin, A. A. Zhukov) were initiated. The regular series Africana (African Ethnographic Working Papers) was edited by Olderogge and published until 1982. After the death of D. A. Olderogge in 1987, the department was headed by A. A. Zhukov (until 2006), a well-known specialist in Swahili language and literature (Zhukov 1997).

In 1959 a scientific research centre for the comprehensive study of Africa was established in Moscow – the Africa Institute of the Academy of Sciences of the USSR. It became the largest centre for African research in the field of politics and social science, but it never dealt with languages.

The ongoing tradition of teaching and studying African languages in Leningrad (now St Petersburg) helped to establish related institutions in Moscow. In 1960 an independent unit – the Chair of African Studies – came into existence as a branch of the Institute of Oriental Studies at Moscow University, renamed in 1972 as the Institute of Asian and African Studies, a leading Russian centre for training specialists in Oriental and African studies. The first was a group of Swahili students. The department is headed by a graduate of Leningrad University, N. V. Gromova, a well-known specialist in Swahili. Among other publications, textbooks of Swahili and Hausa and extended Swahili–Russian, Russian–Swahili dictionaries were published. In 1965, another graduate of Leningrad University, N. V. Okhotina, who was a specialist in Bantu languages, established the Department of African Languages in the Institute of Linguistics of the Academy of Sciences of the USSR. She headed the department until 1988 when she was succeeded

---

[2] According to the Soviet academic system, research institutes belonged to the Academy of Science, while universities were run under the Ministry of Education.

by V. A. Vinogradov, a recognized specialist in the phonology and typology of African languages. Among other publications of the department, the influential series Fundamentals of African Linguistics is worth mentioning.

All these Leningrad/St Petersburg and Moscow institutions have been working in close cooperation in publishing and organizing conferences. An example of such cooperation is a work called *Historical Comparative Vocabulary of Afrasian* by a group of Moscow specialists in Afrasian languages who have gained international recognition (A. G. Belova, A. S. Chetverukhin, A. Y. Militarev, V. Y. Porkhomovsky, O. V. Stolbova), headed by the famous Leningrad/St Petersburg scholar I. M. Dyakonov (Diakonoff et al. 1994–1997).

At the early stage, African studies as a university discipline in Poland focused on studies in Semitic languages (Geez and Amharic). Courses in other African languages (Hausa and Swahili) were made possible when Nina Pilszczikowa, a former student of D. A. Olderogge from St Petersburg, and Rajmund Ohly from Krakow, joined the staff. Since 1977, three languages, i.e. Amharic, Hausa, and Swahili, have been taught as the main languages in the programme offered by the Department of African Languages and Cultures. Linguistic studies on particular topics were initiated within the university degree procedures, and topics include the verbal system in Amharic (Joanna Mantel-Niećko), Arabic loans in Amharic (Witold Brzuski), abstract nouns in Swahili (Rajmund Ohly), word formation in Swahili (Eugeniusz Rzewuski), and constructions expressing spatial relations in Hausa (Nina Pawlak), among others (Piłaszewicz 2007). Along with linguistic analyses, work was also conducted with a view to the preparation of grammars and teaching materials in Polish.

In Krakow, at the Institute of Oriental Studies (a chair until 1972), there were regular courses in Swahili and Cushitic languages. The first Swahili–Polish dictionary for teaching purposes appeared in 1966 (Stopa, Garlicki). Research on Afroasiatic (Hamito-Semitic) linguistics was developed by Andrzej Zaborski (1942–2014). Significant steps in his academic career were marked by his PhD dissertation on biconsonantal verbal roots in Semitic and the post-PhD dissertation on the verb in Cushitic (Zaborski 1975). These were grounded in the Polish and East European tradition of diachronic studies based on Indo-European and Semitic languages represented by prominent scholars such as Jerzy Kuryłowicz and Robert Hetzron. Zaborski's work entitled *The Morphology of Nominal Plural in the Cushitic Languages* (1986) remains the main bibliographic reference of Cushitic and Afroasiatic studies.

A particularly dynamic development of studies in African languages in the period 1960–1989 created opportunities for scholars to go to Africa and do field research. Scholarships offered within cooperation programmes signed at the state level enabled the researchers (occasionally also students) to stay in Ghana, Nigeria, and Ethiopia. The work of some Polish scholars (as experts) conducted abroad in African countries (Rajmund Ohly in Tanzania and Namibia, Eugeniusz Rzewuski in Mozambique, Stanisław Piłaszewicz in Nigeria) contributed to the studies in African languages in Warsaw and to the development of the university centres of African studies in Africa. On the other hand, students from Africa (studying medicine or other subjects in Poland) were engaged as native speakers in teaching and research programmes.

Following the events of 1968 in Poland, some scholars left the country (Stefan Strelcyn, Nina Pilszczikowa, Zygmunt Frajzyngier). As a result of this, the number of scholars working on African languages in Warsaw was significantly reduced. Zygmunt Frajzyngier's further research activities in African linguistics, including the descriptions of Chadic languages, were affiliated to the University of Boulder, Colorado.

A representative of the Eastern Bloc until 1989/1990, the German Democratic Republic was also active in the development of African studies conducted in partnership with other countries of Eastern Europe. The Afrika-Institut was founded in 1960 at the Karl Marx University of Leipzig as an extension of the earlier department of African studies within the Oriental Institute. It became the main centre for teaching African languages as well as linguistic and sociolinguistic studies in African languages (in 1966–1990 it functioned as the Teaching and Research Centre for Africa and the Near East). The works published in German constituted coursebooks of African languages, such as Hausa (Brauner & Ashiwaju 1966), Swahili (Herms & Brauner 1979), and Amharic (Richter 1987). Also dictionaries of Swahili and Hausa for German-speaking users were published (Höftmann & Herms 1979; Legère 1990; Herms 1987). Along with linguistic and sociolinguistic aspects of Amharic, Hausa, and Swahili, also other African languages were subject to more detailed investigations (e.g. Bambara and Songhay in reference to tonality). Among the prominent scholars, Karsten Legère is worth mentioning in this context. For a long period (from 1975 to1979) he was working at the University of Dar es Salaam. In 1986 he became Associate Professor of Bantu linguistics at the Karl Marx University of Leipzig. After German reunification, he worked at various universities, including Windhoek, Gothenburg (see section 3.3.3.1), and Vienna as a renowned scholar specializing in sociolinguistics and language policy, language endangerment, language description and documentation in the area of Bantu linguistics (with regional focus on Tanzania and Namibia).

In the former Czechoslovakia, the 1960s are also seen as a dynamic period in the development of African studies, African linguistics in particular. At that time, studies on African languages were conducted with international cooperation and supported by institutional links between the Oriental Institute and Western institutions (such as SOAS in London, INALCO in Paris, and the Institut für Ägyptologie und Afrikanistik in Vienna). Petr Zima, a prominent Czech linguist specializing in West African linguistics, conducted fieldwork in Ghana and Nigeria; he was also awarded a research fellowship at the Department of Linguistics at the University of Ghana. His earliest publications focused mostly on the structural features of Hausa grammar in the typological perspective (genitive constructions, aspect system), gradually extending to studies on the particular linguistic and sociolinguistic aspects of Hausa (Zima 1972), especially in the context of its use in the function of a lingua franca in West Africa.

The important centre of studies in African languages in Czechoslovakia was the Department of Asian and African Studies at the Faculty of Arts, Charles University, Prague. Karel Petráček, a Semitist and expert on Ethiopia (dealing with Amharic and Cushitic languages), extended his main interest to sub-Saharan Africa. The results of work on African languages were published mostly in foreign languages (German, English). The *Archiv Orientální* journal (founded in 1929) was the main forum for the presentation of linguistic analyses. Other publications were also written in Czech (see, e.g. Růžička 1968; Zima 1973; Petráček 1989).

In Hungary, a common interest in Africa from the 1960s put African studies at the forefront of research activities within many disciplines. The linguist István Fodor made an attempt to evaluate Greenberg's classification of African languages (Fodor 1966). By raising questions of interest for general linguists and linguists working in Indo-European, Finno-Ugric, and other special branches, he drew attention to theoretical and methodological objections to Greenberg's theses. The only Hungarian researcher with a degree in African studies (because he graduated in the Soviet Union) was Géza Füssi Nagy (d. 2008). He wrote the first Hungarian–Swahili grammar book (Füssi Nagy 1987) and compiled the first Hungarian dictionaries for Swahili (Füssi Nagy 1985; 1986). Robert Hetzron (1938–1997), a linguist of Hungarian origin, is internationally recognized for his works on the comparative study of Afroasiatic languages, as well as for his study of Cushitic and Ethiopian Semitic languages.

In other East European countries (Bulgaria, the former Yugoslavia), many scientific research centres were founded either within the structures of the Academy of Sciences or at the universities, but studies on Africa did not pave the way for the establishment of the discipline of African linguistics.

During the communist period, African studies in Eastern Europe were closely connected with the political situation, which determined relations between the countries of the Eastern Bloc and Africa. However, African linguistic studies also functioned across political boundaries, and collaboration with scholars from abroad flourished. The conference *Unwritten Testimonies of the African Past*, held in Ojrzanów, near Warsaw, on 7–8 November 1989, is symbolic in this context. The fall of the Berlin wall happened just when scholars from the East and the West were meeting to discuss current topical issues of African linguistics.

3.2.5   The Current Situation

In the post-1989 period, especially after the integration of Poland, the Czech Republic, Slovakia, and Hungary into the European Union in 2004, there has been a change in international relations within East European countries. As a part of this process, the study of African languages in Eastern Europe has gained a new dimension. New concerns in reference to European integration brought new ties through collaborative programmes between institutions and programmes of staff exchange (such as the SOCRATES-ERASMUS scheme). All centres had to revise their programmes with regard to teaching African languages as a part of university teaching goals. Within research programmes, the knowledge of African languages has been more commonly used for solving linguistically defined problems rather than for descriptive works.

In Poland, African linguistics is one possible specialization at the master's and doctoral levels. In Warsaw, courses in Swahili, Hausa, and Amharic, as well as in African linguistics in a comparative perspective are offered, with reference to the grammars and other publications in Polish (Łykowska 1998; Ohly et al. 1998; Pawlak 1998, 2010). Individual research works on Bantu, Semitic, and Chadic linguistics are inclined towards topics relevant for theoretical aspects in the field of phonology, syntax, ethnolinguistics, cognitive linguistics, and lexicography. Some particular projects involving the analyses of African languages in a comparative perspective have gained support from the national system of financing scholarly activities (e.g. the linguistic embodiment by Iwona Kraska-Szlenk; lexicographic Swahili studies by Beata Wójtowicz; symbolic values of the language of emotions by Nina Pawlak). The results of research works are presented mostly in foreign languages (English, French), but they are also published in Polish, in the periodical *Afryka*, for example. The journal *Studies of the Department of African Languages and Cultures* (published since 1984, renamed *Studies in African Languages and Cultures* in 2018) presents the results of scholarly works in linguistics and in other disciplines related to Africa. The research programme at the Department of African Languages and Cultures, University of Warsaw, functions in cooperation with universities in Africa, in particular with Bayero University, Kano, in Nigeria.

In Krakow, the Chair of Afroasiatic Linguistics, headed by Professor Andrzej Zaborski, was established in 2000. It has become a centre of comparative linguistics in the Semitic and Afroasiatic fields. The journal *Folia Orientalia*, published since 1959 by the Oriental Committee, Polish Academy of Sciences – Krakow Branch, is a forum for researchers from around the world. It is devoted to Oriental studies and publishes contributions on African linguistics, most frequently on Afroasiatic languages and linguistics.

In the Czech Republic, African studies as a discipline has been offered within MA programmes at the Charles University, but only in combination with another discipline. Knowledge of one African language is required – usually it is Swahili. However, at present courses are not conducted and African linguistics functions as a research programme only. Some initiatives (seminars, lectures on Africa and African languages in particular) are undertaken by institutions representing the Czech Academy of Sciences or other academic units (e.g. the Centre for the Studies of Contacts and Conflicts).

Czech studies on African languages are better known through the achievements of some prominent researchers dealing with linguistics. Among them, Petr Zima, who has worked closely with many linguists abroad (mostly from Germany, France, Austria) and coordinated projects granted either by Charles University, or by the Grant Agency of the Czech Republic (which today is known as the Czech Science Foundation). The projects oriented towards more general problems of communication, contacts, and barriers in different cultures have made a significant contribution to linguistic studies in areal influences and language contact in Africa (Zima & Tax 1998; Zima 2010). Areal features were the subject of particular interest in his other projects dealing with the horizons of the *Sprachbund* (Zima 2009) and problems of language classification in Africa (Zima 2000). New languages have become the subject of descriptive works, namely Songhay (Nicolaï & Zima 1997).

Another scholar, Václav Blažek, a historical linguist affiliated to Masaryk University (Brno), specializes in Afroasiatic (mostly Cushitic) and Nilo-Saharan languages. He also contributes to the development of a new Czech centre of African studies in Pilsen. His works on comparative linguistics include the data from languages representing African and Indo-European language families, e.g. the topic of numerals (Blažek 1999).

The journal *Linguistica Brunensia*, published (in Czech and English) by the Faculty of Arts of the Masaryk University in Brno since 2009, focuses on general linguistics and invites contributions on African languages made from this perspective.

African studies in Hungary are not distinguished as an academic specialization at any level, but it is possible to focus on African languages within linguistic studies. At the Eötvös Loránd University in Budapest, research work on comparative linguistics within Afroasiatic, with a focus on the relationship between Egyptian and other branches of the family, is conducted by the renowned scholar Gábor Takács. With reference to his Egyptological and Semitic background, he conducts studies on Cushitic and Chadic within Afroasiatic in the field of comparative linguistics. He is the author of two dictionaries: *Etymological Dictionary of Egyptian* (1999) as well as the *Comparative Dictionary of the Angas-Sura Languages* (2004).

Research on Africa is also conducted in the Africa Research Centre, Faculty of Humanities at the University of Pécs, and in the Hungarian Academy of Sciences. The only Hungarian scholarly journal on Africa, the *Afrika Tanulmányok* (Africa Studies), has been published in Pécs since 2007.

The 1990s was a period of very dynamic change in Russia, too. The ideological basis for many fields in the humanities was lost, and science faced severe financial difficulties. Many spheres of the humanities also suffered from an ideological and theoretical crisis. However, African linguistics was never strictly ideologically oriented, and therefore this change was not crucial. Perhaps more crucial were the financial problems, which had a negative impact on human resources. If previously employment at a university or Academy institution was a prestigious and comparatively well-paid endeavour (and it offered institutions the opportunity to replenish staff with the best graduates), this sphere of activity lost its appeal for many who could have been an asset to the field. This 'brain drain', whether external (i.e. to foreign institutions) or internal (through loss of personnel to other spheres of activity) was especially significant for a field like African linguistics, in which relatively few scholars covered a huge academic area, and in which every specialist is unique. Despite this difficult situation, those who remained in the field managed to keep the institutions alive and even developed some new trends.

A significant realignment of the earlier ties and interests in African languages has strengthened the linguistic orientation of African studies. K. I. Pozdniakov, trained as a linguist both in Leningrad (graduate student) and Moscow (postgraduate student), contributed much to this orientation, promoted cooperation between St Petersburg and Moscow, and opened up a new avenue for studying Atlantic languages (Pozdniakov 1993).

The efforts of D. A. Olderogge and A. A. Zhukov ensured that even in Soviet times African studies in Leningrad were not absolutely isolated from the rest of the world, but from the 1990s onwards, the Department of African Studies established much more intensive and regular contact with many centres abroad. Many students and practically all the teachers visited Africa (earlier it was either impossible or rather problematic). In this respect, the Mande project, organized and headed by V. F. Vydrine, played the most important role. This ongoing project was of great value not only as a source of first-hand field data but also as a perfect training school for students. Moreover, scholars from St Petersburg managed to visit many centres of African studies abroad (such as Leipzig, Frankfurt, Bayreuth, Hamburg, Helsinki, London, Paris, later Gothenburg, Berkeley, and Dar es Salaam). It not only helped to establish regular contacts with colleagues but also improved access to the publications which appear all over the world. All this led to much better inclusion and integration into the general research process and helped to overcome a certain isolation of Soviet African studies. Six issues of the *St Petersburg Journal of African Studies* (1993–1997) were published in English. This journal, edited by V. F. Vydrine, enabled the papers by Russian scholars to be read by foreign colleagues.

Among some recent important projects, two are worth particular mention: corpora of Manden languages available online and a huge (1,140-page) volume on the Mande language (Vydrine 2017). Both projects are headed by V. F. Vydrine and are made in collaboration with linguists mostly from St Petersburg and Moscow.

Great attention in the curriculum is devoted to language teaching, and some courses in historical linguistics and linguistic typology of African languages are also provided. Currently, the languages taught as the main subjects include Amharic, Bamana, Hausa, and Swahili, while Geez, Maninka, Kinyarwanda, and Arabic are taught as the second language. Among other activities of the Department of African Studies (headed since 2006 by A. Y. Zheltov, who trained as a Bantuist and specialist in the typology of African languages (Zheltov 2008)) is the conference on African Studies in memoriam of D. A. Olderogge (the so-called Olderogge readings), which takes place in St Petersburg every two years. The volume of the proceedings, the *African Collection* (a sort of heir to the series Africana), edited by V. F. Vydrine (2007, 2009) and A. Y. Zheltov (2011, 2013, 2015) has been published regularly since 2007. Among other important publications, the *Textbook of Bamana* (Vydrine 2008) and *Dictionnaire Dan–Française (dan de l'Est)* by V. F. Vydrine (Vydrine & Kességbeu 2008) may be mentioned. In 2012–2014 the purpose of a linguistic expedition to the Adamawa province in Nigeria, organized and headed by A. Y. Zheltov, was to provide a description of certain Adamawa languages.

At the Department of African Studies of Moscow University (for many years headed by a recognized specialist in Swahili, N. V. Gromova), the list of languages taught as main subjects includes four African languages: Hausa, Swahili, Amharic, and Afrikaans, while other languages, such as Zulu, are offered as complementary courses. Recently Fula was added as one of the languages that may be studied. In research work, some other African languages and language groups (families) are subjects of interest, namely Bantu, Afroasiatic, and Nilotic. Besides some research publications, the department publishes authoritative textbooks and dictionaries used not only in Moscow but also in St Petersburg (e.g. Gromova & Okhotina 1995). N. V. Gromova was a participant in the Complex Expedition of the Institute of Africa in Tanzania.

The Russian Academy of Sciences includes research institutions which have only doctoral students. The Department of African Languages of the Institute of Linguistics (now headed by A. B. Shluinsky, a specialist in Kwa and Mande languages and linguistic typology) is the main research centre for African languages. Linguistic studies are conducted in Bantu, Afroasiatic, Mande, and Kwa languages, as well as Fula and Songhay. Research topics also cover other languages, e.g. Ekoid languages. A. I. Koval has been a leading specialist in Fula for many years. V. Y. Porkhomovsky is one of the specialists in Afrasian languages of world renown who is involved in various international projects.

I. N. Toporova, I. S. Ryabova, and A. D. Lutskov contributed much to Bantu studies.

Some important articles about African languages have also appeared in special issues on general typology under the editorship of V. S. Khrakovskiy (e.g. Khrakovskiy 1989, 1992).

There are also researchers working on Afroasiatic languages in the Department of Asian and African Languages in the Institute of Oriental Studies of the Russian Academy of Sciences. The St Petersburg branch was reorganized into the Institute of Oriental Manuscripts; it maintains the tradition of studies in manuscripts, including those from Africa.

African languages are also taught and investigated at some other institutions located in various research institutes and universities. They have a more specialized orientation; for example, Swahili and Amharic courses are taught in the Moscow State Institute of International Relations, and Amharic and Geez at St Tikhon's Orthodox University. Recently Swahili was introduced into the curriculum of Kazan State University.

Many graduates of Russian universities specializing in African linguistics work abroad, for instance, K. I. Pozdniakov and V. F. Vydrine are professors at INALCO, D. Idiatov and T. Nikitina are researchers at LLACAN, Paris, D. G. Bondarev works on Kanuri manuscripts, and D. A. Nosnitsin collaborated with the *Encyclopedia Ethiopica* project in Hamburg, whereas O. A. Ivanova taught at the University of California, Los Angeles.

3.3   Contributions to the Study of African Languages from the Nordic Countries (Arvi Hurskainen)

3.3.1   Introduction

This section gives an outline of the study of African languages currently going on in various Nordic countries. The description is limited to the work of individual researchers as far as it was/is financed by these countries. Therefore, the work of each researcher is included only as far as the above criterion is fulfilled.

Research on African languages has been and often is carried out as part of study on general linguistics, or other such research areas that have made it possible to study African languages too. Only the University of Gothenburg in Sweden has a professorship dedicated to the study of African languages. In Norway and Denmark, African languages are studied mostly in departments of general linguistics. In Finland, the professorship at the University of Helsinki is defined as African studies, covering a wider research field, which also makes it possible to study subjects that normally would be studied in other departments, such as anthropology and history, for instance.

3.3.2   Early Initiatives

The motivation for studying African languages emerged initially as part of missionary activities. There was a need to be able to communicate using local languages. Missionaries had to learn the languages, and this was made possible by producing grammars and dictionaries. The pioneers seldom had formal linguistic training. Yet they produced valuable resources for many languages, which have remained standard language resources of those languages till today. The work of missionaries also included the creation of orthographies and production of teaching materials for schools. Finally, their contribution extends to such achievements as the translation of Bible or its parts into local languages. Today the Bible translations constitute the most important, and sometimes the only, resource for computational applications such as machine translation.

Among the earliest pioneers was the Danish scholar Rasmus Rask (1828), who wrote an introduction to the Accra language on the Guinea Coast (modern Ghana). Finland made its contribution in northern Namibia with regard to local Bantu languages. The earliest major achievement was the translation of the Bible into Oshindonga by Martti Rautanen. The first draft of the whole Bible was ready in 1920, but it took more than 30 years before it was published in 1954 in London. Later, Toivo Tirronen worked on teaching materials, such as a grammar (1977) and a dictionary (1986) of Oshindonga. These were written from the viewpoint of Finnish users. Tirronen also published the Ndonga–English dictionary (1986). Based on the material left by Tirronen, Lahja Lehtonen, in collaboration with Eljas Suikkanen, edited the English–Ndonga dictionary (Lehtonen 1996).

3.3.3   Current Academic Contributions

African linguistics in the Nordic countries has largely been a matter of individual contributions of rather recent vintage. What follows is a country-by-country description of individual academic contributions to African language studies.

3.3.3.1   Sweden
Research on African languages in Sweden is concentrated at two universities, one in Uppsala and one in Gothenburg.

Uppsala University   In Uppsala, the research was mostly in the hands of Abdulaziz Lodhi, an immigrant from Tanzania. He started as a lecturer of Swahili in 1974 in the Faculty of Arts, Department of Linguistics and Philology (currently Faculty of Languages, Department of Semitic Languages). He became Associate Professor in 2002 and Full Professor in 2008. Lodhi later also studied various aspects of Swahili language and culture, including foreign influences on the language. He pointed out lexical loans from a number of Asian languages, and also the structural influences of those languages on Swahili (Lodhi 2000). He pioneered Swahili–Swedish lexicography (Lodhi et al. 1973; Lodhi & Otterbrandt 1987) and contributed to the compilation of Oxford dictionaries of Swahili (Lodhi et al. 2007). His research interests include aspiration in Swahili adjectives and verbs as well as verbal extensions in Bantu languages (Lodhi and Engstrand 1985; Lodhi 2004).

Since Lodhi's retirement in 2012, Swahili teaching has continued, led by a lecturer in general linguistics, Swahili teaching being part of the duties.

University of Gothenburg   The first professor studying African languages at Gothenburg University (Faculty of Arts, Department of Oriental and African languages) was Tore Janson. Initially having studied Latin, he then shifted to African languages, concentrating on comparative Bantu studies. After retiring in 2001, he was affiliated with Stockholm University. Karsten Legère followed Janson in the professorship from 2001 until his retirement in 2010. Having received his academic education in Leipzig under the socialist regime, he worked as a researcher at Dar es Salaam University, and later in Windhoek at the University of Namibia, gaining great experience and publishing widely on African languages. The African studies profile in Gothenburg was different from Uppsala. While in Uppsala the emphasis has been on concrete language teaching (Swahili), in Gothenburg the emphasis has been on research on African languages in general, without extensive African language teaching. The major achievement of Legère is the Languages of Tanzania Project (LoT), carried out in collaboration with the University of Dar es Salaam. He has also worked on endangered languages, in part in collaboration with Bernd Heine and Christa König. The Akie, a southern Nilotic language in Northern Tanzania, and Vidunda, a Bantu language in Central Tanzania, have been special foci (Legère 2007; Legère et al. 2015). Legère was a partner in SIDA-funded linguistic cooperation projects with Maputo (2001–2003) and Dar es Salaam (2001–2010).

The following researchers are based in Gothenburg. Christina Thornell had worked within primary education in the Central African Republic (CAR) in various pedagogical tasks, including the project for developing the orthography of the Sango language. The need to understand linguistic processes more deeply led to formal studies in linguistics. From 1998 she worked in a post-doctoral position at the University of Gothenburg. Characteristic of her work is thorough fieldwork, profiting from her long stay among Sango speakers, when she learned to speak that language. In her PhD dissertation she describes the Sango language and its lexicon from a sociolinguistic and lexicosemantic perspective (Thornell 1997). Thornell also conducted linguistic research among the Mpiemo and documented their speech. These recordings were analysed in collaboration with phoneticians at the University of Lund in Sweden. She also made ethnobotanical studies investigating the knowledge and use of wild plants among the Mpiemo people (Thornell 2005). Later, Thornell studied a language and dialect cluster, which she terms Ukhwejo. She studied the phonological and morphological features of these languages with the aim of establishing their linguistic distance from each other, and also from Mpiemo.

Helene Fatima Idris has studied mostly the linguistic situation in Sudan. She has studied the status and use of African languages in environments where the Arabic language dominates. The focus was especially on the Nyala area (in Darfur) and Khartoum (Idris 2008). She has also participated in the study of language policies in selected African countries (Idris et al. 2007).

Malin Petzell's research interests include Bantu languages, language description (documentation and analysis), nominal and verbal morphosyntax, language endangerment, and field methods (Petzell 2012). Petzell has studied Kami, an endangered language in western Tanzania, as part of a larger project on endangered languages. The aim was to document and analyse the language, keeping in mind the interests of the speaker community as well as of the research community. In another project, Petzell studied tense, aspect, and mood (TAM) systems in selected East Ruvu Bantu languages (Kaguru, Kami, Kwere, Kutu, Luguru, and Zaramo) (Petzell & Hammarström 2013). The TAM features were studied in relation to their forms, meanings, functions, and distribution. Especially interesting in the project is the work of producing semantic verb property lists and describing their interaction with TAM markers, a task usually neglected in language descriptions.

Laura Downing followed Legère as a professor of African languages. She studied information structure in Bantu languages (Downing & Hyman 2016). She also headed a research project studying the prosodic system of Somali. This prosodic system falls between stress and tone and is therefore difficult to study.

Eva-Marie Bloom Ström studied morphosyntactic variation in Xhosa dialects in the Eastern Cape area. The project focused on certain grammatical constructions including relative clause formation, the expression of focus, and the so-called temporal mood – areas where variation is expected.

Tolve Rosendal's study aimed at identifying the reasons behind code-switching, the alternation between Ngoni and Swahili, in the Ruvuma Region in south-western Tanzania. The study addressed such questions as the following: is code-switching a sign of language loss or a communication strategy, or both? Do the Ngoni lose their identity in this process or is it possible that new identities are developed?

Jouni Maho has compiled and maintained very extensive bibliographies of African language studies and other collections of sources and made them available on the web (1998).

3.3.3.2 Norway

In Norway, African language studies are concentrated mainly at the University of Oslo and the Technical University of Norway in Trondheim. In Oslo, pure linguistic studies as well as studies on sociolinguistics and language policy are represented. In Trondheim, courses on Swahili language and culture have been offered since 1980. In addition, the Department of Linguistics has been involved in supporting linguistic research in Africa by providing scholarships for African students and by taking part in various research projects in Africa.

University of Oslo Rolf Theil Endresen was appointed as Associate Professor of African Languages (Hausa, Fulfulde) at Oslo University in 1978, and as Professor of African Languages in 1994. Around 2000, the position was changed to Professor of General and African Linguistics. Endresen retired in 2017. The position is attached to the Department of Linguistics and Philosophy (currently Department of Linguistics and Scandinavian Studies) of the Historical-Philosophical faculty. From 1990 until 2000, Endresen taught Fulfulde and Hausa, with an emphasis on Fulfulde, and most of the research was concentrated on African linguistics, mostly Fulfulde (West Africa) and the non-Bantu Bantoid Nizaa (Cameroon). From 2000, he taught general linguistics, as he had before 1990, but he gave courses in African linguistics until around 2010. He continued to do research on African linguistics, and since 2002 primarily on Omotic languages. His study on phonology included, for example, Nizaa, Kafa, and Koorete (Endresen 1990/1991, 2007, 2011). He carried out grammatical studies on Fulfulde and Subiya, such as on the etymological relationship between benefactive and causative suffixes (Endresen 2008). Endresen has supervised nine PhD students, seven of them from Africa. Edgar Mberi studied the status and functions of auxiliaries in Shona (2002). Langa Khumalo focused on Ndebele passive constructions (2007). The subject of Emmanuel Chabata was the causative in Nambya (2007). Sisay Binyam concentrated on Koorete verbal morphology (2008). Kjelsvik Bjørghild studied emerging speech genres of teaching and learning interaction in Cameroonian schools and villages (2008). Nomalanga Mpofu focused on the Shona adjective (2009). The subject of Ngoshu Debela was the semantics of Oromo frontal adpositions (2011). Bizuneh Gebre studied Shinasha noun morphology (2014).

Kjell Magne Yri studied mostly Ethiopian languages at Oslo University, with special focus on Amharic and Sidaamu/Sidama Afoo. On Sidaamu, he studied the copula and case marking as well as nouns and adjectives, and also the phonology and orthography of the language (Yri 2013). On Amharic, he compared the relative and genitive constructions and their assumed semantic relatedness (Yri 2009).

Ingse Skattum's research area is sociolinguistics, language policy, multilingualism, and orally transmitted literature. In Africa, she studied mainly Bambara and its use in various roles (Skattum 2008). The majority of her publications deal with the role of national languages in education in an environment where the colonial language (French) functions as official language. Particular emphasis is placed on developments in Mali. Together with Birgit Brock-Utne (Brock-Utne and Skattum 2009) and others, she studied the introduction of national languages into primary schools in Mali, and its consequences on training. Mali works as a case study, but the lessons learned there have a bearing on other parts of Africa as well. Skattum has supervised several PhD and MPhil students in the above-mentioned fields. In her PhD dissertation, Kristin Lexander (2010) studied a mixture of Wolof and French, but also Fulfulde, Arabic, Spanish, and English, mainly in SMS, from both a quantitative and a qualitative point of view. The study was carried out among students in Dakar, Senegal. Anne Knutsen (2007) discussed and rejected the claim that French in the Ivory Coast can be considered a pidgin. However, she showed it to be very deviant from standard French and to borrow extensively from African languages. She studied language choice, French morphosyntax, and language attitudes in correspondence with the linguistic profiles of the speakers. Guri Bordal (2012) focused on the influence of the major African language Sango on French prosody.

Marit Lobben is a scholar of the Afroasiatic (Chadic) language Hausa and has worked within major linguistic theories such as Cognitive Grammar, grammaticalization theory, and the prototype theory of linguistic categorization. She is a semanticist as well as a syntactician, and she wrote her PhD dissertation on the polysemous syntactic relationship of causative and benefactive constructions (Lobben 2010). In line with Adele Goldberg's Construction Grammar, she questions the basic tenets of generative syntax, which dissociate syntactic form from meaning. She carried out psycholinguistic fieldwork in Niger, Nigeria, and the Ivory Coast. Her research included studies on the mental storage and memorization techniques of children and adults of the noun plural system in Hausa.

Technical University of Norway, Trondheim   Assibi Amidu is professor at the Norwegian University of Science and Technology (NTNU) in Trondheim, he has given courses in Swahili language, culture, and history since 1980. Born in Ghana, he completed his master's degree at the School of Oriental and African Studies, University of London, in 1976. He completed his PhD degree at the same institution in 1980. The same year he was appointed as a lecturer of Swahili in Trondheim. He has published extensively on various aspects of Bantu languages, using Swahili as the test language. The research subjects include gender and noun classes, transitivity and argument structure, pronouns and pronominalization, as well as lexical and grammatical borrowing (Amidu 2009, 2011).

Adams Bodomo completed his MA degree at the University of Ghana in 1988 and continued his studies at NTNU in Trondheim. In 1993 he completed an MPhil degree in linguistics/African studies, and in 1997 he completed a PhD examination at the same institute (Bodomo 1997). Presently, he is Full Professor and Chair of African Languages and Literatures at the University of Vienna, Austria.

Lars Hellan works at the Technical University of Norway; he has contributed to the development of language technology of African languages through various projects. Based initially on sign theory, he developed approaches for categorizing verbs on the basis of their behaviour in sentences. Together with his colleagues, Dorothee Beermann and Mary Esther Kropp Dakubu, he has even extended the work to include multilingual environments. The MultiVal project, for which Norwegian, Spanish, and Ga (Ghana) were taken as test languages, is an example of such cooperation in this field (Hellan et al. 2013; Hellan et al. 2014). Such work leads to important repositories of structured data in the badly neglected field of verb semantics, benefiting also the study of African languages. Another important initiative is the construction of TypeCraft, a user-driven database for the creation and retrieval of small corpora of Interlinear Glossed Text (Beerman and Mihaylov 2014; Beermann 2015).

Norway has been a counterpart and principal funder in such projects as Computational Lexicography, Typology, and Adult Literacy (The Legon-Trondheim Linguistics Project) in cooperation with the University of Ghana, sponsored by NUFU, for the periods 1996–2000, 2002–2007, and 2007–2009, and MaLEX (Malawi Lexicon Project), computational documentation of three Malawian languages, in cooperation with the University of Malawi, sponsored by NUFU, for the period 2007–2012. The main target here was dictionary compilation, although only one has come out so far (for Ciyawo) and two PhDs.

3.3.3.3 Denmark

Current African linguistic research in Denmark is associated with initiatives by individual researchers, such as Karl-G. Prasse, Torben Andersen, and William McGregor.

Karl-G. Prasse from the University of Copenhagen was born in Hamburg, Germany, in 1929. He stands out as Denmark's eminent scholar of Tuareg (Berber), including grammatical descriptions (1972–1973–1974–2009). He also studied their oral literature (1989–1990) and compiled a Tuareg–French dictionary containing about 40,000 entries and covering the two main Tuareg dialects of Niger, namely those of the Azawagh and Ayr regions, supplemented by a number of notes from the dialects of the Kél-Geres and Mali (Prasse 2003).

Torben Andersen from Aalborg University worked for a number of years as a lecturer in the Department of Communication and Psychology (Faculty of Humanities) while studying African languages as part of his duties. In 2012 he became Associate Professor in Comparative Linguistics. He has studied Nilotic languages, carrying out fieldwork, for example, in Sudan. Individual languages that he has studied include Dinka, Berta, Kurmuk, Jumjum, Mayak, Anywa, and Päri. On Dinka, he studied verbal directionality and argument alternation, interrogative sentences, and auxiliary verbs. On Mayak he studied number inflection, vowel harmony, and vowel alternation. He also compared the phonology and morphophonology as well as morhosyntax of Anywa and Päri languages.

William McGregor at the Department of Linguistics, Cognitive Science and Semiotics at Aarhus University has done research on the Khoisan language Shua (McGregor 2014, 2015).

3.3.3.4 Finland

Finland's contributions to African linguistics also rest with a limited number of individual yet highly productive researchers centred at the University of Helsinki. Full-time teaching and study of African languages at Helsinki University started in 1980, when Arvi Hurskainen was appointed as lecturer of Bantu languages. The subject was enlarged to 'African studies' in 1989, when a professorship was also established. Hurskainen was appointed to this position, where he continued until retirement in 2006, whereupon Axel Fleisch took over the professorship. The lectureship of Bantu languages was continued by Raimo Harjula, and from 2004 onwards by Lotta Aunio (formerly Harjula).

Arvi Hurskainen's major contribution to African linguistics lies in the field of language technology. The principal African language that he used for developing technological tools was Swahili. Among early outcomes of this research was a morphological analyser of Swahili (1992). The work continued by developing the disambiguation component (1996). Later on, the emphasis was on developing rule-based machine translation systems between Swahili and English, as well as on other applications facilitated by rule-based language technology. Major outcomes of these developments include the analysed corpus of Swahili (Helsinki Corpus of Swahili 1.0, Helsinki Corpus of Swahili 2.0),[3] a Swahili spelling checker that was included in Microsoft Word distributions (Hurskainen 1992), a dictionary-compiling system on the basis of text corpus (Hurskainen 2015), an intelligent interactive language learning system (Hurskainen 2010), a vocabulary compiler, and a bilingual corpus tagger.

---

[3] http://urn.fi/urn:nbn:fi:lb-2014032624 (main page of the corpus) http://urn.fi/urn:n-bn:fi:lb-2016011301 (annotated version) http://urn.fi/urn:nbn:fi:lb-2016011302 (not annotated version).

Using language technology methods, he also analysed the performance of five Swahili dictionaries (Hurskainen 2002), trying to find out how well they cover the words used in prose text. Another application of language technology was the programme for converting disjoint writing into conjoint writing, as is the case with such languages as Kwanyama (Hurskainen & Halme 2001) and Northern Sotho (Hurskainen et al. 2005).

In his research, Hurskainen paved the way to developing the type of language technology that might be suitable for most African languages. Machine translation technology has shifted more and more to using methods such as statistical machine translation (Koehn 2010) and neural machine translation (Cho et al. 2014). These technologies require extensive human-translated parallel corpora for training the system. They also require that the morphological structure of the language be fairly simple and that the word order of the source language and target language be similar. None of these requirements is satisfied with most African languages. In contrast to these current approaches, the rule-based methods, such as those developed by Hurskainen, do not need those preconditions. The language technology systems are based on detailed linguistic and lexical description. This method makes it possible to describe exhaustively morphological structures of any complexity and to translate the messages in to another language. The language technology field is aware of the danger that many minority languages, especially those in Africa, are in danger of falling out of the main development trend in translation technology. In many cases Africa has benefited from technology transfer developed somewhere else. In this case, however, the transfer may lead to disaster and disillusionment, because the main trend methods simply do not suit African languages. The danger should be widely acknowledged and measures should be taken in Africa to develop such language technology that is suitable and affordable. By using rule-based translation methods, African languages could be integrated into the global translation system, where any language can be translated into any other language. Each local language would need only one translation system, that is, a quality translation system between that language and interlingua (for practical reasons a variety of English) in both directions. This would facilitate global communication between all languages.

Sponsored by the Ministry of Foreign Affairs, Hurskainen, together with the Institute of Kiswahili Research at the University of Dar es Salaam, carried out the Swahili Language and Folklore research project between 1988 and 1992. The aim was to collect linguistic data on Swahili dialects in Tanzania as well as to collect folklore in these language varieties (Hurskainen 1993). The collection contains wordlists of 610 items from all Swahili dialect areas of Tanzania as well as over 100 hours of recorded speech from those dialect areas. The records were first transcribed into written form, and later they were also digitized into sound files.

Hurskainen also initiated the periodical *Nordic Journal of African Studies* in 1992. The periodical first appeared in printed form, but later the issues were moved to the web, where they are freely available to all.[4]

Lotta Aunio wrote her PhD dissertation on the Ha language in western Tanzania, describing various aspects of the language, including tone (Harjula 2004). Later she undertook a comparative study of Bantu nominal tone, comparing tone in the Ikoma, Nata, and Isenye languages in western Tanzania (Aunio 2015). She also initiated the Mara Project, where she, together with other researchers, studied more extensively the languages of the Mara area in Tanzania. The topic of this study was the comparative grammar of four lacustrine Bantu languages, adding also Ngoreme to the above-mentioned three languages. The project studied the grammar from the perspective of linguistic variation as an indicator of historical relations and language contact (Aunio et al., forthcoming). She also provided an important study on syllable weight and tone in Mara Bantu languages (Aunio 2017).

Axel Fleisch followed Hurskainen on the chair, having received his initial training in African linguistics in Germany. His PhD dissertation was on the morphosemantic analysis of the Lucazi language belonging to a cluster of closely related varieties in south-eastern Angola known as Ngangela. The study focused on the grammatical description of the language in general, but also more specifically on the analysis of the verbal morphology and its interaction with lexical semantics (Fleisch 2000). Fleisch has also studied word order variation in two Berber dialects, Taqbaylit (Kabyle) and Tashelhit (Shilha). He found that although Berber is considered a VSO language, pragmatics trigger the emergence of relatively stable discourse-configurationality, without giving rise to a VSO > SVO shift. In another study of Berber languages, Fleisch (2007) elucidated the problem of classifying these languages along the twofold typology as either verb-framing or satellite-framing, concentrating mainly on Tashelhit (Fleisch 2007).

Fleisch carried out in-depth research on locativizing strategies in Southern Ndebele (Fleisch 2005). While Bantu languages normally have the threefold locative class system (definite, inside, and indefinite), Southern Ndebele has lost it and instead developed a complex system where upper space plays a significant role. The expression of spatial notions is discussed on the basis of the four etymologically related terms *phezu* (*kwa-*+N), *phezulu*, *ngaphezu* (*kwa-*+N), and *ngaphezulu*. These terms serve to express orientational and topological notions referring to upper space. The locatives are best understood as etymologically related radial categories which have undergone different diachronic developments with considerable overlap. The locative structures are context-sensitive and co-occur in certain landmark and trajector noun phrases.

---

[4] www.njas.helsinki.fi; since 2018: www.njas.fi.

Also verbs often have derivational morphology when used with these locatives. Therefore, it is problematic to classify Southern Ndebele as belonging to either verb-framed or satellite-framed languages. Perhaps Southern Ndebele, as well as other Nguni languages, is a borderline case, undergoing diachronic change from a language type that tends to be rather verb-framed to one which tends to be more satellite-framed.

Fleisch also studied recent advances in comparative Bantu studies. He claims that two major trends in recent historical linguistics have found their way into more recent approaches to Bantu language history. One is that traditional philological work with its focus on historical particularities and the wealth of descriptive data has been extended into a line of investigation that is more concerned with the history of semantic change. An important question for this broadened approach is how to account for regularities in historical lexical semantics. The other notion is that if concepts are understood as radial categories, many of the often puzzling relations between different meanings of cognate lexical items can be accounted for in a more satisfactory way than before. By linking divergent meanings in cognitively plausible ways, there is no need to assume an unconvincingly high number of idiosyncratic innovations. It seems that approaches to Bantu historical semantics will have to integrate a notion that allows for similar semantic changes in different languages without necessarily regarding these as shared innovations. Fleisch has also contributed to the study of theories and methods of African conceptual history (Fleisch 2016).

Doctoral and postdoctoral research in Helsinki covers a wide range of topics. Based on the morphological analyser of Swahili (Hurskainen 1992), Seleman Sewangi from Dar es Salaam University wrote his PhD dissertation on the computer-assisted extraction of terms in specific domains (Sewangi 2001). Based on the same analysis system, Wanjiku Ng'ang'a from Nairobi University wrote a PhD dissertation on word sense disambiguation of Swahili using machine learning technologies (Ng'ang'a 2005). Gregory Kamwendo from the University of Malawi wrote his PhD dissertation on language policy and health services in a Malawian referral hospital (Kamwendo 2004). Riikka Halme wrote her PhD dissertation on the tone system of Kwanyama (Halme 2004). The PhD dissertation of Don Killian was on Uduk phonology and morphosyntax (Killian 2015). Jonna Katto wrote her PhD dissertation on the female guerrilla fighters of FRELIMO in northern Mozambique (Katto 2017).

4 African Linguistics in North Africa

Abderrahman El Aissati and Yamina El Kirat El Allame

4.1 Introduction

In this chapter, we are discussing works conducted within local institutions, that is, works whose authors were, or still are, based in North Africa. Admittedly, a large amount of local research has not been published widely and is, consequently, not very well known; this includes work that continues to be done on the Internet. Therefore, the present overview cannot be complete. We have chosen to include all accessible research carried out by agents who were employed by a local institution, regardless of the duration of such employment and the ultimate origin of the researcher. We will deal with any works on language in general, including descriptive studies and grammar books, the compilation of dictionaries, and the development of teaching materials. The reader will find information on the history and development of language studies in North Africa with a double focus on studies of Berber and varieties of spoken Arabic. Clearly, Arabic linguistics has the lion's share of research and publications, given that Arabic is the official language and holds a prominent position in the Islamic world.

For ease of exposition, we have chosen a country-by-country approach and have divided this overview for each country basically into three subsequent historical periods: the precolonial period, the European colonization period, and the post-independence period. Although these periods differ for the respective countries in the area, their significance in shaping different kinds of research interests remains comparable. The precolonial 'Islamic' period was a warranty for interest in Arabic, the colonization period brought about more interest in local varieties, with continuation of interest in Arabic and Islam in general,[1] while independence allowed local universities to have their own research agendas, in many cases starting with a hostile attitude to languages other than Arabic, and sparking debates on national languages and languages of education. Arab nationism has been using Arabic as

---

[1] The Congrès international des Orientalistes, which held its first session in 1873 in Paris, is a good illustration of the interest of colonial powers in the 'Orient'. The proceedings of many of its sessions are available online (e.g. first session at: http://gallica.bnf.fr/ark:/12148/bpt6k65804267/f1.image, accessed 28 December 2016).

a pillar in building new postcolonial states, usually, but not always, with Islam as a common denominator for countries where Arabic is – mostly – the only official language.

4.2   Egypt

Considering any systematic work on language as part of linguistics would take us back about 4,000 years to the time when the Egyptians invented hieroglyphs to render speech in writing.[2] The interest of Ptolemaic Egyptians in phonetics, for example, was noted by Johnson (2013) referring to their 'propensity for punning as well as for other word-play dependent on phonetics'. The language(s) used in antiquity in what has come to be known as Egypt is commonly believed to be an ancestor of Coptic.

Mostly because Coptic was the language of the Coptic Church, especially after the Copts turned away from the Byzantine Church (Rubenson 1996), it remained in use for several centuries, even during the Islamic conquest of the area, and is still in use as a liturgical language today. A Coptic–Greek bilingual lexicon was written in the Middle Ages (see Sidarus 1978 for a general overview of this period). One should expect more on Coptic by indigenous authors because of its importance to the Coptic Church. Some examples of works on the language in the nineteenth century are Lepsius (1835, 1836, 1880), Tattam (1863), and Ludwig (1880). Coptic was already known to Western scholars in the late fifteenth century (Emmel 2004, cited in Grossman et al. 2015:4).[3]

Coptic is a good example illustrating the role of religion in fortifying the position of a language, if the language in question is associated with this religion. As Sidarus (1978:125–126) notes, 'the majority of Coptic philologists will be found to be eminent biblical scholars'. In the twentieth century, Coptic Egyptian vernaculars continued receiving some attention. A number of dialect descriptions and grammar compilations appeared, including Chaîne (1933) on the grammar of Coptic dialects, and Mallon's grammar of Coptic, first published in 1904 (available online), with a fourth edition appearing in 1956. Mallon's grammar focuses on the Boharic dialect of Coptic, with comparisons to other dialects where relevant. In 1948, a Coptic grammar in English was published (Plumley 1948), but more grammar descriptions of Coptic (various dialects) have appeared more recently, such as Reintges (2004), Shisha-Halevy's (1986) structural study of Coptic grammatical categories and his voluminous study (2007) on Coptic syntax, reviewing work on the syntax of the Bohairic dialect.

---

[2] See Appendix I A Brief Survey of the History of Linguistics; www.templeok.com/Appendix%20 I%20A%20Brief%20Survey%20of%20the%20History%20of%20Linguistics%20V2.pdf (accessed 19 October 2016); the non-hieroglyphic systems are left out of consideration.
[3] For a review of studies on the Coptic language, see Hamilton (2006:193–272).

Vergote's *grammaire copte* (1973–1983) is also an illustration of the interest in descriptive grammars of Coptic.

Work on Egyptian Arabic was done by indigenous as well as foreign researchers. The earliest known study of Egyptian Arabic, where the colloquial is recognized as a separate language from Standard Arabic, was by the Egyptian Yusuf al-Maghribi, who discusses the 'impurity' of Egyptian Arabic, which despite its heavy loans from Coptic remains an Arabic variety (Zack 2009). Ayoub (1949), on verbal morphology of Egyptian Arabic, stands out among the few works done on Egyptian Arabic in the first half of the twentieth century.

More recent studies of Egyptian Arabic cover all major fields of language studies, namely syntax, such as Anwar (1979) on the copula 'be' and equational sentences in Egyptian colloquial Arabic, Al-Jundi (1965) on the syntax of Arabic dialects, Saad (1967) on the syntax of Egyptian Arabic, further introductory and/or descriptive grammars, such as Abdel-Massih et al. (2009) and Khalafallh (1969) on Sa'idi Egyptian Arabic, and Abu Farag's (1960) work on the Arabic variety of Tahway (Minufia Province). Important works containing contributions on various linguistic topics are as follows:

- Phonology and phonetics: see Abdallah (1960) on the intonation of Egyptian Colloquial Arabic, Helmy-Hassan (1960) on the phonology of Cairene Arabic, and Abu-Lfadl (1961) on a dialect of the Sharqiyya province in Egypt.
- Morphology: see Ghali's (1960) dissertation on substantive morphology of Egyptian Arabic and Abu-Lfetouh (1961) on the morphology of Egyptian Colloquial Arabic.
- Dictionaries: see, for example, Badawi and Kees (1958).

Al-Jundi (1965) stands out as one of the few PhD dissertations that were defended at an Egyptian University. Language contact between Coptic and Egyptian Arabic was also a topic of research (e.g. Bishai 1959, 1960, 1961).

For an overview of research in Arabic linguistics in general, we recommend a visit to the website of the Arabic Linguistics Society (ALS).[4] The ALS has been organizing an annual symposium on Arabic linguistics since 1987. Selections of papers from these symposia appear regularly in the series Perspectives on Arabic Linguistics, published by John Benjamins. The research interests of the ALS are clearly stated on its website: 'theoretical linguistics (phonetics, phonology, syntax, semantics, morphology), historical linguistics, sociolinguistics, pragmatics and discourse analysis, psycholinguistics, corpus linguistics, and computational linguistics'. The American Association of Teachers of Arabic (AATA) publishes the annual journal *Al-'arabiya*, with contributions spanning

---

[4] www4.uwm.edu/letsci/linguistics/als/.

various fields such as pedagogy, philology, (socio)linguistics (aataweb.org). Both ALS and AATA are oriented towards Arabic in general, be it standard or colloquial, and regardless of the countries where it is spoken.

Egyptian languages other than Coptic and Arabic have received much less attention. Miller (1996) provides an overview of works on Nubian, Beja, and Berber in Egypt. Nubian has had a bigger share in linguistics literature, partly because of its importance in terms of number of speakers. These are more substantial in Sudan than in Egypt, where only speakers of Kenzi (known as Matoki by its speakers) and Fadicca can be found, although these are practically not to be found in Egypt anymore, but in neighbouring Sudan. Interested archeologists and the massive displacement of Nubian populations have also played a major role in this attention.

The language of the Siwa Oasis, commonly referred to as Siwi Berber, caught the attention of Stumme (1914), Walker (1921), Laoust (1931), and Abd al-Khalik (1940; cited in Vycichl 1991). In general, this Eastern-most variety of Berber remains under-represented in Berber studies in general. Recently, however, the *Berber Studies Journal* (published by Rüdiger Köppe, Cologne) has contributed greatly to disseminating research on Berber and other African languages, and on the Siwi Berber variety of Egypt in particular. Volume 10 in the series, edited by Dymitr Ibriszimov and Maarten Kossmann, is a publication of a number of chapters written by Vycichl as part of an ambitious project on Berber historical linguistics. More recent works on Siwi Berber, which appeared in the same series, are Naumann's (2012) dissertation on the acoustic properties of the segments of Siwi Berber and Souag (2013) on language contact between Arabic and Siwi Berber, with numerous examples from Siwi, and complete texts illustrating different genres. The latter also contains an extensive grammar description of Siwi. Souag's (2010) dissertation on language contact in the language islands of Siwa and Tabelbala (Algeria) is a much-needed addition to the studies of language contact in the area.

Beja, an Afroasiatic (Northern Cushitic) language, mostly spoken in Sudan and by a few thousand speakers in the southernmost part of Egypt, has been the object of a few studies, such as Adrob (1986) on the influence of Arabic on the lexicon of Beja, and Vanhove (2006), who presents an overview of the state of affairs regarding research on this language. She notes the work of Almkvist (1881–1885) as the first one on Beja, pointing out its limitations in not being a linguistic work, but more of an account of the history of Bishari dialect. The most substantial work done on Beja is authored by Reinisch (1893–1894), 'which includes a grammatical description mixing elements of the northern and southern varieties (Beni Amer, Bishari and Hadendowa), with a lot of etymological notes, and a collection of texts in phonetic transcription with a translation into German, which was followed by a bilingual dictionary (1895)' (Vanhove 2006:2).

For Nile-Nubian, Miller (1996) recommends consulting Armbruster (1960, 1965); Bell (1970a); Junker and Schäfer (1921); Massenbach (1933, 1962); Mitwalli Badr (1955); Schäfer (1917); Werner (1987).

Examples of works on Nubian are Rouchdy (1980, 1991) on contact between Arabic and Nubian, and Abdel-Hafiz (1988), which is a comprehensive work on the grammar of Kunuz Nubian. Other publications containing contributions on different linguistic topics related to Nubian can easily be found; e.g. Bender (1989), Abu Manga et al. (2006). A general annotated bibliography of Nubian languages is compiled by Jakobi and Kümmerle (1993). A specialized journal in Nubian studies was launched in 2014, under the name of *Dotawo: A Journal of Nubian Studies*. The journal was created to cater for the following:[5]

Nubian studies needs a platform in which the old meets the new, in which archaeological, papyrological, and philological research into Meroitic, Old Nubian, Coptic, Greek, and Arabic sources confront current investigations in modern anthropology and ethnography, Nilo-Saharan linguistics, and critical and theoretical approaches present in post-colonial and African studies.

For more recent publications, numerous resources are available, such as the journal *Zeitschrift für Arabische Linguistik* (from 1978).[6] A more recently released journal on Arabic linguistics is the *International Journal of Arabic Linguistics* (vol. 1 in 2015), edited by Echcharfi (University Mohamed V, Morocco) and Al Batal (University of Texas at Austin).[7]

Issues relating to the sociology of language and sociolinguistics were addressed quite early in Egypt. Awad (1947, 1980) defended the idea that Egyptian Arabic is capable of functioning in all domains, including those assigned to Standard Arabic. This was a rather revolutionary idea at the time, namely to compare a colloquial variety to the Standard, which is deemed to rise above all variations. Sharing this idea of the non-sacredness of Arabic was another scholar, Taha Hussein. He defended Arabic as a national symbol and offered the Coptic Church his help to 'improve' the use of Arabic in its services (Suleiman 2008:37–38).

4.3   Libya

Libyan languages have received less attention in linguistic research compared to other languages in the area (see Behnstedt & Woidich 2013:322 and Benkato & Perreira 2016). Different varieties of Libyan Berber have been

---

[5] See the home page of the journal at: https://punctumbooks.com/titles/dotawo-volume-1-2014/.
[6] Issues up until 2013 are available online at www.digizeitschriften.de/en/dms/toc/?PPN=PPN513339353.
[7] For more info on this journal, see http://arabic-linguistics.com/.

identified in the literature, such as Nefusi and Zuara in the north-west part of the country, as well as Awjila, Sokna, El Fogaha, Tamasheq, and Ghadames. An Indo-European descendant, Domari, is still spoken in Libya, and so is the Nilo-Saharan language Tedaga, which is reported to have a few hundred speakers in the southern part of the country. Benkato and Pereira (2016) report that they could not find a single work on the Libyan varieties of Hausa and Tubu (also referred to as Tibu, Tibbu, Tebu, Tebou), nor on the Greek variety still spoken by the Gritliya community in eastern Libya. Although we know to a certain extent about the languages spoken in the part known as Libya before the Islamic conquest, it is difficult to find any works on these languages in this early era.

A few publications can be found dating back to the nineteenth century, such as Rohlfs (1872) on numerals in Ghadames Berber and Newman's (1882) book on Libyan vocabulary. Hartmann's (1899) collection of poems in Arabic of the Bedouin desert is another example from this period, although not technically a linguistic publication. An interesting compilation of texts from a Libyan language dating from this period is that on Nefoussi Berber of Chenenni by Bossoutrot (1900);[8] Vycichl (1972) is another study on Nefoussi Berber. Ghadames Berber was dealt with by Calassanti-Motylinski (1903, 1904), who also dealt with Nefoussi Berber in a publication dating to 1898. A more recent publication on Ghadames Berber is Vycichl (1966). One publication that stands out is that of Nehlil (1909) on the variety of Ghat, but no extra information could be found about this author.

In general, publications on Libyan matters, including languages, have appeared in specialized journals published in Europe, but also in Algeria, Tunisia, and Morocco. The *Revue du Monde Musulman* (published in Paris by Leroux, between 1908 and 1926) was under the editorship of the Mission Scientifique du Maroc, later the Direction Générale des Affaires Indigènes, Section sociologique, and subsequently the Direction des Affaires Politiques, Section des affaires islamiques.

A few works were done on the Arabic of Libya, especially on the variety of Tripoli, such as Stumme (1898), Farina (1912), Griffini (1913), Scialhub (1913), Rossi (1935), Newman (1936), Cesàro (1939, 1954), and to a much lesser extent on the Arabic of Benghazi , such as Panetta (1943a, 1943b, 1958, 1962a, 1962b), whose work on Benghazi Arabic spans a period of almost four decades.

Regarding Libyan Jewish Arabic varieties, there seems to be very little work done on them. Tripoli Jewish Arabic was dealt with by Cohen (1928), while Benghazi Jewish Arabic was not dealt with at all (Benkato & Perreira 2016). Other varieties that have been scarcely studied are those of Southern

---

[8] A brief review can be found in Brugnatelli (2016).

Libya (Fezzan region). The only substantial work on these is that of Philippe Marçais, which was carried out between the 1940s and 1970 but published posthumously (Benkato & Pereira 2016; see also Marçais 1945, 1956, 1957). Other works cited in the annotated bibliography of Benkato and Perreira are language learning manuals and dictionaries, very likely provided for the benefit of the Italian army (see n.a. 1900, 1911, 1941).

Berber languages of Libya were also treated in a few publications, but to a much lesser extent than Arabic varieties. The only works we could come across for this period, including those cited in Benkato and Pereira (2016), are Farina (1912), Trombetti (1912), Griffini (1913), Beguinot (1914, 1930, 1934, 1935), and Buselli (1921, 1924) on Nefusi Berber.

Benkato and Pereira (2016) have found 37 PhD dissertations by Libyan researchers on Libyan Arabic, one on Berber, and a dozen MA theses, all defended at American and European universities, and unpublished. A few examples are Steita's (1970) MA thesis (at the University of Leeds) on grammatical categories in Cyrenaican Arabic, Laradi's (1972) MA thesis on negation in Tripoli Arabic, Elfitoury's (1976) descriptive grammar of Libyan Arabic, Laradi's (1983) PhD dissertation on pharyngealization in Tripoli Arabic, Abumdas (1985) on the phonology of the variety of Zliten (Western Libya), Harrama's (1993) dissertation on the morphology of the Al-Jabal dialect of Libyan Arabic (Nefussa mountains). The only PhD dissertation on Berber which we could find in the bibliography of Benkato and Perreira is the one by Yedder (1982). It contains a large body of ceremonial chants in the Berber variety of Ghadames (the thesis can be downloaded from the SOAS library website).

Starting from the second decade of the twenty-first century, there has been a significant rise in the number of theses on Libyan Arabic, ranging from phonetics to discourse analysis (see Benkato & Pereira 2016 for more recent publications on Arabic and Berber Libyan varieties).

European-based researchers, especially those with an Italian background, have enriched studies of Libyan languages, such as Serra (e.g. 1964, 1967, 1968a-b) on Zuara Berber, Chiauzzi (1971, 1972, 1974), whose work was more ethnographic than linguistic, but also other orientalists from different nationalities, such as Vycichl (1952, 1954, 1972, 1991, 2005). All in all, in North Africa, Libya remains the country with the least research on its indigenous varieties.

4.4   Tunisia

The oldest reference to a work on Arabic in Tunisia in the bibliography of Youssi (1989) is Stumme (1893), while the oldest references we could find to a study of Berber in Tunisia is Calassanti-Motylinski (1885), cited in Boukous (1989c:150).

Interest in the languages of Tunisia can be seen in a number of publications in the *Revue Tunisienne*. This journal was published by the Institut de Carthage (Association tunisienne des lettres, sciences et arts), between 1894 and 1913 (twenty issues). A complete index of the contents of the different issues has been made available online by the French National Library.[9] The contents of the journal give a good idea of the importance of language issues during the period of its publication. One of the main concerns of contributors was the origin of the languages of North Africa, mainly Arabic and Berber, as can be seen in the articles by Bertholon (1905–1906), and other contributions in Volumes 10, 11, 12, and 13 of the same journal.

Equally important was the study of the structure and lexicon of the different varieties, language borrowing, and language contact, as can be seen from the index of topics of the journal:

- language contact/lexical borrowing, 'Infiltration graduelle de termes français et italiens dans la langue judéo-arabe de Tunis [Gradual infiltration of French and Italian terms in Tunisian Judeo-Arabic]', Volume 11 (1904), p. 499,
- the writing systems of these languages, 'Berbère: plusieurs lettres de ces langues ne peuvent etre figurées que par l'alphabet grec [many letters can be depicted only by means of the Greek alphabet]', Volume 10 (1903), p. 114, Volume 10, p. 72; 'Figuration rationnelle des lettres et signes de la langue arabe, reproduits en caractères latins [Rational depiction of letters and signs of Arabic, reproduced in Latin characters]', Volume 17 (1910), pp. 306, 409, 510, Volume 18 (1911), pp. 54, 327.

What could be termed as a beginning of sociolinguistic studies is illustrated by articles on the functions of languages in different contexts, such as

- 'L'arabe, est-il une language vivante? [Is Arabic a living language?]', Volume 16 (1909), p. 269, and
- 'Notions sur les langues littéraires et vulgaires, mortes et vivantes [Notions on literary and colloquial languages, living and dead]', Volume 16 (1909), p. 181.
- 'Persistence des langues berbère et punique à l'époque romaine [Persistence of Berber and Punic languages during the Roman era]', Volume 10 (1903), p. 370,
- 'Le tunisien, l'algérien, le marocain sont des langues vivantes, filles de langue arabe morte, nécessité de les développer [Tunisian, Algerian, and Moroccan are living languages, daughters of the dead Arabic language, necessity of developping them]', Volume 22 (1913), p. 518,

---

[9] http://gallica.bnf.fr/ark:/12148/bpt6k580392q/f1.image.

- 'La vitalité d'une langue ne peut se mesurer à la facilité d'accroissement de son vocabulaire [The vitality of a language cannot be measured by the ease of growth of its vocabulary]', Volume 15 (1908), p. 302.

One of the earliest substantial studies on Tunisien Berber varieties is Basset (1891). In 1911, Provotelle published a study on the phonology and morphology of the Berber variety of Qal'at Es-sened (Boukous 1989c:144).

A certain similarity between Tunisia and Egypt should be noted; it concerns the interest in a national vernacular. Abdesslam (1956) addresses the relationship of Standard Arabic to colloquial Tunisian Arabic. Khmiri (1958) and Kraief (1959) take up this issue in short articles written in Arabic. Garmadi (1966, 1972) and Skik (1967) provide an analysis of the linguistic situation of Tunisia and the challenges of multilingualism, including French. Hamzaoui (1970) deals with Arabicization within the Tunisian Ministry of the Interior. A general account of the linguistic situation in Tunisia after independence is given in Maamouri (1973).

Language contact and borrowing was also on the agenda of authors such as Baccouche (1966), who examines the language of mechanics, and Ghazi (1958) and Garmadi (1966) on contact between French and Arabic in Tunisia. Attia (1966) addresses a sociolinguistic issue by examining the different registers of the use of Arabic in Tunisia.

Linguistics proper, especially phonology and morphology, had also a share in the interest of indigenous linguists. Attia (1969) contributes to the study of the phonology of the Mahdia variety of Tunisian, Skik (1967) provides a description of the phonology of the Tunisian Arabic variety of Gabès, Baccouche (1972) examines the phoneme /g/ in Tunisian urban centres, and Baccouche (1969) deals with the phonology of the Tunisian Arabic variety of Djemmal.

Language and education was treated in works such as Garmadi (1968a, 1968b). The choice of the instruction language at school, where the competition between French and Arabic was most obvious, both at policy level and in practice (contrastive analysis), was also taken up by different authors, such as El Ayeb (1966) on school language errors in Arabic, and Baffoun (1973) on psychological effects of the type of language of instruction. Nomenclature did not escape the attention of some authors, such as Garmadi (1966) on street signs.

Tunisian Berber has attracted very little interest in linguistic research, seeing the small percentage of its speakers in the country (Boukous 1989c). One of the main sources on Tunisian Berber in the early period of independence is Pencheon (1968). Tunisian researchers are still scarce on the topic of Berber. The entry on Berber of Tunisia in the *Encyclopédie berbère* contains one reference to a North African (Moroccan) linguist (Ahmed Boukous 1989c on

Tunisian Berber), while Boukous (1989c) cites no Tunisian author in his overview of Berber in Tunisia. The most recent reference to a work on Tunisian Berber we could trace is Gabsi (2013), which is the published version of his PhD dissertation *A Concise Grammar of the Berber Language of Douiret (Southern Tunisia)*, defended in 2003 at the University of Western Sydney. In 2011, Gabsi published an article on attrition and maintenance of Berber in Tunisia. An informative entry on Amazigh of Djerba is provided by Chaker (1995).

4.5   Algeria

As early as 1832, the teaching of Arabic and Islamic jurisprudence was allowed by French authorities, and as soon as the Ecole Supérieure des Lettres was founded in 1879, the teaching of Berber became institutionalized.

Chaker (1982:81) notes the advanced state and high quality of linguistic studies in the Maghreb, in comparison to social sciences studies in general, but also underlines the small number of such studies. The scarcity of research on Berber varieties could not be explained by the absence of knowledge of the existence of this language, as texts from different varieties were already in circulation even before 1830, i.e. before Algeria officially became a protectorate of France (de Saporta 1970–1971, in Chaker 1982:82).

Language studies conducted in the nineteenth century in Algeria and in the Maghreb in general were authored by military officials, such as General Hanoteau's description of Kabyle (1858) and Touareg (1860), or religious authorities, such as Père C. Huyghe (1901) on Kabyle and (1906) on Chaouia and Père Charles de Foucauld on Touareg (Chaker 1982:82), while academically oriented researchers remain a small minority.

The end of the nineteenth century saw the appearance of local interest in Berber, the product of which remains of little scientific value but added considerably to lexical studies, such as the work of Boulifa, Ben Khouas, Ben Sedira, and Cid Kaoui (Chaker 1982:82). The twentieth century witnessed a continuation of research on Berber, which ceased to be a monopoly of religious and military institutions, and was taken up by the university, or institutions of higher studies, with an overwhelming majority of French authors in French-controlled zones, and Spanish and Italian authors in zones under Spanish and Italian administration in Morocco and Libya.

Language studies in Algeria (and the Maghreb) were not in line with the contemporary structuralist trends in linguistics at the time. Before the independence of the countries of the Maghreb, the predominant tradition was the French linguistic tradition, inspired by scholars such as Antoine Meillet or E. Vendryes (Chaker 1982:84).

The Arabic varieties of Algeria did not receive as much attention as those of the other countries of the Maghreb. Some of the few indigenous authors are Bencheneb (1905—1907) on Algerian proverbs, (1922) on Turkish borrowings in Algerian Arabic, (1942, 1943) on the varieties of Algiers, and (1946) on the Média variety (south of Algiers). Dhina (1938) deals with phonetics and phonology of the variety of Arba' in southern Algeria. In this connection, we also note Cohen (1912) on Jewish Arabic of Algiers.

In 1931, Marcel Cohen founded the research group GLECS (Groupe Linguistique d'Études Chamito-Sémitiques) at the École des Hautes Études in Paris (Sorbonne), which would deal with Maghreb languages, including Berber and Arabic varieties. As its name indicates, the publication of the GLECS (*Comptes Rendus du Groupe Linguistique d'Études Chamito-Sémitiques*) would consist mainly of works on the languages of North Africa and the Middle East. Local publishing houses have contributed to facilitating publications of all kinds on Algerian and North African matters, including language and literature. The best known of these are the Jourdan, La Typo-Litho and Jules Carbonnel in Algiers. A large number of the works on the languages of the region was published with the support of local authorities and/or that of French authorities. La Typo-Litho and Jules Carbonel published the journal *Bulletin des Études Arabes* (intermédiaire des arabisants) from 1941 to 1952.

After the independence of Algeria in 1962, research on Algerian colloquial languages was not a priority for the newly created universities, such as the University of Algiers. In fact, starting from 1962, the Berber chair was cancelled, even before the creation of the University of Algiers. Some interest in Algerian Arabic could be discerned, as can be seen by publications around this time. These include Djidjelli (1962) and Dziri (1970), both intended for use as teaching manuals for Algerian Arabic.

The first publication in Berber on the grammar of Berber is authored by Mouloud Mammeri in 1976. Work on Berber, and Arabic to a lesser extent, found fertile ground in French universities, which were relatively more accessible to North African students and researchers. A number of theses were defended in French universities on different topics relating to language, such as Chaker (1973) on verbal derivation in Kabyle, and Morsly (1988) on language borrowing between French and Arabic.

There are a number of sociolinguistic investigations on Algerian varieties, such as Dendane (2007) on language attitudes and sociolinguistic variation, Bagui (2012) on the use of Standard Arabic in everyday conversations, and Ammour (2012) on language variation in Nedroma. An analysis of the linguistic situation in Algeria, which focuses in particular on the conflict between Arabic and French but also the rivalry between French and English (Chapter 4 of the book) can be found in Benrabah (2013).

4.6   Morocco

The Arabic varieties in Morocco have received a large amount of scholarly attention. The bibliography of Moroccan Arabic, compiled by Youssi (1989), lists 363 entries, with the absolute majority authored by French researchers. This holds true particularly for the colonization period and up until the 1970s, when Moroccan authors started paying attention to their national languages. Ben Srhir (2013) presents a succinct analysis of dozens of manuals for learning Moroccan Arabic and Standard Arabic spanning more than a century. The Association Internationale de Dialectologie Arabe (AIDA) is an international venue for researchers on Moroccan Arabic and other Arabic varieties (see below for online reference).

While in neighbouring Algeria the linguistic craft was in the hands of religious missionaries and to a lesser extent military authorities, in Morocco it was the military who reigned over the field of language studies from different perspectives (Chaker 1982:82).

Galand (1989:66) points out that Berber studies has attracted more international interest since 1956. Referring to studies conducted during the protectorate, he rightly observes that their merit lay more in documenting the different varieties than in contributing to theoretical linguistics. Paradoxically, the first generation of Berber linguists would be more tempted by theory and would seldom provide large corpora on which their work is based, a fact which Galand deplores as it risks fragmenting our knowledge of Berber in general (1989:70).

In the 1970s, a few Berber researchers authored some pioneering works in different areas of linguistics. Boukous (1974) defended the first master's thesis on Soussi (Tashelhit) prose by a Moroccan Berber researcher in France (Galand 1989:68). Akouaou (1976) prepared his master's thesis on the phonology of the Tashelhit variety of Berber. In the same year, Mohamed Guerssel finished his master's thesis on Berber phonology (see Guerssel 1977), and Saib defended his PhD thesis on the phonology of the Tamazight of Ayt Ndir at UCLA (1976). A few years later, the number of works devoted to Berber dialects rose. Chami (1979) pioneered studies of the Northern Berber varieties by defending a master's thesis on the phonology and morphology of the Guelaya Berber dialect, using the functionalist approach of André Martinet. El Moujahid published an article on the phonology of Tashelhit in 1979, and in 1981 finished his Doctorat de troisième cycle on the nominal morphology of Tashelhit, adopting a generative approach. In 1993 he defended his Doctorat d'Etat (PhD) thesis on the same topic. In 1985, El Medlaoui defended his doctoral thesis on segments and syllabification in Tashelhit Berber, one of the pioneering works in the phonology of Amazigh varieties. It has generated considerable interest in the status of the epenthetic vowel (schwa) and syllabification in the phonology of Amazigh. Most of the works carried out in this period dealt with syntax, phonology, and morphology, but a few dealt also with sociolinguistics (e.g. Boukous 1974, 1979; Abbassi 1977; and Bentahila 1981, 1983).

In the 1980s, Moroccan universities provided some expertise for linguistic research, mostly within departments of French language and literature and later on English language and literature. A newly created graduate programme in linguistics at the Mohamed V University has provided fertile ground for local research, most of which remains unpublished.

Research groups on language and communication are constantly being created in the country, (e.g. Laboratoire Langage et Société URAC56 of the University of Ibn Tofail (Kenitra); Laboratoire Langue, Cultures et Traductions, Mohamed 1 University, Oujda, Équipe de Recherches et d'Etudes Linguistiques, Sidi Mohamed Ben Abdellah, Fes, etc.). These organize international conferences on language-related issues, but unfortunately they are not easily accessible via the Internet. *The Linguistic Society of Morocco* (www.lisaaniyaat.com) also provides information on the state of research in Arabic linguistics worldwide.

A recent development which has contributed to research on Berber was the creation of the Royal Institute for Amazigh Culture (IRCAM) in 2001. A number of researchers trained in linguistics at different Moroccan and foreign universities joined the institute and were given full time research and development jobs. Linguists with different backgrounds joined to carry out the tasks of developing school materials, specialized lexicons, and so on, and in doing so they had to deal with the different varieties of the language. The publications of the institute can be found on its website (www.ircam.ma).

Specialized Berber master's degrees have been created at a number of Moroccan universities in the last decade, where a major part of the curriculum is devoted to linguistics. The traditional venues for linguistics research have thus been extended.

Today, it is practically impossible to provide an inventory of all the research that is being carried out on Moroccan languages, but we can point to the great interest that young researchers are showing in studying the languages of their country. The recent admission of Berber as an official language in the Moroccan Constitution as well as the current debate on the suitability of Standard Arabic and Moroccan Arabic for vital domains such as education and the media have sparked more interest in language planning and sociolinguistics.

For an overview of publications, we recommend Bougchiche (1997), which is unfortunately already outdated. The online *Bibliographie berbère* of the Centre de Recherche Berbère (INALCO, Paris) contains more than 3,000 entries for works published from 1980.[10] A very significant contribution to Amazigh studies is the *Encyclopédie berbère*, which first appeared in

---

[10] www.centrederechercheberbere.fr/bibliographie-berbere.html.

1984, even though the French anthropologist Gabriel Camps had started work on it as early as 1970. The *Encyclopédie* has recently been made available online (https://encyclopedieberbere.revues.org). For Moroccan Arabic, there are numerous resources. In addition to publications in journals of Arabic, the interested reader can follow current research by consulting the website of the *Association Internationale de Dialectologie Arabe.*[11] Of the 29 journal titles listed on the website of Daniel Newman (University of Durham), none is published by a Moroccan university.[12] There are, however, a handful of such journals, such as the *Revue de la Faculté des Lettres et des Sciences Humaines* of Mohamed V University (Rabat), and a similar one published by the University Sidi Mohamed Ben Abdellah (Fez), or the *Revue des Langues, Cultures et Sociétés*, edited by Leila Messaoudi of the Ibn Tofail University (Kenitra).[13] In respect of applied linguistics, Gebril (2017) provides an overview of current research in North Africa and the Middle East.

Research on Moroccan Arabic has had more attention from European scholars than Moroccan scholars, especially in the period of colonization. A relatively large number of works on Moroccan Arabic can be found in different bibliographies and on the Internet. Examples from the early period of colonization are the bilingual dictionaries of Tedjini (1923, 1924), and Sbihi (1933) on the etymology of certain expressions in Moroccan Arabic. The independence period did not bring about an immediate interest in Moroccan Arabic or Berber, but such interest was to be witnessed after about two decades (in the 1970s). For example, Khomsi (1975) dealt with the phonetics and phonology of the Arabic variety of Casablanca, Youssi (1977) addressed secret languages in Morocco, and Benhallam (1980) examined the syllable in Moroccan Arabic. Moroccan universities did not have the capacity to supervise research on Berber and Moroccan Arabic at the time. This is why most of these works were published abroad, mostly in France, where academic research on Moroccan languages was also more accessible. That should not come as a surprise since this country had already established a long tradition of research on local languages of North Africa, and some of the research directors were already well acquainted with the languages of the area.

[11] http://aidabucharest2015.lls.unibuc.ro/.
[12] https://community.dur.ac.uk/daniel.newman/journals.html.
[13] http://revues.imist.ma/?journal=LCS&page=index (accessed March 2017).

5 The Study of African Languages and Linguistics in North-Eastern Africa

Maria Bulakh, Marie-Claude Simeone-Senelle, Wolbert G. C. Smidt, Rainer Voigt, Ronny Meyer, and Angelika Jakobi

5.1   Introduction

This chapter sketches out the history of the study of African languages in North-Eastern Africa: Djibouti, Eritrea, Ethiopia, Somalia (including Somaliland), South Sudan, and Sudan. The focus is on local research traditions and institutions. A separate section deals with Geez studies because of its unique time depth and importance for the development of native linguistic research in Eritrea and Ethiopia.

The Horn of Africa was divided into several spheres of influence during the colonial period. Sudan and British Somalia belonged to the British Empire, Djibouti was the only colony of the French in Eastern Africa, and Eritrea and parts of Somalia were Italian colonies. The first Italian attempt to colonize Ethiopia at the end of the nineteenth century failed. Eritrea remained under the rule of Italy, which eventually occupied the whole of Ethiopia between 1935 and 1941. After liberation, Eritrea was a British protectorate until 1961, when it again became a province of Ethiopia, from which it separated after a referendum to become an independent state in 1993. South Sudan became independent from Sudan in 2011.

5.2   Geez Research History (Maria Bulakh)

5.2.1   Traditional Geez schools

The oldest known Ethiopian language is Geez, which was the main spoken language of the Aksumite Empire, in the first millennium AD. In the second millennium AD, it ceased to be a spoken language but continued its existence as the language of liturgy and as a literary language in religious and secular writings. The necessity of teaching Geez to new generations of church students led to the emergence of a local grammatical tradition with Amharic as the language of instruction. While local schools of Geez have undoubtedly existed since the post-Aksumite period, the written tradition of the so-called *säwasəw* (lit. 'steps, ladder') – Geez vocabularies (mostly Geez–Amharic) accompanied with grammatical information – does not usually pre-date the seventeeth century (Meley 2010).

5.2.2   The Beginning of Geez Studies in the Western Tradition

The history of Western scholarly interest in Geez begins in the sixteenth century, by which time the church of *Santo Stefano (dei Mori)* in the Vatican had become the constant dwelling place of Ethiopian monks in Rome, and thus, communication between Ethiopians well versed in Geez and European scholars became possible. It was in Santo Stefano that the German Johannes Potken was able to hear Geez liturgy, which inspired his interest and resulted in the first printed Geez book: the Ethiopic Psalter, with a brief grammatical sketch and notes on pronunciation (Potken 1513). The most prominent figure among the Ethiopian monks at Santo Stefano was Täsfa Ṣəyon (monastic name P̣eṭros; known as Petrus Aethiops, Pietro Indiano, Petrus Ethiops, Petrus Ethyops), who collaborated intensively with European scholars belonging to the Catholic reformed circle. Thanks to his efforts, the New Testament in Geez was printed (Petrus 1548, 1549). He also provided information and financial support for the first grammar of Geez, composed by the Italian Mariano Vittori (1552). In Potken's and Vittori's works, Geez is labelled 'Chaldaic'. The first dictionary of Geez was published in Rome by Jacob Wemmers (1638), a Dutch scholar, who probably also learned it from the monks of Santo Stefano.

A solid foundation for linguistic research on Geez was laid by the German Hiob [Job] Ludolf [Leutholf], known as the founder of Ethiopian studies. In 1649, he met in Rome *abba* Gorgoryos, a monk from Santo Stefano dei Mori, who taught him Geez. Ludolf's grammar (1661a) and lexicon (1661b) of Geez remained standard reference books for the subsequent two centuries.

The nineteenth century was marked by a renewed interest in Geez, stimulated by a growing number of European travellers and missionaries visiting Ethiopia, who brought Ethiopian manuscripts to Europe. Publication of numerous Geez texts made it possible and necessary to replace Ludolf's works by a new dictionary and grammar, written in accordance with contemporary linguistic standards, based on a large text corpus. This task was carried out by August Dillmann, an outstanding German Orientalist. His grammar (published in 1857, republished with additions and corrections by Carl Bezold in 1899, revised and translated into English by James A. Chrichton in 1907) and *Lexicon* (1865) resulted from lifelong work with Geez manuscripts and surpassed Ludolf's pioneering attempts by far.

5.2.3   Progress after Dillmann

Neither Dillmann's *Lexicon* nor his grammar have been replaced by works of equal dimensions and depth so far. The concise grammatical descriptions which appeared in the subsequent decades are mostly conceived as tutorial material or short encyclopaedic descriptions (Lambdin 1978; Gragg 1997;

Weninger 1999; Prochazka 2004; Bulakh & Kogan 2013; for earlier works, see Leslau 1965a; the most substantial modern description is Tropper 2002). Some aspects of Geez grammar became subjects of special studies (the most prominent are Schneider 1959; Weninger 2001).

Additions to Dillmann's *Lexicon* were published by Sylvain Grébaut (1952). Another important achievement of Geez lexicography is Wolf Leslau's (1987) *Comparative Dictionary*, which, in spite of many deficiencies, is a useful etymological tool. In 2014, the project TraCES: From Translation to Creation: Changes in Ethiopic Style and Lexicon from Late Antiquity to the Middle Ages, headed by Alessandro Bausi, was launched at Hamburg University; among its aims is the creation of a digital dictionary of Geez, with Dillmann's *Lexicon* as a starting point. Within the same project, a digital corpus of selected Geez texts, representative in terms of genres and chronology, with linguistic annotation and links to the digital dictionary, is being compiled, which brings Geez studies into the new stage of computer-aided research (see Bausi 2015).

At the beginning of the twentieth century, a modern Ethiopian school of Geez studies emerged, integrating the local tradition and Western influences. Its most important outcomes are Kidanä Wäld Kəfle's (1955) dictionary with a grammatical sketch and several grammars by Ethiopian scholars (see Leslau 1965a). The Ethiopian tradition itself also became an object of research, and several works on traditional Geez pronunciation appeared, starting with Trumpp (1874) and ending with fundamental monographs by Mittwoch (1926) and Makonnen (1984). Other aspects of the traditional Geez school are rather neglected, but see Muluken (2013).

5.2.4   *Geez Epigraphic Studies*

The nineteenth century marks the beginning of Geez epigraphic studies: a significant number of early Ethiopic inscriptions were copied and published by travellers, followed by a few scholarly publications (notably Müller 1894). The most significant contribution, however, was made at the beginning of the twentieth century by Enno Littmann (1913) in the course of the *Deutsche Axum Expedition*. Afterwards, further Geez inscriptions of various length were discovered and treated in articles (see references in Bernand et al. 1991:529–538; and Marrassini 2014:358–359) and in two important monographs: Drewes (1962) and Bernand et al. (1991) (RIÉ), the latter containing photographs and texts of all Geez inscriptions known at the time of publication. A comprehensive dictionary, concordance, and grammatical description of epigraphic Geez remain desiderata. A further task of Geez linguistics is bringing together the evidence of the epigraphic corpus and of the oldest manuscripts (see Bausi 2005; Bulakh 2014).

5.2.5   Centres of Geez Studies

Geez studies traditionally developed in Europe within classical Semitic studies. Many Semitists (such as Heinrich von Ewald and Theodore Nöldeke in Germany, or Boris A. Dorn [Johannes Dorn] in Russia) included Geez in their research or teaching activities. The establishment of academic centres for Ethiopian studies in Europe at the end of the nineteenth century and in the course of the twentieth century led to the emergence of regular Geez courses in a number of institutions of higher learning (see Krachkovskiy 1955:45–112, 137–145): the École Pratique des Hautes Études in France (initiated in 1879 by Joseph Halévy, succeeded by Marcel Cohen in 1919); the University of Rome (since 1885 by Ignazio Guidi); the Oriental University of Naples (since 1956 by Luigi Fusella); the Oriental Faculty of St Petersburg State University (since 1896 by Boris Turaev); the Berlin Seminar for Oriental Languages (since 1907 by Eugen Mittwoch); the School of Oriental and African Studies of the University of London (since the late 1930s); the Institute of Oriental Studies at Warsaw University (from 1954 to 1969 by Stefan Strelcyn); Hamburg University (since 1970 by Ernst Hammerschmidt); the Department of Near Eastern Languages and Civilizations of Harvard University (since the 1960s by Thomas Lambdin). In Ethiopia, important centres of Geez studies are the Institute of Ethiopian Studies and the Philology Center of the Academy of Ethiopian Languages and Cultures at Addis Ababa University.

5.3   Djibouti (Marie-Claude Simeone-Senelle)

5.3.1   Brief Historical Background

The Republic of Djibouti, eponymous of its seaport capital, was established as the smallest state of the Horn of Africa in 1977. Its French colonization began with the protectorate Territoire d'Obock et de ses Dépendances (Territory of Obock and its Dependences) in 1883, which became the Côte Française des Somalis (CFS) in 1896, with Djibouti city as capital. In 1967 the colony was renamed Territoire Français des Afars et des Issas (TFAI).

5.3.2   Linguistic Background

Two main ethnolinguistic groups are living in Djibouti, Somali and Afar, as well as an Arab minority on the northern coast and in Djibouti city. Each community speaks its language: Somali (afsoomaali) and Afar (qafaraf [ʕafaraf]) (both Cushitic), and a specific Arab variety. French was the only official language of the colony. At present French and Standard Arabic are the two official languages of Djibouti. Both are taught in public schools, but French is the only medium of instruction. Somali and Afar are officially listed as national languages but not taught, while Djiboutian Arabic is considered a regional variety.

Because of its geopolitical situation, Djibouti is a privileged place for linguistic contact. Since 2015 the population influx from Yemen has significantly changed the linguistic landscape in the port cities. Now more than ever the capital is a true melting pot. Besides Somali, Afar, Arabic, French, and English, many other languages of different genetic families are in contact, including Amharic, Oromo, Saho, Wolof, Hindi, and Urdu.

5.3.3   Linguistic Research

Starting from colonization until the 2000s, studies on Djiboutian languages were limited to Somali and Afar (see Morin 2012:45–54; Nilsson 2016).[1] Spoken Arabic and French were hardly considered. The impact of linguistic contact and the emergence of new varieties are not yet the object of linguistic research. Until the early twenty-first century, Djibouti had no official institution for linguistic research, which was carried out by a few local scholars, and by scientists belonging to European institutions.

Just before independence, research on the Afar language began through cultural associations working for the promotion of literacy such as the Union pour le Développement Culturel (UDC), founded in 1973. In 1976, UDC adopted the Latin alphabet developed by Dimis (Hamad b. Abdallah b. Hamad) and Reedo (Gamaladdin Abdoulkadir, then director of the Afar Language Studies and Enrichment Center (ALSEC) in Samara, Ethiopia), which enabled writing in Afar and fostered collaboration between Djibouti and Ethiopia.[2] Subsequently, glossaries, grammar sketches, and primers were prepared for educational purposes for terminology, pedagogy, and lexicography (see references in Morin 2012:51).

In 1978, the Institut Supérieur d'Études et de Recherches Scientifiques et Techniques (ISERST) was founded. It included a Human Sciences section, where Didier Morin (1947–2017) launched linguistic research on Afar, Somali, Saho, and Beja between 1978 and 1982 (see Morin 2012:50–51). In 2002, the Institut des Langues de Djibouti (ILD) was created within the Centre d'Études et de Recherches de Djibouti (CERD), the successor of ISERST. ILD aims at contributing to a better knowledge of the national linguistic heritage (initially for Somali and Afar) by collecting and studying corpora of linguistic and

---

[1] Works missing from Morin (2012:50–52) and Nilsson (2016) include Hassan Kamil (2003, 2007, 2015), Mohamed Hassan (2003), Simeone-Senelle (2007, forthcoming), and Simeone-Senelle and Mohamed Hassan (2013) on Afar; Kassim Mohamed (2012, 2015, 2016) and Simeone-Senelle (2002, 2005a, 2005b) on Djiboutian Arabic; and Mohamed Ismail (2011), Youssouf Elmi (2002, 2003), and Warsama Ahmed (2003) on Somali.

[2] Another script, similar to that of Somali, is used in Eritrea.

traditional literature, and developing and publishing dictionaries (see Saalax Xaashi 2004 and Aadan 2013 in Nilsson 2016). It organizes national and international meetings and collaborates with several institutions in France (Centre National de la Recherche Scientifique, CNRS; Institut National des Langues et Civilisations Orientales, INALCO; and Langage, Langues et Cultures d'Afrique, LLACAN), in Ethiopia (ALSEC and the Afar Language Academy in Samara, and the University of Jigjiga), in Somalia (the Somali Language Academy in Mogadishu), and in Somaliland (Borama University). In 2004 an agreement of cooperation was signed between ILD and LLACAN. Currently, the Afar Section at ILD (Hassan Kamil) and LLACAN (Simeone-Senelle) are carrying out a collaborative project for a dialectal dictionary of halieutic vocabulary, and studying the Arabic and French influence on Afar spoken at the coast. Data are being collected on the Djiboutian and Eritrean coast to build up a specific database of the halieutic domain: fauna, fishing, and navigation techniques, taboos and rites related to the sea.

The Institut des Sciences et des Nouvelles Technologies de Djibouti (ISNTD), established in 2001, is working on automatic Natural Language Processing, i.e. on machine-aided translation and speech recognition, which so far concerns only the Somali language (see Nilsson 2016 for entries under Abdillahi, Nimaan, and Karouah, Abdillahi Nimaan, and also http://somalital .canalblog.com/tag/Thèse).

In accordance with the national language policy, the University of Djibouti (UD) has offered compulsory introductory courses in the national languages, Somali and Afar linguistics to third year BA students since 2006. As there is no full professor in linguistics at UD, postgraduate students are obliged to enrol at foreign universities.

The Centre de Recherches de l'Université de Djibouti (CRUD) opened a linguistics section for the national languages, Somali, Afar, and spoken Arabic (vernacular and lingua franca) in addition to French and Standard Arabic. CRUD publishes the *Revue Universitaire de Djibouti* (RUD) and organizes interdisciplinary scientific days each year.

The new Institut de Recherche Indépendant de la Corne de l'Afrique (IRICA) was founded in Djibouti in June 2016 'to promote indigenous knowledge, provide community for researchers, and conduct applied research in the Horn of Africa' (www.irica-dj.com). It is a multidisciplinary institute embracing natural sciences, earth and life sciences, and human sciences. It publishes a monthly online bilingual bulletin *Recherche-Newsletter*. The first volume of IRICA's *Annals of the Horn of Africa* was scheduled for 2019. Until now linguistic research concerns exclusively the teaching of mother tongues and the use of English by students in Djibouti.

Under the supervision of the Minister of Communication and Culture, two symposia were organized in Djibouti on the Somali language (2002) and on the Afar language (2003) (Morin 2012:52). In December 2012, the Conference on the 40th Anniversary of Somali Orthography was held in Djibouti (Nilsson 2016:95). Since 2006, the annual International Day devoted to the Mother Tongues has brought together specialists in didactics.

The first doctoral theses on languages spoken in Djibouti (Somali, Afar, vernacular Arabic) were defended at INALCO/LLACAN in France between 2011 and 2015: Abdirachid Mohamed Ismail (2011), Souad Kassim Mohamed (2012), and Mohamed Hassan Kamil (2015). Now they have responsibilities in research centres – Abdirachid Mohamed Ismail as vice-president of IRICA, Souad Kassim Mohamed as Senior Lecturer in Linguistics and Didactics at UD and member of CRUD, and Mohamed Hassan Kamil as researcher at CERD and director of ILD – and play a key role in the development of linguistic research in Djibouti.

5.4   Eritrea (Wolbert G. C. Smidt, in cooperation with Rainer Voigt)

5.4.1   Introduction

Research carried out on languages spoken in the territory of today's Eritrea links up with different historical periods and with changes in the engagement of different institutions and professionals. These were, in the nineteenth century, first explorers, focusing on geographical research, and missionaries. As a consequence of improved accessibility of the Red Sea port of Massawa, then capital of the Egyptian 'Governorate Baḥr al-Aḥmar', professional linguists also visited the region, the most important being the Austrian Leo Reinisch in the 1870s. After Egyptian control faded and the lowlands passed into the hands of the Italians in 1885/1887, who created the Colonia Eritrea in 1890, linguistic research was mainly carried out by Italians. It was continued by Protestant missionaries, especially Swedish. During the Second World War, control of Eritrea fell into the hands of the British. A new Eritrean press emerged, with important Eritrean personalities strongly influencing the emergence of a modernized Tigrinya. Research was interrupted during the conflictual integration and annexation of Eritrea by Ethiopia after the mid-1950s, but revived on both sides of the border after the early 1990s by both private and state institutions. Research was then carried out by local linguists and writers.

According to official accounts, nine languages are spoken in Eritrea, namely Tigrinya, Tigre, Kunama, Nara, Bilen, Saho, Afar, To-Bedawi (Beja), and Arabic, while recent linguistic research suggests a greater degree of diversity. Kunama is now seen as a cluster of languages, similar to Tigre.

5.4.2   *Periodization of Linguistics in Eritrea*

5.4.2.1   *Early Linguistic Research in the 'Erythraean' area*

The first written Tigrinya texts date from the nineteenth century. The history of Tigrinya research starts with Protestant missionary activities. Carl Wilhelm Isenberg commissioned the Adwa priest *däbtära* Matewos, in the capital of Tigray in Ethiopia, to translate the Bible into Tigrinya; part of it is published in Praetorius (1871) (Smidt 2009). Unthinkable in other Ethiopian Orthodox areas, this was fostered by the role of Adwa as an international crosspoint, Matewos himself being of partial non-Ethiopian (Greek) descent. These translation endeavours culminated in the publication of the Tigrinya Bible (Voigt 2003a; Smidt 2009), which in turn served as source material for the detailed linguistic studies of Tigrinya by Praetorius, who produced an excellent grammar (Praetorius 1871). Praetorius had never left Europe, he used skills stemming from his classical Semitic language training and Bible studies, and enjoyed the support of a Tigrayan informant, of whose stay in Germany not much is known. Another Tigrinya Bible translation is the one by Nathaniel Pearce, an early nineteenth-century British settler in Tigray, who chose his own transcription system in Latin letters with, however, a very poor understanding of phonology. The first important Tigrinya text collection is the one by Johannes Kolmodin, a Swedish missionary, who had stayed in the Eritrean highlands at a young age and was able to carry out a thorough research on the ancient historiographical oral traditions of Ḥamasen. The texts documented by him belong to the finest examples of early Tigrinya literature, still strongly marked by their oral character, but showing a high degree of consciousness for grammar, spelling, and high language (Kolmodin 1912, 1914).

The Protestant mission established a school in Imkullu (also: Moncullo) at the coast of Massawa, where several languages were spoken, and publications in regional languages were prepared. Likewise, the Catholic mission, with a main centre in Keren, was active in the creation of literature and dictionaries (Francesco [da Bassano] 1918; Coulbeaux & Schreiber 1915, the lost second volume of which has been found by the author and is currently being prepared for publication). Their printing press was one of the first in North-Eastern Africa. Religious literature was also printed in the St Chrischona Pilgrim Mission in Basle, notably a reworked version of the Tigrinya Bible, but also short texts in different languages, and linguistic material prepared by Johann Ludwig Krapf. Massawa was marked by a great multitude of languages, including from inner Ethiopia such as Oromo, because of the regional and international commerce and slave trade. The Oromo Bible translation, a pioneering work in Oromo language documentation and the development of literature, was carried out at Imkullu by Onesimos Nesib. The Amharic Bible printed in St Chrischona contributed to literacy and new religious movements in Ḥamasen, as Amharic was by then used as an inter-regional lingua franca between the Ethiopian centre and the coast. The French-trained specialist of Oriental languages, Werner Munzinger, known especially for his important ethnographic œuvre produced in Keren and Massawa from the 1850s, also published the first detailed word list of Tigre (1865), soon followed by von Beurmann (1868). Likewise, the linguist Reinisch worked in Massawa in the Egyptian period, where he recorded oral texts, the most remarkable being those provided by the local notable *Nugus* of Dankal in the Bôri peninsula in Afar. Reinisch also produced important works on Cushitic and Nilo-Saharan languages of the Erythraean region, such as Bilen, Saho, and Kunama, with oral texts still relevant for cultural and linguistic research due to the exactness of textual scrutiny and transcription (Kießling 2008). During the Italian colonial period, dictionaries and grammars were produced and repeatedly re-edited (e.g. Perini 1893; Camperio 1894; Anon. 1919). Missionaries continued publishing in local languages (e.g. Rodén 1913). The Semitist Carlo Conti Rossini authored a wealth of linguistic works and documentations of oral and written texts, most notably Tigrinya songs and poems, but also some works on Tigre (1894). The most important publication of Tigre texts is Littmann (1910–1915), on the basis of which Höfner finalized his Tigre dictionary (1962).

5.4.2.2   The First 'Eritreanization' of Linguistics
After the establishment of the British, later UN-led administration of the Colonia Eritrea in 1941, a dynamic new Eritrean press emerged. Several Eritrean personalities played a role, publishing mainly in Tigrinya, Tigre, and Arabic, thus creating the basis for literacy and standardization. The journalist and politician Wäldä-Ab Wäldä-Maryam became a prolific Tigrinya writer, who marked the emergence of a modernized Tigrinya based on the variant of the Ḥamasen highlands. He was a member of the *Waʿəla qʷanqʷa Təgrañña* (Tigrinya Language Council), established in 1944 by the British Military Administration after the decision to make Tigrinya the administrative language. It comprised, besides the British officer and trained Semitist Edward Ullendorff, several experienced Eritrean publicists, such as *abba* Yaʿəqob Gäbrä Iyäsus (1889–1969), a Catholic priest (his grammar was published in three editions from 1931 to 1948, his local tales in 1948/1949), who became the president, and a Seventh Day Adventist who became vice-president (Ullendorff 1985, 2010; Ghirmai Negash 1999). Their tasks were the standardization of the language and the introduction of new terminologies for modern phenomena, which was partially successful. Tigrinya newspapers, such as the *Eritrean Weekly News*, documented their discussions. The traditional orthography used by the Protestants, oriented at actual pronunciation, and that used by the Catholic Church, with a stronger focus on etymology, remained un-unified (Voigt 2003a).

This first phase of Eritrean linguistic work has led to new important grammars (a. Ma. Ḥa. = *abba* Matewos Ḥagos 1958/1959, 1960/1961), dictionaries, and text collections (Agosṭinos, Tädla 1994); among the latter, the 'Epic, Tales and Proverbs of the Elders' are of great importance, as they document traditional parlance (Yaʾǝqob Gäbrä-Iyäsus zä-Ḥebo 1948/1949. Tigrinya literature started flourishing (Ghirmai Negash 1999; Voigt 2010, 2019).

5.4.2.3 Modern Linguistics and New Dictionaries

Tigrinya continued to attract the interest of Semitists (Leslau 1941). A few scholars devoted their professional career to it, like Rainer Voigt, who was also one of the first to draw attention to the great diversity of dialects, still ignored by Ullendorff (Voigt 1977, 2003b, 2005). Yaqob Beyyene has contributed considerably to the knowledge of Tigrinya texts through publications on customary law and dialectology. Tigre also continued to be studied (Raz 1983). A rise of linguistic studies in Eritrea was observed in the 1990s after Eritrea had become an independent state (e.g. Tigrinya: Sälomon Gäbrä Krǝstos 1993; cf. Voigt 2019).

The richest Tigrinya dictionary is that of Kane (2000), based on a study of the great bulk of modern Tigrinya literature. Owing to the new Eritrean press, Tigrinya and Tigre literature in particular flourished, which also triggered linguistic discussions (e.g. by Amanuel Sahlä). Both Eritreans in exile and local linguists started to publish voluminous works on Tigrinya and increasingly also on other languages (Musa Aron 2005; Tesfay Tewolde Yohannes 2002, and other grammatical studies 1993, 2005, 2016; Mulugeta Girmay Melles 2001). There are several doctoral and MA dissertations on Tigrinya by Eritreans (e.g. Kiros Fre Woldu 1985; Girmay Berhane 1991; Keffyalew Gebregziabher 2004; Nazareth Amlesom Kifle 2011).

The decision by the Eritrean government that 'all nine languages' should be official languages of the state triggered important research. Linguists working for the Ministry of Education documented dialects and identified those most suitable for education, at times in cooperation with the SIL linguist Klaus Wedekind (Daniel Teclemariam et al. 1997; Alexander Naty 2000). Systematic comparison of grammar and vocabulary reconfirmed that Tigré is to be classified, from a formal point of view, as a spoken dialect of Geez rather than as a separate language. Saho was studied by a group of linguists producing rich material within the Atlas of the Traditional Material Culture of the Saho project, including the documentation of Saho literature; see the extra issue of *Ethnorêma* (Banti et al. 2009 and Banti & Vergari 2013; Vergari 2005; Morin 1994, 1999, 2010). Morin (1999) also includes important studies on Afar; a Nara phonology was developed by Klaus Wedekind and Dawd Abushush. Formerly so-called dialects are now identified as languages, including Illiit and Sokodas within a Kunama language cluster (John Abraha Ashkaba & Smidt 2007). The language spoken on the Dahlak islands was identified by Simeone-Senelle as a separate language (Saleh Mahmud 2005), already described in the seven-teenth century as distinct from mainland Tigre by Olfert Dapper (Smidt 2005). The most important monolingual Tigrinya dictionary is the one by Täkkə'e Täsfay (1999; see also his Tigrinya–English dictionary 2012) with the recent important addition by Danə'el Täklu Rädda (2017/2018); other monolingual dictionaries are Yimesgen Hailegiorgis (2011) and Kidanä-Maryam Zär-'ɘzgi (2008). Increasing tourism and migration of Eritreans to Europe led to the crea-tion of bilingual dictionaries (German–Tigrinya: Zemicael Tecle (2012), ed. by Mussie Tesfagiorgis and Tesfay Tewolde Yohannes, with support by Siegbert Uhlig and the author; an early example is Teclu Lebassi 1991; Russian-Tigrinya: Gutgarts 2017). There are by now numerous smaller language guides (e.g. English–Eritrean Tigrinya, Mesfin Gebrehiwot 1996; Oriolo 1997; for German: Noor 2017; and a German–Tigrinya language guide by the author; for French: Rilliet 2000; for Swedish: Adi Gäbrä 1989; for Russian Gutgarts 2017; see also the manual for translators: Sebhatu Gebremichael Kuflu 2013).

Tigrinya literature also flourished on the Tigrayan side, with new independent works created by Tigrayans in Ethiopia (Danə'el Täklu Rädda 2003/2004). A lan-guage conference in Mekelle [Mäqälä] discussed the modern development of the lan-guage (Maḥbär bahli Təgray (Tigray Culture Association) 1998/1999, 2007/2008). On the Tigrayan side, the most remarkable dictionary is by Kasa Gäbrä-Həywät and Amanu'el [Èmmanuil] Gankin (2007/2008). It is one more step in the attempt to create a standard 'high Tigrinya', oriented on the central Tigrayan language. Kasa Gäbrä-Həywät, before becoming Ambassador of Ethiopia to Russia, had been teaching the Ethiopian languages Geez, Amharic, and Tigrinya to diplomats and then at the State University of Moscow for almost three decades (1954–1983). The dictionary is a result of his cooperation with Gankin, as with their Tigrinya grammar, *Säwasəw Təgrəñña* (2003/2004). In previous decades he had translated numerous Russian authors into Amharic, such as Dostoievski, Gorki, Tolstoi, and Pushkin.

The Tigrinya Language Council of 1944 did not last many years. The institution-alization of language studies was strongly hampered by the conflicts between Eritrea and Ethiopia. It was carried on by foreign institutions, especially Tigrinya, which was regularly taught at Free University (FU) Berlin by Rainer Voigt (with only occasional Tigrinya teaching at the Asia Africa Institute of Hamburg University, at the Universiy of Naples 'L'Orientale', at INALCO in Paris, and at Moscow State University, for example). Missionary institutions, especially SIL and earlier the Swedish Protestant mission, had developed strong linguistic traditions. From the early 1990s, in Eritrea the Curriculum Department of the Department of General Education at the Ministry of Education played a key role in the institutionalization of linguistic research; at the same time, the University of Asmara furthered lin-guistic teaching and research. In Tigray in Ethiopia, the new universities (Mekelle, Addigrat, Axum) established language departments. Mekelle has its own Tigrinya Department, which contributed to the creation of the first local studies on dialectol-ogy of Tigrinya (Daniel Teklu Redda 2013/2014; Danə'el Täklu Rädda 2003/2004).

Studies of Eritrean languages appear in all established linguistic, philological, Orientalist, and Ethiopianist journals, such as *Aethiopica*; a greater number of such studies appear in *Ethnorêma*, published in Naples, the *Rassegna di Studi Etiopici*, in *Africa*, Rome, and in the *Journal of Eritrean Studies* of the University of Asmara; to be mentioned is also the defunct *Quaderni di studi etiopici*, published in Asmara before the 1990s, and *ITYOPIS, Northeast African Journal of Social Sciences and Humanities*, Mekelle. The *Encyclopaedia Aethiopica*, edited in Hamburg (2003–2014), contains articles on all languages of Eritrea and on local cultural terminologies, most of them based on new research (e.g. in Tigrinya).

5.5   Ethiopia (Ronny Meyer)

5.5.1   Introduction

The history of Ethiopian linguistics has been previously described according to either specific periods (e.g. Bender 1970; Abebe & Haileyesus 2001; Shimelis & Binyam 2009) or specific disciplines, like Ethiopian studies (e.g. Ullendorff 1945; Hammerschmidt 1965), Cushitic linguistics (Mous 2012; Sasse 1981), or Omotic linguistics (Azeb 2012). Biographic information cited in this section mainly stems from Uhlig (2003–2014). The publication details of some cited scholars can be found in the above-mentioned works, also in Unseth (1990) and Leslau (1965a). For studies since 1995, see Voigt's *Bibliography of Ethiosemitic and Cushitic Linguistics* (and also Omotic) in the *Aethiopica* (since 1998). Bibliographies on Ethiopian linguistics, which include all four language families, are Pankhurst (1976a) and Lockot (1982, 1998).

5.5.2   Institutionalization of Ethiopian Linguistics

5.5.2.1   Language Academy
In 1942, the imperial government established an institution for developing the Amharic language, from which eventually the National Amharic Language Academy evolved in 1972. Its objectives were to facilitate the use of Amharic in education and administration, to promote Amharic literature, and to preserve Geez literary traditions; other Ethiopian languages were not considered (Fellman 1978a). Under the Derg, it was replaced by the Academy of Ethiopian Languages, whose four units – lexicography, linguistics, terminology, and literature – were supposed to promote Ethiopian languages in general (Moges 2010:32–37). Members of the academies were exclusively Ethiopians, including Merse Hazen Wolde Kirkos, Getachew Haile, Hailu Fulass, Sergew Hable Selassie, Amsalu Aklilu, Demissie Manahlot, Habte Mariam Marcos

(Academy of Ethiopian Languages 1986). After 1991, the academy became the Ethiopian Languages Research Center (ELRC) at Addis Ababa University, later renamed the Academy of Ethiopian Languages and Cultures. As an institution exclusively dedicated to research, it cooperates with local authorities towards the standardization of Ethiopian languages.

5.5.2.2 Department(s) of Linguistics

Since its foundation in 1950, the University College of Addis Ababa – renamed Haile Selassie I University in 1962 and Addis Ababa University (AAU) in 1975 – had a language department, which initially only offered English and French courses. Amharic and Geez were introduced in 1953/1954 through the effort of Wolf Leslau[3] and then continued by Ethiopian scholars (Hailu 1970). At that time, linguistics was a part of individual language courses.

A separate Department of Linguistics (DLING) was established at the new Institute of Language Studies (ILS) in 1978/1979, which also hosted the Departments of Ethiopian Languages and Literature (DELL), Foreign Languages and Literature, and Theatrical Arts. As AAU could award only BA and MA degrees, a PhD had to be obtained from a foreign university. The main concern in the DELL was teaching Amharic, and Amharic oral and written literature, while DLING did research on all Ethiopian languages, mainly from a sociolinguistic or a theoretical linguistic perspective. Between 2000 and 2012, the DELL split into the departments of Amharic, Oromo, and Tigrinya. Several new programmes were established for Applied and General Linguistics (2004), Ethiopian Sign Language (2008), Documentary Linguistics, Experimental Phonetics and Philology (2007), Computational Linguistics (with the School of Information Science).

From the 1990s to 2013, the numbers of both students and staff at DLING increased. In addition to Ethiopian linguists like Baye Yimam, Zelealem Leyew, Abebe G/Tsadik, Hirut W/Mariam, Moges Yigezu (as seniors) and Daniel Aberra, Debela Goshu, Binyam Sisay, and many others (as juniors), the staff included several expatriate linguists. Initially it was only Klaus Wedekind (SIL), who was followed, among others, by Graziano Savà, Orin Gensler, Ronny Meyer, Joachim Crass, Anne-Christie Hellenthal, Tarni Prasad, André Montingea, Izabela Orlowska, Paolo Marrasini, Alessandro Gori, Gianfrancesco Lusini, and Alessandro Bausi. New PhD holders at DLING, such as Shimelis Mazengia, Derib Ado, Feda Negesse, Girma Mengistu, Endalew Assefa, and others, acquired their entire education in Ethiopia. In 2017 DLING had about

---

[3] Wolf Leslau (1906–2006) started to study Ethiosemitic with Marcel Cohen at Paris in 1931–1939. In Ethiopia, Leslau introduced and promoted Ethiopian linguistics through continuous lectures and by facilitating the education of the first modern Ethiopian linguists: Habte Mariam Marcos (1930–1992), Abraham Demoz (1935–1994), and Hailu Fulass; the last two of these linguists were awarded a PhD from UCLA (Leslau 1992; Müller 2007).

30 permanent staff members, almost all Ethiopians.[4] Currently, DLING is involved in two large international collaborative research projects with the University of Oslo, sponsored by NORAD. The Linguistic Capacity Building project (2013–2019)[5] focuses on the promotion of several Ethiopian languages, while the Beyond Access project (2016–2020)[6] is concerned with the improvement of mother tongue education in Ethiopia, South Sudan, and Sudan.

Since the 1990s, 37 new universities have been built all over the country; another 11 will follow soon. A few of them started to offer a BA/MA in linguistics (Mekelle, Wollo, Hawassa, the latter is also about to start a PhD programme). Some regional universities established research centres for the languages spoken in their vicinity, like the Oromo Research Center (inaugurated in 2012 at the Adama Science and Technology University, since 2016 at Arsi University in Asella), or the Institute for the Development of the Amharic Language (established in 2012 at Bahr Dar University).

5.5.2.3   Institute of Ethiopian Studies (IES)

The IES, a part of AAU, aims at the preservation and promotion of Ethiopian history and culture. It hosts a research position for Ethiopian languages, currently filled by Aklilu Yilma. The IES was founded in 1963 by Richard Pankhurst (1927–2017) and Stanislaw Chojnacki (1915–2010), who laid the foundation for a unique library in the Horn of Africa (Chojnacki 2007). As local and visiting researchers commonly archive a copy of their publications at the IES, it hosted the most comprehensive collection on Ethiopian languages in the 1990s, but is currently witnessing a steady decline.

5.5.2.4   Summer Institute of Linguistics (SIL) – Ethiopia Branch

Since 1973, SIL Ethiopia, which is focused on Bible translation and Christian scriptures in Ethiopian languages, is actively involved in research on Ethiopian languages, with a focus on standardization and promotion for mother tongue education. SIL temporarily worked together with DLING and the IES. Some SIL linguists, e.g. Michael Ahland and Colleen Ahland, have defended their PhD theses on Ethiopian languages, typically at the University of Texas at Arlington, which thus has become an important centre for Ethiopian Linguistics, particularly with regard to Nilo-Saharan languages.

---

[4]   See www.aau.edu.et/chls/academics/department-of-linguistics/ (accessed 10 July 2017).
[5]   See www.hf.uio.no/iln/om/organisasjon/tekstlab/prosjekter/Ethiopia/index.html (accessed 10 July 2017).
[6]   See www.aau.edu.et/chls/academics/department-of-linguistics/norad-beyond-access/ (accessed 10 July 2017).

Table 5.1 Ethiopian journals on Ethiopian linguistics

Name	Founded	Current editor
Journal of Ethiopian Studies	1963	IES (founded by R. Pankhurst)
Ethiopian Journal of Languages and Literature	1990 (?)	CHLSJC (former ILS)
Zena Lissan: Journal of the Academy of Ethiopian Languages and Cultures (former Zena Lissan; Lissan: Journal of African Languages and Linguistics)	(?)	Academy of Ethiopian Languages and Culture
ELRC Working Papers	2005	

5.5.2.5 Research Dissemination

Research on Ethiopian languages is regularly disseminated through international and local journals, the ones listed in Table 5.1 being published in Ethiopia.

The International Conference of Ethiopian Studies is a regular interdisciplinary forum for Ethiopian studies in general. The first conference took place in Rome in 1959, followed by 19 other conferences conducted in Europe, Israel, Japan, the United States, and Ethiopia. Until the 1980s, the number of Ethiopian scholars was relatively low at the conferences abroad but has steadily increased since the 1990s (see Assefa 2009:ii). In the 1980s, the Annual Conference of the Institute of Language Studies (since 2012 the Annual Conference of the College of Humanities, Language Studies, Journalism and Communication) was established, which is an important national meeting for linguists. Furthermore, Ethiopian linguistics is represented at regular meetings, like the International Conference of Cushitic and Omotic Languages, the Nilo-Saharan Linguistics Conference, the North Atlantic Conference on Afroasiatic Linguistics, and the World Congress of African Linguistics.

5.5.3   Main Periods in Ethiopian Linguistics

5.5.3.1 Early Period

One of the earliest fundamental linguistic activities by native Ethiopians was the creation of scripts, notably the Ethiopic script (or *fidel*) for writing Geez in about AD 300, which was later modified for other Ethiopian languages (see Meyer 2016). About a thousand years later, Muslim Ethiopians started to use Arabic *Ajam* scripts for writing Harari, and since the eighteenth century also Amharic, Argobba, Oromo, Silt'e (see Pankhurst 1994:257–259; Wetter

2006).[7] Probably in the seventeenth century, the *säwasəw* was developed as an indigenous grammatical tradition to preserve the knowledge of Geez (see section 5.2.1).

During the eighteenth century, research on Ethiopian languages substantially increased through early European explorers and missionaries, mainly from Britain, France, Germany, and Italy (for an overview, see Pankhurst 1976a; also Ullendorff 1945). The first professional scholar involved in empirical research on Ethiopian languages was Leo Reinisch (1832–1919), whose fieldwork in Ethiopia in 1875/1876 and 1879/1880 resulted in the first comprehensive descriptions of several Nilo-Saharan, Omotic, and mainly Cushitic languages (see Pankhurst 1976a:29). Later other scholars followed, like Enno Littmann (1875–1958), who besides his studies in Ethiopian epigraphic languages and modern Ethiopian languages, notably Tigre, facilitated as director of the German Axum expedition (1905–1906) some of the earliest audio recordings in Amharic, Tigre, and Geez (see Ziegler 2005). In the 1880s, Italians started to dominate linguistic field research in Ethiopia, most prominently Enrico Cerulli (1898–1988) and Martino Mario Moreno (1892–1964) with their fundamental works on Cushitic and Omotic (see Unseth 1990; also Bausi 2016).

Ethiopians, who were educated by missionaries or abroad, started with the linguistic description of their native languages. The work of Onesimos Nesib (1856–1913), who studied at the Swedish mission in Munkullo, marks the beginning of indigenous Oromo Studies (see Tasgaraa 2007; and also Pankhurst 1976b). At Munkullo, (Aläqa) Tayye Gäbrä Maryam (1861–1924), who is also the author of *yäʔityop'ya hïzb tarik* 'History of the People of Ethiopia' (1920E.C., i.e. 1927/28G.C.), prepared one of the first native Geez grammars (Alemé 1972). He was sent as first language instructor for Amharic and Geez to the Seminar of Oriental Languages in Berlin from 1905 to 1908, where he met Eugen Mittwoch (1876–1942). Afäwärq Gäbrä Iyäsus (1868–1947) was sent for his education to Italy in 1887, where he then became an Amharic lector at the Istituto Orientale in Naples from 1902 until his return to Ethiopia in 1912. Besides various fundamental grammatical and lexical works on Amharic (see Leslau 1965a), he also composed the first novel in Amharic *ləbb wälläd tarik* (lit. 'heart born history', hence *ləbb wälläd* later became the technical Amharic term for 'novel'), published in Rome in 1908 (see Fellman 1991). Other foreign-educated Ethiopians prepared grammatical sketches and vocabularies for Amharic, Geez, Tigrinya (the last two often bilingual with Amharic). A major work on Amharic is Märse Hazän Wäldä Qirqos's (1899–1978) grammar from 1942/1943 (Sergew 1980:88–90), followed by Täklä Maryam Fantaye's

---

[7] Moreover, Arab scholars prepared the first linguistic descriptions of Ethiopian languages (East Gurage, early Amharic) in vocabularies and grammar sketches from the thirteenth to the fifteenth centuries (Muth 2009; Bulakh & Kogan 2011).

grammar in 1953/1954 and Dästä Täklä Wäld's (1901–1985) monolingual Amharic dictionary in 1970 (for references, see Leslau 1965a). Research on Amharic was fostered by new mass media and the introduction of secular education.

5.5.3.2 Constituting Period

A prominent scholar of this period is Wolf Leslau, who between 1946 and 1974 conducted fieldwork on all Ethiosemitic languages, Kafa (Omotic), and on Highland East Cushitic (see Devens 1991; Müller 2007). The data are published in the series Ethiopians Speak: Studies in Cultural Background, and in separate comparative grammars. The lexical data was compiled in various etymological dictionaries, notably for Gurage (Leslau 1979) and Geez (Leslau 1987). Furthermore, he dealt with language contact phenomena, and Amharic and Gurage argots. Leslau's work on Amharic intensified in 1964 when UCLA started to train US Peace Corps volunteers in Amharic, for which he prepared, among others works, a textbook and a bilingual dictionary (Leslau 1965b, 1976).[8] His reference grammar (Leslau 1995) is still the most comprehensive description of Amharic.[9]

In addition to Europeans, linguists from Japan and the USA also engaged in research on Ethiopian languages, with a certain predominance of linguists from the USA during the 1960s. Beside the establishment of the Peace Corps in 1964 and the work of W. Leslau, another major cause for this trend was the *Language Survey of Ethiopia* in 1968–1969, supported by the Ford Foundation as part of the larger *Survey of Language Use and Language Teaching in Eastern Africa*. The Ethiopian survey team encompassed Charles A. Ferguson (director), J. Donald Bowen, Robert L. Cooper, and M. Lionel Bender. The results of the Ethiopian survey, mainly published in Bender et al. (1976) and Bender (1976), represent a milestone in the development of Ethiopian linguistics. Moreover, the team adopted – and strongly advertised – Harold C. Fleming's (e.g. 1969) proposal to consider the former West Cushitic branch a separate Afroasiatic family, Omotic, which is still controversially discussed (for details see Lamberti 1991:554–558; Theil 2012). The two volumes provide comparable and state-of-the-art grammar sketches for languages from all four families. The strong sociolinguistic component of the language survey fostered research on topics like lingua franca communication and mother tongue education, language use and spread in multilingual areas, linguistic areas (and language typology), registers (avoidance and secret languages, jargons, politeness), and dialectology. Later, societal multilingualism and language

---

[8] The only textbook in Europe and the USA until Appleyard (1995) (with several reprints and a new edition in 2013). Richter's (1987) textbook addresses only German learners.
[9] As Hartmann's (1980) grammar is in German, it remained unrecognized.

policy/planning became primary research topics in socialist countries, particularly the GDR, and also in Ethiopia (Mesfin 1974; Amsalu & Richter 1980; Mulugeta 1988).

After that, work on Ethiopian languages follows either a general descriptive approach (see, e.g. the works of W. Leslau, R. Hetzron, G. Goldenberg, and O. Kapeliuk for Ethiosemitic; or the contributions in Bechhaus-Gerst & Serzisko (1988) and Hayward (1990) for Cushitic and Omotic) or a formal approach with focus on syntax (e.g. Bliese 1981) or phonology (e.g. McCarthy 1983). Among the increasing number of Ethiopian linguists, the generative approach dominates, for example Baye Yimam (1986), or Hailu Fulass's (1973) first formal grammar of and in (!) Amharic. Furthermore, comparative Ethiosemitic studies started to appear, e.g. Hetzron (1977) or Ullendorff (1955).

Another prominent research field was lexicography. Ethiopian linguists were mainly engaged in the lexicographic development of Amharic, for which the Science and Technology Terminology Translation Project was established at the Academy of Ethiopian Languages in the 1980s. Related to this is the publication of a multitude of Amharic dictionaries by Ethiopians and foreigners, among which Amsalu (1985) and Amsalu and Mosback (1981) are most popular in Ethiopia, but Leslau (1976) and Kane (1990) abroad. Dictionaries were prepared for Highland East Cushitic (Hudson 1989), Afar (Parker & Hayward 1985), Oromo (Gragg 1982), and Burji (Sasse 1982).

Research on Geez almost vanished from Ethiopia at the end of this period, while studies on Amharic literature and folklore were intensified (see Taye & Shiferaw Bekele 2000; Fekade 2001). As only Amharic served as an official language, applied linguistic activities on other languages was basically nonexistent, except for the adult literacy campaign. An indigenous research tradition on Oromo developed outside Ethiopia. Since the first grammar completely written in Oromo circulated, most probably compiled by Haile Fida (unpublished typescript 1973, often quoted as 'anonymous'), who was a former Oromo language instructor at the University of Hamburg, native Oromo linguists write the language in an adapted Roman script, known as *qubee*, which met strong opposition from other Ethiopians, particularly when Tilahun Gamta published his Oromo dictionary in Ethiopia in 1989 (see Teferi 2015).

5.5.3.3 Expansion Period

In 1992–1995, the IES in cooperation with SIL conducted the *Survey of Little-Known Languages of Ethiopia* during which lexical and sociolinguistic information on under-described Ethiopian languages was gathered (Aklilu & Wedekind 2002). Moreover, the survey created awareness for language shift and death (Brenzinger 1998), and fostered research on endangered languages, such as Ongota (Savà & Tosco 2000; Fleming 2006) and Kemant (Zelealem 2003).

Various new dictionaries have appeared (e.g. Gutt & Hussein 1997; Appleyard 2006; Turton et al. 2008; Hayward & Eshetu 2014). M. Lionel Bender's comparative work on Omotic and Nilo-Saharan languages is a substantial contribution to research in these families (see Hudson 2008). Often as part of PhD projects, Ethiopian and foreign linguists (see below) produced a multitude of comprehensive grammars for Ethiopian languages, so that today only few, mainly Nilo-Saharan, languages lack a grammatical description. Except for a few Ethiopians, such as Moges Yigezu, research on Nilo-Saharan is dominated by foreign linguists (e.g. Don Killian on Uduk, Torben Anderson on Berta, Colleen Ahland on Gumuz, Andreas Joswig on Majang). Recently, Old Amharic is also getting more attention (e.g. Girma 2014).

Since the 1990s, Ethiopian languages have been taken into account more and more in linguistic reference works (e.g. Hetzron 1997; Heine & Nurse 2000; Weninger 2011; Frajzyngier & Shay 2012; Bulakh, Kogan & Romanova 2013), etymological or comparative dictionaries (e.g. Orel & Stolbova 1995; Ehret 2001; Kogan 2015), and in comparative grammars of Semitic (Lipiński 1997; Goldenberg 2013). These works (or the contributions they contain) are typically prepared by foreign scholars; Ethiopians are rarely involved. A notable exception is the *Encyclopaedia Aethiopica* (Uhlig 2003–2014), which Siegbert Uhlig initiated at Hamburg University in the 1990s.

Ethiopian linguists also rarely work on language classification, which besides classical lexicostatistics (e.g. Hudson 2013) now involves phylogenic models. Girma (2009), who severely questions the 'established' Ethiosemitic classifications, revived older controversies about the African or Arabian origin of Ethiosemitic.

The first two decades of this period also exhibit various research projects in Europe and the USA, probably spurred by the large number of Ethiopian linguists, who pursued their PhD abroad or in a sandwich programme with AAU (see, for instance, Table 5.2).

In general, the typological-descriptive approach currently predominates in Ethiopian linguistics. The more than one hundred in-house PhD dissertations at AAU follow such a framework. Among Ethiopian linguists, Baye Yimam is the most influential proponent of the formal approach. His generative grammar of (and in) Amharic (Baye 1994 with new editions in 2008 and 2017) is so famous that its concepts have become the main component of Amharic grammar lessons at school.

Applied linguistics, language planning, and standardization are central research issues (Heugh 2014). As Ethiopia has a long experience in Amharic mother tongue education, ACALAN selected AAU as one of three African universities for its Pan-African Master's and PhD Programme in African Languages and Applied Linguistics (PANMAPAL) in 2006. Moreover, the introduction of mother tongue education in Ethiopian vernaculars presupposed

Table 5.2 Selection of PhD projects by Ethiopian linguists

University	PhD student	Topic	Defence
Cologne	Zelealem Leyew	Qimant	1998
	Hirut Wolde-Mariam	Haro	2003
	Beniam Mitiku	Harari	2013
Brussels	Moges Yigezu	Phonetics/phonology of Surmic	2002
Leiden	Azeb Amha	Maale	2001
	Mulugeta Seyoum	Dime	2008
	Tolemariam Fufa	Afroasiatic verb derivation	2009
	Ongaye Oda	Konso	2013
	Mulugeta Tarekegn	Psycholinguistics	2017
Oslo	Binyam Sisay	Koreete	2008
	Debela Goshu	Semantics of Oromo prepositions	2011
	Kebede Hordofa	Classification of Oromo dialects	2009
Trondheim	Bedilu Wakjira	Kistane	2010
	Getahun Amare	Argobba	2009
	Wondwosen Tesfaye	Dirayta	2006
Tromsø	Girma Awgichew	Ethiosemitic syntax	2003
Quebec	Mengistu Amberber	Amharic	1997
Montreal	Degif Petros	Chaha	1997
London	Iyasu Hailu	Ethiopian sign language	2010
Jerusalem	Anbessa Tefera	Sidaama	2000

a certain level of status and corpus planning, which typically was done by regional language experts, often supported by the Department of Linguistics or the Academy of Ethiopian Languages and Cultures. As a result, the amount of written material in vernacular languages substantially increased, which also includes their linguistic description by native speakers.

During the last few years, several new research areas have appeared, such as sign language (Pawlos 2015), experimental linguistics (Derib 2011), linguistic landscape (Hirut & Lanza 2014), computer linguistics,[10] and corpus linguistics.[11]

---

[10] The first computer linguist at AAU is Demeke Asres, who successfully defended his PhD in 2016.

[11] As part of collaborative research projects, Ethiopian linguists are currently preparing digital language corpora for Amharic, Oromo, Somali, Tigrinya, Wolaitta, and Gurage (see http://tekstlab .uio.no/ethiopia/ and https://habit-project.eu/wiki).

5.6   Somalia (Ronny Meyer)

Somalia constitutes an almost monolingual area dominated by Somali, which exhibits great dialectal variation; in southern Somalia, the minority languages KiBajuni, Chi-Mwiini, and Mushungulu – which belong to Bantu – are found (see Appleyard & Orwin 2008:283–290). Somali is also spoken in Djibouti and parts of northern Kenya. It probably represents the best-studied Cushitic language (for a bibliograhical overview, see Nilsson 2016) and has a very productive literary tradition.

In 1880–1900, the Somali-speaking area was divided and colonized by Britain, Italy, and France; Ethiopia annexed the Ogaden. The former British and Italian colonies merged to form independent Somalia in 1960; the French colony became independent Djibouti in 1977. Although Somali was spoken by more than 90 per cent of the population in independent Somalia, the choice of an official language became a central political issue. In the decade preceding independence, all attempts to select one of the various indigenous scripts or an Ajam- or Roman-based script for writing Somali failed. Consequently, the former colonial languages, English and Italian, as well as Arabic (which was favoured by Islamic institutions), became official languages. Attempts to resolve the Somali script controversy failed (Griefenow-Mewis 1992:131–132). Eventually, the military government, which came to power in 1969, declared Somali the official language in 1973 and decided to standardize it in a Roman-based script in 1972, which was spread through national literacy campaigns in 1973–1974 (see Johnson 2006). Subsequently, Somali became the sole language in administration and pre-university education, and was used in written mass media. At university level, it was the medium of instruction in the Department of Somali Language and Literature; all other departments used English, Italian, or Arabic. The standardization of Somali was fostered through the then Academy of Culture and the National University of Somalia in Mogadishu (Andrzejewski 1987:75). The expansion of literacy and education in Somali was impeded by a lack of economic resources and increasing political repression in the 1980s, resulting in a large brain drain, and then stopped completely during the civil war in 1991–1992 and the subsequent unrest.

Scientific linguistic research on Somali started with the work of Leo Reinisch (1832–1919), who – through original fieldwork with native speakers – published the first comprehensive description of Somali in 1900–1904. Linguists who have substantially contributed to the study of Somali include Bogumil W. Andrzejewski (1922–1994), Giorgio Banti, Mara Frascarelli, Jacqueline Lecarme, Martino M. Moreno, John Ibrahim Saeed, and Mauro Tosco.

In the 1920s, Cusmaan Yuusuf Keenadiid created an indigenous script (a phonetic syllabary) for writing Somali, the Osmania. It was promoted as a national symbol by the Somali Youth League, who taught it in schools across the country, and it became the most frequently used script for writing Somali by native authors after the Second World War. In the 1950s, Roy C. Abraham (1890–1963) substantially improved Somali lexicography by an English–Somali and a Somali–English dictionary, which was published in 1964 and 1967 (see Nilsson 2016). Later, several mono- and bilingual dictionaries (in English, French, Italian, Russian) were published, notably by Agostini, Puglielli & Siyaad (1985) with about 40,000 lemmata, which were gathered over a period of seven years by a team of 39 scholars from the Somali National University, the Somali Academy of Sciences, Arts and Literature, and the University of Rome La Sapienza (Andrzejewski 1992:106); a large Somali–English dictionary is R. David Zorc and Madina M. Osman (1993). The most comprehensive dictionary, with more than 3 million tagged and grammatically annotated words, is the online Somali Corpus (www.somalicorpus.com) developed by Jama Musse Jama in collaboration with the Redsea Cultural Foundation and the University of Naples 'L'Orientale'. Until the 1990s, a number of Somali grammars and textbooks were also published (see Nilsson 2016); the most comprehensive is John (Ibrahim) Saeed (1993).

A central topic in Somali linguistics is the description and classification of Somali dialects (e.g. Lamberti 1986; for further references, see Nilsson 2016). Another prominent topic in Somali grammar is focus and discourse configurationality (e.g. Tosco 2001), besides a variety of studies on morphology, syntax, and comparative studies (e.g. Banti 1988). In sociolinguistics, studies on the standardization of Somali (e.g. Laitin 1977; Labahn 1984) and on Somali scripts (e.g. Tosco 2010; Banti & Ismaïl 2015) dominate.

The Regional Somali Language Academy, founded in 2013 as a pan-Somali institution with a base in Djibouti, is concerned with the Somali language and culture in Somalia, Djibouti, and Ethiopia. Moreover, Somali linguistics constitutes a part of the broader field of Somali studies, with the Somali Studies International Association as its main body (Cassanelli 2001). The International Congress of Somali Studies was inaugurated in Mogadishu in 1980. Founded in 2014, the Hargeysa Cultural Center, with Jama Musse Jama as director, is an important institution for the study of the Somali language, which is supported by the Redsea Cultural Foundation.

5.7   Sudan and South Sudan (Angelika Jakobi)

5.7.1   Introduction

The aim of this section of the chapter is to trace the development of linguistic research in the Sudan since its beginnings in the late eighteenth century. At that time, the Sudan comprised several political entities, the Shilluk kingdom with its capital at Fashoda, the Funj sultanate of Sennar, the sultanate of Darfur, and the sultanate of Taqali. In 1820 the Ottoman Empire (known as *Turkiya*) began conquering the Sudan and eventually extended its power far to the south, annexing Bahr al-Ghazal and Equatoria. The Mahdist revolt, the so-called *Mahdiya* (1885–1899), did not succeed in ridding Sudan of Egyptian and, later, British rule. After these 18 years of war, the joint-rule state of the Anglo-Egyptian Sudan was established. It existed until the Republic of Sudan became independent in 1956. In 2011 southern Sudan split off, establishing a separate state, the Republic of South Sudan. Keeping this grossly simplified course of history in mind, the term Sudan is used to cover all those distinct political entities.

The linguistic landscape of the Sudan is characterized by (i) the written traces of two ancient indigenous languages, Meroitic and Old Nubian, (ii) the unequal status of the Sudanese African languages on the one hand and of Arabic on the other, and (iii) linguistic diversity, as reflected by some 130 languages representing three language phyla, Nilo-Saharan, Niger-Congo, and Afro-Asiatic (also Afroasiatic). The most linguistically diverse areas are the Nuba Mountains, South Sudan, Darfur, and the Sudan-Ethiopia border area.

5.7.2 Vocabularies of Travellers and Explorers

During the eighteenth and nineteenth centuries, foreign travellers and explorers entered Sudan to search for gold or for the sources of the Nile, to abolish the slave trade, to spread Christianity, or even to explore the largely unknown inner-Sudan, its peoples and languages.

In northern Sudan, the German Ulrich Jasper Seetzen (1816:247–262), the Swiss Johann Ludwig Burckhardt (1819:153–159), and the French Cadalvène and Breuvery (1841:493–517) collected brief vocabularies of 'Berber', 'Dungala', 'Nouba', 'Dar Mahass', and 'Dongolah', which were later identified as varieties of the Nile Nubian languages, Nobiin and Dongolawi (Andaandi).

In eastern Sudan, some varieties of the Beja language were encountered. They comprise word lists of 'Adareb and Bishareen', as recorded by the Englishman Henry Salt (1814:407–408) and 'Sauaken', as recorded by Seetzen (1816:263–279), as well as a grammar sketch of 'To'beḍauie' written up by the Swiss Werner Munzinger (1864:543–551).

On the Sudan–Ethiopia border, Salt (1814:414–416) collected samples of languages later identified as Gumuz (see Tucker and Bryan 1956:148). Other languages in that area – Nuer, Berta, Tabi, Funj ('Fungi') – were recorded by the Austrian Ernst Marno (1874:481–495). His Funj word list has documentary value since this language has become extinct.

In southern Sudan the German explorers Eduard Rüppell (1829:370–373) and Georg August Schweinfurth (1873) recorded a variety of languages, later classified as representing three different groups, Central Sudanic, Ubangi, and Western Nilotic.

As it was difficult in the eighteenth and nineteenth centuries to access Darfur, several Fur wordlists were collected outside of that area. Seetzen (1816:319–333), for instance, recorded a Fur word list in Cairo, Rüppell (1829) in Kordofan. By contrast, Salt (1814:408–410) and the French Orientalist Joseph Halévy (1874) collected vocabularies from Fur pilgrims passing through Ethiopia. Other languages of Darfur, such as the Saharan language Berti (now extinct), the Taman languages Tama and Erenga, the Daju languages (Daju of Darfur, Daju of Dar Sila and Baygo), and the Nubian languages Midob and Birgid remained unknown until the beginning of the twentieth century, when the British colonial administrator Harold MacMichael (1918, 1920) published vocabularies of these languages.

The Nuba Mountains of Kordofan are a linguistically very heterogeneous area. Rüppell (1829:370–373) published vocabularies of seven distinct languages, four of these (Shwai, Koldeji, Tagoi, and Tegali) representing three Nuba Mountain language groups, Heibanic, Kordofan Nubian, and Rashad, respectively. About 100 years later, the MacDiarmids (1931) were able to show that there are, in fact, ten distinct language groups in the Nuba Mountains.

When comparing the vocabularies recorded by the British Arthur Holroyd (1839) and the Austrian Geologist Josef von Russegger (1844:355–360) to samples of Jebel Dair and a Nile Nubian language, Munzinger (1864:543–551) realized that these languages were related. This finding was corroborated by the comparative word lists of Heinrich Brugsch (1864) and Richard Lepsius (1880:lxxvii). Finally, when Midob and Birgid, spoken in Darfur and Haraza of northern Kordofan, were identified as Nubian languages, too, the extent of the widely scattered Nubian language family became apparent (Westermann 1912/1913; MacMichael 1922:119; Bell 1975). For an annotated bibliography of the Nubian languages, see Jakobi and Kümmerle (1993).

Some speakers of African languages were even abducted as slaves from Sudan and taken to Europe where they served as language informants. The story of the Fur, a Dinka, and a Tumale boy is told in 'The Tutschek brothers and their Sudanese informants' (Hair 1969).

5.7.3   The 'Pre-scientific Period'

Unlike the travellers and explorers who commonly collected more or less brief vocabularies from speakers they had coincidentally met, the Christian missionaries aimed at preparing Bible translations and therefore tried to get insights into the grammatical structure of some selected languages. In 1851 at Gondokoro on the upper White Nile, the first missionary station was founded. Soon the first grammars of Dinka and Bari were produced (Kirchner 1861; Mitterrutzner 1866, 1867; Beltrame 1870). Comparing these languages with the vocabularies recorded by Schweinfurth and Marno (see above), the

Austrian linguist Friedrich Müller in his *Grundriss der Sprachwissenschaft* (vol. I, 1876) had already recognized the genetic relationship between Bari, Dinka, Nuer, and Shilluk, which were later classified as Western Nilotic languages.

5.7.4 Increasing Professionalization

Müller was soon followed by other professional Africanists who strived to add new data and deepen the language analyses. The Austrian Leo Reinisch and the German Richard Lepsius initially competed in the field of Nile Nubian language studies; in 1879, a year before Lepsius's *Nubische Grammatik* (1880) appeared, Reinisch managed to publish his *Nuba-Sprache*. Reinisch was later concerned with other languages of North-Eastern Africa, contributing, among other studies, a four-volume study of Beja ('Beḍauye') in 1893–1894.

In 1928 the German Diedrich Westermann – at that time the director of the London-based International Institute of African Languages and Cultures (later the IAI, i.e. International African Institute) – was invited as a linguistic expert to join the Rejaf conference in southern Sudan (Sudan Government 1928). The conference was attended by government representatives and missionaries engaged in educational work; however, representatives of the Sudanese peoples were not invited. The conference decided for a restrictive language policy in the southern Sudan that differed sharply from the policy adopted in northern Sudan where Arabic was promoted, whereas the use of the local African languages was strongly discouraged. In the south, by contrast, six African languages – Dinka, Nuer, Shilluk, Bari, Lotuko, Zande – were selected to be developed for the use in elementary education. Another objective of the conference was to use the International Phonetic Alphabet (IPA) for writing the southern Sudanese languages.

Owing to the application of the IPA and Westermann's Shilluk grammar (1912) that served as a model for grammatical descriptions of Nilotic languages, many missionaries succeeded in considerably improving their studies, as seen in the grammars of Nuer (Crazzolara 1933) and Lotuxo (Muratori 1938) – to mention just two (for more details, see Köhler's history of Nilotic studies of 1955). As for our knowledge of the Central Sudanic and Volta-Kongo languages, we owe much to the work of the Italian missionary Stefano Santandrea (1961, 1976).

The pioneering work of the British Archibald Tucker and Margaret Bryan, from the 1930s to 1950s, brought much progress in the study of Sudanese languages. On behalf of the IAI, they carried out a typological survey of *The Non-Bantu Languages of North-Eastern Africa* (Tucker & Bryan 1956). One of their outstanding publications was *Linguistic Analyses* (Tucker & Bryan 1966), which has become a standard reference work, as it comprises grammar sketches of 33 language groups, some of which are still little known to the present day.

Another pioneer in linguistic research was the British missionary and anthropologist Roland Stevenson. He had carried out studies of a considerable number of languages in the Nuba Mountains (Stevenson 1956/1957; Jakobi 1995) and in other places of the Sudan. Therefore he was able to contribute a substantial amount of data to Tucker and Bryan (1966), comprising grammar sketches of eight distinct Nuba Mountain languages. Three of his manuscript grammars – on the Koman language Uduk and on the Kordofanian languages Tira and Otoro – were posthumously published; see Stevenson and Bender (1999) and Stevenson (2009) edited by Schadeberg.

5.7.5   Academic Institutionalization

In the 1960s, as a response to growing interest in the modern spoken and ancient written languages, Khartoum University set up the Sudan Research Unit. In 1972 it was transformed into the Institute of African and Asian Studies (IAAS). Several publication series were initiated. One of them, the Linguistic Monograph Series, made available hitherto unpublished studies of Fur (Beaton 1968), Nubian (Ayoub 1968), Bagirmi (Stevenson 1969), Uduk (Beam & Cridland 1970), Moro (Black & Black 1971), Murle (Lyth 1971), Dinka (Tucker 1978), as well as Bell's *Place Names in the Belly of Stones* (1970b), and Mutawallī's (undated) primer on Nobiin.

Two volumes in the Sudanese Studies Library series were devoted to linguistic issues, *Studies in Ancient Languages of the Sudan*, edited by Abdelgadir Mahmoud Abdalla (1974) and *Directions in Sudanese Linguistics and Folklore*, edited by Sayyid Ḥāmid Ḥurreiz and Herman Bell (1975).

Stimulated by Björn Jernudd's research for his doctoral thesis (1979) in the 1970s, the IAAS initiated the Language Survey of the Sudan, a sociolinguistic project that was concerned with the use of Arabic and the local African languages in multilingual communities such as the Nuba and Ingessana Mountains. Bell (1995) provides an overview of the aims and scope of that survey. This project has continued to stimulate sociolinguistic studies such as Mahmud (1983), Abu Manga (1986), Mugaddam (2002), Idris (2007), Abdelhay (2007), and Nashid (2014), to mention but a few.

In the 1970s the Summer Institute of Linguistics (SIL) established a branch in Sudan. The SIL missionaries first engaged in studies of southern Sudanese languages such as Surmic, Central Sudanic, and Nilotic (e.g. Arensen 1982; Gilley 1992; Persson & Persson 1991). More recently, they focused on languages spoken in eastern Sudan or the Nuba Mountains, e.g. Beja (Wedekind et al. 2007), Gaahmg (Stirtz 2011), Tira (Watters 1993), and Talodi (Norton & Thomas Kuku 2015). In 1981 SIL established the series Occasional Papers in the Study of Sudanese Languages (OPSL) as an outlet for the publication of Sudanese and non-Sudanese linguists. All issues of OPSL are accessible online.[12]

5.7.6 Current Research

Both the triennial conferences, the Nilo-Saharan Linguistics Colloquium and the Nuba Mountain Languages Conference initiated by Thilo Schadeberg in 1979 and 2011, respectively, and the proceedings of these conferences, have stimulated much of the recent linguistic research in the Sudan. The publication series Nilo-Saharan - Linguistic Analyses and Documentation (NISA), which was established by Franz Rottland and M. Lionel Bender in 1987, provides another outlet for publishing on Sudanese languages such as Nobiin (Werner 1987), Fur (Jakobi 1990 and Waag 2010), Anywa (Reh 1996), Surmic (Dimmendaal & Last 1998), Western Nilotic (Storch 2005), and Belanda Boor (Heyking 2013). A recently established open access journal, *Dotawo*, is exclusively devoted to Nubian studies. It is edited by Vincent van Gerven Oei and Giovanni Ruffini. Their research focuses on medieval Nubia and the Old Nubian language.

Fortunately, various Niger-Congo languages spoken in the Nuba Mountains have also attracted linguistic attention, particularly Koalib (Quint 2009), Tima (Alamin 2012; Schneider-Blum 2013), Dagik (Vanderelst 2016), and Lumun (Smits 2017).

The Afroasiatic language phylum is represented by Sudanese Arabic which is the lingua franca of Sudan. Juba Arabic, by contrast, is an Arabic-based pidgin-creole spoken in South Sudan. Presently Manfredi (2017) carries out research on both languages.

Studies of the ancient written languages, Meroitic and Old Nubian, have started with the ground-breaking works of the British Egyptologist Francis L. Griffith (1909, 1911, 1913). Currently Kirsty Rowan (2006) argues for an Afroasiatic classification of Meroitic, whereas Claude Rilly (2010) concludes that Meroitic is most closely related to Nubian, Tama, Nyimang, and Nara and thus affiliated to the northern branch of Eastern Sudanic, a subgroup of Nilo-Saharan.

Another noteworthy positive development is that there are several native speakers of Sudanese languages who are presently involved in research projects. Angelo Naser, for instance, is engaged in the Moro project initiated by Sharon Rose (University of California, San Diego), Siddig Ali takes part in the Koalib project of Nicolas Quint (LLACAN, INALCO, Paris). Elsadig Omda, in turn, is part of the Zaghawa documentation project of Isabel Compes (University of Cologne).

---

[12] www.sil.org/resources/search/series/occasional-papers-study-sudanese-languages.

Note that recent developments in Nilo-Saharan, Niger-Congo, and Afro-Asiatic language studies in Sudan are also reflected in *The Cambridge Handbook of African Linguistics* (Wolff 2019), chapters 9, 10 and 11.

Acknowledgements

Maria Bulakh acknowledges support of her work by the Russian Foundation for Basic Research (RFBR), grant #17-06-00391.

Marie-Claude Simeone-Senelle is grateful to Fatouma Mahamoud (Research Assistant at ILD), Hibo Moumin Assoweh (Senior Lecturer at UD, Director of CRUD), Amina Said Chireh (Teacher-Researcher at UD, Secretary of IRICA), and Mohamed Hassan Kamil (Researcher, Director of ILD).

Ronny Meyer and Wolbert Smidt are grateful to Giorgio Banti, Joachim Crass, Mauro Tosco, and Rainer Voigt for support with important information and literature on the research history of the Horn of Africa, and to Yvonne Treis and the editor for comments on earlier versions.

6   African Linguistics in Southern Africa

Sonja E. Bosch and Inge M. Kosch

6.1   Introduction

In this chapter we explore the history of African linguistics in the Southern African region (including Botswana, Lesotho, Namibia, South Africa, and Swaziland) on Bantu[1] and formerly so-called Khoisan[2] languages, from an inside-Africa perspective. The focus is on research activities and methodological approaches to the study of African languages which were established and homegrown and are largely conducted *in loco* by African researchers with or without (further) outside stimuli at local universities and research institutions. We address the motivations for copying or maintaining European/Western 'academic culture' and higher education systems in order to 'close the gap' between the formerly so-called First World and what is now called the Global South, if not – in the long run – to establish Africa as a relevant region of global knowledge production.

Such a perspective regards the impact from Europe as more or less imposed or solicited 'academic fertilization' for the growth of local and regional structures and institutions. Furthermore, stories of success and failure on African soil are included, suggesting a clear-cut distinction of the apartheid and post-apartheid periods. In this respect, Poulos (1986:13) comments that

the nature of our discipline is closely intertwined with, and influenced by the socio-political system that is operative in our society. In fact, social and political factors appear to have an effect on the very status and significance of Bantu language studies as a discipline.

---

[1] The term 'Bantu' was introduced in language studies as far back as 1857 by the German philologist Dr W. H. I. Bleek, there being, however, no certainty as to when exactly he first used it. Although this term became stigmatized in South Africa because of its use in contexts other than language, it is used in the international field of linguistics to refer to a particular family of languages that share common linguistic features.

[2] Khoisan refers to four or five groups of non-Bantu click languages spoken in southern and eastern Africa. There is a basic distinction within South African so-called Khoisan, namely Khoe (formerly and derogatively 'Hottentot') and non-Khoe (formerly and derogatively 'Bushman', also known as 'San') according to Wolff (2016:304).

This chapter is roughly divided into three historical periods; these periods should not be regarded as hard-and-fast time spans but as approximate indications of the era that was dominated by a particular model:

1. The exploration years covering pre-scientific (missionary, colonial) studies of African languages (*c.* mid-1800s to 1927).
2. Postcolonial linguistics as dealt with by Southern African institutions (*c.* 1927 to 1975).
3. Modern linguistics reflecting research priorities with regard to a variety of modern linguistic theories (*c.* 1975 to date).

6.2   Pre-Scientific Studies (*c.* Mid-1800s to 1927)

6.2.1   Background

In Africa, Westerners in the person of missionaries were invariably responsible for the development of orthographies for the various African languages, which facilitated further linguistic investigation. By the mid-1800s the spade work for the establishment of orthographies and spelling systems had roughly been done, empowering the missionaries to gain the 'monopoly', as it were, over the development of linguistic analyses and descriptions from a Western viewpoint. The mid-1800s is an arbitrary starting point to the pre-scientific period, while its end can be associated with a more definite milestone in 1927, to be discussed in the next section. There were several noteworthy publications on grammatical issues in African languages before the 1850s (e.g. Bennie 1826; Boyce 1834; Archbell 1837; Casalis 1841; Bryant 1849; to mention but a few), but since then a steady increase in the quality and quantity of contributions could be observed. Colenso, for example, produced a *Zulu–English Dictionary* in 1861, which had a long-term effect on the development of the Zulu language. Apart from well-known languages, lesser-known languages like the Khoisan languages also attracted the attention of scholars (Hahn 1857; Vedder 1910, 1911; Doke 1925; Engelbrecht 1925). Phonetic descriptions were and remained a topic of interest in the studies of the Khoisan languages because of the unique sound systems of these languages.

6.2.2   Research Priorities

The pre-scientific, exploration period was characterized by the production of word lists, dictionaries, and basic grammars by missionaries. Their primary objective was of a practical nature, namely to design lesson manuals for language learners, primers, elementary readers, and Bible translations, to facilitate the communication of the gospel. The translation of the Bible and grammatical work could not be divorced from each other. According to Welmers (1971:567–569), lesson manuals are academically interesting since 'they can be classed as good descriptive grammars which happen to have a pedagogical organization'. The focus was on the acquisition of language and not on the scientific description of individual linguistic phenomena.

Not being trained as language experts in African languages, the missionaries had recourse to patterns of grammars of European languages when drafting their manuals. It is therefore not surprising to find some descriptions in the early grammars that are inaccurately imposed on the structure of the relevant African language. However, it was quite acceptable for linguistics of contemporary and classical languages of the time to serve as paradigm for the linguistics of African languages. This led Wilkes (1978:108) to refer to this period as the classical period of grammatical studies. The influence of the so-called classical approach to the analyses of the Bantu languages is evident, for example, in the following works on the Zulu language: Grout (1893) recognizes three cases of nouns, namely the genitive, the locative, and the vocative, while Schreuder (1850:17) even introduces a fourth case, the 'rodcasusen' which refers to nouns appearing in a subject or object position. Colenso (1903), on the other hand, classifies nouns into three classes, namely the Simple (nominative or accusative), the Vocative, and the Oblique or Locative (dative or ablative). The German missionary Wanger (1917) also relied on grammatical notions of case when referring to the Zulu possessive as the genitive case, and treating locative affixes as prepositions, thereby inappropriately implying nominal declination and formally marked grammatical case categories.

Ziervogel (1956:1–2) remarked:

One may take it as a rule that all these writers superimposed the grammar of their own mother tongue upon the particular Bantu language they were dealing with ... Not only was it the accepted approach at the time, it is the only logical and practical one ... The medium used in the exposition of Bantu languages was quite foreign to the structure of Bantu. It is a fact we have to consider that the language in which we clothe our thoughts has a definite bearing on our approach to a subject.

Once the basics of a grammar had been laid down, missionaries with an interest in linguistics and other scholars invariably shifted their focus to the description of specific linguistic phenomena. With regard to the study of African languages during this period, the following comment describes the developments:

From the fourth decade of the 19th Century right on through into the 20th Century, in increasing numbers, the Bantu languages began to be studied in a more modern method with more attention to their intrinsic structure. It might be stated that the mediaeval Latin approach of the 'Age of Brusciotto' gave way to the imposition of modern European grammatical methods, in which only to a certain extent was 'Bantu grammar' given any free play. Two decades of the 20th century had to pass before any real move was made for the 100 per cent treatment of Bantu languages according to the genius of Bantu grammar.

(Doke & Cole 1969:27)

It is noteworthy that although the Bantu languages were identified as tone languages from an early stage, tone studies hardly featured in the works of early grammarians. The only significant studies on tone during the pre-scientific era, according to Wilkes (1978:110), were those of Endemann (1911) (Northern Sotho), Jones and Plaatje (1916) (Tswana), and Doke (1926) (Zulu).

With regard to phonetics and phonology studies of the Khoisan languages which are characterized by tone as well as clicks, Güldemann (2013:80) reports that considerable research was done in the nineteenth century on |Xam (a now extinct language spoken in the western part of South Africa) by Bleek and Lloyd (1911) and Bleek (1928-1930). Doke's (1925) contribution to the tonological description of Grootfontein !Xung, albeit preliminary, is also noteworthy during this period (Miller 2013:93).

6.2.3   Leading Figures

Most of the scholars who produced material on the African languages were not born in Southern Africa but came as missionaries from Europe. They acquired the language of the people to whom they had been assigned by their missionary society and started producing written material with the help of local informants and converts. Many of these missionaries adopted a Southern African country as their new home.

Missionaries were therefore often the leading figures in the exploration of linguistic phenomena. There were sporadic contributions by native speakers to the development of African languages during this period, but these pertained more to literature than to linguistic issues. Having had first-hand exposure to the structure of the language while compiling basic grammars, some of the missionaries developed into ardent linguists who advocated for the correct spelling and grammatical descriptions of the African languages. A case in point is Endemann (1876), who produced a grammar on the Sotho languages in which he advocated for a scientific approach to the choice of orthographic symbols. His scientifically motivated symbols, however, were impractical and never became popular. His grammar and that of other emerging scholars had vestiges of Western linguistic descriptions.

Some noteworthy academic contributions on specific linguistic aspects of African languages were produced during the pre-scientific time, for example Bourquin (1922a, 1922b) on the prefix of the locative and the adverb in Xhosa, and Eiselen (1924) on the change of consonants through a preceding *i* in the Bantu languages.

Traill (1999:41) observed that Khoisan studies maintained a steady momentum in the last century since the initial investigations of ǀXam by Bleek and Lloyd (1911) mentioned above. The journal *Bantu Studies*, which appeared for the first time in October 1921 (renamed *African Studies* after 1941), afforded scholars based in South Africa a valuable forum for publishing the results of local research in the field of Khoisan linguistics, some of the contributing pioneers being D. F. Bleek, W. H. I. Bleek, C. M. Doke, J. F. Maingard, and G. S. Nienaber.

As more and more languages were being reduced to writing and more information became available, interest in comparative study increased with scholars like Appleyard (1850), Bleek (1862, 1869), Torrend (1891), and Meinhof (1899, 1906) rendering outstanding and leading contributions. Classifications of the Bantu languages were also attempted during this period (e.g. Van Warmelo 1927). In Bleek's *Comparative Grammar* (1869), one of the most important contributions was his classification of the language types in South Africa according to '(a) a South African division of the sex-denoting languages (Nama, !Kora, Cape Hottentot and Eastern Hottentot) and (b) a South African division of the Bantu family' (Doke & Cole 1969:64). Throughout this work, Bleek (1869) particularly compared and contrasted the 'Hottentot' suffix formation with the prefix formation of the Bantu languages.

6.2.4   Impact

Opinions on the impact of the pre-scientific (missionary, colonial) studies of African languages vary. Wilkes (1978:109) concludes that this period contributed some useful reference works with valuable grammatical information that can still be used to this day. He refers in particular to the work of Colenso, Bryant, and Wanger with regard to Zulu; Endemann and Beyer with regard to Northern Sotho; Archbell, Wookey, and Crisp with regard to Tswana; Boyce and Appleyard with regard to Xhosa; and Jacottet with regard to Southern Sotho. However, Dowling and Maseko (1995:100) are of the opinion that although 'missionaries often became the leading scholars of African linguistics, the importance of their work was diminished by their political and ideological allegiances'.

6.3   Postcolonial Linguistics (*c*. 1927 to 1975)

6.3.1   Background

Contributors to postcolonial African linguistics in Southern Africa (*c*. 1927 to 1975) were mainly African-born Africanists, with a broad training in linguistics. Only since the early 1920s have scholars involved with the study of the indigenous South African languages been born in South Africa, lived in the country all their lives, and acquired the Bantu languages at a young age (Ziervogel 1956:2). They generally focused on languages with which they were well acquainted from extended personal experience. Clements (1989:5) points out that this was in contrast with the European Africanists who spent time in Africa carrying out field research. Not only did the European Africanists acquire the new languages they were exposed to but they were also more holistic in their research involving history, society, and culture, true to the tradition of past pursuits of the missionaries, explorers, and colonial administrators.

In the postcolonial period, linguistic investigation in the African languages became an end in itself, after it had played a secondary role during the pre-scientific era (Griesel 1991:246). This period was marked by increased contributions from trained linguists, which ultimately completely replaced the participation of the missionaries (Kosch 1993:29).

The incremental establishment of departments of African languages at tertiary institutions in Southern Africa provided emerging scholars with a conducive and collegial surrounding in which to pursue their linguistic endeavours. Such academic structures did not exist per se during the pre-scientific period. An example of a precursor to such departments was the Department of Bantu Studies at the University of the Witwatersrand which C. M. Doke joined in 1923 (Herbert 1993:4). In 1946 the Department of African Languages at the University of South Africa (Unisa) was established as an independent department after the evolvement of Unisa out of the University of the Cape of Good Hope, which had been functioning as an examining body since 1873 (Kosch & Bosch 2014:51-52).

According to *Studies in Bantoetale* (1980: Preface), the precursor to the creation of the Department of African Languages at the University of Pretoria was the approval of a senate recommendation by the Council of the University on 16 August 1917 that a chair in native languages be established. However, the execution of this recommendation failed to come to fruition for a number of years. In 1923 E. H. Brooks recommended that lectures in Bantu studies be exchanged between the University of Pretoria and the University of the Witwatersrand. C. M. Doke made himself available to teach the isiZulu course, while G. H. S. Roussouw (from Johannesburg) offered a course in Bantu ethnology. Rev. P. E. Schwellnus was approached to act as part-time lecturer. These arrangements of 1923 were the first steps towards the eventual establishment of a fully-fledged Department of African Languages (known at the time as the Department of Bantu Languages) in 1935. In 1936 J. A. Engelbrecht was appointed as the first chair of department.

The University of Botswana, the National University of Lesotho, and the University of Swaziland have a shared history. The National University of Lesotho started out as the Pius XII Catholic University College at Roma,

Lesotho in 1945. In 1964 the university became non-denominational and part of a larger university system, known as the UBBS or University of Bechuanaland, Basotholand and Swaziland. The purpose was 'to reduce the three countries' reliance on tertiary education in apartheid-era South Africa'.[3] After Botswana and Lesotho gained independence in 1966, the University was renamed the University of Botswana, Lesotho and Swaziland (UBLS). The Department of African Languages and Literature (ALL) of the University of Botswana has been in existence since 1971. Both regional and international recognition has been gained over the years since its inception.[4]

In 1975 Lesotho broke away from the partnership and founded its own independent university in 1977–1978. Its Department of African Languages and Literature offers mainly Southern Sotho but other languages such as Zulu, Xhosa, and Tswana have also been part of the course content. In 1982 the universities of Botswana and Swaziland also each became fully-fledged institutions of higher education in their own right.

Research outputs during the postcolonial period include in addition to general grammar works, theses and scientific articles in journals. Researchers were now mainly academics who were susceptible to and in contact with new linguistic approaches internationally, like, for instance, those of Meinhof (1899, 1906) and Guthrie (1948a). The language of publication was mainly English, occasionally Afrikaans, but seldom African languages. A few of the grammars published in the African languages were, for instance, Schwellnus' (1931) Northern Sotho grammar (*Tlhalosa-Polelo: Grammar ya Sesotho se se bolelwaxo dileteng tša Transvaal*), Mojapelo's (1960) Northern Sotho grammar (*Popo-puo ya Sesotho*), Nyembezi's (1956) Zulu grammar (*Uhlelo Lwesizulu*), and Pahl's (1967) Xhosa grammar (*Isixhosa*).

In the case of the Khoisan languages, Dorothea F. Bleek published her *Comparative Vocabularies of Bushman Languages* in 1929, followed by a descriptive grammatical sketch of the language of the /xam-ka-!e/ (Bleek 1928–1930). A re-classification of the Khoisan languages was also attempted by Westphal (1962), whose interest in non-Bantu languages in Angola, Botswana, and Namibia resulted in research findings that the Khoi and the San languages belonged to totally different language families. Interestingly enough, Westphal's so-called 'splitter' approach only gained acceptance in the late 1990s mainly through the work of Tom Güldemann (W. H. G. Haacke, personal communication, 7 March 2017). Cole (1971:18) came to the conclusion that with the challenges experienced in the Khoisan languages at phonological level, 'progress in morphological analysis becomes bogged down and retarded'. It will be shown in the discussion of the next era that there

[3] https://en.wikipedia.org/wiki/University_of_Botswana#History.
[4] www.ub.bw/home/ac/1/fac/12/dep/66/African-Languages-&-Literature.

were nevertheless scholars such as Snyman, Traill, and Haacke who made a breakthrough in this regard. Snyman's main contributions to Khoisan studies were the publication of his master's dissertation 'An Introduction to the !Xũ (!Kung) Language' (1970) in which he 'cracked' or deciphered the phonology of !Khung, and also his PhD thesis 'Zul'hõasi Fonologie en Woordeboek' (1975). Westphal was the supervisor of both these studies.

6.3.2   Research Priorities and Leading Figures

Against the background of Wilkes's (1978:108) observation that the scientific study of the Bantu languages is cumulative, implying that each period is 'more scientific' than the foregoing (see Griesel 1991:25), we will pay attention to leading figures such as Doke, Ziervogel, Cope, and van Wyk and their seminal publications.

In the early years of the 1920s, the phonetic school became popular in linguistic studies. C. M. Doke, born in Bristol, England, in 1893, moved to South Africa with his parents in 1903 as a ten year-old. He was an exponent of this phonetic school in the field of South African Bantu languages. His 'Phonetics of the Zulu Language' (submitted for a DLitt degree in 1924) served as an example for similar studies of various other Bantu languages throughout Africa. In 1927 Doke published his *Textbook of Zulu Grammar*, thereby revolutionizing Bantu linguistic description (Kosch 1993:28). Therefore the year 1927 is generally regarded as the watershed between the exploratory or pre-scientific studies of African languages and the commencement of a new era of grammatical description in the South African Bantu languages. Doke's approach was basically functional as regards grammar, and purely phonetic as regards the definition of a word. Doke (1945:79), who had the insight that a more suitable model of grammatical description for the Bantu languages was called for, described the major contribution of his own work as 'a new grammatical classification and treatment designed to get away from the European and classical preconceptions, and use a mould more naturally suited to the structure of the Bantu languages'. Doke's model of grammatical description is regarded by Van Wyk (1993:21) as a paradigm shift in the African languages brought about by the discarding of inappropriate assumptions and terminology dating from earlier grammatical work in the classical tradition. Examples are superfluous grammatical categories such as 'case', 'preposition', and 'article' (Kosch 1993:33). It is significant, however, that the descriptions of many Bantu grammars are to this day influenced by Doke's terminology, as well as his understanding of 'moods' and 'tenses', a relic of European language grammars (Kosch 1993:33). Regardless of such shortcomings, Doke's approach deserves recognition 'since it was the first in which the identification of words was based not on intuitions stemming from a European background, but on more scientifically motivated criteria' (Kosch 1993:31). Wilkes (1978:112) remarks that the lack of a properly motivated definition of the Bantu word had previously given rise to writers dividing words at their own discretion, leading to different disjunctive and conjunctive methods of word division. Doke's theory regarding the word in Bantu, which he defined as 'that sound or group of sounds which is subject to one main stress and only one' (Wilkes 1978:112), favoured the conjunctive writing method which was adopted for the Nguni languages. Overall, Doke's theories strongly influenced Bantu grammar for at least the next three decades.

During the postcolonial period, several attempts were made by linguists to improve on Doke's scientific investigations. Ziervogel came to the conclusion that the phonetic principle used by Doke to mark word boundaries could not be applied across the board. In his publication *A Grammar of Swazi* (1952), Ziervogel therefore proposed a new approach to the identification of the word in Bantu languages. Based on Meinhof's view of the Bantu word, he adopted the morphological approach to the analysis of the Bantu word in terms of root plus prefixes and suffixes. Later on, Ziervogel worked towards broadening his definition by adding functional, prosodic as well as semantic principles. His work can also be regarded as a variation of Doke's model. Ziervogel's method of analysis did not have a particularly wide-ranging impact on Bantu grammatical works in general, although he applied it to various Southern African Bantu languages including Zulu, Swazi, Northern Sotho, and Northern Transvaal Ndebele. However, according to Kosch (1993:39), the 'School of Ziervogel' can chronologically be regarded as the transition from the Dokeian period to the Van Wyk era.

Cope (1957), in his work on the grammatical structure of Zulu, followed suit by deviating from Doke's prosodic approach. Instead, he offered an alternative to the traditional 'form and function' analysis of Zulu by rigorously applying the principle of form. He chose to follow the syntactically based method propounded by the London linguist Malcolm Guthrie (1948a), who regarded the sentence as the most fundamental building block. Cope's approach was not widely acknowledged or actively applied beyond his own and his students' publications (Griesel 1991:110).

Van Wyk (1958) proposed a new theory with regard to word identification in the Bantu languages particularly in Northern Sotho, as representative of the disjunctively written Sotho languages, and in Zulu, as representative of the conjunctively written Nguni languages. Van Wyk's aim was to address the main objection against Doke's word identification process, which was mainly of a phonological nature, and did not, for instance, make provision for anomalies such as monosyllabic words. He therefore propounded the analysis of words on different levels, with an emphasis on syntax. The grammatical description of Northern Sotho was more affected by Van Wyk's theory than was the case of the analysis of the Nguni languages, which continued to be influenced by the Dokeian structural approach inspired by Doke and Bloomfieldian linguistics.

Griesel (1991:89) regards van Wyk's approach as a new model rather than a new paradigm, which did not completely substitute the Dokeian model in the research community, but rather formed an undercurrent. In addition, Kosch (1993:65) points out that for the most part 'the Bantu languages as a field of scientific investigation benefitted from the theories put forward by Van Wyk. He had indicated the important role of general linguistic science in providing a theoretical foundation which would ensure a more meaningful and systematic approach to Bantu linguistic study.'

Mother tongue speakers contributing to the scientific study of the Bantu languages during the postcolonial period were few and far between. This state of affairs changed notably with the establishment of the formerly so-called black universities. At the University of the North (now University of Limpopo), for example, Mayevu (1973) published an article on the subjectival concord in Tsonga, while Setshedi (1975) investigated the auxiliary and deficient verbs in Tswana in his MA dissertation. Scholars who attempted a scientific treatment of Zulu and Southern Sotho in the medium of the languages were, for instance, Nkobi (1954) and Khaketla (1951). Referring to these works, Ziervogel (1956) points out that 'They simply follow Doke without being in the least critical. Except for the medium, which is Zulu and Sotho respectively, they have brought us nothing new in two languages so well known.' Yet, significant work was done by mother tongue speakers on dialect research, which became essential in newly founded departments of Bantu languages at various South African universities (see Wilkes 1978:145), particularly in the light of the influence that mass media such as the press and the radio had on the standardization of different, but related linguistic varieties. Important contributions were made by Jordan (1942) on Bhaca, Mzamane (1948) on Phuthi, and Mokgokong (1966) on Northern Sotho.

6.3.3   Impact

Kosch (1993:38) argues that over time the impact of the Dokeian model based on the structuralist framework of analysis fluctuated. While some scholars such as Cole (1955), Malcolm (1949), and van Eeden (1956) closely followed the principles of Doke, others such as Ziervogel (1952) and Cope (1957) worked only partially within this framework of analysis.

In 1968 Van Wyk averred that Doke's functional approach had been losing support in South Africa during the preceding couple of years. He based his observation on the fact that African studies in English-medium universities, for instance the University of the Witwatersrand in Johannesburg and the Rhodes University in Grahamstown, had been replacing the Dokeian model with an approach based more on American structural linguistic principles. In contrast, most of the Afrikaans-medium universities had replaced the Dokeian model by a Dutch-inspired structural approach. The University of South Africa adhered to an adapted form of the Dokeian model as implemented by Ziervogel.

Gough (1993:35) goes so far as to say that Doke's methodology continued to impact most of the so-called new approaches. He continues by offering an analogy which could explain Doke's contribution to Bantu linguistics in simple terms: 'a certain (possibly mythical) people ... never quite cleaned their cooking pots, but always left a little bit over. Cooking pots were handed down from generation to generation, so there was, in a sense, a continuity in the pot extending far beyond the immediate meal. Doke's model itself bears some of the hallmarks of European grammatical tradition, and in most "new approaches" Dokean influences continue to remain in evidence. The pot, in a way, has never been scrubbed clean' (Gough 1993:35).

6.4   Modern Linguistics (*c*. 1975 to Date)

6.4.1   Background

A gradual transition took place from about 1975 reflecting research priorities with regard to a variety of modern linguistic theories. The transition entailed a movement from structuralism to the modern period, with 1975 being adopted as an arbitrary boundary (Goslin 1983).

Kosch (1993:74) observes that 'The first of the more sophisticated contemporary theoretical models to offer a challenging new framework to Bantuists was the transformational-generative model.' In an unpublished manuscript, Louwrens (1981b) expressed his views on the so-called Chomskyan revolution, thereby referring to the influence of the transformational-generative grammar (TGG) model of Chomsky (1957) on the practice of Bantu linguistic studies in South Africa. He gives a comprehensive overview of conference presentations, publications in scholarly works and theses within this framework by South African linguistic scholars on South African indigenous languages since 1971. He considered four African language conferences between 1971 and 1981 and found that the few presentations within the Chomskyan theory were negligible and could not serve as a barometer of trends within the field of Bantu linguistics. In addition, the TGG framework in Bantu linguistics was mostly restricted to syntactic studies, which included, amongst others, studies on the adjective, pronouns, and relativization. These studies were primarily confined to the Nguni languages.

As far as publications are concerned, Louwrens considered an article by Lanham (1971) as the first contribution in which clear signs of Chomsky's influence could be detected, fourteen years after the publication of Chomsky's influential work *Syntactic Structures* (1957). Louwrens remarks that a typical feature of Lanham's article and other early contributions was their tentative and highly experimental character. After Lanham, Ainsley (1972) published an article in which some principles of transformational grammar were applied to the sentence in Bantu. Ainsley described his own work as 'an extremely tentative exercise' (1972:32).

Other scholars who experimented with the applicability of the Chomskyan concept on the grammar of the South African Bantu languages in the decade 1971–1981, according to Louwrens (1981b), include Wilkes (1973, 1974, 1976) on Zulu, Hendrikse (1975, 1976, 1978), Hendrikse and Zotwana (1975), du Plessis (1979, 1981), and Visser (1983) on Xhosa. Louwrens found that there was no increase in publications which displayed Chomskyan influence. Some scholars abandoned the Chomskyan model soon after the initial experiments. Scholars worked within the standard theory (ST) and the extended standard theory (EST) and contributors mainly represented only three universities, namely the University of Pretoria (Wilkes), Rhodes University (Hendrikse), and the University of Stellenbosch (Du Plessis and Visser). Since 1980, as observed by Louwrens, contributions were conducted within the framework of the revised extended standard theory (REST) and contributions became confined to one scholarly journal published by the University of Stellenbosch (*Studies in Afrikatale*).

In an unpublished manuscript, Louwrens (1981b) advances some reasons as to what could have curtailed the large-scale impact of the 'Chomskyan revolution' on the study of Bantu linguistics at that time.

• The grip of the taxonomic grammar on Bantu linguistic study: A taxonomic grammar is in essence classificatory, with identification techniques which are mechanistic in character (in opposition to the mentalistic character of the Chomskyan language theory). Following the publication of Doke's *Textbook of Zulu Grammar* (1927), Bantu linguistic study increasingly assumed a taxonomic character, supported further by contributions on Northern Sotho and Zulu by Van Wyk (1958 and 1961), who was a proponent of European structuralism.

• The syntactically oriented character of Chomsky's theory: At the time when Chomsky's *Aspects of the Theory of Syntax* was published in 1965, Bantu linguistics did not have a syntactic tradition and very little had been done in the field of syntax in the Bantu languages. Researchers were taken up by the intricacies of the morphological and phonological systems of the languages and it suited them to work within the taxonomic framework even for syntactic investigations.

• The English-oriented character of Chomsky's theory: It was found that Chomsky's theory failed in certain respects to satisfactorily cater for aspects of the Bantu languages regarding their unique structure.

- The strong mentalistic impact of Chomsky's theory: In contrast to Chomsky's theory, which focused strongly on the cognitive functions of the ideal speaker/hearer, Bantu linguistic studies had a strong practical penchant, which is a further mark of taxonomic descriptive models. The overriding mentalistic character of Chomsky's approach did not appeal to Bantu linguistic scholars.

Louwrens, who adopted a functional approach, found it impossible to work within the framework of Chomskyan grammar, as the latter ignored the role of the context of discourse. As remarked by Louwrens (quoting Givón 1979:41–42), the Chomskyan linguistic theory was backed by 'dreamed-up artificial sentences outside their discourse context and detached from communicative function'.

Unlike previous periods in the description of Bantu grammar, the modern period was not dominated by any specific approach over a prolonged time. According to Kosch (1993:74), 'Bantu linguistic description as a whole opened up to a variety of international developments at approximately the same time, resulting in the co-occurrence of studies conceived within different frameworks.'

The general approach to linguistic investigation became increasingly influenced by changes in social and political conditions in South Africa. Slabbert and Finlayson (1998:289) refer to the process of rapid urbanization together with the legacy of apartheid in South Africa, which led to the development of large townships on the peripheries of the major industrial centres. The people who settled in these townships, as well as their adjoining and multilingual urban centres, represented different language groups. A realization thus emerged that although it was essential to describe languages phonologically and grammatically, the associated patterns of linguistic communication begged to be understood. This insight called for the inclusion of the social aspects of language in the study of linguistics and hence the emergence of the area of applied linguistics, including among others sociolinguistics. There are, however, different schools of thought when it comes to whether the field of sociolinguistics should be regarded as an intrinsic part of linguistics or not.

6.4.2   Contributions by Various Institutions and Academics

As mentioned above, African linguistic studies adopted divergent approaches in the years following 1975. In cases where linguistics was practised within a particular framework or philosophy, the impact was mostly localized and confined to certain universities. Individual researchers set the trend and mentored colleagues who in turn supervised postgraduate students who followed their approach with regard to their philosophy and theoretical inclinations. One could therefore speak of emerging regional 'schools' of African linguistics, which temporarily cast their research within the TGG mould, or adaptations thereof or other frameworks. At the University of Stellenbosch, the theory of government and binding was applied to the study of Xhosa (du Plessis, Visser). This framework was also adopted in a number of publications produced by the Department of African Languages and Literature at the National University of Lesotho (Machobane). At the University of Pretoria, the applicability of case grammar and relational grammar in Zulu and Northern Sotho was investigated (Wilkes, Prinsloo). Research based on typological investigations was produced by scholars at Unisa (Hendrikse, Poulos, Bosch). A noteworthy contributor within the functional approach was Louwrens, who addressed issues like the distinction between old and known information, definiteness and indefiniteness, and concepts like co-reference, focus, contrast, and discourse analysis (1979, 1981a). According to the functional model, 'the grammatical correctness of a sentence is less important than the message being communicated' (von Staden 1986:5). Discourse analysis narrowed the gap between pure linguistics and language as a social phenomenon.

In a contribution on the phonetic and phonological studies of Southern African languages, Lubinda (2012:34) laments that phonetics and phonology research is one of the most neglected fields of language research in Southern Africa and that very few universities in the region have phonetics laboratories or research units devoted to phonetics and phonology. However, it should be emphasized that pockets of excellence can indeed be identified with regard to the scientific study of phonetics and phonology in South Africa. Here we refer in particular to the Research Unit for Experimental Phonology of the University of Stellenbosch (RUEPUS), which contributed to inspiring laboratory phonology and language technologies research and development in South Africa (see Chapter 22 in *The Cambridge Handbook of African Linguistics*, for more details). Examples of significant experimental research on African languages accomplished during this period are Roux (2003) and Jones and Roux (2004) on prosody and perception; Jessen and Roux (2002) and Naidoo (2012) on speech production and transmission; Lewis (1998) on phonology and phonetics; and Roux et al. (2000) on phonetics for speech technology.

Traill (1977:iii) remarked that 'narrow linguistic research on the Khoisan languages is currently being undertaken by an extremely small number of individuals'. Three of the very few locally born scholars were Snyman (Unisa), Traill (University of the Witwatersrand), and Haacke (initially at the Academy for Tertiary Education, and later at the successor institution, the University of Namibia), who emerged as leading figures in the area of Khoisan research. These academics had started publishing in the early 1970s. Snyman's interest in the Khoisan group is reflected in numerous publications in which he, as analytical field linguist, dealt with language classification based on lexical, phonological, and grammatical grounds (e.g. Snyman 1974, 1977). Traill was foremost a phonetician, specializing on the Khoisan language !Xóõ, which is renowned for having an extremely extended consonant inventory in comparison to any other existing language. Traill's publications (e.g. 1977, 1985, 1986) addressed the phonetics and phonology of !Xóõ and also contributed to comparative research on the sound systems in the Khoisan languages. Based in Namibia, Haacke's research interest ranges from grammatical descriptions of Nama (1977) to typological comparisons of northern dialects of Khoekhoegowab (2010). His main interest, however, remains tonology (Haacke 1999), which he also carried over to his work on Khoekhoe lexicography (Haacke & Eiseb 2002) and two glossaries that have been generated out of a customized electronic database with authoritative spelling and complete tone marking. The system he established for Khoekhoe has in essence been adopted by other Khoesanists, also for comparative work.

Some scholars affiliated with the University of Botswana ventured into research on selected Khoisan languages, albeit with a more sociolinguistic focus, for instance Batibo (2010a, 2015) and Chebanne (2010). Chebanne is also involved in the linguistic documentation of Khoisan languages of Southern Africa. Furthermore, Batibo's contributions cover aspects of phonology, tonology and morphology of languages in Botswana and Tanzania, including comparisons between linguistic features of Tswana and Swahili (1996, 2010b). Another scholar who has made contributions to the linguistic study of selected languages of Botswana and Čilubà is Lukusa, while Motse-Mogara has added to existing knowledge on Naro, Jul'hoansi, and !Xóõ, languages which were the focus of her doctoral study (2011). Kari, at the same university, focused on Naro and Degema. Kalanga, a Bantu language of the Shona group spoken in northern Botswana, has amongst others been the object of investigation and description by Mathangwane (1998) and Letsholo (Department of English).

One of the prominent figures in African linguistics at the University of Lesotho is Machobane. Her studies cover a wide range of topics including tense and aspect in Southern Sotho (1985), the passive construction (1987), prefixes, suffixes, word order constraints, and locative constructions.

6.4.3 Institutional Transformation

At Unisa and elsewhere in institutions of higher learning (e.g. the University of Pretoria), the designation 'Bantu' to name a department was increasingly deemed inappropriate in the prevailing political climate, hence the former Department of Bantu Languages at Unisa was renamed the Department of African Languages in 1978, even before the demise of apartheid.

Transformation was also reflected in the naming of modules, for instance in the case of the Department of African Languages at Unisa. Up to 2004 linguistics modules at Honours level bore the name of their exact content; for example, there were five separate modules catering for each of the core areas of research in linguistics, namely Phonetics, Phonology, Morphology, Syntax, and Semantics. From 2005 modules were combined in compliance with the university's imperative that offerings be rationalized. This resulted in the reduction of five modules to two. The new module titles were not to include any references to the traditional descriptions of the disciplines as they were reflective of theories and content advanced by Western thought, whereas the mandate of the university was to 'Africanize' the course content of all offerings. The purpose of the new names was to make the modules more attractive and accessible to students and not to scare them off with nomenclature that they could not identify with. The renaming of modules was done as shown below:

> Phonetics and phonology > Sounds and sound systems.
> Morphology, syntax and semantics > From form to meaning.

Dowling and Maseko (1995:101) explain that universities took over the tasks of teaching the African languages in a more formal and structured way than was the case when these languages were taught by missionaries for evangelical purposes. They are of the opinion, however, that African language departments tended to follow international trends in linguistics, such as structuralism and TGG while neglecting the more relevant area of applied linguistics. Wright (2002:17) confirmed this opinion by stating that:

Rather than focus on African languages as living cultural media, the academic study of African languages in South African universities has in general followed the international pattern of change in the field of general linguistics: briefly, grammatical studies on the lines established by C. M. Doke in the 30s, 40s and 50s were followed (belatedly) in the 60s by structuralism, pioneered in South Africa by E. B. van Wyk. The 70s saw work shaped by the transformational-generative approach (L. W. Lanham, A. Wilkes, D. P. Lombard, H. W. Pahl et al.). The African linguists who now work in the field have generally stayed with this model of academic linguistic enquiry, seeking ever more accurate descriptive and analytical knowledge.

Brock-Utne's (2003:42) recommendation for Africa is 'to develop its own courses, research, and publications, more directly suited to situations in Africa'. A new approach to course content and research would stem 'the alarming decline in registrations at African language departments in South African universities' (Wright 2002:4). Gxilishe (2009) reports that 'The number of student enrolments in official indigenous African languages at universities and technikons has shown a dramatic decline of about 50 percent since 1999.' Consequently, many departments of African languages had to close down or were restructured. It is therefore not surprising that during the past two decades there has been a change in the way African linguistics is taught – at most South African universities, at least, the 'undergraduate course material has been designed with the needs of contemporary African society in mind and in recognition of the development of knowledge that relates to the African continent' (Kosch & Bosch 2014).

The classical sub-fields of linguistics became taboo words. The insistence of doing away with this nomenclature was a demonstration of resistance to the imposed Western approach by teachers who were not the owners of the African languages as study objects. 'Indigenous knowledge' had been left out of the equation and now native speakers wanted to reclaim the study of African languages as their own in all aspects and to recast it in their own mould in pace with post-apartheid reconceptualizations. The 'camouflaging' of the content of modules was not effected in all Southern African teaching institutions. At the National University of Lesotho, the University of Swaziland as well as the University of Namibia, the traditional terms for the linguistic disciplines continue to be used unapologetically.

It is interesting to note that the number of contributions dealing with the five core areas of linguistic investigation (phonetics, phonology, morphology, syntax, and semantics) submitted to the *South African Journal of African Languages* (*SAJAL*) for publication is constantly surpassed by contributions in other fields such as literature, language planning, language in education, translation studies, terminology development, and sociolinguistics (see Figure 6.1 below). The journal was first published in 1981 and has since attracted national and international contributions by scholars from all parts of Africa and abroad.

The same tendency is observed among master's and doctoral students in the Department of African Languages at the University of South Africa, who are less likely to choose topics within the field of linguistics for their research. Interestingly enough, most of those who have explored linguistic topics have

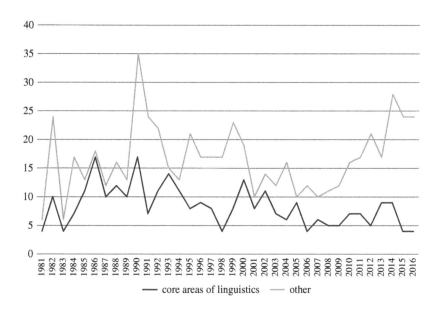

Figure 6.1 *SAJAL* statistics 1981–2016

hailed from countries outside of South Africa. It would appear that such students are more exposed to and comfortable with linguistics than students at South African institutions in their education leading up to postgraduate level.

The South African Constitution provides for equal status of the eleven official languages and the principle of multilingualism – therefore a new trend has emerged, namely linguistics offered through the medium of the language being taught (up to now, this was mainly the case of literature studies). This provides the opportunity for more focused development of linguistics terminology, as stated in Phillipson (1996:162): 'The challenge is to promote the development and elaboration of the indigenous languages and harness them to the nation-building process in ways that are democratic and not ethnically divisive.'

Interdisciplinary applied linguistics studies such as computational linguistics and corpus linguistics have increasingly come to the fore in African linguistics since about 2000 but will not be dealt with in this chapter. See Chapter 22 in *The Cambridge Handbook of African Linguistics* for more details.

6.5   Conclusion

We presented three main phases in the development of the linguistic descriptions of African languages in Southern Africa. Academically based research output emerged during the missionary or pre-scientific period from about the middle of the 1800s. Doke's contribution in 1927 can be taken as a transition to the so-called postcolonial period when the dominance of the Western framework was challenged with new insights regarding the unique structure of the African languages. As the previous phase, this phase was also marked by seminal publications of prominent figures who had a long-term influence on succeeding research. The advent of the modern period from *c.* 1975 saw a deviation from the mainly structural investigation to more diversified approaches such as TGG and several related and other theories. This led to pockets of specialization within selected theories at different tertiary institutions.

Whereas during the initial period of linguistic investigation, missionaries had a free hand in the study and teaching of the languages, in later periods the approach was shaped by changes in social and political conditions, as summarized by Clements (1989:8): 'New fields of study do not emerge out of a vacuum, but respond to specific research needs and social conditions.' Over time African linguistics in Southern Africa has become a field of specialization in its own right.

Acknowledgements

The authors gratefully acknowledge Professor Wilfred Haacke for valuable information on non-Bantu click languages research provided by personal communication.

7   African Linguistics in Eastern Africa

Amani Lusekelo

7.1   Introduction

In this chapter, I explore the history of African linguistics in the Eastern African region. The twelve East African countries dealt with in this chapter include Kenya (plus Mombasa Islands) and Tanzania (including the Zanzibar Islands), the native home of Swahili. Other countries, with dominant indigenous languages in brackets, involve Burundi (Rundi), Comoro (Ngazidja), Madagascar (Malagasy), Malawi (Chewa or Nyanja), Mauritius (Morisyen), Rwanda (Nyarwanda), Seychelles (Seselwa), Uganda (Ganda), Zambia (Bemba), and Zimbabwe (Shona) (Batibo 2005:23). Much attention is paid to the dominant (national) languages such as Bemba, Chewa (Nyanja), Ganda, Nyarwanda, Shona, and Swahili, which have remained at the centre of research for the past 176 years.[1] Their history begins with earlier recorders (missionaries, explorers, and colonial administrators) and native linguists, who concentrated their research on these major African languages. Minority languages are mentioned but are not focused on in this chapter.

This chapter is organized into four convenient epochs. Section 7.2 provides background information on the rise of linguistics in Eastern Africa on the basis of groundwork, mainly dictionaries and grammar books compiled by missionaries for the period of 100 years between 1840 and 1940. Section 7.3 offers a detailed description of the contributions of institutions on the research and documentation of East African languages, as well as the mentorship of local linguists for the period of 30 years between 1940 and 1970. During this period, colonial language centres were transformed into university institutions. Section 7.4 constitutes the third phase (from 1970s to date). It comprises the emergence of the indigene academics, with some theoretically inclined research agendas, mainly on their mother tongues.

---

[1] Many other languages of the four language phyla exist in Eastern Africa: the Niger-Congo (Bantu family), such as Yao in Malawi, Nkore-Kiga in Uganda, and Karanga in Zimbabwe; Nilo-Saharan languages such as Acholi in Uganda, Datooga in Tanzania, and Luo of Kenya and Tanzania; Afroasiatic languages such as Iraqw and Burunge in Tanzania; and the Khoisan phylum, e.g. Hadzabe and Sandawe of Tanzania.

7.2   A Hundred Years of Pre-Scientific Studies (1840–1940)

7.2.1   *Literacy in Arabic and Swahili*

According to Nurse and Spear (1985) and Massamba (2002), different peoples settled along the East African coast in the course of history. Persians from the Gulf Coast and Arabs from Oman had migrated to Zanzibar and Mombasa by the eleventh century. By 1500 CE, Bantu speakers had settled along the coast. The Portuguese from Europe travelled to the Indian Ocean coast in Eastern Africa by 1650. Therefore, prior to pre-scientific studies of the Swahili coast, the spread of Swahili literacy emerged.

An outstanding contribution involves literacy studies provided in Arabic and Swahili by Moslems. Mukuthuria (2009a:40) highlights Sultan Seyyid Said and Arab slave trader Hemed Mohammed El Murjebi (better known as 'Tippu Tip') as prominent figures in that execution. The setback for the emergence of linguistics during this period lies in the negligence of such contributors to the documentation of East African languages. It is a pity that, in consequence, our knowledge of the contribution of Arabic and Islam to the development of literacy, particularly in Swahili and, of course, in African languages (e.g. Chewa, Ganda, Ngazidja, Rundi), is not known today (Knappert 1996; Mukuthuria 2009a).

During the Portuguese invasion between 1650 and 1730, there were documents generated within the realm of Swahili culture. However, most of the old Swahili texts in Arabic had been destroyed during the invasion (Zhukov 2004). The existing documents are presumably stored at the University of Dar es Salaam (Pawlikova-Vilkanova 2006a). The oldest Swahili texts in Arabic are letters stored at Goa (dated 1711–1728) and *tendi* 'poems' from Mombasa and Zanzibar (dated 1652–1728) (Zhukov 2004). After the 1750s, many famous poets emerged in Lamu, Mombasa, and Zanzibar, but Mohammed Kijumwa from Lamu, Muyaka Haji al-Ghassaniy from Mombasa, and Fumo Liyongo from Zanzibar deserve particular mention (O'Fahey 2008:340).

Despite the destruction caused by the Portuguese invasion of the East African coast, some language-oriented issues emerged. First, the poetic works in Swahili impacted on the grammar of the language. Zhukov (2004:6) opines that 'the enrichment of the poetic vocabulary with Arabic words affected the phonological structure of the language and contributed to the appearance of new rhythms and consonances'. Second, it marked the rise and recognition of the Swahili dialects. Zhukov (2004) comments that Swahili developed on its own dialect base, which included three groups of dialects: the northern (Kiamu), the central (Kimvita), and the southern (Kiunguja). Lastly, Swahili literacy was obtained in the hinterlands such as western Kenya and eastern Uganda (Were 1967).

7.2.2   Documentation and Promotion of Local Languages for Purposes of Christianity

7.2.2.1   Early Dictionaries and Grammar Books in German and British East Africa

British East Africa primarily comprised present-day Kenya, though Uganda became a British protectorate. German East Africa consisted of three states, namely Tanganyika (now Tanzania), Rwanda, and Burundi. Along the coast of Kenya and Tanzania, the Swahili language became the well-known lingua franca (Ashton 1944; Polomé 1967; Whiteley 1969), which was adopted as a national language at independence (Batibo 2005).

Burundi and Rwanda have a similar linguistic background. The history of languages there emerged after independence on 25 September 1961. Siboma (1997:xv) comments that since the penetration of Europeans was not felt in the whole of German East Africa, the formation of both Burundi and Rwanda began with the German explorers, who identified Rwanda in 1894. In fact, the White Fathers of the Roman Catholic Church created the first mission in 1900.

In German and British East Africa, the history of linguistics emerged with the devotion of two missionary societies, which participated in the writing of grammars, the compilation of dictionaries, and the translation of Christian texts (Frankl 1992; Griefenow-Mewis 1996; Pawlikova-Vilkanova 2006b; Mangwa 2008; Togarasei 2009). First, the Church Missionary Society, under the auspices of the University's Mission to Central Africa, had earlier influence on the emergence of Eastern African linguistics through the Anglican and Lutheran churches of Mombasa and Zanzibar. Second, the Society of Missionaries of Africa (White Fathers) of the Catholic Church engaged later in the development of local languages in Eastern Africa.

The scholarly linguistic works in Swahili began in the 1840s with the publications by the German priest Ludwig Krapf (CMS), who compiled a dictionary between 1844 and 1848 in Mombasa, Kenya, and a Swahili grammar book, published in 1882 and 1850 respectively. From Zanzibar in Tanzania, the major contributions by the missionaries to the emergence of Eastern African linguistics were vested in grammar books by the priest Edward Steere (CMS) (Steere 1894, 1918), and dictionaries and a grammar book by the priest Charles Sacleux of the White Fathers (Sacleux 1891, 1909a, 1909b, 1939). The usefulness of these earlier publications is recognized by many scholars (e.g. Ashton 1944; Polomé 1967; Mtavangu 2013). The production in written form of oral works produced by Africans began with missionaries such as the priest William Ernest Taylor, who collected Swahili poetry such as *Utenzi wa Fumo Liyongo* (Frankl 1999) and published groundwork for Swahili (Taylor 1891, 1897).

For Uganda, the history begins with the Ganda language, which had been the centre of attention for missionaries and explorers. Porter (1997:379) comments that 'after 1885, British alliances in East Africa meant that Luganda was adopted as the chief language of church and state'. However, the presence of Swahili in Uganda preceded the dominance of Ganda. In fact, during the reign of kabaka Mutasa (1856–1884), the kingdom of Buganda entertained trade with merchants from the Swahili coast, mainly from the Sultanate of Zanzibar (Pawlikova-Vilkanova 2006b; Mukuthuria 2009a). Swahili became the main vehicle of communication in trade and Islamic activities in the kingdom.

Since Swahili was equated to Islam, later on Christian priests started teaching literacy in both Swahili and Ganda to members of the kingdom of Buganda under kabaka Mutesa (Pawlikova-Vilkanova 2006b:200). Then the documentation of Ganda became necessary. Numerous efforts were put in place in order to write the grammar and dictionary of the language. In addition, Baganda customs were studied and documented under the auspices of the CMS.

The pioneer missionary to Uganda was the Scot Alexander Murdock Mackay (CMS) in the years 1878 to 1892. In teaching Christianity and establishing the church within the kingdom of Buganda, he translated religious texts into Ganda (Mullins 1904). Another priest, George Lawrence Pilkington (CMS), translated biblical stories and religious hymns and wrote a draft of Luganda grammar. Joseph Dennis Mullins was another CMS missionary; in his 1904 book (re-published in 1908), he provides reference to the publications *Handbook of Luganda* (Pilkington 1891) and *Luganda–English and English–Luganda Vocabulary* (Pilkington 1892).

7.2.2.2   Church Clergymen: Emergence of Indigene Scholars in German and British East Africa (1890s–1930s)

The famous author in Uganda is Apollo Kaggwa (1864–1927). As a servant of the Mutasa's palace, he was converted to Christianity by the CMS in 1886 and obtained literacy classes in Arabic, Ganda, and Swahili. Later, he devoted himself to the production of Christian materials in the Ganda language for the kingdom of Buganda. With regard to the emergence of East African linguistics, Apollo Kaggwa is well known for his publications written in the Ganda language, which include these important historical volumes: *Ekitabo kye Basekabaka be Buganda* (The Kings of Buganda) (Kaggwa 1900), *Ekitabo kya basekabaka beBuganda, nabeBunyoro nabeKoki, nabeToro, nabeNkole* (The Kings of Buganda, Bunyoro, Koji, and Toro) (Kaggwa 1901), *Ekitabo kye mpisa za Baganda* (The Customs of the Baganda) (Kaggwa 1907), and *Ebika bye Buganda* (Clans of Buganda) (Kaggwa 1912). *The Customs of the Baganda* (Kaggwa 1934) and *The Kings of Buganda* (Kaggwa 1971) have been translated into English.

Another important person in the development of Ugandan languages is the Anglican clergyman Reverend Henry Wright Kitakule Duta (CMS). He translated Christian texts, including sections of the old and new testaments into Ganda (Duta et al. 1899a, 1899b, 1902). He also documented the customs of the Baganda as expressed in the Ganda language (Duta et al. 1902). In addition, Rev. Duta participated in the writing of a pedagogical grammar book for Ganda (Duta & Hattersley 1904).

The contribution of Father Alexis Kagame (1912–1981) of the Roman Catholic Church to the promotion of Nyarwanda cannot be overlooked. Father Alexis Kagame was a Rwandan poet, linguist, historian, and philosopher who wrote in French and his own language, Nyarwanda (Ukwamedua 2011:251). As a graduate of Georgian University in Rome (1951–1955), Father Alexis Kagame returned home in 1958 and became a teacher at a Catholic seminary and then a professor at the University of Rwanda in 1963 Father Kagame collected numerous cultural and linguistic materials for Nyarwanda and published important resources such as *La philosophie Bantu-Rwandaise de l'être* (Kagame 1956), *Introduction aux grands genres lyrics de l'ancien Rwanda* (Kagame 1969), and *La philosophie Bantu comparée* (Kagame 1976).

In Tanzania, the Anglican Church trained Mathias E. Mnyampala (1917–1969). He published important books about the Gogo, his ethnic group, including *Historia, mila na desturi za Wagogo wa Tanganyia* (Mnyampala 1954). For the history of Swahili, Mnyampala and Chiraghdin (1977) is essential.

7.2.2.3   Promotion of Vernaculars in Rhodesia and Nyasaland (1890s–1930s)

In Northern Rhodesia (now Zambia), between 1885 and 1945, many mission stations were established in order to teach the gospel (Posner 2003). To fulfil this mission, early missionaries devoted much energy to writing grammars, compiling dictionaries, and translating religious texts, which were used in teaching the gospel. However, since local languages were many in Zambia, early missionaries chose some languages and developed them as vehicles of communication across ethnic groups, whose local languages were not developed. Consequently, Zambia became linguistically divided into four zones based on the primary endoglossic lingua franca: Tonga in the southern parts, Bemba in the north, Nyanja (Chewa) in the eastern parts, and Lozi in the west.

During the colonial period, school materials were produced in these languages. Gordon (2014:50) reports that by 1924 the education system of Zambia was in three tiers, namely the first two years were taught in the local language, the next five years in a regional language (Bemba, Lozi, Nyanja, and Tonga), and any further education being offered in English. As a result, by 1937, 92 per cent of all study materials produced in Northern Rhodesia and Nyasaland were in Bemba, Lozi, Nyanja, Tonga, or English (Posner 2003:133). At independence in 1964, two more languages became prominent. Consequently, for the linguistic situation in Zambia today, 'emphasis has shifted towards the promotion of Zambia's seven national languages, Bemba, Nyanja, Tonga, Lozi, Lunda, Luvale, and Kaonde' (Marten & Kula 2008:292).

The pioneer of Bantu linguistics who studied the Lamba language of Zambia is the South African Professor Clement M. Doke (1893–1980) (Mangwa 2008; Togarasei 2009; Mufanechiya & Mufanechiya 2015). Doke got interested in Lamba because he lived in the area. He obtained a master's degree from Johannesburg University College, with a thesis titled 'The Grammar of the Lamba Language' (Doke 1917).

In Southern Rhodesia (now Zimbabwe), the picture obtained in Zambia appears to be similar to the missionary patterns in this territory. In fact, the main contributors to the early development of Zimbabwean linguistics are the church organizations, later supported by the colonial government. Serious evangelization in Southern Rhodesia tallied with the colonization of the country between the 1890s and 1940s. For example, in Mashonaland, Togarasei (2009) reports that the translations of the Bible and religious books into Shona were undertaken on the basis of the missionaries available in the Shona-speaking areas.

Across Mashonaland, the distribution of different mission societies was obvious. The Catholic Church occupied the north-east parts, the Methodist Church occupied the eastern parts, the Anglican Church concentrated in the eastern region, the Lutheran Church concentrated in the south-western side, the Dutch Reformed Church were in southern parts, and the Salvation Army went to the north. Consequently, each church translated the Bible and Christian texts into a different Shona dialect. For instance, in the southern areas, the Dutch Reformed Church and the Lutheran Church operated in the Karanga-speaking community, and hence Reverend Andrew A. Louw of the Dutch Reformed Church translated the Bible into Karanga. Again, by 1898 the Methodist Church published *Ivangeri ya Marako* (the Gospel of Mark) in the Zezuru dialect. Between 1905 and 1908, E. H. Etheridge translated the New Testament into the Manyika dialect of Shona (Togarasei 2009).

In Nyasaland (now Malawi), the Scottish Missionary Society dominated the development of Malawian vernaculars. The mission opened up a printing press called Hetherwick Press in Blantyre in 1884 for the publication of religious materials in the vernacular languages (Kamwendo 1998). Chewa/Nyanja received much attention, and publications in it outnumbered other vernaculars. In northern parts of Malawi, the Livingstone Mission of the Church of Scotland contributed significantly to the growth of secular literature in Tumbuka, mainly before independence (Kamwendo 1998:34).

The influence of missionaries in Zimbabwe, Zambia, and Malawi is primarily on the documentation of major languages such as Bemba, Chewa/Nyanja, and Shona. In addition, their impact is witnessed in areas related to the compilation of dictionaries and writing of grammar books.

7.3   Earlier Language Institutions in Eastern Africa (1940–1970)

7.3.1   Emergence of the Swahili Committee in East Africa

The Inter-Territorial Language (Swahili) Committee for East African Dependencies (later the Swahili Committee) existed between 1930 and 1970 with member territories being Kenya, Tanzania, Uganda, and Zanzibar. The Swahili Committee was held at intervals of ten years between Mombasa (Kenya), Kampala (Uganda), and Dar es Salaam (Tanzania) (Mulokozi 2005; Legère 2006; Mbaabu 2007). It was established in order to standardize the language and encourage research in Swahili. Operating from Dar es Salaam, the committee came under the supervision of Frederick Johnson between 1930 and 1937. During his time in office, the history of dictionaries of Standard Swahili began with the compilation of three volumes, namely *Kamusi ya Kiswahili* (Johnson 1935), *Standard Swahili–English Dictionary* (Johnson 1939a), and *Standard English–Swahili Dictionary* (Johnson 1939b). These volumes set the fundamental structure of the dictionaries produced for Standard Swahili by TUKI (2004, 2014).

Between 1930 and 1963, the Swahili Committee encouraged research on the grammar of the language. Mulokozi (2005:8) mentions many scholars who were supported by the committee. For Eastern Africa, I will mention a few important university affiliates in Kenya and Tanzania. First, the morphology of Swahili was examined by the German scholar Bernhard Krumm. In his research, much attention was paid to the influence of foreign words on the grammar of Swahili (Krumm 1940). From the School of Oriental and African Studies, London, the comprehensive pedagogical grammar book by Ethel O. Ashton was written in the late 1930s and early 1940s with the support of the Swahili Committee (Ashton 1944). This grammar book is still a useful tool today in learning the Swahili language. Another researcher was Wilfred H. Whiteley, the fifth secretary of the Swahili Committee (1953–1958), who conducted research on the syntax of the language and wrote a book (Whiteley 1968).

Apart from linguistics, the committee promoted research on Swahili literature. Jan Knappert (initially from the School of Oriental and African Studies), being the secretary of the Swahili Committee between 1961 and 1964 (Mulokozi 2005:26), examined the oral wealth of Swahili people. Knappert recorded and transformed oral verses into written forms for the many genres of Swahili literature (Zhukov 2004; Mukuthuria 2009a). His important books include *Traditional Swahili Poetry* (Knappert 1967), *Myths and Legends of Swahili* (Knappert 1970), *Four Centuries of Swahili Verses* (Knappert 1979), and *Epic Poetry in Swahili and Other African Languages* (Knappert 1983).

Under the auspices of the Swahili Committee, Shaaban Robert (1909–1962) is one of the Tanzanian scholars who was promoted by the committee (Mulokozi 2005). As a civil servant in the colonial government between 1926 and 1960, he became interested in Swahili poetry and novels. He composed a number of novels and poems which are used in the education system in Tanzania, e.g. *Kusadikika* (Robert 1951), *Kufikirika* (Robert 1967), and *Siku ya Watenzi Wote* (Robert 1968). In addition, his letters are contained in a useful collection called *Barua za Shaaban Robert* (Mulokozi 2002).

7.3.2   Standard Unified Shona Orthography in Southern Rhodesia

Togarasei (2009) reports that the need for a common Bible in Shona arose from the proliferation of the translations into different dialects of the Shona language. Thus, the Standard Unified Shona Orthography (SUSO) was conceived at the Southern African Missionary Conference for all church organizations working in Zimbabwe, which was held from 1903. The conference spearheaded the standardization and harmonization of the various Shona dialects (Fortune 1969; Mufanechiya & Mufanechiya 2015). Both the church organizations and colonial government needed a standard orthography for Shona language to be used in schools and church services across Mashonaland. Though the unified standard orthography does not cater for variation in spoken dialects such as Karanga, Korekore, Manyika, Ndau, Nambya, it is well suited for use in the conventional written form (Mangwa 2008).

The South African scholar Professor Clement M. Doke of the University of the Witwatersrand was commissioned to lead the committee to standardize the orthography of Shona. In the committee, Reverend Andrew A. Louw of the Dutch Reformed Church and Father Barnes of the Catholic Church contributed much in the writing of the orthography, which was not fully approved by the government in 1931 (Togarasei 2009). The orthography was accommodated in SUSO (Mufanechiya & Mufanechiya 2015). George Fortune of the University of Zimbabwe is another important scholar who contributed to the orthography of Shona (Togarasei 2009). While at the University Zimbabwe, he published several works on Shona, including *Elements of Shona* (Fortune 1967) and *A Guide to Shona Spelling* (Fortune 1972).

Since 1981, both Ndebele and Shona have become important languages, which were used in colonial schools particularly for the Zimbabwe Junior Certificate Examination Level (Mufanechiya & Mufanechiya 2015). In 1987, more minority languages were introduced on the lower level of education, and Shona remained an important subject up to tertiary level. Since it was successfully promoted, today Shona is a comparatively advanced language; it unites about 75 per cent of Zimbabweans (Mufanechiya & Mufanechiya 2015).

7.3.3   The Chichewa Board in Malawi

Three prominent African linguists published extensively on the Chichewa Board in their motherland Malawi, namely Kamwendo (1998, 2008, 2010), Kishindo (2000, 2001), and Mtenje (2002). This report is a summary of the many statements about the board.

The Chichewa Board was founded by the President Dr Hastings Kamuzu Banda (1898–1997). The passion for Chewa was conceived when Dr Banda was an informant for the Chewa language at the University of Chicago in the 1930s and at the University of London in the 1940s. From 1958, Dr Banda became interested in linguistics and the development of the dialect of Nyanja called Chewa into the national language. In 1968, Chewa was elevated to the status of national language.

The Chichewa Board was established in 1972 and it was declared a statutory board by 1977, with the three responsibilities: (i) to develop and approve the new Chewa orthography rules, (ii) to provide the national dictionary of the Chewa language, and (iii) to develop the Chewa language. One of the merits of the board was the establishment of the standard orthography of the language. Also, the Chichewa Board checked the use of the language in newspapers and magazines as well as on the radio across the country (Malawi Broadcasting Cooperation) and in translations.

During the formulation of the Chichewa Working Group of the board in 1975, there was no dictionary in Chewa; rather, the existing dictionary was in Nyanja. The working group failed to produce a good dictionary within 25 years of service. With regard to the writing of a standard Chichewa grammar, the board managed to release the instructions in 1991. Nonetheless, such instructions were never used in writing a grammar book. After Dr H. K. Banda lost the elections in 1994, the Chichewa Board was dissolved in 1995.

A new horizon for all languages of Malawi emerged. For instance, Kamwendo (2010:276) reports that 'the Chichewa Board was transformed into the Centre for Language Studies, a linguistically more inclusive academic and research institution'. Also, the new language policy allowed promotion of all Malawian languages. Consequently, the Malawi radio became a multilingual station in Chewa, English, Lomwe, Sena, Tonga, Tumbuka, and Yao.

7.4   Modern Linguistics as Generated by African Scholars (1970 to Date)

7.4.1   Conspicuous Research Themes

Within the period between 1970s to date, generally, research priorities in the region had been changing slightly. Six major themes have been apparently dominant: (i) sociolinguistics of language-in-education, (ii) lexicostatistics, (ii) Bantu tone and phonological theory, (iv) predicate structures of Bantu languages, (v) development and modernization of African languages, and (vi) endangerment and documentation of local languages. Each of these themes has been dominant at a given period in time.

Right at the dawn of African independence, native linguists engaged in research into the sociolinguistics of the language of education. In the late 1960s and early 1970s, scholars such as Abdulaziz (1972), Kashoki (1978), and Mbaabu (1973, 1978) highlighted the importance of mother tongue education. Later, this significant field of research dominated the period between 1980s and 1990s, mainly on the role of English in the East African education system, e.g. Banda (1996) for Zambia, Kamwendo (1998) for Malawi, Rubagumya (1990), and Batibo (1995) for Tanzania, among others.

The divide is obvious for the region. On the one hand, in Kenya, Tanzania, and Uganda, Swahili and Ganda were also examined. In Kenya, a country with over 40 indigenous languages, Abdulaziz (1982:95) highlights that 'there are two *lingua francas*, English and Swahili, that play an important functional roles at the national level'. In fact, the education system in Kenya allows both languages to be the MoI, though English dominates. In Tanzania, most scholars are in favour of Swahili over English as MoI. Rubagumya (2003:164) opines:

In any case, is English the best weapon for Tanzania to be competitive in the global market? Shouldn't we instead take advantage of what we can do better, like teaching Kiswahili here and abroad to people who need it?

Moreover, the research focused on the impact of Swahili and Ganda over smaller languages such as Luo, Gusii, and Gikuyu (Mbaabu 1973, 1978; Abdulaziz 1982; Batibo 1990, 1995).

On the other hand, the situation in Zambia, Zimbabwe, and Malawi warranted the research agenda to be on the contribution of mother tongue education to the prospering of pupils in schools. For instance, the Government of Zambia permitted a two-tier education system in that seven regional languages (Bemba, Lomwe, Lozi, Lunda, Luvale, Nyanja, and Tonga) are used as MoI in lower education levels and thereafter English is used as MoI (Kashoki 1978; Banda 1996, 2009; Marten & Kula 2008).

The next epoch began in 1970s through to the 1990s. Lexicostatistics formulated the main research agenda in Eastern Africa. In attempts to undertake a proper classification of African languages, broader surveys of the lexicon were conducted mainly using Swadesh's 200 word list. The motivation for the lexicostatistics surveys of East African languages emanated from not only the shortfalls of the previous publications but also the views of the community members. Massamba (1977:2-3) comments:

The most unfortunate thing about the different views held by these people, however, is that none of them has been substantiated by any linguistic evidence. These conclusions have been surely assumed through reasons which are outside the scope of linguistic proper. To the best of my knowledge there is no literature, within the realm of linguistics, which can be used as a basis of comparing these languages.

For this period, native and expatriate linguists conducted studies in individual countries across the region. For instance, Massamba (1977) conducted a comparative study of the Ruri, Jita, and Kwaya languages of Tanzania. Another case is by Mubanga Kashoki and Michael Mann, who conducted a study for the classification of Zambian Bantu languages (Kashoki & Mann 1978). Derek Nurse in collaboration with students and staff at the University of Dar es Salaam conducted comparative researches of Bantu languages in Tanzania, e.g. the Bantu languages of south-western Tanzania (Nurse 1988). These lexicostatistical studies deciphered the cognates at the level of vocabulary and similarities and differences in sound patterns at the level of morphophonology.

During this period, non-Bantu languages in Eastern Africa were also studied. However, most of the scholars were of foreign origin, e.g. Christopher Ehret and Bonny Sands (Maho & Sands 2002; Ehret 2011). The exception is Lucia N. Omondi and Duncan O. Okombo, who studied Nilotic languages, mainly Luo (Omondi 1975; Okombo 1982). Ehret is the champion of research on comparative linguistics for the Nilotic family (1971) and Afroasiatic (Cushitic) languages (1974, 1980). Sands examined the sound patterns in Hadza and compared the language with members of the Khoisan family in Southern Africa (Sands 1998a, 1998b). Her main contribution to Khoisan linguistics is to say that unlike Sandawe, Hadza is not related to Khoisan languages and hence needs to be treated as an isolate language.

The connection between linguistic facts and the history of the African past had been the subject of research in Eastern Africa (Nurse 1997). Comparative research had been conducted in Eastern Africa to decipher the nexus of the African communities. Both local and foreign researchers made contributions to this research theme (Ehret 2011). For instance, open cases for Bantu include language contact in north-eastern Tanzania (Nurse 2000), Chasu and Gweno contact in Tanzania (Mreta 2000), and lexicostatistical and historical survey of Bantu F languages (Masele 2001), to mention but a few.

The third epoch, which splits three ways, emerged in the 1980s and 1990s. It begins with the studies of tone in Bantu languages mainly after the formulation of Autosegmental Theory by John Goldsmith. They focused on the contribution of Bantu tone to phonological theories. Bantu tone was at the heart of this research agenda; for example, while the tone system in Chewa was examined by Mtenje (1986), mainly with the prosodic morphology, Batibo (1985) examined tone shift in Sukuma nouns. The contribution of the Nilotic language Luo was examined by Okombo (1986).

It was followed by studies on the status of the object NPs in Bantu clauses. Sam Mchombo from Malawi and Lioba Moshi from Tanzania are pioneers in this topic. They argue that Bantu languages behave differently with regard to the status of the object marker(s), word order, and co-occurrence of lexical NPs within a clause. The dichotomy is between symmetrical and asymmetrical Bantu (Bresnan & Mchombo 1987, 1995; Bresnan & Moshi 1990; Alsina & Mchombo 1993; Bukuru 1998; Moshi 1998, among others). The dichotomy is confirmed in numerous Bantu languages (Marten et al. 2007). However, Rugemalira (1993) rejects some of the suggestions, particularly when verbal extensions are involved.

The application of the theory of predicate structure is examined further in relation to the functions of verb extensions and the resulting thematic roles. The productive verbal extensions tend to increase and/or decrease the number of NPs within a clause, hence distorting the word order in Bantu (Alsina & Mchombo 1993; Rugemalira 1995). A formal pattern is attested (Ngunga 2000) which encompasses the CARP pattern (Hyman 2003).

Studies of the argument structure involved examination of word order patterns in clauses. Africanists examined word order patterns in numerous Bantu languages, e.g. Swahili (Vitale 1981), Chewa (Corbett & Mtenje 1987; Mchombo 2004), Gikuyu (Mugane 1998), Nyakyusa (Lusekelo 2009), to mention but a few. With regard to the status of word order, a few comparative works exist for noun phrases of Bantu languages (Rugemalira 2007; Lusekelo 2013). The main thesis defended is that canonical word order for Eastern Bantu is N > DEM/POSS > A/NUM, with exceptions that yield semantic changes.

The next epoch re-emerged in the 1990s, focusing on the theme of the development and modernization of the major African languages, namely Bemba, Chewa, Swahili, and Shona. It will be recalled that in the 1970s standard orthographies had been established for these languages. However, incorporation of new terms turned out to be necessary. Therefore, scholars recorded the standardized vocabularies for the languages, e.g. term development in Swahili (Massamba 1997), development of terminologies in Chewa (Kishindo 2000, 2001), development of the Shona language (Mangwa 2008; Madzimbamuto 2012). In Kenya and Tanzania, TUKI and BAKITA created and disseminated the terminologies (King'ei 2002; Legère 2006; Mbaabu 2007; Mukutharia 2009b). Perhaps I should reiterate here that the Institute of Kiswahili Studies, which is an amalgamation of the Institute of Kiswahili Research and the Department of the Kiswahili at the University of Dar es Salaam, has taken over the role of TUKI and it plays a central role in both terminology development and terminology dissemination in the country and outside. It facilitates teaching, funding research, and publishing research findings from fieldworks (Mulokozi 2009). It also promotes using Standard Swahili by publication of grammar books (e.g. Massamba et al. 2003, 2004) and Swahili–English and English–Swahili dictionaries (e.g. TUKI 2014) and specialized dictionaries (e.g. TUKI 1995, 2004).

Legère (2006:179) highlights that,

In the late eighties and nineties the terminology development in Tanzania shifted to TUKI. This institute had a long tradition of coining terms for a number of subjects. Its predecessor, the Interterritorial Language (subsequently Swahili) Committee, since its formation in 1930, had disseminated in the *Bulletin* (and later in the *Swahili* journal) a number of terms that reflected the rich potential of Kiswahili to cope with modern concepts. In recent years TUKI discussed and subsequently published terminology lists for e.g. literature, biology (approx. 1175 entries), chemistry (approx. 1450 entries), physics (approx. 1220 entries), etc.

The last epoch began in the 1990s and crystallized in the 2000s. The research theme emanated from UNESCO's call for linguistic rights (Brenzinger 1992, 2007). In Africa, national languages such as Bemba, Chewa, Swahili, and Shona, and ex-colonial languages such as English exerted detrimental pressure on minority languages. Hence there emerged the need to promote minority languages.

As a result, some research output focused on the documentation of minority languages. In Malawi, after the fall of Dr Kamuzu Banda, many minority languages were promoted (Kamwendo 2010). Other publications focused on language revival. For instance, Rottland and Okombo (1992) discuss the situation of Suba society in relation to the influence of neighbouring Bantu and lexification by Luo in Kenya. In the Suba area, four language layers exist in this order: Suba, Swahili, Luo, and English, a situation which permits changing language attitudes in favour of major languages such as Luo and Swahili (Okombo 1999). In Tanzania, scholars are engaged in language documentation through the writing of grammar books and dictionaries (e.g. Rugemalira 2005, 2009) under the auspices of the Languages of Tanzania Project.

These epochs are apparent in the many publications by indigene linguists. Perhaps the *Kiswahili* journal, which commenced in 1930 as *Bulletin*, should be used to demonstrate the research agendas published and the dispersal of contributors across the globe between 1976 and 2016. Of the more than 400 publications in the *Kiswahili* journal, articles for linguistics outnumber the rest, as captured in Figure 7.1.

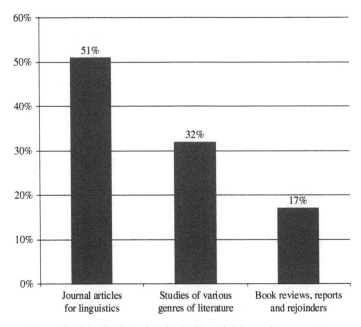

Figure 7.1 Distribution of topics in *Kiswahili* journal

The themes of research published by the *Kiswahili* journal differ in value, as summarized in Figure 7.2.

The authorship is another fascinating issue. More than half of the authors (65%) come from Tanzania. Another major contribution (17%) comes from Europe (e.g. Germany, Russia, and Austria). Kenyans constitute 13%, and the remaining 4% comes from various nations, namely Canada, Japan, Libya, Nigeria, and the USA (Figure 7.3).

7.4.2   Prominent Figures and their Research Outputs

A few African linguists, who trained in the 1960s, emerged in the 1970s.[2] These academics were recruited by and co-worked with European scholars in university colleges in Eastern Africa. Three prominent linguists emerged in the 1960s.

First, Mubanga E. Kashoki, the Zambian professor of African languages of the Institute of Economic and Social Research (University of Zambia), is

---

[2] Many indigene experts conduct research on African languages, but I purposefully present a few pioneers who impacted on the main themes herein. Where available, I provide a footnote giving young linguists mentored by these pioneer scholars.

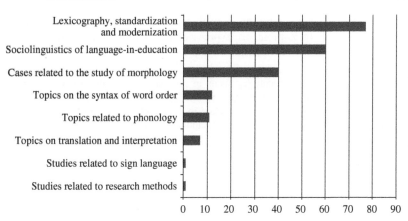

Figure 7.2 Contents of articles in *Kiswahili* journal

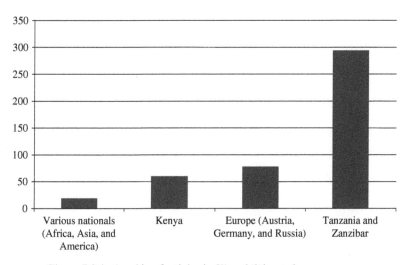

Figure 7.3 Authorship of articles in *Kiswahili* journal

the pioneer of Eastern Africa linguistics. Professor Kashoki graduated from Michigan State University in 1967; he engaged in research on Bemba and generated influential publications on MoI (e.g. Kashoki 1968, 1978, 1990).[3] His involvement with the politics of language planning in Zambia cannot be

---

[3] Mubanga E. Kashoki worked with young linguists such as Felix Banda on the development of orthographies of Zambian languages.

underestimated here, including contributions to sociolinguistic and demographic research in Zambia, as expressed in the following quote (Kashoki 1978:33):

Invariably, the highest percentages occur in provinces where the official languages besides being linguae francae are also spoken as mother tongues, or where several other languages related to them are spoken in the area by the majority of the people, e.g. Bemba (98.3% and 88.2%) in the Luapula and Northern Province respectively; Nyanja (84.3%) in the Eastern Province; Tonga (98.0%) in the Southern Province; Lozi (93.0%) in the Western Province; and Lunda, Luvale and Kaonde (46.2%, 46.9% and 41.5% respectively) in the Northwestern Province.

On the study of Bantu languages, Kashoki has published influential works which deal with the impact of loanwords on Bantu morphology (Kashoki 1995, 2012).

Second, Mohamed H. M. Abdulaziz (graduate of University College, London, 1967) emerged as the earliest indigenous scholar to examine and offer a detailed description of multilingualism in the region, mainly in the 1960s and 1970s (Abdulaziz 1971, 1972, 1982). For instance, he stipulates that Tanzania is diglossic in that Kiswahili and English are the official languages in the country. However, the large populations of rural Tanzanians used vernaculars (recently called ethnic community languages) by then, and thus the working cadre maintained a third language, the mother tongue (Abdulaziz 1972). Even now, however, English remains in so-called higher domains such as education, the high court, and international commerce (Campbell & Qorro 1997; Rubagumya 2003). In addition, Abdulaziz made tremendous contributions to the language planning policy in Kenya and Tanzania (e.g. Abdulaziz 1981, 1982). His publications advocate the use of local languages such as Swahili and Sheng, together with English. He also had influence on the standardization of African languages such as Swahili (Abdulaziz 1982) and other African languages (Abdulaziz 1988, 2000).

Apart from sociolinguistics and language-in-education, Abdulaziz carried out research on general linguistics. For instance, he examined the syntax of Swahili (Abdulaziz 1996) and the standardization of Kenyan languages (Abdulaziz 1991).[4]

The third scholar who trained at Makerere University and made outstanding contributions on East African linguistics in the 1970s and 1980s is the Ugandan Francis X. Katamba (Emeritus Professor at Lancaster University). He is the champion of Bantu morphology who uses Ganda and Swahili data in

---

[4] Abdulaziz's influence on the linguists of Eastern African is apparent for his students, who examined Swahili dialects (Bakari 1982), word order patterns and syntax (Okombo 1982; Mberia 1993; Sikuku 2001), and discourse analysis (Habwe 1999), to mention but a few. These doctoral students of Mohamed H. M. Abdulaziz are lecturers and professors of linguistics at the University of Nairobi. Therefore, his impact is still felt today.

a seminal volume (Katamba 1993) and in a book chapter (Katamba 2003). His main contribution is on the status of the augment in Bantu languages. Hyman and Katamba (1993) claim that the augment marker, which is invariably a V, rather than a CV as previously claimed by De Blois (1970), functions as a definite marker. This claim is substantiated by the fact that it occurs in linguistic environments which provide the distinctions of (in)definiteness.

The second wave of indigenous linguists in Eastern Africa were recruited in the 1970s and 1980s by other African linguists. Lucia N. Omondi is a Kenyan linguist who trained at the University of London and wrote a thesis on the syntax of the Nilotic language Luo (Omondi 1975). Previously, Professor Omondi obtained a bachelor's degree in 1968 and postgraduate degrees in 1971, both from the University of Nairobi. Her contributions surround the Nilotic languages (e.g. Omondi 1981, 1993, 1995/2007, and Rottland & Omondi 1993).[5] Apart from syntax, which is her major area of research, Omondi does research on reduplication (1986) and language policy in Africa (e.g. Omondi 1999).

The Tanzanian Herman M. Batibo trained in general linguistics at Sorbonne University in Paris and wrote a thesis on Sukuma in 1976, published as Batibo (1985). He began a career in African linguistics by specializing in the study of phonology and morphology. Thus, at the University of Dar es Salaam, he conducted research on Bantu languages, with particular attention to tone in Sukuma (Batibo 1976, 1991), sound patterns in Swahili (Batibo 1990, 1996, 2002), and lexical borrowing and historical linguistics (Batibo & Rottland 2001). Therefore, some of his main contributions include the position of tone in Bantu languages and the adaptation of new syllable structures in Swahili, mainly at word-initial position in loanwords such as *stesheni* 'station'. Later on, he developed an interest in language-in-education (Batibo 1990), conducted research on language endangerment, and, since the 1990s, has published works on the fate of minority languages of Tanzania (Batibo 1992, 1995) and endangered languages and historical changes of languages in Africa (Batibo 2005).[6]

The pioneer of African linguistics in Malawi is Sam A. Mchombo, who mentored many Malawian linguists in the 1970s (Mtenje 2002). He received a doctoral degree from the University of London in 1978 and is now Professor of African Studies at the University of California. On the theory of lexical-functional grammar, this Malawian scholar contributed tremendously. I should also mention two theoretical matters that are frequently cited. First, syntactic issues on object marking in Bantu languages as emanating from Bresnan and Mchombo (1987, 1995) and Alsina and Mchombo (1993) have remained significant to date. The symmetrical–asymmetrical dichotomy is still debated today,

---

[5] Lucia N. Omondi's doctoral students at the University of Nairobi specialize in Nilotic languages, mainly Luo, e.g. Duncan O. Okombo, J. H. A. Uduol, and the syntax of Bantu, e.g. N. Mwaniki on Gikuyu.
[6] Currently, Herman Batibo works in the Department of African Languages and Literature (University of Botswana), where he conducts research on Khoisan languages and sociolinguistics.

mainly with regard to the status of the object marker, as an agreement marker or pronominal element (Marten & Kula 2012). Sam Mchombo maintains the (a)symmetricity in Bantu, as he highlights (2004:80–81):

Languages such as Kinyarwanda and Kichaga, for which the 'two object analysis' appears to hold, have been called 'symmetric languages', whereas languages such as Chichewa and Siswati in which the NPs behave differently are referred to as 'asymmetric languages'. Some languages (e.g. Sesotho) seem to be of mixed types in that they have both asymmetric and symmetric object marking, depending on semantic roles.

Second, using the lexical integrity principle, Bresnan & Mchombo (1995) analysed the role of nominal prefixes within Bantu NPs. They criticize ideas advanced previously that nominal classes designate number, case, and gender. Bresnan and Mchombo argue that the far-left element within the morphology of Bantu nouns has numerous functions. In addition, derived nouns, which bear a secondary nominal prefix, behave like other nouns with regard to number indication.

David P. B. Massamba began a career with comparative and historical linguistics (1977) and managed to document the history of Swahili (2002). This is one of the major areas of research in which he participated from 1972 to date. Massamba, who trained in autosegmental phonology under the influence of John Goldsmith at Indiana University, researched on tone in Bantu languages with particular attention to his mother tongue Ciruri. Most of his publications have been on tone and accent in this language (e.g. Massamba 1984, 1992). His influence on graduate students resulted in research output on tone in Bantu languages such as Makua (Ismail 2011) and Giha (Bichwa 2016). In addition, Massamba contributed to the history of phonology, particularly on phonological issues in Bantu languages (1996). Thus, his main areas of influence is seen in the application of autosegmetal phonological theory as well as in contributing to the theories on the origin of Swahili in Kilwa, Lamu, Mombasa, and Zanzibar.

The contribution of Nilotic languages to linguistic theory is made possible through the research output of Duncan Okoth Okombo. After graduating from Nairobi University, where he wrote a thesis on constituent order in Luo under the supervision of Mohamed H. M. Abdulaziz (Okombo 1986), Okombo researched and published on language vitality and general linguistics. Specifically, both generative grammar (Okombo 1982) and functional grammar (Okombo 1997) had been applied to the analysis of the Dholuo language.[7]

One of the students of Professor Mchombo is the Malawian Alfred J. D. Mtenje, a graduate of University College London with a thesis on Chichewa (Mtenje 1986). Since then, many of his contributions surround the tonology

---

[7] Duncan O. Okombo influenced students such as Jane A. N. Oduor to examine the phonology of Dholuo at the University of Nairobi (Oduor 2000).

of Malawian Bantu (Mtenje 1987, 1988). Specifically, he contributes to the theoretical analysis of Bantu tone with regard to the theory of linear order phonology (Mtenje 1988) and tone shift due to reduplication (e.g. Mathangwane & Mtenje 2010). In addition, his writings focus on prosodic morphology in relation to tone (e.g. Hyman & Mtenje 1999) and prosodic phrasing in relation to relativization (e.g. Downing & Mtenje 2010; Mtenje 2011). Many of his contributions can be read in a current publication on the phonology of Chichewa (Downing & Mtenje 2017). Apart from phonology, he has had an impact on language documentation (the compilation of dictionaries) and terminology development. In Malawi, Mtenje has had an influence on a number of subtopics related to Bantu phonology.[8]

One eminent scholar represents indigenous linguists who emerged in the 1990s. The Zambian scholar Felix Banda graduated from the Free University of Brussels with a thesis on the use of Zambian English in the education system (Banda 1995); he has had a great impact on Eastern African linguistics. His research interests surround multilingualism and MoI in Tanzania (Mohamed & Banda 2008), language use and identity in Africa (Banda 1996, 2009; Oketch & Banda 2008), language and culture in urban Africa (Banda & Kunkuyani 2015), and literacy in Africa (Banda & Kirunda 2005). He advocates for linguistic rights, as the comment below highlights:

Multilingualism is not just about the use of different languages but also the different varieties of the available languages. A monolingual approach is not only an unrealistic endeavour but also goes against the individual's linguistic rights to multilingualism – that is the right for multilinguals to use their repertoires functionally for different purposes and in communicative events. (Oketch & Banda 2008:10)

Felix Banda's impact on African linguistics is also evident in respect of issues related to multilingualism, mainly through his supervision of numerous doctoral candidates across sub-Saharan Africa.[9]

7.5   Conclusion

Historically, the Church Missionary Society and the White Fathers commenced documentation of Eastern African languages. Early grammar books and

---

[8] Mtenje's students include Winfred Mkochi (director of the Centre for Language Studies, University of Malawi), Pascal Kishindo (Professor of Linguistics, University of Malawi), Jean Chavula and Stella Kachiwanda (lecturers in Linguistics, University of Malawi), to mention but a few.

[9] Topics dealt with by his doctoral students surround multilingualism, e.g. Oketch Omondi (Technical University of Kenya): language use in multilingual settings in Kenya; Kelvin Mambwe (University of Zambia): language use and identity in Lusaka; Hashim I. Mohamed (Sokoine University of Agriculture in Tanzania): classroom discourse in higher education in Tanzania; Rebecca F. Kirunda (Kyambogo University in Uganda).

dictionaries compiled and published by missionaries between 1890 and 1930 remain important tools for understanding languages such as Bemba, Chewa (Nyanja), Ganda, Shona, Tonga, and Swahili. In the period following 1940, foreign language experts, mainly from Europe (Britain, France and Germany), wrote useful grammar books, which provided a foundation for the analysis of Bantu languages in Eastern Africa. Contemporary linguists of African descent took over from European academics, mainly in ex-British university colleges in the region. The benchmark began in the 1970s with such mother tongue speakers as Mubanga Kashoki (Bemba), Mohamed Abdulaziz (Swahili), Herman Batibo (Sukuma), Al Mtenje (Chewa), Sam Mchombo (Chewa) and David Massamba (Ruuri). These were trained in universities in Europe and North America. In the 1980s and 1990s, linguists trained in East African universities took over, e.g. Duncan Okombo (Luo), Josephat Rugemalira (Nyambo), Jane Oduor (Luo), Pascal Kishindo (Chewa), to mention but a few. Generally, the topics dealt with include sociolinguistics, the standardization and modernization of African languages, Bantu tone, argument structure, and language endangerment.

Acknowledgements

I am grateful to David Massamba (University of Dar es Salaam), Felix Banda (University of Western Cape), Jane A. N. Udour (University of Nairobi), Nancy C. Kula (University of Essex), and Al Mtenje (University of Malawi) for valuable information.

Abbreviations Used in This Chapter

BAKITA	Baraza la Kiswahili Tanzania (Swahili Council of Tanzania)
CARP	causative-applicative-reciprocal-passive order
CMS	Church Missionary Services
DEM	demonstrative
MoI	Medium of Instruction
N	(head-)noun
NP	noun phrase
NUM	numeral(s)
POSS	possessive
SUSO	Unified Orthography of a Unified Language called Shona
TUKI	Taasisi ya Uchunguzi wa Kiswahili (Institute of Swahili Research).

8   African Linguistics in Official English-Speaking West Africa

Bruce Connell and Akinbiyi Akinlabi

8.1   The Beginning of Linguistics in Africa

The development of linguistics in what are now the (officially) English-speaking parts of West Africa has followed a path similar to that for Central Africa and the Horn of Africa (see Chapter 5, this volume). It was typically missionaries or scholars with religious interests concerned with scripture translation who developed a more general interest in language study, the development of orthographies, grammars, and dictionaries. The earliest known records of a West African language, though, appear in the records of Portuguese explorers in 1523, in the form of vocabulary apparently from a precursor to present-day Akan (Kwa, Ghana). However, for almost two centuries little more was done outside the collection and publishing of brief word lists, mostly of coastal languages encountered by Europeans. The first major developments in West African language study came almost two centuries later.

Also, like the other regions referred to, little has been written on the history of linguistics in West Africa. D. T. Cole's 'The History of African Linguistics to 1945' (1971) is considered one of the main sources for the early history of linguistics in Africa, but his account is not particularly strong in its discussion of West Africa. Cole acknowledges this, saying that he 'professes Bantu linguistics, with no pretensions to knowledge of other areas, nor to being a historian' (1971:1); he also brings into play the apt metaphor of Africa being a 'bottom-heavy continent'. P. E. H. Hair's (1967) *The Early Study of Nigerian Languages* constitutes an excellent account, though it is restricted in both its temporal and its geographical scope: it covers only up until about 1890 and, as its title suggests, the focus is on Nigeria. Even this, however, must be qualified in that its true focus is more properly described as being the work of the Church Missionary Society (CMS) in Nigeria, and so other work, inspired or initiated by other people and organizations, is omitted from the discussion. It should also be remarked, though, that since much of the work carried out by the CMS at that time was based in Sierra Leone, in Freetown, considerable information is also made available in Hair's account about the early period of language studies in Sierra Leone. Other available sources include Bamgbose

(1994) and Emenanjo (2007); Bamgbose (2007, 2011) add to these, though they are from a somewhat different perspective, not primarily intended as historiography. They do, however, describe a view that determined the shape of a major strand of linguistic work at least in Nigeria during the author's time, if not also elsewhere in West Africa. Information about the more recent, modern, history of linguistics in (officially) English-speaking West Africa can be found in such sources as Yankah et al. (2014), the introduction to which discusses the growth of linguistics at the University of Ghana, or the brief histories of linguistics departments occasionally found at departmental websites for different universities in the region.

There are many gaps. In focusing on 'English-speaking' West Africa and the contributions of African scholars, this chapter is a first attempt at filling in some of the gaps that exist in the historical record of the region. Other contributors to the present volume focus on 'French-speaking' parts of West Africa (and elsewhere), and on the contributions of non-Africans to the development of linguistics in Africa. We recognize that the focus on 'English-speaking' West Africa may be artificial in some respects. On the one hand, languages do not respect political boundaries.[1] Often one finds not just related languages on either side of an 'Anglo-Franco' border (languages of the Sehwi-Ahanta cluster on both sides of the Ghana–Côte d'Ivoire border, for example), but indeed even the same language, e.g. Yoruba (West Benue-Congo) in Nigeria and Benin Republic, or Mambila (Bantoid) in Nigeria and Cameroon. Chumbow and Tamanji (cited in Bamgbose 2011) mention some 45 languages found on both sides of the Nigeria–Cameroon border. It must also be noted that some of the important structures and institutions that have served linguistics and language study in West Africa have explicitly and deliberately disregarded the Anglo-Franco divide. One thinks here especially of the West African Language Survey and the West African Linguistics Society – Société Linguistique d'Afrique Occidental (WALS/SLAO) which grew from the Survey. On the other hand, in defence of the approach adopted here, one might point out that the practices of the British and French as colonial masters differed, not least in their academic traditions, and within these in their approaches to language study. This has had no small influence on the development of linguistics in the different parts of West Africa.

As indicated, our focus is intended to be largely on the contributions African scholars have made to the development of linguistics in the region. This cannot be done without acknowledging and discussing to some extent the contributions of non-Africans to this development. Many of the most influential African linguists received their training abroad, while other 'non'-African linguists spent

[1] More accurately, political boundaries (i.e. their creators) did not respect language or linguistic regions.

sufficiently long periods of their careers in Africa as working linguists, training the early generation of African linguists that their contributions must be acknowledged. Other contributors to this volume address the contributions of Western scholars directly. Language study in West Africa by African scholars, however, pre-dates the colonial period that established the anglo-francophone divide, at least in the person of Samuel Ajayi Crowther (1809–1891), so it is with him and the CMS in Sierra Leone that our history begins. Following discussion of this work, we proceed to look briefly at other aspects of language study in Freetown, where he was situated, and then to look at the true beginnings of modern linguistics in West Africa, with the contribution of the West African Language Survey, the establishment of the WALS/SLAO and the growth of linguistics departments in, especially, Ghana and Nigeria.

8.2   The Church Missionary Society, Samuel Ajayi Crowther, and Yoruba

The Sierra Leone Company founded the British colony of Freetown in 1792, bringing over 1,100 freed slaves from Nova Scotia. Many of the key figures involved in the company were also involved in founding the Society for Missions to Africa and the East, which was later to become the Church Missionary Society.[2] Its West Africa mission was established in what is now Guinea (Conakry) in 1804 and in 1816 in Freetown. Its members came mostly from the Clapham Sect and included William Wilberforce, who was prominent as an abolitionist. Many of their missionaries to West Africa came from the Evangelical Lutheran Church in Württemberg, Germany, and had trained in seminaries in both Germany and Britain. These included James Schön, who was instrumental in establishing the mission in Freetown; Schön was also a linguist and later produced both a grammar and dictionary of Hausa (1862, 1876). As discussed below, he also worked closely with Samuel Ajayi Crowther, the first Yoruba linguist.

Today Yoruba is among the best described of African languages, and research on Yoruba has contributed considerably to linguistic theory generally. Discussion of Yoruba here is all the more pertinent because on the one hand, as Hair (1967) points out, unlike other widely spoken languages of the West African sub-region (e.g. Akan, Ewe, Duala, Fulfulde, Hausa, Igbo, Malinke, Wolof), Yoruba was 'not even known to language scholars of the world' (Hair 1967:4) at the beginning of the nineteenth century. The brief word lists and language fragments that had been published for these languages were invariably

---

[2] A brief history of the CMS can be found at the CMS website: http://churchmissionsociety.org/our-history with further information available at https://en.wikipedia.org/wiki/Church_Mission_Society; Murray (1985) provides a more detailed discussion.

collected by foreign travellers and traders in the region and, for reasons which cannot be explored here, the Yoruba region was not often visited by Europeans prior to the nineteenth century (Hair 1967:4–5). In the first decades of the nineteenth century, collected Yoruba word lists began to appear, typically under the name 'Aku' or 'Akoo'. Most notable of these is the collection of word lists from some 30 languages, including Yoruba, at the newly established colony for freed slaves at Freetown, in Sierra Leone, by the Quaker Hannah Kilham, in 1827–1828. Kilham worked with two other missionaries to gather the Yoruba material. One of the missionaries was John Raban; in his account, Hair speculates that the Yoruba speaker they worked with was likely Samuel Ajayi Crowther. Raban published three small pamphlets on Yoruba (1830, 1831a, 1831b), again as Hair suggests, perhaps with the encouragement of Kilham and the assistance of Crowther.

Samuel Ajayi Crowther was born in Osogun, in Ibarapa Local Government of what is now Oyo State in Nigeria.[3] He was taken as a slave at the age of 12, in 1821. The ship on which he had been enslaved was captured by the British, who by then opposed the slave trade. The liberated people were taken to Freetown, where Crowther met the above-mentioned missionaries, Kilham and Raban, as well as James Schön. In 1826 Crowther was sent to London for a year, where he studied at St Mary's Church School, studies which reportedly included Latin and Greek. It is also apparent from his work, as discussed later in this report, that he knew something of Chinese. Though we find no statement as to where he picked up this knowledge, it was quite likely to have been during his stay in London. It was on his return to Freetown that he began assisting Kilham and Raban. Hair reports that Crowther attempted to learn Temne and speculates that it was this experience, rather than helping Raban as his informant, that sparked his interest in studying his own language. This work began around 1838. Around this time a growing number of educated Yoruba speakers at Freetown were interested in their language, particularly in developing a written literature in Yoruba, but Crowther is clearly the most important of these. In 1841 he was sent, along with the linguist missionary Schön, on the Niger Expedition. Crowther's selection for the mission was based in part on his being a Yoruba speaker, though since most of the country covered was not Yoruba speaking, it also involved his learning Hausa (Chadic, Nigeria); it was assumed that Hausa would be used in the interior. This proved not to be the case, and on the expedition Crowther was exposed to both Nupe (West Benue-Congo, Nigeria) and Igbo (West Benue-Congo, Nigeria), among other languages. As for the broader goals of the Niger mission, it is fair to say that while not all of

---

[3] A lively account of Crowther's life, and especially his early years, is given in the Dictionary of African Christian Biography, https://dacb.org/stories/nigeria/legacy-crowther/ (accessed 14 February 2019).

these aims were realized,[4] it was successful in studying the distribution of languages along the Niger River, up to and around the confluence with the Benue. It is difficult to say to what extent Schön influenced or inspired Crowther, or vice versa, though Hair notes that they remained friends and collaborators well into old age; he further suggests that Schön may have assisted Crowther in a number of ways in his work, ranging from linguistic points to proof-reading. In 1843 Crowther's first major work on Yoruba appeared, *A Vocabulary of the Yoruba Language: Part I English and Yoruba; Part II Yoruba and English; to Which Are Prefixed Grammatical Elements of the Yoruba Language.* A revised edition of the vocabulary appeared in 1852, with an expanded Grammar published separately in the same year. In 1864 he published *A Grammar and Vocabulary of the Nupe Language,* and in 1882 *A Vocabulary of the Ibo Language.* Crowther's work also included many primers and numerous translations of parts of the Bible into these three languages.

It may be noted that Crowther was not the only indigenous linguist or language scholar in Freetown at the time. Others, such as John Christopher Taylor, were engaged in writing primers and translating portions of the Bible. Taylor himself was Igbo, though born in Sierra Leone, and collaborated with Crowther on several occasions, including joining him on the Niger Expedition of 1857. For the most part, these others, such as Taylor, were concerned not so much with the linguistic study of African languages but with developing a literature for their language. Crowther too was involved in these efforts, and he is frequently referred to as the 'father of Yoruba literature'. He can also fairly be honoured as the first indigenous West African linguist. Crowther died in 1891 in Lagos.

As for Schön, beyond collaborating with Crowther, he is also known for his work on Hausa; he produced both a grammar (1862) and a dictionary (1876); an earlier version, a 'Vocabulary', appeared in 1843) as well as other materials. Schön's was not the only work carried out on languages situated to the north of the Niger and Benue rivers; work was carried out on Kanuri, especially by Sigismund Koelle (see Chapter 2, this volume). Other work in Freetown in the nineteenth century includes Koelle's monumental opus *Polyglotta Africana* (1854). We leave further discussion of this to Chapter 2 (this volume).

However, the work carried out by the CMS, including that of Crowther, while the focus of Hair's (1967) history was not the only linguistic work done during the nineteenth century in this part of West Africa. East of the Niger River, in the Cross River region, similar work was carried out by missionaries of the United Presbyterian Church of Scotland. While there is no record of indigenous scholars contributing to the description and development of the languages of this

---

[4] The expedition stalled at the confluence of the Niger and Benue Rivers, as discussed in Hair (1967).

region comparable to the work of Crowther, the contributions of native-speaker authorities are often acknowledged in works that were published.

The language that benefited most from these efforts was Efik (Cross River, Benue-Congo; Nigeria), which for a time rivalled, if not outshone, other West African languages with regard to development and description. Early important work on Efik includes, by Hope M. Waddell, *A Vocabulary of the Efik or Old Calabar Language, with prayers and lessons* (1852, revised in 1859), and, by Reverend Hugh Goldie, *Principles of Efik Grammar* (1857) and a *Dictionary of the Efik Language (in Two Parts)* (1862). Waddell acknowledges King Eyo Honesty, Mr Egbo Young, and Young Eyo Honesty as 'the best native authorities'.

It is interesting to note that neither Goldie nor Waddell seemed aware of tone, which carries a high functional load lexically and especially grammatically in Efik; stress, or what was apparently perceived as stress is indicated, often, though not regularly or consistently, corresponding to High tone. Yet despite this failing they clearly managed to communicate in the language, and their work is both creditable and useful.

At the same time, and in a similar vein, Johann Gottlieb Christaller[5] of the Basel Evangelical Missionary Society was working in Ghana, with mission-educated David Asante and Theophilus Opoku, among other African scholars. Christaller published, in 1875, his *A Grammar of the Asante and Fante Language Called Tshi (Chwee, Twi)* and followed this, in 1881, with his *Dictionary of the Asante and Fante Language Called Twi*. An earlier, *English–Tshi–Akra Dictionary* (1874), and *A Collection of 3,600 Tshi Proverbs* (1879) were also published. Both the grammar and the dictionary remain useful to this day. One of the most notable and striking aspects of his work from the perspective of linguistic scholarship was the implicit recognition of the tonal phenomenon downstep, though it was not until much later, with the work of Dennis Winston (1960) on Efik, in particular, that the downstep 'nut was cracked'.

8.3   The Colonial Period

From the late nineteenth century until the early 1960s, when the British colonies in West Africa gained their independence, linguistic research and the study of the languages of the region continued, though there is little evidence to suggest much in the way of contribution from local scholars. To be sure, there were efforts directed at orthography design, though these, often for quasi-political reasons and also because their developers were untrained in the task, were almost completely destined to not gain acceptance. Work of a linguistic

---

[5] Details of Christaller's life and work can be found at https://dacb.org/stories/ghana/christaller-j/ (accessed 14 February 2019).

academic nature carried out by Western or other foreign scholars is treated elsewhere in this volume (see Chapter 2), so here we mention just briefly one or two notable scholars and their works. The first of these is Ida C. Ward, whose *The Phonetic and Tonal Structure of Efik* (1933) rectified the weakness of the work of Goldie and Waddell, at least in beginning to come to grips with tone. Ward's analysis refers to a mid tone in Efik, along with high and low tones, though she recognized a relationship between high and mid tone (perhaps influenced by Christaller's work on Fante; see above).

Ward followed this up some two decades later with an *Introduction to the Yoruba Language* (1952); the intervening period saw her contribute numerous publications to journals such as the *Bulletin of the School of Oriental and African Studies*, both as a solo author and in collaboration with others, on a number of languages including Igbo and Bamum. One of the scholars with whom she collaborated was a German linguist by the name of Diedrich Westermann; together they wrote *Practical Phonetics for Students of African Languages*, first published in 1930 and which has undergone several reprints. The importance of Westermann and his contributions to African linguistics cannot be overstated as they not only covered phonetics and descriptive grammar but also established the foundations of historical linguistics and the classification of African languages, and spanned several geographical and political regions of Africa (see Chapter 2, this volume).

8.4   The Expansion of Modern Linguistics in the Postcolonial Period

Independence for Britain's colonies in West Africa – Ghana in 1957, Nigeria in 1960, Sierra Leone in 1961, and The Gambia in 1965 – coincided with a substantial change in direction in linguistics as a discipline. This observation, obviously, is not intended to suggest a connection between the two, and it was well over a decade before the new views in linguistic theory began to show much influence on linguistics in West Africa generally (some notable exceptions are mentioned below). However, it does allow us to refer to independence as opening a period we can conveniently refer to as 'modern linguistics' in West Africa, even though there was little immediate change in interest or direction from the preceding few decades. There was, however, greatly increased incentive for linguistic research, partly due to the interests of new African governments and partly due to the contribution of the Ford Foundation, a private foundation based in the United States, which had the goal of advancing human welfare.

The West African Languages Survey was established in 1961 with a five-year grant of $176,000 from the Ford Foundation, under the direction of Professor Joseph H. Greenberg (see Chapter 11, this volume). The purpose of the grant was twofold: the endowment of fellowships and grants for research on West

African Languages, and English and French as second languages, and the organization of an annual West African Languages Congress. The dedicated fellowship programme sponsored research on specific languages, some of which was published in book form in the West African Language Monographs series. Many of these monographs took the form of descriptive grammars, based in some cases on modern linguistic theory. The five such grammars that were included in the series, in order of appearance, were as follows: *A Grammar of the Kolokuma dialect of Ijo* (Williamson 1965); *A Grammar of Diola-Fogny* (Sapir 1965); *A Grammar of Yoruba* (Bamgbose 1966); *Transformational Grammar of Igbo* (Carrell 1966); and *The Kanakuru Language* (Newman 1974). Other volumes included Ladefoged's (1964) *Phonetic Survey of West African Languages*, a survey of 61 languages which had a second edition published in 1966, Innes's (1967) *Grebo–English Dictionary*, Crabb's (1969) *Ekoid Bantu Languages of Ogoja*, and Hair's (1967) *The Early Study of Nigeria Languages*, referred to earlier.

The inaugural West African Languages Congress, initiated by the West African Languages Survey, was held at the University of Ghana, Legon, in 1961. The congresses have continued up until the time of writing, though since 1970 on a biennial basis, under the auspices of the WALS/SLAO, with host institutions alternating between anglophone and francophone locales. WALS/SLAO is itself by far the most important legacy of the West African Languages Survey. The Society was instituted at the end of the mandate of the Survey, at the Fifth West African Languages Congress, held at the University of Ghana, Legon, on 6–10 April 1965. Its main objectives were (and remain) to foster linguistic research in the region and to establish an ongoing forum for the exchange of ideas among African language scholars in both anglophone and francophone areas in West Africa. WALS/SLAO assumed the activities of the Survey and proceeded to set up working groups for areas of special interest, such as different language families of the region (e.g. Benue-Congo, Kwa, and Chadic), oral literature, and sociolinguistic problems, in particular the problems of language in relation to education. The impetus of the Society resulted in the accelerated development of linguistics and linguistic studies, cooperation across the francophone and anglophone divide, and the establishment and publication of the *Journal of West African Languages* (*JWAL*), which first appeared in 1964. The Monograph series mentioned above, as well as the *Benue-Congo Word List Vol. 1* (1968); *Vol. 2* (1973), and the *West African Language Data Sheets Vol. 1* (1976); *Vol. 2* (1980) were also important early initiatives of the Society.

The importance of the West African Languages Survey is seen not only in terms of the linguistic research it supported and carried out during the five years it was active, but in three other respects: its support for the training of African linguists, both as researchers and teachers; the emergence of departments of linguistics (discussed below), and the founding of the West African Linguistic Society, which, as mentioned, took over and expanded the activities previously carried out by the Survey. When the Survey was initiated, there was no West African linguist with a PhD in linguistics; by the end of its five-year term, there were at least eight linguists with PhD degrees. When the Survey was initiated there was no West African university with a linguistics department, but by the time it evolved into WALS/SLAO in 1965, departments had been established in Dakar (Senegal), Abidjan (Côte d'Ivoire), Accra (Ghana), Ibadan (Nigeria), and Yaoundé (Cameroon).

The mission of the *JWAL* was laid out in an editorial in its first issue, stating that 'material is becoming available on languages of which ... not even the existence was known. It seems appropriate that a journal devoted mainly to such material should be edited from West Africa itself' (*JWAL* 1, 1964:3). The journal was first published at the Institute of African Studies of the University of Ibadan under the editorship of L. Frank Brosnahan, Robert G. Armstrong, Carl Hoffman, and John Spencer, all but the last of whom were based at Ibadan. A letter from the editors which accompanied the first issue of *JWAL* amplified the sentiments of the editorial, stating, 'We are particularly interested in articles devoted to languages about which little is so far known, and we are therefore prepared to publish fragmentary material wherever this is presented methodically and with due scientific rigour.'[6]

Among the working groups set up within the Society was the Benue-Congo Working Group, whose output included two volumes of compiled comparative word lists of languages (Williamson 1968, 1973), many of which were previously unrecorded, and for which the only available data were the word lists included. The *West African Language Data Sheets*, a collection of basic word lists and sentences following a template established at the Fifth West African Languages Congress, took longer to reach publication (Vol. 1, 1976, Vol. 2 1980) but covered in total 83 West African languages; seven of the descriptions were authored or co-authored by West African scholars.

8.4.1   Linguistics as an Academic Discipline

8.4.1.1   Ghana
Modern linguistics in Ghana has its roots in the Phonetics Department of the University of the Gold Coast, later the University of Ghana (Yankah et al. 2014), not unlike the situation described below for the University of Ibadan. The Phonetics Department, however, was non-degree granting, its principal purpose being to assist students to achieve pronunciation of English at a level consistent with that found throughout educated communities elsewhere in the

---

[6] A copy of this letter is in the possession of one of the present authors.

British Commonwealth. This department became the Department of Linguistics and Ghanaian Languages in 1964. Yankah et al. (2014) list its founding members as Mrs McCallien, Lindsay Criper, Alan Duthie, and Lawrence Boadi; Florence Dolphyne and Helmut Truteneau joined later. Of the founders, Boadi and Dolphyne were Ghanaian; both completed their PhDs at the University of London. The department began offering courses in 1965, including courses in general linguistics and stylistics. Its first two graduates, honours BA students one of whose degree combined Twi and Russian, came in 1968.

The 1970s were a period of growth and development for the department, for linguistics, and what the role of the discipline was on the national stage in Ghana. Course offerings were expanded to include sociolinguistics, psycholinguistics, and applied linguistics as well as postgraduate degree and diploma programmes. This period also saw increased focus on Ghanaian languages, especially Akan, Ewe, and Ga. The first PhD student to graduate from the department was a Commonwealth student from Australia, K. C. Ford.

The objectives of the department, as stated currently on the departmental website,[7] but first elaborated in 1970, were threefold:

- to produce knowledge through research on all aspects of language and language use including language teaching, language and business, language and society, language policy, language and the deaf, language and culture, language and law, language and politics etc.;
- to train students to appreciate the nature of language in general and Ghanaian languages in particular, and their role in the development of the society;
- to prepare students to take up prominent roles and provide solutions in all aspects of public life where language expertise in all forms is called for.

These aims were reiterated on the occasion of the 50th Anniversary of the department by Professor Kweku Osam, emphasizing the role of the department in developing indigenous Ghanaian languages both in research and teaching, and in helping to mitigate the gradual loss of domain of indigenous languages to English.[8]

While the linguistics department at Legon was and continues to be the centre of linguistics in Ghana, departments or programmes in linguistics are also now found in three other Ghanaian universities: the Department of Modern Languages, Kwame Nkrumah University of Science and Technology, Kumasi (1973); the Department of Applied Linguistics, University of Education, Winneba (2003); and the Department of Ghanaian Languages and Linguistics at the University of Cape Coast; the last of these departments was set up in

---

[7] www.ug.edu.gh/linguistics/about/vision (accessed 14 February 2019).
[8] www.ug.edu.gh/news/department-linguistics-launches-50th-anniversary (accessed 10 December 2017).

1974, with the aim of training teachers for Ghanaian languages and of expanding interest in and study of Ghanaian languages beyond Akan and Ewe. Programmes in linguistics were restricted to Government universities, and the study of linguistics was intended to go hand in hand with the study of Ghanaian languages. None of the more recent private universities has established a linguistics programme.

Outside university departments and their mandates, linguistics has had both an academic and a non-academic presence in Ghana. The Linguistic Circle of Accra, which later evolved into the Linguistic Association of Ghana, was founded in 1967 by linguists from the department at Legon, including Boadi and Dolphyne, along with Gilbert Ansre, Mary Esther Kropp Dakubu, and John M. Stewart, all of the Institute of African Studies at the University of Ghana. Ansre, an ordained minister in the Evangelical Presbyterian Church of Ghana as well as an academic, was also active in the development of several Ghanaian languages ranging from orthography development to Bible translation.

8.4.1.2 Nigeria

Linguistics in Nigeria has developed in a series of waves, corresponding to expansions of the university system. The University of Ibadan was, in colonial times, affiliated with the University of London, and by virtue of this came to be Nigeria's premier university. As a result, linguistics in Nigeria was first established there. We focus our discussion first on linguistics in Ibadan and then summarize its growth elsewhere in the country together with accompanying developments.

Linguistics in Ibadan   Parallel to early developments in Ghana in the 1960s, linguistics began in Nigeria, at the University of Ibadan, in part through the impetus of the West Africa Language Survey. Like the University of Ghana, the University of Ibadan was established as a college of the University of London in 1948. With the founding of the university came a department of English, with one of its primary foci being the training of students to acquire a 'good command of English both written and spoken' (a 1952 report of the visitation panel to the University College). This led to the establishment of the sub-Department of Phonetics in 1954. The sub-Department of Phonetics became the Department of Linguistics and Nigerian Languages in 1962 because of the need to not only teach English pronunciation but to widen coverage of phonetic theory, acoustic phonetics, and phoneme theory and its application to features of Nigerian languages. At the same time, a phonetics laboratory was established for teaching and research on Nigerian languages. After linguistics became a full department in 1963, a postgraduate certificate course in Phonetics and Linguistics was established. It became a postgraduate 'diploma' in 1965, and in 1969 it was renamed a Postgraduate Diploma in Linguistics. This diploma was targeted at graduate language teachers and was intended to serve as background training for graduates who did not already have adequate training in linguistics to proceed to a higher degree in the discipline. The first set of linguistics majors was admitted in 1966; and the first four students to graduate with bachelor degrees in linguistics came in 1969. This first graduating set consisted of three female students – Helen A. Akinseye, Olayinka O. Euler-Ajayi, and Ruth O. Molomo – and one male student, Benjamin O. Elugbe. Of these, Elugbe continued on to earn a PhD in 1973; Elugbe was later to become professor and head of department, in 1984.

There were three founder members when the Department of Linguistics was established in 1962–1963, all in the lecturer cadre: Elizabeth Dunstan, Carl Hoffmann, and Kay Williamson. Robert G. Armstrong, whose official position was director of the Institute of African Studies, and who was the first scholar to be appointed Research Professor of Linguistics in a Nigerian University in 1963, maintained some relationship with the department. Ayo Bamgbose joined them later in 1963, also as a lecturer. Hoffmann was appointed acting head of the new department and served in this capacity until 1966, when he became a professor and head of department. He remained head of department until 1969. Ayo Bamgbose became professor in 1968, and in 1969 took over from Carl Hoffmann as head of department, thus earning the distinction of being the first West African to become head of a linguistics department.

The foci of linguistics in Ibadan, from its foundation, and subsequently elsewhere in Nigeria, were principally descriptive and historical, an appropriate approach in a country with over 500 languages, the majority of which are undocumented or undescribed. For each set of graduating students at the University of Ibadan, an undescribed language was selected and the different parts of the grammar of the language, that is, phonetics, phonology, morphology, syntax, were described by the students in satisfaction of the requirements for their bachelor's degree in linguistics. The students worked with native-speaker language consultants. Early in its existence, the University of Ibadan adopted a proposal from the Linguistics Department which required every student admitted to the university to complete a form on which they entered their native language. The native speakers of the languages used for study in the graduating linguistics class were chosen either from the students' entries of their native languages or from a member of the junior staff of the university.

The Department of Linguistics and Nigerian Languages (now Linguistics and African Languages) at Ibadan also published a mimeographed journal, *Research Notes*. It first appeared in 1967, with the following stated editorial policy: 'The object is not to publish finished articles and papers but rather word lists, texts or folktales and short notes on West African languages.' The first head of department, Professor Carl Hoffmann, oversaw its publication. He was at the same time, as already noted, an editor of the *JWAL*, which had its editorial office in Ibadan. *Research Notes*, volume 5 (1972) was the first volume with a named editor, Isaac George (later known as Isaac Saba George Madugu), and an editorial board consisting of Ben Elugbe, Mona Lindau, and Kay Williamson.

One of the main preoccupations of the Linguistics Department in Ibadan was the development of orthographies for Nigerian languages, intended crucially as national service, to ensure that oral literature (e.g. stories, folktales) could be written and published in the authors' languages so that these languages could be used in education. The National Language Centre of the Nigerian Federal Ministry of Education sponsored manuals devoted to the orthographies of Nigerian languages. The manuals, titled 'Orthographies of Nigerian Languages', were 'an effort by the National Language Centre to aid the standardization of the orthographies of about two dozen of the most widely-spoken indigenous Nigerian languages' (Banjo 1985). Three manuals appeared under the series. The first volume (1981), edited by Ayo Bamgbose, was on Efik, Hausa, Igbo, and Yoruba. The second volume (1983), edited by Kay Williamson, covered Edo, Fulfulde, Kanuri, Tiv, Nembe, and Ijo. The third volume (1985), edited by Ayo Banjo, covered Berom, Ibibio, Nupe, Idoma, Kalabari, and Igala. In most cases, the orthographies produced as a result of this effort became the official orthographies for the languages in question, because they were supported by the government. In addition, the National Language Centre published a journal, *Nigerian Language Teacher*, which also pursued the aims of language development. The National Language Centre has since been reconstituted as a university-level institution called the National Institute for Nigerian Languages.

The National Institute for Nigerian Languages   The National Institute for Nigerian Languages (NINLAN), Aba, was set up by Decree 117 of 30 December 1993 (now CAP N50 laws of the Federation of Nigeria 2004). It is an autonomous institution under the regulation of the National Universities Commission (NUC). NINLAN is an Inter-University Centre for Nigerian Language Studies. Its functions include 'research, teaching, documentation, and coordination of studies in Nigerian languages' (www.ninlan.edu.ng/). The institute offers undergraduate degrees in education, combining linguistics with Hausa, Igbo, and Yoruba (or Kanuri). In addition, it offers degrees in communication studies in combination with one or more of the Nigerian languages. The institute is always headed by a linguist. Its first executive director was Professor Nolue Emenanjo, followed by Professor Ben Elugbe and, at the time of writing, Professor Chinyere Ohiri-Anichie.

Expansion   Other Nigerian universities existed at independence (e.g. University of Nigeria, Nsukka, and Amadu Bello University at Zaria), but it was not until some years after, in the mid- to late 1970s, that a substantial expansion of the federal university system occurred. Many of the new universities included linguistics programmes, typically in departments of linguistics and Nigerian languages, or African languages. The Centre for the Study of Nigerian Languages (now the Centre for Research in Nigerian Languages and Folklore) at Bayero University, Kano, was established in the early 1970s and still exists, with Sammani Sani as director. The Centre, whose first Nigerian director was Professor Dandatti Abdulkadir, has supported research on languages spoken in the north, primarily Hausa and Fulfulde, but Kanuri and minority languages as well. It has published monographs and conference proceedings, as well as a journal, *Harsunan Nijeriya* (Nigerian languages), which includes articles written in Hausa as well as English. Linguistics at the University of Nigeria started in 1974 as a sub-department of the Department of Foreign Languages and Literatures and became a fully-fledged department in 1981 as the Department of Linguistics and Nigerian Languages with Professor Philip A. Nwachukwu as its first head of department. In 2005 it was renamed the Department of Linguistics, Igbo, and Other Nigerian Languages. The Department of Languages and Linguistics at the University of Calabar came into being in 1976 and by 1984 had its first indigenous head of department, Professor Okon E. Essien. The Linguistics Department at the University of Benin was established in 1979, though it had existed as a programme for some years before within the Department of Foreign Languages. Similarly, the University of Ilorin began its linguistics programme in 1979. Among the other universities included in this wave were Port Harcourt, with Kay Williamson moving from Ibadan to start the programme there, Ife, Jos, Maiduguri, and Bayero University in Kano, each of which also developed linguistics programmes.

A third wave of expansion of linguistics in Nigeria came about in the early 1990s, following the redrawing of state boundaries in Nigeria and the creation of new states. Among these were the Department of Linguistics and Nigerian Languages at the University of Uyo, established in 1992, and later, Adekunle Ajasin University Linguistics, in Akungba, in 1999. In total, over 30 Nigerian universities had linguistics programmes, whether as autonomous departments or, more usually, combined with language study in the first decade of the twenty-first century. Like the flagship linguistics programme at Ibadan, there were two common themes that ran across linguistics programmes in other Nigerian universities. The first was that they often started as part of other programmes, such as programmes for modern European languages or English. Second, these programmes often combined linguistics with Nigerian languages, African languages, communication studies, or literary studies. Third, linguistics programmes were only found in public universities, whether federal or state, and not in private ones. This was in part due to the fact that private universities concentrated mainly on so-called professional courses. Therefore, concerning language they tended to have English departments but not linguistics departments.

The Linguistic Association of Nigeria   The growth of academic linguistics programmes was accompanied by the birth of the Linguistic Association of Nigeria in 1980; its aims were similar to those of WALS/SLAO, listed in Emenanjo (2007: 22) as the following:

a. to offer membership to and ensure permanent contact among all who are engaged in the scholarly study of the languages of West Africa/Nigeria, of their literatures, and of any other national or regional linguistic associations;
b. to initiate, encourage, and support scholarly research in this field both for scientific purposes and to assist African nations/Nigeria with the linguistic aspects of development of West Africa/Nigerian educational and social development;
c. to organize annual/biennial meetings, conferences, congresses as may be thought desirable in furtherance of the aims of these associations;
d. to establish and publish regularly the *Journal of the Linguistic Association of Nigeria* (*JOLAN*) and to assist with the publication of relevant materials from scholarly research in these areas;
e. to offer grants for research in these areas whenever practicable and desirable;
f. to cooperate with or establish association with any international body as may seem desirable and, in particular with the International Council for Philosophy and Humanistic Sciences, thereby entering into official relationship with UNESCO in furtherance of the aims of these associations.

The first meeting was held at the University of Ibadan. The Linguistic Association's journal, *JOLAN*, was established in 1982, with Philip A. Nwachukwu and Victor B. Manfredi as founding editors. It continues to hold annual conferences; its proceedings are published regularly, along with festschrifts and other special editions under the editorship of Ozo-mekuri Ndimele, professor and former president of LAN as well as a former head of the Department of Linguistics & Communication Studies at the University of Port Harcourt. *JOLAN* continues to publish.

8.4.1.3   Other Countries
While Ghana and Nigeria may be considered as constituting the heart of linguistics in officially English-speaking West Africa, other countries also fall within the geopolitical realm of 'anglophone West Africa'; these are Sierra Leone, to which we have already devoted some attention though not in its modern, post-independence form, The Gambia, and the anglophone region of Cameroon, all of which are former British colonies. To these can be added Liberia, which, while English-speaking, was not a British colony but came into being through the resettlement of liberated slaves and freeborn African Americans from the United States.

Despite its auspicious beginning with Freetown as the centre of linguistics and language study in precolonial West Africa, linguistics as an academic discipline in Sierra Leone was diminished, if not dormant, in the latter part of the twentieth century and the early years of the twenty-first. This can be attributed to two main factors; first, it would seem that Fourah Bay College, the main academic centre in Sierra Leone (and now part of the University of Sierra Leone), did not receive the same attention immediately following independence from either the former colonial rulers or the new government as did the University of Ibadan and the then University of the Gold Coast (now University of Ghana), both of which were affiliated with the University of London during the colonial era. Fourah Bay College was affiliated with the University of Durham. As a result it did not fall within the immediate scope of the West Africa Language Survey in the same way as did the other universities. The second, and perhaps more critical reason for the slow (or arrested) development of linguistics – and academics generally – in Sierra Leone was the civil war that devastated the country in the last decade of the twentieth century. Finally, because of the economic downturn, university staff development was non-existent, unless the individual faculty member happened to receive an offer of external sponsorship. With the return of stability, linguistics has gradually begun to grow, with African scholars such as Edward Kenny and Taziff Koroma being prominent.

The Gambia, too, has seen little in the way of development of linguistics as an academic discipline. As in Sierra Leone, this may be attributable, to some extent, to the lack of attention it received as an academic centre during the colonial era, which itself can probably not be divorced from the overall situation of The Gambia, the fact that it is the smallest country in Africa and is essentially surrounded by Senegal, a French-speaking country.

While Cameroon is frequently considered to be part of Central Africa, its English-speaking region is a former British colony; it borders Nigeria and many of its languages are found on both sides of the international frontier. For our purposes, then, it is useful to consider the English-speaking region of Cameroon together with the other parts of West Africa we have looked at. It will be noted, too, that Cameroonian linguists and linguistics programmes were brought under the umbrella of WALS/SLAO from the outset, with the establishment of linguistics at Université Yaoundé I in the early 1960s, where courses are offered in both French and English. (See also Chapter 9, this volume.) Our attention here, however, is on the more recent development of linguistics at the University of Buea, which is the major academic centre in Cameroon's anglophone region. The University of Buea was established in 1993, explicitly intended to follow the English tradition. Its linguistics programme produced its first graduates in 1999. During the first years of the twenty-first century, it established itself as an important centre for linguistic research, with a focus on languages of Western Cameroon and the Grassfields region, led by scholars such as Pius Akumbu, Gratien Atingdogbe, and Ayu'nwi Neba, and in this respect strong research links with international scholars were developed. In 2012 the Seventh World Congress of African Linguistics was hosted by the University of Buea, marking the first occasion the premier international meeting of African linguistics had been held in an English-speaking country of West Africa.

8.4.1.4 First Indigenes

As already noted, Ayo Bamgbose became professor and head of the Department of Linguistics at the University of Ibadan in 1969, at the age of 37. He thus became the first indigenous professor and chair of linguistics anywhere in Africa. In Ghana, Lawrence Boadi was appointed associate professor and head of linguistics in 1974, becoming the first Ghanaian linguist to have that rank and occupy that position. Others followed, Nwachukwu and Essien among them. This first wave of indigenous leaders were all foreign trained; Boadi and Dolphyne at London, while Bamgbose and Essien both earned their PhDs at Edinburgh. Professor Dandatti Abdulkadir became the director of the Centre for the Study of Nigerian Languages at Bayero University, Kano, in 1975.

8.4.2 Contributions of Africans and Non-Africans to African Linguistics in English-Speaking West Africa

There are a great many interesting developments and ways in which linguistics in English-speaking West Africa have contributed not only to the understanding of African languages and linguistics but to linguistics more generally. It is not possible to examine all of these here, so we instead look at two, which are arguably among the most significant, tone and the nature of vowel systems.

8.4.2.1 The Study of Tone

As briefly discussed earlier, Crowther recognized and marked tone early on in his work, as can be seen in his *Vocabulary* (1843). He describes his marking conventions thus in the front matter to that work: 'The acute (´) and grave (`) accents are simply marks of intonation – i.e. the rise or fall of the voice – often, as in the Chinese language, affecting the signification.' The wording of this statement suggests he didn't have a full understanding of how tone operates in Yoruba, but rather one that reflects the intuitions of the native speaker that he was, that is, someone who had studied other languages and was aware enough to know Yoruba shared this characteristic with Chinese, but not English. This knowledge and approach can be compared to the work of Goldie and Waddell on Efik; as we have seen, they were not aware of tone in Efik, but they did hear 'something' (at least Goldie did). Goldie's work pre-dated that of Crowther, so he could not have benefited from the latter's insights; it is not clear whether Goldie would have had access to Crowther's work, though he was aware of it, since the *Vocabulary* is included in a comprehensive list of all language-oriented work by missionaries in West and Central Africa in the Introduction to Goldie's *Dictionary*. Christaller, publishing his work on Fante a decade or more later, may well have had access to Crowther's work and may thus have benefited from it in his analysis of Fante.

In studies that came later, such as Arnott (1964), Green & Igwe (1963), Ward (1936), and Winston (1960), much attention was paid to the description of tone and morphophonemic tonal alternations. Green and Igwe's description of Igbo tone was so illuminating that it made later theorizing on autosegmental phonology by Goldsmith (1976) possible. Finally, Hausaists like Abraham (1941) and Greenberg (1941) proposed that Hausa contour tones are sequences of H and L tones on a single syllable long before Autosegmental Theory (Goldsmith 1976, 1990a) made the same proposal.

8.4.2.2 The Study of Vowel Systems, in Particular ATR Vowel Harmony Systems

Unlike tone, which is typically contrastive in the languages of West Africa, vowel harmony is rather different in the sense that it is a prosodic feature that spans a specific domain, and therefore may be more elusive than tone. While early writers like Crowther did not discuss vowel harmony in Yoruba, Ward discussed Igbo harmony in her 1936 study, and Yoruba harmony in her 1952 study. Boadi (1963) was an early description of Twi harmony. Together with Berry (1957a), Carnochan (1960) on Igbo, and Fromkin (1965) on Twi, these studies represent contributions to the Firthian approach to prosody. None of these studies, however, observed that the type of vowel harmony found in Akan or Igbo is the advanced versus retracted tongue root harmony (or ATR harmony) until Stewart (1967, 1971:199). Stewart also noted that this type of vowel harmony is found 'nowhere outside Africa south of the Sahara' (Stewart 1971:198). This major discovery has formed the basis of the description and analysis of vowel harmony in West African languages ever since.

8.5   West African Linguistics in the Twenty-First Century

Linguistics continued to grow and thrive in the early years of the twenty-first century in those parts of West Africa that are 'English speaking'. The collaborations witnessed between Africans and non-Africans in the decades following independence, both with Africans going abroad to study and work at major centres of linguistic research and returning to their home universities (Bamgbose, Boadi, Dolphyne, Emenanjo, Essien, among others) and with non-Africans coming to study, teach, and do their research at West African universities and becoming de facto Africans (Kropp Dakubu, Williamson), have led to the establishment of a solid academic linguistic tradition in the region. Linguistics programmes were by then training and producing graduates capable in their own right not only of training the next generation of linguists but of contributing on the international stage. The days of linguistics departments or programmes being staffed mainly by expatriate linguists had passed. Instead, scholars such as Akinbiyi Akinlabi, Felix Ameka, Adams Bodomo, and Samuel Obeng are established international figures, based in American and European universities, who return regularly to West Africa to organize schools such as the two summer schools on language documentation: one is held, under the direction of Ameka, at the University of Winneba in Ghana (2008, 2010), and the other is the biennial African Linguistics Summer School, organized by Akinlabi et al., held on a rotating basis at different universities and without regard for the anglophone/francophone divide. And there are, of course, numerous African scholars who, in maintaining and developing programmes in their home universities, have also developed and maintained strong ties with universities and colleagues abroad (Francis Egbokhare, Eno-Abasi Urua among others).

8.6   Language Development

One of the distinguishing characteristics of linguistics in English-speaking West Africa since its very beginnings in the early to mid-nineteenth century has been a focus on language development. In Crowther's time this was motivated by evangelization, the need to be able to write African languages in order to translate religious writings. But this was not the only motive; recall that in Freetown in those days, there were other indigenous scholars whose principal interest, according to Hair (1967), was in developing a literature for their language and, as noted earlier, Crowther himself has been referred to as the 'father of Yoruba literature'. With his focus on the Church Missionary Society, Hair offers no information on what was produced outside of religious translation together with the dictionaries and grammars mentioned. In the modern era the concern with language development has continued, though in the hands of indigenous linguists the focus has been squarely on education and nation building. This approach has been well described in Bamgbose (e.g. 2007) and Emenanjo (2007), in contrast to the theoretical interests found in mainstream (generative) linguistics. Indeed Bamgbose, having established himself in his early years with descriptive and theoretical work (his 1966 *A Grammar of Yoruba* has already been noted), dedicated the last half of his long career more to issues pertaining to the role of language (and thus the linguist) in society and the importance of supporting African languages. His writings in this period range from the monograph *Language and the Nation* (1991) to his plenary at the 40th Annual Conference on African Linguistics, 'African Languages Today: The Challenge of and Prospects for Empowerment under Globalization' (Bamgbose 2011).

The following paragraphs outline just some of what has been done in the way of language development, primarily by indigenous West African linguists, most of whom have also left their mark on linguistics in an international perspective.

8.6.1   Language Development in Ghana

The Akan Orthography Committee was set up in 1952 to develop a unified orthography for the Akan language. In 1978 a common orthography began to be used in primary education, but it was only later, in the 1980s, that a unified orthography suitable for the three major dialects, Akuapem, Asante, and Fante, began to gain acceptance. Among the earliest work by Ghanaians on Ghanaian languages, Akrofi (1937) in particular bears mention as perhaps the first grammar of a West African language written in the language being described (namely, the Twi-Fante variety of Akan). Akrofi together with collaborators (e.g. E. L. Rapp) also produced other materials, such as their 1939 work on spelling materials. A comparative or multilingual dictionary of Akan dialects and English was produced by Berry (1957b), and in 1988 Dolphyne produced a detailed description of the sound system of Akan. Other scholars contributed in a more general perspective, such as Samuel Obeng with his work in the area of pragmatics.

On languages other than Akan, the Dagaare Language Committee produced in 1982 an orthography and other materials, and for the same language Bodomo's work, both descriptive and theoretical (Bodomo 1997), must be mentioned. The standard orthography used by the church in Ghana is based on the Central dialect of Dagaare, but there are several alternative orthographies particularly for dialects in Burkina Faso and Ivory Coast.

Westermann's early work on Ewe (1928, 1930) set a solid foundation for later work on this language. Felix Ameka and James Essegbey have worked in the direction of mitigating the threat to endangered African languages (see below) through a range of efforts both practical/developmental (e.g. Ameka et al. 2011) and theoretical/descriptive.

8.6.2   Language Development in Nigeria

The three largest languages in Nigeria, Hausa, Yoruba, and Igbo, have not surprisingly received the greatest amount of attention over the years.

The writing of Hausa in Latin script (termed bookoo) was introduced by colonial officers (British and French) at the beginning of the twentieth century. Prior to that, Hausa had been written for a century or more using the Arabic script (termed àjàmi), with minor modifications, and this script is still commonly employed by people with a good Islamic education. While a number of early dictionaries have been compiled for Hausa, including Schön (1876), Robinson (1899–1900), 4th edition 1925, and Mischlich (1906), the most substantial works are those of Bargery (1934), Abraham and Mai Kano (1949; 2nd edition Abraham 1962), R. M. Newman (1990), and P. Newman (2007). A remarkable achievement in Hausa lexicography is the monolingual Hausa-Hausa dictionary compiled by the staff of the Centre for the Study of Nigerian Languages in Kano (CSNL 2006). With four recent comprehensive reference grammars compiled by expatriate linguists (Caron 1991 in French of a non-standard variety in Niger, Wolff 1993 in German, Newman 2000 and Jaggar 2001 in English, all three on Standard Hausa and dialectal variation), Hausa today ranks among the best-described African languages.

The earliest formal attempts at devising an orthography for Yoruba came in the context of Crowther's work and had a direct influence on the development of Karl Richard Lepsius's orthography for African languages. While the missionaries in Freetown and in Abeokuta (Nigeria) already referred to (e.g. Schön and Raban, along with Crowther) were likely directly responsible for its development, according to Hair (1967) Schön discussed the proposed orthography with Lepsius while on a visit to London, leading the latter to adopt certain of its conventions. This original orthography survived with little change for over a century. In 1875, a conference on the Yoruba language (chaired by Crowther), which primarily discussed and resolved a number of anomalies in the orthography, was held in Lagos, Nigeria. The orthography was further revised in 1963, 1966, 1969, and 1974. The orthography currently in use is the one approved by the government in 1974, with minor modifications.

Given the substantial dialect variation found in Igbo, attempts to develop a standard, common orthography have been fraught, though Eze and Manfredi (2001:323) report that 'The current official orthography ... was accepted from the Onwu Committee by the Eastern Nigerian government in 1961.' In addition to the work of the nineteenth-century linguistics, among modern linguists, Enemanjo's work (e.g. 2015) deserves particular mention, as do the dictionaries, each of different dialects, of Echeruo (1998) and Williamson (1972).

Despite its auspicious beginning as the object of missionary linguists' attention in the nineteenth century and the early work of Ward (e.g. 1933), Efik has since received scant attention. However, at least two other dictionaries have appeared, that of Adams (1952, in two volumes), and one volume of a planned three-volume learner's dictionary by the Efik scholar E. U. Aye (who was not a linguist by training). Other important work on Efik by T. L. Cook remains unpublished. The situation is somewhat different for the very closely related Ibibio. The leading Ibibio linguist, Okon Essien, mentioned above in his capacity as first African to be head of the linguistics programme at the University of Calabar, was the driving force of Ibibio language development, being responsible for the creation of its orthography (Essien 1984a, 1984b) and other development materials (e.g. mathematical terminology) as well as a descriptive grammar (Essien 1990). Essien published numerous descriptive and theoretical articles on Ibibio in addition to his grammar. In the present century Eno-Abasi Urua, at the University of Uyo, has assumed Essien's mantle, leading work on Ibibio (e.g. Urua 2000; Urua et al. 2012) as well as on the documentation of endangered languages in south-eastern Nigeria. Another language closely related to Efik and Ibibio, Obolo (Cross River, Benue-Congo, Nigeria), was the subject of two descriptive grammars in the modern era, that of Faraclas (1984), who also produced other descriptive and theoretical linguistic work on Obolo, and the Obolo linguist Rowland-Oke (2003). The work of a second Obolo linguist, Uche Aaron, should also be mentioned. Not ony was Aaron instrumental in developing the Obolo orthography (1990), but he also produced work on discourse and pragmatics (e.g. Aaron 1992, 1999).

The standard Kanuri orthography was developed as a joint effort by the staff of the Centre for the Study of Nigerian Languages at Bayero University, Kano, the Kanuri Language Board, and the Borno State Ministry of Education. It was approved by the Kanuri Language Board in 1975. Like many Nigerian language orthographies, the Kanuri orthography did not include tone marking.

Discussion of efforts at language development in Nigeria would be incomplete without mention of the work of Kay Williamson. Although an expatriate, Williamson spent her entire career in Nigeria, first at the University of Ibadan as a founder member of the linguistics programme there and subsequently as a founder member of the linguistics programme at the University of Port Harcourt. Some of her contributions to West African linguistics came about via the West African Language Survey and WALS/SLAO. While in Port Harcourt, she also undertook what was known as the Rivers Readers Project: the development of orthographies and primers for many of the small languages in the then Rivers State. For this work together with her role in training numerous Nigerian linguists, Williamson was dubbed the 'mother of Nigerian linguistics' in the popular press.

8.7   Language Endangerment and Language Documentation

Like their colleagues around the world, African linguists in the final years of the twentieth and the early decades of the twenty-first century showed an increasing awareness of the threatened state of many African languages. A Cameroonian linguist, the late Pius Tamanji (2008) described the overall situation as a threat to Africa's linguistic diversity. Along with Urua, Nigerian linguists such as Francis Egbokhare (in collaboration with the American R. P. Schafer) concentrated on languages in southern Nigeria; Roger Blench, in collaboration with Nigerian linguists such as Selbut Longtau, has maintained a focus on languages in central Nigeria. The concern for threatened languages, rooted in the more general social and political concerns surrounding language development, led to two Summer Schools in Documentary Linguistics in West Africa, the first in 2008 and another in 2010. Both were sponsored by the Hans Rausing Endangered Language Documentation Programme at the School of Oriental and African Studies of the University of London, and both were held at the University of Education in Winneba, Ghana. They were organized by Felix Ameka and featured a cohort of international and African scholars as instructors/resource people; students were drawn from across West Africa, both anglophone and francophone countries, though all instruction was in English.

8.8 African Linguistics School

A similar development, though oriented more towards theoretical linguistics, was the African Linguistics School (ALS). The ALS was co-founded in 2008 by Enoch Aboh (University of Amsterdam), Akinbiyi Akinlabi (Rutgers University), and Chris Collins and John Singler (both of New York University). It was a two-week long school, which introduced current work in core areas of linguistics to students from African universities. The school has been held four times up until the time of writing: in Accra, Ghana (2009); Porto-Novo, Benin Republic (2011), Ibadan, Nigeria (2013), and Yammoussukro, Côte d'Ivoire (2016). The areas of focus are syntax, semantics, phonology, sociolinguistics, and phonetic fieldwork. As many as 16 internationally recognized linguists, coming from North America, Europe, and Africa, formed the teaching cohort, with all faculty teaching *pro bono publico*. Like the school in documentary linguistics, students came from both anglophone and francophone countries, though in this case from universities from all over Africa. About 70 students were chosen from over 300 applications for each school, with a small number of students admitted from universities in Europe or North America. Funding for the school came from a variety of sources: organizations such as the US National Science Foundation, the Carnegie Corporation of New York, the Council for the Development of Social Science Research in Africa (CODESRIA); universities, including New York University, Rutgers University, and the University of Amsterdam; and linguistics associations such as Generative Linguistics of the Old World (GLOW) and the Association of Contemporary African Linguistics (ACAL).

8.9 Conclusion

This brief sketch of the history of linguistics in official English-speaking West Africa is an attempt to fill some of the gaps in our collective knowledge of how linguistics developed in this region, and in particular the contributions of

West African scholars to this development. It is in itself, though, only a stop-gap. Time and space considerations determine that inevitably important people and important contributions have been missed out. And just as inevitable has been an inadvertent focus on what the authors know best from their own involvement and interaction with many of the key people from the modern era discussed here.

We conclude with an observation on what appear to be three general trends over the 200 or so years in which linguistics and language study has developed in this part of West Africa. The first is an abiding concern with language development manifested first, in the nineteenth century, in the motivation for evangelization, and more recently in a recognition of the role language development has to play in social development through, for example, developing materials for mother tongue education. While in the modern era interest in theoretical linguistics has grown, it has not been at the expense of recognizing the role language plays in society. Even those many indigenous linguists who contributed on the international stage continued to contribute in substantive ways to the maintenance and development of languages at home, together with the development of linguistics as a discipline in the region. This is true also of a number of expatriate linguists working on languages of the region.

The second trend is the cooperation between Africans of the region and non-Africans. In the modern era in particular this has been multifaceted. As noted, at the outset funding came from foreign sources, and to a lesser extent this was also the case in the early years of the twenty-first century. Similarly, at the outset the linguistic expertise came from outside Africa, with non-African linguists involved in all three aspects of the development of linguistics in West Africa: training local scholars, language development, and producing descriptive works on local languages and theoretical contributions to general linguistics. At the beginning of the twenty-first century, this cooperation was still present, though with the balance redressed; only rarely now does one find non-Africans in full-time or tenured teaching positions in linguistics programmes in the region, which are staffed almost entirely by indigenes; it is more usual to find West African scholars more or less permanently on the faculty of universities in North America, Europe, and other parts of the world.

A third and unfortunate trend, however, remains the persistent unidirectional drain of results from much of expatriate field research in the region, which feeds into researchers' degree work and academic publications outside Africa with little or no immediate and practical feedback to the community of speakers, for example in terms of assisting language development through readable grammars and dictionaries, suggestions for orthographies, or provision of literacy and post-literacy materials by which to make mother tongue education viable. Notable exceptions, however, do exist, such as, for instance, much of the work of the late Russell Schuh on languages of Yobe State of Nigeria, of Norbert Cyffer and John Hutchison on Kanuri, and of Ekkehard Wolff on Lamang in the Nigerian states of Borno and Adamawa.

Acknowledgements

We would like to acknowledge here the contributions made by a number of scholars, colleagues who through having been a part of the development and expansion of linguistics in West Africa lived the history we have discussed: Nana Aba A. Amfo, Offeibea Awuku, Regina Caesar, G. Tucker Childs, Charlotte Fofo Lomotey, Ozo Mekuri Ndimele, and Amo Ofori all provided information not available to us through either published sources or our own recollections.

9 African Linguistics in Official French-Speaking West and Central Africa

Philip Ngessimo Mathe Mutaka

9.1 Introduction

Wherever names of African-origin linguists appear in bibliographical references on African linguistics, their work is likely to be associated with Western universities. This links up with the observation that many scholars in Africa have PhDs obtained from Western universities, or from African universities, whose professors were trained in Western universities. This could lead to the false assumption that there are very few genuine contributions coming out of Africa. This general impression may hold in particular for so-called Francophone West and Central Africa. However, as will be shown in this chapter, at variance with that impression is a considerable wealth of contributions by African linguists, although some of it tends to be little known due to unfavourable circumstances, such as limited access to publishing agencies, limited distribution of locally published material, and limited funding for linguistic research in African countries in general.

This chapter focuses on the contributions of African linguists in officially French-speaking (so-called francophone) West and Central African countries. It will consist of the following subsections: the pre-academic state of African linguistics, the import of African linguistics under the impact of missionaries and in universities, the current state of African linguistics in various domains of linguistics, and an outlook on perspectives concerning African linguistics in Africa.

9.2 The Pre-academic State of African Linguistics

Current research and teaching of African linguistics in so-called Francophone Africa, like elsewhere on the continent, is largely based on Western academic traditions, from both Europe, in particular from the former colonial motherlands, and the United States of America. It has its roots in European colonialism. Given the historical fact of colonialism, what could have been genuine African roots of African linguistics have had practically no chance to grow and have never been made a topic of research by itself, as far as I am aware.

178

Certain research domains, like surrogate languages and the study of tone, for instance, might have entered general linguistic debate much earlier than actually happened, if 'African' African linguistics had had its chance. Also, since African verbal art allows for various types of creative manipulations of linguistic structure, like alliterations, assonances, tonal rhymes, etc. (as, for instance, described in some detail in Wolff 1980, 2001, 2012, 2014b), these too could have fostered culture-specific schools of 'African' linguistics as forerunners, so to speak, of Western-type academic linguistics. For the sake of argument, let this be illustrated below with a few examples.

It must be noted, further, that African societies and cultures have a long tradition of being based on orality rather than literality. There are only a few exceptions to this in Africa, like, for instance, Ancient Egypt and the Axumite Empire preceding modern Ethiopia and Eritrea, and the use of the Tifinagh script among the Tuareg. Therefore, African intellectuality lacks the characteristic Western obsession with written texts, i.e. the study of philology, which has boosted the literary traditions of so-called Western societies. Rather, a fair number of African cultures have developed abstractions from their spoken languages that allow for the creation of surrogate languages, like drumming (compare the notion of 'talking drums'), whistling, or blowing long trumpets (for instance, among the Songhay and Hausa known as *kakaki*), not forgetting the so-called 'gong' in some Cameroonian villages used by the town crier to announce a meeting at the public place of the village. 'Drum languages', for instance, work on the intuitive knowledge of the people about the existence of different pitch levels, whose combinations in drumming sequences are reflections of words in their languages. A complex use of the drum beats has been developed by the Baluba Shankadi of Katanga, DRC, as reported in Kalonji wa Mpoyo and Demolin (2011:21–38). The drum beats are able to communicate, among other things, messages related to the royal court and the colonial administration, to hunting, death, religion, and messages among family members. Apparently, the drum beats use two tones, High and Low, and their combination is interpreted by the hearers in terms of words conveying a specific message. See the following excerpt (Table 9.1) from Kalonji and Demolin (2011:28; the English translation is mine; B stands for Low tone and is marked by a grave accent, H for High tone, which remains unmarked; HB is a combined Falling tone, marked by a circumflex accent; # marks word boundaries).

The segmentation of the drum beats into small units could be equated to words of the language. The overall structure and length of the phrases in the language helps the hearers decode the drum beat sequences and thus understand the message that the drums convey. In other contexts, tone patterns may also be used to create tonal rhymes in songs, riddles, and proverbs and add to the aesthetic beauty of African verbal art.

Table 9.1 Drum beat message of the Baluba Shankadi

Drum beat	Translation in Kiluba and in English
# B H B H # B H B H # B # H H# B # B B B #	Bùbaìle, bùbaìle bù Ngoyi yà Màlèmbà
# H H # B B # H H # B B #	Muntu pàndì, muntu pàndì
# B H B # B # H B B #	Wàkapìt pà mukwàbò
# BHH # HB H #	Wàbingwa mwânda
Message: It is forbidden to walk at night.	This is the night, the night of Ngoyi of clouds Let each person go home, each person at home, The one who passes through his neighbour's Will be considered guilty.

Another linguistic dimensin is manipulated with proverbs among the Lega of the Democratic Republic of the Congo (DRC). This refers to the use of symbolic objects that are attached to a rope called *mutanga* and that serve the speaker to recall the specific proverb and remember the message linked to that proverb. As reported by Luis Beltrán, one symbolic object can transmit various messages and is thus polysemic. The following two examples of proverbs related to both a concrete object and a symbolic value triggering a specific proverb illustrate this special kind of polysemy (Beltrán 2011:47).

kizugo 'grelot (a small bell that is attached around the neck of a dog)'
  Mpimbi za kizugo izikie mubale ku Manila
  Le son du grelot du chien causa la mort de l'antilope [the sound of the small bell attached around the neck of the dog caused the death of the antelope].
  Tu te comporteras comme l'antilope si tu agis impulsivement: affronte les problèmes et ne fuis pas devant les difficultés de la vie. [You will behave like an antelope if you act impulsively: face the problems and do not flee the difficulties of life.]
musanga 'cowries'
  Ikumi la musanga agungumala ntakongie giziko
  Tu peux avoir la dot à la maison, mais elle ne passera jamais à la cuisine pour te préparer à manger. [You can have the dowry at home, but it will never get to the kitchen to cook you food.]
  Bien que tu sois riche, sans épouse, tu es voué à l'échec : sans épouse (conjointe) même riche on n'atteindra pas le bonheur [Although you may be rich, without a woman, you are bound to be a failure. Without a wife, even though you are rich, you will never be happy.]

Other areas of creative manipulation of language that are based on speaker intuition and awareness of linguistic structure include name-giving and/or naming ceremonies when, for instance, the name of a child may be a reconstruction of his genealogical lineage as is the case among the Aghem of Cameroon (Tschonghongei & Ezigha 2011).

Attention may also be drawn to the innovative work of King Ndam Njoya of the Bamun in Cameroon, who devised an alphabet for a new language that he allegedly created. This is the Shumon that is mostly spoken in the king's palace, while the rest of the Bamun population speaks Shupamem.

One could, for the sake of argument, propose that 'African' African linguistics, in complementarity to its received Western foundations, would have hitherto widely neglected roots in African cultural usages of languages. The domains of research in question, however, are largely covered by ethnolinguistics (or anthropological linguistics) in the Western tradition but would nevertheless profit immensely from the input of African linguists, who have intimate knowledge of these languages and the cultures into which these are embedded.

Taking up another African stream of dealing with linguistics would lead us to the name of Cheikh Anta Diop of Senegal, who is very popular in francophone Africa. Strictly speaking, he is not a linguist but is best described as an Afrocentric historian, anthropologist, physicist, and politician, who became particularly interested in the study of human origins and precolonial African culture. He attempted to make use of linguistic arguments to demonstrate a relationship between ancient Egypt and the African languages (Diop 1974, 1977, 1997), which gained considerable popularity in parts of Africa, but not in Western expert circles; for a critique of Diop's ideas by a highly regarded scholar, see Schuh (1997).

9.3   The Import of African Linguistics

The 'Africa Year', 1960, symbolizes the period when most African officially French-speaking countries got their independence from France and Belgium. During the colonial period that preceded independence, colonizers came hand in glove with Christian missionaries, whose main objective was to 'spread the word of God'. Thus they became interested in African languages and started learning them in order to translate the Bible and preach to illiterates. In order to support this endeavour, early dictionaries and grammar books were written by missionaries, which laid some foundations for Western-type African linguistics in Africa.

Elsewhere, where large areas of French-speaking African countries had been conquered or culturally impacted by Arabs with the simultaneous spreading of Islam, Muslim missionaries established Qur'anic schools where they would teach their followers to memorize the Qur'an by heart. This, however, had no impact on the development of African linguistics in Africa. Contrary to widely held beliefs, Qur'anic schools did not necessarily foster the spreading of spoken Arabic as a lingua franca in sub-Saharan Africa.

Under the colonial regime, Western education brought schools and universities to Africa. The first teachers often came from the countries of the colonizers, that is, France for countries emerging from former French West Africa and French Equatorial Africa, and from Belgium for the later DRC. Students who became interested in languages and linguistics were given scholarships to study in Western countries, mostly Belgium, France, Germany, the Netherlands, and the United States. They wrote their doctoral theses (*doctorat de 3e cycle, doctorat d'état*) at these Western universities. On their return to Africa, they automatically imported the various schools of linguistics to which they had been exposed while studying in Western countries.

Not only for Francophone Africa but here as well, one needs to emphasize the role of SIL International, a non-profit organization dedicated to promoting language-based development within indigenous communities through linguistic research, translation, and practical service, primarily in order to foster and spread Evangelical Christian texts and scriptures. In this work, SIL International has been a collaborator of African linguists working on their own languages within their countries, through the creation of language committees, as is the case of the National Cameroonian Languages Committee (NACALCO) in Cameroon. Linking up with the purely scientific African West African Linguistic Society/*Societé Linguistique de l'Afrique Occidentale* (WALS/SLAO), SIL has also become instrumental in publishing the *Journal of West African Languages* (*JWAL*), which is the research outlet of this oldest academic linguistic society in West Africa. In countries such as Chad, Congo, Cameroon, Gabon, the Central African Republic, Burkina Faso, Benin, and Côte d'Ivoire, linguists affiliated to SIL have done linguistic surveys and written on some languages, for instance, as topics for their PhD theses at Western universities, or they have worked in close collaboration with native speakers to produce primers for use in local schools. To take Cameroon as an example, one could single out SIL-related prominent expatriate researchers and their research output, such as Watters (1982), Anderson (1983), Bird (1999a, 1999b), and Hedinger (2008).

In the sections to follow, primary focus will be on the works of African linguists publishing on African languages, whether affiliated to African authorities and universities, or working from academic institutions outside Africa. Outstanding and influential contributions by non-African linguists will also be mentioned as far as they pertain to so-called Francophone Africa.

9.4   The Current State of African Linguistics

The history of African linguistics in officially French-speaking West and Central Africa has partly been treated in Clements (1989) and Doneux (2003). They contain a Western perspective on the early history of African linguistics until the 1980s, including the history of African linguistics in so-called francophone countries. This chapter complements the previous work by Clements

and Doneux, mainly based on what I was able to find on the Internet on relevant authors and their works, in order to represent what has been achieved by
contemporary African linguists. Another valuable published source is Bostoen
and Maniacky (2005). It includes a number of doctoral dissertations, dictionaries, and grammars written by African and non-African researchers on African
languages. For the categorization of the works, I borrowed from the domains
of linguistics as synthesized in Clements (1989).

A preliminary remark should put the following account into perspective.
African scholars, who have been trained as linguists in Western universities do
not necessarily pursue research on the specific topics for which they have been
trained overseas. Very often, the local situation pushes them to pursue research
on topics that may not be of their primary specialization in a bid to respond, as
linguists, to the local needs of their universities or of their countries. A case in
point is the highly respected Professor Beban Sammy Chumbow of Cameroon,
who was trained as a phonologist but has become involved mostly in language
planning. If I may also speak about myself: I was trained as a phonologist at
the University of Southern California but have been led to also publish books
dealing with AIDS prevention and African culture, besides my publications in
linguistics (Mutaka 1994, 2000, 2001, 2003, 2011a, 2012).

9.4.1   Works on Historical Linguistics, Comparative Linguistics, Language
Classification

Under this heading, reference must be made, first of all, to Capo's works (1988,
1989), in which he explores a number of languages spoken in Benin. Kadima
(1969) is a seminal contribution on the class system of Bantu languages.
Bakume Nkongho Ojong (2012) deals with the reconstruction of the proto-
language of the Nyang dialects of Cameroon. Other important works under
this heading are mostly done by Africanists from Western universities either in
the form of dissertations (e.g. Voeltz 1977; Pozdiniakov 1978; Stallcup 1978;
Grégoire 1990; Janssens 1993; Vydrine 2001) or as part of their (postdoctoral)
research on African languages (e.g. Welmers 1958; Caprile and Jungraithmayr
1978; Bouquiaux 1980; Hyman and Voorhoeve 1980; Bastin 1983; Hombert
1988; Creissels 1991; Egner 1992; and Botne 1994).

9.4.2   Descriptive Works

9.4.2.1   Grammars
Works in terms of descriptive grammars are often doctoral dissertations, e.g.
Bokula (1966), Djarangar Djita Issa (1989), Takassi (1996), and Lébikaza
(1999), or works whose authors have benefited from a Humboldt grant from
Germany, as in the case of Tamanji (2009) and Akumbu and Fogwe (2012) for

their work on the grammars of Bafut and Babanki respectively, or an ILCAA grant from Japan, as in the case of Diouf (2001). Works by Africanists from Western universities include Coupez (1955), Vansina (1959), Dugast (1971), Meeussen (1971), Stappers (1973), and Benoist (1977).

9.4.2.2   Phonetics, Phonology, Morphology
Most work under this heading is on phonology and morphology. Authors of both African and non-African background were involved, e.g. Coupez (1955), Vincke (1966), Guarisma (1969), Leroy (1977), Rialland (1979), Coulibali (1983), Achie Brouh (1996), Gbeto and Möhlig (1997), Essono (2000), Akumbu (2012). Grégoire (1976, 1990) is the only author I found who specifically mentions phonetics and tonetics in the titles of her dissertations.

Some of Motingea Mangulu's works were published in Tokyo, which implies that he has been receiving grants from Japan for his linguistic research (e.g. Motingea Mangulu 2005, 2008, 2010, 2012). For the supportive role of ILCAA in Japan for the linguistic studies on African languages, see Chapter 12 of this volume.

9.4.2.3   Syntax, Semantics, Lexicon
Works under this heading would appear to consist mostly of papers, e.g. Bassène and Creissels (2011). Book publications, which are not readily identified even on the Internet, include Edmond Biloa's syntax books (1995, 1998, 2004, 2005) and Bassong (2013).

9.4.3   Sociolinguistics and Applied Linguistics

9.4.3.1   Sociolinguistics, Language Planning, and Ethnolinguistics
Sociolinguistics and language planning are among the areas in which several African linguists have published. The topics explored include language planning (Kamwangamalu et al. 2013), language contact (Bitjaa Kody 2004; Heine, Kuteva & Salikoko 2005 et al.), transborder languages (Chumbow 1999), bilingualism (Essizewa 2011), ethnolinguistics of individual names (Mangulu 2014), tales and proverbs (Dugast 1975), and narratives of pygmies (Bahuchet 1989).

9.4.3.2   Applied Linguistics, Contrastive Linguistics, Orthography
Orthography is a major domain that African linguists address as they face the need to develop writing systems for the numerous languages on the continent. Norbert Nikiéma is one of the rare US-trained linguists who specialized in orthography as he wrote his doctoral dissertation (Nikiéma 1976). Tadadjeu and Sadembouo (1984) offer an attempt to harmonize the orthography of the more than 200 languages spoken in Cameroon. Other works within the domain of applied linguistics

include Nikiéma (1979, 1980, 1982), Nikiema and Kinda (1997), Diki-Kidiri (2008), Mba and Sadembouo (2012), and Kamwangamalu (2016).

9.4.4   Other Topics

Many scholars in or from so-called Francophone Africa have published on a wide range of other topics like pragmatics, discourse analysis, language acquisition, loanwords, place names, speech perception, language and ethnicity. These include publications by Ousseina Alidou, currently professor at Rutgers University, on gender and Islam (Ousseina 2005; Ousseina & Sikainga 2006). While Bokamba and Bokamba (2005) studied the learning of Lingala, Adouakou (2009) and Adouakou and Ahoua (2009) wrote on the learning of some languages spoken in Côte d'Ivoire. Tchagbale and Lallemand (1982) worked on tales of Togo, as did Ahoua (2002) on tales in Côte d'Ivoire. Musanji's research (2011) was on oral texts and the future of African cultures. Ndoma Ungina (1977, 1998) worked on literacy and language planning in the DRC, Afeli (2003) on multilingualism in Togo, and Mbaya Maweja (2005) on linguistic attitudes in Senegal. Gbeto and Möhlig (2000) studied linguistic loanwords from European languages to languages spoken in Benin. Kiango (2000) worked on Bantu lexicography. Traoré (2000) did research on tribalism in Africa, Goyvaerts (2000) on conflict and ethnicity in central Africa.

A number of works have been published by ILCAA in Japan by Japanese researchers, e.g. Kagaya (1992) on Bakweri vocabulary, and Yukawa (1992) on Yambasa tonology. Kagaya and Nobuko (2006) provided a bibliography of African studies. See also Chapter 12, this volume.

9.4.5   Linguistic Atlas

Several officially French-speaking countries have promoted linguistic atlases that may have been initiated by Western linguists but involve African linguists as active collaborators in their compilation and elaboration. This is the case of the linguistic atlases of Cameroon and of the DRC, in which the late Professor Marcel Kadima Kamuleta was involved. Issa Takassi (1983) was responsible for publishing a sociolinguistic atlas for Togo.

9.4.6   Further References

Bostoen and Maniacky (2005) cover languages spoken in Francophone Africa; the following references include further relevant theses, grammars, dictionaries, and atlases that can be gathered from this source.

Grammars include Capus (1898), Whitehead (1899), Calloc'h (1911), Gauthier (1912), Vandermeiren (1912), De Clercq (1921), Gilliard (1928),

Walker (1950), Tessières and Dubois (1957), Meeussen (1959), Vansina (1959), Jacobs (1964), Doneux (1968), Prost (1968), Dugast (1971), Carrington (1972), Polak-Bynon (1975), Coupez (1980), and Mateene (1992).

Dictionaries include Van Acker (1907), Raponda-Walker (1934), De Clercq (1936), Guthrie (1951), Hagendorens (1956), Galey (1964), Dugast (1967), Rodegem (1970), Gusimana (1972), Helmlinger (1972), Gastines and Lemb (1973), Benoist (1977), Gillis (1981), Kaji (1985, 1992), Van Everbroeck (1985), Nguma (1986), Wendo (1986), Fal et al. (1990), Blanchon (1994), Vanhoudt (1999), Van der Veen et al. (2002), Tymian et al. (2003), Coupez (2005).

Dissertations or master's theses include Bunduki (1965), Furere (1967), Angenot (1971), Chelo (1973), Mutombo (1973), Niyonkuru (1978), Boum (1981), Asangama (1983), Geslin-Houdet (1984), Aramazani (1985), Nsuka Nkutsi (1982), Niyibizi (1987), Boukka (1989), Mfonyam (1989), Van der Veen (1991, 1999), Dodo-Bounguendza (1992), Ondo-Mebiame (1992), Essono (1993), Manfoumbi (1994), N' Landu (1994), Tassa (1994), Mouguiama-Daouda (1995), Atindogbé (1996), Mabiala (1999), Baka (2001), Rekanga (2001), Bostoen (2005c).

Papers include Hulstaert (1950), Beckett (1951), Meeussen (1952), Coupez (1954), Dugast (1954), Mamet (1955), Nsuka Nkutsi (1986), Willems (1955), Kadima (1965), Hombert (1976), Prost (1967), Stappers (1971), Clark (1973), Bolli (1976), Hyman (1976, 1979), Jacquot (1976), Carrington (1977), Hopkins (1982), Mous et al. (1986), Creissels (1988), Blanchon (1990, 1991), and Yukawa (1992).

Atlases are Halaoui et al. (1983) and Hérault (1982). There is also one work on ethnography (Forde 1954) and one on language acquisition (Idiata 1998).

9.5   Outlook on African Linguistics in Africa

African linguists working in Africa tend to be caught between a rock and a hard place when their specialization as linguistic experts, often received abroad, does not immediately meet the practical needs of local policies and politics. When expatriate linguists first came in contact with African languages, they introduced concepts, schools of thought, and research priorities for these languages that were the same as those used to analyse and describe non-African, including Western languages at that time. Likewise, African students were sent to Western universities to be trained as linguists, which led to the perpetuation of Western ideological concepts on linguistics. Coming back to their countries, these African scholars found themselves in the role of proponents of the different Western schools of thought that they were trained in in their own schools or universities. National governments, however, often do not give priority to the type of studies these researchers had pursued in Europe or in the United States. Rather, they urge them to become involved in language planning studies, in producing literacy materials for local populations, in identifying the specific languages in their territories, and eventually in compiling linguistic atlases.

Second, in order to be part of the international scientific community, African researchers also need to identify with current streams in international, i.e. Western-dominated, scholarship. Even if they are in a position to develop approaches of their own that would reflect the immediate needs of their countries, insufficient funding of linguistic studies by African governments creates a serious impediment to the production of studies that would reflect a new and genuine African perspective on applied linguistics in consonance with the immediate practical needs. Moreover, research is largely funded by foreign organizations, and African linguists doing research under such grants will therefore produce the type of work that these organizations expect.

A case in point is advancing literacy in African languages. Because literacy is defined as primarily reading and writing in a language, sophisticated materials have been designed by African linguistic experts to teach people how to read and write in their languages. This is a sublime goal. On the other hand, for many children in the dynamically growing urban agglomerations, the primary need would be, first, to learn to speak their African languages with confidence and competence before they are taught the phonemes and morphology of the language. Oral skills, however, are rarely on the agenda of Western-trained experts in African linguistics.

Third, there is also concern with empowerment and the intellectualization of African languages in the domain of writing and publishing academic works in these languages. African academics face a dilemma: If they want to be recognized by the international scholarly community, they cannot write their PhD dissertations, or any books, in an African language because of the language barrier that excludes a potential international readership. Hence, they feel forced to write in a language of wider communication, which most often is the ex-colonial language. Admirably, some African linguists make a point of providing at least extensive abstracts or summaries in an African language of works produced in French or English. The issue of dissemination and recognition explains why some of the brightest African linguists leave their home countries and work abroad. As much as this brain drain negatively affects African institutions of higher learning, it may result in the production of better work for the benefit of their countries, while and because their authors live abroad.

Another serious problem that students in African linguistics face is scarcity of employment opportunities. The areas of linguistics as taught in Western universities and reproduced in African universities cannot guarantee enough jobs. Africa cannot afford to waste her best human resources. Recently, the rector of the University of Yaoundé 1 decided that departments must propose tracks that give the students who graduate from those departments the opportunity to be directly employed in the job market. This puts a different kind of pressure on university departments in Africa, as compared to the situation elsewhere.

Taking local practical needs and job creation potential seriously, the most obvious tracks for applied African linguistics in Africa, therefore, should be in the wider domain of the intellectualization of African languages, and on the following aspects in particular:

1. Orthographies and corpus planning. This refers to the development of writing systems in local languages as well as lexical engineering, that is, the creation of new terminology for concepts not found in these local languages along with the establishment and sustainable support of local language academies.
2. Literacy and post-literacy in African languages. This refers to the development of didactic and literacy materials for multilingual and multicultural contexts, including books to be read for pleasure. The aim of this track would essentially be to train students to become writers or editors of literature materials (including textbooks and novels, tales, epics, and so on) in their native languages. This material would facilitate the transition of acquiring knowledge from local languages to exoglossic official languages such as French and English.
3. Language pathology (in French: *linguistique clinique*). Students from this training track would be able to identify language pathologies in both oral and written speech and give orientations to the patient, including the need for further medical treatment. Such pathologies include dyslexia, dysorthography, dysgraphy, vocal and articulation problems, fluency troubles, and aphasia.
4. Linguistics and socioeconomic local development. The aim for this track would be to make sure that local development projects funded either by the government or by non-governmental organizations are fully understood by the targeted communities. Explanations to the communities of such projects are best done in their local languages. There is a need for students to be trained in the translation of literacy materials from the official languages, such as English and French, into the various local languages, and also in interpreting (Gabriel Mba, personal communication; see also Wolff 2016).

Acknowledgement

The author acknowledges the input of the editor in giving this chapter its final shape.

10 African Linguistics in Official Portuguese- and Spanish-Speaking Africa

Anne-Maria Fehn

10.1 Introduction

In this chapter, I review past and present contributions to the study of African languages and linguistics from six African countries using Portuguese or Spanish as their official language. These include the five former Portuguese colonies Mozambique, Angola, São Tomé e Príncipe, Guinea-Bissau, and Cabo Verde, as well as the former Spanish colony Equatorial Guinea. Despite their shared colonial experience, the linguistic situation differs between these countries, affecting the political and academic landscape, which dictates the individual status of local languages and the measures to ensure their study and development.

Five of the countries discussed in this chapter form part of an organization of Portuguese-speaking countries in Africa, also known as PALOP (Países Africanos de Língua Oficial Portuguesa (Officially Portuguese-speaking African Countries)). PALOP was founded in 1992 to create an institutional link between the Portuguese ex-colonies Mozambique, Angola, São Tomé e Príncipe, Guinea-Bissau, and Cabo Verde, based on their shared historical experiences and lusophone language policies. In 2010, the former Spanish colony Equatorial Guinea adopted Portuguese as its official language besides Spanish and French in order to become a member of CPLP (Comunidade dos Países de Língua Portuguesa (Community of Portuguese Language Countries)).

All presently lusophone countries were discovered by Portuguese seafarers during the 1400s and colonized in the subsequent centuries. Until the abolition of slavery in the Portuguese colonies in 1869, the slave trade and slave-based plantation economy were central to the exploitation of the indigenous African peoples by the Portuguese colonizers. While de facto slavery continued to exist under the label 'forced paid labour', the colonies gradually shifted to new economies based on the exploration of natural resources and crops like cocoa and coffee. Despite their growing economic importance, none of the colonies, including Spanish Equatorial Guinea, managed to attract a significant number of settlers from the European motherland (Keese 2007). Only after the Berlin Conference of 1884–1885 demanding 'effective occupation' from

189

the participating nations, a change in policy, accompanied by limited investment in infrastructure and education, can be observed. From 1914 onwards, the Department of Native Affairs classified the indigenous population of Angola, Mozambique, and Guinea into those considered 'assimilated', in terms of language, religion, and customs (*assimilados*), and the 'non-civilized' *indígenas* (Keese 2007; Rocha 2017). As the Portuguese deemed the Africans, their culture and languages to be inferior to their own and hence regarded their mission as one bringing 'civilization' to the locals, the study of local languages and customs was of little importance to colonial administration and education policies. During the 1920s, the use of African languages was altogether banned from schools and Catholic missions, although after some protest, oral language use was declared acceptable (Stroud 2007).

With Salazar's rise to power, the colonies became central to the self-conception of the Estado Novo as a legitimate successor to the former glory of the Portuguese Empire. While the first years of the dictatorship mostly continued previous policies, the global rise of anti-colonial movements and decolonization endeavours after the Second World War enforced a paradigmatic shift in Portuguese colonialism. The ideological backdrop of this new policy was constituted by so-called luso-tropicalism, a concept coined by the cultural anthropologist Gilberto Freyre in describing certain characteristics of multiracial Brazilian society (Rocha 2017). In 1951, the Portuguese colonies were rebranded 'overseas provinces', and their status as fully recognized parts of Portugal was reinforced. Under this umbrella, anthropology, including ethnographical and linguistic studies, started to blossom. During the 1960s, a new institution, the Junta de Investigações do Ultramar (now Instituto de Investigação Científica Tropical), was established in Lisbon to administer and publish research undertaken in the Portuguese colonies. Under the political leadership of Adriano Moreira, Minister of Overseas from 1961 to 1963, the study and recognition of cultural and ethnic diversity was declared a central element of the Portuguese colonial empire and triggered the rise of imminent Portuguese scholars, such as geographer Orlando Ribeiro, the ethnographer Jorge Dias, and the physical anthropologist António de Almeida (Rocha 2017). Notwithstanding the number of scholarly works produced, research on non-European languages and cultures remained firmly in the hands of the colonizers. Africans had only limited access to the educational system, which, until independence, remained underdeveloped and focused on applied studies. Research undertaken by researchers independent from the colonial framework was rare and remained restricted to missionary works and amateur studies receiving little international attention.

The 1960s and 1970s were characterized by the outbreak of wars of independence in Angola, Mozambique, and Guinea-Bissau. While Equatorial Guinea obtained independence from Spain in 1968, the Salazar regime in

Portugal held on to its oversea territories until the peaceful revolution in 1974, which was accompanied by the dissolution of the colonial empire. Immediately after independence, violent civil wars firmly embedded within the geopolitical framework of the Cold War continued to shake Angola and Mozambique, destabilizing both countries with after effects lasting until the present day. Guinea-Bissau and Equatorial Guinea did not suffer a civil war but were subjected to autocratic politicians and frequent regime changes effectively preventing sustainable development, including a modern system of education and independent research institutions. With Portuguese remaining the sole official language in all former colonies, little has been done to study and develop indigenous languages, with Cabo Verde constituting a notable exception. Nevertheless, the institutionalization of African studies, often combined with language planning activities, is progressing in all countries, with relevant works by indigenous scholars being produced almost everywhere. At the same time, international collaboration and a growing economic and social stability provide a promising environment for further development and the strengthening of local institutions and researchers.

In the following sections, I will provide a short overview of the study of African languages in the PALOP countries. Each chapter is divided into two sections, one dealing with the study of African languages during the colonial period, and another outlining the situation after independence, combined with a short assessment of ongoing developments.

10.2   Mozambique

Mozambique is located in south-east Africa, covering a surface area of 801,590 km². It lies on the shores of the Indian Ocean and shares borders with Tanzania, Malawi, Zambia, Zimbabwe, Swaziland, and South Africa (Azevedo 1991). The country is linguistically and ethnically diverse, with the number of languages spoken in Mozambique varying according to the sources used. Estimates count around 20 different Bantu languages belonging to Guthrie's zones G, P, N, and S, plus the country's official language Portuguese and various Asian languages spoken by immigrants. The most widespread language is Makhuwa, which is spoken by approximately 25 per cent of the population, followed by Sena and Changana (c. 12 per cent each) (Lopes 1998).

10.2.1   Colonial Period

Following Vasco da Gama's arrival in 1498, subsequent years saw a continuous spread of trading posts and small settlements all along the coastline of Mozambique. In spite of this development, the presence of Portuguese settlers remained negligible and did not penetrate far inland, thereby effectively limiting the contact between the indigenous Bantu-speaking groups and the colonizers. However, by the end of the nineteenth century, a change in Portuguese overseas policies led to the formation of trading companies and the enforced exploitation of local resources and labour. During the 1950s and 1960s, Portuguese emigration was encouraged, leading to an increase in the European presence in Mozambique which rose to a population count of 200,000 by 1974 (Azevedo 1991).

Owing to the limited importance of Mozambique as a settlement colony for most of its history, educational institutions were established only relatively late and mainly focused on the colonizers (Azevedo 1991). Primary education was almost solely provided by missionary schools, and higher education became available only with the establishment of the country's first university, then called Universidade de Lourenço Marques, in 1962.

Apart from anthropological and linguistic research by scholars acting under the guise of the Junta de Investigações do Ultramar in Lisbon, a small amount of more or less independent research was undertaken in the country itself. The first grammars of local languages were drafted by various missionaries, who came to Mozambique in order to spread the gospel amongst the indigenous population. As early as the seventeenth century, Dominican priests are reported to have written catechisms in Tete and Sena that by now have been lost (Moser 1986). Around the same time, an anonymous Jesuit wrote a description of Sena titled *Arte da lingua de Cafre*, which was translated into German and republished by Schebesta (1919). Additional works from the late nineteenth and early twentieth centuries include António Lourenço Farinha's (1917) *Elementos de gramática landina (shironga): dialecto indigena de Lourenço Marques* and *An Introductory Grammar of the Sena Language* by British missionary W. G. Anderson (1897).

A notable character in the research history of colonial Mozambique is the Portuguese scholar António Rita-Ferreira. Having completed a degree in Bantu studies at the University of Pretoria in South Africa, he entered the colonial service of Mozambique in 1942 and after independence became a professor of precolonial history at the Universidade Eduardo Mondlane in Maputo. Based on his travels around Mozambique during the colonial period, he extensively published about the country's ethnographical landscape (e.g. Rita-Ferreira 1958, 1959, 1975).

10.2.2   After Independence

After the war of independence (1964–1974) that eventually led to the formation of the Republic of Mozambique, the country was drawn into a civil war lasting from 1977 to 1992. As a consequence of the ongoing fighting and social disruption, the establishment of institutions promoting education and scientific research was a slow and tedious process which lasts until today. The country's primary institution of higher education remains the Universidade de Lourenço Marques, which was founded during colonial times and renamed Universidade Eduardo Mondlane in 1976. One of the first academic departments devoted to the study of African cultures became the Centro de Estudos Africanos (Centre of African Studies) with a strong focus on researching and promoting indigenous cultures for the benefit of education and development. The linguistic diversity of Mozambique first featured in the university's curriculum when in 1980, the linguist and later ambassador of Poland in Angola, Eugeniusz Rzewuski, then a professor in Maputo (1977–1983), founded a department dedicated to the study of the country's indigenous languages. This institution, known as Núcleo de Estudos de Línguas Moçambicana (Institute for the Study of Mozambican Languages, NELIMO), was promoted to the status of a research centre in 2000 and describes its mission as 'researching, expanding, teaching and disseminating Mozambican languages'. Right after its establishment, the first aim of the institute became the creation of a comprehensive bibliography of Mozambican Bantu, followed by the collection of expanded glossaries of scientific and technical terms (Lopes 1998). These activities may be seen as predecessors of a growing pressure to introduce Mozambican languages into the educational system. After Portuguese had remained the sole language of education in post-independence Mozambique, the Instituto Nacional de Desenvolvimento da Educaçao (National Institute for Education Development, INDE) collaborated with Stockholm University in establishing a mother tongue education project for the use of Bantu languages in adult education (1992–1997). Subsequently, NELIMO and INDE worked together in describing languages with the aim of creating standardized orthographies and teaching materials, such as manuals, primers, and supplementary readers (Lopes 1998).

The description and standardization of Mozambican languages have also been supported by researchers from the Summer Institute of Linguistics (SIL), linked to the Wycliffe Bible Translation Society, which has been collaborating with Mozambican institutions like the Universidade Eduardo Mondlane since 1986. Their current research activities include work on Mwani, Sena, and Makonde, which is frequently coupled with standardization and alphabetization endeavours (SIL 2017).

10.3 Angola

Located on south-west Africa's Atlantic coast, Angola covers an area of 1,246,700 km² and borders on Namibia, the Democratic Republic of Congo, and Zambia. *Ethnologue* (Simons & Fennig 2017) counts 38 languages, including the official language Portuguese, various Bantu languages from Guthrie's zones H, K, and R, as well as endangered minority languages from the Kx'a and Khoe-Kwadi families. The most widespread Bantu language is Umbundu, spoken by 23 per cent of Angolans, followed by Kikongo (8.24%) and Ibinda (2.9%) (INE 2014).

10.3.1   Colonial Period

Angola was first reached by explorer Diogo Cão in 1482; in subsequent centuries it became gradually colonized by the Portuguese. The first settlement was established in 1575 in modern-day Luanda, followed by others along the coastline and, by the eighteenth century, also in the country's interior. For most of its colonial history, settlements and infrastructure in Angola were poorly developed and did not attract many colonists, despite the country's growing importance as a supplier of slaves (Broadhead 1992). Although the end of the nineteenth century saw an attempt to exploit other resources, it was not until after the Berlin Conference (1884–1885) that the Portuguese occupation became more organized and aimed at attracting settlers from the European motherland (Broadhead 1992). Angola counted 350,000 Portuguese after the war of independence had started in 1961, mostly due to Portugal's attempt to maintain its colonies by increased investment in development and infrastructure, and by a growing presence of militaries and civil servants (Bender & Yoder 1974; Bender 1978).

New efforts to attract people to Africa also included the formation of institutions of higher education during the 1960s. In 1962, a University of General Studies was founded in Luanda (Pimenta 2014); however, it was not authorized to hand out degrees until 1968, when it obtained the status of a university and was subsequently renamed the University of Luanda. During its brief existence in a colonial framework, courses offered at the university mostly focused on applied studies such as medicine, teaching, and engineering, with research remaining a privilege of institutions from Portugal. Academic research on the peoples and languages of Angola was carried out by the *Junta de Investigações do Ultramar* in Lisbon. Among the scholars producing linguistic and ethnographic descriptions for the Portuguese colonial authorities, the physical anthropologist António de Almeida (see, e.g. 1994, for a collection of articles) is notable for his survey undertaken during the 1950s, which included many understudied minority groups of southern Angola. Almeida also collaborated with the South African linguist Ernst O. J. Westphal, who left a wealth of recordings and field notes on Bantu, Kx'a, and Khoe-Kwadi languages now held at the archives of the University of Cape Town (www.digitalcollections .lib.uct.ac.za/ernst-westphal-san-languages).

Unlike colonial policies focusing on acculturation and a fostering of the Portuguese language, rather than the study and development of indigenous languages, the church – in particular Jesuit missionaries – displayed a big interest in documenting and writing Angolan Bantu languages of wider communication for preaching the gospel. The earliest works in a Bantu language of the area were two catechisms in Kikongo, written by Gaspar da Conceição (1555) and Mateus Cardoso (1624); later, a grammar of Kimbundu was published as *Arte de gramática da língua de Angola* by the Brazilian Jesuit Pedro Dias in 1697 (Zwartjes 2011).

Descriptions from cultural anthropology not incorporated into the administrative framework of Portuguese colonial studies are hard to come by. The German missionary Karl 'Carlos' Estermann (1896–1976) lived and worked in south-western Angola from 1924 to his death and devoted his time to the ethnographic documentation of the peoples of the area, among them !Xun, Kwepe (Kwadi), the Bantu-speaking foragers known as Kwisi and Twa, as well as all major Southwest Bantu groups from Angola (Kuvale, Herero, Ambo, Nyaneka-Nkhumbi). Although his major work, the *Etnografia do Sudoeste de Angola* (Ethnography of Southwestern Angola) in three volumes (Estermann 1956, 1961a, 1961b) was published under the umbrella of the Junta de Investigações do Ultramar, it can be considered an independent work based in Angola, rather than in Portugal.

Another important character is José Redinha (1905–1983) who came to Angola as a civil servant in 1927 and subsequently shifted to the national diamond company Diamang in the Lunda region. From 1936 to 1946, he travelled about 15,000 km during various expeditions for territorial, ethnic, and cultural recognition, collecting more than 20,000 ethnographical artefacts. His work centred on the Lunda-Chokwe, of whom he became an honorable *soba* (traditional leader) in 1938. Redinha acted as a director of the museum of Angola (1959–1961) and later as a researcher of the Instituto de Investigacao Científica de Angola, a local branch of the Junta de Investigações do Ultramar (1961–1970). After independence, he remained in Angola and became a consultant ethnologist for the Ministry of Education and Culture (1979–1983). His best-known book, *Distribuição étnica de Angola*, was first published in 1962 and has since been reprinted multiple times.

10.3.2 After Independence

The Angolan educational and scientific system was established as part of the infrastructure reforms undertaken by Portuguese colonial authorities during the war of independence (1961–1975), and was expanded and adapted to the new social and administrative realities of an independent state during the civil war (1975–2002). The main institution of higher education remained the University of Luanda, which was first renamed University of Angola, and in 1985 became Universidade Agostinho Neto. During the 1980s, various other institutions with a focus on teacher training were founded throughout the country, with the Instituto Superior de Ciências da Educação (Higher Institute for Educational Studies, ISCED) in Luanda being of particular importance to the emergence of African linguistics in Angola.

However, in the years following independence, the study of the languages of Angola was not undertaken at university level but remained in the hands of the Instituto Nacional de Línguas (National Institute of Languages), which was founded in 1976. The institute devoted its limited capacities to the applied study of the six national languages with the widest distribution (Kikongo, Chokwe, Umbundu, Kimbundu, Ganguela, Kwanyama), culminating in the creation of orthographies first released in 1980. Only after the civil war, in 2004, was the first department of African languages and linguistics established at an institution of higher education, ISCED, under the label Departamento de línguas e literaturas africanas (Department of African languages and literature).

The relatively late interest in African languages in post-independence Angola is of course explained by the disastrous impact of the long-lasting civil war on Angolan society, but also by the limited importance of regional languages for governance and education, compared to other lusophone countries in Africa. Irrespective of their ethnic identities, more than 70 per cent of Angolans speak and understand Portuguese, 39 per cent even consider it their mother tongue (INE 2014). The study and development of indigenous languages, especially for educational purposes, was therefore not given priority until after the war. Recently, in the constitution of 2010, the 'study, teaching and use of other Angolan languages' has been promoted, along with the goal to 'protect, value and dignify Angolan languages of African origin' (UNICEF 2016). The Departamento de línguas e literaturas Africanas, along with other institutions offering training for teachers, is considered instrumental in implementing these policies, as it focuses on both the study and the teaching of the national languages. With the help of Pearson Education, a British publishing service, textbooks have been published in seven Angolan Bantu languages, and mother tongue education projects have been established throughout the country (UNICEF 2016).

Within academia, one of the main personalities promoting research on Angolan languages is Zavoni Ntondo, now a professor at ISCED and the Universidade Agostinho Neto, who has published on various Angolan Bantu languages (e.g. Ntondo 2006, 2015). ISCED-Luanda as well as other academic institutions of Angola also entertain a range of partnerships with researchers and institutions from all over the world. In the field of African studies, recent collaborations include SIL (e.g. Jordan 2016), as well as a TwinLab between ISCED-Huíla in Lubango and CIBIO/InBIO: Research Centre in Biodiversity and Genetic Resources in Vairão, Portugal (e.g. Pinto et al. 2016). Both research collaborations include projects focusing on understudied pastoral and foraging communities from south-western Angola and involve local researchers as well as international scholars from Europe and the United States.

10.4 São Tomé e Príncipe

The two islands forming the Democratic Republic of São Tomé and Príncipe are located about 300 km off the coast of Gabon and together cover an area of 1,001 km². Apart from the country's official language, Portuguese, which is spoken by the entire population, *Ethnologue* (Simons & Fennig 2017) lists three Portuguese-based creole languages which, together with Fa d'Ambô spoken in Equatorial Guinea, form the so-called Gulf of Guinea creoles (Hagemeijer 2011): Santome (São-Tomense, Forro), Angolar (Ngola, Lunga Ngola), and Principense (Lung'ie). While Santome and Angolar are both vigorous, Principense is considered moribund (Maurer 2009). In addition to the indigenous creole languages, Cabo Verdean Creole was introduced on the islands by immigrants (Nascimento 2003).

10.4.1 Colonial Period

After their discovery by Portuguese sailors in 1471–1472, the instalment of a plantation complex based on sugarcane led to the previously uninhabited islands becoming populated by slaves from the West African mainland. When the sugar economy declined in the sixteenth century, São Tomé and Príncipe turned into hardly more than a transit point for the slave trade exporting West Africans to the New World. By the nineteenth century, the introduction of new cash crops, namely coffee and cocoa, led to a renewed colonization of the islands, accompanied by an economic boom (Tenreiro 1961). A revolt of forced laborers leading to the massacre of Batepá in 1953 constituted a turning point in the country's history, giving rise to a new nationalist movement which ultimately led to its independence in 1975 (Seibert 2001).

Despite various attempts to instigate European settlement, the Portuguese were always a minority in the archipelago. Recent studies from molecular anthropology have shown that their contribution to the gene pool of the islands is, in fact, less than 10 per cent (Tomás et al. 2002). While it was possible for non-Europeans, especially for the admixed 'crioulos', to obtain a limited amount of education and hold minor positions within the colonial administration, the educational system and infrastructure of São Tomé and Príncipe itself was severely underdeveloped, with higher education being possible in Portugal only (Seibert 2001).

The peoples and languages of the archipelago received only limited scientific attention during colonial times. While the existence of creolized varieties of Portuguese was mentioned from the seventeenth century onwards, written testimonies appear only in the second half of the nineteenth century, especially in the works of São Tomean writers Fransisco Stockler and Almada Negreiros (Negreiros 1895; Araújo & Hagemeijer 2013). The first linguistic descriptions of the Gulf of Guinea Creoles were provided by the creolists

Schuchardt (1882, 1889) and Coelho (1880–1886). Santome was first used as a literary language by São Tomean writer Francisco de Jesus Bonfim, also known as Faxicu Bêbê Zaua, who from the 1920s onwards wrote texts for the journal *A Liberdade* and various pamphlets (Araújo & Hagemeijer 2013).

The Portuguese anthropologist António de Almeida (1956, 1962), best known for his work on Angola, also undertook an expedition to São Tomé in order to study the Angolar-speakers whose language has an unusually high proportion of Bantu words (Maurer 2009). This observation was linked to the popular belief that they were the descendants of the wreck of a slave ship from Angola just off the south-eastern shore of São Tomé around 1540–1550 (Seibert 2007). Their history has since received much attention, including a recent study from human genetics which confirms their genetic distinctiveness (Coelho et al. 2008).

10.4.2 After Independence

São Tomé and Príncipe gained independence from Portugal in 1975 and, until 1990, was a socialist one-party state. Owing to the decline of the plantation system and the slow development of new economic sectors, the investment in education and infrastructure remained limited. An institution of higher education, the Instituto Superior Politécnico (Polytechnical Institute) was founded on the island of São Tomé in 1994 and only reached the status of a university in 2014. To date, no information on the availability of a department of African linguistics or related courses could be obtained.

As the official language Portuguese is universally spoken in the archipelago, few language planning activities have been undertaken with regard to the country's minority languages. While a growing corpus of linguistic works on the Gulf of Guinea Creoles produced in Portugal, Brazil, and elsewhere has become available (e.g. Ferraz 1974, 1975, 1979; Hagemeijer 2003, 2007, 2011, and others), only a small set of language materials to be used in mother tongue education or language revitalization has been created. Based on experiences made in the Latin American context (Araújo & Agostinho 2010), linguists from Brazil and Europe have made propositions for the standardization of the country's related creole languages, including a standard orthography, Alfabeto Unificado para a Escrita das Línguas Nativas de S. Tomé e Príncipe (Unified Alphabet for Writing the Native Languages of S. Tomé and Príncipe, ALUSTP), which was approved by the government in 2013. There are publications using it (e.g. Araújo & Hagemeijer 2013), and further materials to be used in teaching the languages and training teachers are in preparation (see, e.g. Araújo & Agostinho 2010; Agostinho et al. 2016). At present, some attempts to revitalize Principense are under way, currently involving eight teachers who meet regularly to establish a preliminary curriculum for teaching youngsters, albeit without considering the standard orthography and with no official teaching materials at hand (Agostinho et al. 2016).

10.5   Guinea-Bissau

Covering a surface of 36,125 km², Guinea-Bissau is delimited by the Atlantic Ocean to the West, by Senegal to the north, and by Guinea to the east and south. Apart from the country's official language, Portuguese, *Ethnologue* (Simons & Fennig 2017) lists 22 African languages, most of which can be classified as belonging to either the Atlantic or the Mande subfamilies of Niger Congo. None of these languages is spoken by a substantial part of the population, rendering the Portuguese-based Crioulo spoken by more than 80 per cent of Bissau-Guineans the most important language of inter-ethnic communication (Kohl 2011).

10.5.1   Colonial Period

Guinea-Bissau was discovered in 1446, and in 1588 the first Portuguese settlement was established. Despite the country's importance for the Portuguese slave trade and accompanying presence of traders, officials, and militaries, it never became a settlement colony. African empires like Mali and Gabu gained control of parts of Guinea-Bissau without Portuguese intervention, and only during the first half of the twentieth century, did the European motherland establish full administrative and military control over the country (Eínarsdóttir 2013).

During the final decades of Portuguese colonialism, the ethnic and linguistic heterogeneity of Guinea-Bissau attracted a limited amount of scholarly research, albeit closely monitored by the colonial authorities. In 1945, the governor of the colony, Sarmento Rodrigues, launched the *Boletim Cultural da Guiné Portuguesa* (Cultural Bulletin of Portuguese Guinea), a journal that reached 110 volumes from 1946 to 1973 and thereby became the major bulletin of cultural sciences in the Portuguese colonies. The journal was published by the Centro de Estudos da Guiné Portuguesa (Centre for the Studies of Portuguese Guinea) located in the capital Bissau and featured articles from various fields, ranging from agriculture to cultural anthropology and linguistics. All volumes have been digitized and can be assessed online (http://memoria-africa.ua.pt /Library/BCGP.aspx).

Politically, no measures were undertaken to strengthen or develop the indigenous languages of Guinea-Bissau. Crioulo, in particular, was suppressed by the colonial authorities who feared its potential as an African lingua franca uniting the multilingual ethnic landscape. However, with infrastructural development taking place from the 1920s onwards, it rapidly spread to the urban centres and ultimately became the language of the anti-colonial movement (Kohl 2011).

10.5.2   After Independence

In 1956, a party uniting the independence movements from Cabo Verde and Guinea-Bissau was established under Amílcar Cabral, leading to the liberation war, which started in 1963 and ended with the independence of Guinea-Bissau in 1974. After a brief period during which the same party ruled both countries, they separated in 1980. Since then, Guinea-Bissau has been characterized by political instability, involving a series of successful and attempted coups, which culminated in the war of 1998–1999 (Kohl 2011). After several attempts to return to constitutional rule, yet another *coup d'état* in 2012 resulted in an internationally non-recognized military government (Eínarsdóttir 2013).

   The political upheavals following independence did not allow for the establishment of a modern educational and scientific framework. In 1999, the first public institution of higher education named Universidade Amílcar Cabral was established in the capital Bissau; after a brief period in which the university operated under the umbrella of the Portuguese-based 'Lusófona' group, it was closed, restructured, and reopened in 2010 in collaboration with a Brazilian institution. In addition to the Universidade Amílcar Cabral, there are several private institutions of higher education offering courses (e.g. Universidade Lusófona da Guiné, Universidade Colinas de Boé) (Sanhá 2010), but the study of the country's many African languages does not appear to feature prominently in their curriculum.

   The only language of Guinea-Bissau that has received attention from international researchers, combined with some minor attempts at language planning, is the Crioulo or Bissau-Guinean Creole. The language is attested in the country from at least the sixteenth century and shares a common ancestor with the Crioulo dialects of Cabo Verde where it most likely emerged before being spread to the mainland by immigrants (Jacobs 2010). It has been the subject of a number of publications dealing with aspects of its grammar (e.g. Wilson 1962; Couto 1994) and lexicon (Rougé 1988; Nicoleti 2012), with the Italian missionary Luigi Scantamburlo (e.g. 1981) acting as a major proponent of research on the language in Guinea-Bissau itself. Although Guinea-Bissau has a language policy focusing on Portuguese as sole language of administration and instruction (Cá 2015), some attempts were made to introduce Crioulo, the country's most widespread lingua franca, into the educational system. The Ministry of Education of Guinea-Bissau in cooperation with Dutch and Portuguese institutions launched an experimental project (1987–1997) for the use of Crioulo as the medium of instruction for the first two grades (Hovens 2002:253). Along similar lines, the aforementioned Luigi Scantamburlo started a bilingual teaching project in the Bijagós archipelago (Cá 2015). An overview of ongoing projects using Crioulo as a language of instruction is provided by Martins et al. (2016). Incanha Intumbo, a mother tongue speaker of Crioulo and student of Scantamburlo is currently working at the University of Coimbra in Portugal and has published on his language (e.g. Intumbo 2006).

10.6   Cabo Verde

Cabo Verde, also referred to under the English designation Cape Verde, is an archipelago consisting of ten volcanic islands located 570 km off the coast of West Africa measuring 4,033km^2 in total. Virtually the entire population speaks Cabo Verdean Creole (or Crioulo) as their mother tongue, and Portuguese – the country's official language – as a second language (Simons & Fennig 2017).

10.6.1   Colonial Period

When they were discovered in 1456, all the islands were completely uninhabited. After the establishment of the first settlement at Ribeira Grande (now Cidade Velha) in 1462, Cabo Verde became an important intermediary in the Atlantic slave trade during the sixteenth and seventeenth centuries. The islands attracted merchants, plantation owners, and pirates who gradually admixed with the country's slave population consisting mainly of West Africans. In the sixteenth century, a creole language using Portuguese as lexifier emerged on the island of Santiago and gradually spread to the other islands and to the African mainland to what is now Guinea-Bissau (Carreira 2000:268).

During the nineteenth century, Portugal increased administrative control in the islands and began establishing an institutionalized system of education, including several primary schools, and, in 1866, the Seminary-High School of São Nicolau (Ferreira 1974). Portuguese was, in the beginning, the language of education only for a small part of the population. However, Crioulo gradually became relegated to informal domains, a situation that has effectively lasted until the present day.

As the Portuguese colonial policy became more concerned with the 'assimilation' of the locals in the occupied territories, the devaluation of their native languages and culture accompanied the movement. When the Portuguese linguist Francisco Adolfo Coelho published the first description of the creole of Cabo Verde (Coelho 1880–1886), he called it 'broken Portuguese'. This interpretation persisted throughout colonial times (see also Lyall 1938), and it was not until the study of the local linguist and poet Baltasar Lopes da Silva (1957) that Crioulo began to be perceived as a language in its own right, governed by rules quite distinct from Portuguese.

During the times of the Estado Novo, the number of educational institutions in the country increased. Primary school enrolment quadrupled from 1960 to

1970 (Meintel 1984), and technical schools were introduced, albeit with an almost exclusive focus on agriculture (Ferreira 1974). At the same time, the use of Crioulo in writing and education, as well as in government buildings, was strictly forbidden (Lobban 1995). Intriguingly, the stigmatization of the language during the colonization period did not prevent the rise of Crioulo to a language of music, literature, and poetry. Crioulo-speaking intellectuals like Jorge Barbosa (1902–1971), Eugénio Tavares (1867–1930), and the aforementioned Baltasar Lopes da Silva (1907–1989) created an impressive corpus of written literature in their mother tongue that defied the prohibition of the colonial authorities. During the 1960s, the use of Crioulo also became an important marker of the anti-colonialist movement led by Amílcal Cabral.

10.6.2   After Independence

Cabo Verde became independent in 1975 and entered a period referred to as *Primeira República* (First Republic), which lasted until 1990. Although Portuguese remained the country's official language, there is a strong movement of people supporting the promotion of Crioulo to the status of a co-official language. As a first step towards this goal, linguists of Cabo Verdean origin attended a colloquium held by the Direcção Geral da Cultura (Administration of Culture) in 1979 to work on the development of a unified orthography (Veiga et al. 2000). This orthography was subsequently used by some writers but did not become unanimously accepted, mostly due to dialectal differences in spoken Crioulo which speakers found difficult to unite in a single set of orthographic rules (Duarte 1998). Despite these persisting problems in standardizing the language, a group of linguists headed by Manuel Veiga (b. 1948) keep fighting for the use of Crioulo in official contexts and as a language of instruction in schools and institutions of higher education. In 1994, a new orthography was created based on the 1979 version and became known as ALUPEC (Alfabeto Unificado para a Escrita do Cabo-Verdiano (Unified Alphabet for writing Cabo Verdean)). ALUPEC was approved in 1998 and recognized by the government in 2005. Nevertheless, like its predecessor, it never managed to satisfy all speakers and to this date is neither official nor mandatory.

The comparatively large number of trained linguists with a Cabo Verdean background may seem surprising considering the country's lack of a university, let alone a department of linguistics, until the formation of the Instituto Superior de Educação (ISE) in 1995. However, it has to be kept in mind that the majority of Cabo Verdeans live in the diaspora and many scholars active in the debate actually received their training in Portugal, France, the United States, or Brazil. In consequence, there is a considerable corpus of linguistic descriptions, sociolinguistic treatments, and dictionaries on varieties of Crioulo from Cabo Verdean linguists, only a small subset of which can be quoted in this paper (e.g. Cardoso 1989; Veiga 1996, 2000, 2002; Mendes et al. 2002; Delgado 2008).

Making use of these works, the Universidade de Cabo Verde, founded in 2006 as a union of smaller institutions of higher education such as ISE, offers a comprehensive course titled Línguas, Literaturas e Culturas – Estudos Cabo-Verdianos e Portugueses (Languages, Literature, and Culture – Cabo Verdean and Portuguese Studies), which combines Portuguese and Cabo Verdean Linguistics with an overview of the rich literary tradition available in both languages.

10.7   Equatorial Guinea

The Republic of Equatorial Guinea covers an area of 28,051 km^2 and is composed of Río Muni on the West African mainland and several islands in the Gulf of Guinea, including Bioko (formerly Fernando Po), Annóbon, and Corisco (Serrano 2016). The country is culturally and linguistically diverse (Simons & Fennig 2017), being home to ten Bantu languages from Guthrie's zones A and B, plus two creole languages (Fa d'Ambô and Equatorial Guinean Pidigin). In addition, Spanish, French, and Portuguese hold official status, but only Spanish is used as an actual lingua franca. The two most widely used African languages are Fang (by c. 80 per cent of the population) and Bube (Johnson 2013).

10.7.1   Colonial Period

Equatorial Guinea was discovered in 1471 by the Portuguese explorer Fernando Po and formally belonged to Portugal until it was traded to Spain in 1778, becoming the country's sole sub-Saharan African colony (Johnson 2013). Spanish colonization effectively started from the mid-nineteenth century onwards (Lipski 2004) and mostly focused on the production of palm oil, cocoa, coffee, and timber (Serrano 2016). Spanish became the exclusive language of the colony and was used as a language of administration in government schools and by the Claretian missionaries (Lipski 2004; Castillo-Rodríguez 2014). The Claretians began their mission work in Equatorial Guinea in 1883 and, from 1903 to 1947, published a bimonthly journal entitled *La Guinea Española* which frequently featured articles on the right instruction of the natives in the Spanish language. One section, 'About the Black Race', regularly dealt with indigenous cultures and languages, but there was no actual interest in studying the latter for the purpose of mother tongue education. When, by 1920, three Equatorial Guineans asked for permission to teach in public schools, they were turned down, as it was believed that they did not have the competence to teach in Spanish (Castillo-Rodríguez 2014).

However, other missionaries were less hostile towards the indigenous languages and created detailed descriptions and teaching materials (Bolekia Boleká 1988). The Baptist missionary John Clarke lived on Bioko (then Fernando Po) from 1840 to 1843 and wrote the first description of Bube. His work was followed by that of the Methodist missionary William N. Barleycorn, who was himself of Equatorial Guinean descent and in 1875 created the first Bube primer *Bubi na English*. The first work in Castilian, the *Primer paso a la lengua bubi*, was authored by Joaquín Juanola in 1890 (Bolekia Boleká 1988), and during the 1920s, several linguistic works about the lexicon and grammar of the Bube language were published in Spanish (e.g. Aymemí 1928; Abad 1928). Other works that appeared during the colonial period include descriptions of Fang (e.g. Aranzadi 1962) and the Portuguese-based creole of Annóbon, Fa d'Ambô (e.g. Barrena 1957, 1965).

10.7.2   After Independence

Owing to growing pressure from within and outside the country, Equatorial Guinea reached independence in 1968. A democratic constitution was drafted but was discarded after Francisco Macias Nguema turned the country into an autocratic one-party state lasting from 1970 to 1979. During his reign, infrastructure and economy declined, education practically ceased, and one-third of the entire population was killed (Johnson 2013). The ruling elite also tried to prohibit Spanish and promote Fang as the national language (Lipski 2004), but the new language policy never became implemented. Despite some democratization attempts and the legalization of political parties in the 1990s, the country remains in the hands of the Nguema family who, after the discovery of oil reserves in 1996, struck a deal with influential oil companies from Europe and the United States (Johnson 2013; Serrano 2016). This led to a growing importance of English, which became a preliminary for obtaining a good job in the oil industry (Johnson 2013). In consequence, the teaching of languages within the Universidad Nacional de Guinea Ecuatorial (established in 1995) is more focused on the acquisition of European languages of wider communication than on the study of the indigenous African languages (Johnson 2013). Despite a lack of actual speakers, Portuguese was elevated to the status of an official language in 2010 to enable Equatorial Guinea to become a member of CPLP.

The Agencia Española de Cooperación Internacional (Spanish Agency for International Cooperation) is supporting the local cultural scene through the Centro Cultural de España en Malabo (Spanish Cultural Centre in Malabo) and the Centro Cultural de España en Bata (Spanish Cultural Centre in Bata), established in 1982 as Centro Cultural Hispano-Guineano (Hispanic-Guinean Cultural Centre). The organization further publishes the quarterly magazine *África 2000* and the monthly magazine *El Patio*, both of which feature works from local writers. Among the Equatorial Guinean intellectuals and scholars working abroad, Justo Bolekia Boleká (b. 1954), from the University of Salamanca, is noteworthy for his poetry, essays, and linguistic work on his native language Bube (e.g. Bolekia Boleká 1988, 1991).

11 African Linguistics in the Americas

G. Tucker Childs and Margarida Petter

11.1 African Linguistics in North America (G. Tucker Childs)

11.1.1 Introduction

North American[1] scholarship on African languages has never achieved the same intensity and breadth of research found in Europe, where the interest in African languages is long-standing and extensive. The reasons for these differences are historical and ideological, and perhaps institutional. However, there was a period after the Second World War and African independence when the United States became the hub of (African) linguistics, attracting a fair number of expatriate scholars and students from Africa. In those days, *Studies in African Linguistics* (*SAL*) was considered the major journal in the field, and the Annual Conference of African Linguistics (ACAL) was *the* African linguistics conference to attend. Leading universities were, for instance, UCLA, Indiana, Illinois, Wisconsin, and UQAM. In recent years, African linguistics has seen a decline, including the closing down of many teaching programmes for African languages. Nonetheless, North American scholarship maintains a prominence in the field, particularly on the formal-theoretical side. This work, however, has a focus that is different from purely descriptive work, often relying on second-hand accounts rather than original fieldwork, but it has nonetheless served as an important impetus for the study of African languages and linguistics.

In terms of historical explanations for the differences, neither the United States nor Canada has ever had any African colonies, except for the rather unusual relationship that the United States has had with Liberia. Moreover, since the nineteenth century American linguists have been preoccupied with the description of disappearing Native American languages, having shown little interest in languages beyond their shores.

---

[1] 'North American' will be used as a term referring to Canada and the United States; 'America(n)' will refer only to the United States. My thanks to many Canadian colleagues, in particular, Bruce Connell, Doug Pulleyblank, and Sharon Rose, for their assistance on this paper, especially with the section on Canadian research projects in section 11.2.3.4.

In the middle of the twentieth century, however, descriptive work was eschewed or even abandoned in favour of linguistic 'theory', primarily formal issues arising with the advent and eventual dominance of the generative paradigm. Only recently has the pendulum swung back to more descriptive work with the awareness that we will soon lose many of the world's languages. Study in Africa is also characterized by this generalization, and the subsequent availability of funding for the documentation of endangered languages has promoted scholarship. These mood swings have had implications for the study of African languages, but just as importantly African languages have had a significant impact on linguistic theory and linguistic thinking.

My purpose in what follows is to characterize the scholarly research on African languages in North America, understood to include both the United States and Canada. Because neither of these countries had any African colonies, there was no felt need on the governmental level to study African languages. This was true for the Americans until the advent of the Cold War and the launching of Sputnik in 1958, yet Africa persists in representing a low priority compared to other areas of the world.

The key factor that puts North America far behind Europe in terms of the breadth and longevity of European research on African languages is the lack of a colonial history, pointed out above. Canada also has nothing close to such a history, being a colony itself for many years and today still part of the British Commonwealth. American colonial interests ranged southward to the Caribbean and Central America, and eastward to the Pacific. Africa posed no great attraction to North Americans, least of all the Canadians, and had already been divided up by the Europeans with colonial domains well established early on. The closest thing the United States has to a colony is Liberia, a small country on the coast of West Africa.

Liberia was the site of a back-to-Africa colony, a number of neocolonial enterprises, notably the Firestone Rubber Company, and a sizeable military outpost. Consequently, Liberia has been the site for much important research by Americans on African languages. The small country features the convergence of three important language families Atlantic (Mel (Childs, forthcoming-a)), Mande, and Kru, all typologically distinct groups, and has been the object of intense missionary work. The special relationship between Liberia and the United States illustrates how self-interest at the state level would historically guide the study of African languages. It led to the highest concentration of missionaries and Peace Corps on the African continent in Liberia, an important fact for the study of African languages. It was also the site of much American intelligence gathering for Africa as a whole. It is these same strands, the intelligence community (IC) and by extension the American government, Christian missions, Peace Corps, and numerous research initiatives that form the brand of North American scholarship on African languages throughout the continent.

Mainstream North American linguistics, however, continued to be relatively uninterested in Africa until recently, being preoccupied either with the native languages of North America or with the formal side of linguistic theory. African languages became of some interest when they proved relevant to linguistic theory, exhibiting features that caused theoreticians to reformulate their thinking. Interest was further stimulated when funding became available for the documentation of endangered languages. These two relatively recent developments have created the current state of North American scholarship on the academic side. Missionaries, however, have been more constant in their attentions, although that work has changed to converge with an academic focus as missionaries, too, focused on literacy, language documentation, and linguistic analysis.

The separate strands of African linguistics in North America are here briefly characterized in roughly chronological order, beginning with missionary work that continues to this day. Motivation for the study of African languages has ranged from Bible translation to the recent concern with saving dying languages. Nonetheless, the study of African languages in North America pales beside what has been done and what is being done in Europe.

11.1.2   The Missionaries

The role of Christian missionaries in the study of African languages is considerable (Welmers 1971) but relatively focused with regard to linguistics until recently. Their first forays were limited to learning enough of the local languages to convert non-believers and translate the Bible into local languages. The missionary effort of at least SIL International (SIL),[2] the major North American organization, has expanded its focus. SIL has now been realigned to deal with literacy and the documentation of endangered languages, as can be seen in the following blurb from their website (www.sil.org/).

SIL International is a faith-based nonprofit organization committed to serving language communities worldwide as they build capacity for sustainable language development. SIL does this primarily through research, translation, training and materials development. SIL works alongside ethnolinguistic communities and their partners as they discover how language development addresses the challenging areas of their daily lives – social, cultural, political, economic and spiritual.

SIL has recently sought to monetize its products, e.g. limiting the number of free views of *Ethnologue* (www.ethnologue.com), their compendium of the

---

[2] The organization was formerly known as the Summer Institute of Linguistics; it originated as a summer training programme in Arkansas in 1934 (www.sil.org/about/history, accessed 28 December 2016).

world's languages (Lewis et al. 2015), much to the dismay of at least the Africanist community. This was not the case in the past, when SIL freely shared their expertise and technology. *Ethnologue* has indeed served as the standard reference for languages of the world for the past 60 years. Nonetheless, the contribution to scholarship on African languages by SIL and other missionary organizations has been considerable. Many prominent linguists in both the United States and Canada have a former or ongoing SIL relationship.

Founded in 1934 and led for many years by Kenneth Pike (see below for some of his contributions to African linguistics), SIL has trained many fine linguists of African languages, a great number of whom have contributed significantly to the field in terms of both support and individual scholarship. Nonetheless, there is some unease between missionaries and their non-missionary counterparts, both American and African linguists specializing in African languages. For example, a recent conference on African languages was relocated from the University of Texas at Arlington, a center for SIL training, because of objections from the conference membership. Nonetheless, linguists have long been dependent on missionaries for support, especially when in a country where missionaries have an established presence that will continue far longer than the linguist's (see Dobrin & Good 2009). SIL has been important in terms of field technology, developing and sharing software useful in analysing languages and developing language products. An excellent summary and review of the complicated politics of missionary work can be found in Gilmour (2007); some questions as to the future of missionary work are raised in Peterson and Allman (1999). I turn now to some representative contributions by North American missionary-oriented linguists in the past and present.

Kenneth Pike, a leader of SIL as mentioned above, was a pioneer in developing field methodology. Although Pike's work did not concentrate on African languages, except for some work in Nigeria, his work was crucial in identifying the phonemic importance of tone (Pike 1948). Similarly, William Welmers had missionary ties and was probably the most accomplished field worker of his time, producing many first descriptions of African languages beginning with his dissertation (1946).[3] His work in Africa began in Liberia where he did work for the Lutheran Mission. He also trained many Africanists during his time at UCLA (two of whom later joined the faculty). His magnum opus, *African Language Structures*, where he recorded many of his personal experiences and discoveries in deciphering African languages, long served as an introduction to African languages (Welmers 1973).

---

[3] His primary consultant was Mr Francis N.-K. (Kwame) Nkrumah, a leader of the independence movement in Ghana and its first head of state in 1957; his Penn dissertation was supervised by Zellig Harris, who also oversaw the studies of Noam Chomsky.

Although I have focused on SIL, there are other missionary groups that deserve mention with regard to work on African languages: the affiliated Wycliffe Bible Translators, the Lutheran Bible Translators (LBT), Pioneer Bible Translators, and United Bible Societies (UBS). For example, William J. Samarin, now an emeritus professor at the University of Toronto, is a Pentecostal preacher, whose work in central Africa involved both preaching and linguistics. His work goes back to Samarin (1950)[4] and begins a long history of work on African languages. Samarin is well known for his work on Gbaya and Sango (Samarin 1966, 1967a), as well as for a fieldwork guide (Samarin 1967b) that for many years served as a standard in the field.

Current linguists associated with missionary work have produced important research on African languages and hale from both Canada and the United States, for example, Lynell Marchese Zogbo (on Kru), Doris Payne (Nilotic), John R. Watters (Bantu). More recent work based on African languages, specifically vowel harmony, comes from Miles Leitch and Rod Casali (e.g. Leitch 1997 and Casali 2008), while important work on tone and labialvelars comes from Mike Cahill, the head of research for SIL (e.g. Cahill 2017). Relatively recent publications consisting of full grammars are Stanley (1991), Carlson (1994), Hopkins (1995), Van Otterloo and Van Otterloo (2011), and Nicolle (2014), all of which contain rich descriptions and firm grounding in linguistic theory.

Another source of support has been the governments of both Canada and the United States. As with contributions to foreign aid, Canada on a per capita basis far outstrips its southern neighbour in terms of both interest and measurable scholarship.

11.1.3   Governmental Entities

This section looks at support that has emanated from the Canadian and American governments. The support varies as to nationality both quantitatively and qualitatively. In Canada, generally speaking, support has been given to major research projects, following the European model. In America it has been given to individuals. Research in Canada has been more focused and involved groups of scholars. In the United States the support has typically been more diffuse with the study of African languages often relegated to secondary importance in pursuit of some larger goal or associated end. I start with some American institutions.

---

[4] See https://tspace.library.utoronto.ca/handle/1807/67119 for a complete listing (accessed 27 December 2016).

11.1.3.1 The Foreign Service, Fulbright Fellowships

The Foreign Service has played a role in fostering research on African languages through its Language Studies training division. Its language manuals for some of the major languages of Africa (Amharic, Chinyanja, Fula, Hausa, Igbo, Kirundi, Kituba, Lingala, Luganda, Moré, Swahili, Twi, Yoruba) sometimes represented the only research and descriptive work done on an African language. In 1958, however, the study of African languages received a considerable impetus, as part of the reaction to the Soviet Union's successful launch of Sputnik. A number of 'National Resource' (Title VI) centres were established around the United States. An important aspect of all of these centres was a focus on the learning of foreign languages, a concentration that was sorely lacking in the American educational system. Support was specifically dedicated to research abroad, including Africa.

Another contribution to the study of African languages is the Fulbright-Hays Program in the United States Department of Education. Although limited, their awards have been important for researchers on African languages in terms of international exchange.

11.1.3.2 National Resource Centres

Title VI programmes in the US Department of Education[5] have supported area studies in the United States. Because there are generally no academic lines directly associated with these centres, scholars come from various academic departments around the campus to which their first allegiances are paid. There is nothing like the Africa-oriented centres of European scholarship specializing in African studies, such as the School of Oriental and African Studies (SOAS) at the University of London, and Langage, Langues et Cultures d'Afrique (LLACAN), and Langues et Civilisations à Tradition Orale (LACITO), both affiliated with the Centre National de Recherche Scientifique (CNRS) in Paris, or the various centres of *Afrikanistik* in Germany. Area studies come second to disciplinary studies in the American academic scene.

The brief of the National Resource Centres is to provide the following for both graduate and undergraduate students:

- instruction in fields and topics that provide full understanding of areas, regions, or countries;
- research and training in international studies;
- work in the language aspects of professional fields and research;
- instruction and research on issues critical to current world affairs.[6]

---

[5] Officially International Education Programs Service, Title VI Programs: Building a US International Education Infrastructure, www2.ed.gov/about/offices/list/ope/iegps/title-six.html?exp=6 (accessed 1 April 2017).

[6] See www2.ed.gov/programs/iegpsnrc/index.html for full details (accessed 29 December 2016).

A complete list of the Title VI African Resource Centres is given in (1), located at some of the country's most prestigious research universities. Because the awards have to be renewed every three years, the awardees may change from year to year, as some centres lose their funding and others gain funding. For example, the joint Stanford-Berkeley Center is no longer funded, nor is the centre at the University of California, Los Angeles, which for many years was one of the most important centres in the country. The African Studies Center at UCLA, its related faculty, including a giant of African linguistics, William Welmers (see section 11.1.2), and many African students for many years provided a locus of significant and productive scholarship. Because of the critical mass of Africanists at UCLA, it was the hosting site for *Studies in African Linguistics*, the leading journal in the field. Note that the Title VI centres were devoted to African *studies*, not African languages and linguistics. They were also sometimes coupled with African American studies, as is the case at the University of Minnesota.

(1) Title VI African National Resource Centres FY 2014–2017

> Boston University, African Studies Center
> Harvard University, Committee on African Studies
> Howard University, Department of African Studies
> Michigan State University, African Studies Center
> University of Florida, Center for African Studies
> University of Illinois, Champaign, Center for African Studies
> University of Minnesota, African-American and African Studies
> University of North Carolina, Chapel Hill, African Studies
> University of Wisconsin-Madison, African Studies Program
> Yale University, Council on African Studies

Because language is such a key component of African studies, the study of African languages was promoted either as an instrument of inquiry or as a linguistic object, though the former was much favoured. At each of the centres listed above, there is at least one Africanist linguist and usually more than one, often including an African. Each centre is provided with a number of Foreign Language and Area Studies (FLAS)[7] grants to students studying African languages.[8] Title VI FLAS fellowships were highly important to the growth and development of African linguistics in the United States, both for Americans

---

[7] For several years in the 1980s, these were known as National Resource Fellowships, but they differed in no significant way from the FLAS award.
[8] In the interests of full disclosure I admit that I benefited from four years and one summer of support from FLAS fellowships in Swahili and Kisi. I also benefited from Title VI support at the Joint Center of Stanford-Berkeley for two years as the language coordinator overseeing the study of African languages at UCB.

who took classes in African languages because of these FLAS fellowships and for the many African students who earned PhDs in the States because of the funding they received through the graduate assistantships teaching African languages. In addition to supporting students and administrative staff, Title VI funds were used for outreach and to sponsor various public events and visiting scholars.

11.1.3.3 Peace Corps

Another important milestone in the study of African languages was the launching of the Peace Corps in 1961. President Kennedy and his brother-in-law Robert Sargent 'Sarge' Shriver, the first head of the Peace Corps, moved quickly to place volunteers. By the end of 1961, Peace Corps volunteers were serving in two African countries, Nigeria and Ghana, with a total of more than 500 volunteers around the world.[9]

The number of countries served has grown to include nearly every country in Africa. The countries where Peace Corps volunteers have served include Benin, Botswana, Burkina Faso, Burundi, Cameroon, Côte d'Ivoire, Ethiopia, The Gambia, Ghana, Guinea, Kenya, Lesotho, Liberia, Mali, Mauritania, Morocco, Mozambique, Namibia, Niger, Nigeria, Sierra Leone, Rwanda, Somalia, South Africa, South Sudan, Swaziland, Tanzania, Togo, Tunisia, Uganda, Zambia, Zimbabwe. Only a few countries in Africa have not had any volunteers at all, all in North Africa. This tally represents countries where volunteers have served since 1961, not where there are volunteers now.

The Peace Corps in Africa has had a rocky history not just because of the instability and turmoil in various states, e.g. civil wars or *coups d'état*, but also because of political currents and various faux pas by volunteers. For example, in Nigeria a 1961 postcard from a volunteer occasioned calls for the expulsion of the Peace Corps because of its unflattering description of living conditions in Nigeria.

Importantly for the study of African languages, Peace Corps volunteers were trained in local languages using manuals developed by linguists and others, including linguists who were former Peace Corps volunteers, e.g. Dwyer (1985). That the Peace Corps stressed learning local languages was crucial. Volunteers typically received intensive language training before being posted to their assigned villages. Additional support was also available. During my years as a volunteer in Liberia in the Kisi-speaking area near the borders with Sierra Leone and Guinea, I was given funds to pay a Kisi language instructor for the two years of my tour.

A number of former Peace Corps volunteers ended up doing research on African languages as professors in Europe, Africa, and North America. A list of the names of the early volunteers turned Africanist linguists reads like a who's who in African linguistics (I give only a few examples from the first batch of Peace Corps volunteers in the sixties): Tom Cook, David Dwyer, John Hutchison, Will Leben, Paul Newman, and Russell Schuh.[10] Thus the contribution of former Peace Corps volunteers was significant from the organization's founding and continues to this day.

The Canadian equivalent of the US Peace Corps, Cuso International (Canadian University Students Overseas), is not nearly so ambitious nor of the same order of magnitude. Created by students in 1961, the organization focuses on 'building skills and transferring knowledge'.[11] Likely its small size is the reason it has not produced linguists in the same large numbers as the Peace Corps has done. There is also the Canadian Volunteer Cooperation Program (CVCP), functioning as part of the more general CIDA (Canadian International Development Agency), but it places volunteers in only a limited number of countries.[12]

11.1.3.4 Government-Underwritten Funding Agencies

The National Science Foundation in the United States has been supportive more of individuals than of wide-ranging, multi-year projects on the model of the Europeans (and Canadians). Support for the study of African languages has gone to graduate and undergraduate students as FLAS awards (see section 11.1.3.2) or for projects that only incidentally involve language.

One exception to this generalization is Larry Hyman's CBOLD project at the University of California, Berkeley. Here is a description from the project's web site.[13]

The CBOLD project was started in 1994 by Larry Hyman and John Lowe to produce in Berkeley a **lexicographic database** to support and enhance the theoretical, descriptive, and historical linguistic study of the languages in the important Bantu family. The database includes a substantial list of reconstructed Proto-Bantu roots (based on Guthrie and Meeussen's reconstructions), several thousand additional reconstructed regional roots (called BLR 2 based on the current work of scholars in Tervuren and elsewhere), and reflexes of these roots for a substantial subset of the 500+ daughter languages. Published and unpublished dictionaries of selected Bantu languages have been scanned, converted to test, and entered into the database. Working with colleagues and students

---

[10] The Peace Corps tends to nurture linguists in general. In my (Applied Linguistics) department at Portland State University, we have four of nine tenure-track lines held by former Peace Corps volunteers, all of whom rather surprisingly served in Africa (Guinea, Lesotho, Liberia (where I served 1970–1972), and Tunisia).
[11] www.cusointernational.org/about/about (accessed 27 April 2017).
[12] In a 2005 review of the programme, there were interviews with volunteers only in Ghana and Burkina Faso: www.acdi-cida.gc.ca/inet/images.nsf/vLUImages/Performancereview6/$file/VCP%20English%20Final.pdf, albeit with the distinct programmes worldwide criticized in the report as having 'no unified goal' (accessed 25 December 2016).
[13] www.cbold.ish-lyon.cnrs.fr/ (accessed 30 March 2017).

from the United States, France, Belgium, the Netherlands, Cameroon, Tanzania and other countries, organized into the Bantu Working Group (BWG), the projects primary goals are to:

- set up a collaborative, accessible database for the use of researchers in Bantu languages;
- establish a unified format for computational lexicographic work in the Bantu languages; and
- input extensive (annotated) dictionaries and wordlists of Bantu languages.

It was funded by the NSF for two consecutive three-year periods, 1994–1997 and 1997–2000. In its focus (and its longevity) it approximated the models for research on African languages in Canada and Europe but is considered exceptional in the United States.

Research on the Canadian side has been much more productive, perhaps because it has been more focused. The research has been constrained institutionally by its funding, provided primarily by the Social Sciences and Humanities Research Council of Canada (SSHRC) and in Quebec by the Fonds Québécois de la Recherche sur la Nature et les Technologies (FQRNT, formerly FCAR) and the Fonds Québécois de la Recherche sur la Société et la Culture (FQRSC). The Canadians follow a European rather than an American pattern in concentrating scholarship on a particular issue or topic, as can be seen in the characterizations of the three projects described below. At the least these three have contributed significantly to the scholarship on African languages, including the production of a great number of MAs (*mémoires*) and PhDs (*thèses*).

The African Languages Project (Projet de Linguistique Africaine) at L'Université du Québec à Montréal (UQAM) was started by Jonathan Kaye in 1981 and continued by Jean Lowenstamm after Kaye left for the United Kingdom in 1988. The project received SSHRC and FCAR (now FQRNT – see above) funding, produced several reports, hosted ACAL twice, and was responsible for numerous publications. Kaye focused on West African languages, in particular the Kru languages of Côte d'Ivoire, but also languages spoken in Burkina Faso (Moore) and Cameroon (Bamileke). There was also a great number of Africa-oriented researchers associated with the project: Hilda Koopman, Dominique Sportiche, Isabelle Haik, and Laurie Tuller. Kaye also arranged for many African students to study at UQAM, as has been the case with the other major Canadian projects. PhD dissertations by African students include Moussa Bamba's dissertation on tone, with a focus on Mahou (or Mau) (1992), Emmanuel Nikiema's theoretical dissertation (1993), and Moses Nyongwa's thesis on Bamileke (1994).

In the late 1980s, Jean-François Prunet joined the project, and he and Lowenstamm began focusing on Ethiopian languages, in particular Gurage languages. Once Mohand Guerssel was hired, there was also more of a focus on Berber and Moroccan Arabic (Kaye had a long-standing interest in Moroccan Arabic). Four Ethiopians studied at UQAM during that time, one writing an MA and the three others PhD dissertations. Sharon Rose joined the project in 1990, writing an MA on Chaha before transferring to McGill where she wrote her PhD on Ethio-Semitic, focusing primarily on Gurage languages. This also started the trend to write in English, as the Ethiopians knew no French when they arrived – Degif and Berhanu learned French, Berhanu well enough to complete a BA at UQAM, and Degif well enough to write an MA thesis. Theses on Semitic/Berber from this time period include Berhane (1991) on Tigrinya, Halefom (1994) on Amharic, Banksira (1997) on Chaha, and a related thesis on templatic morphology (Idrissi 2001), all by Africans, which is a significant fact.

The third of the major Canadian research projects supporting research on African languages comes from the field of pidgin and creole studies and is related to the Creolist Hypothesis discussed below. The central question examined by the project was the role of the substrate in the formation of a Caribbean creole, namely, the input provided by African languages, and the issue of relexification. Was Haitian (known formerly as 'Haitian Creole') truly an African language that had simply begun using French words to replace rough African equivalents in creating a new language? The central hypothesis was that French 'phonetic strings' were used as Haitian's building blocks to completely relexify an African language (here read Fongbe).

The Haitian Project ran for many years at UQAM, directed by Claire Lefebvre and later jointly with John Lumsden (e.g. Lefebvre 1998). Not only did it analyse African languages, but it also had a number of Africans working on the project. There were MA theses and a dissertation on Haitian, and in the 1990s, the directors brought two Fongbe-speaking students from Benin to work on the parallels between Fongbe and Haitian Creole: Maxime da Cruz and Aimé Avolonto. Both of these individuals produced theses on the language (da Cruz 1993 and Avolonto 1995), as did Anne-Marie Brousseau (1993), which was eventually published as a Mouton grammar. There were other African scholars (Juvénal Ndayiragije and Kasangati Kinyalolo) and American Africanists (John Singler) involved. Their participation on the project produced further publications, e.g. Ndayiragije (1993), Singler (1993). Thus, as with the two other major research projects, there was considerable support for the study of African languages.

11.1.4 Non-Governmental Entities

The study of African languages has received some important if relatively minor support from non-governmental and non-missionary agencies. These are non-profit entities supported generally by the community of Africanist scholars with occasional institutional support.

11.1.4.1 Annual Conferences on African Linguistics (ACAL)

An important annual gathering that has promoted the study of African languages in North America is ACAL, an acronym also used for the sister organization, Association of Contemporary African Linguistics.

The Annual Conference on African Linguistics (ACAL) was first convened in 1970 and has since been held every year at various sites throughout North America. The affiliated Association of Contemporary African Linguistics, founded in 2013 as a 501(c)(3) non-profit public charity, has the same mission: to advance and sustain the linguistic study of African languages. The Association (with the same acronym) seeks to continue and provide stability to that tradition and to the conference itself. The Association solicits support from ACAL's attendees to guarantee the conference's stability into the future.[14]

ACAL has been critically important in supporting junior scholars in North America, Europe, and Africa. The conference moves around the United States and Canada as part of its regular schedule.

Its international counterpart is the World Conference on African Linguistics (WOCAL) on whose board several North Americans serve (including the author).

11.1.4.2 Studies in African Linguistics

Studies in African Linguistics (SAL) was founded in 1970 at UCLA (an important Title VI centre at the time) as an outlet for research on African languages, both descriptive and theoretical. The current characterization reflects the sentiment of its founders.

Studies in African Linguistics is a peer-reviewed, academic journal ... [which] seeks to publish African language data and analysis that might not find a place easily or suitably in more general journals. Contributions are not expected to adhere to any particular theoretical framework or linguistic theory ... but should be data-oriented and of potential theoretical interest. Contributions may also take the form of short, descriptive grammatical sketches of endangered African languages.[15]

SAL was created specifically in reaction to the preoccupation with formalism as part of the dominant generative paradigm reigning in 1970. A second major impetus was to raise the visibility and status of African languages. Early generative grammar was preoccupied with English (Harris 1995).[16] After some time journals such as *SAL* and its European counterpart, *Journal of African*

---

[14] http://acal.linguistlist.org/ (accessed 31 March 2017). I served on the Steering Committee 2001–16.

[15] http://sal.research.pdx.edu/ (accessed 26 December 2016). This website also features electronic copies of all papers published by *SAL* since its founding.

[16] As has often been waggishly remarked, Universal Grammar in its early days looked a lot like English.

Languages and Linguistics (*JALL*), founded a few years later, provided much data and even theorizing for the burgeoning interest in linguistics. It was also the case that bastions of generative thinking such as MIT began to enrol students interested in languages other than English, and the theory began to change. African languages quickly came to the forefront of linguistic theorizing, especially in phonology.

Talmy Givón was the founder and first editor of *SAL*; other early editors were Tom Hinnebusch, Larry Hyman, and Russ Schuh. All were associated with the Linguistics Department and the Center for African Linguistics at UCLA, a Title VI centre for many years (see section 11.1.3.2), until 1992 when the journal moved to Indiana University, a long-established and current Title VI centre, under the editorship of Robert Botne. The journal *SAL*, nested in the Africanist milieu of UCLA, provided a major and significant outlet for research on African languages. See the following list of editors of *SAL*:

1970 *SAL* founded, Talmy Givón the first editor.
   vol. 1 (1970) – vol. 3, no. 2 (1973), published by Department of Linguistics and African Studies Center, UCLA.
1973 Larry Hyman took over; vol. 3, no. 3 devoted to Givón.
   vol. 3 no. 3 (1973) – vol. 4, no. 2 (1974), published by Department of Linguistics and African Studies Center, UCLA.
1974 Givón and Tom Hinnebusch take it over jointly.
   vol. 4, no. 3 (1974) – vol. 5, no. 2 (1975), published by Department of Linguistics and African Studies Center, UCLA.
1975–1976 Hinnebusch assumes sole editorship.
   vol. 5, no. 3 (1975) – vol. 6, no. 3 (1976), published by Department of Linguistics and African Studies Center, UCLA.
1976-1979 Russ Schuh joins Hinnebusch as co-editor; they alternate numbers.
   vol. 7 (1977) – vol. 9 (1979), published by Department of Linguistics and African Studies Center, UCLA.
1980–1991 Schuh the sole editor.
   vol. 10 (1980) – vol. 22 (1992), published by Department of Linguistics and African Studies Center, UCLA.
1992–2002 Robert Botne becomes editor (with Schuh assisting on first volume).
   vol. 23, 1992–1994 (one vol. for three years) and vols. 24–26 (1995-1997), published by Department of Linguistics and African Studies Center, UCLA.
   vol. 27 (1998) – vol. 31 (2002), publisher changed to African Linguistics and Languages and African Studies Program, Indiana University, Bloomington, IN.

2003–2008 David Odden takes over.
  vol. 32 (2003) – vol. 37 (2008), published by Ohio State University
  Department of Linguistics and the Center for African Studies,
  Columbus, OH.
2006 Festschrift for Russ Schuh, ed. Paul Newman & Larry Hyman
  (Sup. 11)
2009–present Tucker Childs assumes editorship.
  vol. 38 (2009) – present, published by Studies in African Linguistics,
  Inc. (an incorporated non-profit entity), Portland, OR.
  vol. 40 (2011) – present, journal adopts online open-access format
  while maintaining print format for on-demand requests.

In addition to this institutional support for African languages, there were societal and academic currents that promoted interest in African languages.

11.1.5   Leading Figures

As comparatist and typologist, linguist cum anthropologist, Joseph H. Greenberg (1915–2001) stands out as one of the most influential figures in North American African linguistics, to whom we owe a seminal reclassification of *The Languages of Africa* (1963), which still serves as a convenient and widely accepted reference. William Welmers has been mentioned as a central figure at UCLA, responsible for producing the next generation of African linguists represented by scholars such as Paul Newman, Russell Schuh, Larry Hyman, Talmy Givón, Charles Bird. Charles Bird created African linguistics at Indiana, energizing the field and also producing that early generation of African linguists, e.g. John Hutchison, Linda Dresel, Eyamba Bokamba. Similarly, Paul Newman at Indiana, after returning from positions in Nigeria and the Netherlands, recruited several students from Nigeria and Niger and supervised their PhD dissertations, including Mustapha Ahmad, now vice-chancellor in Kano and Professor Ousseina Alidou at Rutgers. Other relevant names come to mind, like Will Leben (Stanford), David Odden (Ohio State), Poland-born Zygmunt Frajzyngier (University of Colorado at Boulder), and Charles Kisseberth (Illinois).

11.1.6   Intellectual Currents

The anti-behaviourist sentiment that fostered the generative movement and its pre-occupation with rationalism combined with a focus on the indigenous languages of North America has not allowed for much support for the study of far-away, under-studied African languages. Nonetheless, there have been some intellectual developments that have stimulated an interest.

General linguistic interest is the first source. Phoneticians and phonologists have always been interested in African languages because of their typologically unusual features (e.g. Ladefoged 1964; Lindau 1978; Traill 1973; and much work by Ian Maddieson and Bruce Connell). Other sub-disciplines were slower to come around. When they did, however, the scholarship was extensive. American interest in formal representations grew rapidly with the study of tone as a phonological phenomenon (e.g. Leben 1971; Goldsmith 1976),[17] and later morphology using some of the same mechanisms (e.g. McCarthy 1981), and syntax (e.g. Bresnan & Mchombo 1987; a summary in Bresnan 1990).[18]

Because research in North America is more discipline- than area-oriented, particular topics rather than *Africanistik* in general have encouraged scholarship on African languages. Chief among these is tone. For example, Autosegmental Theory began with a paper (Williams [1971] 1976) and later expanded into a thesis (Leben 1973). The study of tone continued under the leadership of such scholars as Larry Hyman (USC, UCB) and Russ Schuh (UCLA), Doug Pulleyblank (UBC), Lee Bickmore (SUNY, Albany), and David Odden (Ohio State). Other areas of interest have been vowel harmony, syllable weight, noun class systems and verb extensions, serial verbs, ideophones, topic and focus, argument structure in general, and sociolinguistic topics such as language policy and multilingualism.

In what follows I present and briefly discuss several intellectual currents that promoted the study of African languages. Interest in former black studies (African American studies) in the late 1960s led to the establishment of African American study centres or even departments, which often involved a component of Africanist study, including the learning of African languages. Both the Creolist Hypothesis and the Ebonics Controversy had some links to black studies and the civil rights movement promoted interest in African languages.

Pidgin and creole studies grew interested in African and other substrate languages in reaction to universalist positions, especially as articulated in the work of Derek Bickerton (e.g. 1981, 1984). His proposal, known as the Language Bioprogram, posited *semantic* structures as something like innate Chomskyan syntactic structures, which manifested themselves in newly formed languages such as pidgins and creoles. These semantic structures appeared most notably as distinctions of tense, mood, and aspect. Much work was devoted to show the importance of the African substrate rather than innate structures. For example, in a detailed paper showing the importance of a Kru substrate in Liberian English, John Singler showed the persistence of a highly marked feature in the pidgin used by Kru speakers (Singler 1988).

---

[17] A summary of the importance of African languages to phonological theory can be found in Goldsmith (1990b).
[18] An update appears in Henderson 2011.

A considerable impetus for the study of African languages came from the Creolist Hypothesis (e.g. Rickford 1997, 1998). The hypothesis emerged as a way to explain the considerable divergence found between African American Vernacular English (AAVE) and mainstream varieties (as documented, for example, in the papers in Fasold et al. 1987). Supporters advanced the thesis that the significant differences were attributable to a creole history in the past for AAVE. The implication was, then, that it was not so much extant white dialects that were important in the formation of AAVE but rather the African substrate. The hypothesis was never widely accepted (see Labov 2001) but was important politically and for its stimulation of interest in African languages.

The same assessment holds for the original statement by the Oakland School Board in December of 1999, which set in motion the ensuing Ebonics Controversy. The claim was that AAVE, or Ebonics, was in fact an African language. This statement similarly received little empirical justification but at least raised people's consciousness as to what constituted an African language.[19]

Much more significant in the study of African languages was the interest taken in threatened African languages as part of the general concern for endangered languages. The funding of language documentation has, in fact, been a boon for the study of African languages and marks the swing of the discipline's pendulum towards the descriptive.

Americans and the US government have been concerned with the demise of many of the less widely spoken languages of the world, as articulated in works such as Hale et al. (1992). The interest in North America, however, has been primarily with Native American (USA) and First Nations (Canada) languages, though support for the documentation of dying languages is also available for research on African languages

The forces at work on such marginalized languages have been well known for some time, e.g. empire building, proselytizing (Childs 2007), and colonialization (Connell 2007), and lately threats of globalization (Bromber and Smieja 2004), but the extent to which African languages are threatened is extreme and seems to me to be underestimated (Childs, forthcoming b). The study of *endangered* African languages has been supported by both private and governmental funding agencies available to researchers in North America, as listed below.

• Documentation of Endangered Languages Program (DOBES), funded by the Volkswagen Foundation (http://dobes.mpi.nl/)
• The Hans Rausing Endangered Languages Documentation Programme (ELDP) (www.eldp.net/)

---

[19] The website, http://web.stanford.edu/~rickford/ebonics/ (accessed 27 April 2017), contains much of John Rickford's writing on the controversy, including academic papers as well as many letters to various editors.

- Documenting Endangered Languages (DEL), supported by the National Science Foundation and the National Endowment for the Humanities (www .nsf.gov/funding/pgm_summ.jsp?pims_id=12816)
- Social Sciences and Humanities Research Council (SSHRC) of Canada (www.sshrc-crsh.gc.ca/home-accueil-eng.aspx).

Other funding entities exist, but these are the ones that have funded major language documentation and sometimes revitalization projects in Africa.

11.1.7   Conclusion

Both Canada and the United States began their study of African languages well after the Europeans had established themselves as part of their colonial expansionism. In addition to the differences in history with Europe, North America is far away from Africa, separated by a wide ocean, which is much more challenging to travellers, as the recent influx of African refugees to Europe attests. Thus, North America starts well behind Europe in terms of early scholarship.

North Americans have had to play catch-up and have done so in a number of ways. Various government initiatives such as the SSHRC initiatives in Canada, the Title VI area centres, and the establishment of Peace Corps in the United States have allowed for some connections with Africa to be established. Because of the European orientation of Canadian academe, the study of African languages has perhaps flourished more there (at least per capita) than in the United States. What has been important about the Canadian initiatives is the extent to which they have involved Africans in the scholarship, as the wave of theses and publications attests.

The recent funding for language documentation projects has helped further research on the continent, but in the end the scale is so limited that the result is rather minimal, however important it may be. Whether these initiatives and earlier ones will continue into the future remains to be seen. Unfortunately, the future is dependent on governmental support and is ultimately resolvable into a question of political will, both of which seem in short supply in the United States under the present regime.

Although the support for documenting endangered languages has been a tonic for the study of African languages, that support cannot be expected to last. Current political developments in the United States are not encouraging. For the immediate future we have an administration that is promoting a policy called 'America First', whose only goal seems to be shutting down all foreign affairs except those that will make money for the head of state's family. The opposite is true of Canada with a forward-looking head of state. Canada's contribution to scholarship on African languages is well intentioned, motivated by an outward-looking and international perspective, but the resources are more limited in Canada, and there are no historical or natural connections to the continent.

The other place that must be considered in predicting the future of North American scholarship on African languages is, of course, Africa itself. Here the projections are not terribly encouraging and obtain for scholarship on African languages in general. Poverty, civil unrest, and political instability characterize more of the continent than one would like. South Africa seems to be losing its direction, and kleptocracies are prevalent where there is stability, e.g. in Sierra Leone, a country which, despite an abundance of resources, remains at the bottom of every socioeconomic ranking of states in Africa and even the world.

Globalization, including global warming, poses a threat to scholarship and a threat to African languages themselves. Radical Islamist movements also constitute an important factor. Threats to endangered languages no doubt have an effect on all languages, even ones that would be considered 'safe' and 'stable'. Africans, however, are pragmatic and recognize the instrumental value of language above all else. They do not have the emotional attachment to language that is found elsewhere in the world (Grinevald 2006). Any possibility of local support, synergistic and cooperative ventures such as those proposed in Childs et al. (2014) would be welcome.

Political currents such as nationalism and tribalism, while powerful, do not seem so tied to language as in Europe or North America. Language does not form such a perceived component of identity. While this has favoured multilingualism on the continent, it has not supported languages as linguistic objects. Speakers of the less widely spoken languages are more likely to learn a dominant language. The causal relationship of this practice is unclear. Have speakers of minority languages adopted such a stance as a defence mechanism, or has it been forced on them by the more militant majority? The trend seems impossible to resist.

11.2   African Linguistics in Latin America (Margarida Petter)

The African populations that were transferred by human trafficking to Latin America during the period of the trans-Atlantic slave trade between the fifteenth and nineteenth centuries initially instigated the study of historians and anthropologists. Only rarely, and in an indirect way, were the African languages spoken by the enslaved blacks mentioned in works about the formation periods of the Latin American nations. However, in the nineteenth century there were literary records and stories of travellers who portrayed the speech of Africans trying to express themselves in the languages of the colonizers, many times in a caricatured way. Thus, the somewhat secondary role attributed to academic studies of African languages in this region can be partially explained by the scanty documentation about the African languages that were transplanted and used in Latin America. In addition, colonial practice induced the enslaved Africans to communicate preferentially in the European languages of the colonizers. As a consequence, Latin American linguistic varieties arose from contact between European, African, and indigenous local languages, which are scholarly recognized as Afro-Hispanic and Afro-Brazilian.

Despite the bibliographical invisibility of the African languages, linguists make the best of the Latin American social context by following two lines of research: the study of the survivals/vestiges of African languages in certain cultural communities of practice, and the study of linguistic contact involving the European languages. These two lines of research will be addressed in this chapter, which attempts to present a brief survey of the available historical documentation, and to describe the current state of research on African languages in the region.

11.2.1   Historical Records of African Languages

Among the scarce documentation on African languages in Latin America, two works about the presence and use of these languages stand out, both produced in Brazil – one from the seventeenth century and another one from the eighteenth century. In 1697, the work considered to be the first grammar of Kimbundu was published, *Arte da lingua de Angola* (Art of the language of Angola), *oeferecida* a *Virgem Senhora N. do Rosario, Mãy & Senhora dos mesmos Pretos* (as an offering to the Holy Virgin of Our Lady of the Rosary, Mother & Lady of the same Black people), written by the Priest Pedro Dias of the Company of Jesus. Although it was published in Lisbon, it was written in Brazil, in Salvador, Bahia. Its author was of Portuguese origin, but he lived in Brazil from his infancy; he was a Jesuit, jurist, and doctor. His work, which consisted of 48 pages, is a grammar of the Kimbundu language spoken in Salvador by the enslaved Africans brought from Angola. The book was intended as an aid to the work of the Jesuits who dealt with the blacks, with the objective of facilitating the learning of this language, since there was no grammar of it.

The immense scientific importance of this work is twofold. First, for Africa, because it is the first systematic description of Kimbundu, and second, for Brazil, for several reasons. This work testifies to the use, at that time, of an African language by the enslaved brought from Angola, who could not have been native speakers of that language but probably made use of if for their interactions with other Africans. The described language is fully African, very close to the one spoken today in Angola, and it must not be confused with a pidgin or with a creole language (Bonvini 2008: 38). This document discloses that, in the seventeenth century in Bahia, where the largest black population of the time was concentrated, an African language was used by the enslaved blacks, to the point of calling the attention of the Jesuits who desired to know it in order to indoctrinate its speakers.

Kimbundu is no longer spoken in Brazil. It remains interesting to note that many grammatical aspects noticed by Dias still attract the attention of scholars who investigate the contact between the Portuguese and the African languages in Brazil, such as the existence of a double negation (Dias 1697:41) and the absence of the passive forms (p. 43).

The second outstanding document about African languages in Brazil is *Lingoa gᵃl de Mina, traduzida ao nosso Igdioma, por Antonio da Costa Peixoto, Curiozo nesta Siencia, e graduado na mesma faculdade E.ᵒ*, according to the title that appears in the frontispiece of the manuscript *Obra Nova da Língua Geral de Mina* (A New Work about the General Language of Mina). It was written in Ouro Preto by Antonio da Costa Peixoto and published in 1731, with a second edition in 1741. This document portrays a particular linguistic situation in the quadrilateral mining of Vila Rica - Vila do Carmo - Sabará - Rio dos Montes, which resulted from the concentration of 100,000 enslaved blacks – regularly renewed during a period of 40–50 years – originally from the coast of Benin (called Mina and situated, in a wide sense, between Ghana and Nigeria). This situation engendered a vernacular variety that is typologically close to the African languages of this same coast. Currently, the languages spoken in the region of origin of the enslaved blacks are classified in the subgroup Gbe, of the Kwa group, from the Niger-Congo family. In this subgroup there are about 50 languages, of which the most well known are Ewe, Fon, Gen, Aja, Gun, and Mahi, which could have been present in the mining region by the time that the Língua Geral (Common language) was registered.

The emergence of the African vernacular language can be explained by the necessity of neutralizing the differences of diverse African speeches, typologically very close to one another, used in the mines, in the eighteenth century. This manuscript, which was published only in 1945, in Lisbon, testifies to the existence of a vernacular African language called Língua Geral, probably in reference to the indigenous Língua Geral (Common language).

The manuscript of Antonio da Costa Peixoto was written with the intention of facilitating the learning of the language used in the mines by the slave masters. It unmasks a change in the African linguistic scenery in Brazil: in the eighteenth century, the languages of the coast of Benin were the most evident ones, at least in the more economically active regions. This manuscript is presented as a list of words in the African language, translated into Portuguese, organized by semantic fields; it also contains some dialogues and phrases necessary for immediate communication.

Castro (2002) published a critical essay with an ethnolinguistic matrix about the manuscript of Peixoto, considering it to be of multi-purpose character, which 'gathers true elements for the history and the sociology of the black Brazilians in colonial times' (2002:25). The author identifies the language as 'Mina-Jeje', basically as a Fon lexically based language. For Bonvini (2008:45), the language Mina was, in fact, a vernacular language based on Gbe languages (a set of languages spoken in Togo and Benin) in a phase of pidginization. This 'language', or better, its vocabulary, did not survive in the Portuguese spoken in Brazil, not even in the mining region. However, according to Castro (2002: 27), 'these speeches ... ended-up implanting the bases of the conventual structure of the "terreiros" of the Mina-Jeje tradition in Brazil'.

11.2.2   Current Sources of Research

More recently, research has focused on the religious rites of African origin, and on the study of the languages spoken by rural communities of Afro-descendants. Although the sources are diverse, many of them point, even though in different degrees, to facts of lexical (words borrowed from African languages) and grammatical order (phonetic alterations and rules of agreement that are different from the Spanish and the Portuguese standard varieties), which can be attributed to an interference of African languages.

The study of the influence of African languages on Brazilian Portuguese goes back to the middle of the twentieth century when the identity of the national language was under discussion. The contact between Portuguese, African, and indigenous languages was used as an argument to defend the specificity of Brazilian Portuguese. Two works are considered pioneering efforts in investigating the influence of African languages in Brazil (Raimundo 1933 and Mendonça 1933). They highlighted grammatical features which can be attributed to the impact of African languages and present a list of words which are considered to be of African origin.

Lexicon, being the most perceptible evidence of contact between languages, figures predominantly in the research of features of African languages in Latin America. Nowadays of concern is not only the number of words borrowed from African languages that we find today in the Spanish and the Portuguese languages spoken in Latin America, but also understanding the relevance and vitality of the African words that have resisted for more than four centuries. Even in countries where the Afro-descendant population is more reduced today, such as Argentina, current use of terms of African origin are attested, such as *candombe, marimba, tango, matungo, mandinga, mucama, mondongo, pachanga, malambo*, among others (Buffa & Bezerra 2014:179). In Uruguay, there are vocabularies and glossaries (Pereda Valdés 1965) which mark the presence of words of African origin in the lexicon of the local Spanish. In a recent study, Magdalena Coll published a work about the lexicon of African origin found in the stories of José Monegal (1892–1968), which portray a rural setting, located on the Uruguayan–Brazilian border, from the end of the nineteenth century and the beginning of the twentieth century, which have as protagonists popular human types and many descendants. The author affirms that the words used by the writer 'are not words taken from dictionaries, grammars or orthography; they are words heard by someone who knows to listen', such as *batuque, bombear, bunda, cachimba, cacunda, cafondó, candombe, capanga, catinga, mandinga, marimba, mulambos, muleque, quilombo, quitandera,* and *yimbo* (Coll 2015:237). All the terms are of Bantu origin and all, except the last one, are also common in Brazilian Portuguese.

The words with African origin in Cuban Spanish, originally from Kikongo, Ewe-Fon, Yoruba, Efik-Ibibio, may be classified as 'socio-linguistically neutral' or 'with strong religious cultural origin which prevail in the popular and marginalized Cuban Spanish' (Bernal 2009:61–62). They belong to the first group of words such as *malanga* 'name of a species of plants', *quimbombó* 'a type of plant and fruit', *ñame* 'yam', *bongó* 'a type of drum', *conga* 'a type of dance'. In the second type we find the terms *iriampo* 'head', *butuba* 'food', *bilongo* 'witchcraft', *embó* 'religious sacrifice'. For this author, the lexicon is the sole linguistic level of Cuban Spanish that was influenced by African languages.

In Brazil, the tradition of surveying the lexicon for words of African origin is associated with the quest for defining the specificity of Brazilian Portuguese. It was in the nineteenth century that this question was given prominence, in a debate favoured by the social and political context that preceded and persisted after the independence of the country in 1822. In 1826, the Visconde de Pedra Branca, in a text taken as one of the first reflections on the nature of Brazilian Portuguese (Pinto 1978:xv), designates the vocabulary realm as one of the main differences between the Portuguese spoken in Brazil and the one spoken in Portugal. Pedra Branca presents a list with 49 words used in Brazil and unknown in Portugal. Of the 49 cited words, 16 are of African origin: *quindim, quitute, batuque, cochilar, xingar, muxingueiro, caçula, fuxicar, mocotó, mungangas, muxoxo, mulambo, mandinga, muxiba, quitanda, senzala.*

The most recent inventory appears in the work of Yeda Pessoa de Castro (2001), which lists 3,517 terms with African origin in her survey realized in Bahia but that, in general lines, can be extended to Brazilian Portuguese as a whole. Most of these terms relate to the religious universe, followed by terms related to food and cooking, music, dances, and so on. It deals, therefore, with a specialized lexicon, many times of restricted regional use. The vocabulary effectively used for general purposes is less extensive. In order to verify the more general use of this lexicon, i.e. independent of specific contexts, Alkmim and Petter (2008) have conducted, from the work of Castro (2001), a survey of the words with African origin pertaining to common vocabulary, trying to evidence their integration, mobility, and vitality. The analysis led to the identification of 56 words which the authors organized in three categories:

category 1 includes terms that can be used in any social interaction (30 words), for example *caçamba* 'dumpster' and 'truck', *caçula* 'youngest child', *carimbo* 'official seal or the tool to stamp', *cochilar* 'nap', *xingar* 'offend with words';

category 2 consists of informal, colloquial terms that, depending on the situation, are replaced by others (9 words), for example: *bamba/bambambã* 'expert', 'experienced', *cafuné* 'caress somebody's hair with the tip of your fingers', *muamba* 'merchandise illegally commercialized';

category 3 includes very informal terms, whose usage is more restricted (17 words). Ex: *bunda* 'buttocks', *cafundó* 'faraway place', *quizumba* 'confusion', *ziquizira* 'bad luck, undefined disease'

(Petter 2012)

According to the etymology indicated by Castro (2001), all the terms selected by the research, except *abadá* and *gibi*, originate from Bantu languages. This can be explained by the fact that speakers of Bantu languages have the longest presence and were superior in number and geographic distribution in the Brazilian territory under the slavery regime. Hence resulted the incorporation of a vocabulary with general-purpose use that proved to be more resistant to changes. The languages of the West African area – spoken in the north of the equator – arrived later (eighteenth and nineteenth centuries) and belonged to specific domains and specialized uses, such as religion, music, dance, food/cooking; they were not considered in the research by Alkmim and Petter (2008).

The incorporation of the lexicon of African origin is perceived as a positive aspect of the contact between languages, in the sense that it enriches the linguistic repertoire of the transplanted European languages, characterizing them as varieties that distinguish them from their colonial matrices. On the other hand, the interference of the African languages in the pronunciation of certain sounds or the modification of grammatical structures is considered as harmful to the integrity of Portuguese or Spanish languages. The handling of the language of the colonizer was used in the past to distinguish two important categories of enslaved Africans, *ladinos*, who could already express themselves well in the languages of America, and *bozals*, who could not command perfectly the languages of the masters and, as a consequence, transferred features of their mother tongues to these languages.

In Latin America, there are references to the *bozal* Spanish in the middle of the seventeenth century, in poems and songs. The first documents stem from the mining areas of Peru, Mexico, Colombia, Bolivia, and Guatemala. There are also a few documents of Afro-Hispanic speeches from the eighteenth century, but from Cuba and Mexico only. The geographic distribution of the existing texts reflects the profile of the human traffic in Latin America. The texts from the nineteenth century come from three regions: Cuba (and Rich Port), the coast of Peru, and the region of Buenos Aires/Montevidéu (Lipski, n.d.:10).

11.2.3 Languages in Contact: The Afro-Hispanic and Afro-Brazilian Speeches

With regard to the Spanish spoken by Africans in Latin America, the available information points to situations similar in some aspects to the Brazilian situation. According to Lipski (2015:93), there are three ways to get trustworthy samples of Afro-Hispanic speeches from the past: the collective memory of speeches of the last Africans taken to America; the survival of *bozals* elements in the Afro-Hispanic religious and folkloric rites, and the post-*bozals* linguistic vestiges found in the more isolated Afro-Latin-American communities of speech. The author considers that the first way, which was viable in Cuba until the second half of the twentieth century, is no longer a fruitful source of data. As to the *bozal* language of Afro-Cuban ceremonies, which appears in situations where the adepts are in a state of trance, Lipski believes that the data are not very trustworthy as real instances of Afro-Hispanic speeches from the past, where the writers tried to represent the speech of the African population (2015:93). Currently, the data collected by fieldworkers in communities of Afro-Hispanic and Afro-Brazilians speeches are of great relevance because they can still bring information about distant language contacts in the past.

Even if one considers that the features of African languages found in the religions with African matrix do not reflect the speech of Africans in the past, they are excellent records of the languages that were in contact with the European varieties that were transplanted to Latin America. In this manner, in Cuba and Brazil religious rites became identified as 'nation', that is, according to the predominant African language that is used in the cult. In Cuba, sub-Saharan languages mixed with the Spanish language and became an important part of the linguistic features of the four Afro-Cuban cults that persist until today in that country (Bernal 2009:60–61): (i) Regla de Palo Monte, with Bantu cultural and linguistic elements, of Kikongo origin; (ii) Regla de Ocha and Ifá, known as Santería or Lucumi, with cultural and linguistic models of Yoruba, Ewe, and Fon, languages of the south of Nigeria and Benin; (iii) Regla Arará, with cultural and linguistic models from Ewe-Fon and Abakwa Society; (iv) a reconstitution in Cuba of the Egbo society of Efik and Ibibio of Old Calabar, in Nigeria.

The Spanish spoken in states of trance and/or sung during the ceremonies of Palo Monte resembles the structures of Creole languages, thus supplying evidence that in social spaces where the African presence was and still is remarkable, such as in Cuba and Brazil, the languages of the colonizers have changed after the contact with the speakers of African languages (Cunha 2008).

In terms of comparison, the closest to the language of Palo Monte is the speech of 'preto-velho' (old black), a very popular entity in Umbanda (see below), which represents the aged blacks who lived in the time of slavery in Brazil and that still speak, in states of trance, a well-restructured Portuguese, similar to a pidgin or creole (Petter 2012).

African religions are found in different regions of Brazil and in different rites and under local names: Candomblé in Bahia, Xangô in Pernambuco and Alagoas, Tambor de Mina in Maranhão and Pará, Batuque in Rio Grande do Sul, Macumba in Rio de Janeiro. More recently, in the twentieth century, Umbanda appeared, which is identified as Brazilian religion par excellence, in the sense that it emerged as the meeting point of African cults and indigenous traditions with Spiritism and Catholicism. The 'Candomblés' of the different 'nations' – Nagô-Ketu, Jeje, Angola – make use of different languages: Yoruba, in all the cults and mainly in the nation Nagô-Ketu; Ewe-Fon, in the cults Jeje; Kimbundu and Kikongo, in the Candomblé of Angola. In Maranhão, in Tambor de Mina, there is a mixture of Mina-Nagô languages.

The ritual languages are used in communities of adepts of the cult, who use in their liturgies mixed forms of Spanish/Portuguese and the lexicon of diverse African languages. In Brazil, in profane environments, there is a similar situation, in which words of African languages, of the Bantu group specifically, mix with the local Portuguese, characterizing the so-called private languages of Cafundó and Tabatinga.

Cafundó, a rural quarter of the city of Salto de Pirapora, is located about 150 km from São Paulo, its population consisting largely of African descendants who have conserved the use of a reduced Bantu-based lexicon, a use embedded in the morphosyntactic structure of the regional rural dialect. The lexicon of African origin contains about 160 lexical items, with 15 verbs and 2 adverbs. The majority of its speakers possess a passive knowledge of this repertoire, since its effective use has been decreasing, being used only in the speech of some adults. The children today learn some words sporadically, such as names of foods and some animals. For the cafundoenses (inhabitants of Cafundó), the most important function of the 'language', or *Cupópia*, as they identify it, is that of a secret code, restricted to the members of the community. The secret use of this language fulfils, in the real sense, a playful function, used to deceive the uninformed ones. In this way, the speakers distinguish themselves as African descendants, giving them a sense of superiority over all the social and economic degradation that they are victims of (Vogt & Fry 1996).

Tabatinga, an area on the outskirts of Bom Despacho, in Minas Gerais, was the subject of Sônia Queiroz's (1983) master dissertation that was published only in 1998. Analysing the 'língua da Costa' and comparing it to that of Cafundó, with which it shares – besides the use as form of 'occultation' – many lexical and grammatical elements, the author concludes that the Língua do

Negro da Costa functions as 'a diacritic signal that marks the group of blacks of Tabatinga in opposition to the downtown whites' (Queiroz 1998:106). The 'Língua do Negro da Costa' or 'língua da Tabatinga' is spoken by a group of blacks of the city of Bom Despacho (MG), located about 140 km from Belo Horizonte. This 'language' is grammatically very close to the 'Brazilian popular Portuguese', more specifically to the dialect of the region; it bears a very small vocabulary of Bantu origin, with many terms similar to those of Cafundó. It uses Portuguese derivational and inflection morphemes, even though a diachronic analysis could identify, in a remote time, prefix terms of African origin, morphemes indicating nominal classes, such as, for example *ca-* of *camona* 'child', recognized in the languages of the Bantu group as a mark of the diminutive (Queiroz 1998:79).

It should be noted that these 'languages' did not spread out to the neighbouring communities; they were confined in their environments of use, since they were nurtured with a volition of occultation. There are no records of communities with similar characteristics to those of Cafundó and Tabatinga in other Latin America countries.

Calunga is the name given to the speech found in Patrocínio, a city located in the west of the Triângulo Mineiro (Mining Triangle), in Minas Gerais, used by a small group of speakers, who consider it as a type of secret language. In the same way as Cupópia and the language of Tabatinga, Calunga presents a small lexicon from Bantu languages (Kimbundu, Umbundu, and Kikongo) and morphsyntactic structure of the local vernacular Portuguese (Byrd: 2006:62).

Data from Afro-Hispanic communities, little studied until today, of Paraguay, Ecuador, Panama, Colombia, Mexico, and Bolivia, permit, according to Lipski (2015:94), the reconstruction of some grammatical standards that moulded the Afro-descendant communities during the period of formation of the Hispanic-American dialects, demonstrating in an empirical way the Afro-Hispanic speech of the past. The features mentioned by the author are present in most of the investigated communities: lack of subject-verb agreement; lack of grammatical gender, with a predominance of masculine forms (*comida sabroso*); presence of plural markers only on the first element of the noun phrase (*los patron*); absence of definite articles; paragogic vowels (as a support), as in *Rioso (Dios)*, *siribi (servir)* in Palenquero (Lipski 2015:115–116), among others. The same linguistic features are observed in Brazilian Portuguese spoken in Maroon communities.

The communities of Vale do Chota, in Ecuador, a country that counts a population of African origin of about 25 per cent of its total population, provide a rich source of morphosyntactic phenomena. In Paraguay, the data are rare, in view of the degree of invisibility that the Afro-descendant populations that speak Guaraní as well as the remaining Paraguayans were submitted to. In Mexico, even though the linguistic features of the Afro-Mexican communities are among the most marginalized sociolects of the Spanish language, inter-action between African languages and the *bozal* speech can still be observed (Lipski 2015:94–99).

Panama has communities of speech that conserve residual elements of the Spanish spoken by enslaved African in colonial times. They are recognized as Negros Congos (black Congos), a population distributed throughout the Panamanian Coast, which conserves a ceremonial language that brings much information about the *bozal* speech of the last centuries. According to Lispski (2015:100), the play of the Congos that is carried out nowadays during the carnival refers to events of the history of the enslaved blacks of Panama, to the Hispanic inheritance (music and the dance, in part), and to the African pres-ence (the drum and the costumes). Many anthropological, folkloric, historical, and musical studies were conducted about the Congos, but little was studied in terms of their linguistic properties. The Congo Hablar (Congo speech) imposes deformations and systematic changes on Spanish, which hinders understand-ing by uninitiated ones. This speech contains phonetic deformations and mor-phosyntactic elements that come from the *bozal* language of past centuries (Lispski 2015:100). From the point of view of its usage, the Congo speech resembles the 'Brazilian Cupópia and Calunga ethnolects ... [which] were formed by means of deliberate acts of creation with the purpose of occulting the meaning of the prayers and as an expression of revolt against the white masters' (Lipski 2015:101).

The linguistic situations found in some Afro-Hispanic communities resem-ble the Maroon communities of Brazil. There are convergence points between the Afro-Hispanic variety of Bolivia and the community of Helvécia (Ferreira 1984) in terms of circumstances surrounding their formation (Lipski 2006) while the speech of the Congos of Panama would fit among the Afro-Brazilians 'cryptolects' of Cafundó, Tabatinga, and Calunga (Lipski 1997, 2011).

A different situation from the one described above is found with Palenquero – or Lengua, as it is called by its speakers. It is a creole language spoken in the Columbian town of San Basilio de Palenque, to the south of Cartagena of India (Schwegler 1996). It emerged during the seventeenth century when groups of Maroons (*Cimarrones*) fled from Cartagena to establish fortified communities in the inner regions of Colombia. Apparently, some founders of the palenques were *bozal* and some others that may have had knowledge of the Portuguese Creole of São Tomé. There is evidence that the Palenqueros were bilinguals and that they kept Lengua as an affirmation of their identity (Lipski 2015:102). The verbal system, with invariable root and preverbal particles, second and third person of plural pronouns of Bantu origin (Kikongo), the per-sonal pronoun in postposition in possessive structures (*casa suto* 'our house') are evidence that Palenquero is neither a dialectal variant nor a restructured speech of the Spanish language (Lipski 2015:116). It is a Creole, the only one lexically based on Spanish, except for Papiamento, which is lexically based Ibero-Romanic, spoken in Aruba, Curaçao, and Bonaire.

11.2.4 Closing Remarks

The study of African languages in Latin America was mainly done in support of research that had in focus the Spanish and Portuguese varieties spoken in former European colonies. In Brazil, research on African languages gave first priority to the lexicon and subsequently also discussed the possibility of Brazilian Portuguese having undergone a Creolization process in a distant past (Baxter 1992, among others). This hypothesis has been refuted by authors who used to defend the continuity of the drift brought from Europe, even though recognizing the changes due to the different linguistic contacts that occurred in the new continent (Naro & Scherre 2007). In the other countries of Latin America, the situation is similar, in the sense that, except for the Creole of Colombia, the African presence was considered to be found only in the lexicon, which did not significantly modify the Hispanic varieties of the continent.

In Brazil, research is currently dedicated to the study of the Afro-Brazilian Portuguese spoken by Afro-descendant communities (Lucchesi et al. 2009) and to syntactic facts that can be attributed to the contact with Bantu languages. From this perspective we find the works of Negrão and Viotti (2008, 2011), Avelar et al. (2009), and Avelar (2015), who deal with syntactic constructions of the Brazilian Portuguse which show similarities to structures found in Bantu languages and in the Portuguese spoken in Africa. In the remaining Latin American countries, research has a focus on the Afro-Hispanic varieties, in the attempt to identify morphosyntactic features which would be indicative of African influence (Lipski 2015; Sessarego 2015).

In addition to the search for grammatical features of African languages in the linguistic varieties spoken in Latin America, there is still a strong interest in the identification of lexical elements mainly of Bantu origin (Garcia González 1978; Angenot et al. 2010; Valdés Acosta 2013).

In Latin America, centres whose research focus is on African languages without immediate reference to the contact with the local languages are scanty. In Brazil, the University of São Paulo was the first to introduce courses in African linguistics at both undergraduate and graduate levels, in 1998. The produced works deal with different aspects of the Africanist research, with special attention to West African and Bantu languages. Among the theses defended here, there are two worthy of reference (they were published outside the country), namely Oliveira (2005) and Xavier (2012). There is also another group of researchers recently instituted in this university, working with Creole languages of São Tomé and Príncipe (Araújo & Agostinho 2010; Agostinho et al. 2016) (see Chapter 10, this volume).

12 African Linguistics in Asia and Australia

Shigeki Kaji, Sun Xiaomeng, Yang Chul-Joon,
and John Hajek

12.1 Introduction

Africa is distant from most Asian countries and from Australia, both geographically and historically. With respect to Asian language studies (such as Sino-Tibetan and Japanese/Korean linguistics), we find academic meetings in Asia. However, there are no such meetings related to African language studies in Asia. Thus, it is difficult to grasp an understanding for the whole picture of African linguistics in Asia.

In this regard, Japan is an exception in that studies of African languages are actively conducted there. It has many specialists in African languages, with a relatively long history of research. Japan in terms of research on African languages is followed by China and South Korea, each country with fewer specialists. Australia has devoted effort to supporting the study of African languages, in part due to the growing number of African migrants into the country. Indian settlements in East and South Africa are well known, but there are also several African settlements in India. The Department of African Studies at the University of Delhi, for example, offers certificate and diploma courses in Swahili.

12.2 African Linguistics in Japan (Shigeki Kaji)

Among the Asian countries, Japan stands out regarding the number of researchers, past and present, involved in African language studies. Currently, about 30 such specialists can be identified by name, not counting PhD students, and most of them are affiliated with linguistics or African studies departments at universities, which are scattered all over the country.

It is important to mention two academic societies in Japan, the Linguistic Society of Japan and the Japan Association for African Studies, because African linguistics is the intersection of these two societies. The Linguistic Society of Japan has nearly 2,000 individual members. Although Japanese and English occupy a special status in the research, judging from the number of scholars and the variety of studies conducted in these areas, the intellectual curiosity of Japanese scholars also drives them to study languages from all over the world. The Japan Association for African Studies comprises about 900 individual members (and includes the disciplines of human and social sciences as well as natural sciences). African studies in Japan are driven mostly by academic interest rather than political or economic concerns.

One important characteristic of Japanese African linguistics is that all the researchers in this field conduct fieldwork, and they are more data oriented than theory oriented. The research in this field began after the Second World War, with a few exceptions here and there.

Among the many universities in Japan, the University of Tokyo and Kyoto University are noteworthy. They are the two big national universities in Japan with a long history, and their linguistics departments have produced many specialists in African languages. However, as far as research in African languages in itself is concerned, the Research Institute for Languages and Cultures of Asia and Africa (ILCAA) of the Tokyo University of Foreign Studies (TUFS) is by far the most important.

12.2.1   *The Research Institute for Asian and African Languages and Cultures (ILCAA)*

This research institute was founded in 1964 at the Tokyo University of Foreign Studies (then called the Institute for the Study of Languages and Cultures of Asia and Africa) on the recommendation of the Science Council of Japan for the purpose of acquiring direct knowledge of Asian and African languages and cultures through field research. It is an inter-university research institute and has recruited young researchers and sent them to various countries to pursue fieldwork. Its publications on African languages in the form of dictionaries/ vocabularies, grammars, folktale texts, and so forth are extremely valuable for the scholarship and noteworthy for the number of volumes published and the variety of languages they discuss.[1] The institute offers a PhD programme in African languages and also intensive summer courses in African languages. The languages taught so far include Swahili, Hausa, Yoruba, Wolof, Akan, Lingala, Haya, Chaga-Rombo Amharic, Egyptian Arabic, Malagasy, Afrikaans, and African sign language.

Yukio Ishigaki (1931–1983) was among the first generation of African language researchers in Japan. He graduated from Nagoya University and became a professor at the ILCAA and studied Amharic and other Semitic languages besides Somali. Tsuneo Morino (1933–2003), a Swahili specialist, compiled six volumes of a Swahili dictionary (1990–1997) in collaboration with Hisashi Nakajima, of the Osaka University of Foreign Studies. Akio Nakano (1937– 2008), who graduated from the University of Tokyo, became a professor at

---

[1] For ILCAA publications, see www.aa.tufs.ac.jp/documents/publ/ ILCAApubl2018.pdf.

the ILCAA. He was an eminent fieldwork scholar whose work covered all the areas of Northern Africa and who studied Hebrew, various Arabic dialects, Berber, Amharic, Tigre, Somali, and so on. Yasutoshi Yukawa (1941–2014) also graduated from the University of Tokyo and worked successively at the ILCAA, the University of Tokyo, Kumamoto University, and Teikyo Heisei University. After studying Tibetan, he turned to Africa and did research on more than one hundred Bantu languages throughout the Bantu area stretching from Kenya to Cameroon through DR Congo, and to South Africa through Tanzania, Zambia, and Namibia. His main research focus was tonal matters, and he published an integrative book on Bantu languages in 2014. Shuji Matsushita, also of the University of Tokyo, studied Hausa and other Chadic languages. Ryohei Kagaya, a graduate of Tokyo Denki University, is a phonetician who investigated the Khoisan languages of Botswana and the Bantu languages of Eastern and Southern Africa, such as Kikuyu and Shona. Shigeki Kaji, who graduated from Kyoto University, investigated the Bantu languages of DR Congo and Uganda, such as Tembo, Nande, Hunde, and Nyoro, among others. He mentored several students, among whom are Nobuko Yoneda, Toshiro Kamiya, Yuko Abe, Kyoko Koga, and Ethelbert Kari of Nigeria. Yoneda, Kamiya, and Abe study Bantu languages; Koga Akan languages; and Kari his native Degema of Nigeria. Kari now holds a position as a professor at the University of Botswana. Daisuke Shinagawa, a specialist in the Chaga languages of Tanzania, moved from Kagawa University to the ILCAA in 2016. Abe, whose research area is the Bende/Tongwe languages of Tanzania, moved from the ILCAA to Tokyo Women's Christian University in 2017. Koga is now at Kochi University.

Hiroshi Nakagawa, a specialist in Khoisan languages, is affiliated with the TUFS, and his wife, Hitomi Ono, also specializes in Khoisan languages at Reitaku University, which is located in Chiba Prefecture near Tokyo. Kiyoshi Shimizu graduated from the TUFS and studied Nigerian languages. His Jukun grammar (1980) is well known. He spent his career mainly at the University of Vienna, Austria, and then took a position at Kumamoto University in Japan. Masayuki Nishie (1937–2015) worked at the TUFS before moving to Waseda University, his graduating school. He is an author of excellent field essays based on his experience in Swahili, Masai, Kikuyu, and others. Haruko Sakaedani graduated from the TUFS and studies Egyptian Arabic from pedagogic and sociolinguistic points of view.

12.2.2   The University of Tokyo

The Department of Linguistics of the University of Tokyo is the oldest among the linguistics departments in Japan, and it has produced many specialists in African languages. However, it is not a centre of African language studies. Most of its graduates who wanted to study African languages went to other universities, mainly to the ILCAA, as, for example, did A. Nakano, Y. Yukawa, and S. Matsushita, but also to other universities: Y. Tsuge attended Kanazawa University; M. Wakasa attended Meisei University; and a scholar we cannot forget, R. Kikuzawa, is now associated with the National Museum of Ethnology.

12.2.3   Kyoto University

Kyoto University has a long tradition of African studies, and its Department of Linguistics has produced several specialists in African languages. The first was Masaoki Miyamoto, who studied Swahili and African novels written in Swahili and English. He held the first chair in Swahili when the Department of Swahili and African Languages was first created in 1986 in Japan at what was then the Osaka University of Foreign Studies. Kazuhisa Eguchi (1942–2008), who got a position at the National Museum of Ethnology, carried out a descriptive study of Chadic languages such as Hide in northern Cameroon in the sixties, and later devoted his energy to the Fulfulde language and folktales. He published volumes of Fulbe folktale texts. Shigeki Kaji was the third scholar to study African languages at Kyoto University. He first got a job at the ILCAA, and then took a position in the Graduate School of Asian and African Area Studies (ASAFAS) at Kyoto University. He now works at Kyoto Sangyo University. Osamu Hieda also graduated from Kyoto University. He studied Nilotic languages such as Datooga, Acholi, and Kumam. He was a member of the Department of Swahili and African Languages at the Osaka University of Foreign Studies. Later he joined the ILCAA. Maya Abe, of the ASAFAS, studies Ma'a, a mixed language of Tanzania, from descriptive and sociolinguistic points of view. Shuichiro Nakao, a researcher in Juba Arabic moved from the ASAFAS to Osaka University in 2017. Toshiro Kamiya, a specialist in Zulu and related languages, now works as a research administrator at Kyoto University.

12.2.4   Other Universities

The Department of Swahili and African Languages at Osaka University is the sole department where undergraduate students can specialize in Swahili. At present there are three scholars in this department, namely Nobuko Yoneda, Junko Komori, and Keiko Takemura. Although they all teach Swahili, they also do research on other languages: Yoneda on Bantu Matengo and Herero, Komori on Yoruba of Nigeria and Kerewe of Tanzania, and Takemura on the Swahili dialects of Zanzibar as well as Swahili literature. Katsuhiko Shiota holds a part-time position at Osaka University. He is a specialist in Chadic languages who studies Hausa and Bura as well as Yoruba. The above-mentioned M. Miyamoto, H. Nakajima, and O. Hieda were once affiliated with this university, but all are now retired.

The Osaka University of Foreign Studies merged with Osaka University in 2007. Tadahisa Goto (1911–2010) was a professor of English, and he published an *Introduction to Swahili Grammar* (1972), which was among the first Swahili grammars written in Japanese.

Tenri University is a religious-affiliated university and it missionizes in Africa from its base in Brazzaville. Toshio Jikihara, Professor of French, compiled a series of African language textbooks, mainly for religious purposes, including *Introduction to Lingala* (1965a) and *Lingala Vocabulary* (1965b). Yoichi Wazaki (1920–1992), an anthropologist at Tenri University who lived and did research in the Lake Eyasi area in Tanzania for a long time, deserves mention for the significant *Swahili–Japanese Dictionary* (1980) he published, which is based on the *Oxford Swahili Dictionary*.

Mitsuo Kowaki studies Ethiopian languages in addition to his main area – Hebrew and Akkadian. Since retiring from Kumamoto University, he has been at Kyoto Sangyo University. Yoichi Tsuge, of Kanazawa University, investigates the Omotic Ari language of Ethiopia as well as Amharic. Hideyuki Inui, of Yamaguchi University, conducts a typological study of Ethiopian languages through field surveys. Jun Ikeda, a specialist in Semitic languages, especially Hebrew and Akkadian, at the University of Tsukuba, investigates Semitic languages of Ethiopia, such as Mesqan of Southern Ethiopia. Motomichi Wasaka, adjunct instructor at Meisei University, works in the area of Semitic and Cushitic languages of Ethiopia, such as Wollaitta. Hiroshi Yoshino, who now has a position at an academic recruitment company, studies East Cushitic languages of Ethiopia, such as 'Ale (also known as Dullay or Gawwada). Ritsuko Miyamoto is a professor at Akita University. She studied Fulfulde of Nigeria and Suba of Kenya and now concentrates on the sign language of Kenya. Nobutaka Kamei, of Aichi Prefectural University, extensively studies sign languages in Africa. Kazuhiro Kawachi, a professor of English at the National Defence Academy, does fieldwork on Sidaama of Ethiopia and Kupsabinyi of Uganda from a theoretical syntactic point of view. Yukitoshi Sunano, a professor of French at Kumamoto Prefectural University, engages in the study of multilingualism in Africa and edited, with S. Kaji, a book on multilingualism covering the whole of Africa. Sumiyo Nishiguchi studies Dhaasanac, a Cushitic language of Ethiopia and Kenya, at Tokyo University of Science. Yukiko Morimoto, of Humboldt University of Berlin, studies Bantu languages from a theoretical perspective. Yasuko Nagano-Madsen, a professor of Japanese at the University of Gothenburg, Sweden, carries out phonetic studies on Asian and African languages including Mpiemo of the Central African Republic.

Regarding Malagasy languages/dialects, researchers include Ritsuko Kikuzawa, of the National Museum of Ethnology; Nobukatsu Minoura, of the TUFS; and Noa Nishimoto, of Kyoto University.

12.2.5   Research Budget

Most Japanese universities have no, or almost no, funding for fieldwork in foreign countries, with the exception of some privileged institutions like the ILCAA, which has ample funds for fieldwork and the publication of research. The most important aspect of the research budgets on which researchers rely is grants-in-aid for scientific research from the Japan Society for the Promotion of Science, an organization affiliated with the Ministry of Education and Research. Scholars submit research proposals that are peer reviewed. If accepted, the grants enable them to go abroad every year for a period of four or five years without worrying about funding. The total amount awarded for research projects increases in spite of the economic difficulties of the country, for which the researchers are grateful.

12.3   African Linguistics in China (Sun Xiaomeng)

12.3.1   Introduction

The earliest contact between China and the African continent can be traced back to the Han Dynasty (206 BCE–220 CE), but systematic African studies in China only began in modern times and were not institutionalized until the founding of the People's Republic of China. At the initial stage, the motivation for these studies was pragmatic and political rather than academic. Following this logic, African linguistics in China was quite marginalized, and academic achievements in this field are more limited than, for example, studies of Sino-African relations and contemporary African issues. Nevertheless many achievements are worth mentioning and some of the aspects will be highlighted in this chapter.

12.3.2   African Languages Teaching in China

Undoubtedly African language teaching in China has been quite impressive. From a historical perspective, both Beijing Foreign Studies University (BFSU) and the Communication University of China have done pioneering work, which can be considered the precursor for African linguistics. In 1960, the Beijing Broadcasting Institute (now the Communication University of China) launched a Swahili programme, and one year later, with the establishment of the Department of Asian and African Languages, Beijing Foreign Languages Institute (now the School of Asian and African Studies, BFSU) started a Swahili degree programme, followed by Hausa in 1964. The languages were taught despite a lack of adequately trained lecturers, published language-teaching materials, and dictionaries. The first batch of Hausa students at BFSU was selected from elite undergraduate students of English and French departments. They learned Hausa from some Niger foreign expatriates of China

Radio International (CRI), with the aid of internally circulated language materials and Hausa–French dictionaries, and sometimes through body language. Tanzanian lecturer Aysha Ali Sudan taught Swahili at BFSU during 1962–1963 and received a special commendation by Premier Zhou Enlai for her special contribution to education. Much in the same way, the Beijing Broadcasting Institute started Hausa and Zulu programmes in 1965. The motivation was shared, that is, to meet the demands of diplomatic corps as China also dispatched several batches of diplomats to acquire African vernacular language proficiency, mainly in Swahili, Hausa, Amharic, Lingala, Somali, and Malagasy. In 1965, Premier Zhou Enlai made a state visit to Africa, and during his visit to Tanzania he used Swahili translation on all public occasions. One leading figure of this period is Ge Gongshang (nicknamed Ndugu Ge in Tanzania), who was trained at the Department of Oriental languages, Leningrad University, for the acquisition of Swahili from 1960 to 1963 and afterwards served as the chief Swahili translator of *Selected Works of Mao Tse-Tung*. In 1979 he began to engage in academic research at the Institute of Ethnology and Anthropology, Chinese Academy of Social Sciences, and contributed abundantly to African ethnology. His achievements can mainly be attributed to his Swahili competence and long-term, in-depth fieldworks in Tanzania. Ge's trajectory can be considered as a vivid reflection of the national transition in African studies from a more pragmatic and political orientation to an academic one.

With the turn of the millennium, a fast development of Sino-African relations was witnessed. Especially after the establishment of the Forum on China–Africa Cooperation (FOCAC) in October 2000, the dialogues between China and Africa become more significant, and African studies in China become consequently reinforced. More universities joined the initiative of language degree programmes and language courses. Besides the two pioneer universities mentioned above, the Swahili BA programme is now also available at the Tianjin Foreign Studies University, the Luoyang Foreign Languages Institute, and the Shanghai International Studies University. The most comprehensive work is located at BFSU, which has developed into a university of international reputation for language teaching and research, covering the most important languages of the African continent: Swahili, Hausa, Amharic, Malagasy, Zulu, Somali, and Yoruba. Beijing University has also provided an Igbo language course since 2010. The substantial increase in African languages teaching makes a strong contribution to this field.

12.3.3   Publications and Achievements

During the initial stage of African linguistics in China, focus was placed on the translations of works by foreign scholars, introducing general information about African languages, the classification of African languages, and language policy of particular nations (Brosnahan 1965). Ideological concerns contributed to more translations of Soviet scholars' work (Olderogge 1962; Kobishchanov 1983). In order to understand and explore the field of African languages, Chinese scholars started to publish some introductory papers (Shi Ling 1964; Xin Shui 1966; Zong Fei 1966a, 1966b; Huang Changzhu 1978; Dong Tianqi 1981; Ning Sao 1983; Huang Zequang & Dong Hongyuan 1984), all of which laid a foundation for further research in Chinese academia, and their importance should not be underestimated.

Considering the importance of African language teaching in China, the publication of teaching materials, including textbooks and grammar books, is an integral part of the achievements in this field. In order to provide resources for language instruction to support students' listening, speaking, reading, and writing competence, some textbooks were planned and published with national subsidy (Feng Yupei 2003; Sun Xiaomeng 2008; Sun Xiaomeng & Cheng Ruxiang 2010; Cao Qin & Rui Jufen 2015). Cao Qin and Feng Yupei complied *Kiswahili 1–4*, which gained national acclaim. Several grammar books and dictionaries were also compiled. Cheng Ruxiang's *Takaitaccen Nahawun Hausa* (A Concise Hausa Grammar) and Zhang Peizhi's *Sarufi ya Kiswahili* (Swahili Grammar) are very instructive for both teachers and learners. Some examples will demonstrate the scale, ambition, and scholarship of this field. In 1971, *Kamusi ya Kiswahili–Kichina* (Swahili–Chinese Dictionary) was compiled and published by Foreign Languages Press. Funded by the national publication foundation, the Commercial Press published *Kamus na Sinanci zuwa Hausa* (Chinese–Hausa Dictionary) in 2012, containing some 30,000 entries. The press also organized the compilation of Swahili and Hausa versions of *The Illustrated Chinese Dictionary*.

In more detailed research, some of the prominent typological features in African languages are analysed in comparison to Chinese language and dialects or the communities' languages in China, for instance, in such areas as serial verb constructions (as compared to their Chinese counterparts), noun classification, and categorization in Bantu (as compared to Sino-Tibetan measure words or classifiers), focus prominence in Somali (as compared to topical preference), and logophors in North African languages (as compared to long-distance anaphora). Data for these studies are also taken from previous typological studies conducted by foreign linguists rather than the results of primary empirical studies of African languages.

Other prominent topics in current research include multilingualism (Luo Meina 2011), language policy (Mo Haiwen 2011, Sun Xiaomeng 2014a or 2014b), language and nation building (Li Wengang 2008; Sun Xiaomeng 2013), and language and development (Liu Haifang 2004; Ren Hong 2009). Language and Sino-African relations is another topic being discussed (Luo Yuanyuan 2008). Some of the contributions are embraced in the monographs of language planning and language policy. In the field of sociolinguistics, the first Chinese student to have been awarded an MA in Hausa by Ahmadu Bello

University was Sun Xiaomeng, who published her PhD dissertation entitled *Language Power: the Application of Hausa in Northern Nigeria during the British Colonial Administration*. The thesis examines the interaction between African vernacular languages and colonial power, focusing on the debates over the introduction of a standard orthography and the colonial language policy, and addresses the ways of Hausa dissemination in Northern Nigeria. It concludes that Hausa as a symbolic power played a vital role in the successful implementation of indirect rule in the colony. Li Dan's PhD dissertation mainly discusses African educational language policy from the perspective of language conflict, focusing on South Africa, Nigeria, and Tanzania. In 2014, Kwesi Kwaa Prah, a distinguished Ghanaian sociologist and anthropologist visited the Institute of West-Asian and African Studies of the Chinese Academy of Social Sciences as visiting fellow and gave talks to Chinese academics and the wider public on issues relating to African languages and language policy.

12.3.4   Challenges and New Trends

Despite the achievements mentioned above, challenges remain. These include, first, while maintaining a dynamic equilibrium, China should reorient African linguistics in terms of disciplinary setting and capacity building of expertise, addressing both philological and linguistic concerns. Second, due to the language barrier, linguists in China frequently use second-hand sources as mentioned above. Third, the range of thematic foci and disciplinary coverage should be expanded, fieldwork with vernacular language ability is much needed, and it is necessary to establish systematic and in-depth research agendas. Besides, some tensions exist between student demand, the national interest, and academic coherence. The vulnerable nature of the subject needs long-term strategic planning for development, more government funding, and relevant policy assurance.

It is also very inspiring to mention some new trends. On the national level, the Ministry of Education has set the goal of offering all the official languages of countries that have established diplomatic ties with China, stimulating considerable capacity building in African languages. BFSU takes this initiative forward, and Tigre, Shona, Tswana, Comorian, Kinyarwanda, Kirundi, Wolof, Sesotho, Berbers, and Creole language programmes are on the university's agenda and will be offered in the coming five years There are also some interactions between Chinese intellectuals and their counterparts globally, on both individual and institutional levels. BFSU is collaborating with the School of Oriental and African Studies (SOAS), University of London, to nurture language-based expertise in linguistics, anthropology, literature, and interdisciplinary area studies, an indication for future development in this field.

Meanwhile, young Chinese scholars show their academic capacity inside and outside of China, and their research is built significantly on the command of vernacular African languages. For example, Deng Yanting is an assistant research fellow of the Division of African Studies in the Institute of West-Asian and African Studies of the Chinese Academy of Social Sciences, the premier and the most comprehensive academic research organization on philosophy and social sciences in China. Deng's BA degree is in Hausa language from BFSU, and he was trained as a political scientist afterwards. Most of his research is very African language based. Zhao Lei, lecturer in Swahili, BFSU and PhD candidate of the State University of Zanzibar, focuses on Swahili oral tradition, and most of his research is Swahili based. Cheng Ying, from Beijing University, focuses in her PhD thesis on the transformation of popular theatre culture in urban Nigeria since the 1990s. She examines the linguistic repertoires of a youth theatre troupe based in Lagos and discusses how language, especially Nigerian Pidgin English, is deployed as an essential vehicle of social identification and political activism in popular culture productions.

Several other students are also engaged in African linguistics as part of transnational education, either as Chinese students abroad or as African students in China. At the University of Hamburg, Chinese student Shen Yuning focuses on the analysis of transitivity in Swahili. Liu Shaonan, a PhD candidate in African history at Michigan State University, uses Twi, Igbo, and Hausa for his fieldwork in Ghana and Nigeria. Xu Liang, a PhD candidate in history at Harvard University, uses his language skills in Afrikaans and isiZulu for his dissertation on industrial decentralization in KwaZulu-Natal, South Africa. On the other hand, there is also a strong contribution by students from African countries trained by Chinese universities. This research mainly focuses on comparative linguistics studies between Chinese and the researcher's African language. Olabinjo Yewande, from Soochow University, focuses on the comparative analysis of three personal pronouns in Chinese and Yoruba. Noordin Shariffa Begam from Tianjin Normal University compared Chinese tones with Kiswahili tones, and at the same university, Waina Peter Wamagata's MA dissertation is about the application of Swahili in Chinese language teaching.

China's growing engagement in Africa will generate more demand for African linguistics. It is a very promising field, and there are many opportunities for future development and collaboration.

12.4   African Linguistics in South Korea (Yang Chul-Joon)

12.4.1   *From Swahili Studies to African Linguistics in South Korea*[2]

It would be quite hollow to deal with the historiography of African linguistics in South Korea without mentioning Swahili studies in its entirety. In 1983 the

[2] Financial support provided by the National Research Foundation of Korea (NRF) is gratefully acknowledged (Grant Number: 2010-362-B00003).

first department of Swahili was established in Korea. The establishment of
this department was a significant precursor for African studies in general and
African linguistics in particular. The department was oriented towards training specialists who would be proficient in Swahili for largely practical purposes and have a profound understanding of the continent as a whole. Hankuk
University of Foreign Studies (HUFS)[3] where presently 45 languages of the
world are taught, took the initiative in introducing Swahili. The university itself
was founded in 1954 for promoting the study of foreign languages. It was not
until 1983 that Swahili, considered as one of the most important indigenous
languages of Africa, was introduced as an academic discipline at the departmental level. Since then, the department has seen a range of significant changes
that include the addition of two more African languages, namely Hausa and
Zulu.

It needs to be noted that instrumentality was the principal source of motivation for learning African languages. But the very notion of instrumentality
in its rather ambivalent sense was not solely confined to academia, but also
to officialdom. At the time, Africa was perceived as a diplomatic battlefield
between two Koreas. Those who had a position of authority, especially in
government, also may have been aware of the fact that teaching African languages could be a strategic decision to make in the long term. In this historical and circumstantial context, teaching African languages took root in
South Korea.

The germinal stage of Swahili studies has gradually evolved into the
systematic, scientific study of African languages. Researching African
languages and linguistics in Korea is not yet on a par with European and
American universities both on the individual and institutional levels. The reason is that the general public does not recognize the importance of learning
or investing in African languages as an academic discipline. In addition, an
insufficient number of scholars are engaged in researching African languages
and linguistics due to resource limitation and the lack of institutional support. Another remarkable misconception in relation to the study of African
languages is linked with the monoglot Herderian one-language, one-nation
ideology, which ties language to homogeneous national identity and location
on a defined national territory.[4]

This section will begin with a brief historiography of Swahili studies in particular and African linguistics in general and will end with a discussion of the
limitations and challenges facing the study of African languages for a more
constructive and productive outcome.

---

[3] HUFS is a private university located both in Seoul and Yongin. The university is widely
recognized as the front-runner in the field of foreign language teaching and research in South
Korea.
[4] Johann Gottfried Herder (1744–1803).

12.4.2   The Heyday of Swahili Studies

In the initial stage, much emphasis was placed on the importance of a practical and pragmatic knowledge of Swahili. Students were encouraged to improve the four essential language skills of listening, reading, speaking, and writing, which are known as 'receptive' and 'productive' skills respectively. To substantiate the enhancement of these Swahili language skills, concerted efforts were soon directed to writing books designed for improving the languages skills one needs for effective communication.

Myong-Shik Kwon, widely known as Korea's authority on the Swahili language, has been a prolific writer. Books produced as instructional materials for quality learning include *A Study of the Swahili Language* (Kwon 1986), *A Syntactic Analysis of Swahili* (Kwon 1987), *Mazungumzo ya Kiswahili* (Swahili Conversation) (Kwon 1989), *Lugha ya Magazeti ya Kiswahili* (Swahili in Mass Media) (Yang 1990), *Swahili Grammar* (Yang, in prep.). The publication of these materials for teaching Swahili as a foreign language was subsequently followed by dictionary compilation. A Swahili–Korean Dictionary (Kim and Kwon 1999) was edited with examples of actual usage.

The instrumentality of these materials in the process of language learning cannot be overemphasized. In addition to these concerted efforts for developing teaching materials, Swahili language experts from both Kenya and Tanzania were invited to teach at the department.

The Department of Linguistics at Seoul National University (SNU) also started offering Swahili language courses. The introduction of Swahili as an optional subject was aimed at giving students an opportunity to understand the grammatical structure of the Swahili language largely from a comparative perspective.

12.4.3   Departmental Reorganization and Expansion into a Sub-faculty

The Department of Swahili was renamed in 1988 as the Department of African Languages in order to reflect the departmental course syllabi, which by then included other African languages. A major turning point occurred in 2008 when the Department of Swahili was reshaped and expanded to become a sub-faculty comprising three divisions: East African, Southern African, and West African Studies. Those who choose to study at the Division of Southern African Studies were required to study Zulu, and likewise their counterparts at the Division of West African Studies had to learn Hausa as a compulsory subject.

Learning major African lingua francas at these three divisions has been considered to be a fundamental step for developing studies in various other disciplines such as anthropology and literature produced in indigenous African languages.

Tae-Sang Jang (2012), though not a linguist by training, has written a Hausa grammar, containing authentic and copious reading materials. This book helps students to acquire an excellent grasp of Hausa grammar. The compilation of a Hausa–Korean dictionary is yet to be done.

Compared with Swahili and Hausa, an elaborate and systematic plan of action has not been made yet for developing Zulu language skills. At present, an anthropologist who conducted ethnographic and anthropological field research among the Zulu in the KwaZulu-Natal province is teaching Zulu.

12.4.4   Individual Works Done and Recent Trends in African Linguistics in South Korea

Recent research in theoretical and non-theoretical issues relating to the study of African languages in South Korea has to do with the reorganization and expansion of the department. Specifically the introduction of three major African lingua francas has given a renewed impetus and motivation to scholars involved in the study of African languages to broaden their scope of research on other African languages having genetic and linguistic affinity with these three lingua francas.

Myong-Shik Kwon (2004, 2011) has steadily carried out theory-oriented research in such fields as comparative-historical linguistics, linguistic typology, grammaticalization, contact linguistics, and non-Niger-Congo African languages. His pioneering works *Introduction to the Study of African Languages* (Kwon 2004), *The Grammatical Structure of the Swahili Language* (Kwon 2011b), and *Sociolinguistics* in Africa (2011a) have laid a solid foundation in the field of African linguistics.

Kim (2006, 2013) has concentrated his efforts on linguistic typology, paying particular attention to the Chadic languages of the Afroasiatic language family. In addition, he is working on a grammatical description of the Guduf language (belonging to the Biu-Mandara subdivision of Chadic). His description is based on field research in Nigeria and has paved the way for future research on Chadic languages.

Yang (2014, 2016) has been working on field-based and corpus-driven grammatical analyses of language variation in Swahili, be they social (sociolect), regional/areal, or ethnic (ethnolect), from a functionalist perspective. His works include corpus-based analyses of linguistic variation. He has also conducted extensive sociolinguistic field work in Swahiliphone East African countries (Yang 2013) and focused on the use of corpora in sociolinguistic research in terms of recent trends of sociolinguistic interests. Much work in sociolinguistics is solidly empirical and based on the analysis, be it quantitative or qualitative, of data of language use in actual social contexts.

12.4.5   Challenges Facing African Linguistics in South Korea

Cognizant of the fact that the study of African languages is a fertile ground for deepening our understanding of the very essence of language in itself and that language is elemental to the collective expression of shared norms and values in any given society, South Korea faces several challenges that must be duly addressed for the continuous advancement of African linguistics.

First and foremost, African linguistics is facing a stagnant, if not dwindling, number of students who commit themselves to the study and promotion of African languages.

Second, lack of fieldwork-based primary data gathering for the study of African languages has resulted in lack of originality and resourcefulness. By addressing and overcoming this problem researchers need to collect primary empirical data for the specific purposes of their study. The questions the researchers need to raise are specifically personalized and tailored to elicit appropriate data that will contribute to their study. Instead of being dependent on secondary data for linguistic analysis, it is of crucial importance to secure various types of primary data by conducting field research.

Third, multiple forms of institutional support for the promotion of African linguistics in South Korea need to be implemented to ensure that the systematic study of African languages remains an essential area of research for a better understanding of African languages in particular, and of Africa as a whole.

Fourth, the need to cross traditional disciplinary boundaries between the social sciences and humanities to address changing research topics and objectives is widely recognized. The growing need to place the focus on interdisciplinarity comes from the thematic diversity in African linguistics. Language and culture are intrinsically intertwined with education, philosophy, participatory democracy, and economic development. Therefore, those who are involved in these issues in one way or another are in need of having critical language awareness and conscious sensitivity, to which African linguistics has a lot to contribute.

12.5   African Linguistics in Australia (John Hajek)

It is not surprising that African linguistics has not been a particularly visible discipline in Australia. Australian-based linguists have for the most part focused their efforts on languages of Australia and the wider Asia-Pacific, as well as on English and other European languages. Distance and lack of significant contact have traditionally been important limiting factors with respect to most areas of academic activity on Africa in Australia. Matters have changed somewhat in recent times, at least in terms of linguistics, given the consistent presence of a small number of linguists with experience in African languages as well as the arrival of large numbers of African-born refugees and, more recently, of African-born students and professionals in Australia. This movement from Africa to Australia has resulted in unexpected levels of linguistic diversity that officialdom has only just begun to record more accurately, e.g. through improved census data collection and identification. There is certainly ample scope now for Australian-based linguists to work on a wide range of African languages with speakers resident in Australia, although the take-up remains low.

There has never been in Australia an academic programme or institute dedicated specifically to African languages. Instead, Australian activity in African linguistics must be drawn together through a series of different threads, some of which overlap, and are described below.

With respect to Australian academic associations potentially most relevant to African linguistics, we have the Australian Linguistic Society (ALS) and its journal, the *Australian Journal of Linguistics* (*AJL*). There are also the Applied Linguistics Association of Australia (ALAA), which publishes the *Australian Review of Applied Linguistics* (*ARAL*), and the more general African Studies Association of Australasia and the Pacific (established in 1978) with its journal, the *Australasian Review of African Studies* (*ARAS*). With rare exceptions, it is overwhelmingly the case that African language-related publications in these journals focus on Australia rather than Africa itself.

12.5.1   Bringing African Linguistics to Australia

In the first instance, we note the activity of a small number of linguists who have worked on African languages in addition to their work on other languages for which they are often much better known. In all cases that we are aware of, they have published on African languages while in Australia. In some cases, these are linguists with Africanist experience who came to Australia to take up academic positions, especially in the earlier days of linguistics in this country. These include (a) Britons, Patrick McConvell and Kevin Ford, and American, Paul Black, who completed PhDs on African languages overseas in the early 1970s before eventually working on Australian languages at the School of Australian Linguistics at Batchelor and elsewhere. McConvell worked on Hausa (Nigeria) at SOAS, Ford on Avatime (Ghana) at the University of Ghana, and Black on Lowland East Cushitic (Ethiopia) at Yale University; (b) American Edith Bavin, who first published on Lango (Uganda), before arriving in Australia in 1981. She took up a post in Canberra, before moving to La Trobe University in 1982, where she has also published on Acholi (Uganda); and (c) Keith Allan, who spent extended periods at African universities before arriving at Monash University in 1978.

Mary Laughren (PhD, Nice 1973), most recently at the University of Queensland, appears to have been the first Australian to have completed a doctoral dissertation on an African language, in this case Senufo (Côte d'Ivoire), under the supervision of Gabriel Manessy, before returning to Australia to work on Australian indigenous languages. Somewhat later, Bruce Donaldson, also Australian, completed his PhD on Afrikaans and language contact while in South Africa, before publishing descriptive and pedagogical grammars of the language once back in Australia.

More recent contributions to different aspects of African linguistics have come from other non-African linguists permanently employed in Australia, such as Steven Bird and John Hajek (University of Melbourne), Simon Musgrave (Monash University), Anikó Hatoss (University of New South Wales), and Donna Starks (La Trobe University). Bird published extensively on Cameroonian languages in the 1990s. His work is mostly on questions of phonology as well as of orthography, mainly with respect to Dschang/Bamileke. Hajek has worked with Ken Olson on the typology of the labio-dental flap, a segment most often found in Africa. He has also collaborated with Musgrave on different aspects of South Sudanese languages in Melbourne (including the identification of at least 40 such languages), where the speakers of these languages in Australia are most likely to have settled. Hatoss has also focused on language maintenance and attitudes amongst the South Sudanese – this time mainly in regional Australia, while also collaborating with Starks and South African born Henriette van Rensburg on language maintenance and identity amongst Afrikaans speakers in Australia.

12.5.2   Linguists of African Origin Working in Australia

A small number of linguists of African origin previously or currently resident in Australia are particularly well known for their work in African linguistics. Felix Ameka, originally from Ghana, completed his MA (1986) and PhD (1991) on Ewe at the Australian National University in Canberra, before taking up a permanent appointment in Europe. Ameka is also the first linguist to publish – in 1988 – on an African language in the *AJL*. He remains a frequent return visitor to Australia. Paulin Djité was for many years (1989–2011) at the University of Sydney and then at the Western University of Sydney. During this time he published extensively on language policy issues in Africa and elsewhere before returning to Côte d'Ivoire. Likewise, Ibrahima Diallo currently at the University of South Australia and Finex Ndhlovu at the University of New England have also been very active in the areas of language policy and identity issues in Africa. Both of these scholars completed their doctoral studies on African language issues in Australia – at Griffith and Monash universities respectively. Ndhlovu, originally from Zimbabwe, has more recently also worked extensively on language identity issues among African migrant communities in Australia. Mengistu Amberber, originally trained in Addis Ababa and at McGill in Montreal but now at the University of New South Wales, has published extensively on different aspects of Amharic grammar, especially with respect to argument structure.

12.5.3 Postgraduate Research on African Languages

A small number of linguists associated with the Summer Institute of Linguistics (SIL), either in Africa or through its Australian headquarters just north of Melbourne, have also worked on African languages. Apart from Steven Bird, previously mentioned, a small number of SIL-linked students have undertaken postgraduate research at Australian universities. These include Cathie Bow on the phonology of Moloko (Cameroon) at the University of Melbourne; Rosmarie Moser and Melanie Viljoen who completed their PhDs on Kabba (Central African Republic and Chad) and Buwal (Cameroon) respectively at La Trobe University, which is located close to SIL's Australian headquarters. To these we can also add the following students, who are without any SIL affiliation: Jonathan Moodie and Rosie Billington are completing PhDs on different aspects of Lopit, a South Sudanese language that was originally the subject of a field methods course at the University of Melbourne. However, it has to be said that in general postgraduate research on African languages has been limited over the years.

12.5.4 Language Typology Research Centres

Since the late 1990s, the most consistent source of activity on African linguistics in Australia at a more general level has been through the Research Centre for Linguistic Typology (RCLT), based first in Canberra (1996–1999) and then at La Trobe University in Melbourne (2000–2011). Its activities have continued partly through the Centre for Research on Linguistic Diversity (CRLD) at La Trobe University, but more directly through the Language and Culture Research Centre (LCRC, first established as the Language and Culture Research Group in 2009) at James Cook University (JCU). Many well-known Africanists, such as Felix Ameka, Mechtild Reh, Anne Storch, Gerrit J. Dimmendaal, Mauro Tosco, Paul Newman, and Zygmunt Frajzyngier, among a long list, have been visitors at the RCLT and LCRC. In particular, they have often contributed to annual international workshops and the edited volumes that have resulted from these. For instance, the 2010 international workshop held at JCU on possession and ownership included contributions on Hone (Storch (Nigeria)), Likpe (Ameka (Ghana)) and Wandala (Frajzyngier (Cameroon/Nigeria)), which then appeared in the subsequent volume edited by Aikhenvald and Dixon (2013).

Unusually for Australia, the three centres have also hosted a small number of trained Africanists as postdoctoral fellows. Birgit Hellwig and Yvonne Treis had previously completed doctoral dissertations on Goemai (Nigeria) and Kambataa (Ethiopia) respectively before coming to Australia. Hellwig held fellowships to investigate Katla and Tabaq (South Sudan), while Treis was instead charged with describing Baskeet (Ethiopia). Both continued also to work primarily on their first African languages while in Australia and published extensively on different African languages before returning overseas. In the case of other research fellows, e.g. Knut Olawsky (Dagbani (Ghana)), Renée Lambert-Brétière (Fon (Benin)), and more recently at the LCRD/LCRC, Anne Schwarz (Buli and other Gur languages (Ghana)), they continued to publish on African languages they had originally trained in, while formally working on grammatical descriptions of non-African languages. Schwarz, for instance, also co-edited a volume on information structure in African languages. Of these three linguists, only Olawsky remains in Australia, where he works on Australian languages.

Acknowledgements

Yang Chul-Yoon gratefully acknowledges the financial support provided by the National Research Foundation of Korea (NRF; Grant number 2010–362-B00003).

References

a. Ma. H . [= *abba* Matewos H agos]. 1951 a.-mə. [= 1958/1959] –1953 a.-mə. [= 1960/1961]. *Säwasəw-Təgrəñña*. 2 vols. [Asmara]: Francescana (in one vol.: Rome 1991).

Aadan, Aadan Xasan (ed.). 2013. *Qaamuus Afsoomaali*. Djibouti: Soo Maal.

Aaron, Uche E. 1992. Reported speech in Obolo narrative discourse. In S. J. Huang & W. R. Merrifield (eds.), *Essays in Honor of Robert E. Longacre*, 227–240. Dallas, TX: Summer Institute of Linguistics.

1994. Tense and aspect in Obolo grammar and discourse. Doctoral dissertation, University of California, Santa Barbara.

1999. *Tense and Aspect in Obolo Grammar and Discourse*. Dallas, TX: Summer Institute of Linguistics.

Abad, Isidoro. 1928. *Elementos de la gramática bubi*. Madrid: Editorial del Corazón de María.

Abbassi, Abdelaziz. 1977. A sociolinguistic analysis of multilingualism in Morocco. PhD dissertation, University of Texas at Austin.

Abdalla, Abdelgadir Mahmoud (ed.). 1974. *Studies in Ancient Languages of the Sudan* (Sudanese Studies Library, 3). Khartoum: Khartoum University Press.

Abdallah, Albert G. 1960. An instrumental study of the intonation of Egyptian colloquial Arabic. PhD dissertation, University of Michigan.

Abdel-Hafiz, Ahmed Sokarno. 1988. A reference grammar of Kunuz Nubian. PhD dissertation, State University of New York at Buffalo.

Abdelhay, Ashraf Kamal. 2007. The politics of language planning in the Sudan: the case of the Naivasha language policy. PhD dissertation, University of Edinburgh.

Abdel-Massih, Ernest T., N. Zaki, El-Said M. Badawi Abdelmalek & Ernst N. Mccarus. 2009. *A Reference Grammar of Egyptian Arabic*. Washingon, DC: Georgetown University Press.

Abdesslam, Ahmed. 1956. Al-fusha wa al-ʿaammiya (Classical and dialectal Arabic). Paper read at the Arab Congress in Damascus. (Cited in Youssi 1989.)

Abdulaziz, Mohamed H. Mkilifi. 1971. Tanzania national language policy and the rise of political culture. In Wilfred H. Whiteley (ed.), *Language Use and Social Change: Problems of Multilingualism with Special Reference to Eastern Africa*, 160–178. London: Oxford University Press.

1972. Triglossia and Swahili-English bilingualism in Tanzania. *Language in Society* 1(2): 197–213.

1981. *Language Planning with Special Reference to East African Countries*. Washington, DC: University of Washington Seattle.

251

1982. Patterns of language acquisition and use in Kenya: Rural-urban differences. *International Journal of the Sociology of Language* 34: 95–120.

1988. Development of scientific and technical terminology with special reference to African languages. *Kiswahili* 56: 32–49.

1991. Standardization of the orthography of Kenyan languages. In Norbert Cyffer et al. (eds.), *Language Standardization in Africa*, 189–206. Hamburg: Helmut Buske.

1996. *Transitivity in Swahili*. Cologne: Rüdiger Köppe.

2000. Some issues of concern in the linguistics of African language. In H. Ekkehard Wolff & Orin D. Gensler (eds.), *Proceedings of the 2nd World Congress of African Linguistics*, 3–18. Cologne: Rüdiger Köppe.

Abdulaziz, Mohamed H. Mkilifi & Ken Osinde. 1997. Sheng and English: Development of mixed codes among the urban youth in Kenya. *International Journal of the Sociology of Language* 125: 43–63.

Abebe, Gebre Tsadik & Engdashet Haileyesus. 2001. A decade of research in Ethiopian Linguistics (1990–2000). *Journal of Ethiopian Studies* 34(1): 87–107.

Abraham, Roy C. 1941. *A Modern Grammar of Spoken Hausa*. London: Crown Agents for the Colonies (Published on Behalf of the Nigerian Government).

Abraham, Roy C. & Mai Kano. 1949. *Dictionary of the Hausa Language*. London: The Crown Agents for the Colonies (Published on Behalf of the Nigerian Government). 2nd ed. 1962.

Abu Farag, M. A. 1960. A grammatical study of the Arabic of Tahway (Minufia Province, Egypt). PhD dissertation, SOAS, University of London.

Abu Manga, Al-Amin. 1986. *Fulfulde in the Sudan: Process of Adaptation to Arabic*. Berlin: Reimer.

Abu-Manga, Al-Amin, Leoma Gilley & Anne Storch (eds.). 2006. *Insights into Nilo-Saharan Language, History and Culture: Proceedings of the 9th Nilo-Saharan Linguistic Colloquium, Institute of African and Asian Studies, University of Khartoum, 16–19 February 2004*, 295–308. Cologne: Rüdiger Köppe.

Abu-Lfadl, Fahmi. 1961. Volkstümliche Texte in arabischen Bauerndialekten der ägyptischen Provinz Šarqiyya mit dialektgeographischen Untersuchungen zur Lautlehre. PhD dissertation, Universität Münster.

Abu-Lfetouh, Hilmi Mohamed. 1961/1968. *A Morphological Study of Colloquial Egyptian Arabic*. The Hague: Mouton.

Abumdas, Abdul Hamid Ali. 1985. Libyan Arabic phonology. PhD thesis, University of Michigan at Ann Arbor.

Academy of Ethiopian Languages. 1986. *The Academy of Ethiopian Languages: Facts and Figures*. Addis Ababa: Graphic Printers.

Achie Brouh, Patrice. 1996. *Prosodic Aspects of Baule with Special Reference to the German of Baule Speakers*. Cologne: Rüdiger Köppe.

Adams, R. F. G. 1952. *Efik–English Dictionary*. Liverpool: Philip Son & Nephew.

Adi Gäbrä [Adi Ghebre]. 1989. *Säwasəw Təgrəñña: Tigrinja grammatik med kort kontrastiv grammatik på svenska och engelska*. Sundbyberg: Statens Institut för läromedel. 2nd ed. 2000.

Adouakou, Sandrine. 2009. *Parlons akyé bodin suivi d'un lexique alphabétique akyé-français, français-akyé*. Paris: L'Harmattan.

Adouakou, Sandrine & Firmin Ahoua. 2009. *Parlons agni indénié, Côte d'Ivoire: En appendice, choix de textes*. Turin: L'Harmattan.

Adrob, Uhaj M. 1986. *Mu'jam Bejawi-'arabi* [A Beja-Arabic Lexicon]. MA thesis, Institute of Afro-Asian Studies, Khartoum.

Afeli, Kossi Antoine. 2003. Politique et aménagement linguistique au Togo: Bilan et perspectives. Thèse de doctorat d'Etat, Université de Lomé.

Agostinho, Ana Lívia dos Santos, Manuele Bandeira de Andrade Lima & Gabriel Antunes de Araújo. 2016. O Lung'ie na educação escolar de São Tomée Príncipe. *Trabalhos em Linguística Aplicada* 55(3): 591–618.

Agostini, Francesco, Annarita Puglielli & Ciise Maxamed Siyaad. 1985. *Dizionario somalo–italiano*. Rome: G. Gangemi.

Agostino [da Hebo (d.i. Ḥebo)]. 1955. *Grammatica amarica*. Asmara: Scuola Tipografia Francescana.

Agosṭinos Tädla. 1994. *La lingua abissina: Qwanqwa Ḥabäša*. Asmara: Adveniat Regnum tuum.

Ahoua, Firmin. 2002. *Contes et textes documentaires kwa de Côte d'Ivoire*. Cologne: Rüdiger Köppe.

Aikhenvald, A. & R. M. W. Dixon. 2013. *Possession and Ownership: A Cross-linguistic Typology*. Oxford: Oxford University Press.

Ainsley, A. D. 1972. The Bantu sentence. *Limi* (Bulletin of the Department of African Languages, University of South Africa) 13: 39–52.

Aklilu, Yilma & Klaus Wedekind. 2002. *Sociolinguistic Report on the Survey of Little-Known Languages of Ethiopia*. Dallas, TX: SIL International.

Akrofi, C. A. 1937. *Twi Kasa Mmara* [Twi Grammar]. Longman: London.

Akrofi, C. A. & E. L. Rapp. 1939. *Twi Nsem Nkorɛnkorɛ Kyerɛwbea* [Twi Spelling Book]. Accra: Government Printing Office.

Akumbu, P. W. 2012. *Njém Tonology*. Dallas, TX: SIL International e-Books 45.

Akumbu, P. W. & E. Fogwe. 2012. *A Pedagogic Grammar of Babanki*. Cologne: Rüdiger Köppe.

Alamin, Suzan. 2012. *The Nominal and Verbal Morphology of Tima: A Niger-Congo Language Spoken in the Nuba Mountains*. Cologne: Rüdiger Köppe.

Alemé, Esheté. 1972. Alaqa Taye Gabra Mariam (1861–1924). *Rassegna di Studi Etiopici* 26: 14–30.

Alexander Naty [= Aläksandär Nati]. 2000. Linguistic diversity in Eritrea. *Africa: Rivista trimestrale di studi e documentazione dell'Istituto italiano per l'Africa el'Oriente* 55(2): 267–279.

Al-Jundi, Ahmad. 1965. Al-lahajat al-3arabiyya kama tusawwiruha kutubu al-nahwi wa al-lughati [Arab dialects as perceived by Arab grammarians]. PhD dissertation, University of Cairo.

Alkmim, Tania & Margarida Petter. 2008. Palavras da África no Brasil de ontem e de hoje. In José Luiz Fiorin & Margarida Petter (eds.), *África no Brasil: A formação da língua portuguesa*, 145–178. São Paulo: Contexto.

Almeida, António de. 1956. Contribuição para o estudo da antropologia física dos 'Angolares'. *Actas da Conferência Internacional dos Africanistas Ocidentais. 6a sessão*, vol. V, 11–20. Lisbon: Ártica.

1962. Da origem dos angolares habitantes da ilha de S. Tomé. In *Memórias da Academia das Ciências de Lisboa*, vol. VIII, 283-301. Lisbon: Academia das Ciências de Lisboa.

1994. *Os Bosquimanos de Angola*. Lisbon: Instituto de investigação tropical.

Almkvist, Herman. 1881–1885. *Die Bischari-Sprache Tuu-Bedaawie in Nordost-Afrika*. Uppsala: Kaiserliche Akademie der Wissenschaften.

Alsina, Alex & Sam A. Mchombo. 1993. Object asymmetries and the Chichewa applicative construction. In Sam A. Mchombo (ed.), *Theoretical Aspects of Bantu Grammar*, 17–45. Stanford, CA: CSLI Publications.

Amanuel Sahlä. 1979 a.-m. [= 1987]. *Ḥaṣṣir säwasəw Təgrəñña (məs mällamädi)*. Asmara: Institute of African Studies.

1998. *Säwasəw Təgrəñña bə-säffiḥu - A comprehensive Tigrinya grammar*. Lawrenceville, NJ/Asmara: Red Sea Press.

Amberber, Mengistu. 2012. Differential case marking of arguments in Amharic. In Andrej L. Malchukov & Andrew Spencer (eds.), *The Oxford Handbook of Case*, 742–755. Oxford: Oxford University Press.

Ameka, Felix K. 1987. A comparative analysis of linguistic routines in two languages: English and Ewe. *Journal of Pragmatics* 11: 299–326.

1988. The grammatical coding of the terminal viewpoint of situations in Ewe: a semantic perspective. *Australian Journal of Linguistics* 8: 185–217.

1991. Ewe: Its grammatical constructions and illocutionary devices. PhD dissertation, Australian National University, Canberra. Published in 2012 by LINCOM Europa, Munich.

2002. Cultural scripting of body parts for emotions: on 'jealousy' and related emotions in Ewe. *Pragmatics & Cognition* 10: 27–55.

2004. Grammar and cultural practices: the grammaticalisation of triadic communication in West African languages. *Journal of West African Languages* 30(2): 5–28.

Ameka Felix K., A. S. Duthie, J. A. B. K. Essegbey, K. Dorrvlo, E. Amuzu, K. A. G. Ofori, P. Agbedor, A. Dzameshie & Y. Agbetsoamedo (eds.). 2011. *Ewe Encyclopedia Dictionary of Health*. Legon-Accra: Department of Linguistics, University of Ghana.

Amidu Assibi A. 2009. *Matrix Nominal Phrases in Kiswahili Bantu: A Study of their Effects on Argument Syntax*. Cologne: Rüdiger Köppe.

2011. *Reflexive and Reciprocal Syntax Revisited: Apologia for Internal Evidence in Kiswahili*. Cologne: Rüdiger Köppe.

Ammour, Naima. 2012. A sociolinguistic investigation of language variation in the speech community of Nedroma. Master's thesis, University of Tlemcen.

Amsalu Aklilu. 1985. *Amharic–English Dictionary*. Addis Ababa: Kuraz.

Amsalu Aklilu & G. P. Mosback. 1981. *English–Amharic Dictionary*. Addis Ababa: Oxford University Press.

Amsalu Aklilu & Renate Richter. 1980. Zur Funktion nationaler Sprachen im Prozeß der nationaldemokratischen Revolution in Äthiopien: Ergebnisse einer soziolinguistischen Untersuchung in der Zuckerfabrik Wonji. In Dimitri A. Olderogge & Siegmund Brauner (eds.), *Sozialer Wandel in Afrika und die Entwicklung von Formen und Funktionen afrikanischer Sprachen*, 92–119. Berlin: Akademie Verlag.

Anderson, Stephen C. 1983. Tone and morpheme rules in Bamileke-Ngyemboon. PhD dissertation, University of Southern California.

Anderson, W. G. 1897. *An Introductory Grammar of the Sena Language*. London: Society for Promoting Christian Knowledge.

Andrzejewski, Bogumil W. 1987. Reinisch's work on Somali and its significance today. In Hans G. Mukarovsky (ed.), *Leo Reinisch: Werk und Erbe*, 67–83. Vienna: Verlag der Österreichischen Akademie der Wissenschaften.

1992. Reflections on R. C. Abraham's Somali–English dictionary. *African Languages and Cultures*. Supplement 1 (Papers in honour of R. C. Abraham (1890–1963)): 99–109.

Andrzejewski, Bogumił Witalis & Ioan M. Lewis. 1964. *Somali Poetry*. Oxford: Clarendon Press.

Angenot, Jean-Pierre. 1971. *Aspects de la phonétique et de la morphologie de l'ewondo*. Leiden: Leiden University.

Angenot, Jean-Pierre, Luis Beltran & Daniel Mutombo Huta-Mukana. 2010. L'état de la recherche étymologique des bantouismes afro-ibéroaméricains: bilan, diagnostic et perspectives offertes par le Programme UNIR-Alcalá / AECID. In M. A. D. Teixeira, Dante R. da Fonseca & Jean-Pierre Angenot (eds.), *Afros, & Amazônicos: Estudo sobre o Negro na Amazônia*, 55–65. Porto Velho: EDUFRO/Rondoniana.

Anon. 1919. *Grammatica della lingua Tigrè con annesso Vocabolario Tigrè-Italiano e Italiano-Tigrè*. Asmara: Francescana.

Anwar, Mohamed Sami. 1979. *Be and Equational Sentences in Egyptian Colloquial Arabic*. Amsterdam: John Benjamins.

Appleyard, David. 1995. *Colloquial Amharic: The Complete Course for Beginners*. London: Routledge.

2006. *A Comparative Dictionary of the Agaw Languages*. Cologne: Rüdiger Köppe.

Appleyard, David & Martin Orwin. 2008. The Horn of Africa: Ethiopia, Eritrea, Djibouti, and Somalia. In Andrew Simpson (ed.), *Language and National Identity in Africa*, 267–290. Oxford: Oxford University Press.

Appleyard, J. W. 1850. *The Kafir Language: Comprising a Sketch of its History: Remarks upon its Nature and a Grammar*. London, King William's Town: J. Mason.

Aramazani, B. 1985. Description de la langue havu (bantou J52). 3 vols. PhD dissertation, Université Libre de Bruxelles.

Aranzadi, I. X. 1962. *En el bosque fang*. Barcelona: n. p.

Araújo, Gabriel Antunes de & Ana Lívia Agostinho. 2010. Padronização das línguas nacionais de São Tomé e Príncipe. *Língua e Instrumentos Linguísticos* 26: 49–81.

Araújo, Gabriel Antunes de & Tjerk Hagemeijer. 2013. *Dicionário livre do Santome-Português*. São Paulo: Hedra.

Archbell, W. 1837. *A Grammar of the Bechuana Language*. Grahamstown: Meurant & Godlonton.

Arensen, Jon. 1982. *Murle Grammar* (Occasional Papers in the Study of Sudanese Languages, 2). Juba: Summer Institute of Linguistics.

Armbruster, C. H. 1960. *Dongolese Nubian: A Grammar*. Cambridge: Cambridge University Press.

1965. *Dongolese Nubian: A Lexicon Nubian English. English Nubian*. Cambridge: Cambridge University Press.

Armstrong, R. G. 1964. Roy Clive Abraham, 1890–1963. *JWAL* 1(1): 49–53.

1983. Abraham, Roy Clive. In Herrmann Jungraithmayr & Wilhelm J. G. Möhlig (eds.), *Lexikon der Afrikanistik*, 17–19. Berlin: Dietrich Reimer,

Arnott, David W. 1964. Downstep in the Tiv verbal system. *African Language Studies* 5: 34–51.

Arnott, David W. & Michael Mann. 1974. A. N. Tucker: a bibliography. *African Language Studies* 15: vii–xii.

Asangama, N. 1983. *Le budu, langue bantu du nord-est du Zaïre : esquisse phonologique et grammaticale*. 2 vols. PhD dissertation, Université Sorbonne Nouvelle, Paris.

Ashton, Ethel O. 1944. *Kiswahili Grammar, Including Intonation*. London: Longmans.
Assefa, Woldemariam. 2009. *Bibliography of the International Conferences of Ethiopian Studies (I–XV), 1959–2003 and the first National Conference of Ethiopian Studies, 2000*. Addis Ababa: Institute of Ethiopian Studies.
Atidongbé, G. 1996. Bankon (A40). *Éléments de phonologie, morphologie et tonologie* (Grammatische Analysen Afrikanischer Sprachen, Band 7). Cologne: Rüdiger Köppe.
Attia, Abdelmajid. 1966. Differents registres de l'emploi de l'arabe en Tunisie. *Revue Tunisienne des Sciences Sociales* 8: 115–150.
    1969. Description phonologique du parler arabe de Mahdia (Tunisie). *Revue Tunisienne des Sciences Sociales*.
Aunio, Lotta. 2015. Typological perspective on Bantu nominal tone: the case of Ikoma-Nata-Isenye in western Tanzania. *Southern African Linguistics and Applied Language Studies* 33(3): 359–371.
    2017. Syllable weight and tone in Mara Bantu languages. In Paul Newman (ed.), *Syllable Weight in African Languages*, 191–214. Amsterdam: John Benjamins.
Aunio, Lotta, Holly Robinson, Timothy Roth, Oliver Stegen & John B. Walker. Forthcoming. *A Comparative Grammar of South Mara Languages*.
Avelar, J., S. Cyrino & C. Galves. 2009. Inversion and agreement patterns: parallelisms between Brazilian Portuguese and Bantu languages. In Margarida Petter & Ronald Beline Mendes (eds.), *Proceedings of the Special World Congress of African Linguistics: Exploring the African Language Connection in the Americas*, 207–222. São Paulo: Humanitas.
Avelelar, Juanito. 2015. Sobre a emergência das construções de tópico-sujeito no português brasileiro: mudança desencadeada por contato? In Juanito Avelar & Laura Álvarez-López (eds.), *Dinâmicas Afro-Latinas: Língua(s) e História(s)*, 127–148. Frankfurt am Main: Peter Lang,
Avolonto, Aimé Bienvenu. 1995. Pour une approche minimaliste des verbes à objets inhérents en fongbè. Thèse de doctorat, Université du Québec à Montréal.
Awad, Louis. 1947. *Plutoland, wa qasa'id min shi'r al-xassa* [Plutoland and Poems from the Elite]. Cairo: al-hay'a 'al misriya al-'amma li-lkitab.
    1980. *muqaddimah fi fiqh al-lughah al-'arabiya* [Prolegomenon to the Foundations of the Arabic Language]. Cairo: Sina li-al-nashr.
Aye, E. U. 1991. *A Learner's Dictionary of the Efik Language*. Vol. I. Ibadan: Evans Brothers.
Aymemí, A. 1928. *Diccionario español-bubi; compuesto por el R.P. Antonio Aymemí. Impresión encargada por la Presidencia del Consejo de Ministros, Dirección General de Marruecos y Colonias*. Madrid: Editorial del Corazón de María.
Ayoub, Abd al-Rahman. 1968. *The Verbal System in a Dialect of Nubian* (Linguistics Monograph Series, 2). Khartoum: Sudan Research Unit, University of Khartoum.
Ayoub, Abdel Rahman E. R. 1949. The verbal piece in the Egyptian language (a morphological study). MA thesis, University of London.
Azeb, Amha. 2012. Omotic languages. In Zygmunt Frajzyngier & Erin Shay (eds.), *The Afroasiatic Languages*, 423–504. Cambridge: Cambridge University Press.
Azevedo, Mario. 1991. *Historical Dictionary of Mozambique* (African Historical Dictionaries 47). Metuchen, NJ/London: The Scarcrow Press.
Baccouche, Taieb. 1966. La terminologie des mécaniciens, spécimen de contacts linguistiques. *Revue Tunisienne des Sciences Sociales* 8: 151–164.

1969. Description phonologique du parler arabe de Djemmal (Tunisie): avec choix de textes, transcription et traduction. *Les Cahiers du CERES*, 23–82.

1972. La phonème /g/ dans les parlers arabes de Tunisie. *Proceedings of the Seventh International Congres of Phonetic Sciences*. The Hague: Mouton.

Badawi, Ahmed & Hermann Kees. 1958. *Handwoerterbuch der aegyptischen Sprache*. Cairo: National Publishing House.

Baffoun, Alya. 1973. Le rôle du langage dans le développement psychologique: contribution à l'étude du choix de la langue d'enseignement. *Revue Tunisienne des Sciences Sociales* 32–35: 11–42.

Bagui, Hayet. 2012. Aspects of Modern Standard Arabic use in everyday conversation. Master's thesis, University of Tlemcen.

Bahuchet, S. 1989. Les Pygmées Aka et Baka (Contribution de l'ethnolinguistique à l'étude des populations forestières d'Afrique centrale). PhD dissertation, Université René Descartes (Paris V).

Baka, J. 2001. L'adjectif en bantu. PhD dissertation, Université Libre de Bruxelles.

Bakari, Mohamed. 1982. The morphophonology of Kenyan Swahili dialects. Doctoral thesis, University of Nairobi.

Bakume Nkongho Ojong, Magdaline. 2012. Proto-reconstructions of the Nyang Languages. PhD dissertation, University of Yaoundé 1, Cameroon.

Bamba, Moussa. 1992. De l'interaction entre tons et accent. PhD dissertation, Université du Québec à Montréal.

Bamgbose, Ayo. 1966. *A Grammar of Yoruba*. Cambridge: Cambridge University Press.

1991. *Language and the Nation*. Edinburgh: University of Edinburgh Press.

1994. Three decades of African linguistic research. In A. Akinlabi (ed.), *Theoretical Approaches to African Linguistics*, 1–17. Trenton NJ: Africa World Press.

2007. Linguistics and social responsibility: the challenge for the Nigerian linguist. In O.-M. Ndimele (ed.), *Nigerian Languages, Literatures, Cultures and Policy Reforms: Festschrift for Ayo Bamgbose*, 1–16. Port Harcourt: Linguistic Association of Nigeria in collaboration with M. & J. Grand Orbit Communications & Emhai Press.

2011. African languages today: the challenge of and prospects for empowerment under globalization. In Eyamba G. Bukuma, Ryan K. Shosted & Bezza Tesfaw Ayalew (eds.), *Selected Proceedings of the 40th Annual Conference on African Linguistics*, 1–14. Somerville, MA: Cascadilla Proceedings Project.

Banda, Felix. 1995. The 'meaning-to-grammar hypothesis' of Zambian English: implications for classroom language instruction in multilingual context. PhD dissertation, Université Libre de Bruxelles.

1996. In search of the lost tongue: prospects for mother-tongue education in Zambia. *Language, Culture and Curriculum* 9(2): 109–119.

2009. Accounting for the notion of multilingualism in Africa. *Stellenbosch Papers in Linguistics*, 1–17.

Banda, Felix & Rebecca F. Kirunda. 2005. Factors affecting the initial literacy development of urban and rural learners in the Iganga district, Uganda. *Per Linguam* 21(2): 1–23.

Banda, Felix & Thokozani E. Kunkuyani. 2015. Renegotiating cultural practices as result of HIV in the eastern region of Malawi. *Culture, Health and Sexuality* 17(1): 34–47.

Banjo, Ayo (ed.). 1985. *Orthographies of Nigerian Languages: Manual III*. Lagos: Federal Ministry of Education.

Banksira, Petros Degif. 1997. The sound system of Chaha. PhD dissertation, Université du Québec à Montréal.

Banti, Giorgio. 1988. 'Adjectives' in East Cushitic. In Marianne Bechhaus-Gerst & Fritz Serzisko (eds.), *Cushitic – Omotic: Papers from the International Symposium on Cushitic and Omotic Languages, Cologne, January 6–9, 1986*, 205–259. Hamburg: Helmut Buske.

Banti, Giorgio (main ed.) et al. 2009. *Ethnorêma, lingue, popoli e culture, Rivista annuale dell' associazione Ethnorêma* 5 [Special Issue on the Atlas of the Traditional Material Culture of the Saho (ATMCS)]. Online publication: www.ethnorema.it/rivista-presentazione-link/numero-5-2009.

Banti, Giorgio & Abdirachid M. Ismaïl. 2015. Some issues in Somali orthography. In Cabdirashiid M. Ismaaciil, Cabdalla C. Mansuur & Saynab A. Sharci (eds.), *Afmaal: Proceedings of the Conference on the 40th Anniversary of Somali Orthography (Djibouti, 17–21 December 2012)*, 36–48. Djibouti: The Intergovernmental Academy of Somali Language.

Banti, Giorgio & Moreno Vergari. 2013. The Saho of Eritrea and the documentation of their language and cultural heritage. In *Annali, Dipartimento Asia, Africa e Mediterraneo, Sezione Orientale* (Current Trends in Eritrean Studies vol. 70), 83–108. Naples: Università degli Studi di Napoli 'L'Orientale'.

Bargery, G. P. 1934. *A Hausa–English Dictionary and English–Hausa Vocabulary*. London: Oxford University Press.

Barrena, Natalio. 1957. *Gramàtica annobonesa*. Madrid: Consejo de Investigaciones Científicas.

1965. *La isla de Annobón*. Barcelona: Instituto Claretiano de Africanistas.

Barth, Heinrich. 1862–1866. *Sammlung und Bearbeitung Central-Afrikanischer Vokabularien*. Gotha: Justus Perthes.

Bassène, Alain-Christian & Denis Creissels. 2011. *Impersonal Constructions: A Cross-Linguistic Perspective*. Amsterdam/Philadelphia: John Benjamins.

Basset, André. 1952. *Handbook of African Languages. Part 1: La Langue Berbère*. London: Oxford University Press.

Basset, René. 1891. *Notice sur les dialectes berbères des Harakta et du Djerid tunisien*. London: 9e Congrès International des Orientalistes.

Bassong. 2013. *Information structure and the Basa'a left peripheral syntax*. PhD dissertation, University of Yaoundé 1, Cameroon.

Bastin, Yvonne. 1978. Les langues bantoues. In Daniel Barreteau (ed.), *Inventaire des études linguistiques sur les pays d'Afrique Noire d'expression française et sur Madagascar*, 123–185. Paris: Conseil International de la Langue Française.

1983. *La finale verbal -ide et l'imbrication en Bantou*. Tervuren: RMCA.

1986. Les suffixes causatifs dans les langues bantoues. *Africana Linguistica* 10: 55–145.

1994. Reconstruction formelle et sémantique de la dénomination de quelques mammifères en Bantoue. *Afrikanistische Arbeitspapiere* 38: 5–132.

2001. Les thèmes pour 'os' en Bantoue: perspectives diachroniques. *General Linguistics* 38(1–4): 1–40.

Bastin, Yvonne, André Coupez, Evariste Mumb & Thilo C. Schadeberg (eds.). 2002. *Bantu Lexical Reconstructions 3*. Tervuren: RMCA.

Batibo, Herman M. 1976. A new approach to Sukuma tone. In Larry M. Hyman (ed.), *Studies in Bantu Tonology*, 241–257. Los Angeles: University of Southern California.

1985. *Le Kesukuma (Langue Bantu de Tanzanie): Phonologie et morphologie*. Paris: Editions Recherche sur les Civilisations, Cahier 17.

1990. English language teaching and learning in Tanzanian primary schools. In Casmir M. Rubagumya (ed.), *Language in Education in Africa: A Tanzanian Perspective*, 54–74. Bristol: Multilingual Matters.

1991. The tone structure of the Sukuma nominal forms. In Francis Katamba (ed.), *Lacustrine Bantu Phonology*, 31–54. Cologne: Rüdiger Köppe.

1992. The fate of ethnic languages in Tanzania. In Matthias Brenzinger (ed.), *Language Death: Factual and Theoretical Explorations, with Special Reference to East Africa*, 85–98. Berlin: Mouton de Gruyter.

1995. The growth of Kiswahili as a language of education and administration in Tanzania. In M. Pütz (ed.), *Linguistic Inequality in Africa: Perspectives on the Namibian Experience*, 57–80. Berlin: Mouton de Gruyter.

1996. Loanword clusters nativization rules in Setswana and Kiswahili: a comparative study. *South African Journal of African Languages* 16(2): 33–41.

2002. The evolution of the Swahili syllable structure. *South African Journal of African languages* 22(1): 1–10.

2005. *Language Decline and Death in Africa: Causes, Consequences and Challenges*. Clevedon: Multilingual Matters.

2010a. Integration and identity among Khoesan speakers of Botswana. In Matthias Brenzinger & Christa König (eds.), *Khoisan Languages and Linguistics*, 284–295. Cologne: Rüdiger Köppe.

2010b. A comparative study of Kiswahili and Setswana syllable structures. In M. Matondo (ed.), *Studies in Bantu Linguistics and Languages: Papers in Memory of Professor Rugatiri Mekacha*, 57–73. Bayreuth: Bayreuth African Studies.

2015. Patterns of identity loss in trans-cultural contact situations between Bantu and Khoesan groups in Western Botswana. *Journal of Studies in Literature and Language* 11(1): 1–6.

Batibo, Herman M. & Franz Rottland. 2001. The adoption of Datooga loanwords in Sukuma and its historical implications. *Sprache und Geschichte in Afrika* 16/17: 9–50.

Bausi, Alessandro. 2005. Ancient features of Ancient Ethiopic. *Aethiopica* 8: 149–169.

2015. TraCES: From translation to creation: changes in Ethiopic style and lexicon from Late Antiquity to the Middle Ages, with an annex by C. Vertan. In Alessandro Bausi, Alessandro Gori, Denis Nosnitsin & Evgenia Sokolinski (eds.), *Essays in Ethiopian Manuscript Studies. Proceedings of the International Conference Manuscripts and Texts, Languages and Contexts: The Transmission of Knowledge in the Horn of Africa, Hamburg, 17–19 July 2014*, 11–15. Wiesbaden: Harrassowitz.

2016. The Encyclopaedia Aethiopica and Ethiopian studies. *Aethiopica* 19(1): 188–206.

Bavin, Edith L. 1983. Morphological and syntactic divergence in Lango and Acholi. In R. Vossen & M. Bechaus-Gerst (eds.), *Nilotic Studies: Proceedings of the International Symposium on Languages and History of the Nilotic Peoples, Cologne, January 4–6, 1982*, 147–168. Berlin: Dietrich Reimer.

Baxter, A. A. 1992. Contribuição das comunidades afro-brasileiras isoladas para o debate sobre a crioulização prévia: um exemplo do Estado da Bahia. In E. d'Andrade & A. Khim (eds.), *Actas do Colóquio sobre Crioulos de Base Lexical Portuguesa*, 7–36. Lisbon: Colibri.

Baye Yimam. 1986. The phrase structures of Ethiopian Oromo. PhD dissertation, University College London.

260   References

1994. አማርኛ ሰዋሰው [Amharic Grammar]. Addis Ababa: Elleni Publishing.
Beam, Mary S. & Elizabeth A. Cridland. 1970. *Uduk Dictionary* (Linguistics Monograph Series, 4). Khartoum: Sudan Research Unit, University of Khartoum.
Bearth, Thomas. 2008. Language as a key to understanding development from a local perspective: A case study from Ivory Coast. In Henry Tourneux (ed.), *Langues, cultures et développement en Afrique*, 35–116. Paris: Karthala.
Bearth, Thomas & Fan Diomandé. 2006. The local language: a neglected source for sustainable development. In Ernest W. B. Hess-Lüttich (ed.), *Eco-semiotics: Umwelt- und Entwicklungskommunikation*, 273–293. Tübingen/Basel: A. Francke.
Beaton, Arthur C. 1968. *A Grammar of the Fur Language* (Linguistics Monograph Series, 1). Khartoum: Sudan Research Unit, University of Khartoum.
Becher, Jutta. 2003. Experiencer constructions in Wolof. *Hamburger Afrikanistische Arbeitspapiere (HAAP)* 2: 1–89.
Bechhaus-Gerst, Marianne. 1996. *Sprachwandel durch Sprachkontakt am Beispiel des Nubischen im Niltal*. Cologne: Rüdiger Köppe.
Bechhaus-Gerst, Marianne & Fritz Serzisko (eds.). 1988. *Cushitic-Omotic: Papers from the International Symposium on Cushitic and Omotic Languages, Cologne, January 6–9, 1986*. Hamburg: Helmut Buske.
Beck, Rose Marie. 2001. *Texte auf Textilien in Ostafrika. Sprichwörtlichkeit als Eigenschaft ambiger Kommunikation*. Cologne: Rüdiger Köppe.
     2006. 'We speak Otjiherero but we write in English', 'Doing Elite' at the grass-roots (Herero, Namibia). In Martin Pütz, Joshua Fishman & JoAnne Neff-van-Aertselaer (eds.), *Along the Routes to Power: Explorations of the Empowerment through Language*, 305–332. New York/Berlin: Mouton de Gruyter,
     2010. Urban Languages in Africa. *Africa Spectrum* 45(3): 11–41.
     2011. *Bridging the Language Gap: Approaches to Herero Verbal Interaction as Development Practice in Namibia*. Cologne: Rüdiger Köppe.
     (ed.). 2013. *Language and Development* (Frankfurter Afrikanistische Blätter 20, 2008). Cologne: Rüdiger Köppe.
Beck, Rose Marie & Frank Wittmann (eds.). 2004. *African Media Cultures: Transdisciplinary Perspectives/Cultures de médias en Afrique: perspectives trans-disciplinaires*. Cologne: Rüdiger Köppe.
Beckett, H. W. 1951. *Handbook of Kiluba (Luba-Katanga)*. Mulongo: Garenganze Evangelical Mission.
Beermann, Dorothee. 2015. Data management and analysis for endangered languages. In Mari C. Jones (ed.), *Endangered Languages and New Technologies*, 81–94. Cambridge: Cambridge University Press.
Beermann, Dorothee & Pavel Mihaylov. 2014. TypeCraft collaborative databasing and resource sharing for linguists. *Language Resources and Evaluation* 48(2): 203–225.
Beguinot, Francesco. 1914. *L'area linguistica berbera*. Rome: Ministero delle Colonie.
     1930. Per gli studi di toponomastica libico berbera. In *Atti dell'XI Congresso Geografico Italiano*, vol. III, 243–247. Naples.
     1934. A proposito di Arabi e Berberi in Libia. *Africa Italiana*, n.n.: 1–2.
     1935. Studi linguistici nel Fezzân. *Bollettino della Reale Società Geografica Italiana* 12: 660–665.
Behnstedt, Peter & Manfred Woidich. 2013. Dialectology. In Jonathan Owens (ed.), *The Oxford Handbook of Arabic Linguistics*, 300–325. Oxford: Oxford University Press.

Belcher, Max, Svend E. Holsoe, Bernard L. Herman & Rodger P. Kingston. 1988. *Land and Life Remembered: Americo-Liberian Folk Architecture*. Athens/London: University of Georgia Press.

Bell, Herman. 1970a. The phonology of Nobiin Nubian. *African Language Review* 9: 115–139.

1970b. *Place Names in the Belly of Stones* (Linguistics Monograph Series, 5). Khartoum: Sudan Research Unit, University of Khartoum.

1975. Documentary evidence on the Ḥarāza Nubian language. *Sudan Notes and Records* 56: 1–36.

1995. The Nuba Mountains: who spoke what in 1976? In *Sudanic Africa, Text and Sources Archive, 1* (http://org.uib.no/smi/sa/tan/Nuba.html, accessed 1 August 2017).

Beltrame, Giovanni. 1870. *Grammatica della lingua Denka*. Florence: Civelli.

Beltrán, Luis. 2011. Le système d'écriture d'un peuple négro-africain à tradition orale: la 'mutanga' des Lega. In N. M. Mutaka (ed.), *Glimpses of African cultures / Échos des cultures africaines*, 39–51. Paris: L'Harmattan.

Ben Khouas, Ahmed. 1881. *Notions succinctes de grammaire Kabyle*. Alger: Jourdan.

Ben Sedira, B. 1887. *Cours de langue kabyle*. Alger: Jourdan.

Ben Srhir, Khalid. 2013. Étude comparative des manuels d'arabe en usage dans le Maroc sous protectorat français (1912–1956). In Sylvette Larzooul & Alain Messaoudi (eds.), *Manuels d'arabe d'hier et d'aujourd'hui*, 110–131. Éditions de la Bibliothèque nationale de France.

Bencheneb, Mohamed. 1905–1907. *Proverbes arabes de l'Algérie et du Maghreb*. Alger: Publication de l'Ecole des Lettres d'Alger; Paris: Leroux.

1922. *Mots turcs et persans conservés dans le parler algérien*. Thèse complémentaire. Alger: Carbonel.

Bencheneb, Rahal. 1942. L'argot des Arabes d'Alger. *Revue Africaine* 86: 72–101.

1943. Textes arabes d'Alger. *Revue Africaine* 87: 219–243.

1946. Trois récits de chasse de la région de Médéa. *Revue Africaine* 184–193.

Bender, Gerald J. 1978. *Angola under the Portuguese: The Myth and the Reality*. Berkeley/Los Angeles: University of California Press.

Bender, Gerald J. & P. Stanley Yoder. 1974. Whites in Angola on the eve of independence. *Africa Today* 21(4): 23–37.

Bender, M. Lionel. 1970. Current status of linguistic research in Ethiopia. *Rural Africana* 11: 90–96.

1971. The languages of Ethiopia: a new lexicostatistic classification and some problems of diffusion. *Anthropological Linguistics* 13(5). 165–288.

(ed.). 1976. *The Non-Semitic Languages of Ethiopia*. East Lansing, MI: African Studies Center, Michigan State University.

(ed.). 1989. *Topics in Nilo-Saharan Linguistics*. Hamburg: Helmut Buske.

2000. Nilo-Saharan. In Bernd Heine & Derek Nurse (eds.), *African Languages: An Introduction*, 43–73. Cambridge: Cambridge University Press.

Bender, Lionel Marvin & Robert L. Cooper. 1971. Mutual intelligibility within Sidamo. *Lingua* 27: 32–52.

Bender, M. Lionel, J. Donald Bowen, Robert L. Cooper & Charles A. Ferguson (eds). 1976. *Language in Ethiopia*. London: Oxford University Press.

Benhallam, Abderrafi. 1980. Syllable structure and rule types in Arabic. PhD dissertation, University of Florida.

Benkato, Adam & Christophe Perreira. 2016. An annotated bibliography of Arabic and Berber in Libya. *Libyan Studies* 47: 149–165. www.cambridge.org/core/journals/libyan-studies/article/div-classtitlean-annotated-bibliography-of-arabic-and-berber-in-libyadiv/DE76BB8D3F9BFB6E7A6D8E5ECB479EB4/core-reader (Retrieved 21 January 2017).

Bennett, Patrick R. & J. P. Sterk. 1977. South Central Niger-Congo: a reclassification. *Studies in African Languages* 8: 240–273.

Bennie, J. 1826. *Systematic Vocabulary of the Kaffrarian Language in Two Parts; to which Is Prefixed an Introduction to Kaffrarian Grammar*. Lovedale: Glasgow Mission Press.

Benoist, J.-P. 1969. *Grammaire gouro (groupe mandé – Côte d'Ivoire)*. Lyon: Afrique et Langage 3.

1977. *Dictionnaire gouro-français*. Zuénoula: s.n.

Benrabah, Mohamed. 2013. *Language Conflict in Algeria: From Colonialism to Post-Independence*. Clevedon: Multilingual Matters.

Bentahila, Abdelali. 1981. Attitudinal aspects of Arabic–French bilingualism in Morocco. PhD dissertation, University of Wales.

1983. *Language Attitudes among Arabic–French Bilinguals in Morocco*. Clevedon: Multilingual Matters.

Berhane, Girmay. 1991. Issues in the phonology and morphology of Tigrinya. Thèse, Linguistique, Université du Québec à Montréal.

Bernal, S. V. 2009. Exploring the African language connections in the Americas: the case of Cuban Spanish. In Margarida Petter & Ronald Beline Mendes (eds.), *Proceedings of the Special World Congress of African Linguistics: Exploring the African Language Connection in the Americas*, 57–70. São Paulo: Humanitas.

Bernand, Étienne, A. J. Drewes & Roger Schneider. 1991. *Recueil des inscriptions de l'Éthiopie des périodes pré-axoumite et axoumite*. 3 vols. Paris: Diffusion de Boccard.

Berry, Jack. 1957a. Vowel harmony in Twi. *Bulletin of the School of Oriental and African Studies* 19: 124–130.

1957b. *English, Twi, Asante, Fante Dictionary*. London: Macmillan.

Bertholon, J. L. 1905. Origines européennes de la langue berbère. *Extraits des comptes rendues de l'Association Française pour l'Avancement des Sciences, Congrés de Cherbourg*, 617–624. Paris: Secrétariat de l'association (Hôtel des Sociétés Savantes).

Beurmann, Moritz von. 1868. *Vocabulary of the Tigre Language, Published with a Grammatical Sketch by Adalbert Merx*. London: Trübner & Co.

Beyer, Klaus & Henning Schreiber. 2013. Intermingling speech groups: morphosyntactic outcomes of language contact in a linguistic area in Burkina Faso (West Africa). In Isabelle Leglise & Claudine Chamoreau (eds.), *The Interplay of Variation and Change in Contact Settings: Morphosyntactic Studies*, 107–134. Amsterdam/Philadelphia: John Benjamins.

Bichwa, Saul. 2016. Toni katika vitenzi vya lugha ya Giha. MA dissertation, University of Dar es Salaam.

Bickerton, Derek. 1981. *Roots of Language*. Ann Arbor, MI: Karoma.

1984. The language bioprogram hypothesis. *Behavioral and Brain Sciences* 7: 173–221.

Bierschenk, Thomas. 2003. Brauchen wir mehr Afrika-Politologen und weniger Äthiopisten? *Africa Spectrum* 38(2): 245–250.

Biloa, Edmond. 1995. *Functional Categories and the Syntax of Focus in Tuki* (Lincom Studies in African Linguistics 2). Munich/Newcastle: Lincom Europa.
1998. *Syntaxe générative: La théorie des principes et des paramètres* (Collection Linguistique). Munich/Newcastle: Lincom Europa.
2004. *Cours de linguistique contemporaine* (Lincom Coursebooks in Linguistics 9). Munich/Newcastle: Lincom Europa.
2005. *Grammaire générative: La théorie minimaliste de Noam Chomsky.* Yaoundé: Cameroon University Press (CAMUP).
Binyam, Sisay Mendisu. 2008. Aspects of Koorete verb morphology (Acta humaniora 363). PhD thesis, Department of Linguistics and Scandinavian Studies, University of Oslo.
Bird, Steven. 1999a. Strategies for representing tone in African writing systems. *Written Language and Literacy* 2(1): 1–44.
1999b. When marking tone reduces fluency: an orthography experiment in Cameroon. *Language and Speech* 42: 83–115.
Bishai, Wilson B. 1959. The Coptic influence on Egyptian Arabic (a morphological study). PhD dissertation, Johns Hopkins University.
1960. Notes on the Coptic Substratum in Egyptian Arabic. *Journal of the American Oriental Society* 80, 225–229.
1961. Nature and extent of Coptic influence on Egyptian Arabic. *Journal of Semitic Studies* 6: 175–182.
Bitjaa Kody, Z. D. 2004. La dynamique des langues camerounaises en contact avec le français: approche macrosociolinguistique. Thèse de doctorat d'Etat, Université de Yaoundé I.
Black, K. & K. Black, 1971. *The Moro Language: Grammar and Dictionary* (Linguistics Monograph Series, 6). Khartoum: Sudan Research Unit, University of Khartoum.
Black, Paul David. 1975. Lowland East Cushitic: subgrouping and reconstruction. PhD thesis, Yale University.
Blanchon, J. A. 1990. Noms composés en massango et enzebi de Mbigou (Gabon). *Pholia* 5: 31–48.
1991. Le pounou (B43), le mpongwè (B11a) et l'hypothèse fortis/lenis. *Pholia* 6: 49–83.
1994. *Dictionnaire ipunu-fançais.* Available at www/cbold.ddl.islyon.cnrs.fr/ CBOLD_Lexicons/Punu.Blanchon 1994/.
Blažek, Václav. 1999. *Numerals: Comparative-Etymological Analyses of Numeral Systems and their Implications.* Brno: Masarykova Univerzita.
Bleek, Dorothy F. 1928–1930. Bushman grammar: a grammatical sketch of the language of the /xam-ka-!k'e. *Zeitschrift für Eingeborenen-Sprachen* 19: 81–98, 20: 161–174.
1929. *Comparative Vocabularies of Bushman Languages.* Cambridge: Cambridge University Press.
Bleek, Wilhelm Heinrich Immanuel. 1862. *A Comparative Grammar of South African Languages. Part 1: Phonology.* Cape Town/London: Trübner.
1869. *A Comparative Grammar of South African Languages. Part 2: The Concord. Section 1: The Noun.* Cape Town/London: Trübner.
Bleek, Wilhelm Heinrich Immanuel & L. C. Lloyd. 1911. *Specimens of Bushman Folklore.* London: G. Allen.
Bliese, Loren. 1981. A generative grammar of Afar. PhD dissertation, SIL and University of Texas at Arlington.

Boadi, Lawrence. 1963. Palatality as a factor in Twi vowel harmony. *Journal of African Languages* 2: 133–139.

Bodomo, Adams B. 1997. Paths and pathfinders: exploring the syntax and semantics of complex verbal predicates in Dagaare and other languages. PhD dissertation, Norwegian University of Science and Technology, Trondheim.

1997. *The Structure of Dagaare* (Stanford Monographs in African Linguistics). Stanford: CSLI Publications.

Böhme, Claudia. 2006. *Der swahilisprachige Videofilm Girlfriend: Eine Sprachanalyse.* Mainz: Institut für Ethnologie und Afrikastudien, Arbeitspapiere 63.

Bokula, F. X. 1966. Éléments de grammaire et de vocabulaire de la langue bodo. Thesis, Université Lovanium, Kinshasa.

Bolekia Boleká, Justo. 1988. *Lingüística Bantú a través del Bubi.* Salamanca: Ediciones Universidad Salamanca.

1991. *Curso de lengua bubi.* Malabo: Centro Cultural Hispano-Guineano.

Bolli, M. 1976. *Étude prosodique du Dan (Blossé).* Abidjan: SIL.

Bondarev, Dmitry. 2014. Multiglossia in West African manuscripts: a case of Borno, Nigeria. In Jörg B. Quenzer, Dmitry Bondarev & Jan-Ulrich Sobisch (eds), *Manuscript Cultures: Mapping the Field,* 113–155. Berlin: De Gruyter.

Bonvini, Emilio. 2008. Línguas africanas e português falado no Brasil. In José Luiz Fiorin & Margarida Petter (eds.), *África no Brasil: a formação da língua portuguesa,* 15–62. São Paulo: Contexto.

Bonvini, Emilio & Margarida Petter. 1998. Portugais du Brésil e langues africaines. *Langages* 32(130): 68–83.

Bordal, Guri. 2012. Prosodie et contact de langues: le cas du système tonal du français centrafricain. PhD dissertation, University of Oslo.

Bossoutrot, A. 1900. Vocabulaire Berbère Ancien (dialecte du Djebel Nefoussa). *Revue Tunisienne* 28: 489–507.

Bostoen, Koen. 2002. Osculance in Bantu reconstructions: a case study of the pair -kádang/-káng (fry, roast) and its historical implications. *Studies in African Linguistics* 30(2): 121–146.

2005a. *Étude comparative et historique du vocabulaire relatif à la poterie en Bantoue.* Frankfurt: Peter Lang.

2005b. A diachronic onomasiological approach to early Bantu oil palm vocabulary. *Studies in African Linguistics* 34(2): 113–158.

2005c. *Des mots et des pots en bantou: Une approche linguistique de l'histoire de la céramique en Afrique* (Schriften zur Afrikanistik/Research in African Studies, Band 8). Frankfurt am Main: Peter Lang.

Bostoen, Koen & Jacky Maniacky (eds.). 2005. *Studies in African Comparative Linguistics with Special focus on Bantu and Mande.* Tervuren: RMCA.

Botne, Robert. 1994. *A Lega and English Dictionary with an Index to Proto-Bantu Roots* (East African Languages and Dialects 5,3). Cologne: Rüdiger Köppe.

Bougchiche, Lamara. 1997. *Langues et littératures berbères des origines à nos jours: Bibliographie internationale.* Paris: Ibis Press.

Boukka, L. Y. 1989. Éléments de description du kaamba, parler bantou de la République Populaire du Congo, groupe coongo (H17b). Mémoire de licence spéciale (troisième cycle), Université Libre de Bruxelles.

Boukous, Ahmed. 1974. Etude socio-linguistique de la prose soussie. Thèse de troisième cycle, Université Paris V (René Descartes).

1979. Le profil sociolinguistique du Maroc. *Bulletin Economique et Social du Maroc* 140: 5–31.

1989a. La dialectologie berbère pendant la période coloniale au Maroc. In A. Youssi, A. Benahallam, A. Boukous & M. Dahbi (eds.), *Langue et société au Maghreb: Bilan et perspectives* (Publication de la Faculté des Lettres et des Sciences Humaines: Série Colloques et Séminaires, 13), 119–134. Rabat: Université Mohamed V.

1989b. *Les études de dialectologie berbère en Algérie.* In A. Youssi et al. (eds.), *Langue et société au Maghreb: Bilan et perspectives* (Publication de la Faculté des Lettres et des Sciences Humaines: Série Colloques et Séminaires, 13), 135–141. Rabat: Université Mohamed V.

1989c. *Le berbère en Tunisie.* In A. Youssi et al. (eds.), *Langue et société au Maghreb: Bilan et perspectives* (Publication de la Faculté des Lettres et des Sciences Humaines: Série Colloques et Séminaires, 13), 143–150. Rabat: Université Mohamed V.

Boulifa, Said. 1913. *Méthode de langue kabyle.* Alger: Jourdan.

Boum, M. A. 1981. Le syntagme nominal en modèle. PhD dissertation, Leiden University.

Bouquiaux, Luc. 1980. *L'expansion Bantoue: Actes du Colloque International du CNRS Viviers (France), 4–16 avril 1977.* Vol. II. Paris: SELAF.

Bouquiaux, Luc & Jacqueline Thomas (eds.). 1976. *Enquête et description des langues à tradition orale.* Paris: SELAF.

Bourquin, W. 1922a. The prefix of the locative in Kafir. *Bantu Studies* 1(1): 17–19.

1922b. Adverb und adverbiale Umschreibung im Kafir. *Zeitschrift für Kolonialsprachen* 3/4.

Boyce, W. B. 1834. *Grammar of the Kafir Language.* Grahamstown: Wesleyan Mission Press.

Brahm, Felix & Adam Jones. 2009. Afrikanistik. In Ulrick von Hehl, John Uwe & Manfred Rudersdorf (eds.), *Geschichte der Universität Leipzig 1409–2009*, vol. IV, 1, 295–324. Leipzig: Leipziger Universitätsverlag.

Brauner, Siegmund & Michael Ashiwaju. 1966. *Lehrbuch der Hausa-Sprache.* Leipzig: Hueber.

Bremond, Claude. 1980. Morphologie d'un conte africain. *Cahiers d'Études Africaines* 73–76: 485–494.

Brenzinger, Matthias (ed.). 1992. *Language Death: Factual and Theoretical Explorations with Special Reference to East Africa.* Berlin/New York: Mouton de Gruyter.

(ed.). 1998. *Endangered Languages in Africa.* Cologne: Rüdiger Köppe.

(ed.). 2007. *Language Diversity Endangered.* Berlin/New York: Mouton de Gruyter.

Bresnan, Joan. 1990. African languages and syntactic theory. In Eyamba G. Bokamba, Rick Treece & Dorothy G. Evans (eds.), *The Contribution of African Linguistics to Linguistic Theory*, 35–48. Urbana-Champaign: Department of Linguistics, University of Illinois.

Bresnan, Joan & Lioba Moshi. 1990. Object asymmetries in comparative Bantu syntax. *Linguistic Inquiry* 21: 147–185.

Bresnan, Joan & Sam A. Mchombo. 1987. Topic, pronoun, and agreement in Chichewa. *Language* 63(4): 741–782.

1995. The lexical integrity principle: evidence from Bantu. *Natural Languages and Linguistic Theory* 13(2): 181–252.

Brock-Utne, Birgit. 2003. Formulating higher education policies in Africa: the pressure from external forces and the neoliberal agenda. *Journal of Higher Education in Africa* 1(1): 24–56.

Brock-Utne Birgit & Ingse Skattum (eds.). 2009. *Languages and Education in Africa: A Comparative and Transdisciplinary Analysis*. Oxford: Symposium Books.

Broadhead, Susan H. 1992. *Historical Dictionary of Angola* (African Historical Dictionaries 52). Metuchen, NJ/London: The Scarecrow Press.

Bromber, Katrin & Birgit Smieja (eds). 2004. *Globalisation and African Languages: Risks and Benefits*. Berlin: Mouton de Gruyter.

Brosnahan, L. F. 1965. The linguistic situation in tropical Africa: *Modern Linguistics* 4: 11–12.

Bross, Michael & Ahmad Tela Baba. 1996. *Dictionary of Hausa Crafts: A Dialectal Documentation = Kamus na sana'o'in Hausa*. Cologne: Rüdiger Köppe.

Brousseau, Anne-Marie. 1993. Représentations sémantiques et projections syntaxiques des verbes en fongbè. PhD dissertation, Université du Québec à Montréal.

Brown, Ian. 2016. *The School of Oriental and African Studies: Imperial Training and the Expansion of Learning*. Cambridge: Cambridge University Press.

Brugnatelli, Vermondo. 2016. *Nouveaux matériaux sur le berbère de Cheninni*. Paris: GLECS.

Brugsch, Heinrich. 1864. Aethiopica. *Zeitschrift für allgemeine Erdkunde, N.F.* 17: 1–17.

Brusciotto, Giacinto. 1659. *Regulae quaedam pro difficillimi Congensium idiomatis faciliori captu ad grammaticae normam redactae*. Roma: Typis Sac. Congregationis de Propaganda Fide. Trans. James Mew as *Grammar of the Congo Language as Spoken Two Hundred years ago*, ed. H. Grattan Guinness. London, Harley House, 1882.

Bryan, Margaret A. 1968. The *N/*K languages of Africa. *Journal of African Languages* 7: 169–217.

Bryant, J. C. 1849. The Zulu language. *Journal of the American Oriental Society* 1: 383–396.

Buffa, Diego & Maria José Bezerra. 2014. Pasado y presente de los africanos y sus descendientes en Argentina. *Revista de Estudos, & Pesquisas sobre as Américas* 8(1): 176–189.

Bukuru, Dennis. 1998. Object marking in Kirundi and Kiswahili. MA dissertation, University of Dar es Salaam.

Bulakh, Maria. 2014. Ancient Gəʿəz orthography: evaluation of the fragment of Luke (verses 6:37–6.43) in the manuscript MY–002 from Däbrä Maʿṣo, Təgray. In Alessandro Bausi, Alessandro Gori & Gianfrancesco Lusini (eds.), *Linguistic, Oriental and Ethiopian Studies in Memory of Paolo Marrassini*, 177–212. Wiesbaden: Harrassowitz.

Bulakh, Maria & Leonid Kogan. 2011. South Ethiopian pronouns and verbs in an Arab grammatical text revisited after seventy years. *Journal of the American Oriental Society* 131(4): 617–621.

2013. Geez jazyk [The Geez language]. In Maria Bulakh, Olga Romanova & Leonid Kogan (eds.), *Jazyki mira – Semitskie jazyki: Èfiosemitskie jazyki* [Languages of the World – Semitic Languages: Ethiosemitic Languages], 141–199. Moscow: Academia.

Bulakh, Maria, Leonid Kogan & Olga Romanova (eds.). 2013. *Jazyki mira: Semitskie jazyki* [Languages of the World: Semitic Languages: Ethiosemitic Languages]. Moscow: Nauka.

Bunduki, P. 1965. Esquisse phonologique et morphologique de la langue pheende. Mémoire de licence, Université Lovanium, Léopoldville.

Bunk, Elizabeth Nascimento. 2000. Die Sprachpolitik Portugals in Afrika. Master's thesis, University of Hamburg.

Burckhardt, Johann Ludwig. 1819. *Travels in Nubia*. London: Murray.

Buselli, Gennaro. 1921. Testi berberi del Gebel Nefûsa. *L'Africa Italiana, bollettino della Società Africana d'Italia fasc.* 1: 26–34.

1924. Berber texts from Jebel Nefûsi (Žemmari dialect). *Journal of the African Society* 23: 285–293.

Byrd, Steven. 2006. Calunga: an Afro-Brazilian speech. *Papia* 16: 62–78.

Cá, Virgínia José Baptista. 2015. Língua e ensino em contexto de diversidade linguística e cultural: o caso de Guiné-Bissau. Master's thesis, Universidade Federal de Minas Gerais, Belo Horizonte. www.bibliotecadigital.ufmg.br/ dspace/handle/1843/ BUBD-9XCK5W (accessed 17 April 2017).

Cahill, Michael C. 2017. Labial-velars: a questionable diagnostic for a linguistic area. In Shigeki Kaji (ed.), *Proceedings of the Eighth World Congress on African Linguistics (WOCAL 8), Kyoto, Japan, August 20–24, 2015*. Tokyo: ILCAA.

Calame-Griaule, Geneviève. 1987. *Des cauris au marché: Essais sur des contes africains*. Paris: Mémoires de la Société des Africanistes.

Calassanti-Motylinski, Gustave Adolphe de. 1885. Chanson berbère de Djerba. *Bulletin de correspondence africaine*, 461–464.

1897. Dialogues et textes en berbère de Djerba. *Journal Asiatique* 8 (November/ December): 377–401.

1898. *Le Djebel Nefousa: Transcription, traduction française et notes avec une étude grammaticale*. Paris: Ernest Leroux.

1903. Note sur la mission dans le Souf pour y étudier le dialecte berbère de R'adamès. *Journal Asiatique* 2: 157–162

1904. *Le dialecte berbère de R'édamès*. Paris: E. Leroux.

Calloc'h, J. 1911. *Vocabulaire français-ifumu (Bateke), précédé d'éléments de grammaire*. Paris: Paul Geuthner.

Calvet, Louis Jean. 1992. *Les langues des marchés en Afrique*. Aix-en-Provence: Institut d'Études Créoles et Francophones, Université de Provence.

Camperio, Manfredo. 1894. *Manuale pratico della lingua tigrè*. Milan: Ulrico Hoepli.

Cao, Qin & Rui Jufen, 2015. *Ukalimani wa Kiswahili* [Swahili Interpretation]. Beijing: Foreign Language Teaching and Research Press.

Capo, Hounkpati B. C. 1988. *Renaissance du gbe: Reflexions critiques et constructives sur l'eve, le fon, le gen, l'aja, le gun, etc.* Hamburg: Helmut Buske.

1989. *Linguistique constructive en Afrique noire*. Hamburg: Helmut Buske.

Caprile, J.-P. & H. Jungraithmayr. 1978. *Préalables à la reconstruction du Proto-tchadique*. Paris: SELAF.

Capus, A. 1898. Grammaire de shisumbwa. *Zeitschrift für Afrikanische und Oceanische Sprachen* 4: 1–123.

Cardoso, Eduardo Augusto. 1989. *O crioulo da ilha de São Nicolau de Cabo Verde*. Lisbon/Praia: Instituto de Cultura e Língua Portuguesa.

Carlson, Robert. 1994. *A Grammar of Supyire*. Berlin: Mouton de Gruyter.

Carnochan, Jack. 1960. Vowel harmony in Igbo. *African Language Studies* 1: 155–163.

Caron, Bernard. 1991. *Le haoussa de l'Ader* (Sprache und Oralität in Afrika, 10). Berlin: Dietrich Reimer.

Carreira, António. 2000. *Cabo Verde: Formação e extinção de uma sociedade escraocrata (1460-1878)*. Praia: Instituto de Promocao Cultural.

Carrell, Patricia. 1966. *Transformational Grammar of Igbo*. Cambridge: Cambridge University Press.

Carrington, J. F. 1972. Esquisse de grammaire lokele. Ms. Kisangani.

1977. Esquisse morphologique de la langue likile (Haut-Zaïre). *AL* 7: 65–88.

Carter, Hazel. 1973. Obituary Wilfred Howell Whiteley. *Journal of African Languages* 11: 90.

Casali, Roderic F. 2008. ATR harmony in African languages. *Language and Linguistics Compass* 2/3: 496–549.

Casalis, E. 1841. *Étude sur la langue Séchuana*. Paris: L'Imprimerie Royale.

Cassanelli, Lee. 2001. The Somali Studies International Association: a brief history. *Bildhaan* 1: 1–10.

Castillo-Rodríguez, Susanna. 2014. Glottopolitics and language ideologies in La Guinea Española. Paper presented at Division of Language Theory sessions at the 2014 Modern Language Association, Convention. Session 623. New Work in Language Theory. https://mla.hcommons.org/docs/glottopolitics-and-language-ideologies-in-la-guinea-espanola/.

Castro, Yeda Pessoa de. 2001. *Falares africanos na Bahia: Um vocabulário afro-brasileiro*. Rio de Janeiro: Topbooks/Academia Brasileira de Letras.

2002. *A língua mina-jeje no Brasil: Um falar africano em Ouro Preto do século XVIII*. Belo Horizonte: Fundação João Pinheiro, Secretaria de Estado da Cultura.

Cesàro, Antonio. 1939. *L'arabo parlato a Tripoli: Grammatica, esercizi, testi vari. Grammatiche e lessici delle lingue dell'Africa Italiana*. Rome: Mondadori.

1954. Racconti in dialetto tripolino. *Annali di Istituto Universitario di Napoli* 6: 49–59.

Chabata, Emmanuel. 2007. The Nambya verb with special emphasis on the causative. (Acta humaniora 315). PhD thesis, Department of Linguistics and Scandinavian Studies, Faculty of Humanities, University of Oslo.

Chaîne, Marius. 1933. *Éléments de grammaire dialectale copte: Bohairique, sahidique, achmimique, fayoumique*. Paris: Paul Geuthner.

Chaker, Salem. 1973. Le Système dérivationnel verbal berbère (Dialecte Kabyle). Thèse de doctorat de troisième cycle, Université de Paris III.

1982. Réflexions sur les études berbères pendant la période coloniale (Algérie). *Revue de l'Occident musulman et de la Méditerranée* 34(1): 81–89.

1995. Le berbère de Djerba (Tunisie). *Encyclopédie berbère, fascicule XVI*, 2459–2460.

Chami, Mohamed. 1979. Un parler amazigh du Rif marocain: approche phonologique et morphologique. Thèse de doctorat de troisième cycle, Université de Paris V.

Chebanne, A. 2010. Convergence, identity shifting and language loss in eastern Khoe. In Matthias Brenzinger and Christa König (eds.), *Khoisan Languages and Linguistics*, 296–317. Cologne: Rüdiger Köppe.

Chelo, L. 1973. Phonologie et morphologie de la langue olombo (turumbu). Thesis, Lubumbashi, Université Nationale du Zaïre.

Cheng, Ruxiang. 1997. *Takaitaccen Nahawun Hausa (A Concise Hausa Grammar)*. Beijing: Foreign Language Teaching and Research Press.

Cheng, Ying. 2016. 'Is theatre dying in Nigeria?' Recycling popular theatre in metropolitan Lagos. PhD dissertation, SOAS, University of London.

Childs, G. Tucker. 2007. Trade, Islam, and militarism: contact phenomena and language death in the Atlantic Group. In *The Atlantic Languages: Typological or Genetic Unit?* Hamburg: Asien-Afrika-Institut, University of Hamburg,.

Forthcoming a. Genetically motivated clusters within Atlantic. In Friedrike Lüpke (ed.), *The Oxford Guide to the Atlantic Languages of West Africa*. Oxford: Oxford University Press.

Forthcoming b. Language endangerment in Africa. In Mark Aronoff (ed.), *Oxford Research Encyclopedia of Linguistics*. New York: Oxford University Press.

Childs, G. Tucker, Jeff Good & Alice Mitchell. 2014. Beyond the ancestral code: towards a model for sociolinguistic language documentation. *Language Documentation and Conservation* 8: 168–191.

Cho, Kyunghyun, Bart van Merrienboer, Dzmitry Bahdanau & Yoshua Bengio. 2014. On the properties of neural machine translation: encoder–decoder approaches. In *Proceedings of SSST-8, Eighth Workshop on Syntax, Semantics and Structure in Statistical Translation*, 103–111, October 25. Doha: Association for Computational Linguistics.

Chojnacki, Stanislaw. 2007. A few remarks on collaboration with Richard at the Institute of Ethiopian Studies (IES). *Journal of Ethiopian Studies* 40(1/2): 353–355.

Chomsky, Noam. 1957. *Syntactic Structures* (Janua Linguarum Series Minor, 4). The Hague: Mouton.

1965. *Aspects of the Theory of Syntax*. Cambridge, MA: MIT Press.

Christaller, Johann Gottlieb. 1875. *A Grammar of the Asante and Fante Language Called Tshi (Chwee, Twi)*. Basel: Basel Evangelical Missionary Society.

1881. *A Grammar of the Asante and Fante Language called Tshi (Chwee, Twi)*. Basel: Basler Mission.

Chumbow, Beban Sammy. 1999. Transborder languages of Africa. *Social Dynamics* 25(1): 51–69.

Cid Kaoui, Said ben Mohammed-Akli. 1894. *Dictionnaire français-tamâhaq*. Alger: Jourdan.

Clark, H. 1973. Space, time, semantics, and the child. In T. E. Moore (ed.), *Cognitive Development and the Acquisition of Language*, 27–63. Cambridge: Academic Press.

Clements, George N. 1989. African linguistics and its contributions to linguistic theory. *Studies in the Linguistic Sciences* 19(2): 1–39.

Coelho, Adolfo. 1880–1886. Os dialectos românicos ou neo-latinos na África, Ásia e América. In Jorge Morais-Barbosa (ed.), *Crioulos: Estudos linguisticos*, 3–234. Lisbon: Academia Internacional de Cultura Portuguesa.

Coelho, Margarida, Cíntia Alves Valentina Coia, Donata Luiselli, Antonella Useli, Tjerk Hagemeijer, António Amorim, Giovanni Destro-Bisol & Jorge Rocha. 2008. Human microevolution and the Atlantic Slave Trade: a case study from São Tomé. *Current Anthropology* 49(1): 134–143.

Cohen, Marcel. 1912. *Le parler arabe des juifs d'Alger*. París: Librairie Ancienne H. Champion.

Cohen, Mordekhai. 1928. *Gli Ebrei in Libia: Usi e costume*, trans. and annotated by Martino Mario Moreno. Rome: Sindicato Italiano Arti Grafiche.

Cole, Desmond T. 1955. *An Introduction to Tswana Grammar*. London/Cape Town: Longmans, Green and Co.

1971. The history of African linguistics to 1945. In T. A. Sebeok (ed.), *Current Trends in Linguistics*. Vol. VII: *Linguistics in Sub-Saharan Africa*, 1–29. Berlin: Mouton.

Colenso, J. W. 1861. *A Zulu-English Dictionary*. Rev. and enlarged ed. 1905. Pietermaritzburg: Vause, Slatter & Co.

1903. *First Steps in Zulu: Being an Elementary Grammar of the Zulu Language*. Pietermaritzburg: Vause, Slatter & Co.

Coll, Magdalena. 2015. 'Ni bagres mandingas quedaron!': presencia lingüística africana en la narrativa de José Monegal. In Juanito Avelar & Laura Álvarez-López (eds.), *Dinâmicas Afro-Latinas Língua(s) e História(s)*, 225–242. Frankfurt am Main: Peter Lang.

Connell, Bruce. 2007. Endangered languages in Central Africa. In Matthias Brenzinger (ed.), *Language Diversity Endangered*, 163–178. Berlin: Mouton de Gruyter.

Conti Rossini, Carlo. 1894. Di due nuove pubblicazioni sulla lingua Tigre. *L'Oriente*: 102–114.

1897. (Note etiopiche 2) Leggende tigray. *Giornale della Società asiatica italiana* 10: 143–153.

1903–1906. Canti popolari tigrai. *Zeitschrift für Assyriologie und verwandte Gebiete* 17: 23–52, 18: 320–386, 19: 288–241.

1940. *Lingua tigrina*. [Milan]: A. Mondadori.

1942. *Proverbi, tradizioni e canzoni tigrine*. Rome: Ufficio Studi del Ministero dell'Africa Italiana.

Cook, Thomas L. 1969. *The Pronunciation of Efik for Speakers of English*. Bloomington, IN: African Studies Program and Intensive Language Training Center, Indiana University.

Cope, A. T. 1957. The grammatical structure of Zulu. *African Studies* 16(4): 210–220.

Corbett, Graville G. & Al D. Mtenje. 1987. Gender agreement in Chichewa. *Studies in African Linguistics* 18(1): 1–38.

Coulbeaux, Jean-Baptiste & Julius Schreiber. 1915. *Dictionnaire de la langue tigraï*. Vol. I. Vienna: Kaiserliche Akademie des Wissenschaften (Kommission zur Erforschung von illiteraten Sprachen Aussereuropäischer Völker. Schriften der Sprachenkommission 6). Vol. II (in preparation, ed. Eloi Ficquet & Wolbert Smidt). Vienna: Österreichische Akademie der Wissenschaften.

Coulibali, Bakari. 1983. *Le dioula véhiculaire du Burkina : phonologie, morphologie, syntaxe et règles de transcription*. Thèse de doctorat d'Etat, Université Paris III, Sorbonne.

Coupez, André. 1954. *Études sur la langue luba* (Annales linguistiques 9). Tervuren: RMCA.

1955. *Esquisse de la langue holoholo*. Vol. 12. Tervuren: RMCA.

1980. *Abrégé de grammaire Rwanda*. Butare: Institut National de Recherche Scientifique.

2005. *Dictionnaire kinyarwanda–kinyanrwanda et kinyarwanda–français*. Tervuren: RMCA.

Couto, Hildo Honório. 1994. *O crioulo português da Guiné-Bissau*. Hamburg: Helmut Buske.

Crabb, David W. 1969. *Ekoid Bantu Languages of Ogoja, Part 1*. Cambridge: Cambridge University Press.

Crass, Joachim & Ronny Meyer (eds.). 2007. *Deictics, Copula and Focus in the Ethiopian Convergence Area*. Cologne: Rüdiger Köppe.

2008. Ethiopia. In Bernd Heine & Derek Nurse (eds.), *A Linguistic Geography of Africa*, 228–249. Cambridge: Cambridge University Press.

(eds.). 2009. *Language Contact and Language Change in Ethiopia*. Cologne: Rüdiger Köppe.

Crazzolara, Pasquale J. 1933. *Outlines of a Nuer Grammar* (Anthropos, Linguistische Bibliothek, Internationale Sammlung linguistischer Monographien, 13). Vienna: Anthropos.

Creissels, Denis. 1988. Éléments de phonologie de Koyaga de Mankono (Côte d'Ivoire), *Mandenkan* 16.

1991. *Description des langues négro-africaines et théorie syntaxique*. Grenoble: Ellug.

Crowther, Samuel Ajayi. 1843. *A Vocabulary of the Yoruba Language: Part I English and Yoruba; Part II Yoruba and English; to which Are Prefixed Grammatical Elements of the Yoruba Language*. London: Church Missionary Society.

1864. *A Grammar and Vocabulary of the Nupe Language*. London: Church Missionary Society.

1882. *A Vocabulary of the Ibo Language*. London: Society for Promoting Christian Knowledge.

Crystal, David. 1991. *A Dictionary of Linguistics and Phonetics*. Cambridge, MA: Basil Blackwell.

CSNL. 2006. *Kamusun Hausa na Jami'ar Bayero* [The Bayero University Hausa Dictionary]. Kano: Cibiyar Nazarin Harsunan Nijeriya, Bayero University, Kano.

Cunha, A. S. 2008. Si to lo nfumbe ta sere sere: traços de linguas africanas em mambos e mpuyas em Palo Monte (Cuba). *Africana Studia, Revista Internacional de Estudos africanos* 11: 161–183.

Cyffer, Norbert. 1974. *Syntax des Kanuri, Dialekt von Yerwa (Maiduguri)*. Hamburg: Helmut Buske.

1998. *A sketch of Kanuri*. Cologne: Rüdiger Köppe.

Cyffer, Norbert, Klaus Schubert, Hans-Ingolf Weier & H. Ekkehard Wolff (eds.). 1991. *Language Standardization in Africa*. Hamburg: Helmut Buske.

Czermak, Wilhelm. 1919. *Kordofannubische Studien*. Vienna: Hölder.

1924. *Zur Sprache der Ewe-Neger. Ein Beitrag zur Seelenkunde*. Innsbruck: Rauch.

1951. Sprachgeist und tieferer Wortsinn in Afrika. *Anzeiger der philosophisch-historischen Klasse der Österreichischen Akademie der Wissenschaften* 3: 17–29.

da Cruz, Maxime. 1993. Les constructions sérielles du fongbè: approche sémantique et syntaxique (Thèse). PhD dissertation, Université du Québec à Montréal.

Dagaare Language Committee. 1982. *A Guide to Dagaare Spelling*. Wa: Catholic Press.

Dalby, David. 1977. *Language Map of Africa and the Adjacent Islands*. London: International African Institute.

Danə'el Täklu Rädda. 1996 a.-mə. [= 2003–2004], 2005 a.-mə. [= 2013]). *Zäbänawi säwasəw qwanqwa Təgrəñña*. Addis Ababa: Mega.

2017/2018. Awdawi mäzgäbä - qalat Təgrəñña (dälina), ዓውዳዊ መዝገበ - ቃላት ትግኛ (ደለ), o.O. 2010.

Daniel Teclemariam, Ibrahim Mohammed, John Abraha et al. 1997. *Eritrea Dialect Survey, December 1996–May 1997, Report.* Asmara: Department of General Education, The Ministry of Education.

Daniel Teklu Redda. 2013/2014. *Tigrigna for Beginners.* Mekelle: Tigrai Culture & Tourism.

Debela Goshu Amante. 2011. The semantics of Oromo frontal adpositions. PhD dissertation, Department of Linguistics and Scandinavian Studies, Faculty of Humanities, University of Oslo.

De Blois, Kornelis F. 1970. The augment in Bantu languages. *AL* 4: 87–165.

de Cadalvène, Edmond & J. de Breuvery. 1841. *L'Egypte et la Nubie.* 2 vols. Paris: Bertrand.

De Clercq, Y. 1921. *Grammaire du kiyombe.* Brussels: Goemaere, Bibliothèque Congo V. 1936. *Dictionnaire luba–français.* Léopoldville: Procure des Missions de Scheut.

Delgado, Carlos Alberto. 2008. *Crioulo de Cabo Verde: Situação linguistica da sona do barlavento.* Praia, Cabo Verde: Instituto da Biblioteca Nacional e do Livro.

Dendane, Zoubir. 2007. Sociolinguistic variation and attitudes towards language behaviour in an Algerian context: the case of Tlemcen Arabic. PhD dissertation, Oran University.

Derib, Ado. 2011. An acoustic analysis of Amharic vowels, plosives and ejectives. PhD dissertation, Addis Ababa University.

Derive, Jean. 1975. *Collecte et traduction des littératures orales: Un exemple négro-africain: les contes ngbaka-ma'bo de R.C.A.* Paris: SELAF.

Devens, Monica S. 1991. Annotated bibliography. In Alan S. Kaye (ed.), *Semitic Studies: In Honor of Wolf Leslau on the Occasion of his Eighty-Fifth Birthday.* Vol. I. Wiesbaden: Harrassowitz.

de Wolf, Paul Polydor. 1971. *The Noun Class System of Proto-Benue-Congo.* The Hague: Mouton.

Dhina, Amar. 1938. Notes sur la phonétique et la morphologie du parler des 'Arbâ'. *RA* 82: 313–353.

Diakonoff, Igor M., Anna G. Belova, Alexander S. Chetverukhin, Alexander Ju. Militarev & Viktor Ja. Porkhomovsky. 1994–1997. Historical comparative vocabulary of Afrasian. *St. Petersburg Journal of African Studies* 2: 5–50, 3: 5–26, 4: 7–38, 5: 4–32, 6: 12–35.

Diallo, Ibrahima. 2010. *The Politics of National Languages in Postcolonial Senegal.* Amherst: Cambria.

Dias, Pedro. 1697. *Arte da lingua de Angola, oeferecida a Virgem Senhora N. do Rosario, Mãy, e Senhora dos mesmos Pretos, pelo P. Pedro Dias da Companhia de Jesu.* Lisbon: Officina de Miguel Deslandes, Impressor de Sua Magestade.

Dieu, M. & P. Renaud (eds). 1983. *Situation linguistique en Afrique centrale – Inventaire préliminaire: Le Cameroun. Atlas linguistique de l'Afrique Centrale (ALAC), Atlas linguistique du Cameroun (ALCAM).* Yaoundé: Dgrst/Cerdotola; Paris: ACCT.

Diki-Kidiri, Marcel (ed.). 2008. *Le vocabulaire scientifique dans les langues africaines: Pour une approche culturelle de la terminologie.* Paris: Éditions Karthala.

Dilger, Hansjörg. 2005. *Leben mit Aids. Krankheit, Tod und soziale Beziehungen in Afrika.* Frankfurt am Main: Campus.

Dillmann, August. 1857. *Grammatik der Äthiopischen Sprache.* Leipzig: T. O. Weigel. (2nd ed. Leipzig: Tauchnitz 1899; English trans. London: Williams & Norgate, 1907.) 1865. *Lexicon linguae Aethiopicae cum indice Latino.* Leipzig: T. O. Weigel.

Dimmendaal, Gerrit. 2001. Areal diffusion versus genetic inheritance: an African per-spective. In Alexandra Y. Aikhenvald & R. M. W. Dixon (eds.), *Areal Diffusion and Genetic Inheritance: Problems in Comparative Linguistics*, 358–392. Oxford: Oxford University Press.

(ed.). 2009. *Coding Participant Marking: Construction Types in Twelve African Languages*. Amsterdam: John Benjamins.

Dimmendaal, Gerrit J. & Marco Last. 1998. *Surmic Languages and Cultures* (Nilo-Saharan. Linguistic analyses and documentation 13). Cologne: Rüdiger Köppe.

Diop, Cheikh Anta. 1974. *The African Origin of Civilization: Myth or Reality*, trans. from French by Mercer Cook. New York: Lawrence Hill & Company.

1977. *Parenté génétique de l'égyptien pharaonique et des langues négro-africaines: Processus de sémitisation*. Ifan-Dakar: Nouvelles Éditions Africaines.

1997. *The Peopling of Ancient Egypt & the Deciphering of the Meroitic Script*. London: Karnak House.

Diouf, Jean Léopold. 2001. *Grammaire du Wolof contemporain*. Tokyo: ILCAA.

Djarangar, Djita Issa. 1989. *Description phonologique et grammaticale du bedjond. Parler sara de bediondo, Tchad*, par Thèse de doctorat en Linguistique. University of Paris, Lille.

2014. *Le Dictionnaire pratique du français du Tchad*. Paris: L'Harmattan.

Djidjelli, M. & A. Djidjelli. 1962 (1958). *Premier livre d'arabe dialectal*. Alger: La Typo-Litho.

Djité, Paulin. 2008. *The Sociolinguistics of Development in Africa*. Clevedon: Multilingual Matters.

Dobrin, Lise M. & Jeff Good. 2009. Practical language development: whose mission? *Language* 85(3): 619–629. doi:10.1353/lan.0.0152

Dodo-Bounguendza, E. 1992–1993. Esquisse phonologique et morphologique du gisira, langue bantoue (B41) du Gabon. PhD dissertation, Université Libre de Bruxelles.

Doke, Clement M. 1917. The grammar of the Lamba language. Master's thesis, Johannesburg University College.

1925. *An Outline of the Phonetics of the Language of the Chue: Bushmen of North-West Kalahari*. Johannesburg: University of the Witwatersrand Press.

1926. *The Phonetics of the Zulu Language*. Johannesburg: University of the Witwatersrand Press.

1927. *Textbook of Zulu Grammar*. Johannesburg: University of the Witwatersrand Press.

1945. *Bantu: Modern Grammatical, Phonetical and Lexicographical Studies since 1860*. London: Percy Lund, Humphries & Co.

Doke, Clement M. & Desmond T. Cole. 1969. *Contributions to the History of Bantu Linguistics*. Johannesburg: University of the Witwatersrand Press.

Dolphyne, Florence A. 1988. *The Akan (Twi-Fante) Language: Its Sound System and Tonal Structure*. Accra: Ghana University Press.

Donaldson, Bruce. 1993. *A Grammar of Afrikaans*. Berlin: Walter de Gruyter.

Doneux, Jean-Léonce. 1968. *Esquisse grammaticale du Dan* (Documents linguistiques No. 15). Dakar: Université de Dakar.

2003. *Histoire de la linguistique africaine*. Aix-en-Provence: Publications de l'Uni-versité de Provence.

Dong, Tianqi. 1981. Brief Introduction of Congo Linguistics: *Modern Linguistics* 4: 77–79.

Dowling, T. & P. Maseko. 1995. African language teaching at universities. In K. Heugh, A. Siegrün & P. Plüddemann (eds.), *Multilingual Education for South Africa*, 100–106. Johannesburg: Heinemann.

Downing, Laura J. & Larry M. Hyman. 2016. Information structure in Bantu languages. In Caroline Féry & Shinichiro Ishihara (eds.), *Handbook of Information Structure*, 790–813. Oxford: Oxford University Press.

Downing, Laura & Al Mtenje. 2010. The prosody of relative clauses in Chewa. *ZAS Papers in Linguistics* 53: 53–68.

2017. *The Phonology of Chichewa*. Oxford: Oxford University Press.

Drescher, Martina & Sabine Klaeger (eds.). 2006. *Kommunikation über HIV/AIDS - Interdisziplinäre Beiträge zur Prävention im subsaharanischen Afrika*. Berlin: Lit.

Drewes, A. J. 1962. *Inscriptions de l'Éthiopie antique*. Leiden: Brill.

Du Plessis, J. A. 1979. PS-rules for VP in Xhosa. *Stellenbosch Studies in Afrikatale* 3: 118–158.

1981. Transitivity in Sesotho and Xhosa. *South African Journal of African Languages* 1(1): 50–85.

Duarte, Dulce A. 1998. *Bilinguismo o diglossia?* Praia, Cabo Verde: Spleen.

Dugast, I. 1954. Banen, Bafia and Balom. In D. Forde (ed.), *Ethnographic Survey of Africa: Western Africa*. Vol. IX: *Peoples of the Central Cameroons: Tikar, Bamum and Bamileke, Banen, Bafia and Balom*, 132–167. London: International African Institute.

1967. *Lexique de la langue Tunen (parler des Banen du sud-ouest du Cameroun)*. Paris: Klincksieck.

1971. *Grammaire du Tùnen*. Paris: Klincksieck.

1975. *Contes, proverbes et devinettes des Banen* (Langues et Civilisations à Tradition Orale 12). Paris: SELAF.

Duta, Henry W. 1902. *Engero za baganda 'Proverbs in Luganda language'*. London: Society for Promoting Christian Knowledge.

Duta, Henry W. & C. W. Hattersley. 1904. *Luganda Phrases and Idioms*. London: Society for Promoting Christian Knowledge.

Duta, Henry W., H. Mukasa, N. Mudeka, T. Semfuma & B. Musoke. 1899a. *Ebitabo mwenda ebyomundagano enkade: Bye bitabo okusoka ku Yosuwa okutusa ku Easeka*. London: Society for Promoting Christian Knowledge.

1899b. *Taluleti: Bye bitabo ebitano ebya Musa*. London: British and Foreign Bible Society.

1902. *Endagano empya eya Mukama wa'fe era omulokozi wa'fe Isa Masiya: Ekyakyusibwa mu Luganda okuva mu Luyonani*. London: Society for Promoting Christian Knowledge.

Dwyer, David J. 1985. *African Language Resource Handbook: A Resource Handbook of the Eighty-Two Highest Priority African Languages*. Washington, DC: Department of Education.

Dziri, Larbi. 1970. *L'arabe parlé algérien par l'image*. Paris: Maisonneuve.

Echeruo, M. J. C. 1998. *Dictionary of the Igbo language*. New Haven, CT: Yale University Press.

Egner, I. (ed.). 1992. *Esquisses phonologiques de trois langues ivoiriennes: Beng, dida, yaouré* (Esquisses linguistiques ivoiriennes 1). Abidjan: Institut de linguistique appliquée-ACCT.

Eguchi, Kazuhisa. 1996–1999. *Fulbe Folktales of Northern Cameroon*. 5 vols. Kyoto: Shoukadoh.

Ehret, Christopher. 1971. *Southern Nilotic History: Linguistic Approaches to the Study of the Past*. Evanston, IL: Northwestern University Press.

1974. *Ethiopians and East Africans: The Problem of Contacts*. Nairobi: East African Publishing House.

1980. *Historical Reconstruction of Southern Cushitic Phonology and Vocabulary*. Berlin: Dietrich Reimer.

2001. *A Historical-Comparative Reconstruction of Nilo-Saharan*. Cologne: Rüdiger Köppe.

2011. *History and the Testimony of Language*. Berkeley: University of California Press.

Eiselen, W. W. M. 1924. Die Veränderung der Konsonanten durch ein vorhergehendes in den Bantusprachen. *Zeitschrift für Eingeborenen Sprachen* 14(2): 81–153.

Ekanjume-Ilongo, B. 2005. The phrasal phonology of tones in Akoose: evidence from naturally occurring code-switching data. PhD dissertation, University of Yaoundé 1, Cameroon.

El Medlaoui, Mohamed. 1985. Le parler berbère chleuh d'Imdlawn: segments et syllabation. Thèse de doctorat de troisième cycle, Paris VIII.

El-Ayeb, Ahmed. 1966. Contribution à l'étude des fautes d'arabe chez les élèves du secondaire en Tunisie. *Revue Tunisienne des Sciences Sociales* 8: 63–128.

Elders, Stefan. 2000. *Grammaire mundang*. Leiden: CNWS.

2008. *Grammaire kulango (parler de Bouna, Côte d'Ivoire)*. Cologne: Rüdiger Köppe.

Elfitoury, Abubaker Abdalla. 1976. A descriptive grammar of Libyan Arabic. PhD dissertation, Georgetown University.

Elias, Philip. 1983. Jan Vooerhoeve, 1923–1983. *Journal of African Languages and Linguistics* 5(1): 107–112.

Elias, Philip, Jacqueline Leroy & Jan Voorhoeve. 1984. Mbam-Nkam or Eastern Grassfields. *Afrika & Übersee* 48: 31–107.

Elmoujahid, E. 1979. Présentation des phonèmes de la langue tamazighte: le tachelhiyt d'Igherm (Souss). *Traces* 2: 52–78.

1981. La classe du nom dans un parler de la langue tamazight: le tachelhiyt d'Igherm (Souss-Maroc). Thèse de doctorat de troisième cycle, Université René Descartes Paris V, Sorbonne.

Emenanjo, E. Nolue. 2007. 25 years of the Linguistic Association of Nigeria: some reflections on the achievements and challenges facing Nigerian and African studies. In O.-M. Ndimele (ed.), *Nigerian Languages, Literatures, Cultures and Reforms: Festschrift for Ayo Bamgbose*, 17–32. Port Harcourt: Linguistic Association of Nigeria in collaboration with M. & J. Grand Orbit Communications and Emhai Press.

2015. *A Grammar of Contemporary Igbo*. Port Harcourt: M. & J. Grand Orbit Communications.

Emmel, Stephen. 2004. Coptic Studies before Kircher. In M. Immerzeel & J. van der Vliet (eds.), *Coptic: Studies on the Threshold of a New Millennium* (Orientalia Lovaniensia Analecta 133.1), 1–11. Leuven: Peeters.

Endemann, K. 1876. *Versuch einer Grammatik des Sotho*. Berlin: Wilhelm Hertz.

1911. *Wörterbuch der Sotho-Sprache*. Hamburg: L. Friederichsen.

Endresen, Rolf Theil. 1990/1991. Diachronic aspects of the phonology of Nizaa. *Journal of African Languages and Linguistics* 12: 171–194.

2007. Kafa phonology. *Journal of African Languages and Linguistics* 28: 213–236.

2008. *Fulfulde: Grammatikk over dialekten i 'Aadamaawa*. Institutt for lingvistiske og nordiske studium. Oslo: Unipub AS.

2011. Koorete segmental phonology. *Journal of African Languages and Linguistics* 32: 275–306.

Engel, Ulf. 2003. Gedanken zur Afrikanistik: Zustand und Zukunft einer Regionalwissenschaft in Deutschland. *Afrika Spectrum* 38(1): 111–123.

Engelbrecht, J. 1925. Suffixbildung in den südafrikanischen Bantusprachen, mit besonderer Berücksichtigung hottentottischer Einflüsse. *Mitteilungen des Seminars für Orientalische Sprachen* (Afrikanische Studien) 28(3): 86–131.

Essien, Okon E. 1984a. Towards an Ibibio orthography (part I). *Nigerian Language Teacher* 5: 44–52.

1984b. Towards an Ibibio orthography (part II). *Nigerian Language Teacher* 6: 47–56.

1990. *A Grammar of the Ibibio Language*. Owerri: University Press Limited.

Essizewa, Komlan Essowe. 2011. *Sociolinguistics of Bilingualism in Togo: A Case Study of Kabiye-Ewe Code-Switching*. Saarbrücken: Lambert Academic Publishing.

Essono, J. J. M. 1993. Description synchronique de l'ewondo, bantou (A72a) du Cameroun: phonologie, morphologie, syntaxe. 2 vols. PhD dissertation, Université de la Sorbonne-Nouvelle, Paris III.

2000. *L'Ewondo, langue bantu du Cameroun: Phonologie, morphologie, syntaxe*. Yaoundé: Presses Universitaires d'UCAC & ACCT.

Estermann, Carlos. 1956. *Etnografia do Sudoeste de Angola. Vol I: Os povos não-bantos e o grupo étnico dos Ambós*. Lisbon: Junta de Investigações do Ultramar.

1961a. *Etnografia do Sudoeste de Angola. Vol II: Grupo étnico nhaneca-humbe*. Lisbon: Junta de Investigações do Ultramar.

1961b. *Etnografia do sudoeste de Angola. Vol III: O grupo étnico Herero*. Lisbon: Junta de Investigações do Ultramar.

Eyamba Bokamba & Molingo Virginie Bokamba. 2005. *Tosolola Na Lingala: Let's Speak Lingala* (Let's Speak Series). Urbana-Champaign: National African Language Resources Center, University of Illinois at Urbana-Champaign.

Eze, E. & Victor Manfredi. 2001. Ìgbo. In J. Garry & C. Rubino (eds.), *Facts about the World's Major Languages: An Encyclopedia of the World's Major Languages, Past & Present*, 322–330. New York: H. W. Wilson.

Fal, A., R. Santos & J. Doneux. 1990. *Dictionnaire wolof-français, suivi d'un index français-wolof*. Paris: Karthala.

Faraclas, Nicholas G. 1984. *Obolo Grammar*. Bloomington: Indiana University Linguistics Club.

Farina, Giulio. 1912. *Grammatica araba per la lingua letteraria con un'appendice sul dialetto tripolino*. Bologna: Giulio Groos.

Farinha, António Lourenço. 1917. *Elementos de gramática landina (shironga): Dialecto indigena de Lourenço Marques*. Lourenço Marques: Imprensa Nacional.

Fasold, Ralph W., William Labov, Fay Boyd Vaughn-Cooke, Guy Bailey, Walt Wolfram, Arthur K. Spears & John R. Rickford. 1987. Are black and white vernaculars diverging? Papers from the NWAVE XIV panel discussion. *American Speech* 62(1):1–80.

Fekade, Azeze. 2001. The state of oral literature research in Ethiopia: retrospect and prospect. *Journal of Ethiopian Studies* 34(1): 43–85.

Fekede, Menuta. 2015. *Intergroup Communication among Gurage: A Study on Intelligibility, Inter-Lingual Comprehension and Accommodation.* Saarbrücken: Lambert Academic Publishing.

Fellman, Jack. 1978a. The Amharic Language Academy. *Linguistics* 204: 63–65.

1978b. The beginnings of African linguistics. *African Studies* 37(2): 305–307.

1985. The first grammar of an African tongue. *African Studies* 44(2): 197–198.

1991. Ethiopia's first novel. *Research in African Literatures* 22(3): 183–184.

Feng Yupei. 2003. *Mazungumzo ya Kiswahili (Colloquial Swahili).* Beijing: Foreign Language Teaching and Research Press.

Ferraz, Luiz Ivens. 1974. A linguistic appraisal of Angolar. *Memoriam Antonio Jorge Dias,* vol. II, 177–186. Lisbon: Instituto de Alta Cultura/Junta de Investigações Científicas do Ultramar.

1975. African influences on Principense creole. In Marius Valkho (ed.), *Miscelânea luso-africana,* 153–164. Lisbon: Junta de Investigações Científicas do Ultramar.

1979. *The Creole of São Tomé.* Johannesburg: Witwatersrand University Press.

Ferreira, Carlota. 1984. Remanescentes d um falar crioulo brasileiro. In Carlota Ferreira Carlota et al., *Diversidade do português do Brasil,* 21–32. Salvador: EDUFBA.

Ferreira, Eduardo de Sousa. 1974. *Portuguese Colonialism in Africa: The End of an Era.* Paris: The Unesco Press.

Fiedler, Ines & Anne Schwarz (eds.). 2010. *The Expression of Information Structure: A Documentation of its Diversity across Africa.* Amsterdam: John Benjamins.

Finnegan, Ruth. 1970. *Oral Literature in Africa.* Oxford: Clarendon Press.

Fleisch, Axel. 2000. *Lucazi Grammar: A Morphosemantic Analysis* (Grammatische Analysen afrikanischer Sprachen, 15). Cologne: Rüdiger Köppe.

2005. A cognitive semantic approach to the linguistic construal of UPPER SPACE in Southern Ndebele. *Southern African Linguistics and Applied Language Studies,* 23(2): 139–154.

2007. Orientational clitics and the expression of PATH in Tashelhit Berber (Shilha). In Angelika Mietzner & Yvonne Treis (eds.), *Encoding Motion: Case Studies from Africa* (Annual Publications in African Linguistics, 5), 55–72. Cologne: Rüdiger Köppe.

2008. The reconstruction of lexical semantics in Bantu. *Sprache und Geschichte in Afrika* 19: 67–106.

2016. Theories and methods of African conceptual history. In Axel Fleisch & Rhiannon Stephens (eds.), *Doing Conceptual History in Africa,* 1–20. New York: Berghahn Books.

Fleming, Harold C. 1969. The classification of West Cushitic within Hamito-Semitic. In Daniel F. McCall, N. R. Bennett & J. Butter (eds.), *Eastern African History,* 3–27. New York: Praeger.

1976. Omotic overview. In Marvin Lionel Bender (ed.), *The Non-Semitic-Languages of Ethiopia,* 299–323. East Lansing: African Studies Centre, Michigan State University.

2006. *Ongota: A Decisive Language in African Prehistory.* Wiesbaden: Harrassowitz.

Fodor, István. 1966. *The Problems in the Classification of the African Languages: Methodological and Theoretical Conclusions Concerning the Classification System of Joseph H. Greenberg* (Studies on Developing Countries No. 5). Budapest: Center for Afro-Asian Research, Hungarian Academy of Sciences.

Ford, Kevin. 1971. Aspects of Avatime syntax. PhD thesis, University of Ghana, Legon.

Forde, D. (ed.) 1954. *Ethnographic Survey of Africa. Western Africa, Part IX: Peoples of the Central Cameroons*. London: International African Institute.

Fortune, George. 1967. *Elements of Shona*. Salisbury: Longman.

1969. 75 years of writing in Shona. *Zambezia* 1(1): 55–67.

1972. *A Guide to Shona Spelling*. Salisbury: Longman.

Foucauld, Père Charles de. 1818–1820. *Dictionnaire abrégé Touareg-Français*. Alger: Carbonel.

Frajzyngier, Zygmunt & Erin Shay (eds.). 2012. *The Afroasiatic Languages*. Cambridge: Cambridge University Press.

Francesco [da Bassano]. 1918. *Vocabolario tigray–italiano e repertorio italiano–tigray*. Roma: Casa editrice italiana di O. de Luigi.

Frankl, Peter J. L. 1992. Johann Ludwig Krapf and the birth of Swahili studies. *Zeitschrift der Deutschen Morgenländischen Gesellschaft* 142(1): 12–20.

1999. W. E. Taylor (1856–1927): England's greatest Swahili scholar. *Afrikanistische Arbeitspapiere* 60: 161–174.

Fromkin, Victoria. 1965. On System-Structure Phonology. *Language* 41(4): 601–609.

Furere, M. 1967. Esquisse grammaticale de la langue nande. Thesis, Université Lovanium, Kinshasa.

Furniss, Graham. 1995. *Ideology in Practice: Hausa Poetry as Exposition of Values and Viewpoints*. Cologne: Rüdiger Köppe.

Füssi Nagy, Géza. 1985. *Szuahéli nyelvkönyv (szövegmintákkal és szószedettel)* [Swahili Grammar (Text samples and glossary)]. Budapest: Tankönyvkiadó.

1986. *Szuahéli – magyar kéziszótár* [Swahili–Hungarian Dictionary]. Budapest: Tankönyvkiadó.

1987. *Magyar–Szuahéli kéziszótár* [Hungarian–Swahili Dictionary]. Budapest: Tankönyvkiadó.

Gäbrä Kidan Dästa. 1988/[=] 1996. *Ṣəwṣəway Təgrəñña* ('Təgrəñña Parables'). Mekelle: Mega.

Gabsi, Zouhir. 2003. An outline of the Shilha (Berber) vernacular of Douiret (Southern Tunisia). PhD dissertation, University of Western Sydney.

2011. Attrition and maintenance of the Berber language in Tunisia. *International Journal of the Sociology of Language* 211: 135–164.

2013. *A Concise Grammar of the Berber Language of Douiret (Southern Tunisia)*. Saarbrücken: LAP LAMBERT Academic Publishing.

Galand, L. 1989. Evolution des recherches sur les langues et les littératures berbères du Maroc depuis 1956. In A. Youssi, A. Benahallam, A. Boukous & M. Dahbi (eds.), *Langue et Société au Maghreb: Bilan et Perspectives* (Publication de la Faculté des Lettres et des Sciences Humaines: Série Colloques et Séminaires, 13), 65–70. Rabat: Université Mohamed V.

Galey, S. 1964. *Dictionnaire fang-français et français-fang, suivi d'une grammaire fang*. Neuchâtel: H. Messeiller.

García González, José & Gema Valdés Acosta. 1978. Restos de lenguas bantúes en la región central de Cuba. *Islas, Santa Clara* 59: 4–50.

Garmadi, Salah. 1966. Quelques faits de contacts franco-arabes en Tunisie. *Revue Tunisienne des Sciences Sociales* 3(8): 23–56.

1968a. Etude lexicale de 'Al-Qira'a': 1er livre de lecture arabe. *Les Cahiers du CERES* 1: 17–51.

1968b. La situation linguistique actuelle en Tunisie: problèmes et perspectives. *Revue Tunisiennes de Sciences Sociales* 13: 13–32.

1972. Les problèmes du plurilinguisme en Tunisie. In A. Abdelmalek, A. A.Belal & H. Hanafi (eds.), *Renaissance du monde arabe*, 309–332. Gembloux: J. Duculot, Gastines F. & P. Lemb. 1973. *Dictionnaire basaá-français*. Douala: Collège Libermann.

Gauthier, J. M. 1912. *Grammaire de la langue mpongwée*. Paris: Procure des Pères du Saint-Esprit.

Gbéto, Flavien. 2000. *Les emprunts linguistiques d'origine européenne en fon (Nouveau Kwa, Gbe, Bénin): Une étude de leur intégration*. Cologne: Rüdiger Köppe.

Gbéto, Flavien & Wilhelm J. G. Möhlig. 1997. *Le Maxi du centre-Bénin et du Centre-Togo: Une approche autosegmentale et dialectologique d'un parler gbe*. Cologne: Rüdiger Köppe.

Gebre Bizuneh Guadie. 2014. Shinasha noun morphology. PhD thesis, Department of Linguistics and Scandinavian Studies, Faculty of Humanities, University of Oslo.

Gebril, Atta (ed.). 2017. *Applied Linguistics in the Middle East and North Africa: Current Practices and Future Directions* (AILA Applied Linguistics Series 15). Amsterdam: John Benjamins.

Geider, Thomas. 1990. *Die Figur des Oger in der traditionellen Literatur und Lebenswelt der Pokomo in Ost-Kenya*. Cologne: Rüdiger Köppe.

2003. *Motivforschung in Volkserzählungen der Kanuri (Tschadsee-Region) - Ein Beitrag zur Methodenentwicklung in der Afrikanistik*. Köln: Rüdiger Köppe.

2009. Afrikanische Sprachen und Literaturen an der Universität Leipzig. In Ulrich von Hehl, Uwe John & Manfred Rudersdorf (eds.), *Geschichte der Universität Leipzig: 1409-2009*, 193–205. Leipzig: Leipziger Universitätsverlag.

Gerhard Böhm. 1987. Schriftenverzeichnis von Leo Reinisch. In Hans G. Mukarovsky (ed.), *Leo Reinisch: Werk und Erbe*, 335–339. Vienna: Verlag der Österreichischen Akademie der Wissenschaften,

Gerhardt, Ludwig, Roland Kießling & Mechthild Reh. 2008. Zur Geschichte der Abteilung für Afrikanistik und Äthiopistik. In Ludwig Paul (ed.), *Vom Kolonialinstitut zum Asien-Afrika-Institut: 100 Jahre Asien- und Afrikawissenschaften in Hamburg*, 163–192. Gossenberg: Ostasien-Verlag.

Geslin-Houdet, F. 1984. *Esquisse d'une description du njowi, parler des Mengisa (Cameroun)*. PhD dissertation, Université Paris III.

Ghali, Muhammad Mahmoud. 1960. Substantive morphology of colloquial Egyptian Arabic. PhD dissertation, University of Michigan.

Ghazi, Férid. 1958. Les emprunts dans les parlers arabes de Tunisie. *GLECS* 8: 17–19.

Ghirmai Negash. 1999. *A History of Tigrinya Literature in Eritrea: The Oral and the Written, 1890-1991*. Leiden: Research School of Asian, African and Amerindian Studies (CNWS), Universiteit Leiden.

Gilley, Leoma 1992. An autosegmental approach to Shilluk phonology. Dallas: Summer Institute of Linguistics and the University of Texas at Arlington.

Gilliard, L. 1928. *Grammaire synthétique du lontomba*. Brussels: Éditions de l'Essorial.

Gillis, A. 1981. *Dictionnaire français-kiluba*. Gent: H. Dunantlaan.

Gilmour, Rachael. 2007. Missionaries, colonialism and language in nineteenth-century South Africa. *History Compass* 5(6): 1761–1777. doi:10.1111/j.1478-0542.2007.00472.x.

Gioia, Chiauzzi. 1971. Alcune cantilene relative a ceremonie e ricorrenze libiche. *Studi Magrebini* 4: 77–111.

1972. Materiali per lo studio dei riti agrari in Libia. *Africa* 27(2): 193–230.

1974. Materiali per lo studio dell'abligliamento in Libia. *Studi Magrebini* 6: 73–128.

Girma, Awgichew Demeke. 2009. *The Origin of Amharic*. Addis Ababa: Centre Français d'Études Éthiopiennes.

2014. *A Diachronic Grammar of Amharic*. Princeton, NJ: Red Sea Press.

Girmay, Berhane. 1991. Issues in the phonology and morphology of Tigrinya. PhD dissertation, Université de Québec a Montréal.

Givón, Talmy. 1979. *On Understanding Grammar*. London/New York: Academic Press.

Goddard, Cliff (ed.). 2006. *Ethnopragmatics: Understanding Discourse in Cultural Context*. Berlin/New York: Mouton de Gruyter.

Goldenberg, Gideon. 2013. *Semitic Languages: Features, Structures, Relations, Processes*. Oxford: Oxford University Press.

Goldie, Hugh. 1857. *Principles of Efik Grammar, with Specimens of the Language*. Calabar: United Presbyterian Mission.

1862. *Dictionary of the Efik Language (in Two Parts)*. Edinburgh: United Presbyterian College Buildings.

Goldsmith, John A. 1976. Autosegmental phonology. PhD thesis, Massachusetts Institute of Technology.

1990a. *Autosegmental and Metrical Phonology*. Oxford: Basil Blackwell.

1990b. Phonological theory and African languages. In Eyamba G. Bokamba, Rick Treece & Dorothy G. Evans (eds.), *The Contribution of African Linguistics to Linguistic Theory*, 49–62. Urbana-Champaign: Department of Linguistics, University of Illinois.

Gordon, Rebekah. 2014. Language of education planning in Zambia. *Linguistics Portfolios* 3: 48–57.

Görög-Karady, Veronika. 1992. *Le mariage dans les contes africains: Études et anthologie*. Paris: Karthala.

Görög-Karady, Veronika, Suzy Platiel, Diano Rey-Hulman & Christiane Seydou. 1980. *Histoires d'enfants terribles (Afrique Noire): Études et anthologie*. Paris: Maisonneuve & Larose.

Goslin, Benjamin du Plessis. 1983. *'n Vakdidaktiek Noord-Sotho vir die sekondêre skool*. Pretoria: FJN Harman.

Goto, Tadahisa. 1972. *Introduction to Swahili Grammar*. Tokyo: Daigakushorin.

Gough, D. H. 1993. A change of mood. *African Studies* 52(2): 35–52.

Goyvaerts, Didier. 2000. *Conflict and Ethnicity in Central Africa*. Tokyo: ILCAA.

Gragg, Gene. 1982. *Oromo Dictionary*. East Lansing: Michigan State University.

1997. Ge'ez (Ethiopic). In Robert Hetzron (ed.), *The Semitic Languages*, 242–260. London: Routledge.

Grébaut, Sylvain. 1952. *Supplément au Lexicon Linguae Aethiopicae de August Dillmann (1865) et Édition du Lexique de Juste d'Urbin (1850–1855)*. Paris: Imprimerie Nationale.

Green, M. M. & G. E. Igwe. 1963. *A Descriptive Grammar of Igbo*. Deutsche Akademie der Wissenschaften zu Berlin: Institut für Orientforschung.

Greenberg, Joseph H. 1941. Some problems in Hausa Phonology. *Language* 17: 316–323.

1963. *The Languages of Africa*. Bloomington: Indiana University Press.

Grégoire, H. Claire. 1976a. Étude de la langue gouro (Côte d'Ivoire): phonétique, phonologie, enquête lexicale. PhD dissertation, Université Paris III.

1976b. Le champ sémantique du thème bantou *-bánjá. *African Languages / Langues Africaines* 2: 1–13.

1990. Tonétique et tonologie d'un groupe de langues mandé: étude théorique et expérimentale. Thèse de doctorat en Lettres, Université Paris III.
Griefenow-Mewis, Catherine. 1992. Status change of languages in Sub-Saharan Africa. In Ulrich Ammon & Marlies Hellinger (eds.), *Status Change of Languages*, 100–139. Berlin: Walter de Gruyter.
1996. J. L. Krapf and his role in researching and describing East-African languages. *Afrikanistische Arbeitspapiere* 47: 141–171.
Griesel, G. J. 1991. Aspekte van die linguistiese studie van Zulu, 1849-1991: 'n bydrae tot die linguistiese historiografie. Doctoral thesis, Natal College of Education, Pietermaritzburg, South Africa.
Griffini, Eugenio. 1913. *L'arabo parlato della Libia: cenni grammaticali e repertorio di oltre 10.000 vocaboli, frasi e modi di dire raccolti in Tripolitania; con appendice: primo saggio di un elenco alfabetico di tribù della Libia italiana*. Milan: Ulrico Hoepli. Repr. Cisalpino-Goliardica, Milan, 1985.
Griffith, Francis Ll. 1909. Some Old Nubian Christian texts. *Journal of Theological Studies* 10: 545–551.
1911. *Karanòg: The Meroitic Inscriptions of Shablul and Karanòg*. Philadelphia: University Museum.
1913. *The Nubian Texts of the Christian Period* (Akademie der Wissenschaften, Phil.-Hist. Kasse, Abhandlungen, 8). Berlin: Dietrich Reimer.
Grinevald, Colette. 2006. Worrying about ethics and wondering about informed consent: Fieldwork from an Americanist perspective. In A. Saxena & L. Borin (eds.), *Lesser Known Languages in South Asia: Status and Policies, Case Studies and Applications of Information Technology*, 338–370. Berlin/New York: Mouton de Gruyter.
Gromova, Nelli V. 1999. *Afrikanskoje jazykoznanie v Rossii. 30-ye gody* [African linguistics in Russia in the 30s]. Moscow: Izdatel`skij centr.
Gromova, Nelli V. & Natalia V. Okhotina. 1995. *Teoreticheskaja grammatika jazyka suahili* [Theoretical Grammar of Swahili]. Moscow: Naslediye.
Grossman, Eitan, Martin Haspelmath & Tonio Sebastian Richter (eds.). 2015. *Egyptian-Coptic Linguistics in Typological Perspective*. Berlin/Munich/Boston: Mouton de Gruyter.
Grout, L. 1893. *The IsiZulu: A Revised Edition of a Grammar of the Zulu Language*. London: Kegan Paul, Trench, Trübner.
Guarisma, Gladys. 1969. *Études bafia: Phonologie, classes d'accord et lexique bafia-français*. Paris: Bibliothèque de la SELAF.
Guarisma, Gladys & Wilhelm J. G. Möhlig. 1986. *La méthode dialectometrique appliquée aux langues africaines*. Berlin: Dietrich Reimer.
Guerssel, Mohamed. 1977. Constraints on phonological rules. *Linguistic Analysis* 4(3): 225–254.
Güldemann, Tom. 2008. The Macro-Sudan belt: towards identifying a linguistic area in northern sub-Saharan Africa. In Bernd Heine & Derek Nurse (eds.), *A Linguistic Geography of Africa*, 151–185. Cambridge: Cambridge University Press.
2013. Typology. In R. Vossen (ed.), *The Khoesan Languages*, 25–37. London/New York: Routledge.
Gusimana, B. 1972. *Dictionnaire pende-français*. Bandundu: CEEBA.

Gutgarts, Yaroslav. 2017. *Mämməhari zərəb Təgrəñña–Rusəñña Rusəəñña–Təgrəñña məs mäzgäbä qalat* ['Tigrinya–Russian Russian–Tigrinya phrasebook and dictionary']. Moscow: Wostoknaya Literatura.

Guthrie, Malcolm. 1935. *Lingala Grammar and Dictionary*. Léopoldville: Conseil Protestant du Congo.

1939. *Grammaire et dictionnaire de lingala: la langue actuellement parlée sur les deux rives de la partie centrale du fleuve Congo. Avec un manuel de conversation français-lingala*. Cambridge: Publié pour le Conseil Protestant du Congo par W. Heffer & Sons.

1948a. *The Classification of the Bantu Languages*. London: Oxford University Press.

1948b. *Bantu Word Division: A New Study of an Old Problem* (International African Institute, Memorandum 22). London: Oxford University Press.

1967–1971. *Comparative Bantu*. 4 vols. Farnborough: Gregg.

1973. Obituary Wilfred Howell Whiteley. *Bulletin of SOAS* 36(1): 119–125.

Gutt, Eeva H. M. & Mohammed Musa Hussein. 1997. *Silt'e–Amharic–English Dictionary (with a Concise Grammar of Silt'e)*. Addis Ababa: Addis Ababa University Press.

Gutt, Ernst-August. 1980. Intelligibility and interlingual comprehension among selected Gurage speech varieties. *Journal of Ethiopian Studies* 16: 57–84.

Gxilishe, S. 2009. Afrikaans, African languages and indigenous knowledge systems: the connection. Available at www.litnet.co.za/afrikaans-african-languages-and-indigenous-knowledge-systems/ (accessed on 6 June 2017).

Haacke, W. H. G. 1977. The so-called 'personal pronoun' in Nama. *Khoisan Linguistic Studies* 3: 43–62.

1999. *The Tonology of Khoekhoe (Nama/Damara)* (Quellen zur Khoisan Forschung, 16). Cologne: Rüdiger Köppe.

2010. Naro syntax from the perspective of the desentential hypothesis: the minimal sentence. In Matthias Brenzinger and Christa König (eds.), *Khoisan Languages and Linguistics*, 201–230. Cologne: Rüdiger Köppe.

Haacke, W. H. G. & E. Eiseb. 2002. *A Khoekhoegowab Dictionary with an English-Khoekhoegowab Index*. Windhoek: Gamsberg Macmillan.

Habwe, I. H. 1999. Discourse analysis of Swahili political speeches. PhD dissertation, University of Nairobi.

Hagège, Claude. 1970. *La langue Mbum de Nganha (Cameroun)*. Paris: SELAF.

Hagemeijer, Tjerk. 2003. A negação nos crioulos do Golfo da Guiné: aspectos sincrónicos e diacrónicos. *Revista Internacional de Lingüística Iberoamericana* 2: 151–178.

2007. Clause structure in Santome. PhD dissertation, Universidade de Lisboa.

2011. The Golf of Guinea creoles: genetic and typological relations. In Parth Bhatt & Tonkes Veenstra (eds.), *Creoles and Typology*, 111–154. Amsterdam/Philadelphia: John Benjamins.

Hagendorens, J. 1956. *Dictionnaire français-otetela*. Tschumbe: Ste Marie.

Hahn, C. H. 1857. *Grundzüge einer Grammatik des Hereró*. Berlin: Wilhelm Hertz.

Hailu, Fulass. 1970. The teaching of language and linguistics in universities in Eastern Africa. *Journal of the Language Association of Eastern Africa* 1(2): 45–51.

1973. ሥርዓታዊ ያማርኛ ሰዋሰው *[sərʔatawi yamarəñña säwasəw]* [Rule-governed Amharic Grammar]. Addis Ababa: Department of Ethiopian Languages and Literature.

Hair, Paul E. H. 1967. *The Early Study of Nigeria Languages*. Cambridge: Cambridge University Press.

1969. The Brothers Tutschek and their Sudanese informants. *Sudan Notes and Records* 50: 53–62.

Halaoui, N., K. Téra & M. Trabi. 1983. *Atlas des langues mandé-sud de Côte d'Ivoire.* Abidjan: Institut de Linguistique Appliquée.
Hale, Kenneth L., Colette Craig, Nora C. England, Jeanne LaVerne, Michael E. Krauss, Lucille Watahomigie & Akira Y. Yamamoto. 1992. Endangered languages. *Language* 68: 1–42.
Halefom, Girma. 1994. The syntax of functional categories: a study of Amharic. PhD dissertation, Université de Québec à Montréal.
Halévy, Joseph. 1874. Vocabulaires de diverses langues africaines. *Revue de Philologie et d'Ethnographie* 1: 53–61.
Halme, Riikka. 2004. *A Tonal Grammar of Kwanyama.* Cologne: Rüdiger Köppe.
Hamilton, Alastair. 2006. *The Copts and the West, 1439–1822: The European Discovery of the Egyptian Church.* Oxford: Oxford University Press.
Hammerschmidt, Ernst. 1965. Die äthiopistischen Studien in Deutschland (von ihren Anfängen bis zur Gegenwart). *Annales d'Éthiopie* 6: 255–277.
Hamzaoui, Rachad. 1970. L'arabization au Ministère de l'Intérieur. *Revue Tunisienne des Sciences Sociales. CERES* 3: 11–91.
Hanoteau, Adolphe. 1858. *Essai de grammaire kabyle.* Paris: Challamel.
1860/1896. *Essai de grammaire de la langue Tamachek.* Alger: Librairie Adolphe Jourdan.
Harjula, Lotta. 2004. *The Ha language of Tanzania: Grammar, Texts and Vocabulary* (East African Languages and Dialects 13). Cologne: Rüdiger Köppe.
Harrama, Abdulgialil Mohamed. 1993. Libyan Arabic morphology: Al-Jabal dialect. PhD dissertation, University of Arizona.
Harris, Randy Allen. 1995. *The Linguistics Wars.* Oxford: Oxford University Press.
Hartmann, Josef. 1980. *Amharische Grammatik.* Wiesbaden: Steiner.
Hartmann, M. 1899. *Lieder der libyschen Wüste: Die Quellen und die Texte nebst einem Exkurse über die bedeutenderen Beduinenstämme des westlichen Unterägypten* (Abh. für die Kunde des Morgenlandes, 11:3). Leipzig: Brockhaus. http://gallica .bnf.fr/ark:/12148/bpt6k824335 (accessed 1 January 2017).
Hassan Kamil, Mohammed. 2003. Symposium sur la langue afare. *Sciences et Environnement* 17: 23–27.
2007. Le dynamisme des langues: le cas de l'afar. *Sciences et Environnement* 21: 65–75.
2015. L'afar: Description grammaticale d'une langue couchitique (Djibouti, Erythrée, Ethiopie). PhD dissertation, INALCO/LLACAN, Paris.
Hatoss, Anikó. 2013. *Displacement, Language Maintenance and Identity: Sudanese Refugees in Australia.* Amsterdam: John Benjamins.
Hatoss, Anikó, Donna Starks & Henriette van Rensburg. 2011. Afrikaans language maintenance in Australia. *Australian Review of Applied Linguistics* 34: 4–23.
Haust, Delia. 1995. *Codeswitching in Gambia.* Cologne: Rüdiger Köppe.
Hayward, Richard J. 1984. *The Arbore Language.* Hamburg: Helmut Buske.
(ed.). 1990. *Omotic Language Studies.* London: RoutledgeCurzon.
Hayward, Richard J. & Chabo Eshetu. 2014. *Gamo–English–Amharic Dictionary with an Introductory Grammar of Gamo.* Wiesbaden: Harrassowitz.
Hedinger, Robert. 2008. *A Grammar of Akoose, a Northwest Bantu language.* Dallas, TX: SIL International and the University of Texas at Arlington Publications in Linguistics 143.
Heine, Bernd. 1976. *A Typology of African Languages Based on the Order of Meaningful Elements.* Berlin: Dietrich Reimer.

1978. The Sam languages: a history of Rendille, Boni and Somali. *Afroasiatic Linguistics* 6(2): 1–93.

1985. Concepts of plant taxonomy among the Samburu (Kenya): some preliminary observations. *Afrikanistische Arbeitspapiere* 3: 5–36.

1997. *Cognitive Foundations of Grammar*. New York/Oxford: Oxford University Press.

Heine, Bernd & Derek Nurse (eds.). 2000. *African Languages: An Introduction*. Cambridge: Cambridge University Press.

(eds.). 2008. *A Linguistic Geography of Africa*. Cambridge: Cambridge University Press.

Heine, Bernd & Karsten Legère. 1995. *Swahili Plants*. Cologne: Rüdiger Köppe.

Heine, Bernd & Wilhelm J. G. Möhlig. 1980–1986. *Language and Dialect Atlas of Kenya*. 6 vols. Berlin: Dietrich Reimer.

Heine, Bernd & Mechthild Reh. 1984. *Grammaticalization and Reanalysis in African Languages*. Hamburg: Helmut Buske.

Heine, Bernd, Ulrike Claudi & Friederike Hünnemeyer. 1991. *Grammaticalization: A Conceptual Framework*. Chicago: University of Chicago Press.

Heine, Bernd, Tania Kuteva, Salikoko S. Mufwene & Robert Chaudenson (eds.). 2005. *Language Contact and Grammatical Change* (Cambridge Approaches to Language Contact). Cambridge: Cambridge University Press.

Hellan, Lars, Dorothee Beermann & Tore Bruland. 2013. A multilingual valence database for less resourced languages. In *Proceedings from the Sixth Language Technology Conference (LTC 2013)*, 50–54. Poznan: Fundacja Uniwersytetu im. A. Mickiewicza.

Hellan Lars, Dorothee Beermann, Mary Esther Kropp Dakubu, Montserrat Marimon & Tore Bruland. 2014. MultiVal: towards a multilingual valence lexicon. *University of Ghana Digital Collections*. http://ugspace.ug.edu.gh/handle/123456789/25683.

Hellwig, Birgit. 2011. *A Grammar of Goemai*. Berlin: Mouton de Gruyter.

Helmlinger, P. 1972. *Dictionnaire duala–français suivi d'un lexique français–duala*. (Langues et Littératures de l'Afrique Noire 9). Paris: Klincksieck.

Helmy-Hassan, Salah el-Din. 1960. Verb morphology of Egyptian colloquial Arabic Cairene dialect. PhD dissertation, University of Michigan.

Henderson, Brent. 2011. African languages and syntactic theory: impacts and directions. In Eyamba G. Bokamba, Ryan K. Shosted & Bezza Tesfaw Ayalew (eds.), *Selected Proceedings of the 40th Annual Conference on African Linguistics: African Languages and Linguistics Today*, 15–25. Somerville, MA: Cascadilla Proceedings Project.

Hendrikse, A. P. 1975. Aspects of Xhosa sentential complementation. PhD dissertation, Rhodes University, Grahamstown.

1976. Komplementering of nominalisering: Evidensieële ondersteuning uit Xhosa vir die NP-status van ingebedde sinne van 'n sekere tipe. *Taalfasette* 20(2): 20–37.

1978. The explanatory power of the feature /REFERENTIAL/ in a Xhosa grammar. In E. J. M. Baumbach (ed.), *Second Africa Languages Congress of Unisa*, 105–127. Pretoria: University of South Africa.

Hendrikse, A. P. & S. W. Zotwana. 1975. *Topics in Xhosa Relativization: Some Traditional Analyses Re-examined* (Communication, 4). Grahamstown: Department of African Languages, Rhodes University.

Hérault, G. (ed.). 1982. *Atlas des Langues kwa de Côte d'Ivoire*. Vol. I. Abidjan: Institut de Linguistique Appliquée.

Herbert, Robert K. 1993. Not with one mouth. *African Studies* 52(2): 1–4.
Herms, Irmtraud. 1987. *Wörterbuch Hausa – Deutsch*, Leipzig: VEB Verlag Enzyklopädie.
Herms, Irmtraud & Siegmund Brauner. 1979. *Lehrbuch des modernen Swahili*. Leipzig: VEB Verlag Enzyklopädie. New editions 1982, 1986, 1990.
Hetzron, Robert. 1972. *Ethiopian Semitic: Studies in Classification*. Manchester: Manchester University Press.
   1977. *The Gunnän-Gurage Languages*. Naples: Istituto Orientale di Napoli.
   (ed.). 1997. *The Semitic Languages*. London: Routledge.
Heugh, Kathleen. 2014. Margins, diversity and achievement: system-wide data and implementation of multilingual education in Ethiopia. In Durk Gorter, Victoria Zenotz & Jasone Cenoz (eds.), *Minority Languages and Multilingual Education: Bridging the Local and the Global*, 45–63. Dordrecht: Springer.
Hirut, Woldemariam & Elizabeth Lanza. 2014. Language contact, agency and power in the linguistic landscape of two regional capitals of Ethiopia. *International Journal of the Sociology of Language* 228: 79–103.
Hoff, Rhea. 2014. *Sprachgebrauch und Spracheinstellung zur Herkunftssprache von Akansprecher/innen in Hamburg*. MA thesis, University of Hamburg.
Höftmann, Hildegard & Irmtraud Herms. 1979. *Wörterbuch Swahili–Deutsch*. Leipzig: VEB Verlag Enzyklopädie.
Holroyd, Arthur Todd. 1839. Notes on a Journey to Kordofán in 1836–7. *The Journal of the Royal Geographic Society of London* 9: 163–191.
Hombert, J. M. 1976. Noun classes and Tone in Ngie. In L. M. Hyman (ed.), *Studies in Bantu Tonology* (Southern California Occasional Papers in Linguistics 3), 1–21. Los Angeles: University of Southern California.
   1988. Mammals in the languages of Gabon: a step towards the reconstruction of Proto-Bantu Fauna. Paper presented at the 18th Colloquium on African Languages and African Linguistics, Leiden.
Hopkins, Bradley L. 1982. Étude tonologique du yaouré. *Cahiers Ivoiriens de Recherches Linguistiques* 11: 7–41.
   1995. Contribution à une étude de la syntaxe Diola-Fogny. Thèse de doctorat de troisième cycle, Université de Cheik Ahmed Diop, Dakar.
Hovens, Mart. 2002. Bilingual education in West Africa: does it work? *International Journal of Bilingual Education and Bilingualism* 5(5): 249–266.
Huang Changzhu. 1978. General introduction to African languages: *Dynamics of Linguistics* 2: 2–14.
Huang Zequan & Dong Hongyuan. 1984. The development of Hausa language and its script. *West Asia and Africa* 6: 55–61.
Hudson, Grover. 1989. *Highland East Cushitic Dictionary*. Hamburg: Helmut Buske.
   2000. Ethiopian Semitic overview. *Journal of Ethiopian Studies* 33(2): 75–86.
   2008. In memoriam Marvin Lionel Bender (1934–2008). *Aethiopica* 11: 223–234.
   2013. *Northeast African Semitic: Lexical Comparisons and Analysis*. Wiesbaden: Harrassowitz.
Hulstaert, G. 1950. *La négation dans les langues congolaises*. Brussels: IRCB.
   1957. *Dictionnaire lomongo–français* (Annales du Musée Royal du Congo Belge, commission de linguistique africaine). Tervuren: RMCA.
Hurreiz, Sayyid Ḥāmid & Herman Bell (eds). 1975. *Directions in Sudanese Linguistics and Folklore* (Sudanese Studies Library, 4). Khartoum: Khartoum University Press.

Hurskainen, Arvi. 1992. A two level computer formalism for the analysis of Bantu morphology: an application to Swahili. *Nordic Journal of African Studies* 1(1): 87–122.

1993. *Computer Archives of Kiswahili Language and Folklore*. Final Report. Dar es Salaam: Institute of Kiswahili Research.

1996. Disambiguation of morphological analysis in Bantu languages. In *Proceedings of the 16th International Conference on Computational Linguistics*, vol. I, 568–573. Copenhagen: ACL.

2002. Tathmini ya Kamusi Tano ya Kiswahili [Computer evaluation of five Swahili dictionaries]. *Nordic Journal of African Studies* 11(2): 283–300.

2010. Language learning system using language analysis and disambiguation. *Technical Reports in Language Technology*, Report No. 9. www.njas.helsinki.fi/salama.

2015. Salama dictionary. *Technical Reports in Language Technology*. Report No. 20. www.njas.helsinki.fi/salama.

Hurskainen, Arvi & Riikka Halme, 2001. Mapping between disjoining and conjoining writing systems in Bantu languages: Implementation on Kwanyama. *Nordic Journal of African Studies* 10(3): 399–414.

Hurskainen, A., L. Louwrens & G. Poulos. 2005. Computational description of verbs in disjoining writing systems. *Nordic Journal of African Studies* 14(4): 438–451.

Huyghe, Père G. 1901. *Dictionnaire kabyle–français*. Alger: Jourdan.

1906. *Dictionnaire français–chaouïa*. Alger: Jourdan.

1976. *Studies in Bantu Tonology*. Los Angeles: University of Southern California, SCOPIL 3.

Hyman, Larry M. 1979a. Tonology of the Babanki noun. *SAL* 10: 159–178.

1979b. *Aghem Grammatical Structure*. Los Angeles: University of Southern California, SCOPIL 7.

2003. Suffix ordering in Bantu: a morphocentric approach. In Geert Booij & Jaap van Marle (eds.), *Yearbook of Morphology*, 245–281. Dordrecht: Kluwer Academic.

Hyman, Larry M. & Francis Katamba. 1993. The augment in Luganda: syntax or pragmatics? In S. Mchombo (ed.), *Theoretical Aspects of Bantu Grammar*, 209–256. Stanford CA: CSLI.

Hyman, Larry M. & Al Mtenje. 1999. Prosodic morphology and tone: the case of Chichewa. In René Kegar, Harry va der Hulst & Win Zonneveld (eds.), *The Prosody–Morphology interface*, 90–113. Cambridge: Cambridge University Press.

Hyman, Larry M. & J. Voorhoeve. 1980. *Noun Classes in Grassfields Bantu*. Paris: SELAF.

Idiata, D. F. 1998. *Universaux versus spécificités linguistiques dans l'acquisition du langage chez l'enfant : le cas de la langue isangu (bantu B42)* (Lincom Studies in African Linguistics 34). Munich: Lincom Europa.

Idris, Helene Fatima. 2007. Status and use of languages in Sudan: data and results from Surveys in Nyala and Khartoum. Doctoral dissertation, Göteborgs Universitet.

2008. *Language Use and Language Attitudes in Sudan: Sociolingustic Surveys in Nyala and Khartoum*. Göteborg: University of Gothenburg, Acta Universitatis Gothoburgensis.

Idris, Helene Fatima, Karsten Legère & Tove Rosendal, 2007. Language policy in selected African countries: achievements and constraints. In H. Coleman (ed.), *Language and Development: Africa and Beyond* (Proceedings of the Seventh International Language and Development Conference). Addis Ababa: The British Council.

Idrissi, Ali. 2001. Towards a root-and-template approach to shape-invariant morphology. PhD dissertation, Université de Québec à Montréal.

Innes, Gordon. 1967. *Grebo–English Dictionary*. Cambridge: Cambridge University Press.

Instituto Nacional de Estatistica (INE). 2014. *Censo*. http://censo.ine.gov.ao/xportal/xmain?xpid=censo2014 (accessed 17 April 2017).

Intumbo, Incanha. 2006. Papiamentu, Guiné-Bissau Creole Portuguese, and its substrate, Balanta: a comparison of the noun phrase. *Revista Internacional de Lingüística Iberoamericana* 4(1): 107–115.

Ismail, Joseph H. 2011. A tonological study of Metto-Makua of Southern Tanzania. Doctoral thesis, University of Dar es Salaam.

Jacobs, Bart. 2010. Upper Guinea Creole: evidence in favor of a Santiago birth. *Journal of Pidgin and Creole Languages* 25(2): 289–343.

Jacobs, J. 1964. *Tetela-grammatika (Kasayi, Kongo)*. Gent: Orientala Gandensia.

Jacquot, A. 1976. Étude de phonologie et de morphologie myene. *Études bantoues* 2: 13–78.

Jaggar, Philip J. 2001. *Hausa*. Amsterdam/Philadelphia: John Benjamins.

Jakobi, Angelika. 1990. *A Fur Grammar* (Nilo-Saharan 5). Hamburg: Helmut Buske.

1995. Roland C. Stevenson (1915-1991): Sein Beitrag zur Sprachforschung im Sudan. In M. Wauschkuhn & K. Wohlmuth (eds.), *Die Sudanforschung in der Bundesrepublik Deutschland: Ergebnisse der Bremer Tagung 1993*, 187–200. Münster/Hamburg: LIT.

Jakobi, Angelika & Tanja Kümmerle. 1993. *The Nubian Languages: An Annotated Bibliography* (African Linguistic Bibliographies 5). Cologne: Rüdiger Köppe.

Jang, T. S. 2012. *Hausa Grammar*. Seoul: Hankuk University of Foreign Studies Press.

Janssens, B. 1993. Doubles réflexes consonantiques: quatre études sur le bantou de zone A (Bubi, Nen, Bafia, Ewondo). PhD dissertation, Université Libre de Bruxelles.

Jernudd, Björn H. 1979. The language survey of Sudan: the first phase – a questionnaire – survey in schools. Doctoral dissertation, Umeå University.

Jessen, M. & J. C. Roux. 2002. Voice quality differences associated with stops and clicks in Xhosa. *Journal of Phonetics* 30: 1–52.

Jikihara, Toshio. 1965a. *Introduction to Lingala*. Tenri: Tenrikyo Oversee Mission.

1965b. *Lingala Vocabulary*. Tenri: Tenrikyo Oversee Mission.

John Abraha Ashkaba & Wolbert G. C. Smidt. 2007. Ilit and Sokodas. In Siegbert Uhlig (ed.), *Encyclopaedia Aethiopica*, vol. III, 123–124. Wiesbaden: Harrassowitz.

Johnson, David C. 2013. Oil production and language policy in Equatorial Guinea. In David C. Johnson (ed.), *Language Policy*, 20–24. New York: Palgrave Macmillan.

Johnson, Fredrick. 1935. *Kamusi ya Kiswahili*. London: Oxford University Press.

1939a. *Standard English–Swahili Dictionary*. London: Oxford University Press.

1939b. *Standard Swahili–English Dictionary*. London: Oxford University Press.

Johnson, Janet, H. 2013. Ancient Egyptian linguistics. In Giulio Lepschy (ed.), *History of Linguistics: The Eastern Traditions of Linguistics*, vol. I, 63–75. London/New York: Routledge.

Johnson, John William. 2006. Orality, literacy, and Somali oral poetry. *Journal of African Cultural Studies* 18(1): 119–136.

Jones, D. & S. T. Plaatje. 1916. *A Sechuana Reader: In International Phonetic Orthography (with English Translations)*. London: University of London Press.

Jones, J. & J. C. Roux. 2004. An acoustic and perceptual analysis of queclaratives in Xhosa. *South African Journal for African Languages* 23(4): 223–236.

Jordan, A. C. 1942. Some features on the phonetic and grammatical structure of Baca. Master's dissertation. University of South Africa, Pretoria.

Jordan, Linda. 2016. *A Comparison of Five Speech Varieties of Southwestern Angola.* SIL: SIL Electronic Survey Report 2015-2017.

Juffermans, Kasper. 2015. *Local Languaging, Literacy and Multilingualism in a West African Society.* Bristol: Multilingual Matters.

Juillard, Caroline. 1995. *Sociolinguistique urbaine: La vie des langues à Ziguinchor (Sénégal).* Paris: CNRS.

Jungraithmayr, Herrmann & Dymitr Ibriszimow. 1994. *Chadic lexical roots.* Berlin: Dietrich Reimer.

Junker, Hermann & Heinrich Schäfer. 1921. *Nubische Texte im Kenzi-Dialekt* (Schriften der Sprachenkommission, 8). Vienna: Akademie der Wissenschaften.

Junker, Vasiliy V. 1888-1889. Verzeichnis von Wörtern Centralafrikanischer Sprachen. *Zeitschrift für Afrikanische Sprachen* 2: 35-108.

Kadima, M. 1965. Esquisse phonologique et morphologique de la langue nyanga. *AL* 2: 55-111.

1969. *Le système des classes d'accord en bantou.* Leuven: Vander.

Kagame, Alexis. 1956. *La philosophie Bantu-Rwandaise de l'être.* Paris: Membre Academie Royale Sciences Colon.

1969. *Introduction aux grands genres lyrics de l'ancien Rwanda.* Butare: University of Rwanda.

1976. *La philosophie Bantu comparée.* Paris: Présence Africaine.

Kagaya, Ryohei. 1992. *A Classified Vocabulary of the Bakueri Language.* Tokyo: ILCAA.

Kagaya, Ryohei & Yoneda Nobuko (eds). 2006. *Bibliography of African Language Study: ILCAA 1964-2006.* Tokyo: ILCAA.

Kaggwa, Apollo. 1900. *Ekitabo kye Basekabaka be Buganda.* Kampala.

1901. *Ekitabo kya basekabaka beBuganda, nabeBunyoro nabeKoki, nabeToro, nabeNkole.* London: Luzae.

1907. *Ekitabo kye mpisa za Baganda.* Kampala.

1912. *Ebika bye Buganda.* Kampala.

1934. *The Customs of the Baganda.* New York: Columbia University Press.

1971. *The Kings of Buganda.* Nairobi: East African Publishing House.

Kaji, Shigeki. 1985. *Lexique tembo I: Tembo-swahili du Zaïre–japonais–français* (Asian and African Lexicon 16). Tokyo: University of Foreign Studies, ILCAA, 1992. *Vocabulaire hunde.* Tokyo: ILCAA.

Kaji, Shigeki & Sunano Yukitoshi (eds.). 2009. *Language and Society in Africa: A Study of Multilingualism in Africa.* Tokyo: Sangensha.

Kalonji Wa Mpoyo & Didier Demolin. 2011. Le tambour-téléphone d'Afrique Cas du kyóndo des Baluba Shankádí au Katanga (R. D. Congo). In Ngessimo M. Mutaka (ed.), *Glimpses of African Cultures / Échos des cultures africaines*, 21–38. Paris: L'Harmattan.

Kamwangamalu, Nkonko M. 2016. *Language Policy and Economics: The Language Question in Africa* (Palgrave Studies in Minority Languages). London/New York: Palgrave Macmillan.

Kamwangamalu, Nkonko M., R. B. Baldauf Jr. & R. B. Kaplan (eds.). 2013. *Language Planning in Africa: The Cameroon, Sudan and Zimbabwe.* New York: Routledge.

Kamwendo, Gregory H. 1998. The use of vernacular languages in the Malawian literacy industry. *Alternation* 5(1): 32–38.

2004. *Language Policy in Health services: A Sociolinguistic Study of a Malawian Referral Hospital* (Publications of the Institute for Asian and African Studies, 6). Helsinki: University of Helsinki Printing House.

2008. The bumpy road to mother tongue education in Malawi. *Journal of Multilingual and Multicultural Development* 29(5): 253–263.

2010. Denigrating the local, glorifying the foreign: Malawian language policies in the era of African Renaissance. *International Journal of African Renaissance Studies – Multi-, Inter- and Transdisciplinarity* 5(2): 270–282.

Kane, Thomas Leiper. 1990. *Amharic–English Dictionary*. Wiesbaden: Harrassowitz.

2000. *Tigrinya–English Dictionary*. 2 vols. Springfield, VA: Dunwoody Press.

Kasa Gäbrä-Həywät & Amanuʾel [= Ėmmanuil] Gankin. 1996 a.-m. [= 2003/2004] *Säwasəw Təgrəñña*. Mekelle: Maḥbär bahli Təgray.

Kasa Gäbrä-Həywät & Amanuʾel [= Ėmmanuil] Gankin 2000 a.-mə. [= 2007/2008]. *Mäzgäbä-qalat Təgrəñña*. [no place]: Mega Publishing & Distribution.

Kaschula, Russell H. & H. Ekkehard Wolff (eds.). 2016. *Multilingual Education for Africa: Concepts and Practices*. Pretoria: Unisa Press London & New York: Routledge.

Kashoki, Mubanga E. 1968. *A Phonemic Analysis of Bemba: A Presentation of Bemba Syllable Structure, Phonemic Contrasts and their Distribution*. Manchester: Manchester University Press for the Institute of Social Research, University of Zambia.

1972. Town Bemba: a sketch of its main characteristics. *African Social Research* 13: 161–186.

1978. The language situation in Zambia. In Sirarpi Ohannessian & Mubanga E. Kashoki (eds.), *Language in Zambia*, 9–46. London: International African Institute.

1990. *The Factor of Language in Zambia*. Lusaka: Kenneth Kaunda Foundation.

1995. *Loanwords in Silozi, Cinyanja and Citonga*. Ndola: Mission Press.

2012. *Keeping in Step with Modern Times: A Comprehensive Account of Lexical Adoptives in Icibemba*. Lusaka: Bookworld Publishers.

Kashoki, Mubanga E. & Michael Mann. 1978. A general sketch of the Bantu languages of Zambia. In Sirarpi Ohannessian & Mubanga E. Kashoki (eds.), *Language in Zambia*, 47–100. London: International African Institute.

Kashoki, Mubanga E. & Sirarpi Ohannessian. 1978. *Language in Zambia*. London: International African Institute.

Kassim Mohamed, Souad. 2012. Description du parler hakmi de Djibouti: Arabe vernaculaire de la capitale. PhD dissertation, INALCO/LLACAN, Paris.

2015. Le système de négation chez les locuteurs hakmi et souqi de Djibouti-ville: description et comparaison. *Revue de l'Université de Djibouti* 8: 54–64.

2016. *Berceuses et comptines arabes de Djibouti*. Paris: L'Harmattan.

Kastenholz, Raimund. 1996. *Sprachgeschichte im West-Mande: Methoden und Rekonstruktionen*. Cologne: Rüdiger Köppe.

Katamba, Francis. 1993. *Morphology*. London: Macmillan.

2003. Bantu nominal morphology. In D. Nurse & G. Philippson (eds.), *The Bantu Languages*, 103–120. London: Routledge.

Katto, Jonna. 2017. Beautiful Mozambique: haptics of belonging in the life narratives of female war veterans. PhD dissertation, Department of World Cultures, Faculty of Humanities, University of Helsinki, http://urn.fi/URN: ISBN:978-951-51-2885-0.

Kawada, Junzo (ed.). 1997. *Cultures sonores d'Afrique*. Tokyo: ILCAA.

Keese, Alexander. 2007. *Living with Ambiguity: Integrating an African Elite in French and Portuguese Africa, 1930–61*. Stuttgart: Franz Steiner.

Keffyalew, Gebregziabher. 2004. Relativization in Tigrinya: an HPSG approach. Master's thesis, Technical University of Norway, Trondheim.

Khaketla, B. M. 1951. *Sebopeho sa Sesotho*. Johannesburg: Afrikaanse Pers-Boekhandel.

Khalafallh, Abdelghaniy A. 1969. *A Descriptive Grammar of Ṣạ'idi Egyptian Colloquial Arabic*. The Hague: Mouton.

Khmiri, Tahar. 1958. Al-taqrib bayna lughati al-hadith wa lughati al-kitaba [Narrowing the gap between everyday language and the language of writing]. *Al-Fikr* 24–26.

Khomsi, A. 1975. Étude phonétique et phonologique de l'arabe marocain de Casablanca. Thèse de troisième cycle, Université de Tours.

Khrakovskiy, V. S. (ed.). 1989. *Tipologiya itierativnykh konstrukcij* [Typology of Iterative Constructions]. Leningrad: Nauka.

(ed.). 1992. *Tipologiya imperativnykh konstrukcij* [Typology of Imperative Constructions]. St Petersburg: Nauka.

Khumalo, Langa. 2007. An analysis of Ndebele passive constructions (Acta humaniora. 321). PhD thesis, Department of Linguistics and Scandinavian Studies, Faculty of Humanities, University of Oslo.

Kiango, John Gongwe. 2000. *Bantu Lexicography: A Critical Survey of the Principles and Process of Constructing Dictionary Entries*. Tokyo: ILCAA.

Kidanä, Wäld Kəfle. 1955. *Maṣḥafa sawāsəw wa-gəss wa-mazgaba Ḳālāt ḥaddis*. Addis Ababa: Artistic Printers.

Kidanä-Maryam Zär-'Эzgi. 2003. *Fidälat bə-ḥ addis bəlh at*. 2nd ed. Asmara: Yemane Printing Press.

2008. *Zämänawi mäzgäbä-qalat bə-ḥaddis bəlḥat*. Asmara: Francescana.

Kießling, Roland. 2002. *Die Rekonstruktion der südkuschitischen Sprachen (West-Rift): von den systemlinguistischen Manifestationen zum gesellschaftlichen Rahmen des Sprachwandels*. Cologne: Rüdiger Köppe.

2008. Leo Reinisch. In Siegbert Uhlig & Alessandro Bausi (eds.), *Encyclopedia Aethiopica 4: O-X*, 354–55. Wiesbaden: Harrassowitz.

Kießling, Roland & Maarten Mous. 2003. *The Lexical Reconstruction of West Rift (Southern Cushitic)*. Cologne: Rüdiger Köppe.

2004. Urban youth languages in Africa. *Anthropological Linguistics* 46(3): 303–341.

Kießling, Roland, Britta Neumann & Doreen Schröter. 2011. 'O owner of the compound, those things you are saying – it is the talk of vagueness!': requesting, complaining and apologizing in two languages of the Cameroonian Grassfields. In Gabriele Sommer & Clarissa Vierke (eds.), *Speech Acts and Speech Events in African Languages*, 83–143. Cologne: Rüdiger Köppe.

Kießling, Roland, Maarten Mous & Derek Nurse. 2008. The Tanzanian Rift Valley area. In Bernd Heine & Derek Nurse (eds.), *A Linguistic Geography of Africa*, 186–227. Cambridge: Cambridge University Press.

Killian, Donald. 2015. Topics in Uduk phonology and morphosyntax. Doctoral dissertation, Department of World Cultures, University of Helsinki.

Kim, H. S. 2006. On linguistic characteristics and the languages of the Chadic family from a typological viewpoint. *African Affairs* 20: 61–96.

2013. Linguistic features and Dghwede, Guduf and Gvoko and their internal linguistic relationship (Northern Nigeria). *Journal of the Korean Association of African Studies* 38: 31–66.

Kim, Y. J. & M. S. Kwon (eds.). 1999. *A Swahili–Korean Dictionary*. Seoul: Hankuk University of Foreign Studies Press.

King'ei, Kitula. 1999. Swahili technical terminology: problems of development and usage in Kenya. *Afrikanistische Arbeitspapiere* 60: 147–160.

2002. The challenge of modernising an African language: the case of Kiswahili in East Africa. In K. K. Prah (ed.), *Rehabilitating African languages: Language Use, Language Policy and Literacy in Africa, Selected Case Studies*, 109–124. Cape Town: The Centre for Advanced Studies of African Society.

Kirchner, Matthäus. 1861. Grammatica linguae dincaicae germanice et latina conscripta. Ms., Missione Africanae, Verona.

Kiros Fre Woldu. 1985. The perception and production of Tigrinya stops. Doctoral dissertation, Uppsala universitet.

Kishindo, Pascal J. 2000. Evolution of political terminologies in Chichewa and the changing political culture in Malawi. *Nordic Journal of African Studies* 9(1): 20–30.

2001. Authority in language: the role of the Chichewa Board (1972–1995) in prescription and standardization of Chichewa. *Journal of Asian and African Studies* 62: 261–283.

Kitereza, Aniceti & Wilhelm J. G. Möhlig. 1991. *Die Kinder der Regenmacher: Herr Myombekere und Frau Bugonoka. Eine afrikanische Familiensaga*. Wuppertal: Hammer.

Kjelsvik, Bjørghild. 2008. Emergent speech genres of teaching and learning interaction: communities of practice in Cameroonian schools and villages (Acta humaniora. 369). PhD thesis, Department of Linguistics and Scandinavian Studies, Faculty of Humanities, University of Oslo.

Klein-Arendt, Reinhard. 1992. *Gesprächsstrategien im Swahili*. Cologne: Rüdiger Köppe.

2004. *Die traditionellen Eisenhandwerke der Savannen-Bantu: Eine sprachhistorische Rekonstruktion auf lexikalischer Grundlage*. Frankfurt: Peter Lang.

Knappert, Jan. 1967. *Traditional Swahili Poetry*. Leiden: E. J. Brill.

1970. *Myths and Legends of Swahili*. London: Heinemann.

1979. *Four Centuries of Swahili Verses: A Literary History and Anthology*. London: Heinemann.

1983. *Epic Poetry in Swahili and Other African Languages*. London: Heinemann.

1996. The transmission of knowledge: a note on the Islamic literatures of Africa. *Sudanic Africa* 7: 159–164.

Knutsen, Anne Moseng. 2007. Variation du français à Abidjan (Côte d'Ivoire): étude d'un continuum linguistique et social. PhD dissertation, University of Oslo.

Kobishchanov, Yuri M. 1983. Etnos, religiya i yazyk v Afrike [Ethnic groups, religion and languages in Africa]. *Collection of National Traditions* 1: 32–39.

Koehn, Philipp. 2010. *Statistical Machine Translation*. Cambridge: Cambridge University Press.

Koelle, Wilhelm Sigismund. 1854. *Polyglotta Africana*. London: Church Missionary House. Repr. with historical introduction by P. E. H. Hair, Freetown: Fourah Bay College, 1963.

Kogan, Leonid. 2015. *Genealogical Classification of Semitic: The Lexical Isoglosses.* Berlin: De Gruyter.

Kohl, Christoph. 2011. National Integration in Guinea-Bissau since Independence. *Cadernos de Estudos Africanos* 20: 86–109.

Köhler, Oswin. 1955. *Geschichte der Erforschung der nilotischen Sprachen* (Afrika und Übersee, Beiheft 28). Berlin: Dietrich Reimer.

1975. Geschichte und Probleme der Gliederung der Sprachen Afrikas. In Hermann Baumann (ed.), *Die Völker Afrikas und ihre traditionellen Kulturen. Part I: Allgemeiner Teil und südliches Afrika*, 135–373. Wiesbaden: Franz Steiner.

Kohnen, Bernardo. 1933. *Shilluk Grammar: With a Little English–Shilluk Dictionary.* Verona: Missioni Africane.

Kolmodin, Johannes. 1912. *Traditions de Tsazzega et Hazzega: Textes tigrigna* (Archives d'études orientales 5, 1). Rome: Casa Editrice Italiana di Carlo de Luigi.

1914. *Traditions de Tsazzega et Hazzega, Annales et documents* (Archives d'études orientales 5, 3). Upsal: Imprimerie Edv. Berling.

1915. *Traditions de Tsazzega et Hazzega. Traduction française* (Archives d'Études Orientales 5, 2). Upsal: K. W. Appelberg.

Kosch, Inge M. 1993. *A Historical Perspective on Northern Sotho Linguistics* (Via Afrika Monograph Series 5). Pretoria: Via Afrika.

Kosch, I. M. & S. E. Bosch. 2014. African languages as languages of teaching and learning: the case of the Department of African Languages, University of South Africa. In L. Hibbert & C. van der Walt (eds.), *Multilingual Universities in South Africa: Reflecting Society in Higher Education*, 49–67. Bristol: Multilingual Matters.

Kossmann, Maarten. 1999. *Essai sur la phonologie du proto-berbère*. Cologne: Rüdiger Köppe.

Krachkoskiy, I. Yu. 1955. *Vvedenie v efiopskuyu filologiyu*. Leningrad: Izdatel'stvo Leningradskogo Universiteta.

Kraief, B. 1959. Khataru al-fusha 'ala al-'ammiyya [The danger of Classical Arabic on the Arabic language]. *Al-Fikr* 19–21.

Krapf, Johann Ludwig. 1850a. *An Outline of the Kisuaheli Language with Special Reference to the Kinika Dialect.* Tübingen: Ludwig Friedrich Fuchs.

1882. *A Dictionary of the Suahili Language with Introduction Containing an Outline of the Grammar.* London: Trübner.

Krings, Matthias & Uta Reuster-Jahn (eds.). 2014. *Bongo Media Worlds: Producing and Consuming Popular Culture in Dar es Salaam.* Cologne: Rüdiger Köppe.

Kropf, A. 1899. *A Kaffir–English Dictionary.* South Africa: Lovedale Mission Press.

Kropp Dakubu, M. E. 1977. *West African Language Data Sheets.* Vol. I. Legon: West African Linguistic Society.

1980. *West African Language Data Sheets.* Vol. II. Leiden: African Studies Centre.

Krumm, Bernard. 1940. *Words of oriental origin in Swahili.* London: The Sheldon Press.

Kwon, M. S. 1986. *A Study of the Swahili Language.* Seoul: Myoungji Publishing Co.

1987. *A Syntactic Analysis of Swahili.* Seoul: Myongji Publishing Co.

1988. *Introduction to African Studies: A Comparative-Historical Approach.* Seoul: Myoungji Publishing Co.

1989. *Mazungumzo ya Kiswahili.* Seoul: Myongji Publishing Co.

2004. *Introduction to the Study of African Languages.* Seoul: Hankuk University of Foreign Studies Press.

2011a. *Sociolinguistics in Africa.* Seoul: Hankuk University of Foreign Studies Press.

2011b. *The Grammatical Structure of the Swahili Language.* Seoul: Hankuk University of Foreign Studies Press.

Labahn, Thomas. 1984. Sprachpolitik in Somalia. In Rainer Voßen & Ulrike Claudi (eds.), *Sprache, Geschichte und Kultur in Afrika: Vorträge, gehalten auf dem 3. Afrikanistentag, Köln, 14.–15. Oktober 1982,* 345–356. Hamburg: Helmut Buske.

Labov, William. 2001. Foreword to African American English in the diaspora. In Shana Poplack & Sali A. Tagliamonte (eds.), *African American English in the Diaspora,* xiv–xvii. Malden, MA and Oxford: Blackwell.

Ladefoged, Peter. 1964. *A Phonetic Study of West African Languages.* Cambridge: Cambridge University Press in Association with the West African Languages Survey and the Institute of African Studies, Ibadan.

Laitin, David D. 1977. *Politics, Language, and Thought: The Somali Experience.* Chicago: University of Chicago Press.

Lambdin, Thomas. 1978. *Introduction to Classical Ethiopic (Ge'ez).* Harvard/Missoula: Scholars Press.

Lambert-Brétière, Renée. 2009. Serializing languages as satellite-framed: the case of Fon. *Annual Review of Cognitive Linguistics* 7: 1–29.

Lamberti, Marcello. 1986. *Die Somali–Dialekte: Eine vergleichende Untersuchung mit 35 Karten und zahlreichen Tabellen.* Hamburg: Helmut Buske.

1991. Cushitic and its classification. *Anthropos* 86(4/6): 552–561.

2003. Italian Ethiopian studies in the 20th century. In Rainer Voigt (ed.), *Die äthiopischen Studien im 20. Jahrhundert / Ethiopian Studies in the 20th Century. Akten der internationalen äthiopischen Tagung Berlin 22. bis 24. Juli 2000, Semitica et Semitohamitica Berolinensia 2,* 103–121. Aachen: Shaker Verlag,

Lanham, L. W. 1971. The noun as the deep-structure source for Nguni adjectives and relatives. *African Studies* 30(3/4): 299–311.

Laoust, E. 1931. *Siwa I* (Publications de l'Institut des hautes-études marocaines, 22). Paris: E. Leroux.

Laradi, Widad J. 1972. Negation in colloquial Tripoli Arabic. MA dissertation, University of Leeds.

1983. Pharyngealization in Libyan (Tripoli) Arabic: an instrumental study. PhD thesis, University of Edinburgh.

Laughren, Mary. 1973. Une analyse plérématique du tyebari, un dialecte sénoufo de Côte d'Ivoire. PhD thesis, Université de Nice.

Leben, William R. 1971. Suprasegmental and segmental representation of tone. *Studies in African Linguistics* Supplement 2: 183–200.

1973. Suprasegmental phonology. Doctoral thesis, MIT. Published New York: Garland Press, 1980.

Lébikaza, K. Kézié. 1999. *Grammaire Kabiyè: Une analyse systématique-phonologie, tonologie, et morphosyntaxe.* Cologne: Rüdiger Köppe.

Lefebvre, Claire. 1998. *Creole Genesis and the Acquisition of Grammar: The Case of Haitian Creole.* Cambridge: Cambridge University Press.

Legère, Karsten. 1990. *Wörterbuch Deutsch-Swahili (German Edition).* Leipzig: VEB Verlag Enzyklopädie.

2006. Formal and informal development of the Swahili Language: focus on Tanzania. In O. F. Arasanyin & M. A. Pemberton (eds.), *Selected Proceedings of the 36th Annual Conference on African Linguistics,* 176–184. Somerville, MA: Cascadilla Proceedings Project.

2007. Documenting the Vidunda language of Tanzania. *Working Together for Endangered Languages: Research Challenges and Social Impacts (Proceedings of FEL XI)*. Bath: The Foundation for Endangered Languages.

Legère, Karsten, Bernd Heine & Christa König. 2015. *The Akie Language of Tanzania: A Sketch of Discourse Grammar*. Tokyo: ILCAA.

Lehtonen, Lahja. 1996. *English–Ndonga Dictionary*. Oniipa: ELCIN Printing Press.

Leitch, Myles. 1997. Vowel harmonies of the Congo Basin: an optimality theory analysis of variation in the Bantu Zone C. PhD thesis, University of British Columbia, Vancouver.

Lepsius, Karl Richard. 1880. *Nubische Grammatik, mit einer Einleitung über die Völker und Sprachen Afrika's*. Berlin: W. Hertz.

1936. *Über den Ursprung und die Verwandtschaft der Zahlwörter in der Indogermanischen, Semitischen und der Koptischen Sprache*. Berlin: Ferdinand Dümmler.

Leroy, J. 1977. *Morphologie et classes nominales en mankon (Cameroun)*. Paris: SELAF.

Leslau, Wolf. 1941. *Documents tigrinya (Éthiopien septentrional): grammaire et textes*. Paris: C. Klincksieck.

1965a. *An Annotated Bibliography of the Semitic Languages of Ethiopia*. The Hague: Mouton.

1965b. *An Amharic Conversation Book*. Wiesbaden: Harrassowitz.

1976. *Concise Amharic dictionary*. Berkeley/Los Angeles: University of California Press.

1979. *Etymological Dictionary of Gurage (Ethiopic)*. 3 vols. Wiesbaden: Harrassowitz.

1987. *Comparative Dictionary of Gəʿəz: Gəʿəz-English / English-Gəʿəz with an Index of the Semitic Roots*. Wiesbaden: Harrassowitz.

1992. Introduction. In Wolf Leslau (ed.), *Gurage Studies: Collected Articles*, xiii–xxix. Wiesbaden: Harrassowitz.

1995. *Reference Grammar of Amharic*. Wiesbaden: Harrassowitz.

Lewis, M. Paul, Gary F. Simons & Charles D. Fennig (eds.). 2015. *Ethnologue: Languages of the World*. 18th ed. Dallas, TX: SIL International.

Lewis, P. W. 1998. Phonetic and phonological interference in Xhosa speech communication. D.Litt. thesis, Stellenbosch University.

Lexander, Kristin Vold. 2010. Pratiques plurilingues de l'écrit électronique: alternances codiques et choix de langue dans les SMS, les courriels et les conversations de la messagerie instantanée des étudiants de Dakar, Sénégal. PhD dissertation, University of Oslo, Norway.

Li, Wengang. 2008. An analysis on the language issue during the nation building in Nigeria. *West Asia And Africa* 6: 58–63.

Lindau, Mona. 1978. Vowel features. *Language* 54: 541–563.

Lipiński, Edward. 1997. *Semitic Languages: Outline of a Comparative Grammar*. Leuven: Peeters and Departement Oosterse Studies.

Lipski, John. 1997. El lenguaje de los *negros congos* de Panamá y el *lumbalú* palenquero: función sociolingüística de criptolectos afrohispánicos. *América Negra* 14: 147–165.

2004. The Spanish language of Equatorial Guinea. *Arizona Journal of Hispanic Cultural Studies* 5: 115–130.

2006. Morphosyntactic implications in Afro-Hispanic language: new data on creole pathways. Paper presented at the 35th New Ways of Analyzing Variation Conference (NWAV 35). Columbus, OH, October 2006.

2011. *El habla of los Congos*. Panamá: Instituto Nacional de Cultura.

2015. La reconstrucción de los primeros contactos lingüísticos afrohispánicos: la importancia de las comunidades de habla contemporáneas. In Juanito Avelar & Laura Álvarez-López (eds.), *Dinâmicas Afro-Latinas língua(s) e história(s)*, 93–126. Frankfurt am Main: Peter Lang.

N.d. Spanish world-wide: the last century of language contacts. www: personal.psu.edu/jml34/cr-sch.pd (accessed 2 March 2016).

Littmann, Enno. 1898–1899. Das Verbum der Tigresprache. *Zeitschrift für Assyriologie* 13: 133–178, 14: 1–102.

1910–1915. *Publications of the Princeton Expedition to Abyssinia*. Vols. I–IV A/B. Leiden: E. J. Brill.

1913. *Deutsche Aksum Expedition*. Vol. IV: *Sabäische, Griechische und Altabessinische Inschriften*. Berlin: Dietrich Reimer.

1943. Tigrina Sprichwörter. *Zeitschrift der Deutschen Morgenländischen Gesellschaft* 97 (N.F. 22): 208–238.

Littmann, Enno & Maria Höfner. 1962. *Wörterbuch der Tigre-Sprache, Tigre-Deutsch-Englisch*. Wiesbaden: Franz Steiner.

Liu Haifang. 2004. Africa's development is inseparable from using African languages: Professor Kwesi Kwaa Prah's visit to the Institute of West Asian and African Studies. *West Asia And Africa* 6: 69–70.

Lobban, Richard. 1995. *Cape Verde: Crioulo Colony to Independent Nation*. Boulder, CO: Westview.

Lobben, Marit. 2010. The Hausa causative and benefactive in a cognitive and crosslinguistic perspective. PhD thesis, Department of Linguistics and Scandinavian Studies, University of Oslo.

Lockot, Hans Wilhelm. 1982. *Bibliographia Aethiopica*. Vol. 1. Wiesbaden: Harrassowitz.

1998. *Bibliographia Aethiopica II: The Horn of African in English Literature*, ed. and rev. Siegbert Uhlig & Verena Böll. Wiesbaden: Harrassowitz.

Lodhi, Abdulaziz. 2000. *Oriental influences in Swahili: A Study in Language and Culture Contacts* (Orientalia et Africana Gothoburgensia 15). Göteborg: Acta Universitatis Gothoburgensis.

2004. Strategies of emphasis in Swahili: aspiration, reduplication and gemination. *Africa & Asia: Göteborg Working Papers on Asian and African Languages and Literatures* 4: 142–150.

Lodhi, Abdulaziz & Olle Engstrand. 1985. On aspiration in Swahili: hypothesis, field observations and an instrumental analysis. *Phonetica* 42: 175–187.

Lodhi, Abdulaziz & T. Otterbrandt. 1987. *Kortfattad Swahili–Svensk & Svensk–Swahili Ordbok* [Concise Swahili-Swedish & Swedish-Swahili Dictionary]. Combined new edition in one volume. Uppsala: Nordic Africa Institute.

Lodhi, Abdulaziz, John Gonga Kiango, Abdilahi Nassir & Issac Odeo Ipara. 2007. *Kamusi ya Shule za Msingi* [A Swahili–Swahili Dictionary for Schools]. Nairobi: Oxford University Press.

Lodhi, Abdulaziz, T. Otterbrandt & S. von Sicard. 1973. *Kortfattad Swahili-svensk ordbok*. Uppsala: Nordiska Afrikainstitutet.

Lopes, Armando J. 1998. The language situation in Mozambique. *Journal of Multilingual and Multicultural Development* 19(5): 440–486.

Louwrens, L. J. 1979. Naamwoordfunksies in Noord-Sotho. Doctoral thesis, University of Pretoria.

1981a. The relevance of the notions 'given' and 'new' discourse information in the study of Northern Sotho syntax. *South African Journal of African Languages* 1(1): 21–49.

1981b. Wat spook tans in die Bantoetaalkunde? – 'n Oorsig van enkele taalteoretiese tendense in die Bantoetaalkunde in Suid-Afrika sedert 1971. Ms.

Lubinda, J. 2012. On the phonetic and phonological studies of Southern African languages. In H. S. Ndinga-Koumba-Binza & Sonja E. Bosch (eds.), *Language Science and Language Technology in Africa: A Festschrift for Justus C. Roux*, 33–46. Stellenbosch: SUN Press.

Lucchesi, Dante, Alan N. Baxter & Ilza Ribeiro (eds.). 2009. *O português afro-brasileiro*. Salvador-BA: EDUFBA.

Ludolf, Hiob. 1661a. *Grammatica Aethiopica*. London: Apud Thomam Roycroft.

1661b. *Lexicon Aethiopico-Latinum ...* London: Apud Thomam Roycroft.

Lukas, Johannes. 1965. Afrikanische Sprachen und Kulturen: der Hamburger Beitrag zu ihrer Erforschung. *Mitteilungen der Geographischen Gesellschaft in Hamburg* 56: 149–179.

Luo Meina. 2011. Multilingualism in Africa: *Ethno-National Studies* 2: 76–81.

Luo Yuanyuan. 2008. Analysis on Swahili and Sino-African Relations. *West Asia and Africa* 6: 70–73.

Lüpke, Friederike. 2013. Multilingualism on the ground. In Friederike Lüpke & Anne Storch (eds.), *Repertoires and Choices in African Languages*, 13–76. Berlin: Mouton de Gruyter.

2016. Uncovering small-scale multilingualism. *Critical Multilingualism Studies* 4(2): 35–74.

Lusekelo, Amani. 2009. The structure of the Nyakyusa noun phrase. *Nordic Journal of African Studies* 18(4): 305–331.

2013. Criteria for identification of determiners in Bantu noun phrases. *Journal of the Linguistics Association of Southern African Development Community Universities* 4(1): 4–16.

Lyall, Archibald. 1938. *Black and White Make Brown: An Account of a Journey to the Cape Verde Islands and Portuguese Guinea*. London: W. Heinemann.

Łykowska, Laura. 1998. *Gramatyka języka amharskiego. Ćwiczenia* [Amharic grammar with exercises]. Warsaw: Dialog.

Lyth, R. E. 1971. *The Murle Language: Grammar and Vocabulary* (Linguistics Monograph Series, 7). Khartoum: Sudan Research Unit, University of Khartoum.

Maamouri, Mohamed. 1973. The linguistic situation in independent Tunisia. *The American Journal of Arabic Studies* 1: 50–65.

Mabiala, N. J. N. 1999. Phonologie comparative et historique du koongo. PhD dissertation. Université Lumière-Lyon II.

MacDiarmid, Phoebe A. & Donald N. MacDiarmid. 1931. The languages of the Nuba Mountains. *Sudan Notes and Records* 14: 149–162.

Machobane, M. 1985. Tense and aspect in Sesotho (Studies in African Grammatical Systems 3). Bloomington, IN: Indian University Linguistics Club.

1987. The Sesotho passive constructions. *McGill Working Papers in Linguistics* 4: 33–52.

MacMichael, Harold A. 1918. Nubian elements in Darfur. *Sudan Notes and Records* 1: 33–53.

1920. Darfur linguistics. *Sudan Notes and Records* 3: 197–216.

1922. *A History of the Arabs in the Sudan*. 2 vols. Cambridge: Cambridge University Press.

Madzimbamuto, Farai D. 2012. Developing anatomical terms in Shona language. *South African Medical Journal* 102: 132–135.

Maḥbär bahli Təgray [Tigray Culture Association] (ed.). 1991 ʿa.-mə. [=1998/1999]. *Mäṣṇaʿtətat qäddamay simpoziyäm qwanqwa Təgräñña*. mässänada'ti Täklä-Haymanot Haylä-Səllase (do/r) et alii. Addis Abäba: Maḥbär bahli Təgray (təkkal bet maḥtäm Bərhan-ənna Sälam).

(ed.). 1999 ʿa.-mə. [= 2007] [recte: 2000 ʿa.-mə. [= 2008].] *Wəṣṣəʾit käydi mäbbäl 2 [kaĺaŀy waʿla-n mäṣṇaʿtə-n qwanqwatat Təgray*, preface by Gäbrä-Ab. Mäqälä: Maḥbär bahli Təgray.

Mahmud, Ushari A. 1983. *Arabic in the Southern Sudan: History and Spread of a Pidgin-Creole*. Khartoum: FAL.

Maho, Jouni F. 1998. *Few People, Many Tongues: The Languages of Namibia*. Windhoek: Gamsberg Macmillan.

Maho, Jouni F. & Bonny Sands. 2002. *The Languages of Tanzania: A Bibliography*. Göteborg: ACTA Universitatis Gothoburgensis.

Makonnen, Argaw. 1984. *Matériaux pour l'étude de la prononciation traditionnelle du Guèze*. Paris: Éditions Recherche sur les Civilisations.

Malcolm, D. McK. 1949. *Zulu Manual for Beginners*. Cape Town: Longmans, Green & Co.

Mallon, Alexis. 1904. *Grammaire copte: Avec bibliographie, chrestomathie et vocabulaire*. Beyrouth: Imprimerie Catholique, 1904. www.archive.org/stream/grammairecoptea00maligoog#page/n37/mode/2up (Retrieved March 2017).

Mamet, M. 1955. *La langue ntomba* (Annales Sciences de l'Homme 11). Tervuren: RMCA.

Mammeri, Mouloud. 1976. *Tajeṛṛumt n tmaziɣt (tantala taqbaylit) [Grammar of Amazigh-Kabyle variety]*. Paris: Maspero. First edition, Université d'Alger, 1967.

Manessy, Gabriel. 1961. Le bwamu et ses dialects. *Bulletin de l'Institut Fondamental de l'Afrique Noire* 23: 119–178.

1969. *Les langues gurunsi*. Paris: SELAF.

1975. *Les langues Oti-Volta*. Paris: SELAF.

1979. *Contribution à la classification généalogique des langues voltaïques*. Paris: SELAF.

Manessy, Gabriel & Paul Wald (eds.). 1979. *Plurilinguisme: Normes, situations, stratégies*. Paris: L'Harmattan.

Manfoumbi, R. M. 1994. *Description du pove B22*. PhD dissertation, Université Libre de Bruxelles.

Manfredi, Stefano. 2017. *Arabi Juba: Un pidgin-créole du Soudan du Sud*. Leuven: Peeters.

Mangulu, André Motingea. 2005. *Leboale et lebaate: Langues bantoues du plateau des Uélé, Afrique Centrale*. Tokyo: ILCAA.

2008. *Aspects du bongili de la sangha-Likouala: Suivis de l'Esquisse du Parler Énga de Mampoko, Lulonga*. Tokyo: ILCAA.

2010. *Aspects des parlers minoritaires des lacs Tumba et Inongo: Contribution à l'histoire de contact des langues dans le bassin central congolais*. Tokyo: ILCAA.

2012. *Contributions aux études linguistiques sur le haut Congo: Esquisses du soa, mbesa, tofoké et lokelé*. Tokyo: ILCAA.

2014. *Le nom individuel chez les Ngɔmbɛ de l'Equateur congolais: Etude ethnolinguistique et sociohistorique*. Tokyo: ILCAA.

Mangwa, W. 2008. Language harmonization in Southern Africa: toward a standard unified Shona orthography (SUSO) for Botswana, Mozambique and Zimbabwe. *The Dyke* 3(2): 58–72.

Marçais, Philippe. 1956. Le parler arabe de Djidjelli (Publication de l'Institut d'Etudes Orientales d'Alger). Paris: Adrien Maisonneuve.

1957. Les parlers arabes. In *Initiation à l'Algérie*, 215–237. Paris: Adrien Maisonneuve.

Marçais, William. 1945. Les parlers arabes du Fezzân. In *Travaux de l'Institut de recherches sahariennes*, vol. III, 186–188. Alger: Ernest Imbert.

Marno, Ernst. 1874. *Reisen im Gebiete des blauen und weissen Nil, im egyptischen Sudan und in den angrenzenden Negerländern, in den Jahren 1869 bis 1873*. Vienna: Gerold.

Marrassini, Paolo. 2014. Nota editoriale. In *Storia e leggenda dell'Etiopia tardoantica: Le iscrizioni reali aksumite, a cura di Paolo Marrassini, con un'appendice di Rodolfo Fattovich e una nota editoriale di Alessandro Bausi*, 353–361. Paideia: Brescia.

Marten, Lutz & Nancy C. Kula. 2008. Zambia: 'one Zambia, one nation, many languages'. In Andrew Simpson (ed.), *Language and National Identity in Africa*, 291–313. Oxford: Oxford University Press.

2012. Object marking and morphosyntactic variation in Bantu. *Southern African Linguistics and Applied Language Studies* 30(2): 237–253.

Marten, Lutz, Nancy C. Kula & Nhlanhla Thwala. 2007. Parameters of morphosyntactic variation in Bantu. *Transactions of the Philological Society* 105(3): 1–86.

Martins, Aracy A., Silvestre F. Gomes & Vigínia J. B. Cá. 2016. Letramento(s)/ alfabetização em contextos multilíngues de Angola e Guiné-Bissau. *Educação em Revista* 32(4): 391–412. www.scielo.br/scielo.php?script=sci_arttext&pid=S0102-46982016000400391&lng=en&nrm=iso&tlng=pt (accessed 17 April 2017).

Masele, Balla F. Y. P. 2001. The linguistic history of SiSuumbwa, KiSukuma and KiNyamwezi in Bantu Zone F. Doctoral thesis, Memorial University of Newfoundland, St John's.

Mason, John. 1996. *Tigrinya Grammar*. Lawrenceville, NJ: Red Sea Press.

Massamba, David P. B. 1977. A comparative study of the Ruri, Jita and Kwaya 'languages' of the eastern shores of Lake Nyanza (Victoria). MA thesis, University of Dar es Salaam.

1984. Tone in Ciruri. In George Clements & John Goldsmith (eds.), *Autosegmental studies in Bantu tone*, 235–255. Leiden: Foris Press.

1992. Why Ciruri is an accent language. *Journal and Asian and African Studies* 43: 81–94.

1996. *Phonological Theory: History and Development*. Dar es Salaam: Dar es Salaam University Press.

1997. Problems in terminology development: The case of Tanzania. *Kiswahili* 59: 86–98.

2002. *Historia ya Kiswahili: 50BK hadi 1500BK*. Nairobi: Jomo Kenyatta Foundation.

Massamba, David P. B., Yared M. Kihore & Yohana P. Msanjila. 2004. *Fonolojia ya Kiswahili Sanifu (Sekondari na Vyuo)*. Dar es Salaam: Institute of Kiswahili Research.

Massenbach. G. von. 1933. Wörterbuch des nübischen Kunûzi-Dialektes mit einer grammatischen Einleitung. *Mitteilungen des Seminars für Orientalische Sprachen an der Friedrich-Wilhelms-Universität zu Berlin* 36: 99–227.

1962. *Nübische Texte im Dialekt der Kenuzi und der Dongolawi* (Abhandlungen für die Kunde des Morgenlandes 34,4). Wiesbaden: Franz Steiner.

Mateene, Kahombo. 1992. *Essai de grammaire du kihunde: Syntaxe, morphologie et phonologie mélangées* (Hamburger Beiträge zur Afrikanistik 1). Münster/Hamburg: LIT.

Mathangwane, J. T. 1998. Allomorphy and the morphology–syntax distinction in Ikalanga. In I. Maddieson & T. J. Hinnebusch (eds.), *Language History and Linguistic Description in Africa*, 217–228. Asmara: Africa World Press.

Mathangwane, Joyce & Al Mtenje. 2010. Tone and reduplication in Wandya and Subiya. In Karsten Legère & Christina Thornell (eds.), *Bantu Languages: Analyses, Description and Theory*, 175–189. Cologne: Rüdiger Köppe.

Maurer, Philippe. 2009. *Principense: Grammar, Texts and Vocabulary of the Afro-Portuguese Creole of the Island of Príncipe, Gulf of Guinea*. London: Battlebridge.

Mayevu, G. S. 1973. Preliminary remarks on the subjectival concord in Tsonga. In M. E. R. Mathiva, J. E. S. Setshedi & C. P. N. Nkondo (eds.), *Essays on Literature and Language, Presented to Prof. T. M. H. Endemann by his Colleagues*, 119–125. Turfloop: University of the North.

Mba, Gabriel & Etienne Sadembouo (eds.). 2012. *De l'exploration du multilinguisme dans les villes africaines / Exploring Multilingualism in African Urban Cities*. Paris: L'Harmattan.

Mbaabu, Ireri. 1973. Language planning in Kenya: some practical considerations. *Lugha* 5(3): 13–14.

1978. *Kiswahili lugha ya Taifa*. Nairobi: Kenya Literature Bureau.

2007. *Historia ya usanifishaji wa Kiswahili*. Dar es Salaam: Institute of Kiswahili Research.

Mbaya Maweja. 2005. *Pratiques et attitudes linguistiques dans l'Afrique d'aujour-d'hui: Le cas du Sénégal*. Munich: Lincom Europa.

Mberi, Edgar Nhira. 2002. The categorical status and functions of auxiliaries in Shona. D.Phil. thesis, Department of African Languages and Literature, University of Zimbabwe.

Mberia, Kithaka wa. 1993. Kitharaka segmental morphology with special reference to the noun and verb. PhD dissertation, University of Nairobi.

McCarthy, John J. 1981. A prosodic theory of non-concatenative morphology. *Linguistic Inquiry* 12: 373–418.

1983. Consonantal morphology in the Chaha verb. In Michael Barlow, Daniel P. Flickinger & Michael T. Wescoat (eds.), *Proceedings of the West Coast Conference on Formal Linguistics*, 176–188. Stanford: Stanford Linguistics Association.

McConvell, Patrick. 1973. Cleft sentences in Hausa? A syntactic study of focus. PhD dissertation, SOAS, University of London.

McGregor, William. 2014. Numerals and number words in Shua. *Journal of African Languages and Linguistics* 35(1): 45–90.

2015. Four counter-presumption constructions in Shua (Khoe-Kwadi, Botswana). *Lingua* 158: 54–75.

Mchombo, Sam A. 2004. *The Syntax of Chichewa*. Cambridge: Cambridge University Press.

Meeussen, Achille Émile. 1952. *Esquisse de la langue ombo* (Anales Sciences de l'Homme 4). Tervuren: RMCA.

1959. *Essai de grammaire rundi* (Annales Sciences de l'Homme 24). Tervuren: RMCA.

1967. Bantu grammatical reconstruction. *Africana Linguistica* 3: 79–121.

1969. *Bantu Lexical Reconstructions*. Tervuren: Musée Royal de l'Afrique Central.

1971. *Éléments de grammaire lega* (Archives d'Ethnographie 15). Tervuren: RMCA.

Meinhof, Carl. 1899. *Grundriss einer Lautlehre der Bantusprachen*. Leipzig: F. A. Brockhaus.

1906. *Grundzüge einer vergleichenden Grammatik der Bantu-Sprachen*. Berlin: Dietrich Reimer.

1912. *Die Sprachen der Hamiten*. Hamburg: L. Friedrichsen.

Meintel, Deirde. 1984. *Race, Culture and Portuguese Colonialism in Cabo Verde*. Syracuse: Maxwell School, Syracuse University.

Meley, Mulugetta. 2010. Säwasəw. In Siegbert Uhlig (ed.), *Encyclopaedia Aethiopica*, vol. IV: O–X, 562–564. Wiesbaden: Harrassowitz.

Mendes, Mafalda, Aires Semedo, Fátima Ragageles & Nicholas Quint. 2002. *Dicionário Prático Português-Caboverdiano: Variante de Santiago*. Coimbra: Edições Tenacitas.

Mendonça, R. 1933. *A influência africana no português do Brasil*. Rio de Janeiro: Sauer.

Mengistu, Amberber, Brett Baker & Mark Harvey (eds.). 2010. *Complex Predicates: Cross-Linguistic Perspectives on Event Structure*. Cambridge: Cambridge University Press.

Mesfin Ghebrehiwet. 1996. *Tigrigna for Foreigners and English for Tigrigna Speakers*. [Asmara]: Lissan.

Mesfin, Wolde/Mariam. 1974. The relative distribution of the major linguistic and religious groups in urban areas. In *IV Congresso internazionale di studi etiopici (Roma, 10-15 aprile 1972), Tomo II (sezione linguistica)*, 193–201. Rome: Accademia Nazionale dei Lincei.

Meyer, Ronny. 2006. Bibliography of Renate Richter 1966–2006. *Lissan: Journal of African Languages and Linguistics* 20(1/2). 5–14.

2016. The Ethiopic script: linguistic features and socio-cultural connotations. *Oslo Studies in Language* 8(1): 137–172.

Meyer, Ronny & Lutz Edzard (eds.). 2016. *Time in Languages of the Horn of Africa*. Wiesbaden: Harrassowitz.

Meyer, Ronny, & Renate Richter. 2003. *Language Use in Ethiopia from a Network Perspective: Results from a Sociolinguistic Survey Conducted among High School Students*. Frankfurt am Main: Peter Lang.

Meyer, Ronny, Yvonne Treis & Amha Azeb (eds.). 2014. *Explorations in Ethiopian Linguistics: Complex Predicates, Finiteness and Interrogativity*. Wiesbaden: Harrassowitz.

Meyer-Bahlburg, Hilke & [H.] Ekkehard Wolff. 1986. *Afrikanische Sprachen in Forschung und Lehre: 75 Jahre Afrikanistik in Hamburg (1909–1984)*. Berlin/ Hamburg: Dietrich Reimer.

Mfonyam, J. 1989. Tone in orthography: the case of Bafut and related languages. PhD dissertation. University of Yaoundé, Cameroon.

Miehe, Gudrun, Jonathan Owens & Manfred von Roncador. 2007. *Language in African Urban Contexts*. Münster: Lit.

Miller, A. L. 2013. Northern Khoesan. In R. Vossen (ed.), *The Khoesan Languages*, 92–96. London/New York: Routledge.

Miller, Catherine. 1996. Nubien, berbère et beja: notes sur trois langues vernaculaires non arabes de l'Égypte contemporaine. *Les langues en Egypte*. Première serie 27–28: 411–431.

Mischlich, Adam. 1906. *Wörterbuch der Hausasprache*. Berlin: Georg Reimer.

Mitterrutzner, Johann C. J. 1866. *Die Dinka-Sprache in Central-Afrika*. Brixen: Weger. 1867. *Die Sprache der Bari in Central-Afrika*. Brixen: Weger.

Mittwoch, Eugen. 1926. *Die traditionelle Aussprache des Aethiopischen*. Berlin: Mouton de Gruyter.

Mitwalli Badr, M. 1955. *Study in Nubian Language*. Cairo: Dar Miṣr li'l-Ṭibā'a.

Mnyampala, Mathias E. 1954. *Historia, mila na desturi za Wagogo wa Tanganyia*. Nairobi: Eagle Press.

Mnyampala, Mathias E. & S. Chiraghdin. 1977. *Historia ya Kiswahili*. London: Oxford University Press.

Mo Haiwen. 2011. The dilemma of primary education language policy in Tanzania: *Education Research Monthly* 7: 98–100.

Moges, Yigezu. 2010. *Language Ideologies and Challenges of Multilingual Education in Ethiopia: The Case of Harari Region*. Addis Ababa: OSSREA.

Mohamed Hassan, Saleh. 2003. La morphologie de la langue afare. *Sciences et Environnement* 17: 17–21.

Mohamed Ismail, Abdirachid. 2011. Dialectologie du somali: problématique et perspectives. PhD dissertation, INALCO/LLACAN, Paris.

Mohamed, Hashim I. & Felix Banda. 2008. Classroom discourse and discursive practises in higher education in Tanzania. *Journal of Multilingual and Multicultural Development* 29(2): 95–109.

Möhlig, Wilhelm J. G. 1976. Guthries Beitrag zur Bantuistik aus heutiger Sicht. *Anthropos* 71: 673–715.
  1981. Stratification in the history of the Bantu languages. *Sprache und Geschichte in Afrika* 3: 251–316.
  1986. Grundzüge der textmorphologischen Struktur und Analyse afrikanischer Erzählungen. *Afrikanistische Arbeitspapiere* 8: 5–56.
  2000. Das Studium der schwarzafrikanischen Sprachen. In Sylvain Auroux (ed.), *History of the Language Sciences: An International Handbook on the Evolution of the Study of Language from the Beginnings to the Present* (Handbooks of Linguistics and Communication Science (HSK 18.1)), 980–991. Berlin: De Gruyter Mouton.

Möhlig, Wilhelm J. G. & J. Christoph Winter. 1983. Afrikanistik. In Herrmann Jungraithmayr & Wilhelm J. G. Möhlig (eds.), *Lexikon der Afrikanistik*, 22–23. Berlin: Dietrich Reimer.

Mojapelo, G. P. 1960. *Popo-puo ya Sesotho*. Johannesburg: Afrikaanse Pers Beperk.

Mokgokong, P. C. 1966. A dialect-geographical survey of the phonology of the Northern Sotho area. Master's dissertation, University of South Africa, Pretoria.

Moñino, Y. 1995. *Le Proto-gbaya: Essai de linguistique comparative sur vingt et une langues d'Afrique Centrale*. Paris: SELAF.

Morin, Didier. 1994. Dialectologie de l'afar-saho. In Gideon Goldenberg & Shlomo Raz (eds.), *Semitic and Cushitic Studies*, 252–266. Wiesbaden: Harrassowitz.
1999. *Le texte légitime, pratiques littéraires orales traditionnelles en Afrique du nord-est*. Paris: Peeters.
2010. Saho literature. In Siegbert Uhlig et al. (eds.), *Encyclopaedia Aethiopica* vol. IV, 473–475. Wiesbaden: Harrassowitz.
2012. *Dictionnaire afar-français*. Paris: Karthala.
Morino, Tsuneo & Hisashi Nakajima. 1990–1997. *A Dictionary of the Swahili Language*. 6 vols. Tokyo: Research Institute for Asian and African Languages and Cultures, Tokyo University of Foreign Studies.
Morsly, Dalila. 1988. Le français dans la réalité algérienne. PhD dissertation, Université de Paris V.
Moser, Gerald. 1986. The Portuguese in Africa. In Albert S. Gerard (ed.), *European Language Writing in Sub-Saharan Africa*, vol. I, 43–48. Budapest: Akadémiai Kadó.
Moser, Rosmarie. 2003. Kabba: a Nilo-Saharan language of the Central African Republic. PhD thesis, LaTrobe University. Published in 2004 by Lincom Europa, Munich.
Moshi, Lioba. 1998. Word order in multiple object constructions in Kivunjo-Chaga. *Journal of African Languages and Linguistics* 19: 137–152.
Motse-Mogara, B. G. 2011. A comparative study of the verb structure in Northern, Central and Southern Khoesan: the case of Jl'Hoansi, Naro and !Xóõ. Doctoral thesis, University of South Africa, Pretoria.
Mouguiama-Daouda, P. 1995. Les dénominations ethnoichtyologiques chez les Bantous du Gabon. Étude de linguistique historique. PhD dissertation, Université Lumière-Lyon II.
Mous, Maarten. 1993. *A Grammar of Iraqw*. Cologne: Rüdiger Köppe.
2003. *The Making of a Mixed Language: The Case of Ma'a/Mbugu*. Amsterdam: Benjamins.
2007. John M. Stewart, 1926–2006. *Journal of African Languages and Linguistics* 28(1): 71–74.
2012. Cushitic. In Zygmunt Frajzyngier & Erin Shay (eds.), *The Afroasiatic Languages*, 342–422. Cambridge: Cambridge University Press.
Mous, Maarten & A. Breedveld. 1986. A dialectometrical study of some Bantu languages (A40–A60) of Cameroon. In G. Guarisma & W. J. G. Möhlig (eds.), *La méthode dialectométrique appliquée aux langues africaines*, 177–241. Berlin: Dietrich Reimer.
Mpiranya, Fidèle. 2015. *Swahili Grammar and Workbook*. London: Routledge.
Mpofu Nomalanga. 2009. *The Shona adjective as a prototypical category* (Acta humaniora 407). PhD thesis, Department of Linguistics and Scandinavian Studies, Faculty of Humanities, University of Oslo.
Mreta, Abel Y. 2000. The nature and effects of Chasu-Kigweno contact. In K.K. Kahigi, Y.M. Kihore, & M. Mous (eds). *Languages of Tanzania*, 177–189. Leiden: CNWS (Research School of Asian, African and Amerindian Studies).
Mtavangu, Norbert. 2013. La contribution des Français à l'étude du swahili: le cas de Charles Sacleux (1856-1943). Doctoral thesis, INALCO, Paris.
Mtenje, Al. 1985. Arguments for an autosegmental analysis of Chichewa vowel harmony. *Lingua* 66: 21–52.

1986. Issues in the nonlinear phonology of Chichewa. PhD dissertation, University College London.
1987. Tone shift principles in the Chichewa verb. *Lingua* 72: 169–209.
1988. On tone and transfer in Chichewa reduplication. *Linguistics* 26: 125–155.
2002. The role of language in national development: a case for local languages. Inaugural Lecture, University of Malawi.
2011. On relative clauses and prosodic phrasing in Ciwandya. *ZAS Papers in Linguistics* 55: 121–139.
Mufanechiya, Tafara & Albert Mufanechiya. 2015. Teaching Chishona in Zimbabwe: a curriculum analysis approach. *The Journal of Pan African Studies* 8(8): 35–51.
Mugaddam, Abdelrahim H. 2002. Language maintenance and shift in Sudan: the case of ethnic minority groups in greater Khartoum. PhD thesis, University of Khartoum.
Mugane, John. 1998. Gikuyu NP morphosyntax. In I. Maddieson & T. J. Hinnebusch (eds.), *Language History and Language Description in Africa*, 239–248. Trenton, NJ: African World Press.
Mukarovsky, Hans G. 1976–1977. *A Study of Western Nigritic*. Vienna: Institut für Ägyptologie und Afrikanistik.
1983. Reinisch, Leo. In Herrmann Jungraithmayr & Wilhelm J. G. Möhlig (eds.), *Lexikon der Afrikanistik*, 201–202. Berlin: Dietrich Reimer.
1987. *Mande-Chadic Common Stock: A Study of Phonological and Lexical Evidence.* Vienna: Afro-Pub.
(ed.). 1987. *Leo Reinisch: Werk und Erbe.* Vienna: Verlag der Österreichischen Akademie der Wissenschaften.
Mukuthuria, Mwenda. 2009a. Islam and the development of Kiswahili. *The Journal of Pan African Studies* 2(8): 36–45.
2009b. Uhakiki wa mtafaruku wa isitilahi za kiisimu na nafasi ya usanifishaji katika maendeleo ya Kiswahili. *Mulika* 28: 48–61.
Müller, D. H. 1894. *Epigraphische Denkmäler aus Abessinien nach Abklatschen von J. Théodore Bent.* Vienna: F. Temsky.
Müller, Friedrich. 1876–1888. *Grundriss der Sprachwissenschaft.* 4 vols. Vienna: Hölder.
Müller, Walter W. 2007. Zum Gedenken an Wolf Leslau (1906–2006). *Aethiopica* 10: 210–218.
Mullins, Joseph D. 1904. *The Wonderful Story of Uganda*. London: Church Missionary Society.
Mulokozi, Mugyabuso M. 2002. *Barua za Shaaban Robert 1931-1958.* Dar es Salaam: Institute of Kiswahili Studies.
2005. Miaka 75 ya Taasisi ya Uchunguzi wa Kiswahili (1930–2005). *Kiswahili* 68: 1–28.
2009. Mustakabali wa Kiswahili katika ukanda wa maziwa makuu. *Mulika* 28: 72–87.
Mulugeta, Girmay Melles. 2001. *Tigrinya Reader and Grammar.* Springfield, VA: Dunwoody.
Mulugeta, Eteffa. 1988. Multilingualism as a socio-linguistic factor affecting communication. In Beyene Tadesse (ed.), *Proceedings of the Eighth International Conference of Ethiopian Studies, Addis Ababa, 26–30 November 1984*, 1–21. Addis Ababa: Institute of Ethiopian Studies.
Muluken, Andualem Shiferew. 2013. *Comparative Classification of Geʕez Verbs in the Three Traditional Schools of the Ethiopian Orthodox Church.* Aachen: Shaker.

Munzinger, Werner. 1864. *Ostafrikanische Studien*. Schaffhausen: Hurter.

1865. Vocabulaire de la langue Tigre. In Augustus Dillmann (ed.), *Lexicon linguae Aethiopicae*, 53–64. Lipsiae: Weigel.

Muratori, Carlo P. 1938. *Grammatica Lotuxo*. Verona: Missioni Africane.

Murray, Jocelyn. 1985. *Proclaim the Good News: A Short History of the Church Missionary Society*. London: Hodder & Stoughton.

Musa Aron. 1994. *Mäzgäbä-qalat səmat Ertrawəyan Təgrəñña-n Təgrä-n*. Toronto: Musa Aron.

2005. *Kəbət-qalat həgya təgre*. Asmara: Aḥtämti Hədri.

Musanji, Ngalasso Mwatha. 2010. Décolonisation et devenir culturel de l'Afrique et de ses diasporas, Conférence inaugurale au Colloque international Alioune Diop, l'homme et l'œuvre face aux défis contemporains, Dakar (Sénégal), 3-5 mai 2010; published in *Présence africaine* 181–182 (2011): 41–71.

2011. Textes oraux: littérarité et modernité. In Virginia Coulon and Xavier Garnier (eds.), *Les littératures africaines: Textes et terrains. Hommage à Alain Ricard*, 241–259 Paris: Karthala.

Musgrave, Simon & John Hajek. 2010. Sudanese languages in Melbourne: linguistic demography and language maintenance. In Y. Treis and R. de Busser (eds.), *Selected Papers from the 2009 Conference of the Australian Linguistic Society*, 1–17. www.als.asn.au/proceedings/als2009/musgravehajek.pdf.

Mutaka, [Ngessimo M.] Philip. 2003. *The Fruit of Love*. Yaoundé: Editions Sherpa.

2011a. *Love and AIDS Prevention*. Paris: L'Harmattan.

(ed.). 2011b. *Glimpses of African Cultures / Échos des cultures africaines*. Paris: L'Harmattan.

Mutaka, Ngessimo M. 1994. *The Lexical Tonology of Kinande*. Munich: Lincom Europa.

Mutaka, Ngessimo M. & Beban Sammy Chumbow (eds.). 2001. *Research Mate in African Linguistics: Focus on Cameroon: A Fieldworker's Tool for Deciphering the Stories Cameroonian Languages Have to Tell. In honor of Professor Larry M. Hyman*. Cologne: Rüdiger Köppe.

Mutaka, Ngessimo M. & Kambale Kavutirwaki. 2001. *Kinande/Konzo–English Dictionary with an English–Kinande Index*. Trenton, NJ: Africa World Press.

Mutaka, Ngessimo M. & Pius Tamanji. 2000. *Introduction to African Linguistics*. Munich: Lincom Europa.

Mutaka, Philip. 2012. *Divine Bud: Testimonies of God's Intervention*. Mankon: Langaa RPCIG.

Mutawallī Badr, Muḥammad. N.d. *Iqra' bil-lughat al-nobiyyat / Nobîn nog gery* (Linguistics Monograph Series, 8). Khartoum: Sudan Research Unit, University of Khartoum.

Muth, Franz-Christoph. 2009. Frühe Zeugnisse des Amharischen und der Gurage-Sprachen in einer polyglotten Wortliste von Al-Malik Al-Afḍal (gest. 778/1377). *Folia Orientalia* 45/46:87–109.

Mutombo, H. D. 1973. Ébauches de grammaire de la langue bembe et du dialecte kalambayi de la langue luba-kasayi. Thesis, Université Libre de Bruxelles.

Mzamane, G. I. M. 1948. A concise treatise of Phuthi with special reference to its relationship with Nguni and Sotho. Master's dissertation, University of South Africa, Pretoria.

n.a. 1900. *Piccolo dizionario della lingua araba parlata in Tripoli di Barberia ad uso degli italiani*. Tripoli: Imprimerie Orientale.

n.a. 1911. *Manualetto per l'ufficiale in Tripolitania: Carte e schizzi topografici. Comando del Corpo di Stato Maggiore*. Rome: Laboratorio foto-litografico d'artiglieria.

n.a. 1941. Un pó di arabo tripolino. Manuale pratico di nomenclatura e fraseologia italiana-araba-tripolina. Con pronunzia figurata. Edizioni Guide turistiche. Novi Ligure (S.A. Arti grafiche Panetto, & Petrelli, Spoleto).

N'Landu, K. 1994. Éléments de description du kisundi (H13b). Thesis, Université Libre de Bruxelles.

Naidoo, S. 2012. A Comparative study of explosive [b] and implosive [b] in Nguni. In H. Steve Ndinga-Koumba-Binza & Sonja Bosch (eds.), Language Science and Language Technology in Africa: A Festschrift for Justus C. Roux, 21–32. Stellenbosch: SUN Press.

Naro, A. & M. M. Scherre. 2007. Origens do português brasileiro. São Paulo: Parábola.

Nascimento, Augusto. 2003. O sul d diaspora: Cabo-Verdianos em plantações de S. Tomé e Príncipe e Moçambique. Praia, Cabo Verde: Edição da Presidência da República de Cabo Verde.

Nashid, Sawsan Abdel Aziz Mohammed. 2014. The sociolinguistic situation in Northern Bahr el Ghazal State (South Sudan): a case study of Aweil Town. PhD thesis, University of Khartoum.

Nassenstein, Nico & Andrea Hollington (eds.). 2015. Youth Language Practices in Africa and Beyond. Berlin: De Gruyter Mouton.

Naumann, Christfried. 2012. Acoustically Based Phonemics of Siwi (Berber) (Berber Studies, vol. 36). Cologne: Rüdiger Köppe.

Naumann, Christfried, Steven Moran, Guillaume Segerer & Robert Forkel. (eds.). 2015. Tsammalex: A Lexical Database on Plants and Animals. Leipzig: Max Planck Institute for Evolutionary Anthropology. http://tsammalex.clld.org (accessed 23 February 2017).

Nazareth Amlesom Kifle. 2011. Tigrinya applicatives in lexical-functional grammar. Doctoral dissertation, University of Bergen.

Ndayiragije, Juvénal. 1993. Syntaxe et sémantique du clivage du prédicat en fongbè. PhD dissertation, Université de Québec à Montréal.

Ndhlovu, Finex. 2015. Hegemony and Language Policies in Southern Africa: Identity, Integration, Development. Newcastle upon Tyne: Cambridge Scholars.

Ndoma, Ungina. 1977. Some aspects of planning language policy in education in Belgian Congo: 1906–1960. PhD dissertation, Northwestern University, Evanston, Illinois.

1998. Beginning literacy in Congo: immediate implications. Annales de la Faculté des Lettres 1(1): 157–163.

Negrão, Esmeralda & Evani Viotti. 2008. Estratégias de impessoalização no português brasileiro. In José Luiz Fiorin & Margarida Petter (eds.), África no Brasil: A formação da língua portuguesa, 179–203. São Paulo: Contexto.

2011. Epistemological aspects of the study of the participation of African languages in Brazilian Portuguese. In Margarida Petter & Martine Vanhove (eds.), Portugais et langues africaines: études afro-brésiliennes, 13–44. Paris: Karthala.

Negreiros, Almada José. 1895. Historia Ethnographica da ilha de S. Tomé. Lisbon: José Bastos.

Nehlil, Mohammed. 1909. Etudes sur le dialecte de Ghat (Publications de l'Ecole des Lettres d'Alger, Bulletin de Correspondance Africaine). Paris: E. Leroux.

Newman, Francis William. 1882. Lybian Vocabulary. London: Hertford.

1936. Nomenclatura elementare ed espressioni nelle lingue amharica, galla, araba (dialetto tripolino): Oltre 1400 parole e 400 frasi. Rome: Istituto Coloniale Fascista.

Newman, Paul. 1974. *The Kanakuru Language*. Cambridge: Cambridge University Press

2000. *The Hausa Language: An Encyclopedic Reference Grammar*. New Haven, CT: Yale University Press.

2007. *A Hausa–English Dictionary*. New Haven, CT: Yale University Press.

2010. The making of JALL: its beginnings and intellectual foundations. *Journal of African Languages and Linguistics* 31: 3–11.

Newman, Roxanna M. 1990. *An English–Hausa Dictionary*. New Haven, CT: Yale University Press.

Ng'ang'a Wanjiku. 2005. *Word Sense Disambiguation of Swahili: Extending Swahili Language Technology with Machine Learning* (Publication No. 39). Helsinki: Department of General Linguistics University of Helsinki.

Nguma W. 1986. *Dictionnaire français –Yansi (Rép. du Zaïre)*. Bandundu: CEEBA.

Ngunga, Armindo. 2000. Constraints in suffix ordering in Ciyao. In Vicki Carstens & Frederick Parkson (eds.), *Advances in African Linguistics*, 189–204. Trenton: African World Press.

Nicolaï, Robert. 1990. *Parentés linguistiques: À propos du Songhay*. Paris: Éditions du CNRS.

2001. Gabriel Manessy. In Robert Nicolaï (ed.), *Leçons d'Afrique: Filiations, ruptures et reconstitution de langues. Un hommage à Gabriel Manessy*, 11–19. Louvain-Paris: Peeters.

Nicolaï, Robert & Petr Zima. 1997. *Songhay*. Munich: LINCOM.

Nicoleti, Elizabeth C. 2012. *Substrate Influence on Body-Part Idioms in Crioulo of Guinea-Bissau*. SIL International: SIL e-Books.

Nicolle, Steve. 2014. *A Grammar of Digo: A Bantu Language of Kenya and Tanzania*. Dallas, TX: SIL International.

Nikiema, Emmanuel. 1993. De la légitimation des représentations en phonologie: le palier syllabique. PhD dissertation, Université du Québec à Montréal.

Nikiéma, Norbert. 1976. On the linguistic bases of moore orthography. PhD dissertation, Indiana University, Bloomington.

1979. *La situation linguistique en Haute-Volta: Travaux de recherche et d'application sur les langues nationales*. Ouagadougou: National Commission for UNESCO.

1980. *Èd góm mooré: La grammaire du mooré en 50 leçons*. Ouagadougou: Université de Ouagadougou.

1982. *Moor gulsg sebre: Manuel de transcription du mooré*. Ouagadougou: Presses Africaines.

Nikiéma, Norbert & Jules Kinda. 1997. *Moor gom-biis no-tûur gulsg sebre: Dictionnaire orthographique du moore*. Ouagadougou: SOGIF.

Nilsson, Morgan. 2016. *Somali Language and Linguistics: A Bibliography* (Studia Interdisciplinaria Linguistica et Litteraria 7). Gothenburg: Department of Languages and Literatures, University of Gothenburg. https://gupea.ub.gu.se/handle/2077/51577?locale=en.

Ning Sao. 1983. Languages and scripts in Africa. *West Asia and Africa* 5: 51–54.

Niyibizi, M. S. 1987. Esquisse structurale du sengele. Thesis, Université Libre de Bruxelles.

Niyonkuru, L. 1978. Phonologie et morphologie du giphende. Thesis, Université Libre de Bruxelles.

Nkobi, S. D. 1954. *Incwadi yesizulu yabafundi bezikole ezincane neziphakeme*. Johannesburg: A.P.B.

Noor, Nazrabo. 2017. *Akademisches Wörterbuch, 3000 der wichtigsten Fachbegriffe aus dem Uni-Alltag: Deutsch–Tigrinya, Tigrinya–Deutsch*. Hamburg: Interkultura.

Norton, Russell & Thomas Kuku Alaki. 2015. The Talodi languages: a comparative-historical analysis. *Occasional Papers in the Study of Sudanese Languages* 11: 31–161.

Nsuka Nkutsi, F. 1982. *Les structures fondamentales du relatif dans les langues bantoues* (Annales, 1O8). Lyon: Université Lumière-Lyon II. Tervuren: RMCA.

1986. Formatifs et auxiliaires dans les langues bantoues: critères de détermination. *Africana Linguistica* 10: 339–364.

Ntondo, Zavoni. 2006. *Morfologia e sintaxe do Ngangela*. Lunda: Editorial Nzila.

2015. *Fonologia e Morfologia do Oshikwanyama*. Angola: Mayamba.

Nurse, Derek. 1988. The diachronic background to the language communities of Southwestern Tanzania. *Sprache und Geschichte in Afrika*, 9: 15–115.

1997. The contributions of linguistics to the study of history in Africa. *Journal of African History* 38(3): 364–366.

2000. *Inheritance, Contact, and Change in Two East African Languages* (Language Contact in Africa 4). Cologne: Rüdiger Köppe.

Nurse, Derek & Thomas Spear. 1985. *The Swahili: Reconstructing the History of an African Society 800–1500*. Philadelphia: University of Pennsylvania Press.

Nyembezi, C. L. S. 1956. *Uhlelo Lwesizulu*. Pietermaritzburg: Shuter and Shooter.

Nyongwa, Moses. 1994. Aspects théoriques de la création lexicale: le cas du bamiléké (Thèse). PhD dissertation, Université du Québec à Montréal.

O'Fahey, Sean R. 2008. Arabic literature in the eastern half of Africa. In Shamil Jeppe & Souleymane B. Diagne (eds.), *The Meanings of Timbuktu*, 333–347. Cape Town: HSRC Press.

Oduor, Jane A. N. 2000. A study of syllable weight and its effect in Dholuo phonology. Doctoral thesis, University of Nairobi.

Ohly, Rajmund, Iwona Kraska-Szlenk & Zofia Podobińska. 1998. *Język suahili* [The Swahili language]. Warsaw: Dialog.

Okombo, Duncan O. 1982. *Dholuo morphophonemic in a generative framework*. Berlin: Dietrich Reimer.

1986. The functional paradigm and Dholuo constituent order. Doctoral thesis, University of Nairobi.

1997. *A functional grammar of Dholuo*. Cologne: Rüdiger Köppe.

1999. Language and ethnic identity: the case of the Abasuba. *Kenyan Journal of Sciences* 5(1): 21–38.

Olderogge, Dmitriy A. [1937] 1983a. Opredelenie vremeni i prostranstva v yazykax bantu [Time and space in Bantu languges]. In D. A. Olderogge, *Epigamiya: Izbrannye stat'i* [Epigamia: Selected Writings], 239–253. Moscow: Nauka.

[1977] 1983b. Yazyk kak istoricheskij istochnik [Language as a historical source]. In D. A. Olderogge, *Epigamiya: Izbrannye stat'i* [Epigamia: Selected Writings], 191–220. Moscow: Nauka.

1949. Xamitskaya problema v afrikanistike [The Hamitic problem in Africanistics]. *Sovetskaya etnografiya* 3: 70–84.

1961. *Suahili–russkiy slovar'* [Swahili–Russian Dictionary]. Moscow: Gos. izd-vo inostrannyh i nacional'nyh slovarej.

1962. Sovremennoe sostoyanie i problemy izucheniya yazykov Afriki [The current situation and problems in African linguistics]. *Philology in China* 2: 94–103.

1963. *Kamus na hausa-rashanci ... Hausa-russkiy slovar'* [Hausa–Russian Dictionary]. Moscow: Institut ètnografii AN SSSR.

1993. The study of African languages in Russia. *St Petersburg Journal of African Studies* 1: 113–123.

Oliveira, Márcia. 2005. *Perguntas de constituinte em Ibibio e a teoria do tipo oracional: Aspectos da periferia à esquerda com ênfase em foco.* Munich: Lincom Europa.

Olson, Kenneth S. & John Hajek. 2003. Cross-linguistic insights on the labiodental flap. *Linguistic Typology* 7: 157–186.

Omondi, Lucia N. 1975. The major syntactic structures of Luo: a generative transformational analysis. PhD dissertation, University of London.

1981. The verb *to be* in Dholuo syntax. In Thilo C. Schadeberg & M. L. Bender (eds.), *Nilo-Saharan. Proceedings of the first Nilo-Saharan linguistics colloquium,* 101–107. Dordrecht, Cinnaminson: Foris.

1986. Reduplication as a linguistic phenomenon. *Afrikanistische Arbeitspapiere,* 8: 87–113.

1993. Comp and question words in Dholuo. In Franz Rottland & Lucia N. Omondi (eds.), *Proceedings of the Third Nilo-Saharan Linguistics Colloquium,* 225–237. Hamburg: Hemut Baske.

1995. *Dholuo Emotional Language: An Overview* (Series A: General and Theoretical Paper No. 361). Essen: LAUD. 2nd ed. 2007.

1999. Problems of language policy in East Africa. In Herbert Langthaler (ed.), *Sura za Africa – Voices from Africa,* 345–361. Frankfurt am Main: Peter Lang.

Omondi, Oketch & Felix Banda. 2008. Multilingual discourse practices in community development in Nyanza Province, Kenya. *Southern African Linguistics and Applied Language Studies* 26(1): 1–11.

Ondo-Mebiame, P. 1992. De la phonologie à la morphologie du fang-ntumu parlé à Aboumezok. PhD dissertation, Université Libre de Bruxelles.

Orel, Vladimir E. & Olga V. Stolbova. 1995. *Hamito-Semitic Etymological Dictionary: Materials for a Reconstruction.* Leiden: Brill.

Oriolo, Leonardo. 1997. *The Red Sea Press Tigrinya Phrase Book.* Lawrenceville, NJ: The Red Sea Press.

Orwin, Martin. 1995. *Colloquial Somali.* London/New York: Routledge.

1996. Professor Bogumil Witalis Andrzejewski 1922–1994. *Bulletin of the School of Oriental and African Studies* 59(1): 125–128.

Ouane, Adama & Christine Glanz. 2010. *Why and How Africa Should Invest in African Languages and Multilingual Education: An Evidence- and Practice-Based Policy Advocacy Brief.* Hamburg: UNESCO Institute for Lifelong Learning.

Ousseina D. Alidou. 2005. *Engaging Modernity: Muslim Women and the Politics of Agency in Postcolonial Niger.* Madison: University of Wisconsin Press.

Ousseina D. Alidou & Ahmed Sikainga (eds.). 2006. *Post-Conflict Reconstruction in Africa.* Trenton: Africa World Press.

Pahl, H. W. 1967. *Isixhosa.* Johannesburg: Educum.

Panetta, Ester. 1943a. *L'arabo parlato a Bengasi: I Testi con traduzione e note. II Grammatica. Grammatiche e lessici delle lingue dell'Africa italiana.* 2 vols. Rome: Libreria dello Stato.

1943b. *Forme e soggetti della letteratura popolare libica.* Milan: Istituto per gli Studi di Politica Internazionale.

References 309

1958. Vocabolario e Fraseologia dell'arabo parlato a Bengasi. Lettera A. *Annali Lateranensi (Annali del Pontificio Museo Missionario Etnologico)* 22: 318–369.

1962a. Vocabolario e Fraseologia di Bengasi (continuazione del XXII, 1958). *Annali Lateranensi (Annali del Pontificio Museo Missionario Etnologico)* 26: 257–290.

1962b. Vocabolario e Fraseologia dell'arabo parlato a Bengasi. Lettera B. *Studi Orientali 5 (A Francesco Gabrieli. Studi orientalistici offerti nel sessantesimo compleanno dai suoi colleghi e discepoli)*: 195–216.

Pankhurst, Alula. 1994. Indigenising Islam in Wallo: Ajäm, Amharic verse written in Arabic script. In Bahru Zewde, Richard Pankhurst & Taddese Beyene (eds.), *Proceedings of the Eleventh International Conference of Ethiopian Studies. Addis Ababa, April 1–6 1991*, vol. II, 257–273. Addis Ababa: Institute of Ethiopian Studies.

Pankhurst, Richard. 1976a. Bibliographical sketch. In M. Lionel Bender (ed.), *The Non-Semitic Languages of Ethiopia*, 25–42. East Lansing, MI: African Studies Center, Michigan State University.

1976b. The beginnings of Oromo studies in Europe. *Africa: Rivista trimestrale di studi e documentazione dell'Istituto italiano per l'Africa e l'Oriente* 31(2): 171–206.

Parker, Enid M. & Richard Hayward. 1985. *An Afar–English–French Dictionary (with Grammatical Notes in English)*. London: SOAS.

Parkin, David J. 1974. Language switching in Nairobi. In W. H. Whiteley (ed.), *Language in Kenya*, 189–215. Nairobi: Oxford University Press.

Pasch, Helma. 1994. *Standardisierung internationaler afrikanischer Verkehrssprachen*. Opladen: Westdeutscher Verlag.

Paul, Ludwig (ed.). 2008. *Vom Kolonialinstitut zum Asien-Afrika-Institut: 100 Jahre Asien- und Afrikawissenschaften in Hamburg*. Gossenberg: Ostasien-Verlag.

Paulme, Denise. 1976. *La mère dévorante: Essai sur la morphologie des contes africains*. Paris: Gallimard.

Pawlak, Nina. 1998. *Język hausa* [The Hausa Language]. Warsaw: Dialog.

2010. *Językoznawstwo afrykańskie* [African Linguistics]. Warsaw: WUW.

Pawlikova-Vilkanova, Viera. 2006a. Biblical translation of early missionaries in East and Central Africa: I. Translations into Swahili. *Asian and African* 15: 80–89.

2006b. Biblical translation of early missionaries in East and Central Africa: translations into Luganda. *Asian and African* 15: 198–210.

2011. The role of early 'missionaries of Africa' or 'White Fathers' in the study and development of African languages. *Asian and African* 20(1): 267–288.

Pawlos, Kassu. 2015. *Guide for Teaching Ethiopian Sign Language*. Addis Ababa: Addis Ababa University Press.

Pencheon, T. G. 1968. La langue berbère en Tunisie et la scolarisation des enfants berbérophones. *Revue Tunisienne des Sciences Sociales*, 173–186.

Pereda Valdés, I. 1965. El negro em el Uruguay: pasado y presente. *Revista del Instituto Histórico y Geográfico del Uruguay* 25: 177–185.

Perini, Ruffillo. 1893. *Manuale teorico-pratico della lingua Tigrè*. Rome: La Società Geografica Italiana.

Persson, Andrew M. & Janet R. Persson. 1991. *Mödö-English Dictionary with Grammar* (Bilingual Dictionaries of Sudan, 1). Nairobi: Summer Institute of Linguistics.

Peterson, D. & J. Allman. 1999. Introduction: new directions in the history of missions in Africa. *Journal of Religious History* 23: 1–7. doi:10.1111/1467-9809.00070.

Petraček, Karel. 1989. *Úvod do hamitosemitské (afroasijské) jazykovědy* [Introduction to Hamito-Semitic (Afroasiatic) Linguistics]. Prague: Státní Pedagogické Nakladatelství.

Petrus, Ethiops. 1548, 1549. *Testamentum Novum, cum epistola ad Hebraeos tantum.* Rome: Vaterium Doricum et Ludovioum fratres Brixianos.

Petter, M. 2011. A presença de línguas africanas na América Latina. *Lingüística* 26: 78–96.

2012. African languages in Latin América. In *Proceedings of the Sixth World Congress of African Linguistics, Cologne, 17–21 August 2009*, 29–38. Cologne: Rüdiger Köppe.

Petzell, Malin. 2012. The under-described languages of Morogoro: a sociolinguistic survey. *South African Journal of African Languages* 32(1): 17–26.

Petzell, Malin & Harald Hammarström. 2013. Grammatical and lexical comparison of the Greater Ruvu Bantu languages. *Nordic Journal of African Studies* 22(3): 129–157.

Phillipson, R. 1996. Linguistic imperialism: African perspectives. *ELT Journal* 50(2): 160–167.

Pike, Kenneth L. 1948. *Tone Languages: A Technique for Determining the Number and Type of Pitch Contrasts in a Language, with Studies in Tonemic Substitution and Fusion.* Vol. IV. Ann Arbor: University of Michigan Press.

Piłaszewicz, Stanisław. 2007. Afrykanistyka [African studies]. In Maciej Popko (ed.), *75lat Instytutu Orientalistycznego Uniwersytetu Warszawskiego* [75 years of the Institute of Oriental Studies, University of Warsaw], 23–36. Warsaw: WUW.

Pilkington, George L. 1891. *Handbook of Luganda.* London: Society for Promoting Christian Knowledge.

1892. *Luganda–English and English–Luganda Vocabulary.* London: Society for Promoting Christian Knowledge.

Pimenta, Fernando Tavares. 2014. The Portuguese 'New State' and the reform of the colonial state in Angola: the political behavior of the white elites (1961–1962). *História* 33(2): 250–272.

Pinto, E. 1978, 1981. *O português do Brasil: Textos críticos e teóricos.* Vols. I and II. São Paulo: EDUSP.

Pinto, Joana C., Oliveira, Sandra, Teixeira, Sergio, et al. 2016. Food and pathogen adaptations in the Angolan Namib desert: Tracing the spread of lactase persistence and human African trypanosomiasis resistance into southwestern Africa. *American Journal of Physical Anthropology* 161(3): 436–447.

Plumley, John Martin. 1948. *Introductory Coptic Grammar.* London: Home & Van Thal.

Polak-Bynon. L. 1975. *A Shi Grammar. Surface Structures and Generative Phonology of a Bantu Language* (Annales Sciences Humaines 86). Tervuren: RMCA.

Polomé, Edgar C. 1967. *Kiswahili Language Handbook.* Washington, DC: Centre for Applied Linguistics.

Porter, Andrew. 1997. 'Cultural imperialism' and Protestant missionary enterprise, 1780–1914. *The Journal of Imperial and Commonwealth History* 25(3): 367–391.

Posner, Daniel N. 2003. The colonial origins of ethnic cleavages: the case of linguistic division in Zambia. *Comparative Politics* 35(2): 127–146.

Potken, Johannes. 1513. *Psalterium Davidis et Cantica aliqua: Canticum canticorum*. Rome: Marcellus Silber alias Franck.

Poulos, G. 1986. The study of African languages: misconceptions within a society. Inaugural lecture, University of South Africa, Pretoria, 24 June 1986.

Pozdiniakov, Konstantin I. 1978. Mande languages: a historical comparative analysis. PhD dissertation, Institute of Linguistics, Moscow.

1993. *Sravnitel'naja grammatika atlanticheskikh jazykov* [Comparative Grammar of Atlantic Languages]. Moscow: Nauka.

Praetorius, Franz. 1871. *Grammatik der Tigriñasprache in Abessinien hauptsächlich in der Gegend von Aksum und Adoa*. Halle: Buchhandlung des Waisenhauses.

Prasse, Karl-G. 1972, 1974, 2009. *Manuel de grammaire touarègue*. Copenhagen: Akademisk Forlag.

1989–1990. *Poésies touarègues de l'Ayr*. 2 vols. (with Mohamed Ghabdouane). Copenhagen: University of Copenhagen & Museum Tusculanum Press.

2003. *Dictionnaire touareg–français (Niger)*. Copenhagen: Museum Tusculanum Press.

Prochazka, S. 2004. *Altäthiopische Studiengrammatik*. Fribourg: Academic Press.

Prost, André. 1953. *Les langues mandé-sud du groupe mana-busa*. Dakar: Institut Français d'Afrique Noire.

1964. *Contribution à l'étude des langues voltaïques*. Dakar: Institut Français d'Afrique Noire.

1967. *La langue Loghoma* (Documents Linguistiques 13). Dakar: Université de Dakar.

1968. *La langue bisa: Grammaire et dictionnaire*. 2nd ed. Farnborough: Gregg Press.

Provotelle, Dr. 1911. *Etude sur le tamazir't ou zenatia de Qal'at Es-sened*. Paris: E. Leroux.

Pugach, Sara. 2012. *Africa in Translation: A History of Colonial Linguistics in Germany and Beyond, 1814–1945*. Ann Arbor: University of Michigan Press.

Queiroz, S. M. 1998. *Pé preto no barro branco. A língua dos negros da Tabatinga*. Belo Horizonte: Editora da UFMG.

Quint, Nicolas. *The Phonology of Koalib: A Kordofanian Language of the Nuba Mountains (Sudan)*. Cologne: Rüdiger Köppe.

Raban, John. 1830. *A Vocabulary of the Eyo, or Aku, a Dialect of Western Africa*. Compiled by the Rev. J. Raban, one of the missionaries of the CMS in Sierra Leone. London: Church Missionary Society.

1831a. *A Vocabulary of the Eyo, or Aku, a Dialect of Western Africa*. Compiled by the Rev. J. Raban, one of the missionaries of the CMS in Sierra Leone. Part II. London: Church Missionary Society.

1831b. *The Eyo Vocabulary*. Compiled by the Rev. J. Raban, one of the missionaries of the CMS in Sierra Leone. Part III. London: Church Missionary Society.

Raimundo, J. 1933. *O elemento afro-negro na língua portuguesa*. Rio de Janeiro: Renascença.

Rampton, Ben. 1995. *Crossing: Language and Ethnicity among Adolescents*. London: Longman.

Raponda-Walker, A. 1934. *Dictionnaire mpongwe-français suivi d'éléments de grammaire*. Metz: La Libre Lorraine.

Rask, Rasmus. 1828. Vejledning til Akra-Sproget på Kysten Ginea [Introduction to the Accra language on the Guinea Coast]. www.scribd.com/doc/113833310/Rasmus-Rask-Vejledning-til-Akra-Sproget-på-Kysten-Ginea-med-et-Tillæg-om-Akvambuisk.

Raz, Shlomo. 1983. *Tigre Grammar and Texts*. Malibu, CA: Undena.

Redinha, José. 1962. *Distribuição étnica de angola*. Angola: Centro de Informação e Turismo de Angola.

Reh, Mechthild. 1996. *Anywa Language: Description and Internal Reconstructions* (Nilo-Saharan: Linguistics Analyses and Documentation 11). Cologne: Rüdiger Köppe.

    2003. Plädoyer für eine Stärkung der Afrikaforschung, die afrikanische Sprachen als gesellschaftliches Gestaltungs-, Interpretations- und Ausdrucksmedium ernst nimmt. *Africa Spectrum* 38(2): 251–253.

    2004. Multilingual writing: a reader-oriented typology – with examples from Lira municipality (Uganda). *International Journal of the Sociology of Language* 170: 1–41.

Reh, Mechthild & Bernd Heine. 1982. *Sprachpolitik in Afrika*. Hamburg: Helmut Buske.

Reh, Mechthild, Christiane Simon & Katrin Koops. 1998. *Experiens-Kodierung in afrikanischen Sprachen typologisch gesehen: Formen und ihre Motivierungen*. Hamburg: Institut für Afrikanistik und Äthiopistik.

Reinisch, Leo. 1879. *Die Nuba-Sprache*. 2 vols. Vienna: Braumüller.

    1893–1894. *Die Beḏauye-Sprache in Nordost-Afrika*. 4 vols. (Sitzungsberichte der Akademie der Wissenschaften zu Wien, phil.-hist. Klasse). Vienna: Alfred Hölder.

Reintges, Chris H. 2004. *Coptic Egyptian (Sahidic Dialect): A Learner's Grammar*. Cologne: Rüdiger Köppe.

Rekanga, J. P. 2001. Essai de grammaire himba (langue bantoue du Gabon, B36). 2 vols. PhD dissertation, Université Libre de Bruxelles.

Ren, Hong. 2009. African development needs the integration of African vernacular languages. *Journal of Ningxia University* (Social Science Edition) 5: 179–180. http://linguistics.africamuseum.be/BLR3.html (accessed 16 October 2016).

Reuster-Jahn, Uta. 2002. *Erzählte Kultur und Erzählkultur bei den Mwera in Südost-Tansania*. Cologne: Rüdiger Köppe.

Rialland, Annie. 1979. Une langue à tons en terrasse: Le Gulmancema. Thèse d'état, Université René Descartes, Paris V.

Rice, Keren. 2011. Documentary linguistics and community relations. *Language Documentation and Conservation* 5: 187–207.

Richter, Renate. 1987. *Lehrbuch der amharischen Sprache*. Leipzig: Enzyklopädie-Verlag. 2nd ed. published by Verlag Langenscheidt, Munich, 1994.

Rickford, John R. 1997. Prior creolization of African-American English? Sociohistorical and textual evidence from the 17th and 18th centuries. *Journal of Sociolinguistics* 1: 315–336.

    1998. The creole origins of African-American Vernacular English: evidence from copula absence. In Salikoko S. Mufwene, Guy Bailey, John R. Rickford & John Baugh (eds.), *African-American English: Structure, History, and Use*, 154–200. London/New York: Routledge.

Rilliet, Frédéric. 2000. *Dictionnaire tigrigna-français/français-tigrigna*. Paris: L'Harmattan.

Rilly, Claude. 2010. *Le méroïtique et sa famille linguistique* (Afrique et Langage, 14). Paris/Leuven: Peeters.

Rita-Ferreira, António. 1958. *Agrupamento e caracterização étnica dos indígenas de Moçambique*. Lisbon: Junta de Investigações do Ultramar.

1959. Mozambique ethnic characterisation and grouping. *South African Journal of Science* 55(8): 201–204.

1975. *Povos de Moçambique: História e cultura.* Porto: Afrontamento.

Robert, Shaaban. 1951. *Kusadikika.* London: Nelson.

1967. *Kufikirika.* Nairobi: Oxford University Press.

1968. *Siku ya Watenzi Wote.* London: Nelson.

Robinson, Charles H. 1899–1900. *Dictionary of the Hausa Language.* Cambridge: Cambridge University Press. 4th ed. 1925.

Rocha, Jorge. 2017. Race and society in Portugal: two notes and a remark. *Journal of Anthropological Sciences* 95: 339–343.

Rodegem, F. M. 1970. *Dictionnaire rundi–français* (Annales Sciences Humaines 69). Tervuren: RMCA.

Rodén, Karl Gustav. 1913. *Kəl'e Mansaʿ – dəgəm wa-fətəh wa-ʿadotat, Le tribù dei Mensa – storia, legge e costumi.* Asmara/Stockholm: Nordiska Boktryckeriet.

Rohlfs, Gerhard. 1872. Die Zahlzeichen der Rhadamser. *Ausland* 29: 695–696.

Rossi, Ettore. 1935. Vocaboli stranieri nel dialetto arabo della città di Tripoli. In B. Migliorini & V. Pisani (eds.), *Atti del III Congresso internazionale dei linguisti (Roma, 19–26 settembre 1933),* 186–193. Florence: F. Le Monnier.

Rottland, Franz. 1982. *Die südnilotischen Sprachen.* Berlin: Dietrich Reimer.

Rottland, Franz & Duncan O. Okombo. 1992. Language shift among the Suba of Kenya. In Matthias Brenzinger (ed.), *Language Death: Factual and Theoretical Explorations with Special reference to East Africa,* 273–283. Berlin/New York: Mouton de Gruyter.

Rottland, Franz & Lucia N. Omondi (eds.). 1993. *Proceedings of the Third Nilo-Saharan Linguistics Colloquium.* Hamburg: Hemut Buske.

Rouchdy, Aleya. 1980. Language in contact: Arabic Nubian. *Anthropological Linguistics* 22(8): 334–344.

1991. *Nubian and the Nubian Language in Contemporary Egypt: A Case of Cultural and Linguistic Contacts.* Leiden: Brill.

Rougé, Jean-Louis. 1988. *Petit dictionnaire étymologique du Kriol de Guinée-Bissau et Casamance.* Bissau: Instituto Nacional de Estudos e Pesquisa.

Roux, J. C. 2003. On the perception and production of tone in the Sotho and Nguni languages. In S. Kaji (ed.), *Proceedings of the Third International Symposium on Cross-linguistic studies of Tonal Phenomena,* 155–176. Tokyo: University of Foreign Studies.

Roux, J. C., E. C. Botha & P. H. Louw. 2000. Synthesizing prosody for commands in a Xhosa TTS system. *Proceedings of the Sixth International Conference on Spoken Language Processing ICSLP 2000,* 16-20 October 2000, vol. III, 263–266. Beijing, China.

Rowan, Kirsty. 2006. Meroitic: a phonological investigation. PhD dissertation, SOAS, University of London.

Rowland-Oke, Mary. 2003. *Description systématique de la langue Obolo-Andoni: Langue du groupe Cross River.* Paris: Harmattan.

Roy-Campbell, Zaline M. & Martha Qorro. 1997. *The Language Crisis in Tanzania: The Myth of English versus Education.* Dar es Salaam: Mkuki na Nyota Publishers.

Rubagumya, Casmir M. 1990. *Language in Education in Africa.* Clevedon: Multilingual Matters.

2003. English-medium primary schools in Tanzania: a new 'linguistic market' in education? In Birgit Brock-Utne, Zaline Desai & Martha Qorro (eds.), *Language of Instruction in Tanzania and South Africa (LOITASA)*, 146–169. Dar es Salaam: E&D Vision Publishing.

Rubenson, Samuel. 1996. The transition from Coptic to Arabic. *Égypte/Monde arabe*, Première série, 27–28.

Rugemalira, Josephat M. 1993. Bantu multiple 'objects' constructions. *Linguistic Analysis* 23(3/4): 226–253.

1995. Verbal extensions in Runyambo. *Afrikanistische Arbeitspapiere* 41:51–87.

2005. *A Grammar of Runyambo*. Dar es Salaam: University of Dar es Salaam.

2007. The structure of Bantu noun phrase. *SOAS Working Papers in Linguistics* 15: 135–148.

2009. *Chigogo–Swahili–English Dictionary*. Dar es Salaam: University of Dar es Salaam.

Ruíz, Richard. 1984. Orientations in language planning. *NABE Journal* 8(2): 15–34.

Rüppell, Eduard. 1829. *Reise in Nubien, Kordofan und dem peträischen Arabien*. Frankfurt am Main: Wilmans.

Růžička, Karel. 1968. *Úvod do swahilštiny* [Introduction to Swahili]. Prague: Academia.

Saad, Gamal Eldin M. 1967. *A Syntactic Study of Egyptian Colloquial Arabic*. The Hague: Mouton.

Saalax Xaashi, Carab. 2004. *Qaamuus. Ereykoobe*. Djibouti: ILD/Machadka Affafka ee Xaruuta Cilmibaadhista Jabbuuti.

Sacleux, Charles. 1891. *Dictionnaire Français–Swahili*. Zanzibar: Mission de PP. du St Esprit.

1909a. *Grammaire Swahilie*. Paris: Saint-Esprit.

1909b. *Grammaire des dialectes Swahilis*. Procure des PP. du Saint-Esprit.

1939. *Dictionnaire Swahili–Français*. Paris: Travaux et Mémoires de l'Institut d'Ethnologie.

1939/1941. *Dictionnaire Swahili–Français*. Paris: Institut d'Ethnologie.

Saeed, John I. 1993. *Somali Reference Grammar*. Wheaton, MD: Dunwoody.

Saib, Jilali. 1976. *A Phonological Study of Tamazight Berber, Dialect of the Ayt Ndhir*. PhD thesis, University of California, Los Angeles.

Saleh Mahmud. [2005] 2007. Tigre dialects. *Journal of Eritrean Studies* 4: 45–73.

Sälomon Gäbrä Krəstos. 1985[= 1993]. *Mäṣna'ti qwanqwa Təgrəyna – „ḥarägat Təgrəyna" – na'ta säb qwanqwa* [The Foundations of the Təgrəñña Language – Təgrəñña Idioms – Colloquial Language]. Asmara: Francescana.

Salt, Henry. 1814. *A Voyage to Abyssinia and Travels into the Interior of that Country [...] in the Years 1809 and 1810*. Philadephia: Carey; Boston: Wells & Lilly.

Samarin, William J. 1950. A provisional phonemic analysis of Kisi. *Kroeber Anthropological Society Papers* 2: 89–102.

1966. *The Gbeya Language: Grammar, Texts, and Vocabularies*. Berkeley, CA: University of California Press.

1967a. *A Grammar of Sango*. The Hague: Mouton.

1967b. *A Guide to Linguistic Fieldwork*. New York: Holt, Rinehart, & Winston.

Samatar, Said S. 1998. Remembering B. W. Andrzejewski: Poland's Somali genius. *Research in African Literatures* 29(3): 208–219.

Sands, Bonny. 1998a. The linguistic relationships between Hadza and Khoisan. In Mathias Schladt (ed.). *Language, Identity and Conceptualization among the Khoisan*, 265–283. Cologne: Rüdiger Köppe.

1998b. *Eastern and Southern African Khoisan: Evaluating Claims of Distant Linguistic Relationships*. Cologne: Rüdiger Köppe.

Sanhá, Alberto. 2010. *Educação Superior em Guiné-Bissau*. Porto Alegre: Pontifícia Universidade Católica do Rio Grande do Sul.

Santandrea, Stefano. 1961. *Comparative Outline-Grammar of Ndogo-Sere-Tagbu-Bai-Bviri* (Museum Combonianum, 13). Bologna: Editrice Nigrizia.

1976. *The Kresh Group, Aja and Baka Languages (Sudan): A Linguistic Contribution*. Naples: Istituto Universitario Orientale.

Sapir, J. David. 1965. *A Grammar of Diola-Fogny*. Cambridge: Cambridge University Press.

Saporta, I. de. 1970. Une enquête linguistique au XVIIIe siècle: le vocabulaire arabe et berbère recueilli par L. Chenier, Consul de France au Maroc. *Comptes rendus du Groupe Linguistique d'Études Chamito-Sémitiques (GLECS)* 15: 1–16.

Sasse, Hans-Jürgen. 1979. The consonant phonemes of Proto-East-Cushitic (PEC). *Afroasiatic Linguistics* 7: 1-67.

1981. Die kuschitischen Sprachen. In Bernd Heine, Thilo C. Schadeberg & Ekkehard Wolff (eds.), *Die Sprachen Afrikas*, 187–215. Hamburg: Helmut Buske.

1982. *An Etymological Dictionary of Burji*. Hamburg: Helmut Buske.

Sauvageot, Serge. 1965. *Description synchronique d'un dialecte wolof: Le parler du dyolof*. Dakar: IFAN.

Savà, Graziano & Mauro Tosco. 2000. A sketch of Ongota: a dying language of southwest Ethiopia. *Studies in African Linguistics* 29(2): 59–135.

2008. 'Ex uno plura': the uneasy road of Ethiopian languages toward standardization. *International Journal of the Sociology of Language* 191: 111–139.

Sbihi, Ahmed. 1933. Etymologies réelles de certaines expressions courantes de l'arabe dialectal. *Hésperis* 19(1/2): 523–527.

Scantamburlo, Luigi. 1981. *Gramática e dicionário da língua criol da Guiné-Bissau (GCr)*. Bologna: Editrice Missionaria Italiana.

Schadeberg, Thilo. 1981. *A Survey of Kordofanian (1): The Heiban Group*. Hamburg: Helmut Buske.

1990. *A Sketch of Umbundu*. Cologne: Rüdiger Köppe.

1992. *A Sketch of Swahili Morphology*. Cologne: Rüdiger Köppe.

2002. Progress in Bantu lexical reconstruction. *Journal of African Languages and Linguistics* 23(2): 183–196.

Schäfer, H. 1917. *Nubische Texte im Dialeckt der Kunuzi (Mundart von Abu Hôr)*. Berlin: Akademie der Wissenchaften.

Schebesta, Paul. 1919. Eine Bantugrammatik aus dem 17. Jahrhundert: Arte da lingua de Cafre. *Anthropos* 14/15: 764-787.

Schleicher, August. 1863. *Die Darwinsche Theorie und die Sprachwissenschaft*. Weimar: Böhlau.

Schmidt, Sigrid. 1989. *Katalog der Khoisan-Volkserzählungen des südlichen Afrikas: Catalogue of the Khoisan Folktales of Southern Africa* (2 vols.). Hamburg: Helmut Buske.

Schneider, Roger. 1959. *L'expression des compléments de verbe et de nom et la place de l'adjectif épithète en Guèze*. Paris: Champion.

Schneider-Blum, Gertrud. 2013. *A Tima–English Dictionary: An Illustrated Lexicon of a Niger-Congo Language Spoken in the Nuba Mountains (Sudan)*. Cologne: Rüdiger Köppe.

Schön, James. 1861. *Oku Igbo: Grammatical Elements of the Igbo Language*. London: Watts.

1862. *Grammar of the Hausa Language*. London: Church Missionary Society.

1876. *Dictionary of the Hausa Language: Part I Hausa-English, Part II English-Hausa. With Appendices of Hausa Literature*. London: Church Missionary Society.

Schott, Rüdiger. 1990. Project of comparative analysis of motifs and themes in African tales. *Asian Folklore Studies* 49: 140–142.

(ed.). 1993. *Bulsa Sunsuelima: Folktales of the Bulsa in Northern Ghana*. Münster/ Hamburg: Lit.

Schreiber, Henning. 2008. *Eine historische Phonologie der Niger-Volta-Sprachen: ein Beitrag zur Erforschung der Sprachgeschichte der östlichen Ost-Mandesprachen*. Cologne: Rüdiger Köppe.

2009. Social networks, linguistic variation and micro change in an African context: a case study in the borderland of Mali and Burkina Faso. *Sprache und Geschichte in Afrika* 20: 209–229.

Schreuder, H. P. S. 1850. *Grammatik for Zulu-sproget*. Christiania: W. C. Fabritius.

Schuchardt, Hugo. 1882. Über das Negerportugiesische von S. Thomé. *Sitzungsberichte Wien* 101: 889–917.

1889. Über das Negerportugiesische der Ilha do Príncipe. *Zeitschrift für romanische Philologie* 13: 463–475.

Schuh, Russell G. 1997. The use and misuse of language in the study of African history. *Ufahamu: A Journal of African Studies* 25(1): 36–81.

Schwegler, Armin. 1996. *'Chi ma nkongo': Lengua y rito ancestrales en El Palenque de San Basilio (Colombia)*. Vol. II. Frankfurt am Main: Vervuert.

Schweinfurth, Georg August. 1873. *Linguistische Ergebnisse einer Reise nach Centralafrika*. Berlin: Wiegandt & Hempel.

Schwellnus, P. E. 1931. *Tlhalosa-Polelo: Grammar ya Sesotho se se bolelwaxo dileteng tša Transvaal*. London/Glasgow: Blackie, & Son.

Scialhub, Giuseppe. 1913. *Grammatica italo–arabe con i rapporti e le differenze tra l'arabo letterario e il dialetto libico*. Milan: Hoepli.

Sebhatu Gebremichael Kuflu. 2013. *Ꝫwway fəqərti Təgrəñña hoyä! - Oh! - Cry Profusely Beloved Tigrinian! A Handy Manual for Writers & Translators*. Stockholm: Författares Bokmaskin.

Seetzen, Ulrich Jasper. 1816. *Dr Seetzen's linguistischer Nachlass, und andere Sprachforschungen und Sammlungen, besonders über Ostindien*. In Johann Severin Vater (ed.), *Proben deutscher Volksmundarten*, 245–350. Leipzig: Fleischer.

Segerer, Guillaume & Sébastien Flavier. 2011–2016. *RefLex: Reference Lexicon of Africa*. Version 1.1. Paris Lyon. http://reflex.cnrs.fr/ (accessed 22 February 2017).

Seibert, Gerhard. 2001. Camaradas, clientes es compadres. *Colonialismo, socialismo e democratização em São Tomé e Príncipe*. Lisbon: Vega.

2007. Angolares of São Tomé island. In Philip Havik & Malyn Newitt (eds.), *Creole Societies in the Portuguese Colonial Empire*, 105–126. Bristol: Bristol University Press.

Sergew Hable Sellassie. 1980. Two leading Ethiopian writers. *Journal of Semitic Studies* 25: 85–93.

Serra, Luigi. 1964. Testi berberi in dialetto di Zuara. *Annali dell'Istituto Orientale di Napoli* 14: 715–726.

1967. Su alcune costumanze dei Berberi ibaditi di Zuara (Tripolitania). In *Atti del Terzo Congresso di Studi Arabi e Islamici (Ravello 1966)*, 623–632. Naples: Istituto Universitario Orientale, Naples.

1968a. Due racconti in dialetto berbero di Zuara (Tripolitania). *Studi Magrebini* 2: 123–128.

1968b. Quelques remarques comme suite aux premiers textes en dialecte berbère de Zuara (Tripolitaine). *Annali Istituto Universitario Orientale* 18: 444–447.

Serrano, Alicia Campos. 2016. Equatorial Guinea. *Oxford Bibliographies in African Studies.* https://libraries.indiana.edu/resources/oxford-bib-african (accessed 17 April 2017).

Sessarego, S. 2015. *Afro-Peruvian Spanish Slavery and the Legacy of Spanish Creoles.* Amsterdam/Philadelphia: John Benjamins.

Setshedi, J. E. 1975. The auxiliary verbs and the deficient verbs in Tswana. Unpublished MA dissertation, University of the North (Limpopo), Turfloop.

Sewangi Seleman. 2001. *Computer-Assisted Extraction of Terms in Specific Domains: The Case of Swahili.* University of Helsinki: Institute for Asian and African Studies (Publications, 1).

Seydou, Christiane & Denise Paulme. 1972. Le conte des 'Alliés animaux' dans l'Ouest africain. *Cahiers d'Études Africaines* 45: 76–108.

Shi Ling. 1964. Swahili. *World Knowledge* 2: 33.

Shimelis, Mazengia & Sisay Binyam. 2009. Ethiopian linguistics at the dawn of the 21st century. *Journal of Ethiopian Studies* 42: 69–83.

Shimizu, Kiyoshi. 1980. *A Jukun Grammar* (Beiträge zur Afrikanistik 9). Vienna: Afro-Pub.

Shisha-Halevy, Ariel. 1986. *Coptic Grammatical Categories: Structural Studies in the Syntax of Shenoutean Sahidic* (Analecta Orientalia 53). Rome: Pontificium Institutum Biblicum.

2007. *Topics in Coptic Syntax: Structural Studies in the Bohairic Dialect* (Orientalia Lovaniensia Analecta, 160). Leuven: Peeters Publishers & Department of Oriental Studies.

Siboma, André. 1997. *Hope for Rwanda: Conversation with Laurie Guilbert and Harvé Deguine.* London: Pluto Press.

Sidarus, Adel Y. 1978. Coptic lexicography in the Middle Age: The Coptic Arabic scalae. In R. McL Wilson (ed.), *The Future of Coptic Studies*, 125–141. Leiden: E. J. Brill.

Sikuku, Justin. 2001. Syntactic patterns of anaphoric relations in Lubukusu. PhD dissertation, University of Nairobi.

SIL. 2017. SIL-Mozambique: Trabalhos em Curso. www.sil.org/series/trabalhos-em-curso-sil-mozambique.

Silva, Baltasar Lopes da. 1957. *O dialecto Crioulo de Cabo Verde.* Lisbon: Imprensa Nacional.

Simeone-Senelle, Marie-Claude. 2002. L'arabe, langue maternelle de citoyens djiboutiens du nord de la République de Djibouti (Obock). In A. Youssi & F. Benjelloun (eds.), *Proceedings of the 4th Conference of the International Arab Dialectology Association (AIDA), April 1–4, 2000, Marrakesh, Maroc*, 140–150. Rabat: AMAPATRIL.

2003. Haka na Dahālík. In Siegbert Uhlig (ed.), *Encyclopaedia Aethiopica*, vol. II, 70–71. Wiesbaden: Harrassowitz.

2005a. The Horn of Africa. In Kees Versteegh & O. Köndgen (eds.), *Encyclopedia of Arabic Language and Linguistics*, vol. I, 268–275. Leiden: Brill.

2005b. Djibouti/Eritrea. In Kees Versteegh & O. Köndgen (eds.), *Encyclopedia of Arabic Language and Linguistics*, vol. I, 654–659. Leiden: Brill.

2007. Les relatives en afar. HAL-SHS: Archive ouverte en Sciences de l'Homme et de la Société. http://halshs.archives-ouvertes.fr/halshs-00343529/fr/ (accessed 1 December 2008).

Forthcoming. Property and stative verbs in Afar. In P. Boyeldieu (ed.), *Qualification in the African Languages.* Louvain: Peeters.

Simeone-Senelle, Marie-Claude & Mohammed Hassan Kamil. 2013. *Agreement in ʕAfar: 43rd Colloquium on African Languages and Linguistics*. Leiden, Netherlands. https://halshs.archives-ouvertes.fr/halshs-01112414/fr (accessed 1 December 2016).

Simons, Gary F. & Charles D. Fennig (eds.). 2017. *Ethnologue: Languages of the World*. 20th ed. Dallas, TX: SIL International.

Singler, John Victor. 1988. The homogeneity of the substrate as a factor in pidgin/creole genesis. *Language* 64: 27–51.

1993. The African presence in Caribbean French colonies in the seventeenth century: documentary evidence. *Travaux de recherche sur le créole haïtien* 16–17 :1–236.

Sitoe, Bento. 2001. *Verbs of Motion in Changana*. Leiden: CNWS.

Skattum, Ingse. 2008. Mali: in defence of cultural and linguistic pluralism. In Andrew Simpson (ed.), *Language & National Identity in Africa*, 98–121. Oxford: Oxford University Press.

Skik, Hicham. 1967. Les problèmes linguistiques en Tunisie. *Revue Tunisiennes des Sciences Sociales* 4(9): 169–176.

Slabbert, S. & R. Finlayson. 1998. Comparing Nguni and Sotho: a sociolinguistic classification. In I. Maddieson & T. J. Hinnebusch (eds.), *Language History and Linguistic Description in Africa*, 288–306. Asmara: Africa World Press.

Smidt, Wolbert G. C. 2005. Dahlak ethnography. In Siegbert Uhlig (ed.), *Encyclopaedia Aethiopica*, vol. II, 70. Wiesbaden: Harrassowitz.

2009. Matewos. In *Biographisch–Bibliographisches Kirchenlexikon*, Bd. 30, 971–974. Munich: Traugott Bautz.

Smits, Heleen. 2017. *A Grammar of Lumun: A Kordofanian Language of Sudan*. Utrecht. LOT.

Snyman, J. W. 1970. *An Introduction to the !Xũ (!Kung) Language*. Cape Town: AA Balkema.

1974. The Bushman and Hottentot languages of Southern Africa. *Limi* 2(2): 28–44.

1975. *Zu|'hõasi Fonologie en Woordeboek*. Cape Town: AA Balkema.

1977. Vowels of Zu|Hoasi. *Khoisan Linguistic Studies* 3: 93–106.

Sommerauer, Erich. 2010. Die Afrikanistik in Österreich. 1824–1992. www.afrikanistik.at/pdf/themen/historisch.pdf.

Souag, Lameen. 2010. Grammatical contact in the Sahara: Arabic, Berber, and Songhay in Tabelbala and Siwa. PhD dissertation, SOAS, University of London. http://eprints.soas.ac.uk/13430/1/souag-thesis-final.pdf.

2013. *Berber and Arabic in Siwa (Egypt): A Study in Linguistic Contact* (Berber Studies, 37). Cologne: Rüdiger Köppe.

Spagnolo, Lorenzo M. 1933. *Bari Grammar*. Verona: Missioni Africane.

Stallcup, K. 1978. A comparative perspective on the phonology and noun classification of three Cameroon Grassfields Bantu languages: Moghamo, Ngie, and Oshie. PhD dissertation, Stanford University.

Stanley, Carol. 1991. *Déscription morpho-syntaxique de la langue Tikar (parlé au Cameroun)*. Lille: SIL.

Stappers, L. 1971. Esquisse de la langue lengola. *AL* 5 :257–307.

1973. *Esquisse de la langue mituku* (Annales Sciences Humaines 80). Tervuren: RMCA.

Steere, Edward. 1870. *Swahili Tales as Told by the Natives of Zanzibar, with an English Translation*. London: Bell, & Dalby.

1894. *A Handbook of the Swahili Language as Spoken at Zanzibar*. London: Society for Promoting Christian Knowledge.

1918. *Swahili Exercises: Compiled for University's Mission to Central Africa*. London: Society for Promoting Christian Knowledge.

Steinbrich, Sabine. 1982. *Gazelle und Büffelkuh: Frauen in Erzählungen der Fulbe und Haussa*. Munich: Renner.

Steita, Fathiya. 1970. Clusters in grammatical categories in Cyrenaican Arabic. MA dissertation, University of Leeds.

Stevenson, Roland C. 1956–1957. A survey of the phonetics and grammatical structure of the Nuba Mountain languages. *Afrika und Übersee* 40: 73–84, 93–115; 41: 27–65, 117–152, 171–196.

1969. *Bagirmi Grammar* (Linguistic Monograph Series, 3). Khartoum: Sudan Research Unit, University of Khartoum.

2009. *Tira and Otoro: Two Kordofanian Grammars by Roland C. Stevenson*, ed. Thilo C. Schadeberg. Cologne: Rüdiger Köppe.

Stevenson, Roland C. & Marvin Lionel Bender. 1999. *Uduk Grammar and Lexicon* (Studies in African linguistics, 37). Munich: Lincom Europa.

Stewart, John M. 1967. Tongue root position in Akan vowel harmony. *Phonetica* 16: 185–204.

1971. Niger–Congo, Kwa. In T. A. Sebeok (ed.), *Current Trends in Linguistics*. Vol. 7: *Linguistics in Sub-Saharan Africa*, 179–212. The Hague: Mouton.

1973. The lenis stops of the Potou Lagoon languages, and their significance for pre-Bantu reconstruction. *Papers in Ghanaian Linguistics*, Suppl. 4: 1–49.

Stirtz, Timothy. 2011. *A Grammar of Gaahmg, a Nilo-Saharan Language of Sudan*. Utrecht: LOT.

Stoecker, Holger. 2008. *Afrikawissenschaften in Berlin von 1919 bis 1945: Zur Geschichte und Topographie eines wissenschaftlichen Netzwerkes*. Stuttgart: Franz Steiner.

Stopa, Roman. 1935. *Die Schnalze: ihre Natur, Entwicklung und Ursprung* (Polska Akademija Umiejętności, Prace Komisji Językowej, 23). Kraków: Gebethner, Wolff.

Stopa, Roman & B. Garlicki. 1966. *Mały słownik suahilijsko-polski i polsko-suahili-jski* [A Concise Swahili–Polish and Polish–Swahili Dictionary]. Warsaw: Wiedza Powszechna.

Storch, Anne. 2005. *The Noun Morphology of Western Nilotic*. Cologne: Rüdiger Köppe.

Stroomer, Harry. 1987. *A Comparative Study of Three Southern Oromo Dialects in Kenya*. Hamburg: Helmut Buske.

Stroud, Christopher. 2007. Bilingualism: colonialism and postcolonialism. In Monica Heller (ed.), *Bilingualism: A Social Approach*, 25–49. London/New York: Palgrave Macmillan.

Studies in Bantoetale. 1980. Volume 7.1. Feesuitgawe 1930-1980. 'n Historiese oorsig: Departement Bantoetale – 1917 tot 1980. i – iii.

Stumme, Hans. 1893. *Tunisische Märchen und Gedichte*. Leipzig: Hinrichs. http://menadoc.bibliothek.uni-halle.de/ssg/content/titleinfo/1071301 (accessed 12 August 2017).

1898. Märchen und Gedichte aus der Stadt Tripolis in Nordafrika. *Eine Sammlung transkribierter prosaischer und poetischer Stücke im arabischen Dialekt der Stadt Tripolis nebst Übersetzung, Skizze des Dialekts und Glossar*. Leipzig: Hinrichs.

1914. Eine Sammlung über den Berberischen Dialekt der Oase Siwa. *Berichte der Verhandlungen der Königlichen Gesellschaft der Wissenschaften zu Leipzig, Philologisch-historische Klasse* 66(2): 91–109.

Sudan Government. 1928. *Report of the Rejaf Language Conference*, 1928. London.

Suleiman, Yasir. 2008. Egypt: From Egyptian to Pan-Arab Nationalism. In Andrew Simpson (ed.), *Language and National Identity in Africa*, 26–43. Oxford: Oxford University Press.

Sun Xiaomeng. 2004. Rubutaccen Wasan Kwaikwayo a Rukunin Adabin Hausa: Habakarsa da Muhimmancinsa. MA dissertation, Ahmadu Bello University.

2008. *Colloquial Hausa*. Beijing: Foreign Language Teaching and Research Press.

2009. The political game around the national language of Nigeria. *International Forum* 5: 68–72.

2010. Fifty years of vernacular African languages teaching in China: missions and challenges. *West Asia And Africa* 5: 31–36.

2013. An analysis of Hausa language and the nation building in Nigeria. *International Forum* 3: 67–72.

2014a. An analysis on native language policy during British colonial administration in Northern Nigeria based on power element. *West Asia And Africa* 1: 79–91.

2014b. *Language and Power: The Application of Hausa in Northern Nigeria during the British Colonial Administration*. Beijing: Social Sciences Academic Press.

Sun Xiaomeng & Cheng Ruxiang, 2010. *Harshen Hausa*. Beijing: Foreign Language Teaching and Research Press.

Szabó, Loránd. 2013. Africa studies in Hungary: The African Research Centre of the University of Pécs. *Modern Africa: Politics, History and Society* 1(1): 125–133. https://edu.uhk.cz/africa/index.php/ModAfr/article/view/48.

Tabe, Florence. 2016. Groundwork in generative syntax. Ms. University of Yaoundé 1, Cameroon.

Tadadjeu, Maurice & Etienne Sadembouo (eds). 1984. *Alphabet général des langues camerounaises/General Alphabet of Cameroon Languages*. Yaoundé: SIL.

Takács, Gabor. 1999. *Etymological Dictionary of Egyptian*. Vol. I: *A Phonological Introduction*, Leiden: Brill.

2004. *Comparative Dictionary of the Angas-Sura Languages*. Berlin: Dietrich Reimer.

Takassi, Issa. 1983. *Inventaire linguistique du Togo, Atlas et études sociolinguistiques des Etats de l'entente (ASOL)*. Abidjan: Institut de Linguistique Appliquée (ILA).

1996. Description synchronique de la langue ncam (Bassar), parler de Kabou (Togo). Thèse d'Etat, Université du Bénin.

Täkkə'e Täsfay. 1999. *Zämänawi mäzgäbä-qalat Təgrəñña*. Asmara: Ḥədri.

2012. *Mə'bul mäzgäbä-qalat Ǝnglizəñña-Təgrəñña /Advanced English–Tigrinya Dictionary*. Asmara: Ḥədri.

2014. *Mäba'ta säwasəw-ən sənä-sḥuf-ən Təgrəñña*. Asmara: Ḥədri.

Tamanji, Pius N. 2008. Globalization and African languages: regression in linguistic diversity. In A. S. Bobda (ed.), *Explorations into Language Use in Africa*, 71–94. Frankfurt am Main: Peter Lang.

2009. *A Descriptive Grammar of Bafut*. Cologne: Rüdiger Köppe.

Tasgaraa, Hirphoo. 2007. *Abbaa Gammachiis (Oneesimos Nasib). A Native of Oromiya: Enslaved, Freed, and an Envoy of the Gospel*, trans. Guutaa Magarsaa. Addis Ababa: Asteer Gannoo Literature Society.

Tassa Okombe-Lukumbu, G. 1994. Esquisse de description phonétique, phonologique et morphologique du tofoke (C53). Mémoire de licence, Université Libre de Bruxelles.

Tattam, Henry. 1863. *A Compendious Grammar of the Egyptian Language as Contained in the Coptic, Sahidic, and Bashmuric Dialects*. London/Edinburgh: Williams and Norgate.

Taye Assefa & Shiferaw Bekele. 2000. The study of Amharic literature: an overview. *Journal of Ethiopian Studies* 33(2): 27–73.

Taylor, William E. 1891. *African Aphorisms or Saws from Swahili-Land*. London: Society for Promoting Christian Knowledge.

1897. *Groundwork of the Swahili Language*. London: Society for Promoting Christian Knowledge.

Tchagbale, Zakari & Suzanne Lallemand. 1982. *Toi et le ciel. Vous et la terre. Contes Paillards Tem du Togo*. Paris: SELAF

Teclu Lebassi. 1991. *Wörterbuch Deutsch – Tigrigna*. 2 vols. [Heidelberg]: Research & Information Centre of Eritrea.

Tedjini, Belkacem. 1923. *Dictionnaire marocain-français*. Paris: Société d'Editions Géographiques et Coloniales.

1924. *Dictionnaire français-marocain*. Paris: Société d'Editions Géographiques et Coloniales.

Teferi Degeneh Bijiga. 2015. The development of Oromo writing system. PhD dissertation, University of Kent.

Tenreiro, Francisco. 1961. *A ilha de São Tomé*. Lisbon: Memórias da Junta de Investigações Científicas do Ultramar.

Tesfay Tewolde Yohannes. 1993. Word formation in Tigrinya. MA thesis, University of Addis Ababa.

2002. *A Modern Grammar of Tigrinya*. Rome: Tipografia U. Detti.

2005. A comparative study of Tigrinya pronouns and prepositions. Doctoral dissertation, Università degli Studi di Firenze.

2016. *DPs, Phi-features and Tense in the Context of Abyssinian (Eritrean and Ethiopian) Semitic Languages: A Window for Further Research*. Florence: Firenze University Press.

Tessières, U. & V. Dubois. 1957. *Méthode pratique pour apprendre l'omyene*. Paris: Société des Missions évangéliques de Paris.

Theil, Rolf. 2012. Omotic. In Lutz Edzard (ed.), *Semitic and Afroasiatic: Challenges and Opportunities*, 369–384. Wiesbaden: Harrassowitz.

Thomanek, Karl E. 1996. *Concepts of Urban Language in Africa: Implications and Explications in the Study of the Speech Community and Codeswitching*. Vienna: Afro-Pub.

Thomas, Jacqueline & Anne Behaghel. 1980. *La linguistique africaniste française (en France et en Afrique): Le point de la question en 1980*. Paris: SELAF.

Thomason, Sarah Grey, & Terence Kaufman. 1988. *Language Contact, Creolization, and Genetic Linguistics*. Berkeley: University of California Press.

Thornell, Christina. 1997. *The Sango Language and its Lexicon*. (revised PhD dissertation). Lund: Lund University Press.

2005. Knowledge on wild plant names and uses in the Bantu language Mpiemo. *Cameroon Journal of Ethnobotany* 1: 11–17.

Tilahun Gamta. 1989. *Oromo-English Dictionary*. Addis Ababa: Addis Ababa University Printing Press.

Tirronen, Toivo. 1977. *Ndongan kielen oppikirja (Ndonga grammar)*. Helsinki: Suomen lähetysseura.
1986. *Ndonga–English Dictionary*. Oniipa: Oniipa Printing Press.
Togarasei, Lovemore. 2009. The Shona Bible and the politics of the Bible translation. *Studies in the World Christianity*, 15(1): 51–64.
Tomás, Gil, Luísa Seco, Susana Seixas, Paula Faustino, João Lavinha & Jorge Rocha. 2002. The peopling of São Tomé (Gulf of Guinea): origins of slave settlers and admixture with the Portuguese. *Human Biology* 74(3): 397–411.
Torrend, J. 1891. *A Comparative Grammar of the South African Bantu Languages Comprising those of Zanzibar, Mozambique, the Zambezi, etc.* London: Kegan Paul, Trench, Trübner.
Tosco, Mauro. 2000. Cushitic overview. *Journal of Ethiopian Studies* 33(2): 87–121.
2001. A whole lotta focusin' goin' on: information packaging in Somali texts. *Studies in African Linguistics* 31(1/2): 27–53.
2010. Somali writings. *Afrikanistik Online.* www.afrikanistik-aegyptologie-online.de/archiv/2010/2723 (accessed 10 October 2011).
Tourneux, Henry. 2006. *La communication technique en langues africaines*. Paris: Karthala.
Tourneux, Henry & Léonie Métangmo-Tatou (eds). 2010. *Parler du sida au Nord-Cameroun*. Paris: Karthala.
Tourneux, Henry, C. Seignobos & F. Lafarge. 1986. *Les Mbara et leur Langue (Tchad)*. Paris: SELAF.
Traill, Anthony. 1973. A preliminary sketch of !Xu) phonetics. *Edinburgh University Department of Linguistics Work in Progress* 6:1–23.
1977. Phonological status of !Xoo clicks. *Khoisan Linguistic Studies* 3:107–131.
1985. Phonetic and Phonological Studies in !Xoo Bushman. (Quellen zur Khoisan-Forschung, 1). Hamburg: Helmut Buske.
1986. Click replacement in Khoe. In R. Vossen and K. Keuthmann (eds.), *Contemporary Studies on Khoisan, in Honour of Oswin Köhler on the Occasion of his 75th Birthday* (Quellen zur Khoisan-Forschung, 5), 301–320. Hamburg: Helmut Buske.
1999. Foundations in Khoisan studies: a survey of a selection of papers from Bantu studies and African studies, 1921–1967. In R. Finlayson (ed.), *African Mosaic: Festschrift for J. A. Louw*, 41–58. Pretoria: Unisa Press.
Traoré, Mory. 2000. *Esquisse vers l'Eloge du Tribalisme*. Tokyo: ILCAA.
Treis, Yvonne. [2010] 2012. Purpose-encoding strategies in Kambaata. *Afrika und Übersee* 91: 1–38.
Trombetti, Alfredo. 1912. *Manuale dell'arabo parlato a Tripoli: Grammatica, letture e vocabolario*. Bologna: L. Beltrami.
Tropper, Josef. 2002. *Altäthiopisch. Grammatik des Geʻez mit Übungstexten und Glossar*. Münster: Ugarit.
Trumpp, E. 1874. Ueber den Accent im Aethiopischen. *Zeitschrift der Deutschen Morgenländischen Gesellschaft* 28: 515–561.
Tschonghongei, Nelson & Mercy Ezigha. 2011. Cultural issues related to the matrilineal system of the Aghem. In N. M. Mutaka (ed.), *Glimpses of African Cultures / Échos des cultures africaines*, 161–171. Paris: L'Harmattan.
Tucker, Archibald N. 1940. *The Eastern Sudanic Languages*, vol. I. London/New York/Toronto: Oxford University Press for the International Institute of African Languages & Cultures.

1978. *Dinka Orthography* (Linguistics Monograph Series, 9). Khartoum: Sudan Research Unit, University of Khartoum.

Tucker, Archibald N. & M. A. Bryan. 1956. *The Non-Bantu Languages of North-Eastern Africa* (Handbook of African Languages, 3). Oxford: Oxford University Press for International African Institute.

1966. *Linguistic Analyses: The Non-Bantu Languages of North-Eastern Africa* (Handbook of African Languages, 3). Oxford: Oxford University Press for International African Institute.

TUKI (Taasisi ya Uchunguzi wa Kiswahili). 1995. *Kamusi Awali ya Sayansi na Tekinolojia*. Dar es Salaam: Institute of Kiswahili Research.

2004. *Kanusi ya Biolojia, Fizikia na Kemia (English–Swahili Dictionary of Biology, Physics and Chemistry)*. Dar es Salaam: Institute of Kiswahili Research.

2014. *Kamusi ya Kiswahili–Kiingereza*. 2nd ed. Dar es Salaam: Institute of Kiswahili Research.

Turton, David, Yigezu Moges & Olibui Olisarali. 2008. *Mursi–English–Amharic dictionary*. Addis Ababa: Ermias Advertising.

Tymian, J., J. Kouadjio N'Guessan & J. N. Loucou. 2003. *Dictionnaire baoulé-français*. Abidjan: NEI.

Uhlig, Siegbert (ed.). 2003. *Encyclopaedia Aethiopica*. 5 vols. Wiesbaden: Harrassowitz.

Ukwamedua, Nelson U. 2011. A critique review of Alexis Kagame's four categories of African philosophy. *Origisi: A New Journal of African Studies* 8:248–265.

Ullendorff, Edward. 1945. *Exploration and Study of Abyssinia: A Brief Survey*. Asmara: Il Lunedi dell Eritrea.

1955. *The Semitic Languages of Ethiopia: A Comparative Phonology*. London: Taylor's (Foreign) Press.

1985. *A Tigrinya (Təgrəñña) Chrestomathy, Introduction, Grammatical Tables, Tigrinya Texts, Letters, Phrases, Tigrinya-English Glossary, Select Bibliography*. Stuttgart: Steiner.

2010. Tigrinya Language Council. In Siegbert Uhlig (ed.), *Encyclopaedia Aethiopica*, vol. IV, 593–594. Wiesbaden: Harrassowitz.

UNICEF. 2016. *The Impact of Language Policy and Practice on Children's Learning: Evidence from Eastern and Southern Africa*. New York: UNICEF.

Unseth, Peter. 1990. *Linguistic Bibliography of the Non-Semitic Languages of Ethiopia*. East Lansing, MI: African Studies Center, Michigan State University. http://ema.revues.org/1920.

Urua, Eno-Abasi. 2000. *Ibibio Phonetics and Phonology*. Cape Town: Centre for Advanced Studies of African Societies.

Urua, Eno-Abasi, Moses Ekpenyong, and Dafydd Gibbon. 2012. Nwed Usem Ibibio [Ibibio Dictionary]. Uyo: Fruities' Publications Ltd.

Valdés Acosta, G. 2013. *Diccionario de bantuismos del español de Cuba*. Madrid: Sial/Casa de África.

Van Acker, A. 1907. *Dictionnaire kitabwa-français et français-kitabwa*. Brussels: Annales du Musée du Congo, ethnographie série V, Linguistique.

Van der Heyden, Ulrich. 1999. *Die Afrikawissenschaften in der DDR*. Hamburg: Lit.

Van der Veen, L. J. 1991. *Étude comparée des parlers du groupe Okani, B30 (Gabon)*. PhD dissertation, Université Lumière-Lyon II.

1999. Les Bantous eviya (Gabon-B30), langue et société traditionnelle. PhD dissertation, Université Lumière-Lyon II.

Van der Veen, L. J. & S. Bodinga-bwa-Bodinga 2002. *Gedandedi sa geviya, dictionnaire geviya-français*. Paris: Peeters.

Van Eeden, B. I. C. 1956. *Zoeloe-Grammatika*. Stellenbosch: Die Universiteitsuitgewers en -Boekhandelaars.

Van Everbroeck, R. 1985. *Maloba ma lokota: dictionnaire lingala-français, français-lingala*. Kinshasa: Épiphanie.

Van Otterloo, Karen & Roger Van Otterloo. 2011. *The Kifuliiru Language*. 2 vols. Dallas, TX: SIL International.

Van Warmelo, N. J. 1927. *Die Gliederung der südafrikanischen Bantusprachen*. Berlin: Dietrich Reimer.

Van Wyk, E. B. 1958. *Woordverdeling in Noord-Sotho en Zoeloe: 'n Bydrae tot die vraagstuk van woord-identifikasie in die Bantoetale*. Unpublished DLitt thesis, University of Pretoria.

1961. Die woordklasse van Noord-Sotho. In *Feesbundel vir Prof Dr J. A. Engelbrecht: 'n huldigingsblyk aan hom opgedra deur sy oud-studente ter geleentheid van sy vyf-en-sestigste verjaardag, 27 Augustus 1961*, 69–85. Johannesburg: APB (Afrikaanse Pers-Boekhandel) Publ.

1968. Die invloed van die Europese tale en die Europese linguistiese tradisie op die studie van die Bantoetale. In G. Cronjé (ed.), *Kultuurbeïvloeding tussen Blankes en Bantoe in Suid-Afrika*, 85–105. Pretoria: J. L. van Schaik.

1993. C. M. Doke: a critical review by a believing outsider. *African Studies* 52(2): 21–33.

Vanderelst, John. 2016. *A Grammar of Dagik: A Kordofanian Language of Sudan*. Cologne: Rüdiger Köppe..

Vandermeiren, J. 1912. *Grammaire de la langue kiluba-hemba*. Brussels: Ministère des Colonies.

Vanhoudt, Bettie. 1999. Lexique bisa-français. *Mandenkan* 34: 1–113.

Vanhove, Martine. 2006. The Beja language today in Sudan: the state of the art in linguistics. *Proceedings of the 7th International Sudan Studies Conference April 6th–8th 2006. Bergen, Norway*. CD Rom. Bergen: University of Bergen.

(ed.). 2008. *From Polysemy to Semantic Change*. Amsterdam/Philadelphia: John Benjamins.

Vansina, J. 1959. *Esquisse de grammaire bushing* (Annales Sciences de l'Homme 23). Tervuren: RMCA.

Vedder, H. 1910. Grundriss einer Grammatik der Buschmann-Sprache vom Stamm der !kû Buschmänner. *Zeitschrift für Kolonialsprachen* 1: 5–24.

1911. Grundriss einer Grammatik der Buschmann-Sprache vom Stamm der !kû Buschmänner. *Zeitschrift für Kolonialsprachen* 2: 106–117.

Veiga, Manuel. 1996. *O Crioulo de Cabo Verde: Introdução à Gramática*. Praia, Cabo Verde: ICLD.

2000. *Le créole du Cap-Vert. Etude grammaticale descriptive et contrastive*. Paris: Karthala.

2002. *O Caboverdiano em 45 lições*. Praia, Cabo Verde: INIC.

Veiga, Manuel, Dulce Almada et al. 2000. *Actas do 1º Colóquio Linguístico sobre o Crioulo de Cabo Verde 1979*. Mindelo: Gráfica do Mindelo.

Veit-Wild, Flora (ed.). 2003. *Nicht nur Mythen und Märchen: Afrika-Literaturwissenschaft als Herausforderung*. Trier: Wissenschaftlicher Verlag Trier.

Vergari, Moreno. 2005. *Dikshineeri amneefecituk Saaho labcad: Gerho cibra kin Kalimaat Caalamadde* [Practise Saho Using the Dictionary: A Voyage in the Amazing World of Words]. Asmara: Ethnorêma e Sabur Printing Services.

Vergote, Jozef. 1973–1983. *Grammaire copte*. Leuven: Peeters.

Vierke, Clarissa. 2014. Zur Forschungsgeschichte der deutschen Afrikanistik, ihre Anfänge und Ausrichtung, am Beispiel der Swahili-Forschung. In Michel Espagne, Pascale Rabault-Feuerhahn & David Simo (eds.), *Afrikanische Deutschland-Studien und deutsche Afrikanistik*, 73–92. Würzburg: Königshausen & Neumann.

Viljoen, Melanie. 2013. A grammatical description of the Buwal language. PhD thesis, La Trobe University, Bundoora.

Vincke, J. L. 1966. Aspects de la phonologie et de la morphologie de la langue lunda (ruund). PhD dissertation, Université Officielle du Congo d'Elisabethville.

Visser, M. 1983. 'n Leksikaal-interpretatiewe analise van enkele semantiese relasies in Xhosa. *South African Journal of African Languages* 3(Suppl. 1): 73–130.

Vitale, Anthony J. 1981. *Swahili Syntax*. Dordrecht: Foris Publications.

Vittori, Mariano. 1552. *Chaldeae, seu Aethiopicae linguae Institutiones: Nunquam antea a Latinis visae, opus utile, ac eruditum*. Romae: Impressit Valerio Dorico opera Angelo Oldradi. [*Chaldae, Seu Aethiopicae Linguae Institutiones. Opus Util ac Eruditum*. Roma: Typis Sac. Congregationis de Propaganda Fide.]

Voeltz, E. F. K. 1977. Proto-Niger-Congo extensions. PhD dissertation, University of California, Los Angeles.

Vögele, Hannelore, Uta Reuster-Jahn, Raimund Kastenholz & Lutz Diegner (eds.). 2014. *From the Tana River to Lake Chad: Research in African Oratures and Literatures. In memoriam Thomas Geider*. Cologne: Rüdiger Köppe.

Vogt, Carlos & Peter Fry. 1996. *Cafundó: A África no Brasil: linguagem e sociedade*. São Paulo: Companhia das Letras.

Voigt, Rainer. 1977. *Das tigrinische Verbalsystem*. Berlin: Dietrich Reimer.

2003a. Bible translation into Təgre/Təgrəñña. In Siegbert Uhlig (ed.), *Encyclopaedia Aethiopica*, vol. I, 577–578. Wiesbaden: Harrassowitz.

2003b. Wortfolge und Genitivkonstruktionen im Tigrinischen. *Rassegna di Studi Etiopici* n.s. 2: 77–106.

2005. Südtigrinische Dialekte – das einfache und zusammengesetzte Präsens im Dialekt von May-Cäw (Tigray). In Siegbert Uhlig (eds.), *Proceedings of the Fifteenth International Conference of Ethiopian Studies, Hamburg 20–25 July 2003*, 893–898. Wiesbaden: Harrassowitz.

2010. Təgrəñña literature. In Siegbert Uhlig (ed.), *Encyclopaedia Aethiopica*, vol. IV, 905–908. Wiesbaden: Harrassowitz.

Von Heyking, Beatrix. 2013. *A Grammar of Belanda Boor: Phonology and Morphology* (Nilo-Saharan, 27). Cologne: Rüdiger Köppe.

Von Russegger, Joseph. 1844. *Reisen in Europa, Asien und Afrika [...] unternommen in den Jahren 1835 bis 1841*, vol. 2.2. Stuttgart: Schweizerbart.

Von Staden, P. M. S. 1986. African language teaching: What model? *Journal for Language Teaching* 20(2): 2–10.

Voorhoeve, Jan. 1971. Tonology of the Bamileke noun. *Journal of African Languages* 10(2): 44–53.

Vossen, Rainer. 1982. *The Eastern Nilotes: Linguistic and Historical Reconstruction* (Kölner Beiträge zur Afrikanistik 9). Berlin: Dietrich Reimer.

1997. *Die Khoe-Sprachen*. Cologne: Rüdiger Köppe.

Vycichl, Werner. 1952. Das berberische Ziffernsystem von Ghadames und seine Ursprung. *Rivisti di Studi Orientali* 27: 81–83.

1954. Der Umlaut im Berberischen des Djebel Nefusa in Tripolitanien. *Annali dell'Istituto Universitario Orientale* 6: 145–152.

1966. Etude sur la langue de Ghadames. *Genève-Afrique* 5(2): 248–260.

1972. Berberische Nomina Actoris im Dialekt des Djebel Nefusa (Tripolitanien). *Orientalistische Literaturzeitung* 67(11/12): 533–535.

1991. Sketch of the Siwan language. University of Vienna. Ms. (Cited by Miller 1996.)

2005. *Berberstudien; & A Sketch of Siwi Berber (Egypt)* (Berber Studies, 10). Cologne: Rüdiger Köppe.

Vydrine, Valentine F. 2001. The phonological type and the noun morphology of the Proto-Mande. Doctoral thesis, State University, Oriental Department, St Petersburg.

2008. *Yazyk bamana* [The Bamana Language]. St Petersburg: St Petersburg State University.

(ed.). 2017. *Yazyki mira. Yazyki mande* [Languages of the World. Mande Languages]. St Petersburg: Nestor-Istoria.

Vydrine, Valentine F. & Mongnan A. Késségbeu. 2008. *Dictionnaire Dan – Française (dan de l'Est)*, St Petersburg: Nestor-Istoria.

Waag, Christine. 2010. *The Fur Verb and its Context* (Nilo-Saharan, 26.) Cologne: Rüdiger Köppe.

Waddell, Hope. M. 1859. *A Vocabulary of the Efik or Old Calabar Language, with Prayers and Lessons*. 2nd ed. Edinburgh: Grant & Taylor.

Walker, A. 1950. Essai de grammaire tsogo. *Bulletin de l'Institut d'Études Centrafricaines* 1: 1–69.

Walker, W. Seymour. 1921. *The Siwi Language*. London: K. Paul, Trench, Trubner, and Co.

Wamagata Waina Peter. 2016. The application of Swahili in Chinese language teaching. MA dissertation, Tianjin Normal University.

Wanger, P. W. 1917. *Konversations-Grammatik der Zulu-Sprache*. Mariannhill, South Africa: St Thomas Aquins Druckerei.

Ward, Ida C. 1933. *The Phonetic and Tonal Structure of Efik*. Cambridge: Heffer & Sons.

1936. *An Introduction to the Ibo Language*. London: Heffer & Sons.

1952. *Introduction to the Yoruba Language*. Cambridge: Heffer & Sons.

Warsama Ahmed, Saïd. 2003. La langue somalie et sa transcription. *Sciences et Environnement* 17: 59–75.

Watters, John R. 1982. A phonology and morphology of Ejagham. Doctoral dissertation, UCLA.

Watters, Kathie Swanson. 1993. Status and function of Tone in Tira. MA thesis, University of Nairobi.

Wazaki, Yoichi. 1980. *Swahili–Japanese Dictionary*. Tenri: Yotokusha.

Wedekind, Klaus, Charlotte Wedekind, & Abuzeinab Musa. 2007. *A Learner's Grammar of Beja (East Sudan): Grammar, Texts and Vocabulary (Beja-English and English-Beja)*. Cologne: Rüdiger Köppe.

Welmers, William E. 1946. A descriptive grammar of Fanti (Language dissertation No. 39). *Language* 22(3, Suppl.): 1–78.

1958. *The Mande Languages* (Georgetown University Monograph Series in Languages and Linguistics 11). Washington, DC: Georgetown University Press.

1971. Christian missions and language policies. In Thomas E. Sebeok (ed.), *Current Trends in Linguistics*. Vol. VII: *Linguistics in Sub-Saharan Africa*, 559–569. The Hague and Paris: Mouton.

1973. *African Language Structures*. Los Angeles/Berkeley: University of California Press.

Wemmers, Jacob. 1638. *Lexicon Aethiopicum Ad Eminentiss*. Rome: Principem S.R.E. Card. Antonium Barberinum.

Wendo, N. 1986. *Dictionnaire français-yansi (République du Zaïre)* (CEEBA Publications, Série III, 14). Bandundu: CEEBA.

Weninger, Stefan. 1999. *Gəʿəz*. Munich: Lincom Europa.

2001. *Das Verbalsystem des Altäthiopischen: Eine Untersuchung seiner Verwendung und Funktion unter Berücksichtigung des Interferenzproblems*. Wiesbaden: Harrassowitz.

(ed.). 2011. *The Semitic Languages: An International Handbook*. Berlin: de Gruyter Mouton.

Were, Gideon S. 1967. *A History of Abaluya of Western Kenya c. 1500-1930*. Nairobi: East African Literature Bureau.

Werner, Alice. 1915. *The Language-Families of Africa*. London: Society for Promotion of Christian Knowledge.

1917. The Utendi wa Mwana Kupona. In Oric Bates (ed.), *Varia Africana I* (Harvard African Studies, Vol. 1), 147–181. Cambridge, MA: Peabody Museum.

1930. English contributions to the study of African languages. *Journal of the Royal African Society* 29(117): 509–528.

1933. *Myths and Legends of the Bantu*. London: Harrap.

Werner, Roland. 1987. *Grammatik des Nobiin (Nilnubisch)*. Hamburg: Helmut Buske.

Westermann, Diedrich. 1905–1906. *Wörterbuch der Ewe-Sprache*. Berlin: Dietrich Reimer.

1907. *Grammatik der Ewe-Sprache*. Berlin: Reimer.

1911. *Die Sudansprachen*. Hamburg: Friederichsen.

1912. *A Short Grammar of the Shilluk Language*. Philadelphia, PA: The Board of Foreign Missions of the United Presbyterian Church of N. A. and Berlin: Dietrich Reimer.

1912/1913. Ein bisher unbekannter Nubischer Dialekt aus Dar Fur. *Zeitschrift für Kolonialsprachen* 3: 248–251.

1927. *Die westlichen Sudansprachen und ihre Beziehungen zum Bantu*. Berlin: Walter de Gruyter.

1928. *Ewefiala: Ewe – English Dictionary*. Berlin: Reimer.

1930. *A Study of the Ewe Language*. Oxford: Oxford University Press.

1940. *Afrikanische Tabusitten in ihrer Einwirkung auf die Sprachgestaltung*. Berlin: Verlag der Akademie der Wissenschaften.

1941. *Afrika als europäische Aufgabe*. Berlin: Deutscher Verlag.

1954. *Wörterbuch der Ewe-Sprache*. Berlin: Akademie-Verlag.

Westermann, Diedrich & Ida Ward. 1933. *Practical Phonetics for Students of African Languages*. London/New York/Toronto: Oxford University Press.

Westphal, E. O. J. 1962. A re-classification of Southern African Non-Bantu languages. *Journal of African Languages* 1(1): 1–3.

Wetter, Andreas. 2006. Arabic in Ethiopia. In Kees Versteegh (ed.), *Encyclopedia of Arabic language and linguistics*, 51–56. Leiden: Brill.

Whitehead, J. 1899. *Grammar and Dictionary of the Bobangi Language as Spoken over a Part of Upper-Congo (West Central Africa)*. London: Kegan Paul and Trench, Trübner & Co.

Whiteley, Wilfred H. 1968. *Some Problems of Transitivity in Swahili*. London: School of Oriental and African Studies.

1969. *Swahili: The Rise of a National Language*. London: Methuen.

Wilkes, A. 1973. Werkwoorde met die resiprokale agtervoegsel in Zulu: 'n Grammatiese Studie. *Limi* 1(1): 26–33.

1974. Oor die sogenaamde eksklusiewe kwantitatiewe van Zulu. *Studies in Bantoetale* 1(1): 76–86.

1976. Oor die voornaamwoorde van Zulu met besondere verwysing na die sogenaamde demonstratiewe en absolute voornaamwoorde. *Studies in Bantoetale* 3(1): 60–83.

1978. Bantoetaalstudies in Suid-Afrika sedert 1826. *Studies in Bantoetale* 5(1): 107–167.

Willems, E. 1955. *Le Tshiluba du Kasaï pour débutants*. Luluabourg: Mission de Scheut.

Williams, Edwin. [1971] 1976. Underlying tone in Margi and Igbo. *Linguistic Inquiry* 7: 463–484.

Williamson, Kay. 1965. *A Grammar of the Kolokuma Dialect of Ịjọ*. Cambridge: Cambridge University Press.

(ed.). 1968. *Benue-Congo Comparative Wordlist*. Vol. I. Ibadan: West African Linguistic Society, University of Ibadan.

(ed.). 1972. *Igbo-English Dictionary; based on the Onicha Dialect*. Benin City: Ethiope.

(ed.). 1973. *Benue-Congo Comparative Wordlist*. Vol. II. Ibadan: West African Linguistic Society, University of Ibadan.

Wilson, William A. A. 1962. *The Crioulo of Guiné*. Johannesburg: Witwatersrand University Press.

Winston, F. D. D. 1960. The 'mid' tone in Efik. *African Language Studies* 1: 185–192.

Wolff, H. Ekkehard. 1975. The conceptual framework of Humboldtian ethnolinguistics in German Africanistics. In Robert K. Herbert (ed.), *Patterns in Language, Culture and Society: Sub-Saharan Africa* (Working Papers in Linguistics 19, Dept. of Linguistics), 113–124. Columbus, OH: Ohio State University.

1980. *Sprachkunst der Lamang: Stil, Bedeutung und poetische Dimension in zwei Genres oral tradierter Ein-Satz-Literatur* (Afrikanistische Forschungen 8). Glückstadt: J. J. Augustin.

1981. Die Erforschung der afrikanischen Sprachen: Geschichte und Konzeptionen. In B. Heine, Th. C. Schadeberg & E. Wolff (eds.), *Die Sprachen Afrikas*, 17–43. Hamburg: Helmut Buske.

1993. *Referenzgrammatik des Hausa: Zur Begleitung des Fremdsprachenunterrichts und zur Einführung in das Selbststudium*. Hamburg: LIT Verlag.

1998. Afrikanische Sprachminiaturen: Zur formalen Ästhetik von Kleinformen afrikanischer Sprachkunst unter besonderer Berücksichtigung ihrer Tonalität. *ULPA - Languages and Literatures* 5.

2001. Tonal rhymes in Hausa revisited. In Robert Nicolaï (ed.), *Leçons d'Afrique: Filiations, ruptures et reconstitutions des langues*; un Hommage à Gabriel Manessy, 117–125. Louvain/Paris: Peeters.

2007. Die afrikanischen Sprachen im 21. Jahrhundert: Herausforderungen an Politik und Wissenschaft. In Markus A. Denzel et al. (eds.), *Jahrbuch für europäische Überseegeschichte 7*, 189–219. Wiesbaden: Harrassowitz.

2012. The orature–grammar interface: on 'rhymes' in African oral verbal art. In Hugues Steve Ndinga-Koumba-Binza and Sonja E. Bosch (eds.), *Language Science and Language Technology in Africa: Festschrift for Justus C. Roux*, 100–123. Stellenbosch: Sun Press.

2013. *Was ist eigentlich Afrikanistik? Eine kleine Einführung in die Welt der afrikanischen Sprachen, ihre Rolle in Kultur und Gesellschaft, und ihre Literaturen* (Sprache-Kultur-Gesellschaft 13). Frankfurt am Main: Peter Lang.

2014a. Sprache als Schlüssel – Sprache als Ressource: Eine Positionsbestimmung der deutschsprachigen Afrikanistik. In Michel Espagne, Pascale Rabault-Feuerhahn & David Simo (eds.), *Afrikanische Deutschland-Studien und deutsche Afrikanistik*, 19–48. Würzburg: Königshausen & Neumann.

2014b. Und sie reimen doch: Parallelismus in afrikanischen Oraturen. In Vögele Hannelore, Uta Reuster-Jahn, Raimund Kastenholz & Lutz Diegner (eds.), *From the Tana River to Lake Chad: Research in African Oratures and Literatures: In Memoriam Thomas Geider* (Mainzer Beiträge zur Afrikaforschung Volume 36), 51–73. Cologne: Rüdiger Köppe.

2016. *Language and Development in Africa: Perceptions, Ideologies and Challenges.* Cambridge: Cambridge University Press.

(ed.). 2019. *The Cambridge Handbook of African Linguistics.* Cambridge: Cambridge University Press.

Wolff, H. Ekkehard & Ludwig Gerhardt. 1977. Interferenzen zwischen Benue-Kongo und Tschad-Sprachen. *Zeitschrift der Deutschen Morgenländischen Gesellschaft*, Suppl. 3(2): 1518–1543.

Wolff, H. Ekkehard & Ousseina Alidou. 2001. On the non-linear ancestry of Tasawaq (Niger), or: How "mixed" can a language be? *Sprache und Geschichte in Afrika* 16/17: 523–574.

Wright, L. S. 2002. Language as a 'resource' in South Africa: the economic life of language in a globalising society. *English Academy Review* 19(1): 2–19. www.personal.psu.edu/jml34/cr-sch.pd (accessed 2 March 2016).

Xavier, F. 2012. *Segmental and Suprasegmental Phonology of Kimbundu: Regiolects of Luanda, Bengo, Cuanza Norte and Malanje.* Saarbrücken: LAP Academic Publishing.

Xin Shui. 1965. African linguistics. *Linguistics Data* 4: 46.

Ya'əqob Gäbrä-Iyäsus (zä-Ḥebo). 1923 a.-mə. [= 1931], 1926 a.-mə. [= 1934], 1940 [= 1948]. *Ḥaddis mäžämmäriya ziwåṣ͟ṣ͟ə zällo mäṣḥaf säwasəw – Təgrañña nə-zimmäharu qwåla'u mästämhari.* Asmara: maḥtäm Frančäskana.

1941 a.-mə. [= 1948/49]) *Zənna-n tärät-ən məssəla-n nay qäddamot* (Epic, Tales and Proverbs of the Elders). Asmara: Komboni.

Yang, C. J. 1990. *Lugha ya Magazeti ya Kiswahili.* Seoul: Myoungji Publishing Co.

2013. Sociopragmatic functions of conversational code-switching: some examples from Nairobi, Kenya. *African Affairs* 34: 209–232.

2014. Synesis in grammar: some examples from Swahili mass media. *Journal of the Korean Association of African Studies* 42: 179–196.

2016. Animacy versus rhyming in the grammatical agreement of Swahili augmentatives and diminutives. *Journal of the Korean Association of African Studies* 48: 67–88.

Yankah, Kwesi, Kofi Kora Saah & Nana Aba Amfo. 2014. A Legon reader in Ghanaian linguistics. In *Writing by the Faculty Past and Present of the Department of Linguistics, University of Ghana, Legon, on the Occasion of the University's 65th Anniversary*. Banbury: Ayebia Clarke Publishing.

Yedder, Abdurahman M. 1982. The oral literature associated with the traditional wedding ceremony at Ghadames. PhD dissertation, SOAS, University of London http://ethos.bl.uk/OrderDetails.do?uin=uk.bl.ethos.646019 (accessed 2 January, 2017).

Yimesgen, Hailegiorgis. 2011. *Nay Təgrəñña səwya nəgəgər məṭun mäzgäbä qalat, Concise Tigrinya Figure of Speech Dictionary*. Asmara: Atlas P.P.

Youssi, Abderrahim. 1977. Les parlers secrets du Maroc. *La Linguistique* 13(1): 135–143.

1980. Morphologie verbale en arabe marocain médian. In *Actes du VIéme Colloque de la Société International de Linguistique Fonctionnelle (SILF). Rabat, July 1979*, 187–197.

1982. Emphasis as a prosodic feature in Moroccan Arabic. *Langues et Littérature* 2: 185–208.

1983. La triglossie dans la typologie linguistique. *La Linguistique: Revue de la Société Internationale de Linguistique Fonctionnelle* 19(2): 71–83.

1989. Parlers arabes d'Occident (marocain, algérien, tunisien, andalou, hassane, maltais). Bibliographie annotée et classée. In A. Youssi, A. Benahallam, A. Boukous & M. Dahbi (eds.), *Langue et Société au Maghreb. Bilan et Perspectives* (Publication de la Faculté des Lettres et des Sciences Humaines: Série Colloques et Séminaires, 13), 151–219. Rabat: Université Mohamed V.

Youssouf Elmi, Idris. 2002. Symposium pour les langues nationales. *Sciences et Environnement* 16: 55–59.

2003. La phrase somalie. *Sciences et Environnement* 17: 29–32.

Yri, Kjell Magne. 2009. Amharic - the relative and the genitive: are they related semantically? In Janet Constance, E. Watson & Jan Retsö (eds.), *Relative Clauses and Genitive Constructions in Semitic*, 217–228. Oxford: Oxford University Press.

2013. The phonology of 'Sidaamu Afii Jirte: implications for the orthography of Sidaama. *Journal of Ethiopian Studies* 44: 149–161.

Yukawa, Yasutoshi. 1992. A tonological study of Yambasa verbs. In Rohai Kagaya (ed.), *Studies in Cameroonian and Zairean Languages*, 1–46. Tokyo: ILCAA.

2014. *A General Linguistic Study of Bantu Languages*. Tokyo: Hituzi.

Zaborski, Andrzej. 1975. *Studies Hamito-Semitic: The Verb in Cushitic*. Kraków: Uniwersytet Jagielloński.

1986. *The Morphology of Nominal Plural in the Cushitic Languages*. Vienna: Afro-Pub.

1987. Afar-Saho Linguistics: an overview. In Hans G. Mukarovsky (ed.), *Leo Reinisch: Werk und Erbe*, 85–95. Vienna: Verlag der Österreichischen Akademie der Wissenschaften.

Zack, E. W. A. 2009. Egyptian Arabic in the seventeenth century: a study and edition of Yusuf al-Magribi's 'Daf al-isr 'an kalam ahl Misr'. PhD dissertation, University of Amsterdam.

Záhořík, Jan. 2006. African studies in the Czech Republic: from the early Czech-African contacts until the 21st century. *Afrikanistik-Aegyptologie-Online*. www.afrikanistik-aegyptologie-online.de/.

Zelealem, Leyew. 2003. *The Kemantney language: a sociolinguistic and grammatical study of language replacement*. Cologne: Rüdiger Köppe.

Zemicael Tecle. 2012. *Deutsch-tigrinisches Wörterbuch*. Wiesbaden: Harrassowitz.

Zhang Peizhi. 1990. *Sarufi ya Kiswahili (Swahili Grammar)*. Beijing: Foreign Language Teaching and Research Press.

Zheltov, Alexander Yu. 2008. *Yazyki niger-kongo: strukturno-dinamicheskaya tipologiya* [The Niger-Congo Languages: Structural-dynamic Typology]. St Petersburg: Izdatel'stvo Sankt-Peterburgskogo gosudarsvennogo universiteta [St Petersburg State University Press].

2011. African language studies in St Petersburg. In Christina Thornell and Karsten Legère (eds.), *North–South Contributions to African Languages*, 197–203. Cologne: Rüdiger Köppe.

Zhukov, Andrey A. 1997. *Suahili: Yazyk i literature* [Swahili: Language and Literature]. St Petersburg: Izdatel'stvo Sankt-Peterburgskogo gosudarsvennogo universiteta [St Petersburg State University Press].

2004. Old Swahili-Arabic script and the development of Swahili literary language. *Sudanic Africa* 15: 1–15.

Ziegler, Susanne. 2005. Historical sound recordings from Ethiopia on wax cylinders. In Walter Raunig, & Steffen Wenig (eds.), *Afrikas Horn: Akten der ersten internationalen Littmann-Konferenz, 2. bis 5. Mai 2002 in München*, 322–343. Wiesbaden: Harrassowitz.

Ziervogel, D. 1952. *A Grammar of Swazi*. Johannesburg: Witwatersrand University Press.

1956. Linguistic and literary achievement in the Bantu languages of South Africa. Unpublished Inaugural Lecture, University of South Africa.

Zima, Petr. 1972. *Problems of Categories and Word Classes in Hausa: (The Paradigm of Case)* (Dissertationes orientales). Prague: Academia.

1973. *Hauština* [The Hausa Language]. Prague: SPN.

(ed.). 2000. *Areal and Genetic Factors in Language Classification and Description. Africa South of the Sahara*. Munich/Newcastle: Lincom Europa.

(ed.). 2009. *The Verb and Related Areal Features in West Africa. Continuity and Discontinuity within and across Sprachbund Frontiers*. Munich: LINCOM.

(ed.). 2010. *Oracy and Literacy: Their Autonomy and Complementation in Language Communication*. Munich: LINCOM.

2013. African studies in the Czech Republic: Comments on J. Záhořík's paper. *Afrikanistik online* 10 (urn:nbn:de:0009-10-37540).

Zima, Petr & Vladimir Tax (eds.). 1998. *Language and Location in Space and Time*. Munich: LINCOM.

Zong Fei. 1966a. General introduction to Bantu Language. *Philology in China* 1: 69–76.

1966b. General introduction to Zulu. *General Information of Linguistics* 2: 1–4.

Zorc, R. David & Madina M. Osman. 1993. *Somali–English Dictionary with English Index*. 3rd ed. Kensington, MD: Dunwoody Press.

Zwartjes, Otto. 2011. *Portuguese Missionary Grammars in Asia, Africa and Brazil, 1550–1800* (Studies in the History of Language Sciences 117). Amsterdam/Philadelphia: John Benjamins.

Index – African Languages

Index – Countries

Index – Keywords

African studies, 6, 13, 19, 41, 42, 47, 48, 50,
51, 52, 53, 54, 55, 56, 57, 58, 59, 60, 61,
62, 64, 68, 69, 77, 124, 149, 185, 191,
193, 196, 210, 211, 233, 234, 236, 238,
239, 243
African-American Vernacular English, 220
Africanist, 4, 6, 26, 28, 29, 32, 33, 36, 37, 40,
44, 45, 51, 52, 111, 119, 120, 144, 183,
184, 208, 211, 212, 215, 217, 219, 232,
247, 249, 250
Africanistics, 3, 21, 22, 23, 24, 25, 26, 27, 29,
32, 33, 34, 35, 36, 37, 38, 39, 40, 41, 42,
43, 44, 45, 46, 47, 219
Afro-Brazilian, 223, 228, 231, 232
Afro-Cuban, 228
Afro-descendant, 225, 230, 232
Afro-Hispanic, 223, 227, 228, 230, 231, 232
Afro-Mexican, 230
Akkadian, 237
Ancient Egypt, 48, 50, 179, 181
Ancient Greek, 54
anglophone, 12, 160, 167, 168, 171, 175
anthropology, 28, 29, 32, 34, 38, 44, 49,
51, 53, 62, 77, 190, 195, 197, 199,
241, 244
apartheid, 4, 10, 115, 121, 127, 129
  neo-, 13
  post-, 115, 131
art, 25
Asian languages, 64, 191, 233
Axumite Empire, 179

Berberology, 31, 36
Bible, 22, 50, 63, 94, 100, 110, 116, 138, 140,
157, 163, 181, 207

Chinese, 54, 156, 169, 240, 242
Christian mission, 5, 8, 22, 110, 181, 206,
207
classification, 1, 2, 24, 25, 27, 28, 29, 30, 35,
38, 45, 57, 59, 105, 108, 113, 119, 121,
122, 128, 142, 143, 218, 239
clicks, 27, 52, 118

colonial language, 5, 13, 15, 22, 25, 26, 34,
67, 107, 133, 145, 241
colonial, 2, 4, 5, 6, 7, 9, 10, 11, 12, 13, 15, 16,
17, 18, 19, 21, 22, 23, 24, 25, 26, 27, 29,
31, 37, 38, 44, 45, 46, 47, 48, 87, 95, 110,
116, 119, 120, 133, 137, 138, 140, 154,
155, 163, 168, 172, 178, 179, 181, 189,
190, 191, 192, 193, 194, 195, 197, 199,
200, 201, 202, 204, 206, 221, 223, 225,
227, 231
  anti-, 5, 190, 202
  ex-, 10
  neo-, 13, 206
  post-, 1, 6, 10, 12, 13, 17, 19, 22, 25, 27, 39,
41, 42, 45, 74, 77, 116, 119, 120, 121,
123, 124, 132
  pre-, 8, 19, 22, 73, 168, 181, 192
colonialism, 5, 26, 43, 178, 190, 199
colonization, 73, 90, 91, 138, 190, 197, 202,
203
creole, 35, 113, 197, 198, 201, 203, 204, 215,
219, 220, 223, 228, 229, 231, 232, 241
Czech, 57, 59

dance, 226, 227, 231
dialect, 30, 34, 38, 65, 68, 70, 71, 74, 75, 76,
79, 84, 92, 96, 107, 108, 124, 129, 134,
138, 140, 141, 172, 173, 183, 200, 202,
220, 229, 230, 231, 235, 236, 237, 240
dialectology, 38, 96, 97, 103
dialectometry, 38
discourse analysis, 75, 79, 128, 148, 185
Dutch, 2

Ebonics, 219, 220
education, 3, 5, 10, 11, 12, 13, 14, 16, 17, 37,
43, 64, 67, 73, 81, 85, 96, 98, 99, 100,
102, 103, 105, 107, 111, 115, 121, 131,
137, 140, 142, 148, 149, 151, 160, 165,
171, 172, 173, 176, 181, 190, 191, 192,
194, 195, 196, 197, 198, 200, 201, 202,
203, 204, 212, 239, 242, 246
Egyptology, 34, 46, 51, 53

340

Index – Persons